WILDLY FOXTROT

OTHER FOXTROT BOOKS BY BILL AMEND

FoxTrot
Pass the Loot
Black Bart Says Draw
Eight Yards, Down and Out
Bury My Heart at Fun-Fun Mountain
Say Hello to Cactus Flats
May the Force Be With Us, Please
Take Us to Your Mall
The Return Of The Lone Iguana
At Least This Place Sells T-Shirts

ANTHOLOGIES

FoxTrot: The Works
FoxTrot *en masse*
Enormously FoxTrot

WILDLY FOXTROT

BY BILL AMEND

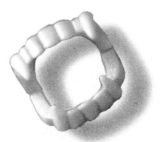

Andrews and McMeel
A Universal Press Syndicate Company
Kansas City

FOXTROT is distributed internationally by Universal Press Syndicate.

Library of Congress Catalog Card Number: 95-77575

ISBN: 0-8362-0416-6

Photos (pages 251-256) by Christina Craver

98 99 00 01 WEB 10 9 8 7 6 5 4

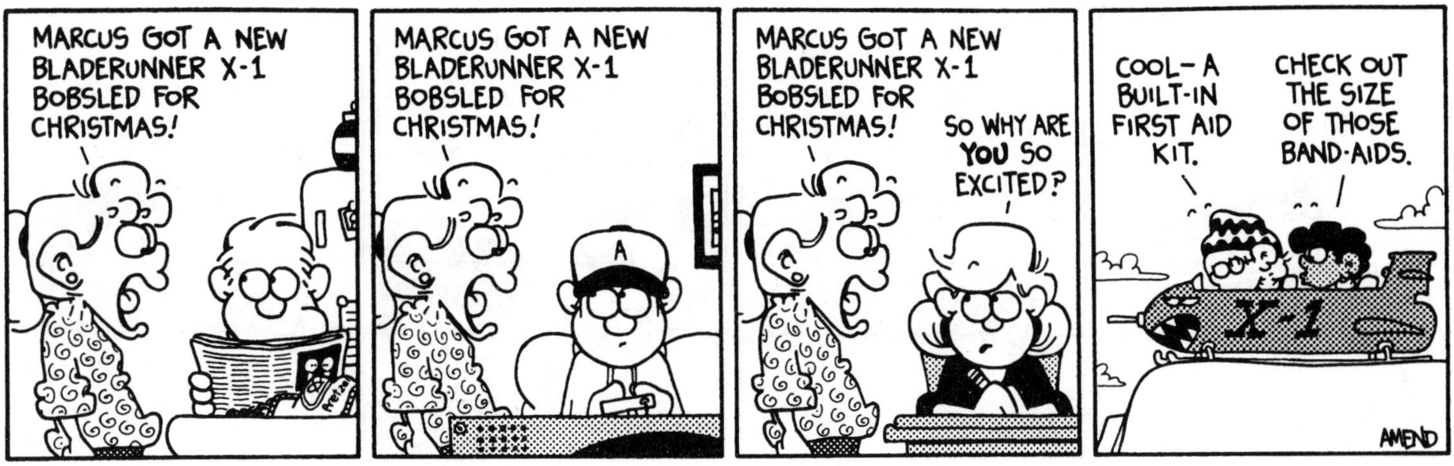
MARCUS GOT A NEW BLADERUNNER X-1 BOBSLED FOR CHRISTMAS!
MARCUS GOT A NEW BLADERUNNER X-1 BOBSLED FOR CHRISTMAS!
MARCUS GOT A NEW BLADERUNNER X-1 BOBSLED FOR CHRISTMAS!
SO WHY ARE **YOU** SO EXCITED?
COOL—A BUILT-IN FIRST AID KIT.
CHECK OUT THE SIZE OF THOSE BAND-AIDS.
X-1
AMEND

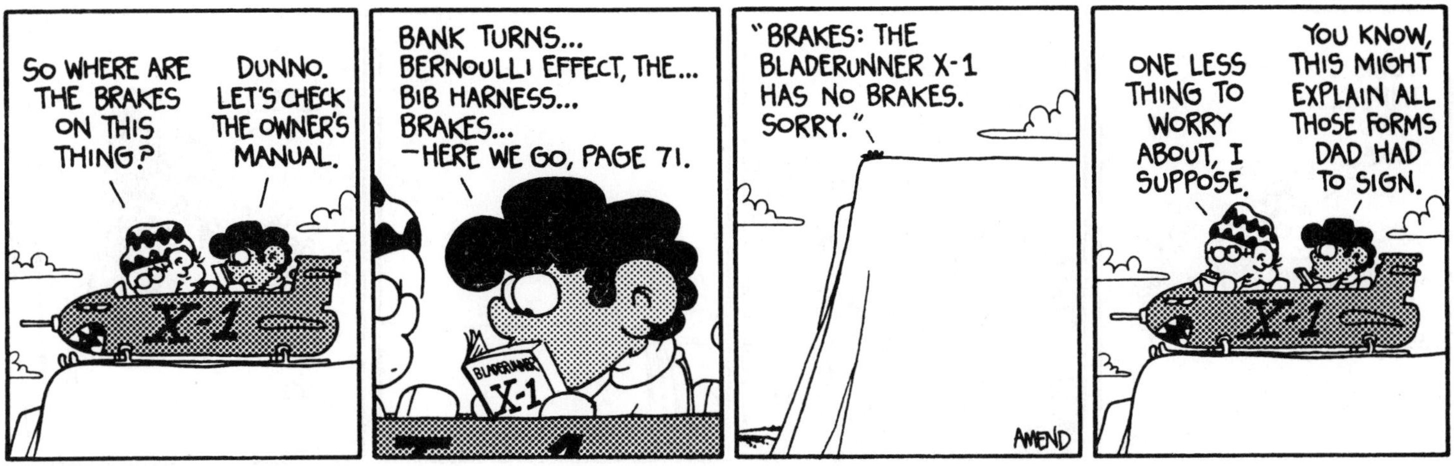
SO WHERE ARE THE BRAKES ON THIS THING?
DUNNO. LET'S CHECK THE OWNER'S MANUAL.
X-1
BANK TURNS... BERNOULLI EFFECT, THE... BIB HARNESS... BRAKES... —HERE WE GO, PAGE 71.
BLADERUNNER X-1
"BRAKES: THE BLADERUNNER X-1 HAS NO BRAKES. SORRY."
AMEND
ONE LESS THING TO WORRY ABOUT, I SUPPOSE.
YOU KNOW, THIS MIGHT EXPLAIN ALL THOSE FORMS DAD HAD TO SIGN.
X-1

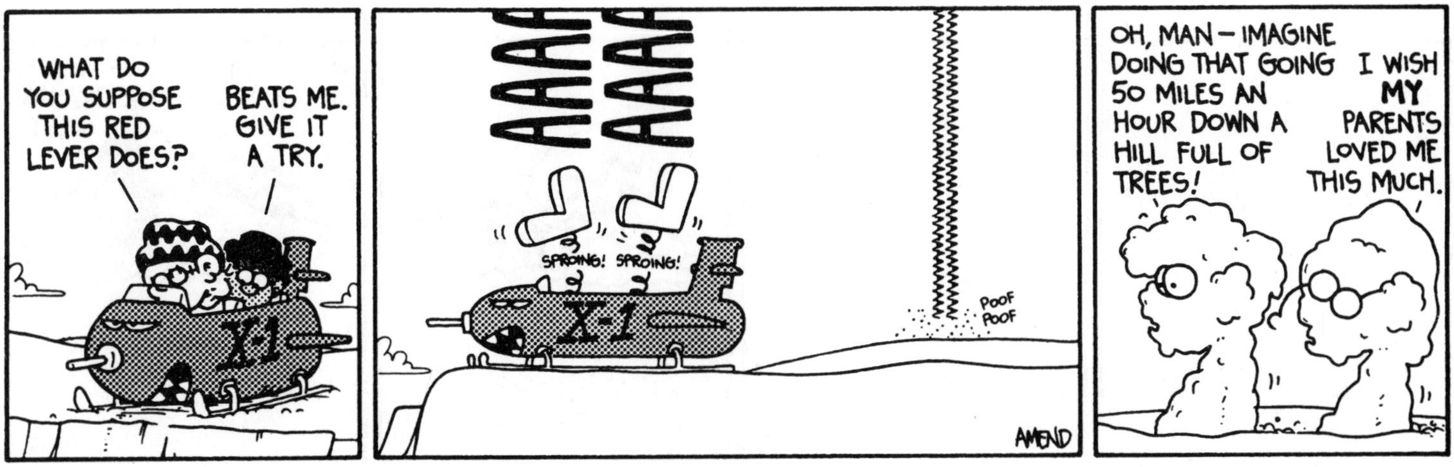
WHAT DO YOU SUPPOSE THIS RED LEVER DOES?
BEATS ME. GIVE IT A TRY.
X-1
SPROING! SPROING!
X-1
POOF POOF
AMEND
OH, MAN—IMAGINE DOING THAT GOING 50 MILES AN HOUR DOWN A HILL FULL OF TREES!
I WISH **MY** PARENTS LOVED ME THIS MUCH.

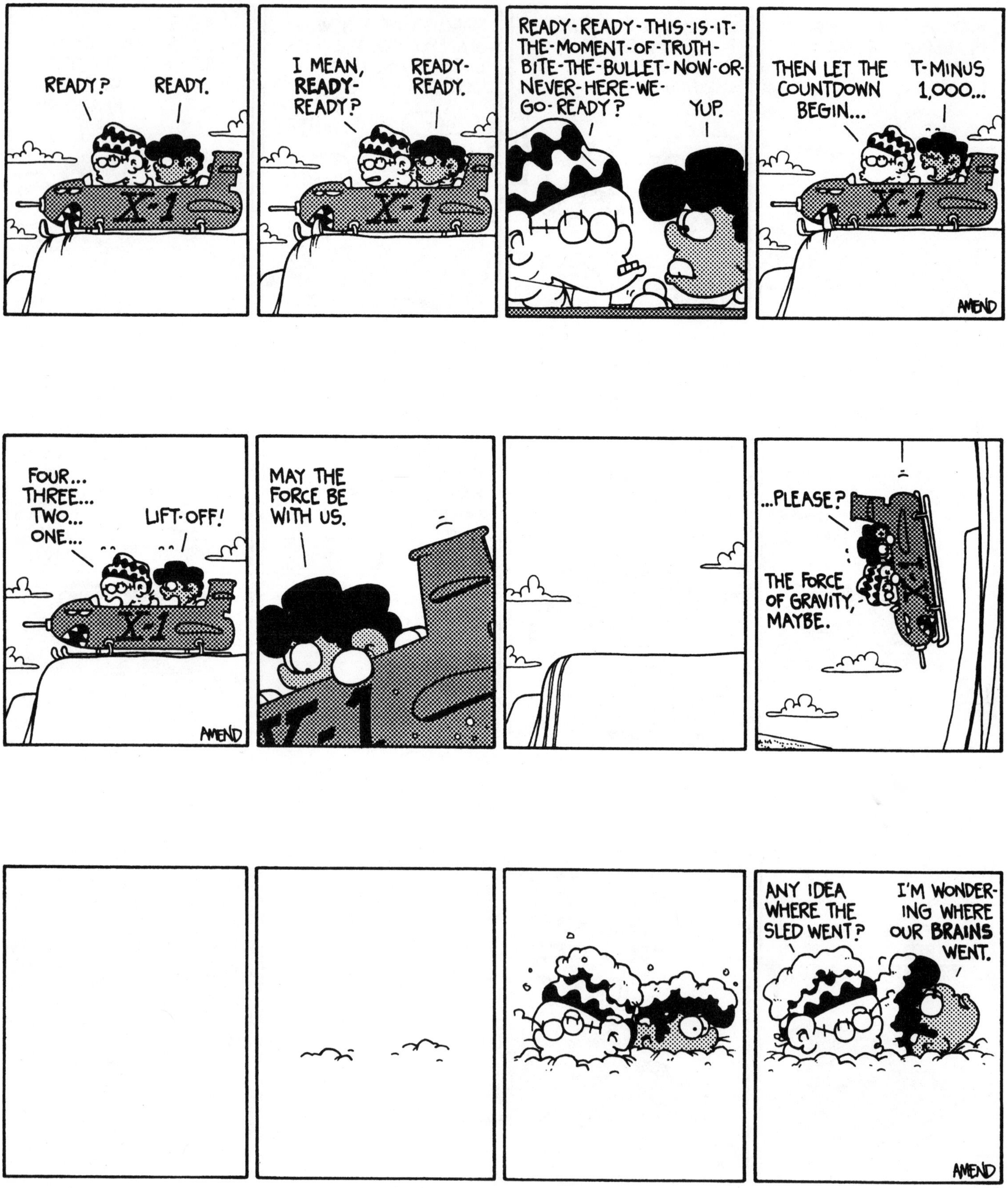

READY?
READY.
I MEAN, **READY**-READY?
READY-READY.
READY-READY-THIS-IS-IT-THE-MOMENT-OF-TRUTH-BITE-THE-BULLET-NOW-OR-NEVER-HERE-WE-GO-READY?
YUP.
THEN LET THE COUNTDOWN BEGIN...
T-MINUS 1,000...
X-1
AMEND
FOUR... THREE... TWO... ONE...
LIFT-OFF!
AMEND
MAY THE FORCE BE WITH US.
...PLEASE?
THE FORCE OF GRAVITY, MAYBE.
ANY IDEA WHERE THE SLED WENT?
I'M WONDERING WHERE OUR **BRAINS** WENT.
AMEND

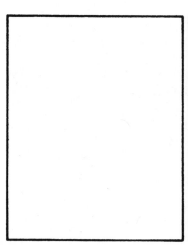

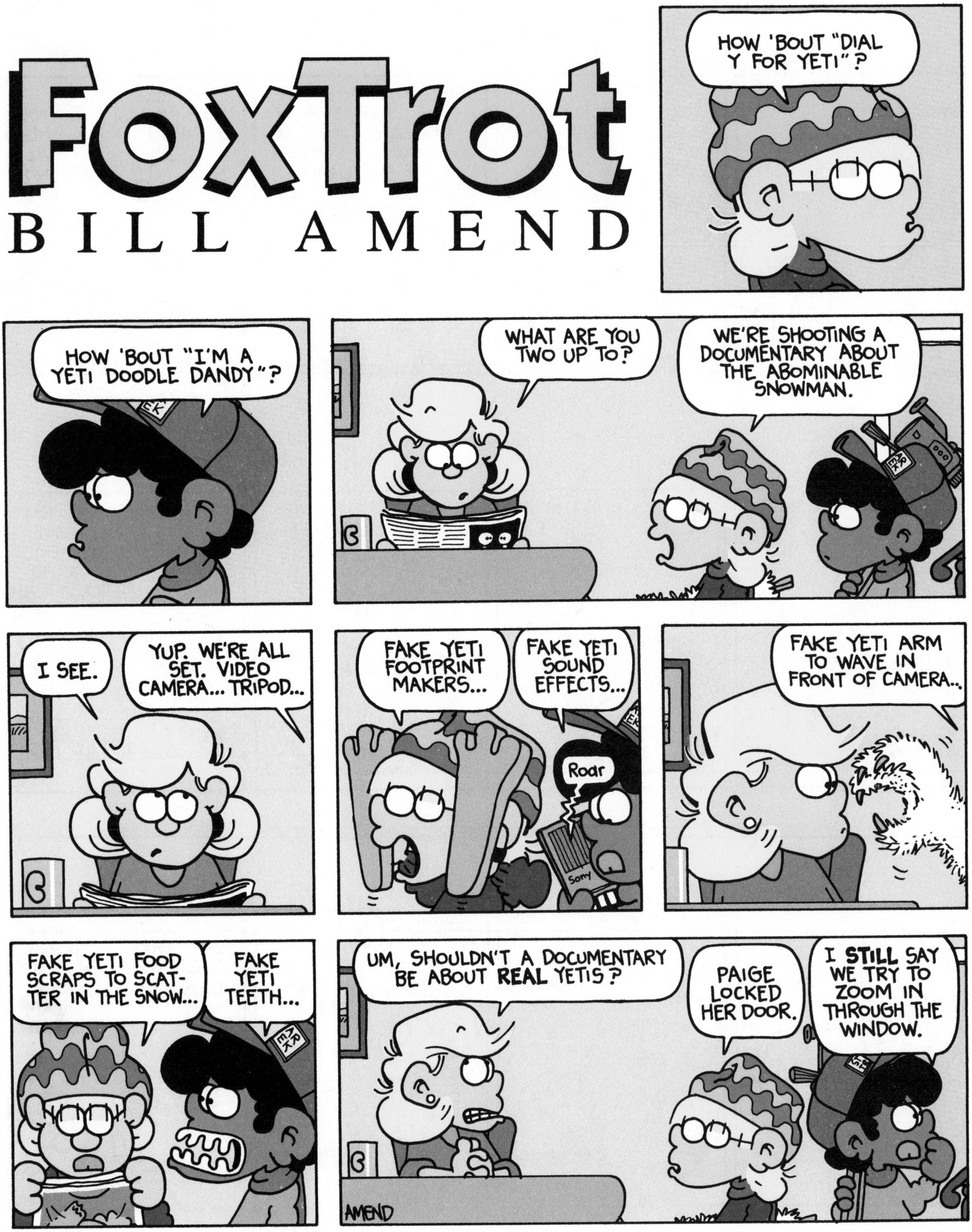
FoxTrot
BILL AMEND
HOW 'BOUT "DIAL Y FOR YETI"?
HOW 'BOUT "I'M A YETI DOODLE DANDY"?
WHAT ARE YOU TWO UP TO?
WE'RE SHOOTING A DOCUMENTARY ABOUT THE ABOMINABLE SNOWMAN.
I SEE.
YUP. WE'RE ALL SET. VIDEO CAMERA... TRIPOD...
FAKE YETI FOOTPRINT MAKERS...
FAKE YETI SOUND EFFECTS...
Roar
Sony
FAKE YETI ARM TO WAVE IN FRONT OF CAMERA...
FAKE YETI FOOD SCRAPS TO SCAT-TER IN THE SNOW...
FAKE YETI TEETH...
UM, SHOULDN'T A DOCUMENTARY BE ABOUT **REAL** YETIS?
PAIGE LOCKED HER DOOR.
I **STILL** SAY WE TRY TO ZOOM IN THROUGH THE WINDOW.
AMEND

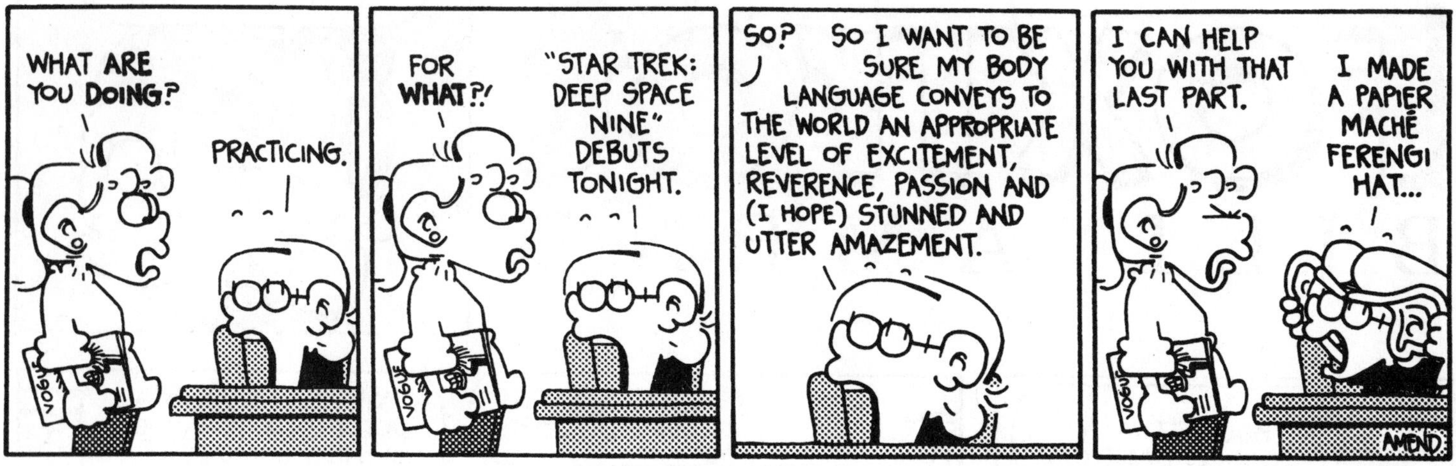
WHAT ARE YOU DOING?
PRACTICING.
FOR WHAT?!
"STAR TREK: DEEP SPACE NINE" DEBUTS TONIGHT.
SO?
SO I WANT TO BE SURE MY BODY LANGUAGE CONVEYS TO THE WORLD AN APPROPRIATE LEVEL OF EXCITEMENT, REVERENCE, PASSION AND (I HOPE) STUNNED AND UTTER AMAZEMENT.
I CAN HELP YOU WITH THAT LAST PART.
I MADE A PAPIER MACHÉ FERENGI HAT...
AMEND

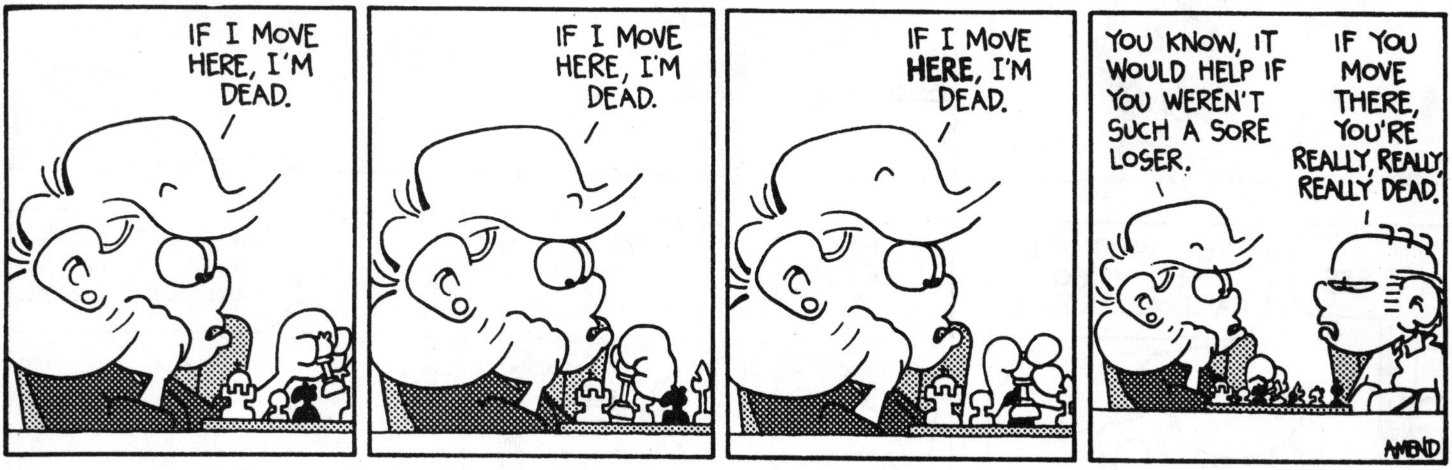
IF I MOVE HERE, I'M DEAD.
IF I MOVE HERE, I'M DEAD.
IF I MOVE HERE, I'M DEAD.
YOU KNOW, IT WOULD HELP IF YOU WEREN'T SUCH A SORE LOSER.
IF YOU MOVE THERE, YOU'RE REALLY, REALLY, REALLY DEAD.
AMEND

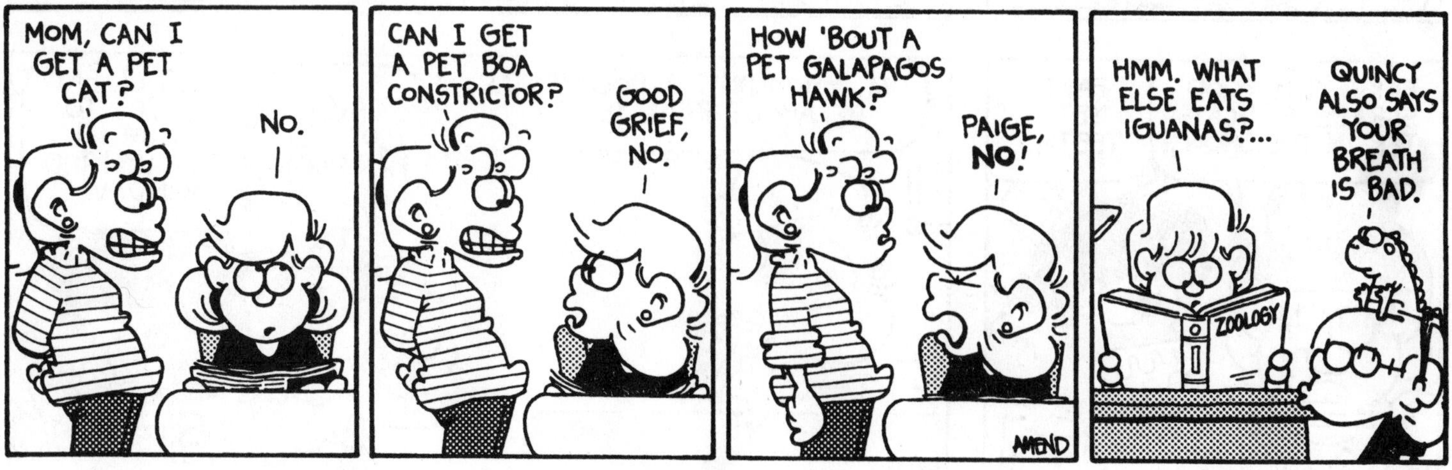
MOM, CAN I GET A PET CAT?
NO.
CAN I GET A PET BOA CONSTRICTOR?
GOOD GRIEF, NO.
HOW 'BOUT A PET GALAPAGOS HAWK?
PAIGE, NO!
AMEND
HMM. WHAT ELSE EATS IGUANAS?...
QUINCY ALSO SAYS YOUR BREATH IS BAD.
ZOOLOGY

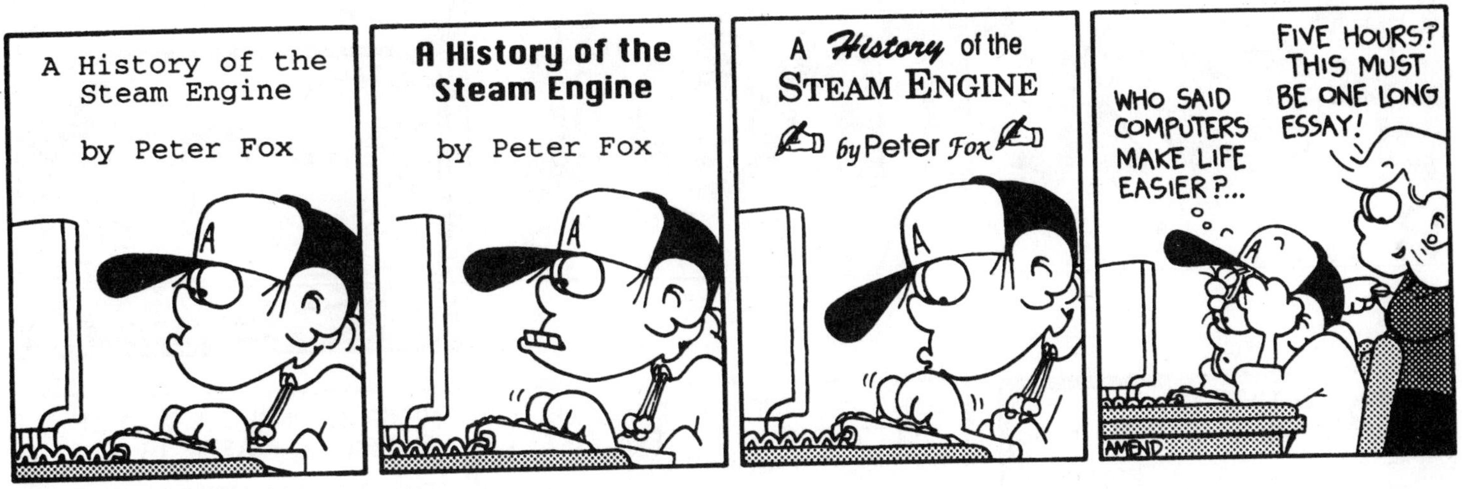
A History of the Steam Engine
by Peter Fox
A History of the Steam Engine
by Peter Fox
A History of the STEAM ENGINE
by Peter Fox
WHO SAID COMPUTERS MAKE LIFE EASIER?...
FIVE HOURS? THIS MUST BE ONE LONG ESSAY!
AMEND

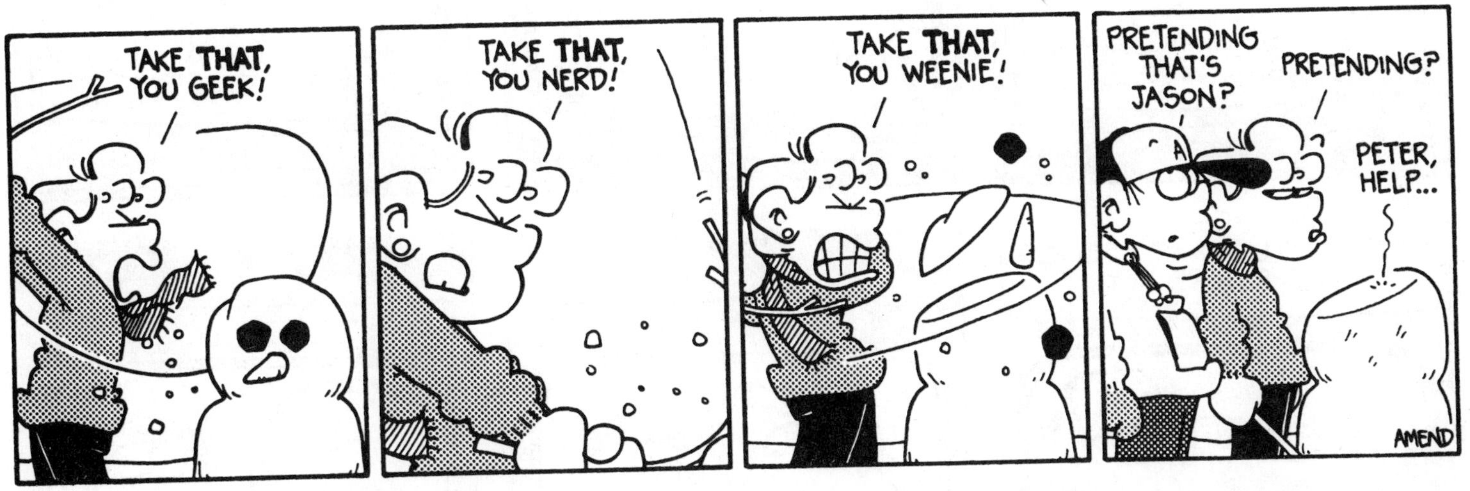
TAKE THAT, YOU GEEK!
TAKE THAT, YOU NERD!
TAKE THAT, YOU WEENIE!
PRETENDING THAT'S JASON?
PRETENDING?
PETER, HELP...
AMEND

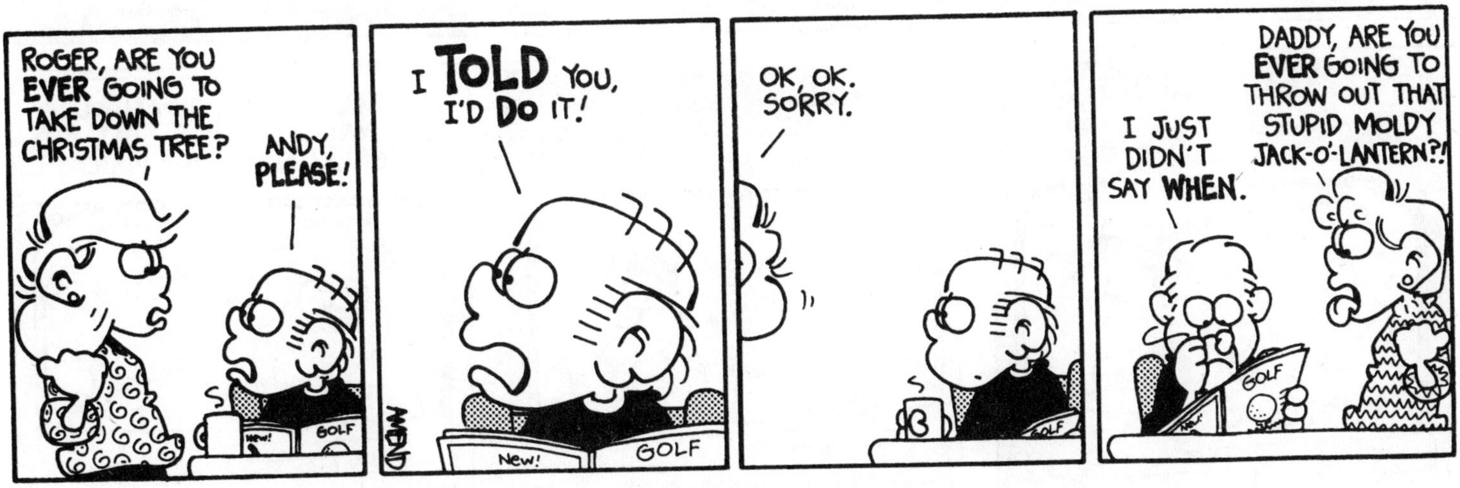
ROGER, ARE YOU EVER GOING TO TAKE DOWN THE CHRISTMAS TREE?
ANDY, PLEASE!
I TOLD YOU, I'D DO IT!
OK, OK. SORRY.
I JUST DIDN'T SAY WHEN.
DADDY, ARE YOU EVER GOING TO THROW OUT THAT STUPID MOLDY JACK-O'-LANTERN?!
AMEND

FoxTrot
BILL AMEND

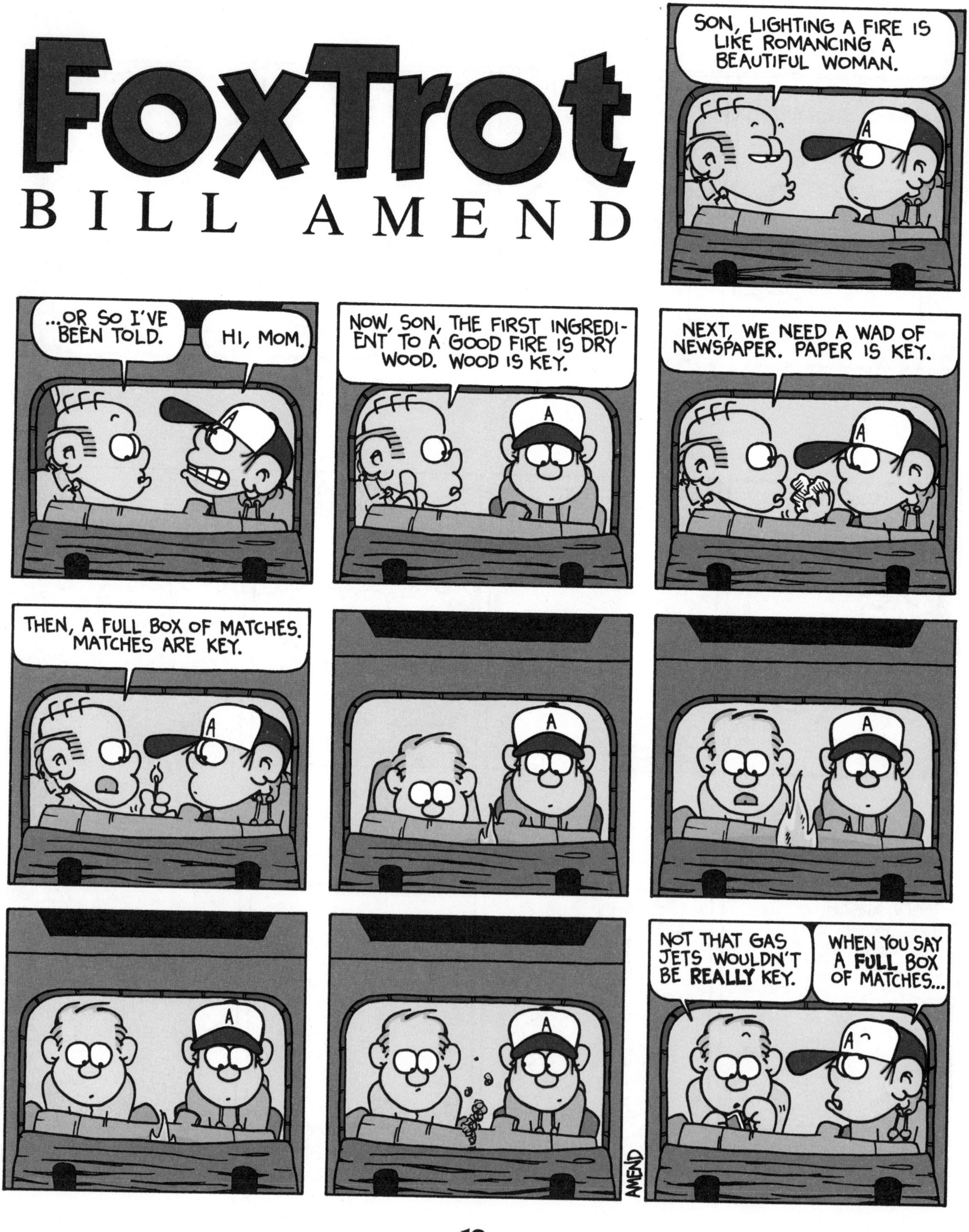
SON, LIGHTING A FIRE IS LIKE ROMANCING A BEAUTIFUL WOMAN.
...OR SO I'VE BEEN TOLD.
HI, MOM.
NOW, SON, THE FIRST INGREDIENT TO A GOOD FIRE IS DRY WOOD. WOOD IS KEY.
NEXT, WE NEED A WAD OF NEWSPAPER. PAPER IS KEY.
THEN, A FULL BOX OF MATCHES. MATCHES ARE KEY.
A
NOT THAT GAS JETS WOULDN'T BE **REALLY** KEY.
WHEN YOU SAY A **FULL** BOX OF MATCHES...
AMEND

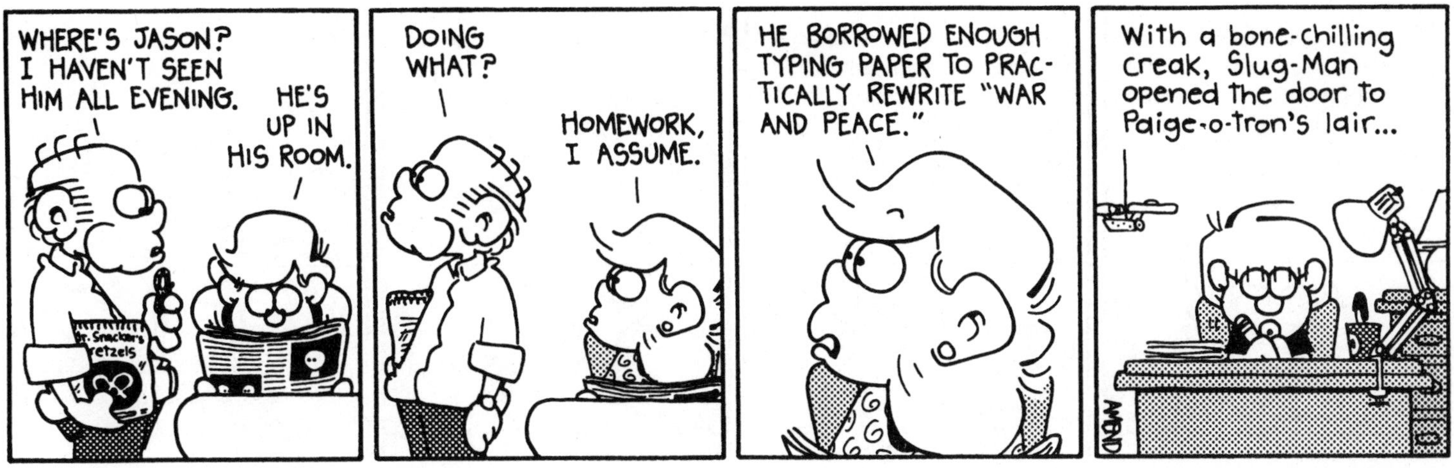
WHERE'S JASON? I HAVEN'T SEEN HIM ALL EVENING.
HE'S UP IN HIS ROOM.
DOING WHAT?
HOMEWORK, I ASSUME.
HE BORROWED ENOUGH TYPING PAPER TO PRAC-TICALLY REWRITE "WAR AND PEACE."
With a bone-chilling creak, Slug-Man opened the door to Paige-o-tron's lair...
AMEND

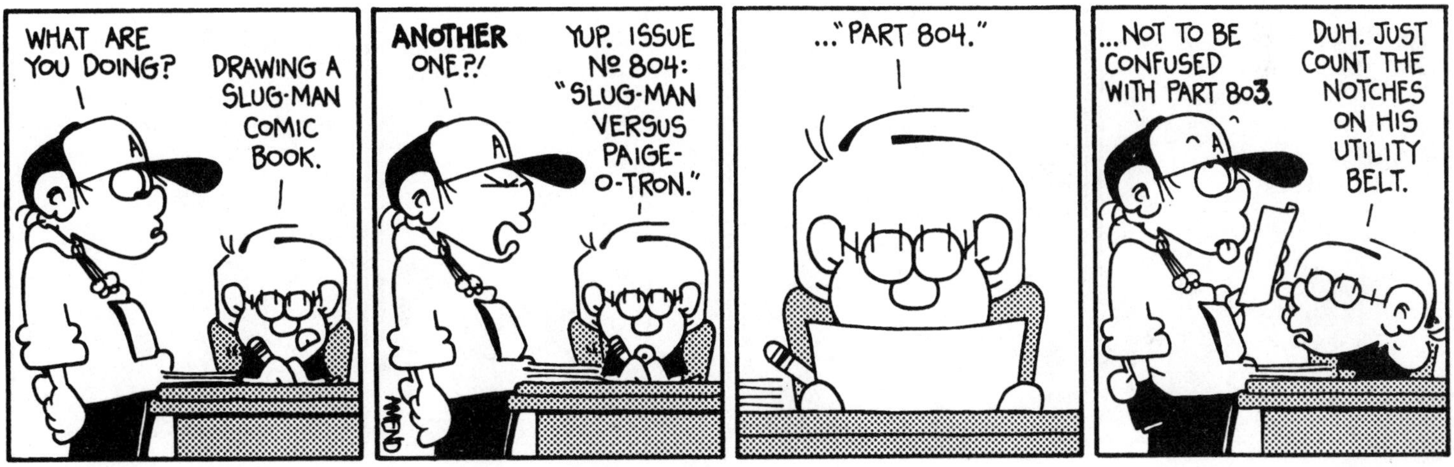
WHAT ARE YOU DOING?
DRAWING A SLUG-MAN COMIC BOOK.
AMEND
ANOTHER ONE?!
YUP. ISSUE № 804: "SLUG-MAN VERSUS PAIGE-O-TRON."
..."PART 804."
...NOT TO BE CONFUSED WITH PART 803.
DUH. JUST COUNT THE NOTCHES ON HIS UTILITY BELT.

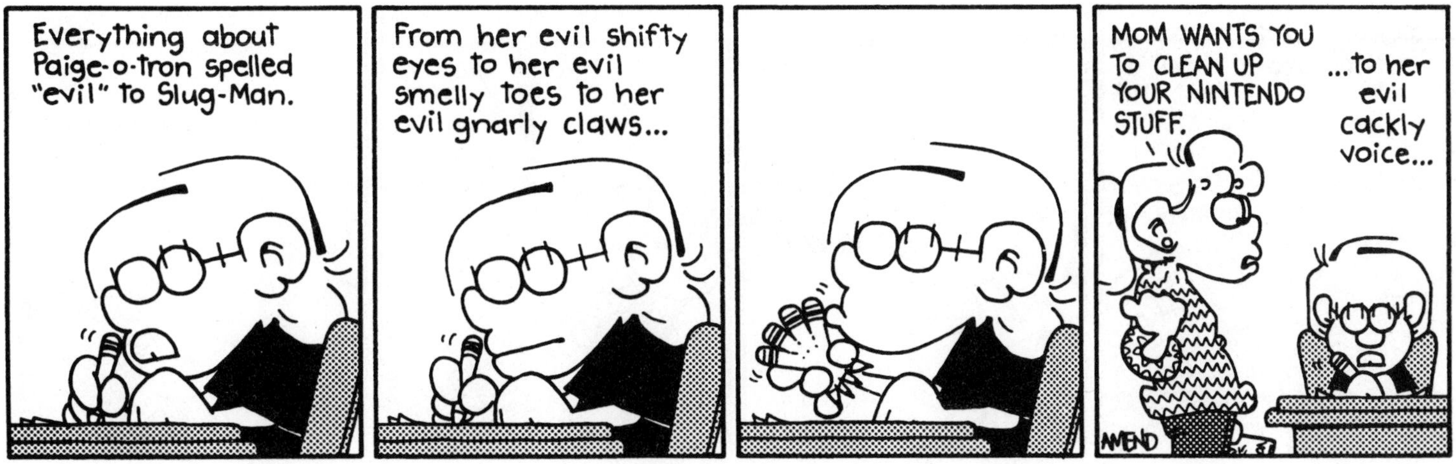
Everything about Paige-o-tron spelled "evil" to Slug-Man.
From her evil shifty eyes to her evil smelly toes to her evil gnarly claws...
MOM WANTS YOU TO CLEAN UP YOUR NINTENDO STUFF.
...to her evil cackly voice...
AMEND

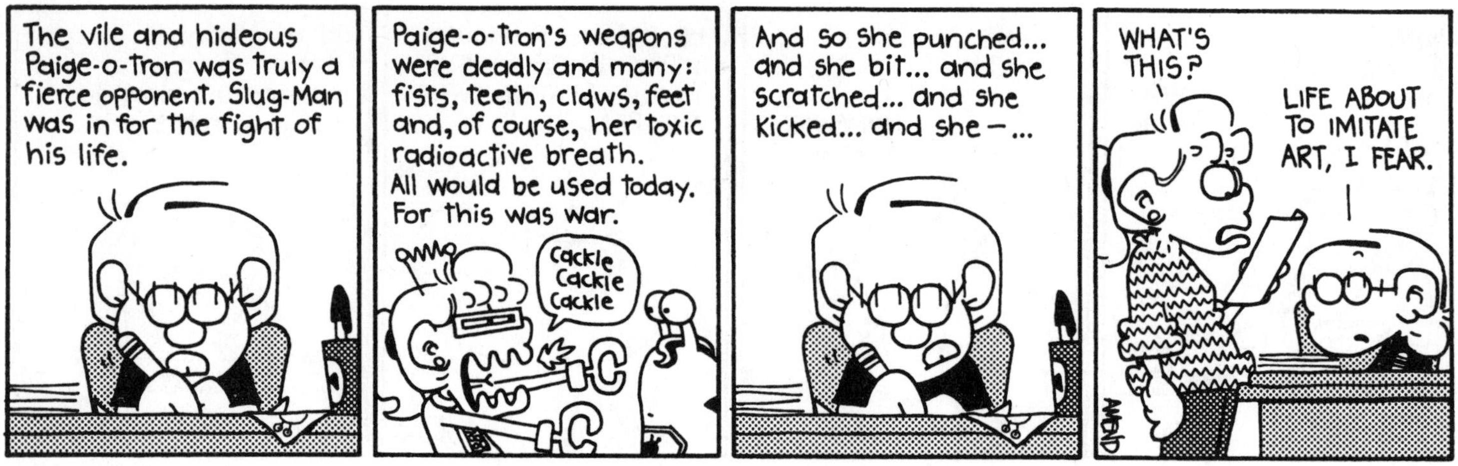
The vile and hideous Paige-o-tron was truly a fierce opponent. Slug-Man was in for the fight of his life.
Paige-o-tron's weapons were deadly and many: fists, teeth, claws, feet and, of course, her toxic radioactive breath. All would be used today. For this was war.
Cackle Cackle Cackle
And so she punched... and she bit... and she scratched... and she kicked... and she –...
WHAT'S THIS?
LIFE ABOUT TO IMITATE ART, I FEAR.
AMEND

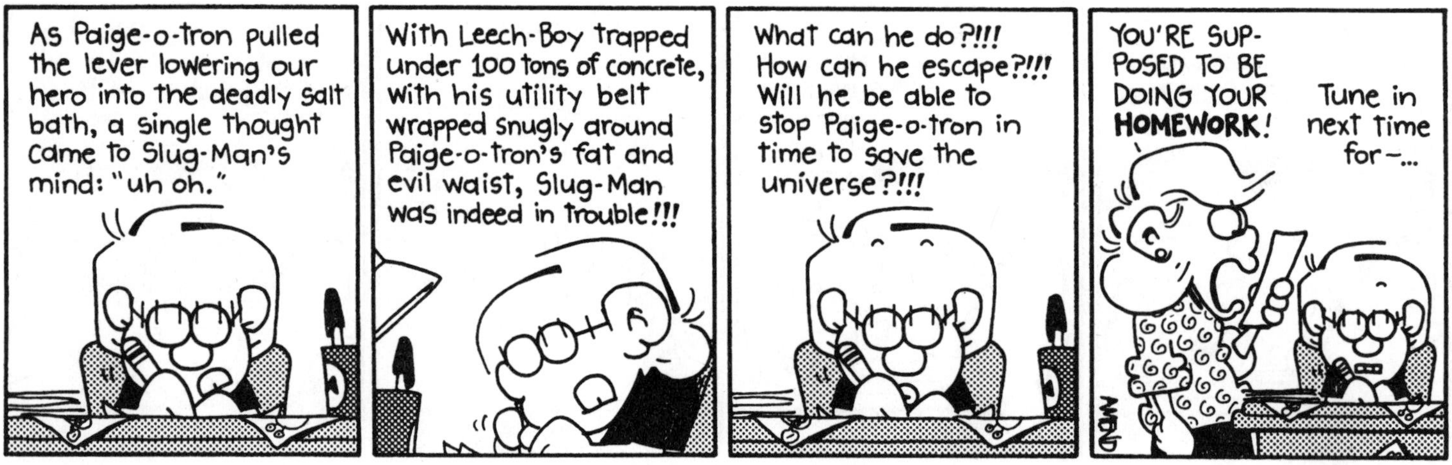
As Paige-o-tron pulled the lever lowering our hero into the deadly salt bath, a single thought came to Slug-Man's mind: "uh oh."
With Leech-Boy trapped under 100 tons of concrete, with his utility belt wrapped snugly around Paige-o-tron's fat and evil waist, Slug-Man was indeed in trouble!!!
What can he do?!!! How can he escape?!!! Will he be able to stop Paige-o-tron in time to save the universe?!!!
YOU'RE SUP-POSED TO BE DOING YOUR HOMEWORK!
Tune in next time for–...
AMEND

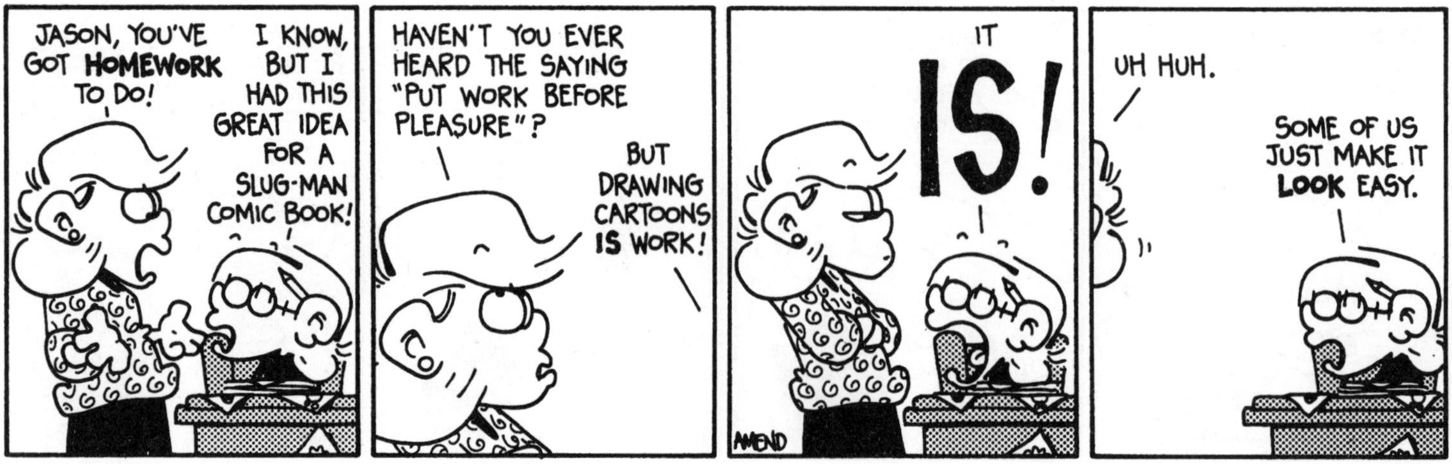
JASON, YOU'VE GOT HOMEWORK TO DO!
I KNOW, BUT I HAD THIS GREAT IDEA FOR A SLUG-MAN COMIC BOOK!
HAVEN'T YOU EVER HEARD THE SAYING "PUT WORK BEFORE PLEASURE"?
BUT DRAWING CARTOONS IS WORK!
IT IS!
AMEND
UH HUH.
SOME OF US JUST MAKE IT LOOK EASY.

FoxTrot

BILL AMEND

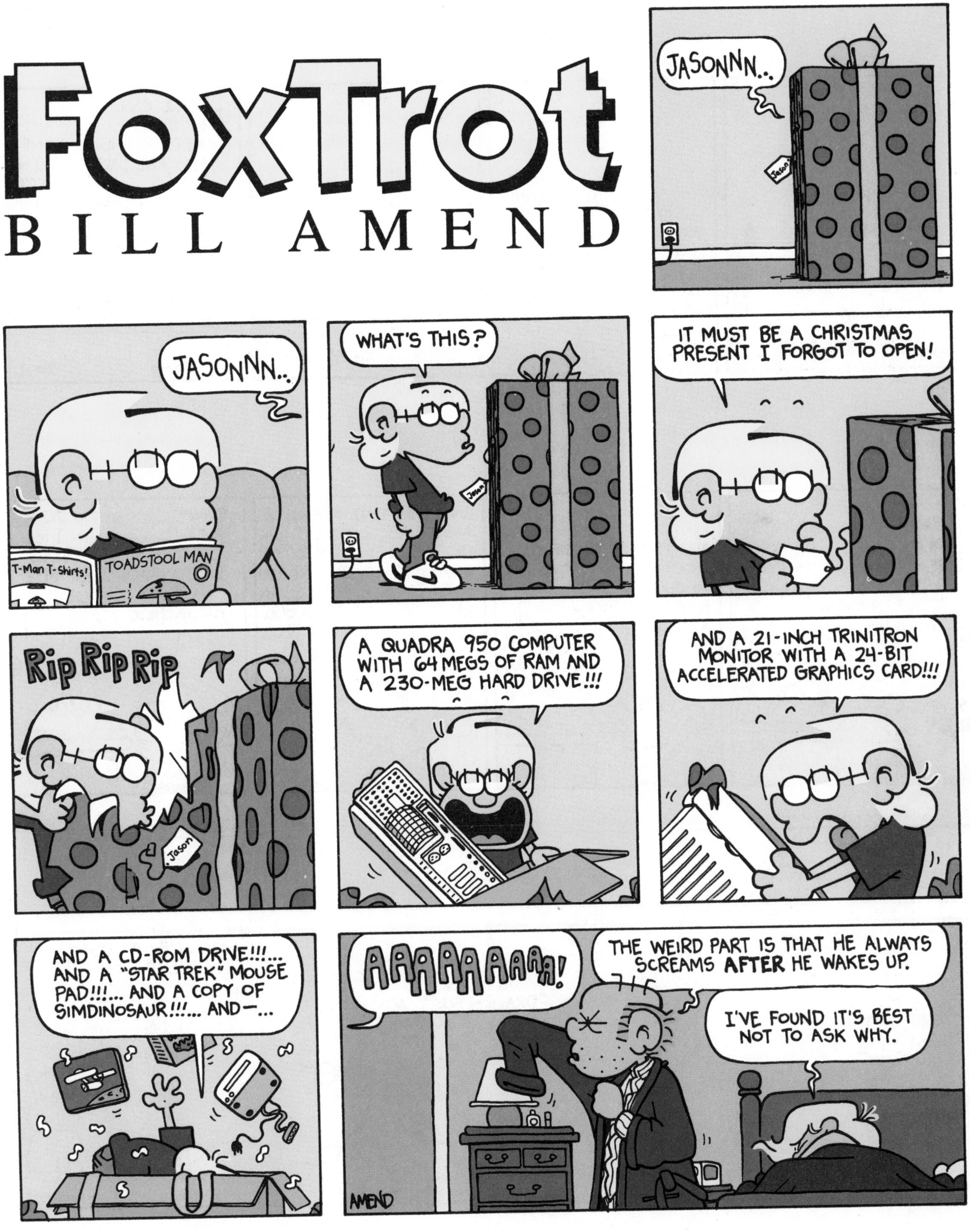
JASONNN...
JASONNN...
T-Man T-Shirts!
TOADSTOOL MAN
WHAT'S THIS?
IT MUST BE A CHRISTMAS PRESENT I FORGOT TO OPEN!
Rip Rip Rip
A QUADRA 950 COMPUTER WITH 64 MEGS OF RAM AND A 230-MEG HARD DRIVE!!!
AND A 21-INCH TRINITRON MONITOR WITH A 24-BIT ACCELERATED GRAPHICS CARD!!!
AND A CD-ROM DRIVE!!!... AND A "STAR TREK" MOUSE PAD!!!... AND A COPY OF SIMDINOSAUR!!!... AND—...
AAAAAAAAAA!
THE WEIRD PART IS THAT HE ALWAYS SCREAMS **AFTER** HE WAKES UP.
I'VE FOUND IT'S BEST NOT TO ASK WHY.
AMEND

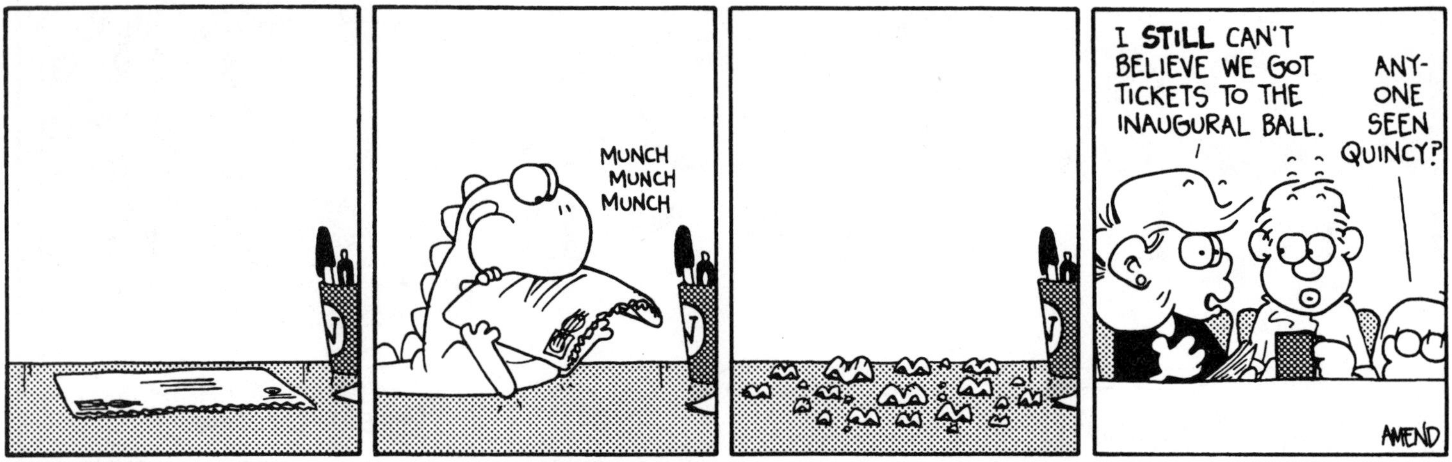
MUNCH
MUNCH
MUNCH
I **STILL** CAN'T BELIEVE WE GOT TICKETS TO THE INAUGURAL BALL.
ANY-ONE SEEN QUINCY?
AMEND

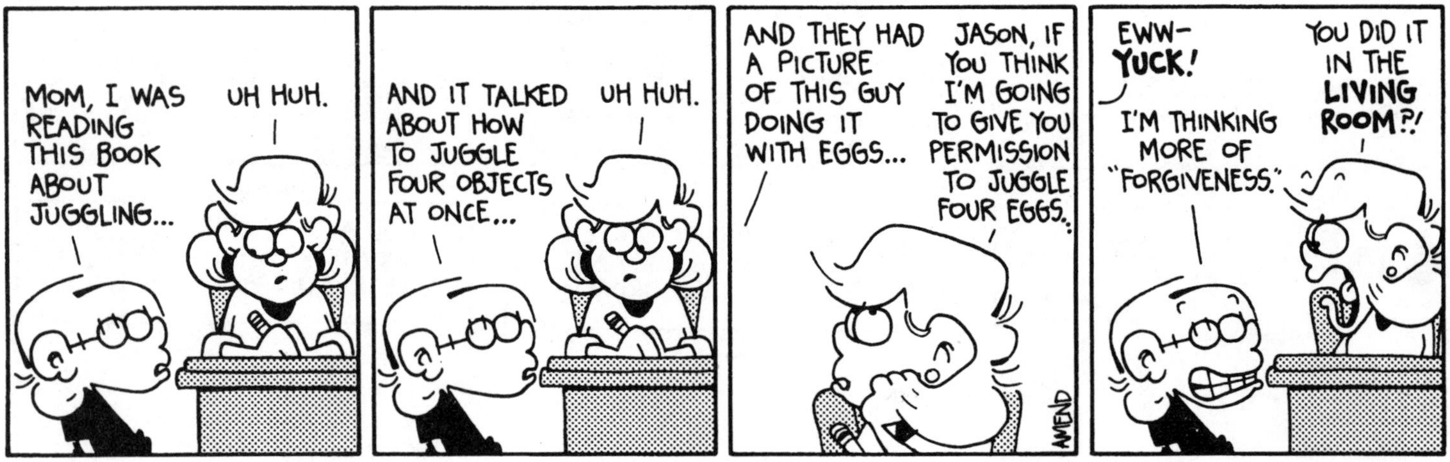
MOM, I WAS READING THIS BOOK ABOUT JUGGLING...
UH HUH.
AND IT TALKED ABOUT HOW TO JUGGLE FOUR OBJECTS AT ONCE...
UH HUH.
AND THEY HAD A PICTURE OF THIS GUY DOING IT WITH EGGS...
JASON, IF YOU THINK I'M GOING TO GIVE YOU PERMISSION TO JUGGLE FOUR EGGS...
AMEND
EWW- **YUCK!**
I'M THINKING MORE OF "FORGIVENESS."
YOU DID IT IN THE **LIVING ROOM**?!

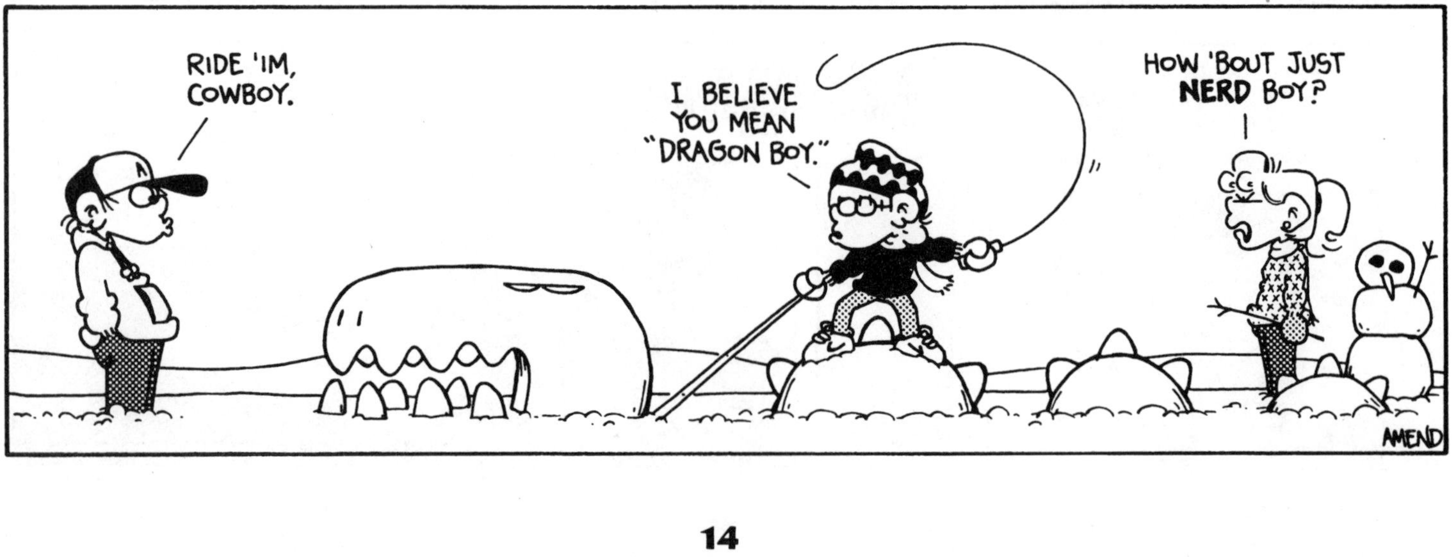
RIDE 'IM, COWBOY.
I BELIEVE YOU MEAN "DRAGON BOY."
HOW 'BOUT JUST **NERD** BOY?
AMEND

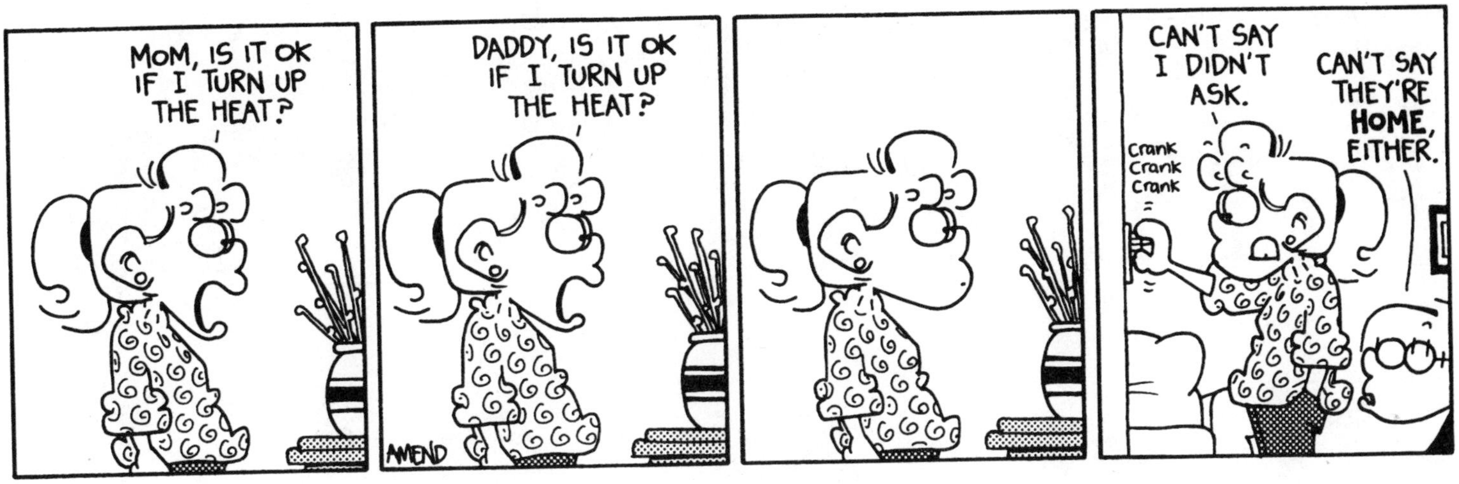
MOM, IS IT OK IF I TURN UP THE HEAT?
DADDY, IS IT OK IF I TURN UP THE HEAT?
AMEND
CAN'T SAY I DIDN'T ASK.
Crank Crank Crank
CAN'T SAY THEY'RE **HOME**, EITHER.

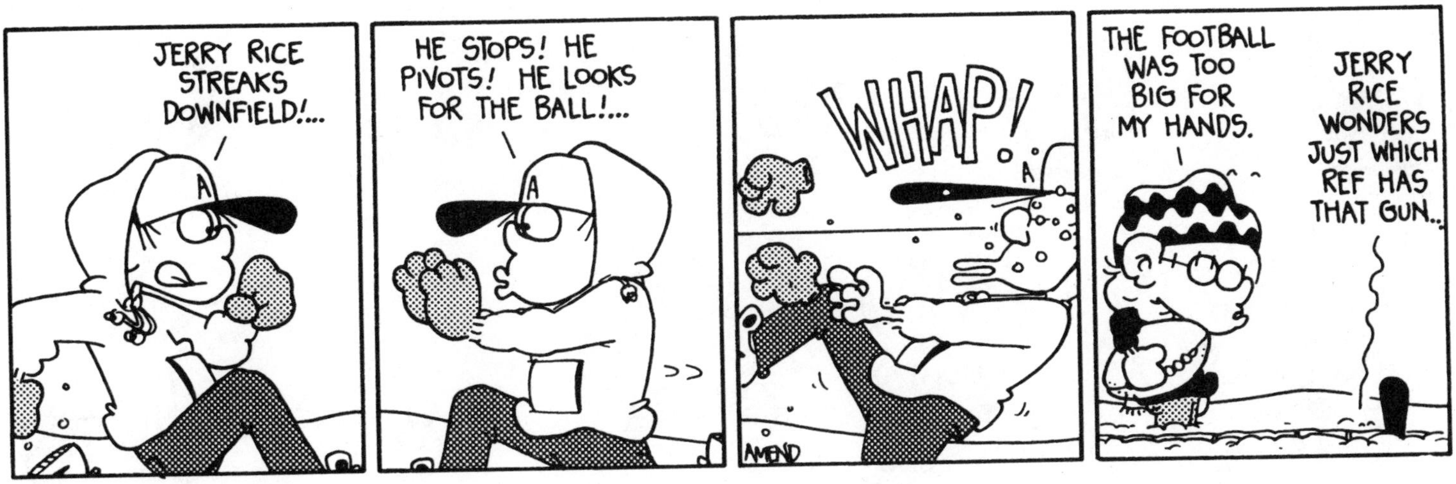
JERRY RICE STREAKS DOWNFIELD!...
HE STOPS! HE PIVOTS! HE LOOKS FOR THE BALL!...
WHAP!
AMEND
THE FOOTBALL WAS TOO BIG FOR MY HANDS.
JERRY RICE WONDERS JUST WHICH REF HAS THAT GUN...

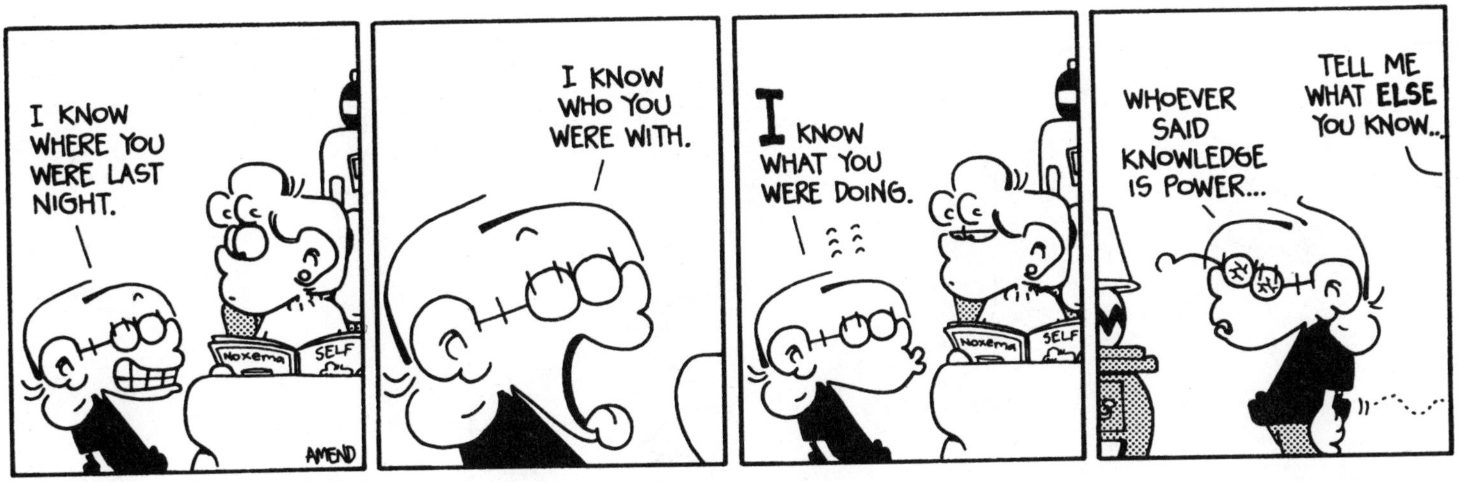
I KNOW WHERE YOU WERE LAST NIGHT.
Noxema
SELF
AMEND
I KNOW WHO YOU WERE WITH.
I KNOW WHAT YOU WERE DOING.
WHOEVER SAID KNOWLEDGE IS POWER...
TELL ME WHAT **ELSE** YOU KNOW...

FoxTrot
BILL AMEND

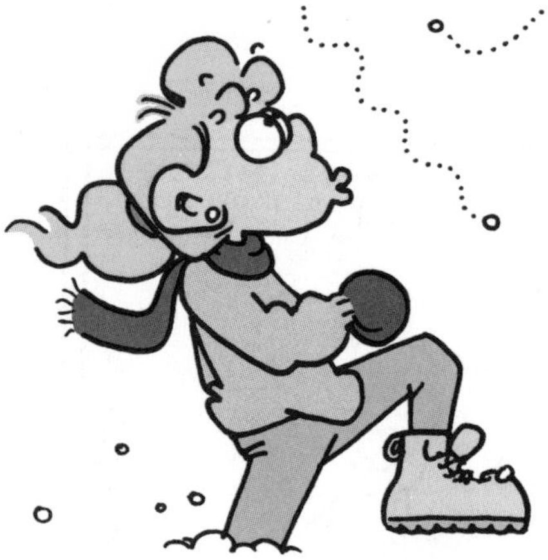

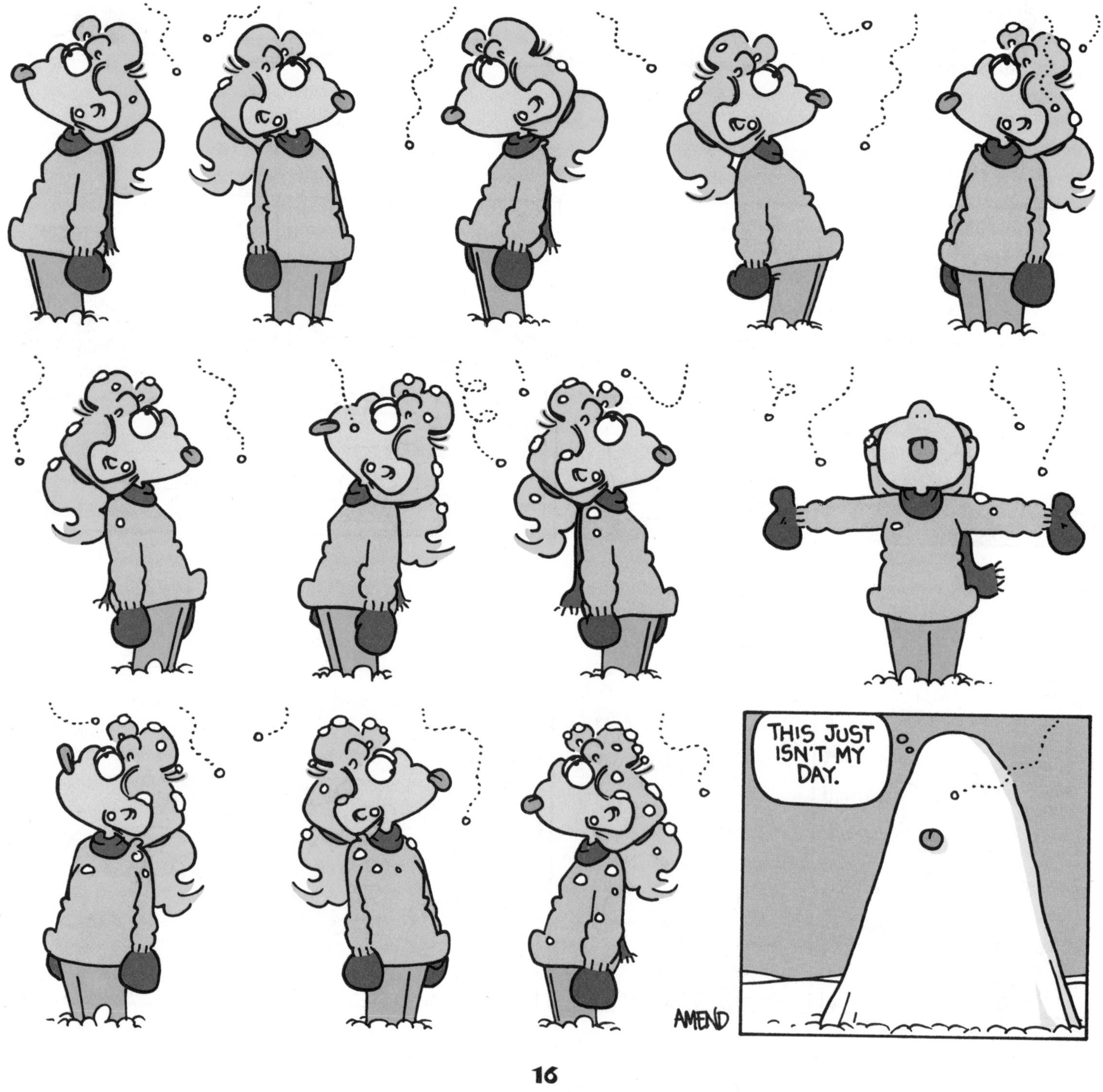
THIS JUST ISN'T MY DAY.
AMEND

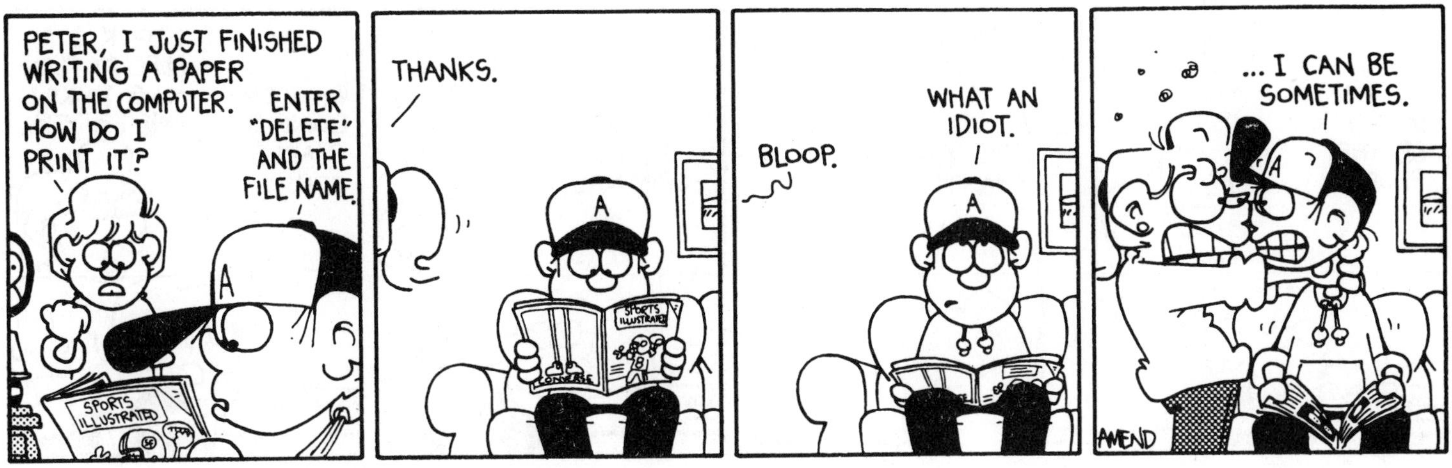

PETER, I JUST FINISHED WRITING A PAPER ON THE COMPUTER. HOW DO I PRINT IT?
ENTER "DELETE" AND THE FILE NAME.
SPORTS ILLUSTRATED
THANKS.
SPORTS ILLUSTRATED
BLOOP.
WHAT AN IDIOT.
...I CAN BE SOMETIMES.
AMEND

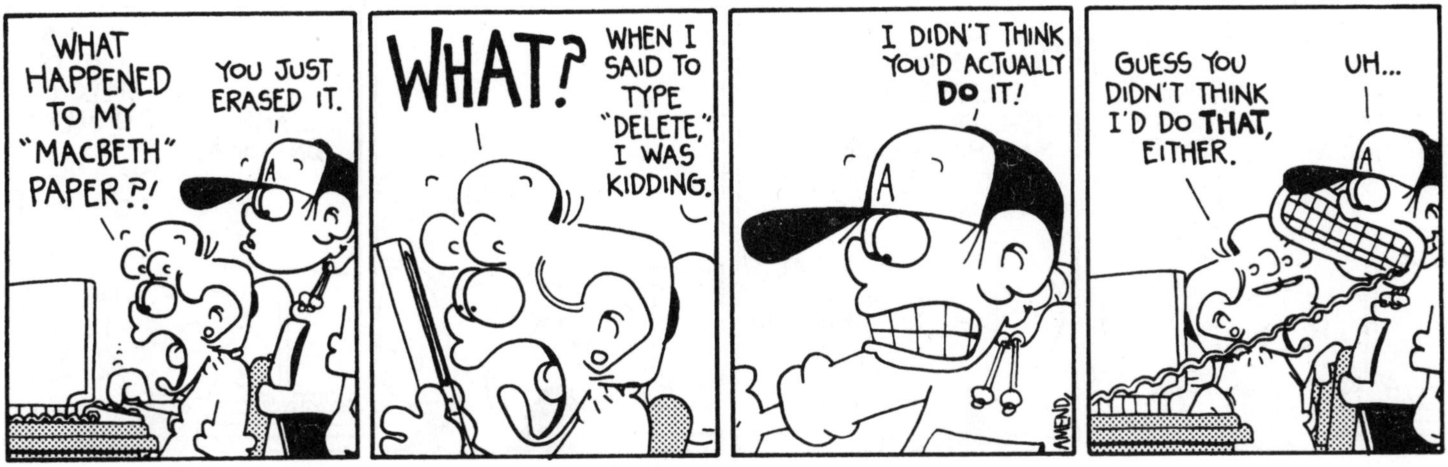

WHAT HAPPENED TO MY "MACBETH" PAPER?!
YOU JUST ERASED IT.
WHAT?
WHEN I SAID TO TYPE "DELETE," I WAS KIDDING.
I DIDN'T THINK YOU'D ACTUALLY **DO** IT!
AMEND
GUESS YOU DIDN'T THINK I'D DO **THAT**, EITHER.
UH...

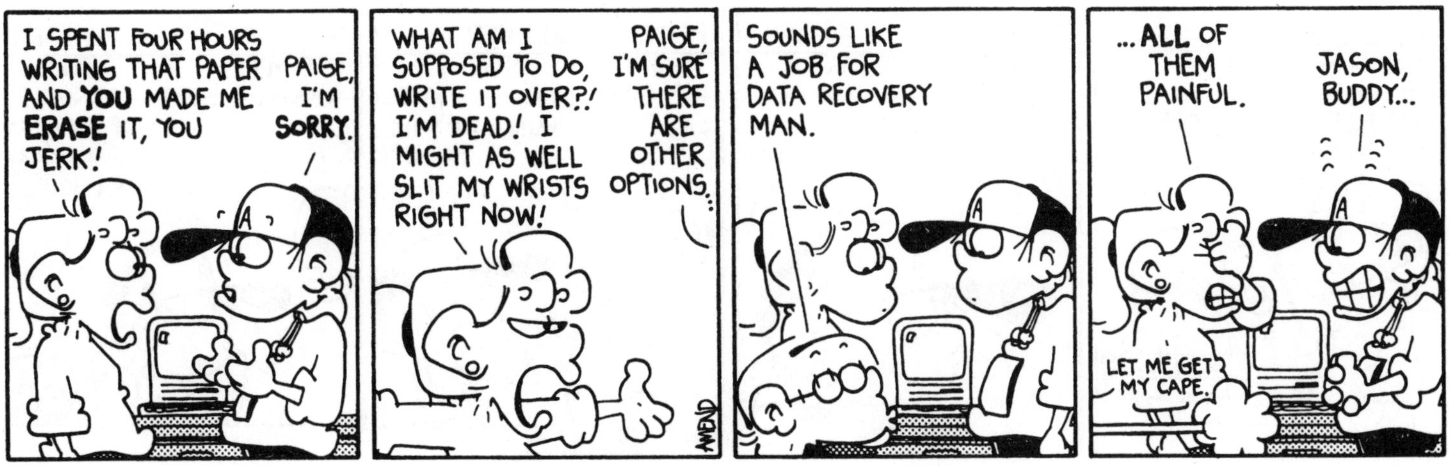

I SPENT FOUR HOURS WRITING THAT PAPER AND **YOU** MADE ME **ERASE** IT, YOU JERK!
PAIGE, I'M **SORRY**.
WHAT AM I SUPPOSED TO DO, WRITE IT OVER?! I'M DEAD! I MIGHT AS WELL SLIT MY WRISTS RIGHT NOW!
PAIGE, I'M SURE THERE ARE OTHER OPTIONS.
AMEND
SOUNDS LIKE A JOB FOR DATA RECOVERY MAN.
...**ALL** OF THEM PAINFUL.
JASON, BUDDY...
LET ME GET MY CAPE.

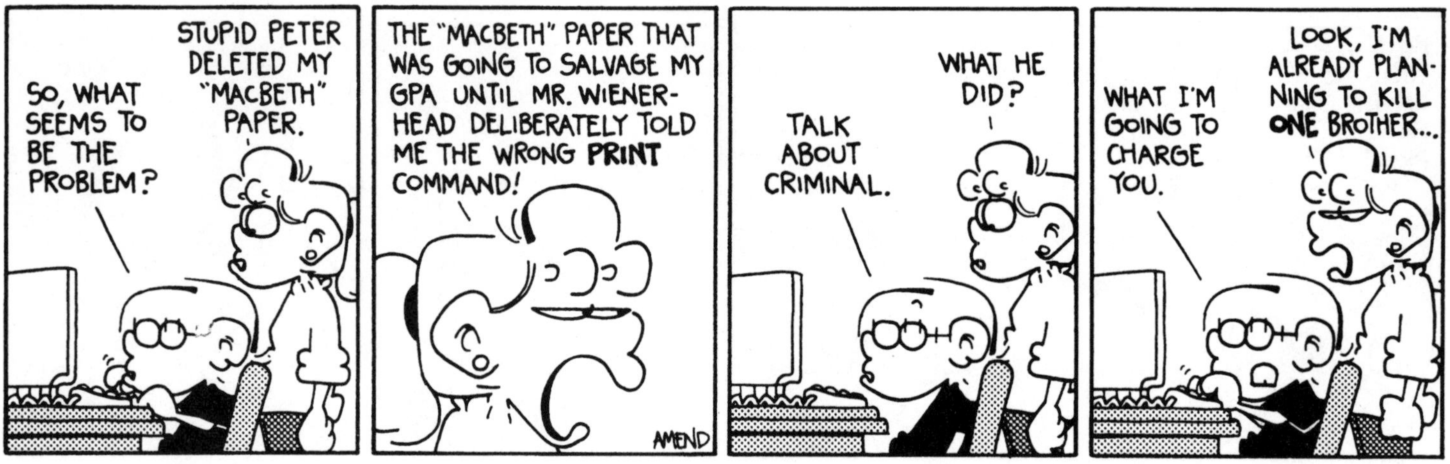
SO, WHAT SEEMS TO BE THE PROBLEM?
STUPID PETER DELETED MY "MACBETH" PAPER.
THE "MACBETH" PAPER THAT WAS GOING TO SALVAGE MY GPA UNTIL MR. WIENER-HEAD DELIBERATELY TOLD ME THE WRONG **PRINT** COMMAND!
AMEND
TALK ABOUT CRIMINAL.
WHAT HE DID?
WHAT I'M GOING TO CHARGE YOU.
LOOK, I'M ALREADY PLAN-NING TO KILL **ONE** BROTHER...

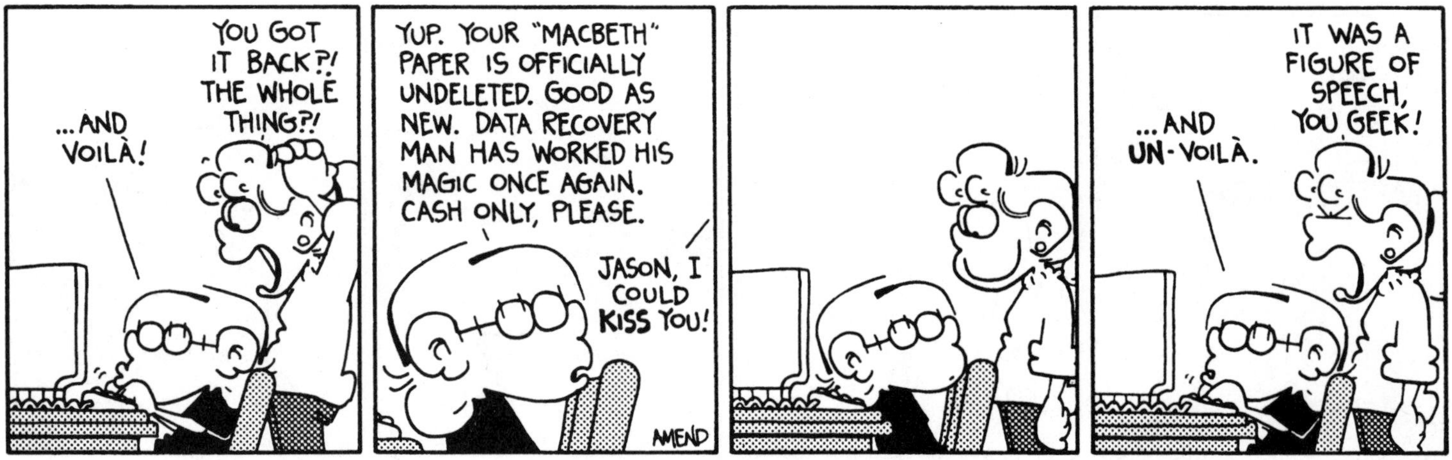
...AND VOILÀ!
YOU GOT IT BACK?! THE WHOLE THING?!
YUP. YOUR "MACBETH" PAPER IS OFFICIALLY UNDELETED. GOOD AS NEW. DATA RECOVERY MAN HAS WORKED HIS MAGIC ONCE AGAIN. CASH ONLY, PLEASE.
JASON, I COULD **KISS** YOU!
AMEND
...AND **UN**-VOILÀ.
IT WAS A FIGURE OF SPEECH, YOU GEEK!

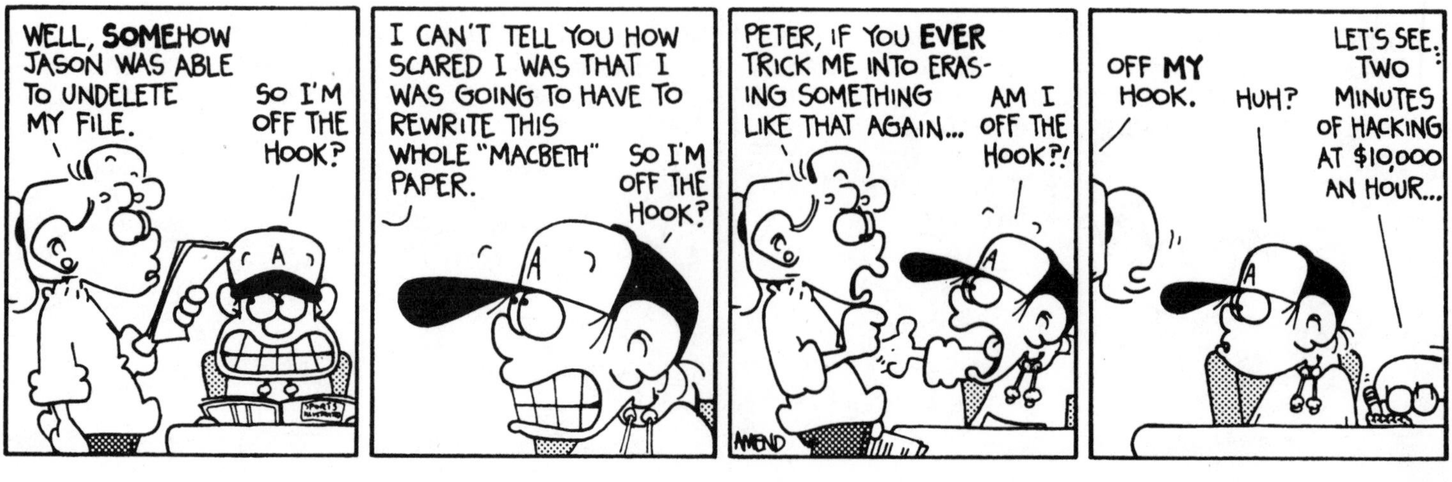
WELL, **SOME**HOW JASON WAS ABLE TO UNDELETE MY FILE.
SO I'M OFF THE HOOK?
I CAN'T TELL YOU HOW SCARED I WAS THAT I WAS GOING TO HAVE TO REWRITE THIS WHOLE "MACBETH" PAPER.
SO I'M OFF THE HOOK?
PETER, IF YOU **EVER** TRICK ME INTO ERAS-ING SOMETHING LIKE THAT AGAIN...
AM I OFF THE HOOK?!
AMEND
OFF **MY** HOOK.
HUH?
LET'S SEE. TWO MINUTES OF HACKING AT $10,000 AN HOUR...

FoxTrot

BILL AMEND

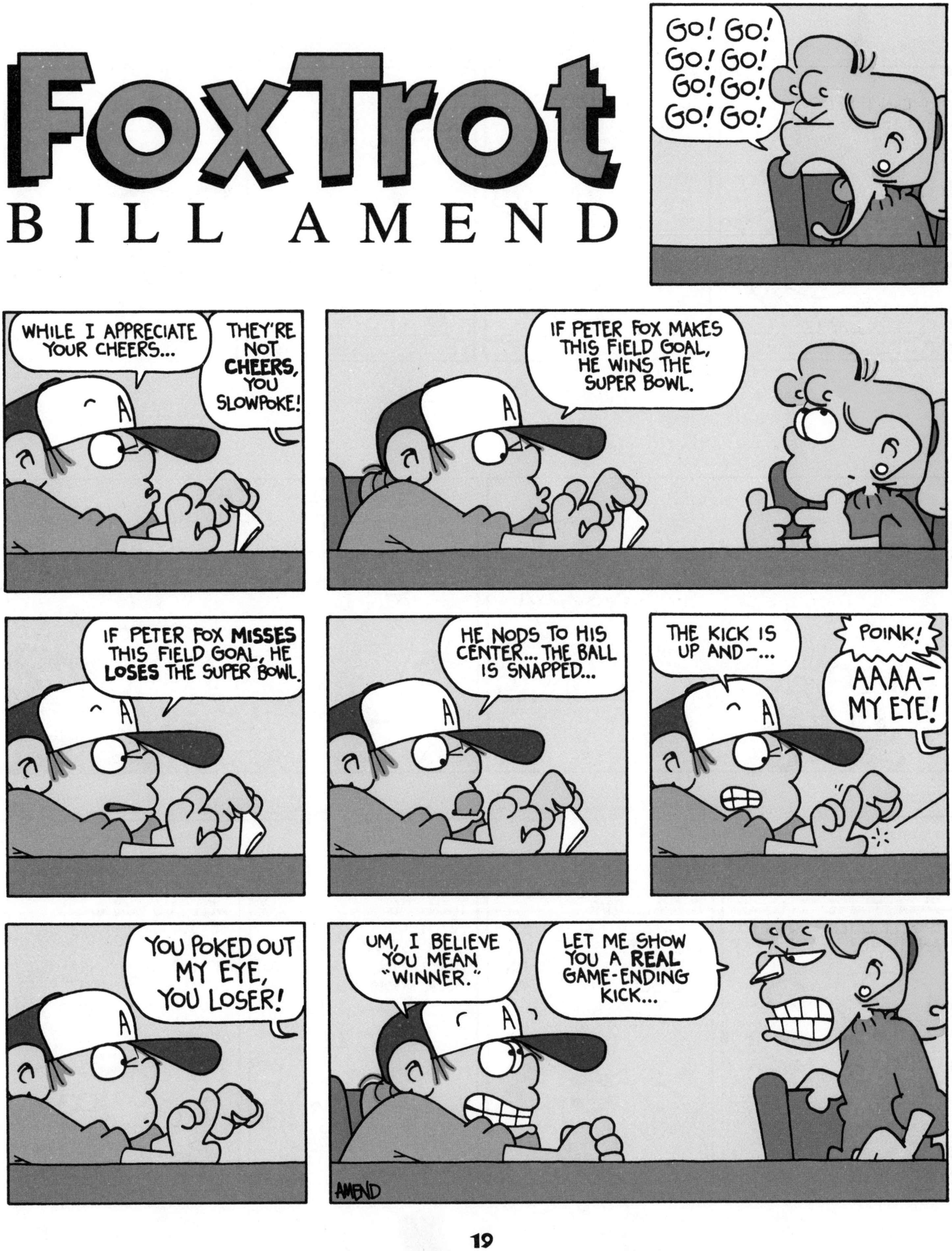

GO! GO! GO! GO! GO! GO! GO! GO!
WHILE I APPRECIATE YOUR CHEERS...
THEY'RE NOT **CHEERS**, YOU SLOWPOKE!
IF PETER FOX MAKES THIS FIELD GOAL, HE WINS THE SUPER BOWL.
IF PETER FOX **MISSES** THIS FIELD GOAL, HE **LOSES** THE SUPER BOWL.
HE NODS TO HIS CENTER... THE BALL IS SNAPPED...
THE KICK IS UP AND–...
POINK!
AAAA– MY EYE!
YOU POKED OUT MY EYE, YOU LOSER!
UM, I BELIEVE YOU MEAN "WINNER."
LET ME SHOW YOU A **REAL** GAME-ENDING KICK...
AMEND

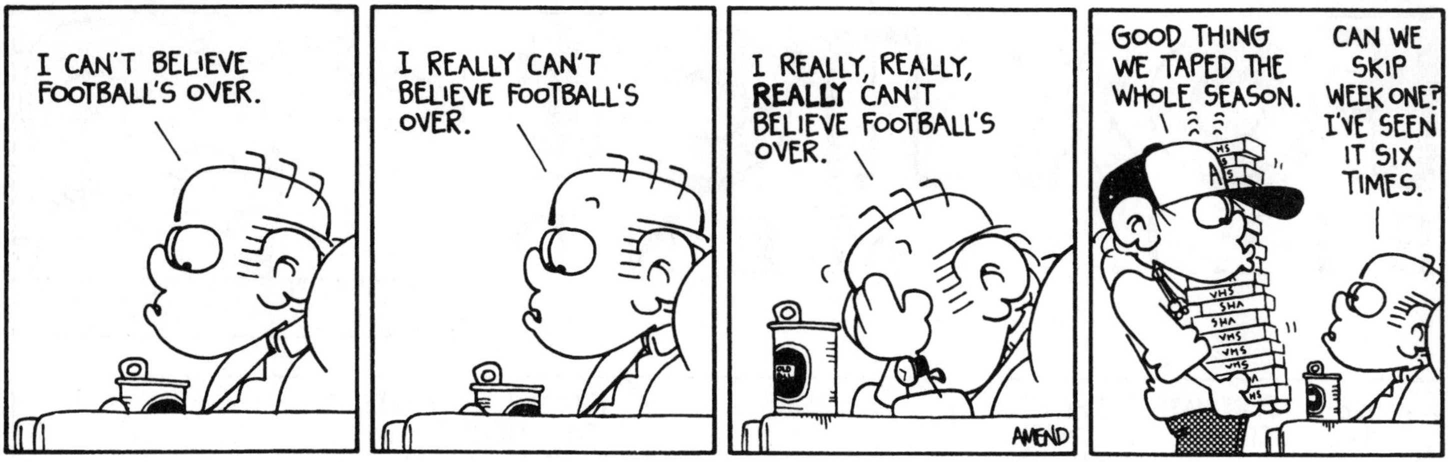
I CAN'T BELIEVE FOOTBALL'S OVER.
I REALLY CAN'T BELIEVE FOOTBALL'S OVER.
I REALLY, REALLY, **REALLY** CAN'T BELIEVE FOOTBALL'S OVER.
AMEND
GOOD THING WE TAPED THE WHOLE SEASON.
CAN WE SKIP WEEK ONE? I'VE SEEN IT SIX TIMES.

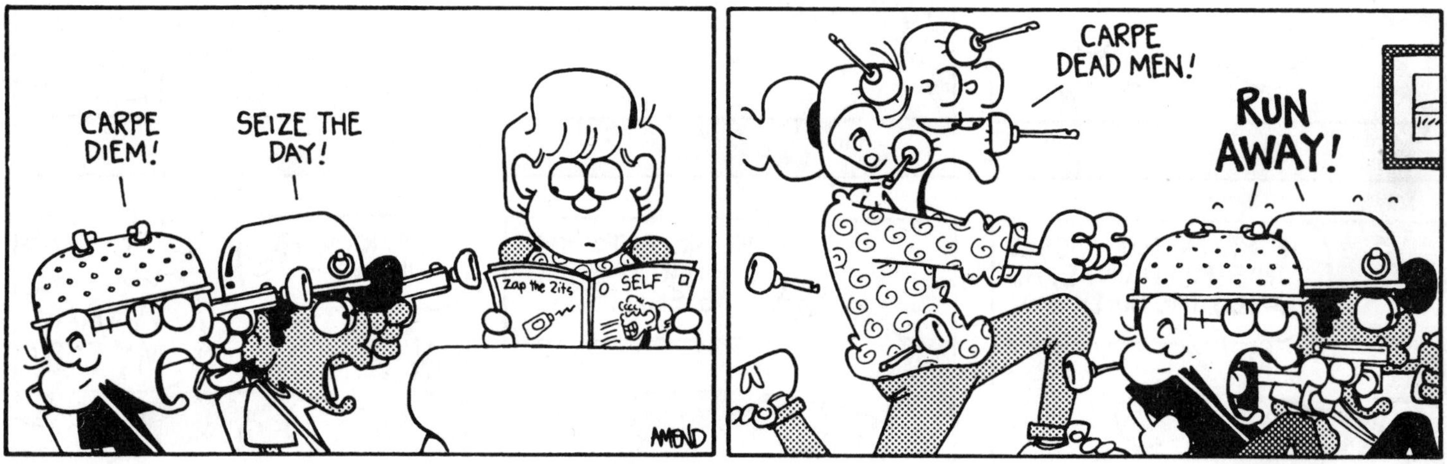
CARPE DIEM!
SEIZE THE DAY!
Zap the Zits
SELF
AMEND
CARPE DEAD MEN!
RUN AWAY!

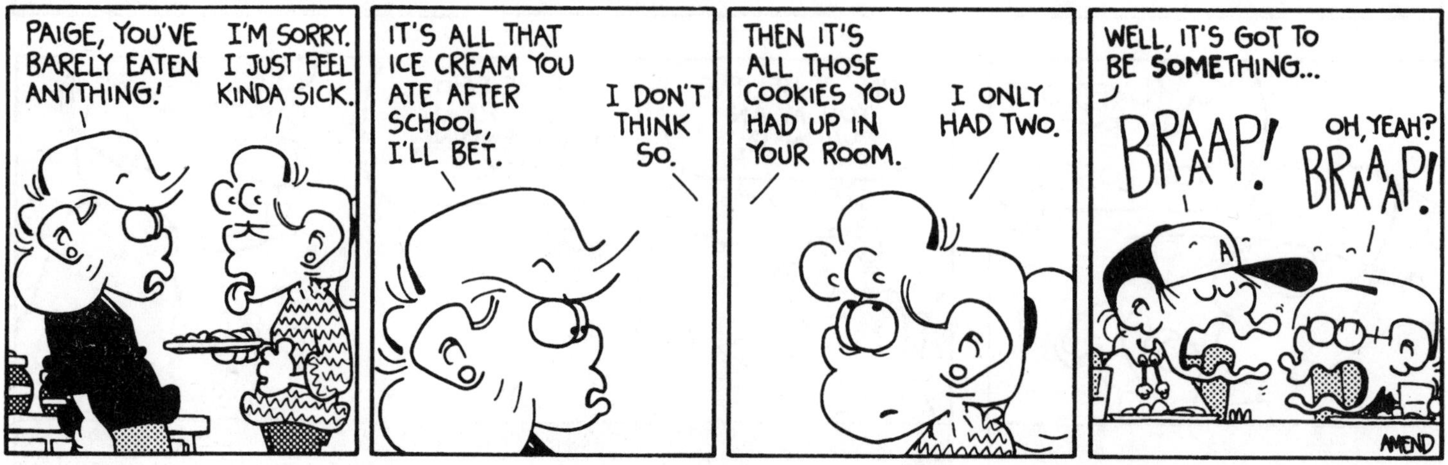
PAIGE, YOU'VE BARELY EATEN ANYTHING!
I'M SORRY. I JUST FEEL KINDA SICK.
IT'S ALL THAT ICE CREAM YOU ATE AFTER SCHOOL, I'LL BET.
I DON'T THINK SO.
THEN IT'S ALL THOSE COOKIES YOU HAD UP IN YOUR ROOM.
I ONLY HAD TWO.
WELL, IT'S GOT TO BE **SOME**THING...
BRAAAP!
OH, YEAH? BRAAAP!
AMEND

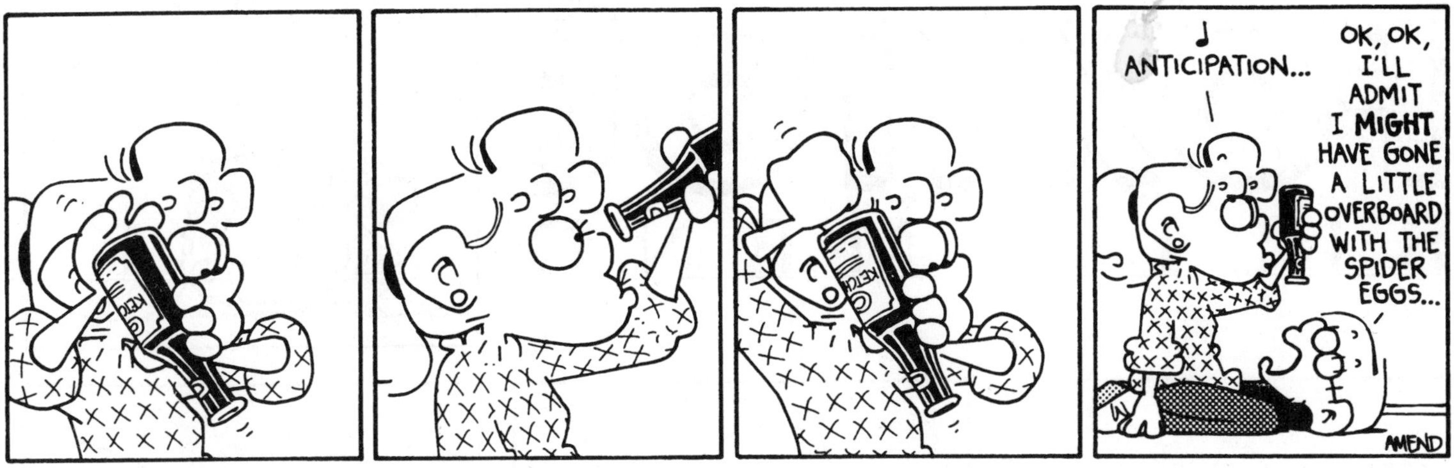
ANTICIPATION...
OK, OK, I'LL ADMIT I MIGHT HAVE GONE A LITTLE OVERBOARD WITH THE SPIDER EGGS...
AMEND

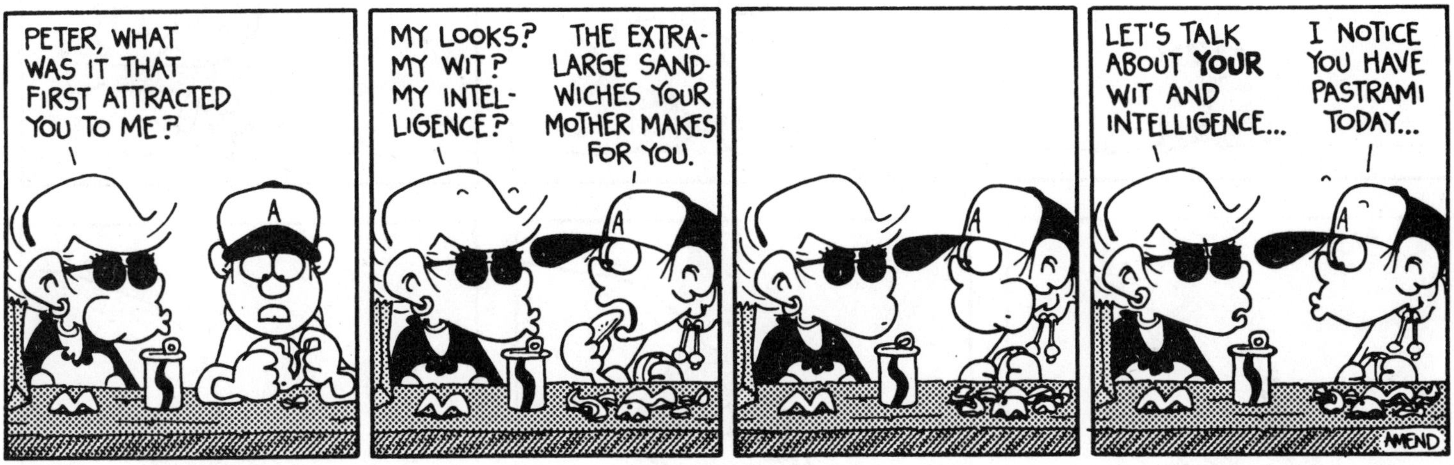
PETER, WHAT WAS IT THAT FIRST ATTRACTED YOU TO ME?
MY LOOKS? MY WIT? MY INTELLIGENCE?
THE EXTRA-LARGE SANDWICHES YOUR MOTHER MAKES FOR YOU.
LET'S TALK ABOUT YOUR WIT AND INTELLIGENCE...
I NOTICE YOU HAVE PASTRAMI TODAY...
AMEND

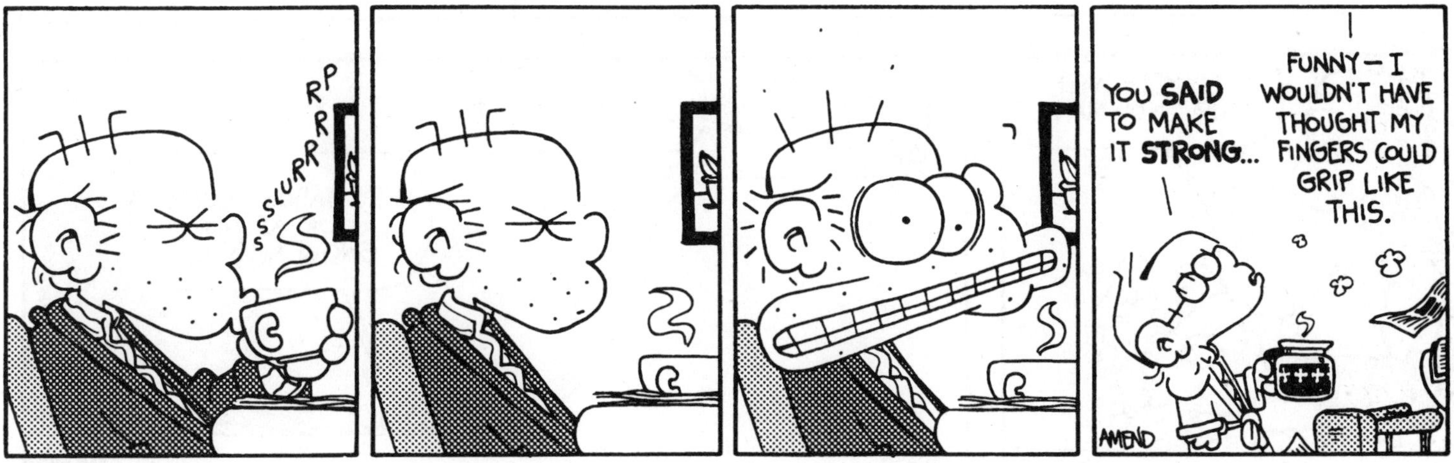
SSSLURRRRP
YOU SAID TO MAKE IT STRONG...
FUNNY—I WOULDN'T HAVE THOUGHT MY FINGERS COULD GRIP LIKE THIS.
AMEND

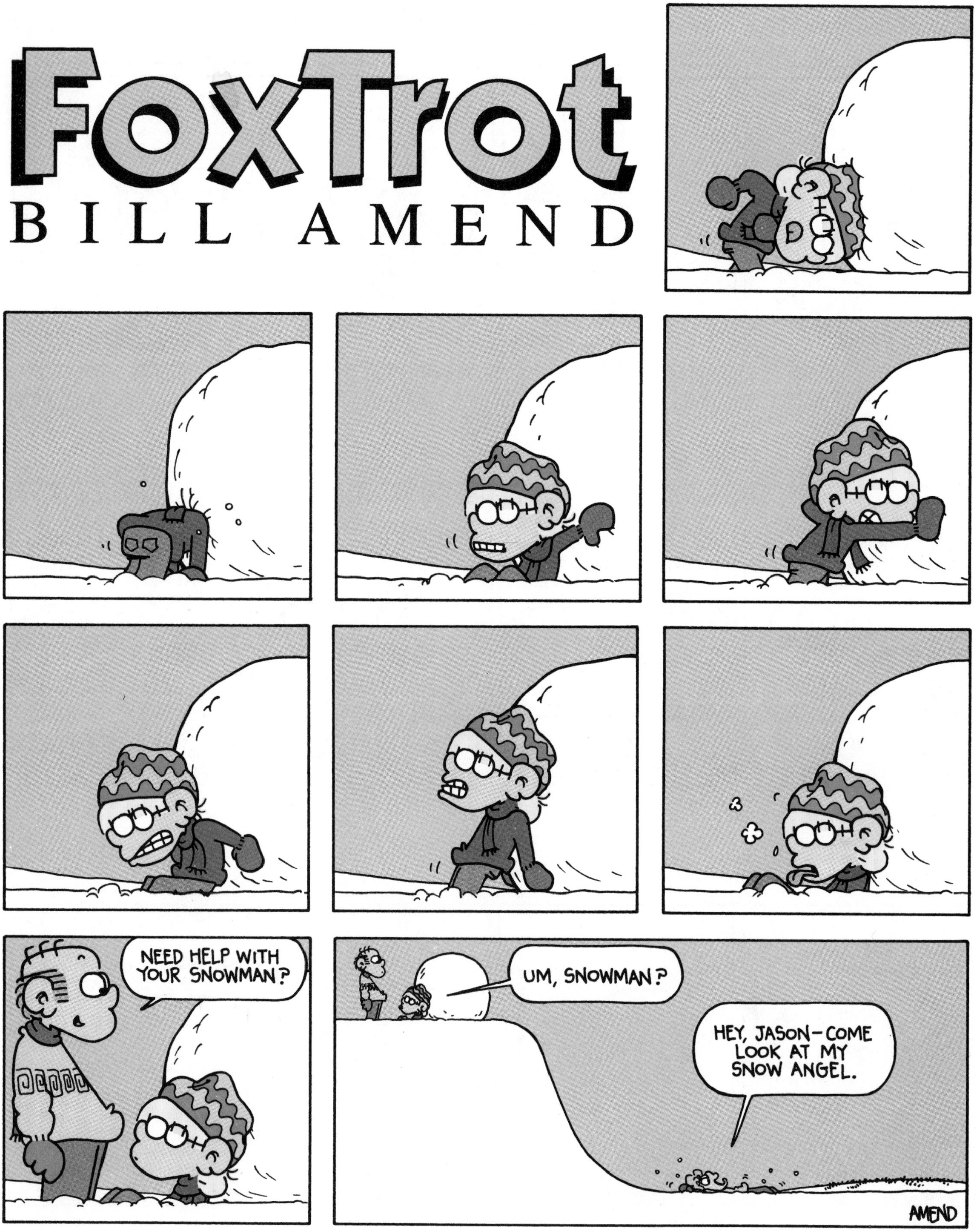
FoxTrot
BILL AMEND
NEED HELP WITH YOUR SNOWMAN?
UM, SNOWMAN?
HEY, JASON—COME LOOK AT MY SNOW ANGEL.
AMEND

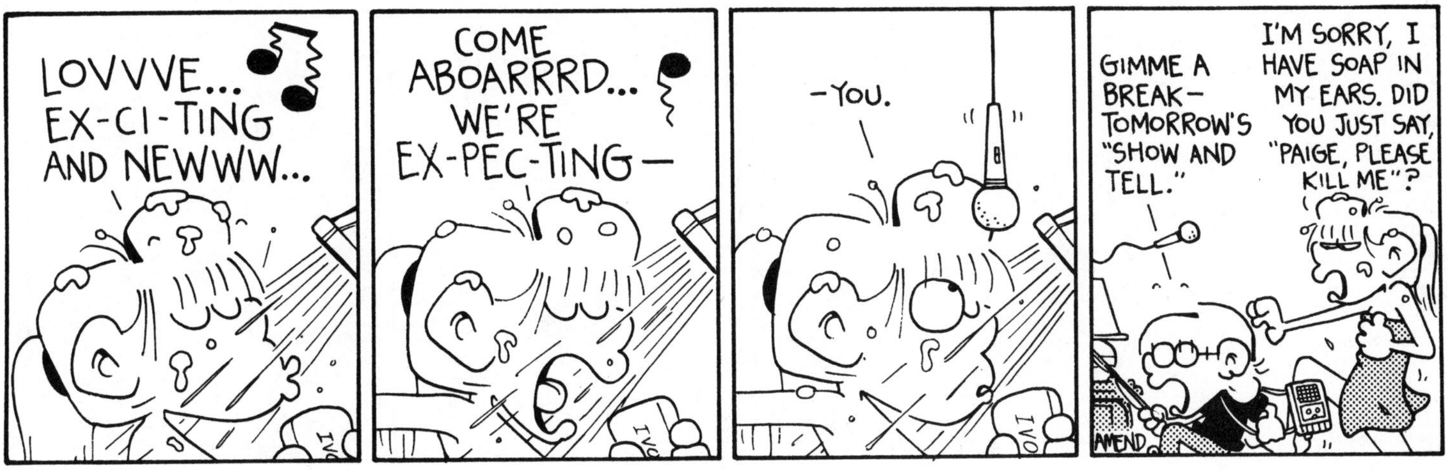
LOVVVE... EX-CI-TING AND NEWWW...
COME ABOARRRD... WE'RE EX-PEC-TING—
—YOU.
GIMME A BREAK— TOMORROW'S "SHOW AND TELL."
I'M SORRY, I HAVE SOAP IN MY EARS. DID YOU JUST SAY, "PAIGE, PLEASE KILL ME"?
AMEND

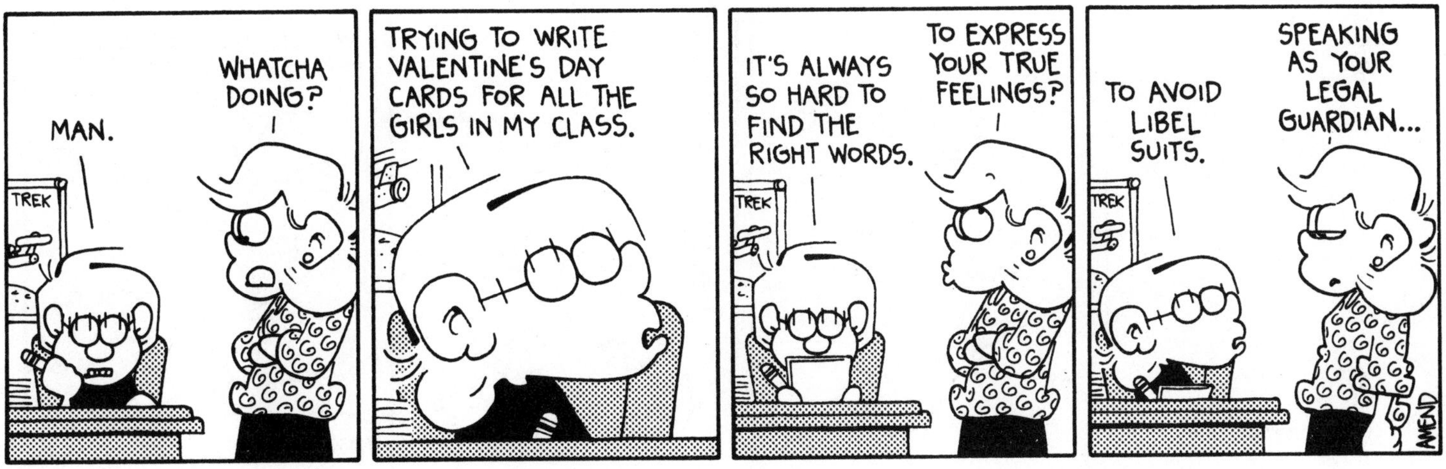
WHATCHA DOING?
MAN.
TRYING TO WRITE VALENTINE'S DAY CARDS FOR ALL THE GIRLS IN MY CLASS.
IT'S ALWAYS SO HARD TO FIND THE RIGHT WORDS.
TO EXPRESS YOUR TRUE FEELINGS?
TO AVOID LIBEL SUITS.
SPEAKING AS YOUR LEGAL GUARDIAN...
AMEND

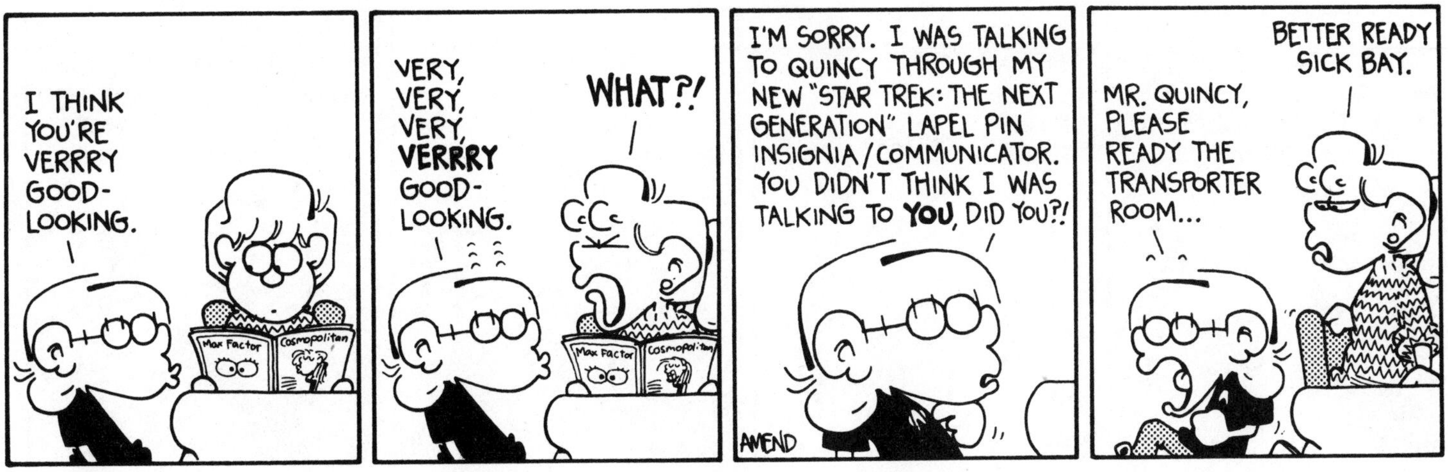
I THINK YOU'RE VERRRY GOOD-LOOKING.
Max Factor
Cosmopolitan
VERY, VERY, VERY, **VERRRY** GOOD-LOOKING.
WHAT?!
I'M SORRY. I WAS TALKING TO QUINCY THROUGH MY NEW "STAR TREK: THE NEXT GENERATION" LAPEL PIN INSIGNIA/COMMUNICATOR. YOU DIDN'T THINK I WAS TALKING TO **YOU**, DID YOU?!
AMEND
MR. QUINCY, PLEASE READY THE TRANSPORTER ROOM...
BETTER READY SICK BAY.

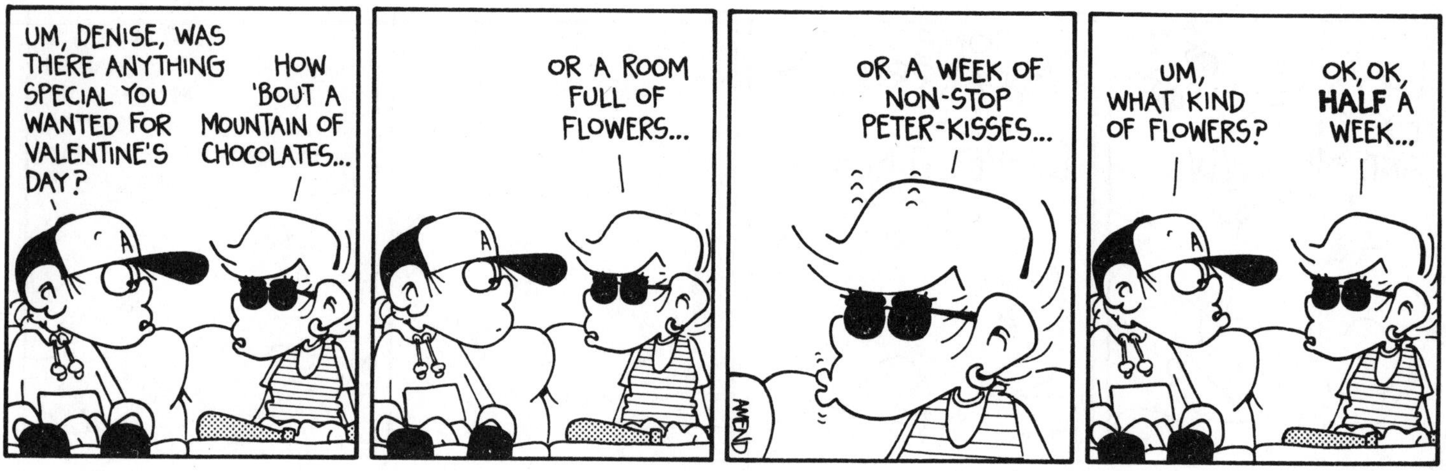
UM, DENISE, WAS THERE ANYTHING SPECIAL YOU WANTED FOR VALENTINE'S DAY?
HOW 'BOUT A MOUNTAIN OF CHOCOLATES...
OR A ROOM FULL OF FLOWERS...
OR A WEEK OF NON-STOP PETER-KISSES...
AMEND
UM, WHAT KIND OF FLOWERS?
OK, OK, HALF A WEEK...

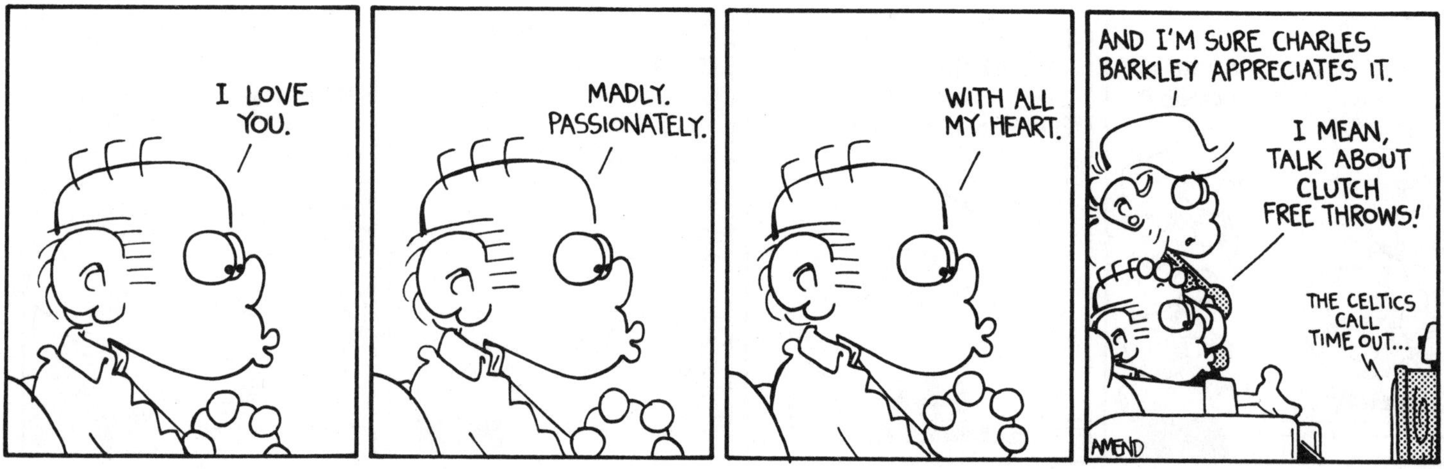
I LOVE YOU.
MADLY. PASSIONATELY.
WITH ALL MY HEART.
AND I'M SURE CHARLES BARKLEY APPRECIATES IT.
I MEAN, TALK ABOUT CLUTCH FREE THROWS!
THE CELTICS CALL TIME OUT...
AMEND

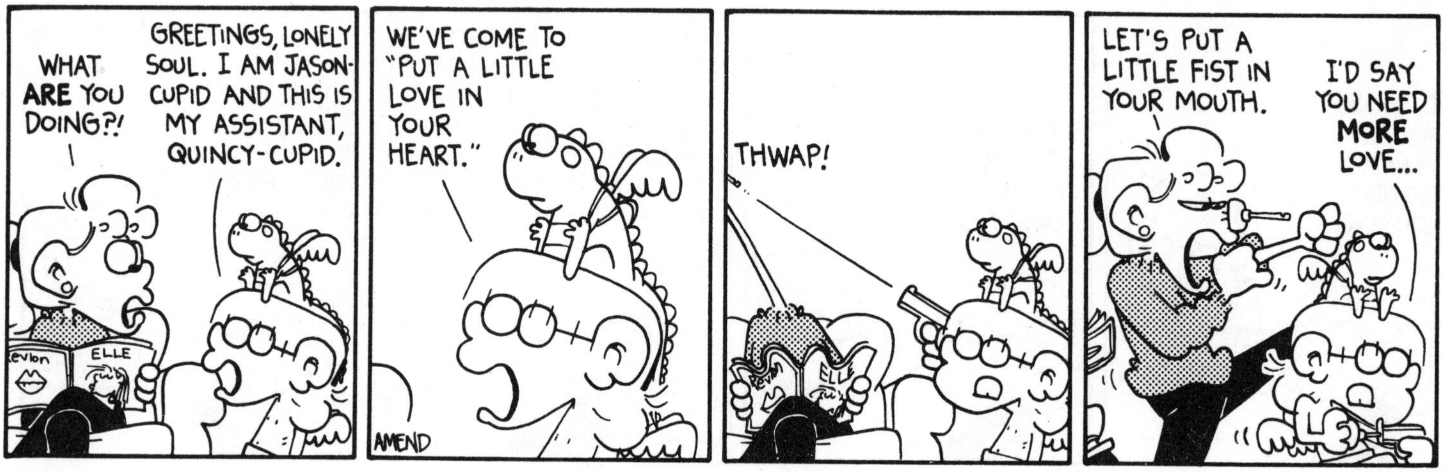
WHAT ARE YOU DOING?!
GREETINGS, LONELY SOUL. I AM JASON-CUPID AND THIS IS MY ASSISTANT, QUINCY-CUPID.
WE'VE COME TO "PUT A LITTLE LOVE IN YOUR HEART."
AMEND
THWAP!
LET'S PUT A LITTLE FIST IN YOUR MOUTH.
I'D SAY YOU NEED MORE LOVE...

FoxTrot

BILL AMEND

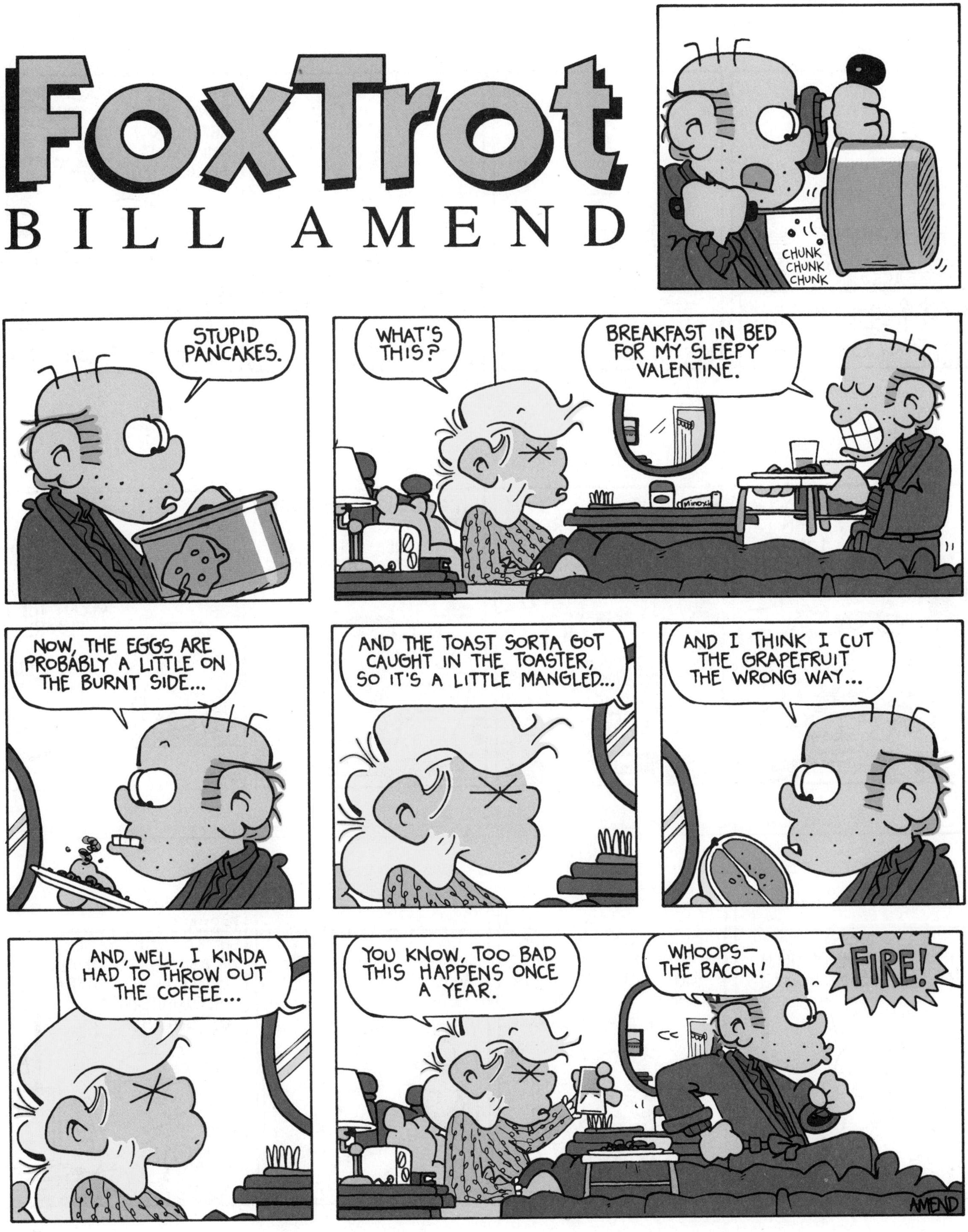

CHUNK CHUNK CHUNK
STUPID PANCAKES.
WHAT'S THIS?
BREAKFAST IN BED FOR MY SLEEPY VALENTINE.
NOW, THE EGGS ARE PROBABLY A LITTLE ON THE BURNT SIDE...
AND THE TOAST SORTA GOT CAUGHT IN THE TOASTER, SO IT'S A LITTLE MANGLED...
AND I THINK I CUT THE GRAPEFRUIT THE WRONG WAY...
AND, WELL, I KINDA HAD TO THROW OUT THE COFFEE...
YOU KNOW, TOO BAD THIS HAPPENS ONCE A YEAR.
WHOOPS— THE BACON!
FIRE!
AMEND

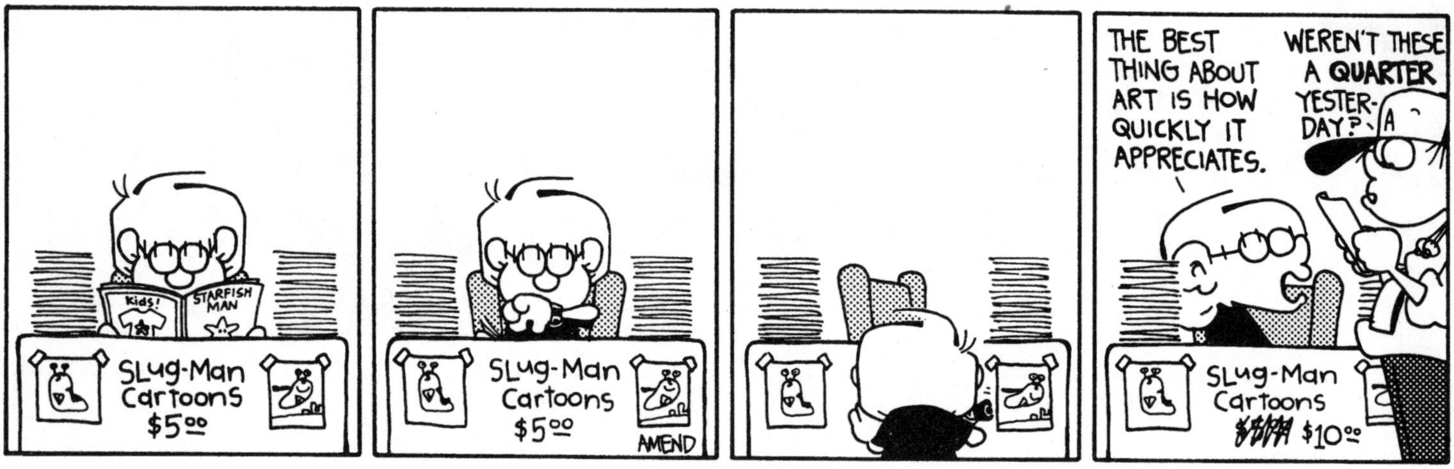
Kids!
STARFISH MAN
SLug-Man Cartoons $5.00
SLug-Man Cartoons $5.00
AMEND
THE BEST THING ABOUT ART IS HOW QUICKLY IT APPRECIATES.
WEREN'T THESE A **QUARTER** YESTERDAY?
SLug-Man Cartoons $10.00

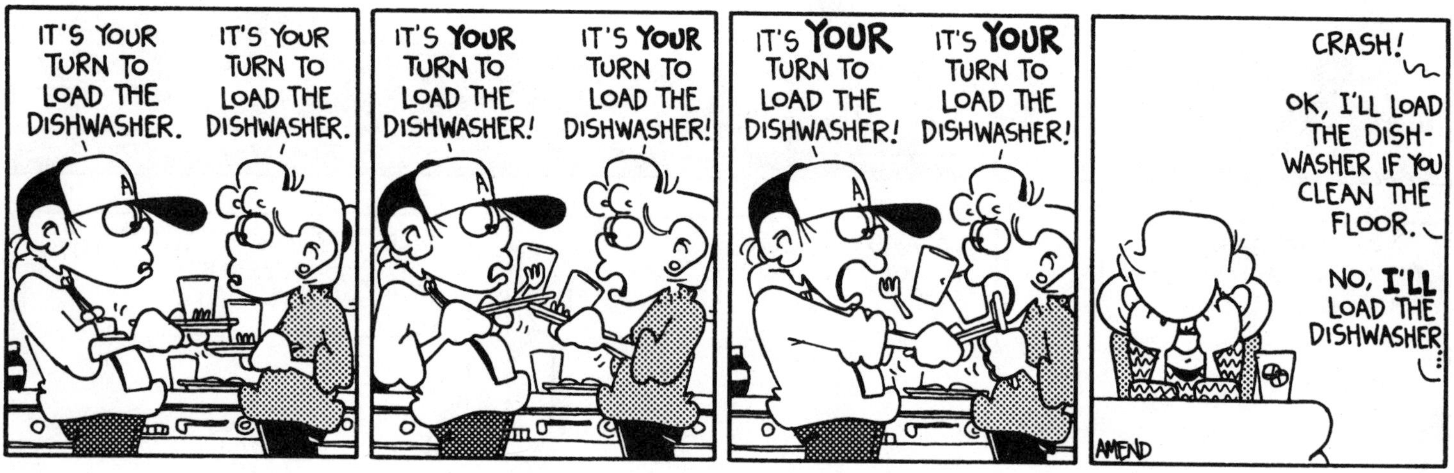
IT'S YOUR TURN TO LOAD THE DISHWASHER.
IT'S YOUR TURN TO LOAD THE DISHWASHER.
IT'S **YOUR** TURN TO LOAD THE DISHWASHER!
IT'S **YOUR** TURN TO LOAD THE DISHWASHER!
IT'S **YOUR** TURN TO LOAD THE DISHWASHER!
IT'S **YOUR** TURN TO LOAD THE DISHWASHER!
CRASH!
OK, I'LL LOAD THE DISH-WASHER IF YOU CLEAN THE FLOOR.
NO, **I'LL** LOAD THE DISHWASHER
AMEND

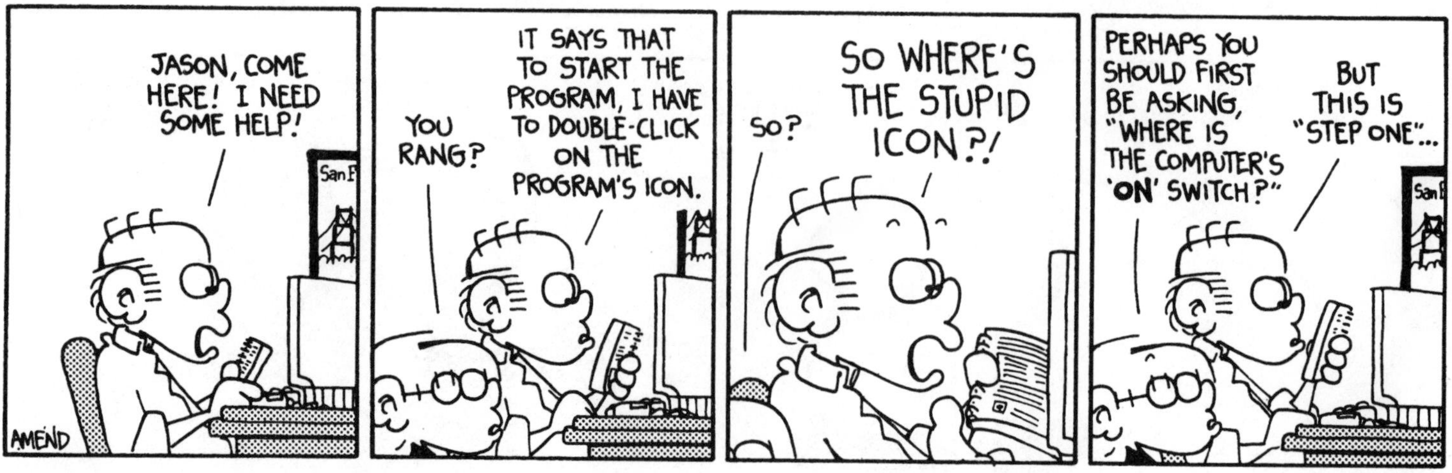
JASON, COME HERE! I NEED SOME HELP!
AMEND
YOU RANG?
IT SAYS THAT TO START THE PROGRAM, I HAVE TO DOUBLE-CLICK ON THE PROGRAM'S ICON.
SO?
SO WHERE'S THE STUPID ICON?!
PERHAPS YOU SHOULD FIRST BE ASKING, "WHERE IS THE COMPUTER'S '**ON**' SWITCH?"
BUT THIS IS "STEP ONE"...

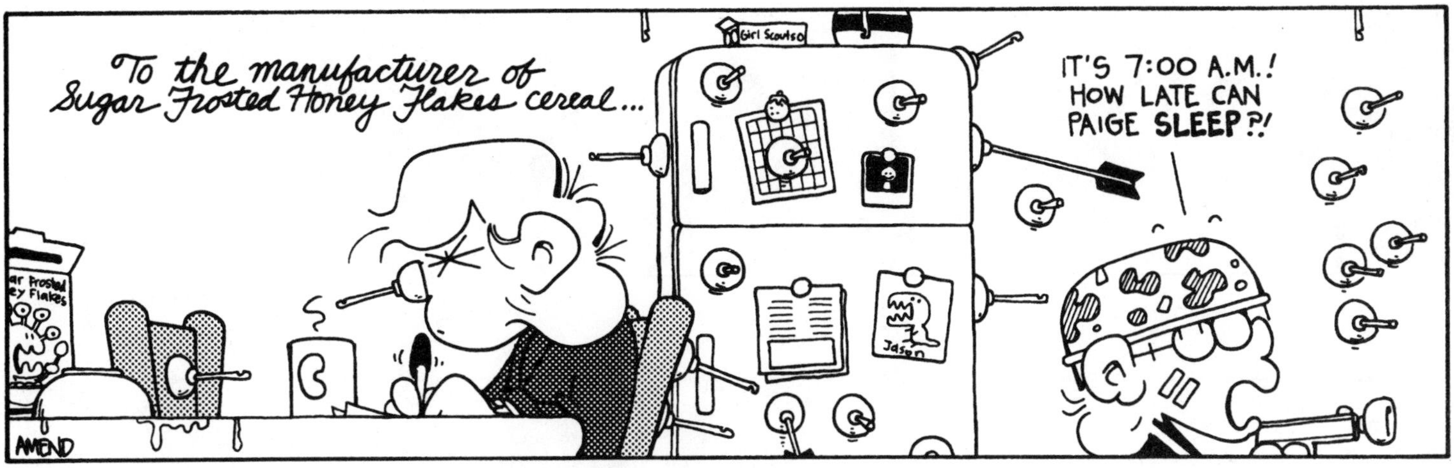

To the manufacturer of Sugar Frosted Honey Flakes cereal...
IT'S 7:00 A.M.! HOW LATE CAN PAIGE SLEEP?!
AMEND

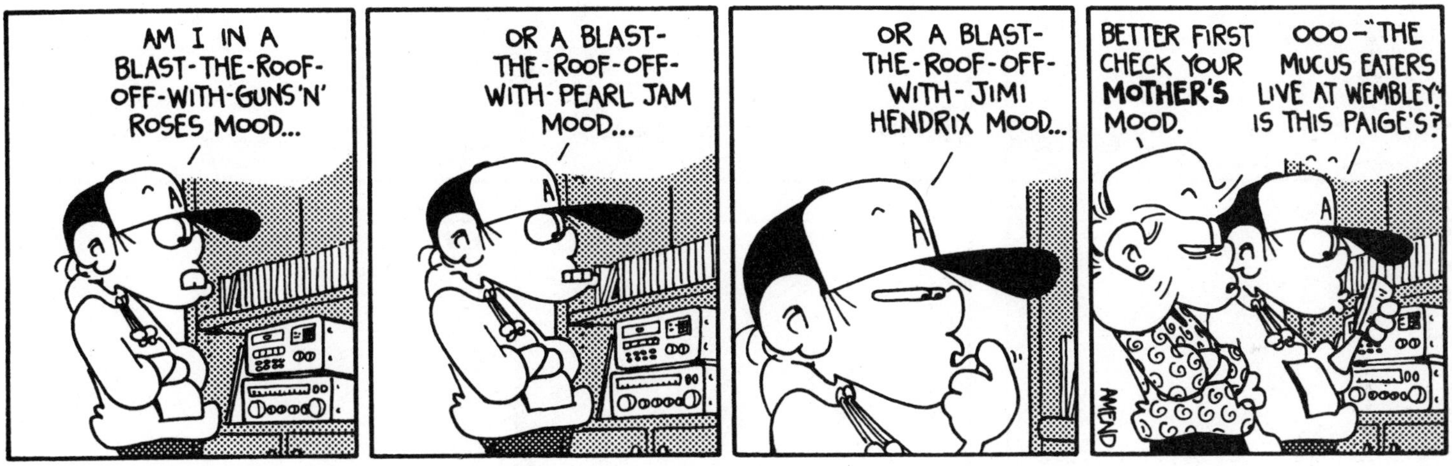

AM I IN A BLAST-THE-ROOF-OFF-WITH-GUNS'N' ROSES MOOD...
OR A BLAST-THE-ROOF-OFF-WITH-PEARL JAM MOOD...
OR A BLAST-THE-ROOF-OFF-WITH-JIMI HENDRIX MOOD...
BETTER FIRST CHECK YOUR MOTHER'S MOOD.
OOO-"THE MUCUS EATERS LIVE AT WEMBLEY." IS THIS PAIGE'S?
AMEND

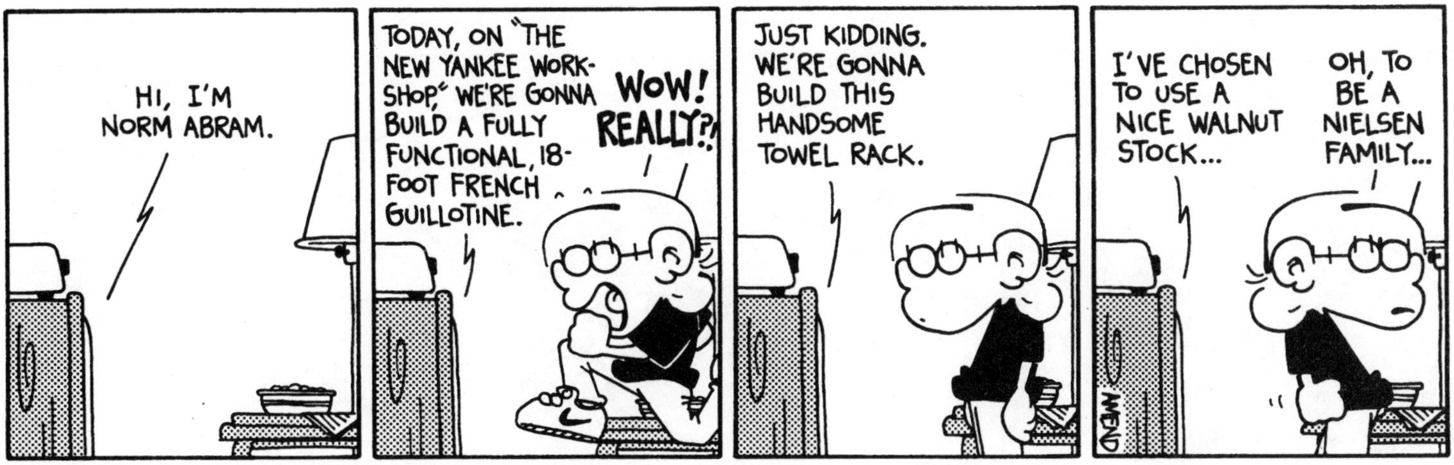

HI, I'M NORM ABRAM.
TODAY, ON "THE NEW YANKEE WORKSHOP," WE'RE GONNA BUILD A FULLY FUNCTIONAL, 18-FOOT FRENCH GUILLOTINE.
WOW! REALLY?!
JUST KIDDING. WE'RE GONNA BUILD THIS HANDSOME TOWEL RACK.
I'VE CHOSEN TO USE A NICE WALNUT STOCK...
OH, TO BE A NIELSEN FAMILY...
AMEND

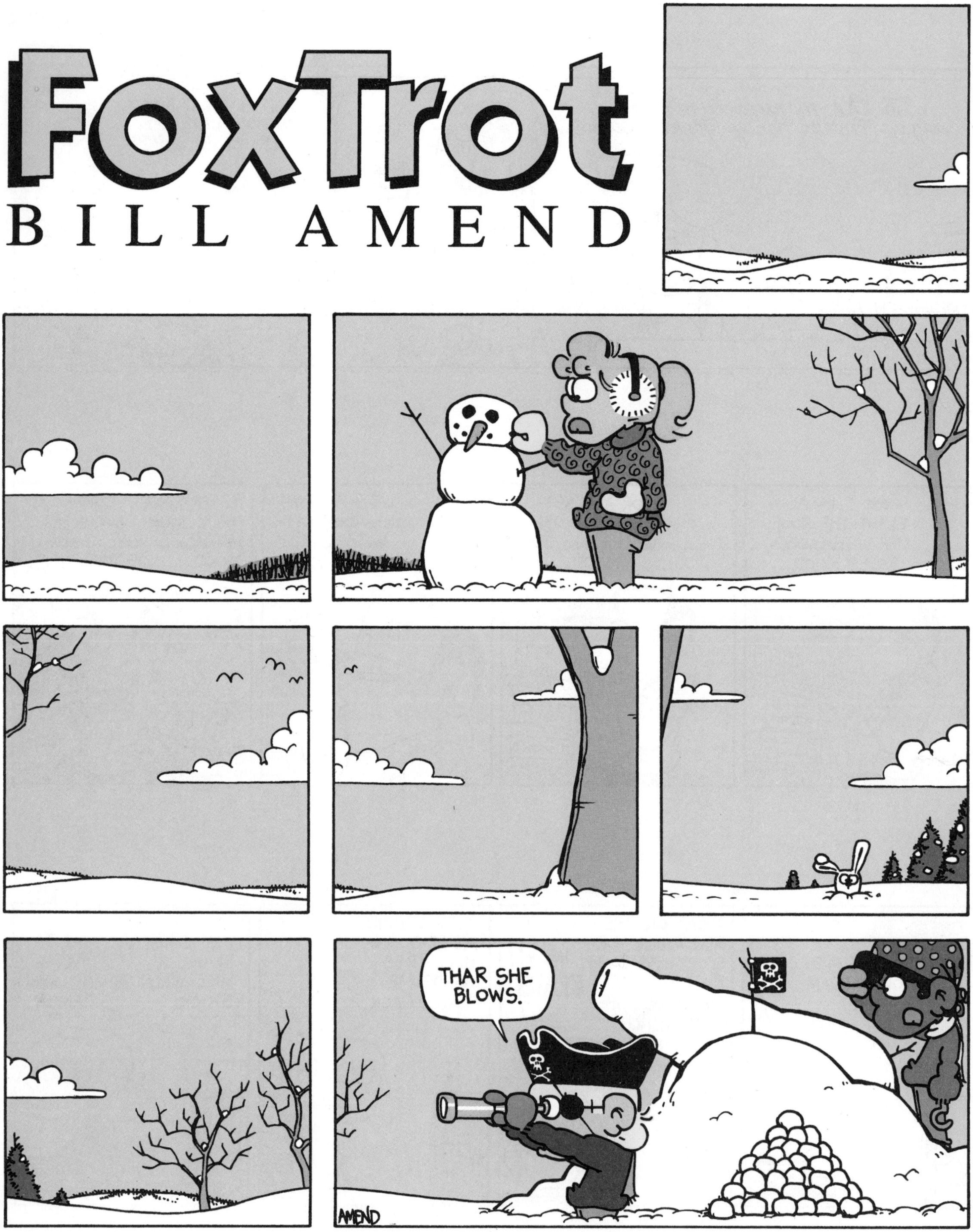
FoxTrot
BILL AMEND
THAR SHE BLOWS.
AMEND

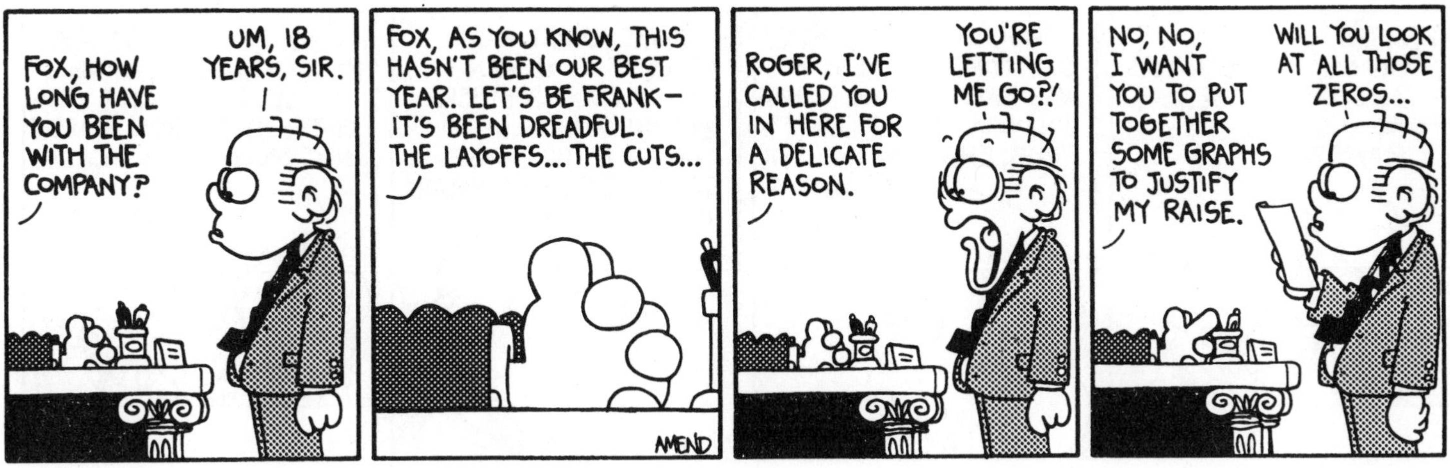
FOX, HOW LONG HAVE YOU BEEN WITH THE COMPANY?
UM, 18 YEARS, SIR.
FOX, AS YOU KNOW, THIS HASN'T BEEN OUR BEST YEAR. LET'S BE FRANK– IT'S BEEN DREADFUL. THE LAYOFFS... THE CUTS...
ROGER, I'VE CALLED YOU IN HERE FOR A DELICATE REASON.
YOU'RE LETTING ME GO?!
NO, NO, I WANT YOU TO PUT TOGETHER SOME GRAPHS TO JUSTIFY MY RAISE.
WILL YOU LOOK AT ALL THOSE ZEROS...

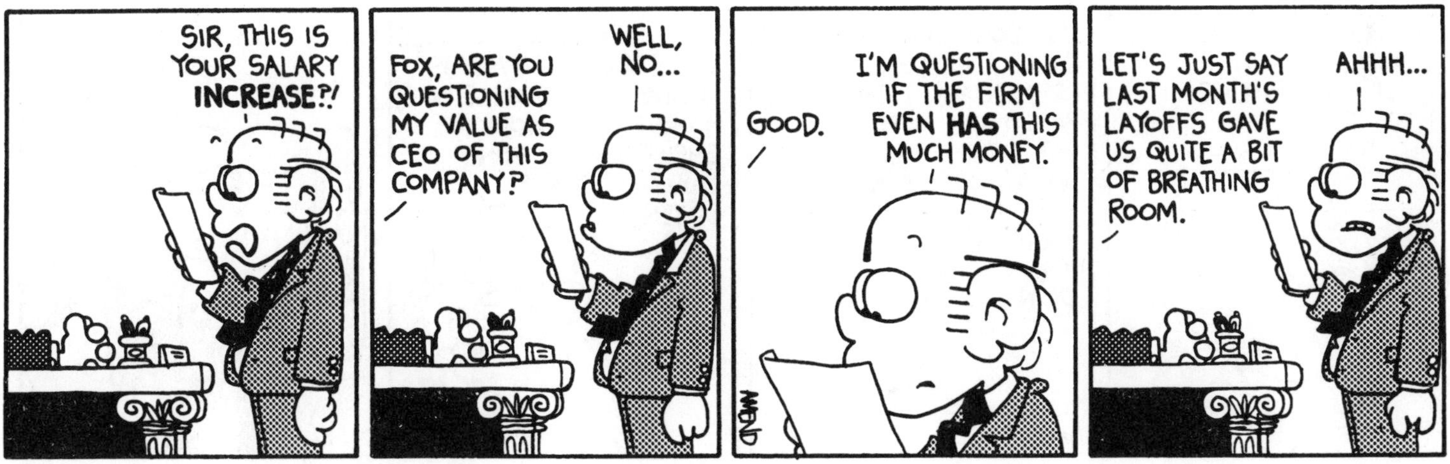
SIR, THIS IS YOUR SALARY **INCREASE**?!
FOX, ARE YOU QUESTIONING MY VALUE AS CEO OF THIS COMPANY?
WELL, NO...
GOOD.
I'M QUESTIONING IF THE FIRM EVEN **HAS** THIS MUCH MONEY.
LET'S JUST SAY LAST MONTH'S LAYOFFS GAVE US QUITE A BIT OF BREATHING ROOM.
AHHH...

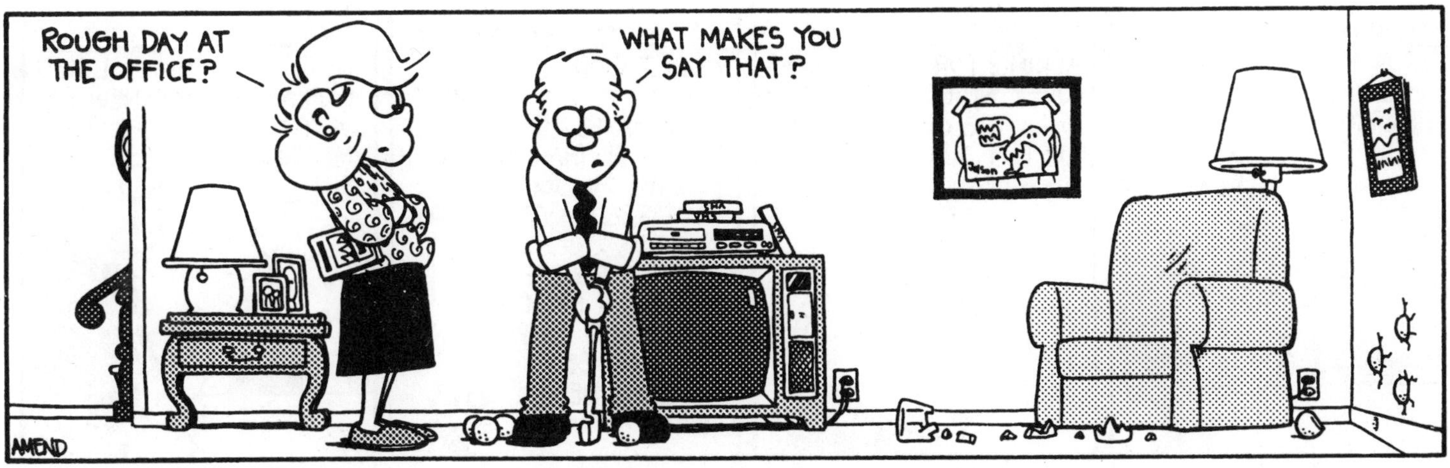
ROUGH DAY AT THE OFFICE?
WHAT MAKES YOU SAY THAT?

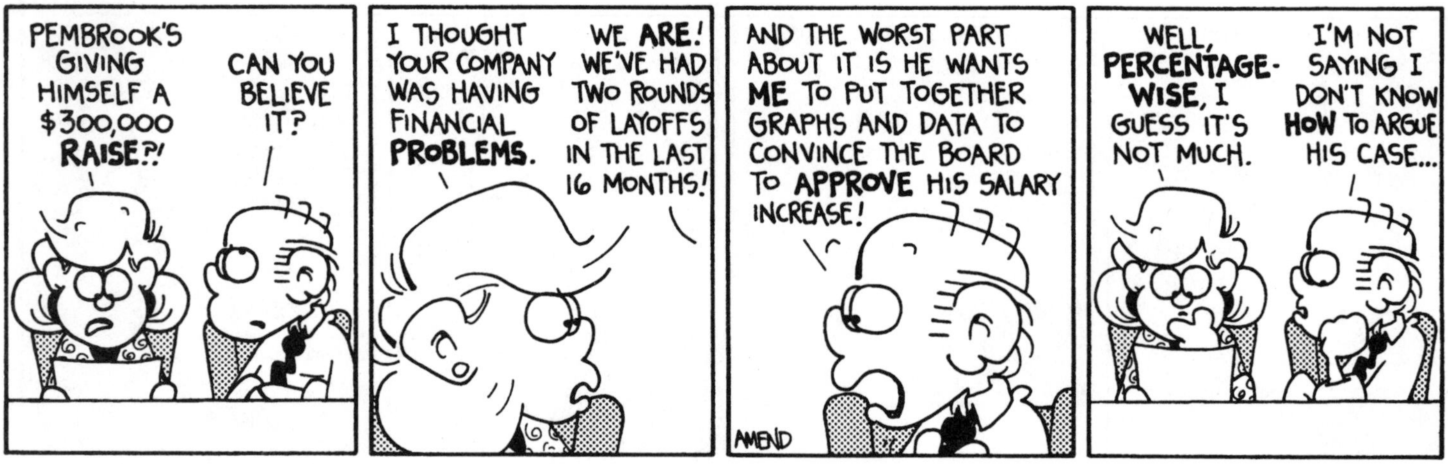
PEMBROOK'S GIVING HIMSELF A $300,000 RAISE?!
CAN YOU BELIEVE IT?
I THOUGHT YOUR COMPANY WAS HAVING FINANCIAL PROBLEMS.
WE ARE! WE'VE HAD TWO ROUNDS OF LAYOFFS IN THE LAST 16 MONTHS!
AND THE WORST PART ABOUT IT IS HE WANTS ME TO PUT TOGETHER GRAPHS AND DATA TO CONVINCE THE BOARD TO APPROVE HIS SALARY INCREASE!
AMEND
WELL, PERCENTAGE-WISE, I GUESS IT'S NOT MUCH.
I'M NOT SAYING I DON'T KNOW HOW TO ARGUE HIS CASE...

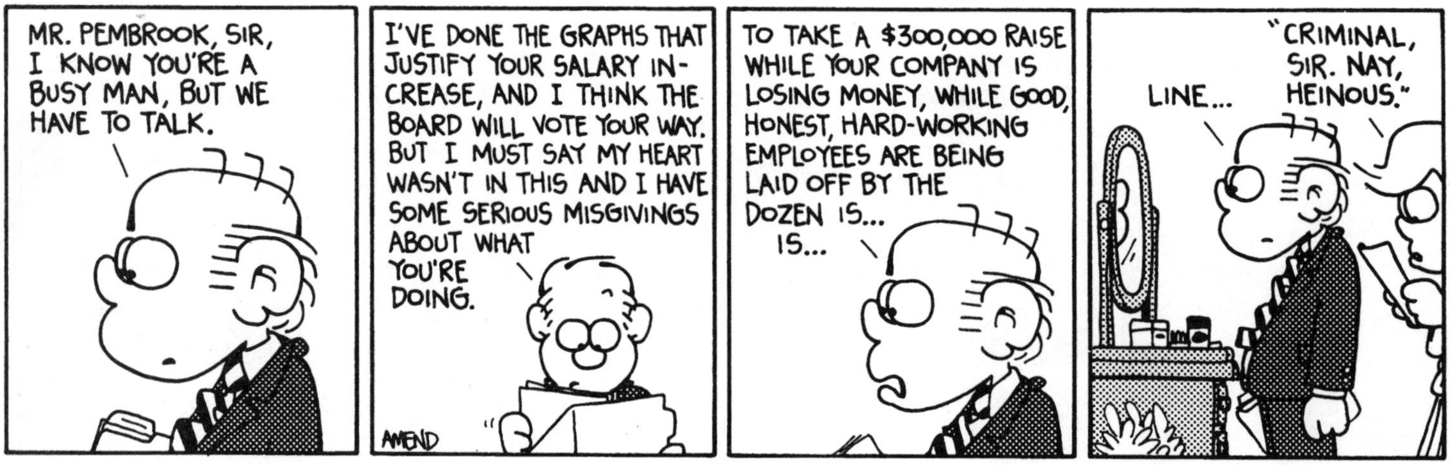
MR. PEMBROOK, SIR, I KNOW YOU'RE A BUSY MAN, BUT WE HAVE TO TALK.
I'VE DONE THE GRAPHS THAT JUSTIFY YOUR SALARY IN-CREASE, AND I THINK THE BOARD WILL VOTE YOUR WAY. BUT I MUST SAY MY HEART WASN'T IN THIS AND I HAVE SOME SERIOUS MISGIVINGS ABOUT WHAT YOU'RE DOING.
AMEND
TO TAKE A $300,000 RAISE WHILE YOUR COMPANY IS LOSING MONEY, WHILE GOOD, HONEST, HARD-WORKING EMPLOYEES ARE BEING LAID OFF BY THE DOZEN IS... IS...
LINE...
"CRIMINAL, SIR. NAY, HEINOUS."

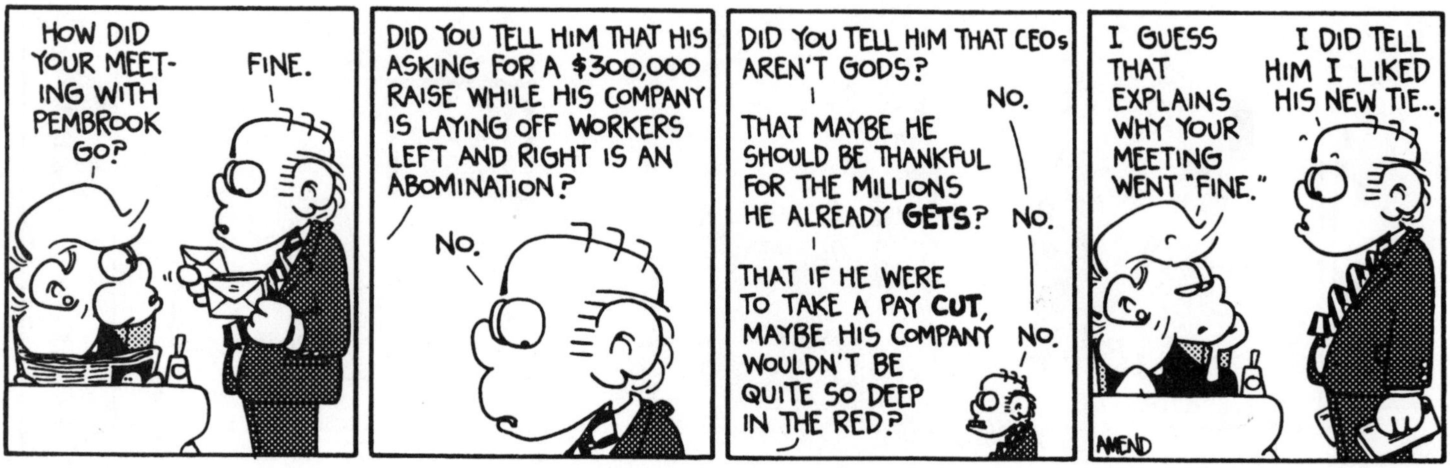
HOW DID YOUR MEET-ING WITH PEMBROOK GO?
FINE.
DID YOU TELL HIM THAT HIS ASKING FOR A $300,000 RAISE WHILE HIS COMPANY IS LAYING OFF WORKERS LEFT AND RIGHT IS AN ABOMINATION?
NO.
DID YOU TELL HIM THAT CEOs AREN'T GODS?
NO.
THAT MAYBE HE SHOULD BE THANKFUL FOR THE MILLIONS HE ALREADY GETS?
NO.
THAT IF HE WERE TO TAKE A PAY CUT, MAYBE HIS COMPANY WOULDN'T BE QUITE SO DEEP IN THE RED?
NO.
I GUESS THAT EXPLAINS WHY YOUR MEETING WENT "FINE."
I DID TELL HIM I LIKED HIS NEW TIE...
AMEND

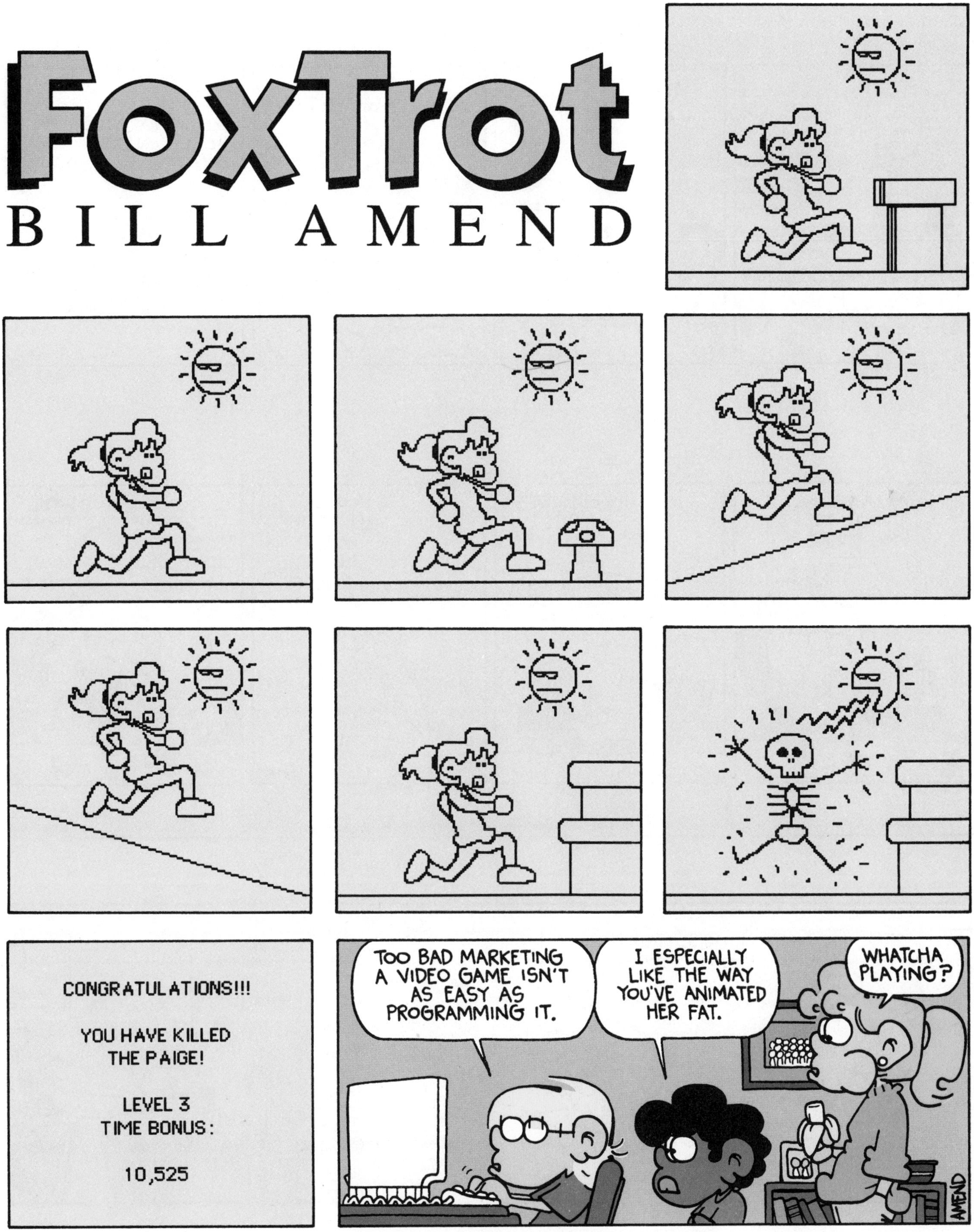
FoxTrot
BILL AMEND
CONGRATULATIONS!!!
YOU HAVE KILLED THE PAIGE!
LEVEL 3
TIME BONUS:
10,525
TOO BAD MARKETING A VIDEO GAME ISN'T AS EASY AS PROGRAMMING IT.
I ESPECIALLY LIKE THE WAY YOU'VE ANIMATED HER FAT.
WHATCHA PLAYING?
AMEND

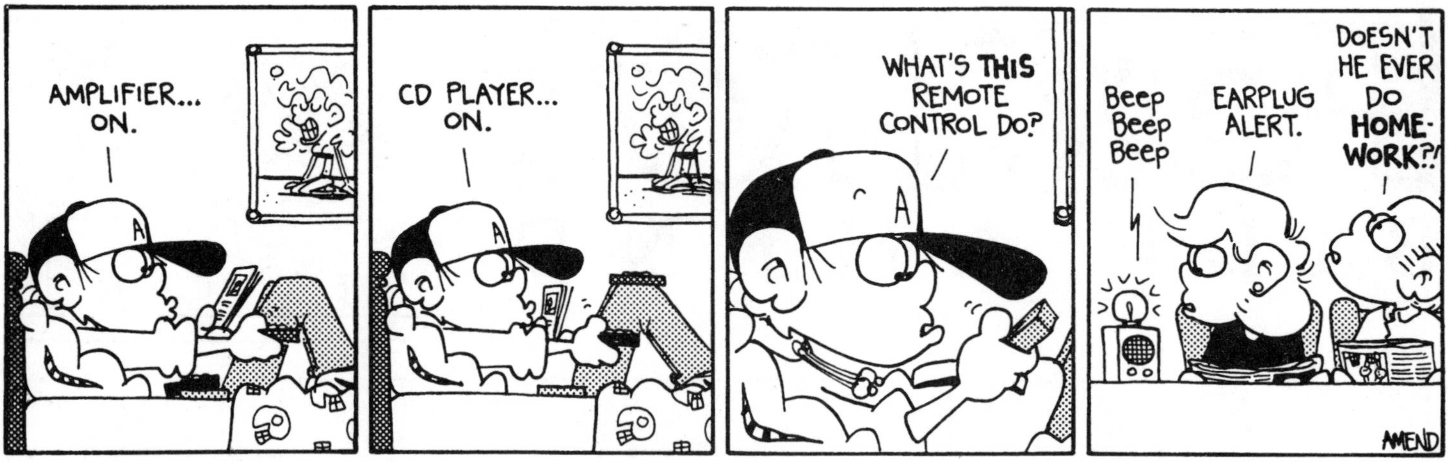
AMPLIFIER... ON.
CD PLAYER... ON.
WHAT'S THIS REMOTE CONTROL DO?
Beep Beep Beep
EARPLUG ALERT.
DOESN'T HE EVER DO HOME-WORK?!
AMEND

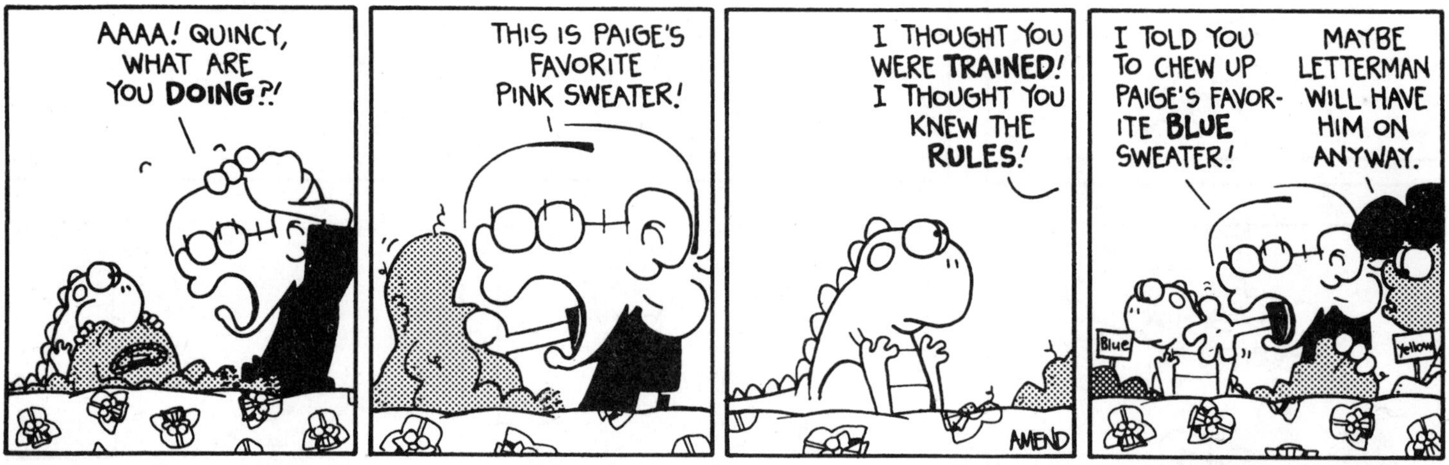
AAAA! QUINCY, WHAT ARE YOU DOING?!
THIS IS PAIGE'S FAVORITE PINK SWEATER!
I THOUGHT YOU WERE TRAINED! I THOUGHT YOU KNEW THE RULES!
AMEND
I TOLD YOU TO CHEW UP PAIGE'S FAVOR-ITE BLUE SWEATER!
MAYBE LETTERMAN WILL HAVE HIM ON ANYWAY.
Blue
Yellow

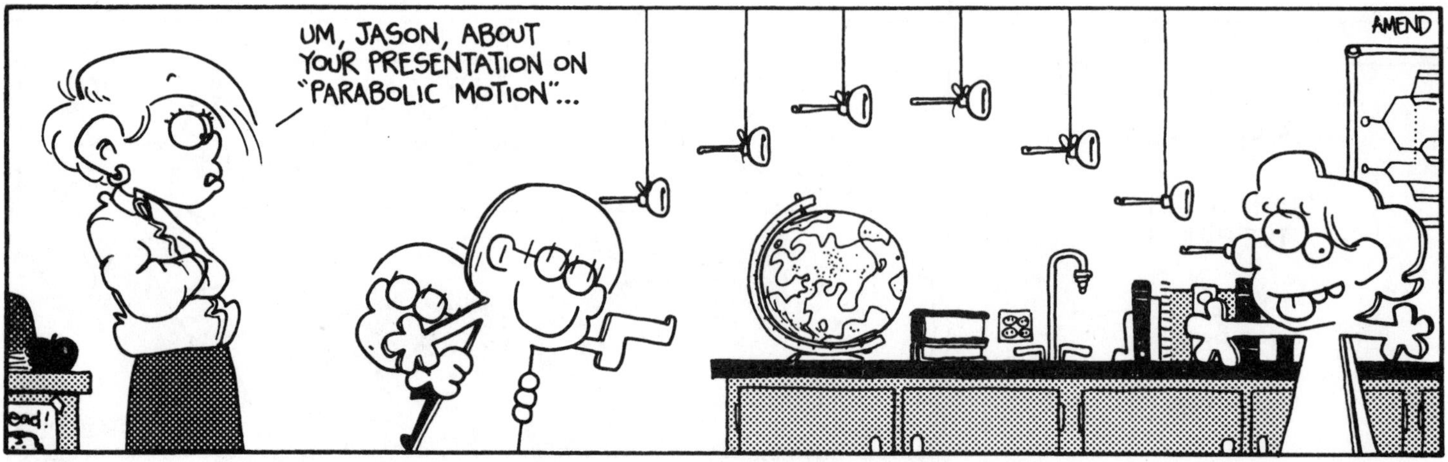
UM, JASON, ABOUT YOUR PRESENTATION ON "PARABOLIC MOTION"...
AMEND

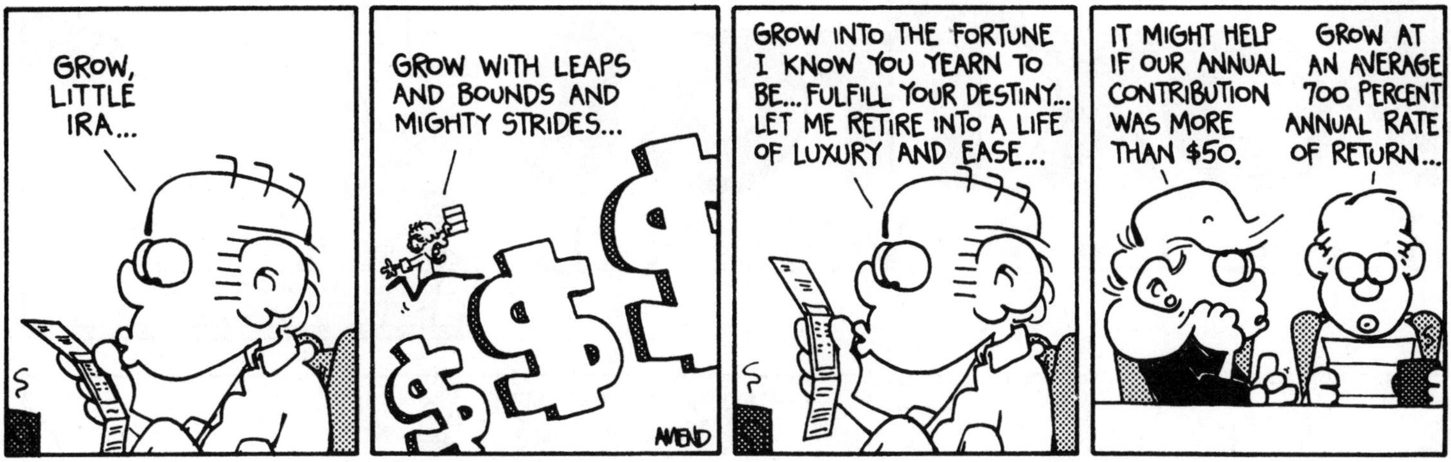
GROW, LITTLE IRA...
GROW WITH LEAPS AND BOUNDS AND MIGHTY STRIDES...
GROW INTO THE FORTUNE I KNOW YOU YEARN TO BE... FULFILL YOUR DESTINY... LET ME RETIRE INTO A LIFE OF LUXURY AND EASE...
IT MIGHT HELP IF OUR ANNUAL CONTRIBUTION WAS MORE THAN $50.
GROW AT AN AVERAGE 700 PERCENT ANNUAL RATE OF RETURN...
AMEND

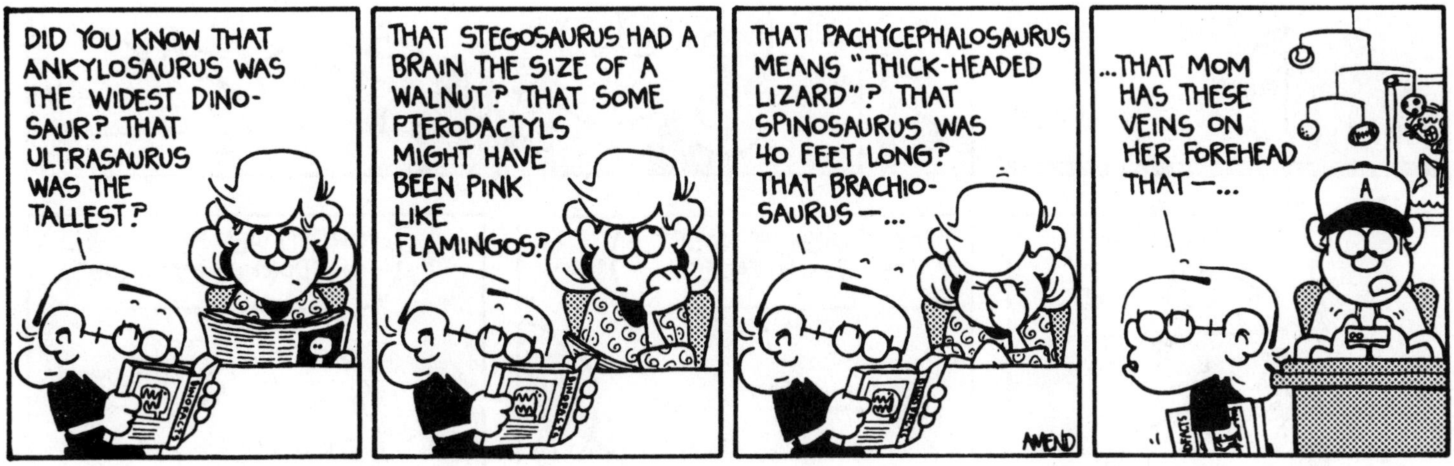
DID YOU KNOW THAT ANKYLOSAURUS WAS THE WIDEST DINOSAUR? THAT ULTRASAURUS WAS THE TALLEST?
THAT STEGOSAURUS HAD A BRAIN THE SIZE OF A WALNUT? THAT SOME PTERODACTYLS MIGHT HAVE BEEN PINK LIKE FLAMINGOS?
THAT PACHYCEPHALOSAURUS MEANS "THICK-HEADED LIZARD"? THAT SPINOSAURUS WAS 40 FEET LONG? THAT BRACHIOSAURUS—...
...THAT MOM HAS THESE VEINS ON HER FOREHEAD THAT—...
AMEND

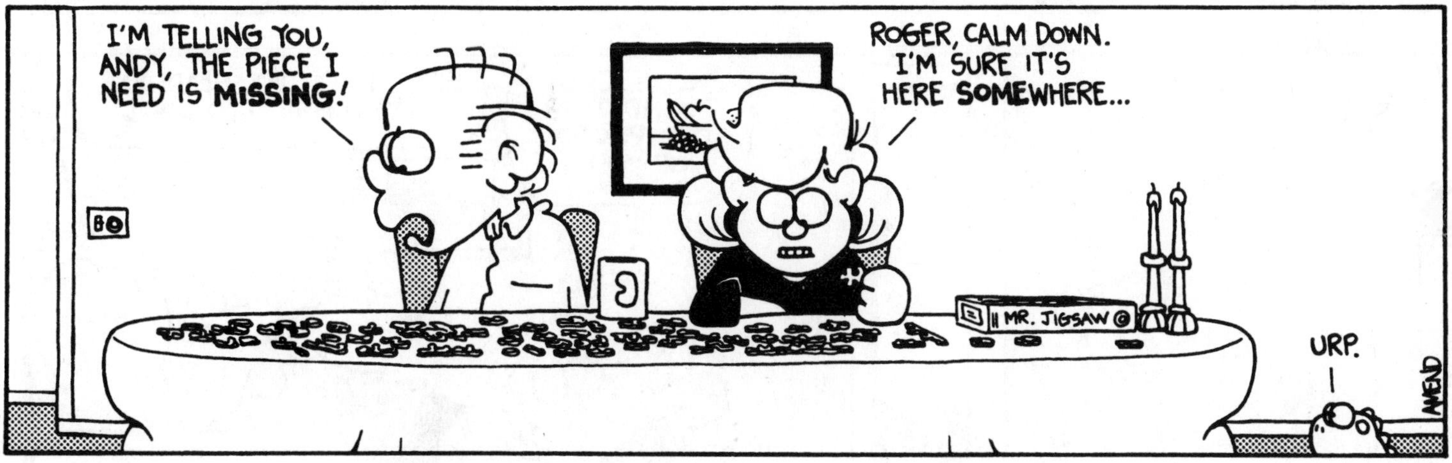
I'M TELLING YOU, ANDY, THE PIECE I NEED IS **MISSING**!
ROGER, CALM DOWN. I'M SURE IT'S HERE **SOME**WHERE...
MR. JIGSAW
URP.
AMEND

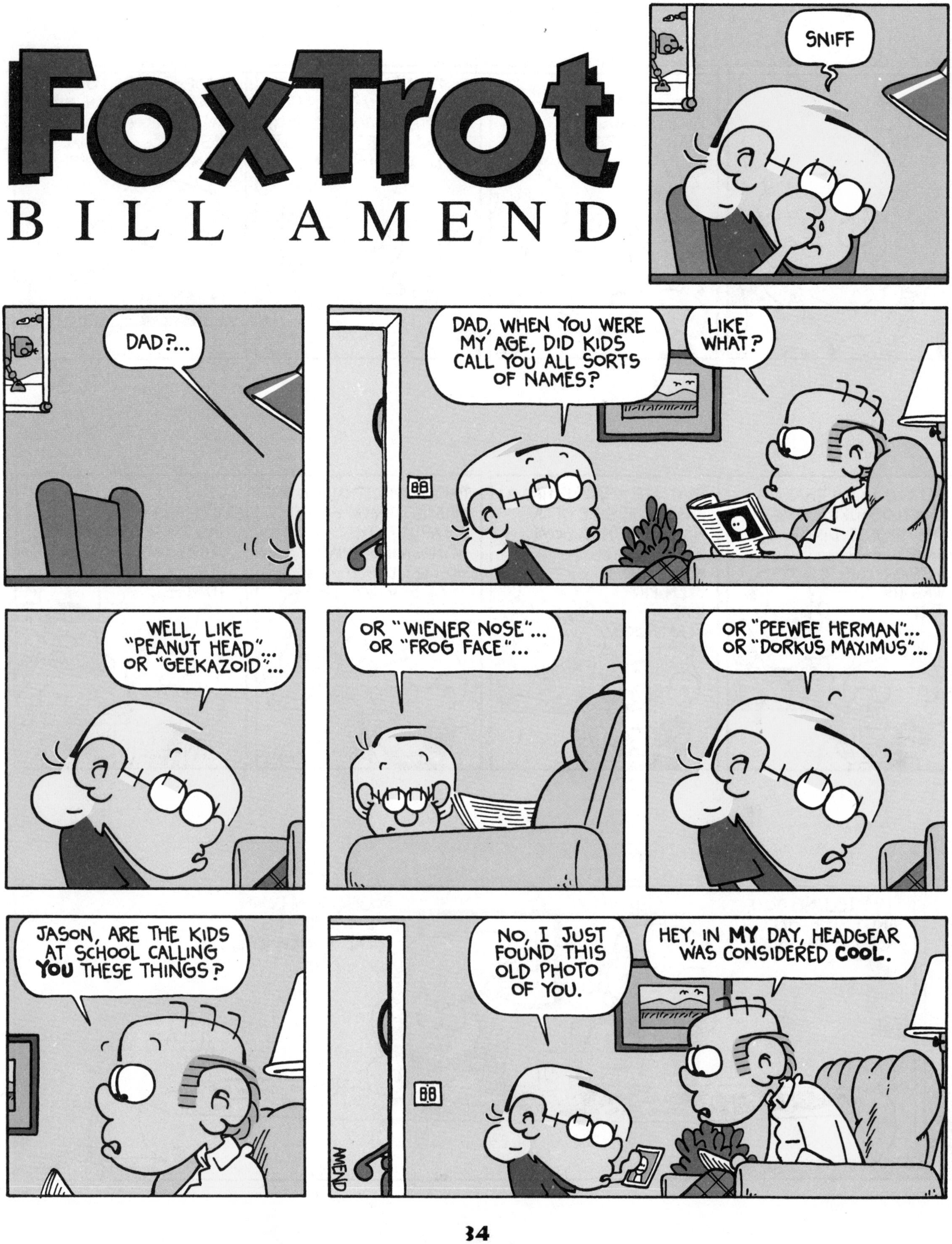
FoxTrot
BILL AMEND
SNIFF
DAD?...
DAD, WHEN YOU WERE MY AGE, DID KIDS CALL YOU ALL SORTS OF NAMES?
LIKE WHAT?
WELL, LIKE "PEANUT HEAD"... OR "GEEKAZOID"...
OR "WIENER NOSE"... OR "FROG FACE"...
OR "PEEWEE HERMAN"... OR "DORKUS MAXIMUS"...
JASON, ARE THE KIDS AT SCHOOL CALLING YOU THESE THINGS?
NO, I JUST FOUND THIS OLD PHOTO OF YOU.
HEY, IN MY DAY, HEADGEAR WAS CONSIDERED COOL.
AMEND

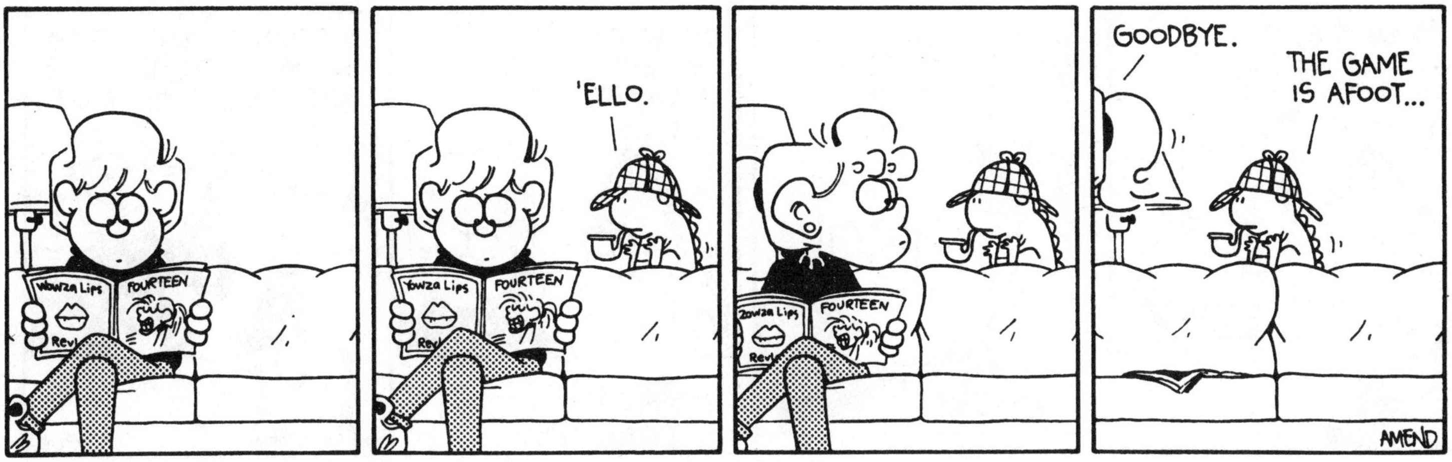
'ELLO.
GOODBYE.
THE GAME IS AFOOT...
AMEND

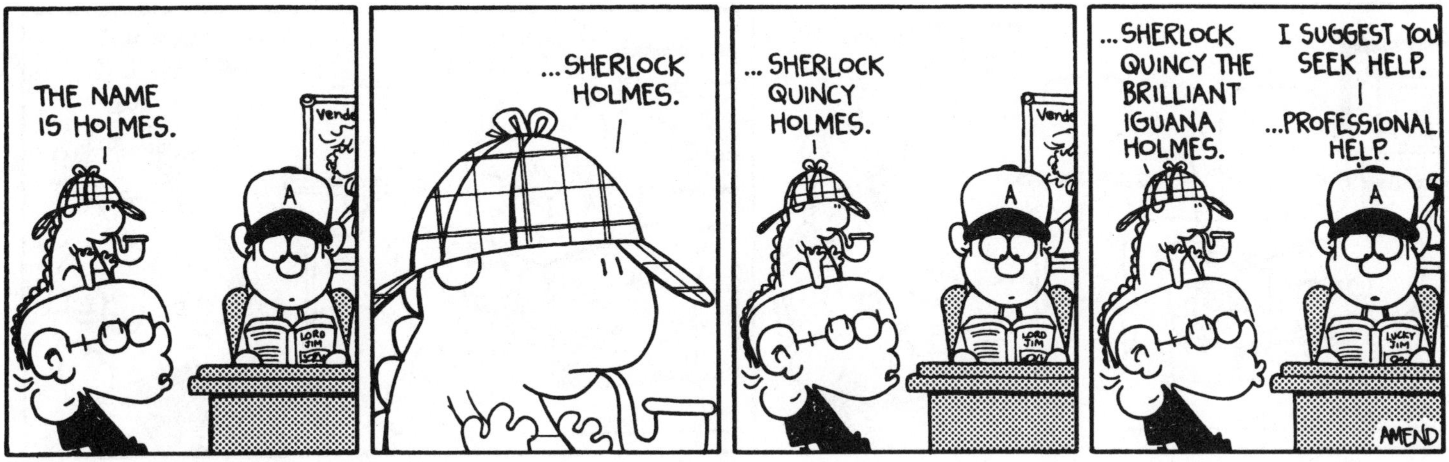
THE NAME IS HOLMES.
...SHERLOCK HOLMES.
...SHERLOCK QUINCY HOLMES.
...SHERLOCK QUINCY THE BRILLIANT IGUANA HOLMES.
I SUGGEST YOU SEEK HELP.
...PROFESSIONAL HELP.
AMEND

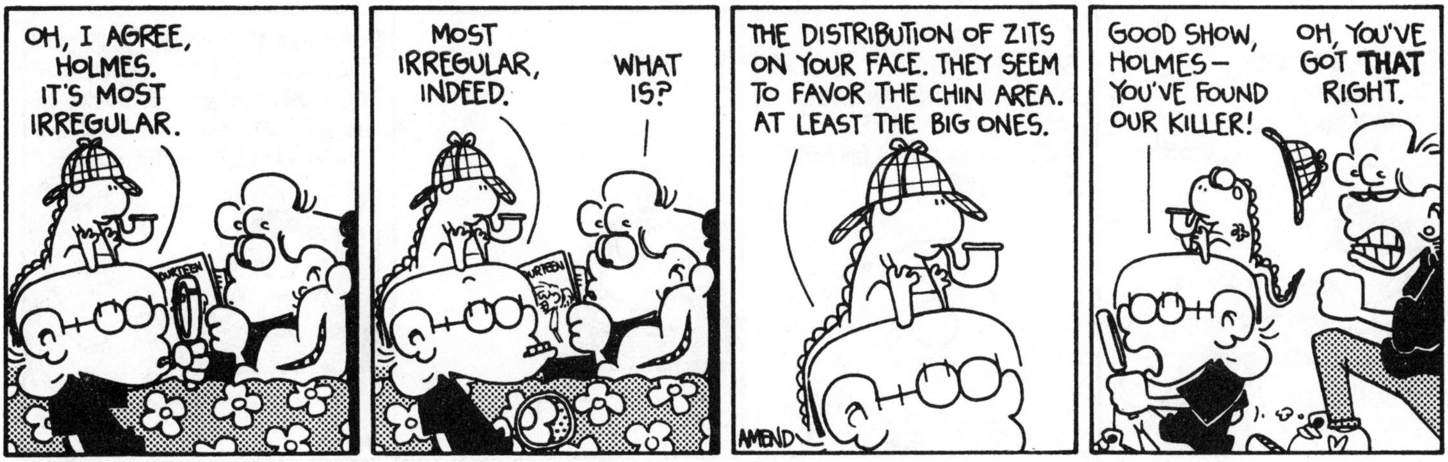
OH, I AGREE, HOLMES. IT'S MOST IRREGULAR.
MOST IRREGULAR, INDEED.
WHAT IS?
THE DISTRIBUTION OF ZITS ON YOUR FACE. THEY SEEM TO FAVOR THE CHIN AREA. AT LEAST THE BIG ONES.
AMEND
GOOD SHOW, HOLMES— YOU'VE FOUND OUR KILLER!
OH, YOU'VE GOT **THAT** RIGHT.

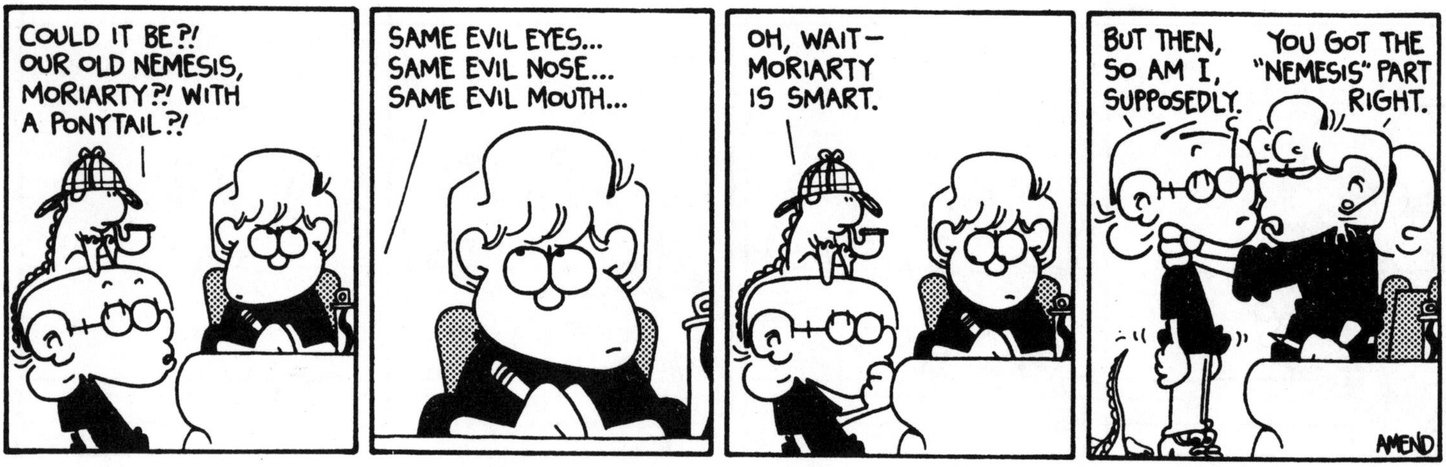
COULD IT BE?! OUR OLD NEMESIS, MORIARTY?! WITH A PONYTAIL?!
SAME EVIL EYES... SAME EVIL NOSE... SAME EVIL MOUTH...
OH, WAIT— MORIARTY IS SMART.
BUT THEN, SO AM I, SUPPOSEDLY.
YOU GOT THE "NEMESIS" PART RIGHT.
AMEND

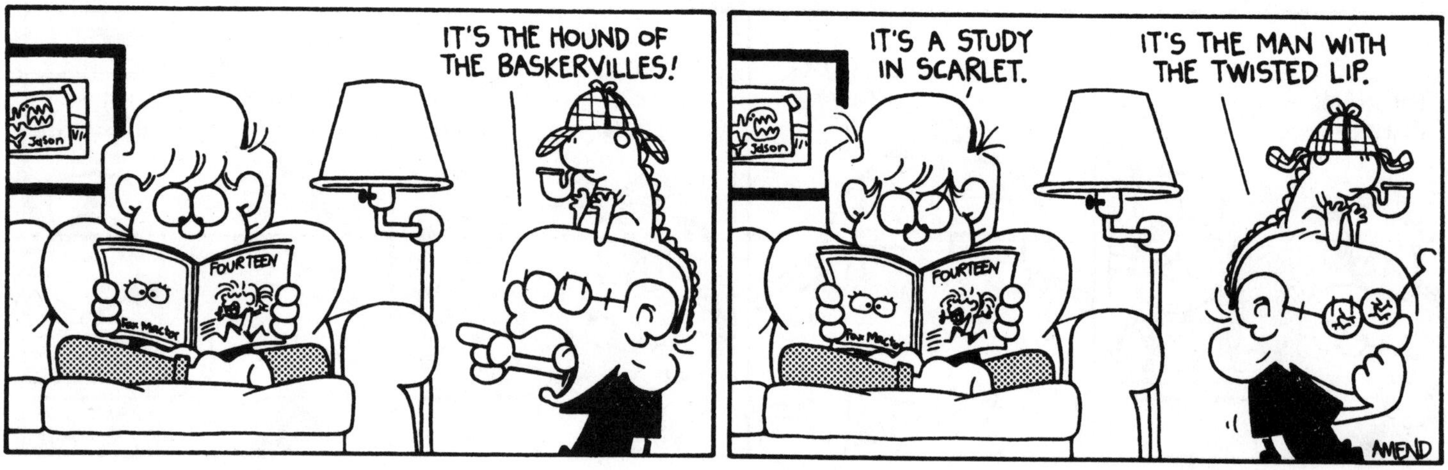
FOURTEEN
IT'S THE HOUND OF THE BASKERVILLES!
IT'S A STUDY IN SCARLET.
IT'S THE MAN WITH THE TWISTED LIP.
AMEND

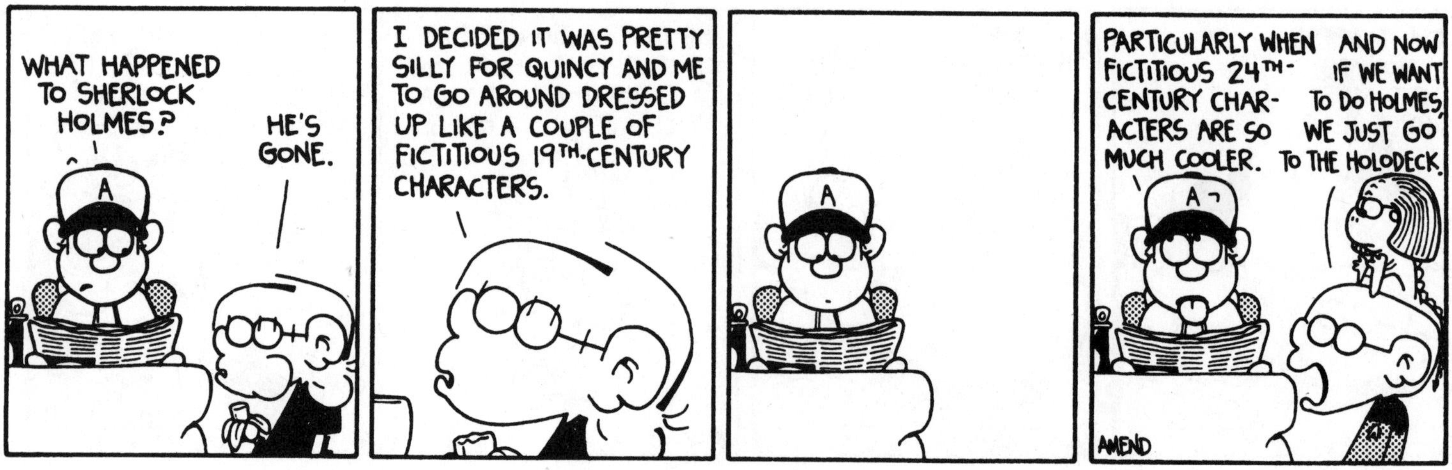
WHAT HAPPENED TO SHERLOCK HOLMES?
HE'S GONE.
I DECIDED IT WAS PRETTY SILLY FOR QUINCY AND ME TO GO AROUND DRESSED UP LIKE A COUPLE OF FICTITIOUS 19TH-CENTURY CHARACTERS.
PARTICULARLY WHEN FICTITIOUS 24TH-CENTURY CHARACTERS ARE SO MUCH COOLER.
AND NOW IF WE WANT TO DO HOLMES, WE JUST GO TO THE HOLODECK.
AMEND

FoxTrot

BILL AMEND

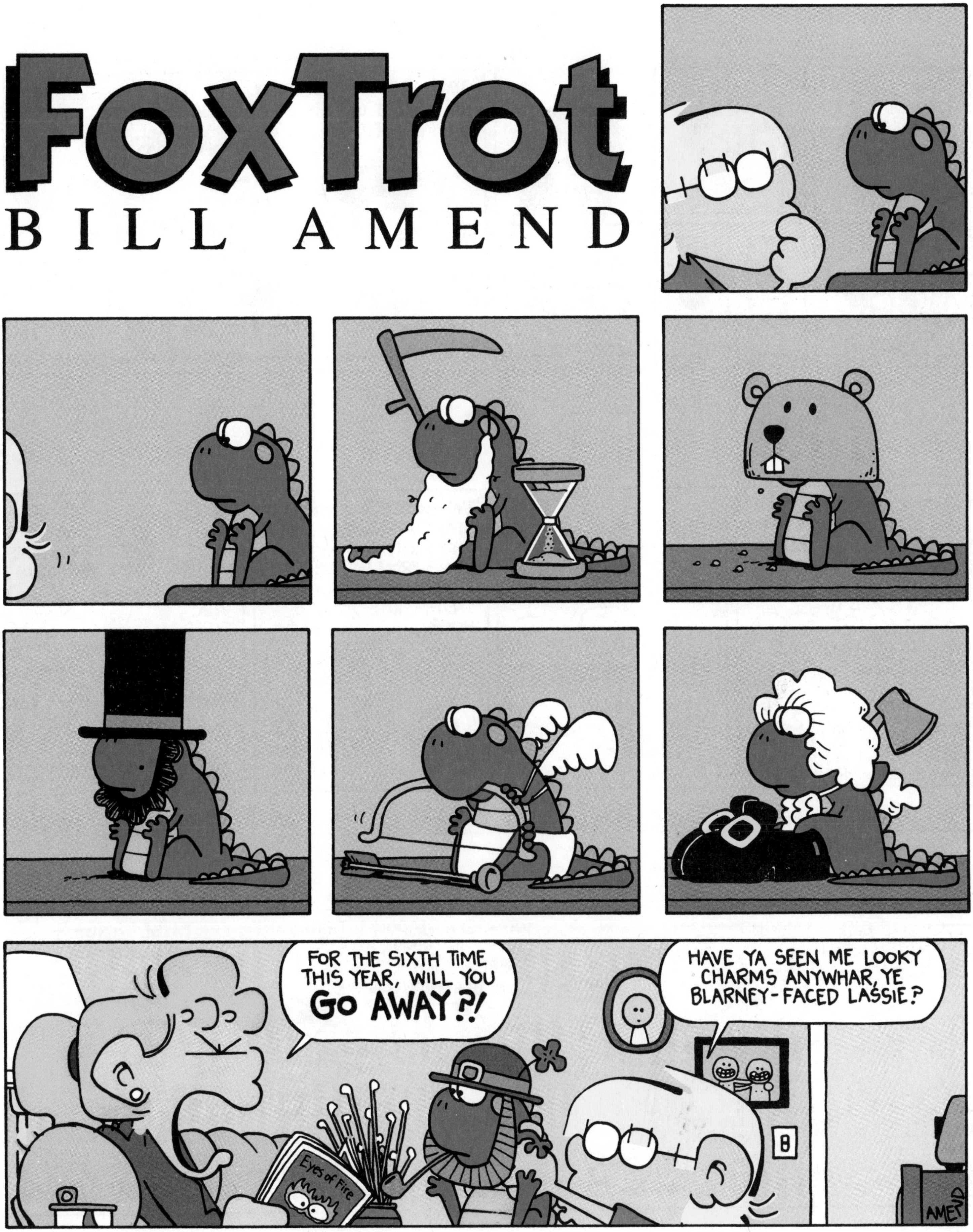

FOR THE SIXTH TIME THIS YEAR, WILL YOU GO AWAY?!
HAVE YA SEEN ME LOOKY CHARMS ANYWHAR, YE BLARNEY-FACED LASSIE?
Eyes of Fire
AMEND

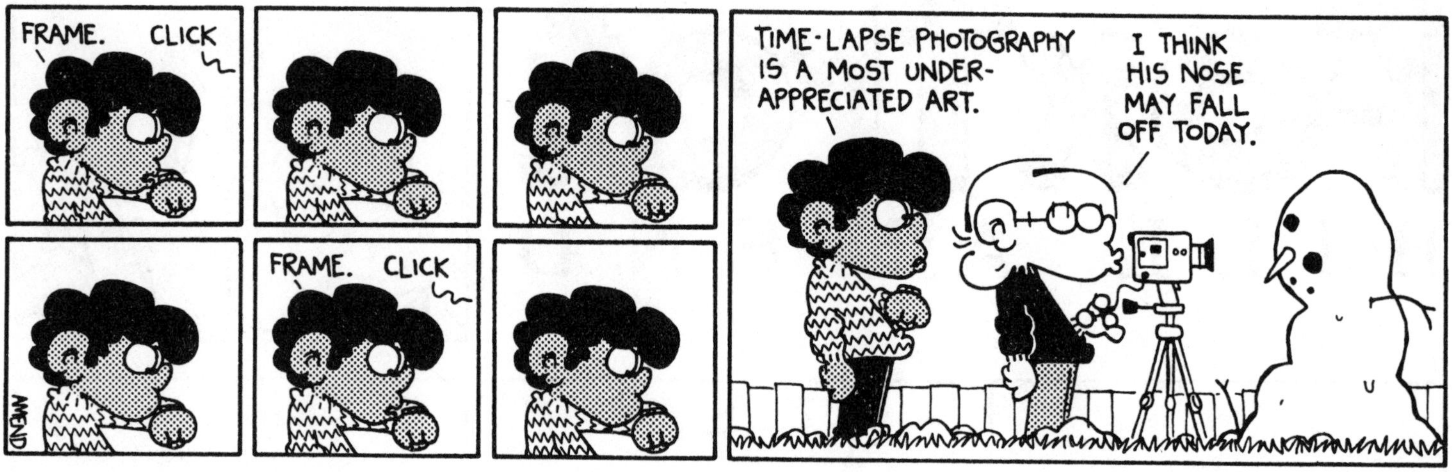
FRAME. CLICK
FRAME. CLICK
TIME-LAPSE PHOTOGRAPHY IS A MOST UNDER-APPRECIATED ART.
I THINK HIS NOSE MAY FALL OFF TODAY.

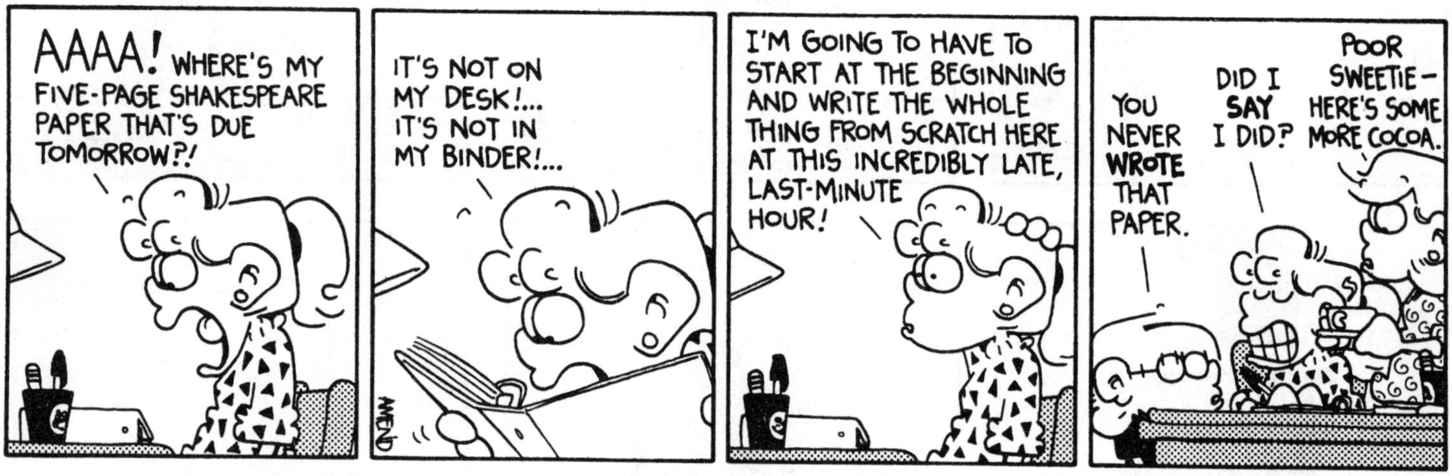
AAAA! WHERE'S MY FIVE-PAGE SHAKESPEARE PAPER THAT'S DUE TOMORROW?!
IT'S NOT ON MY DESK!... IT'S NOT IN MY BINDER!...
I'M GOING TO HAVE TO START AT THE BEGINNING AND WRITE THE WHOLE THING FROM SCRATCH HERE AT THIS INCREDIBLY LATE, LAST-MINUTE HOUR!
YOU NEVER WROTE THAT PAPER.
DID I SAY I DID?
POOR SWEETIE-HERE'S SOME MORE COCOA.

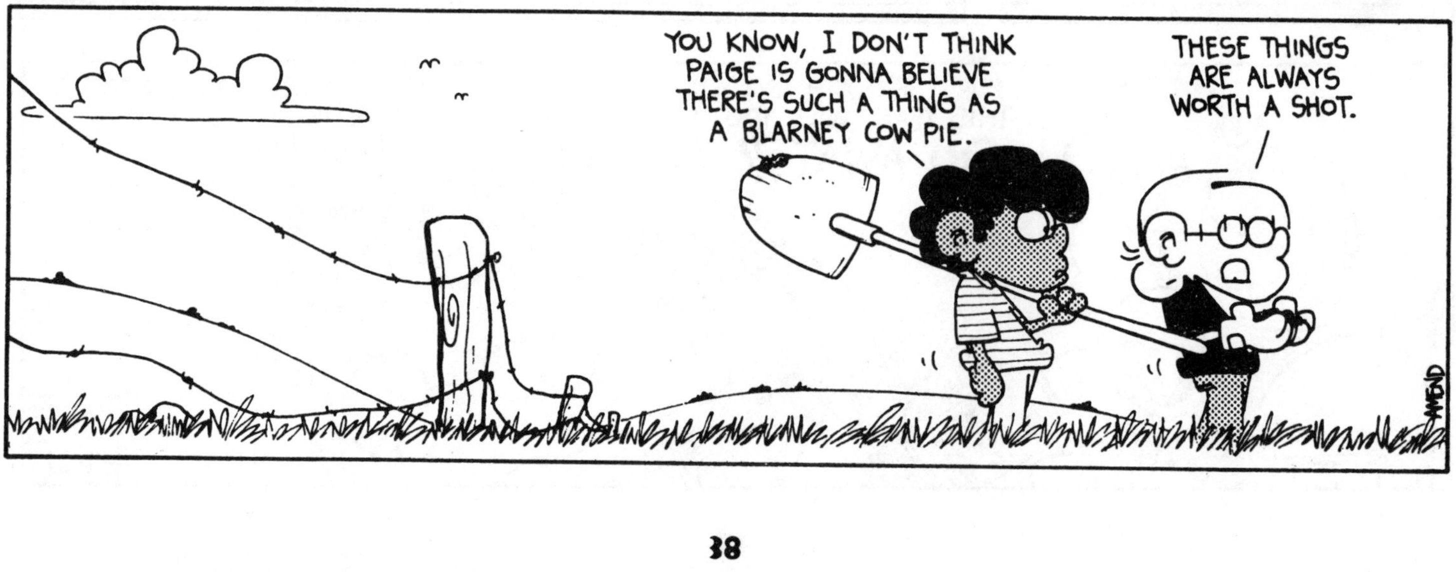
YOU KNOW, I DON'T THINK PAIGE IS GONNA BELIEVE THERE'S SUCH A THING AS A BLARNEY COW PIE.
THESE THINGS ARE ALWAYS WORTH A SHOT.

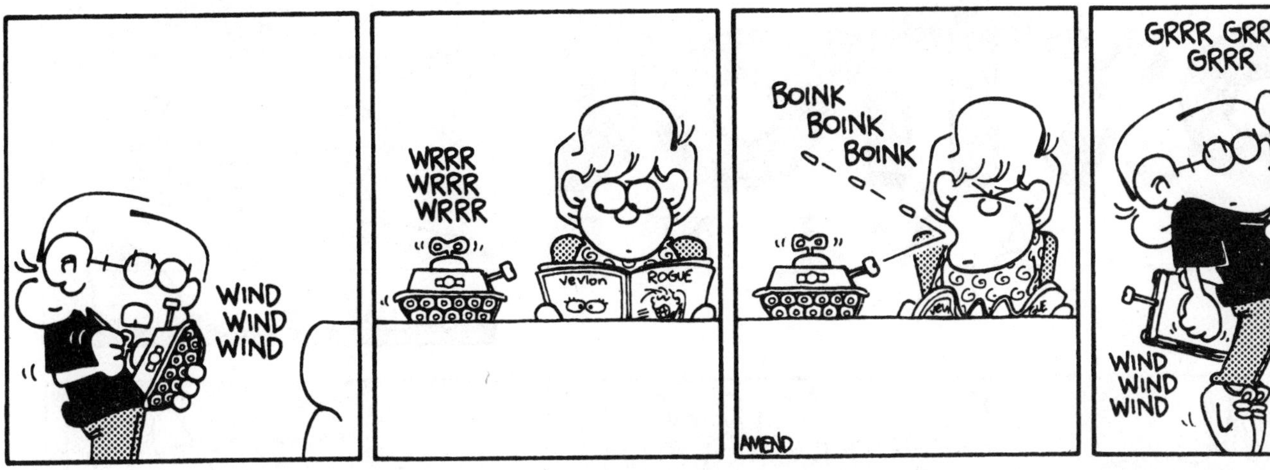

WIND WIND WIND
WRRR WRRR WRRR
Vevlon
ROGUE
BOINK BOINK BOINK
GRRR GRRR GRRR
WIND WIND WIND
AMEND

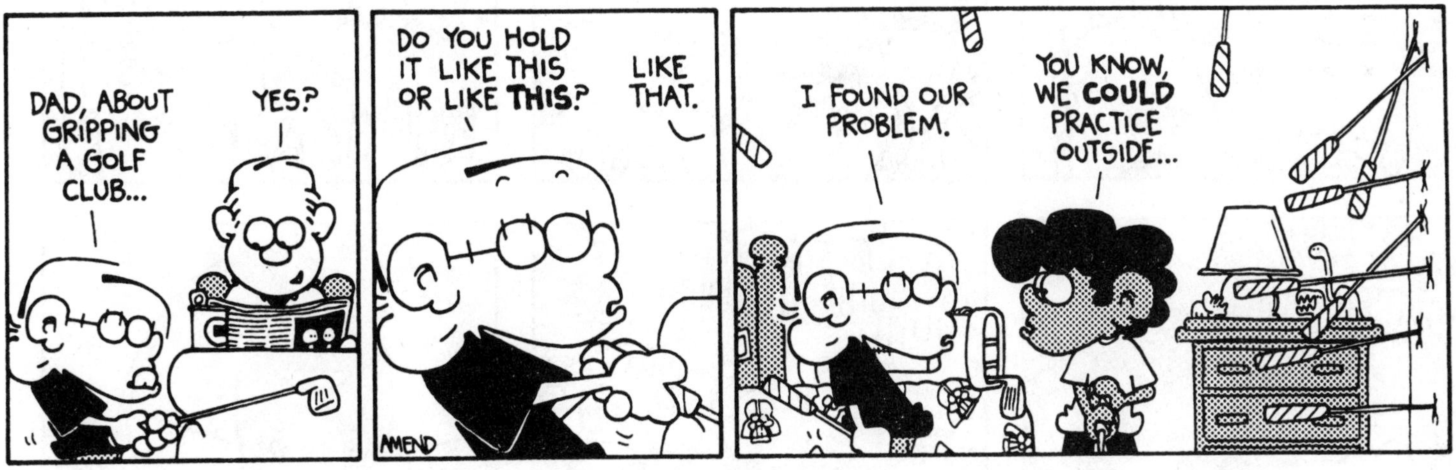

DAD, ABOUT GRIPPING A GOLF CLUB...
YES?
DO YOU HOLD IT LIKE THIS OR LIKE **THIS**?
LIKE THAT.
AMEND
I FOUND OUR PROBLEM.
YOU KNOW, WE **COULD** PRACTICE OUTSIDE...

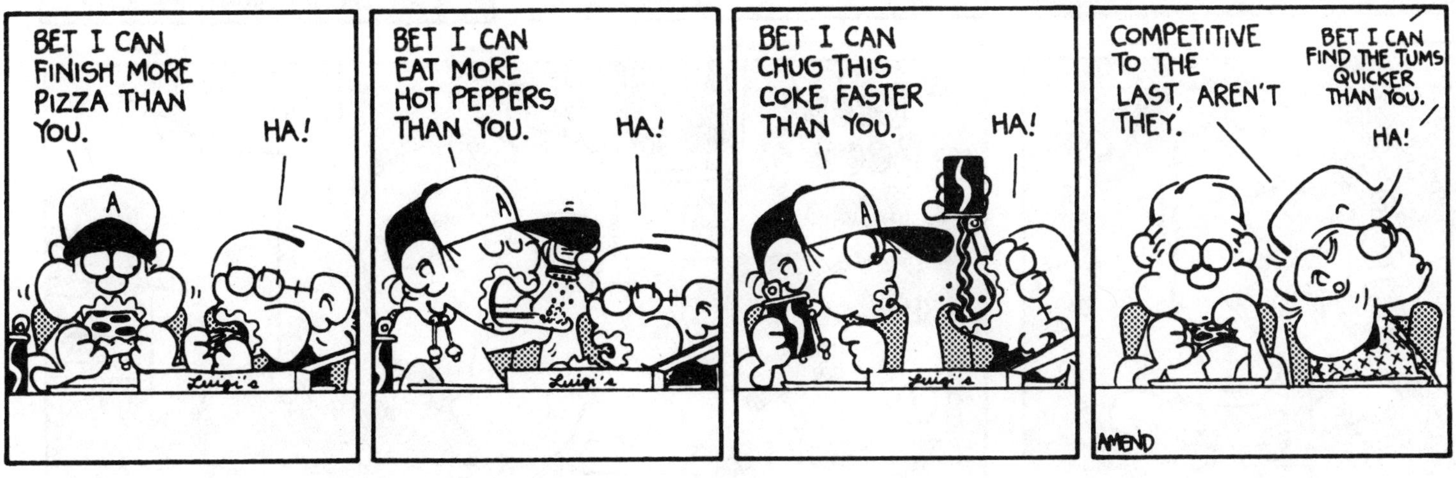

BET I CAN FINISH MORE PIZZA THAN YOU.
HA!
Luigi's
BET I CAN EAT MORE HOT PEPPERS THAN YOU.
HA!
Luigi's
BET I CAN CHUG THIS COKE FASTER THAN YOU.
HA!
Luigi's
COMPETITIVE TO THE LAST, AREN'T THEY.
BET I CAN FIND THE TUMS QUICKER THAN YOU.
HA!
AMEND

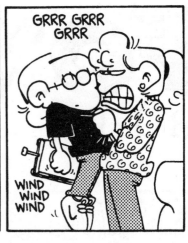

FoxTrot

BILL AMEND

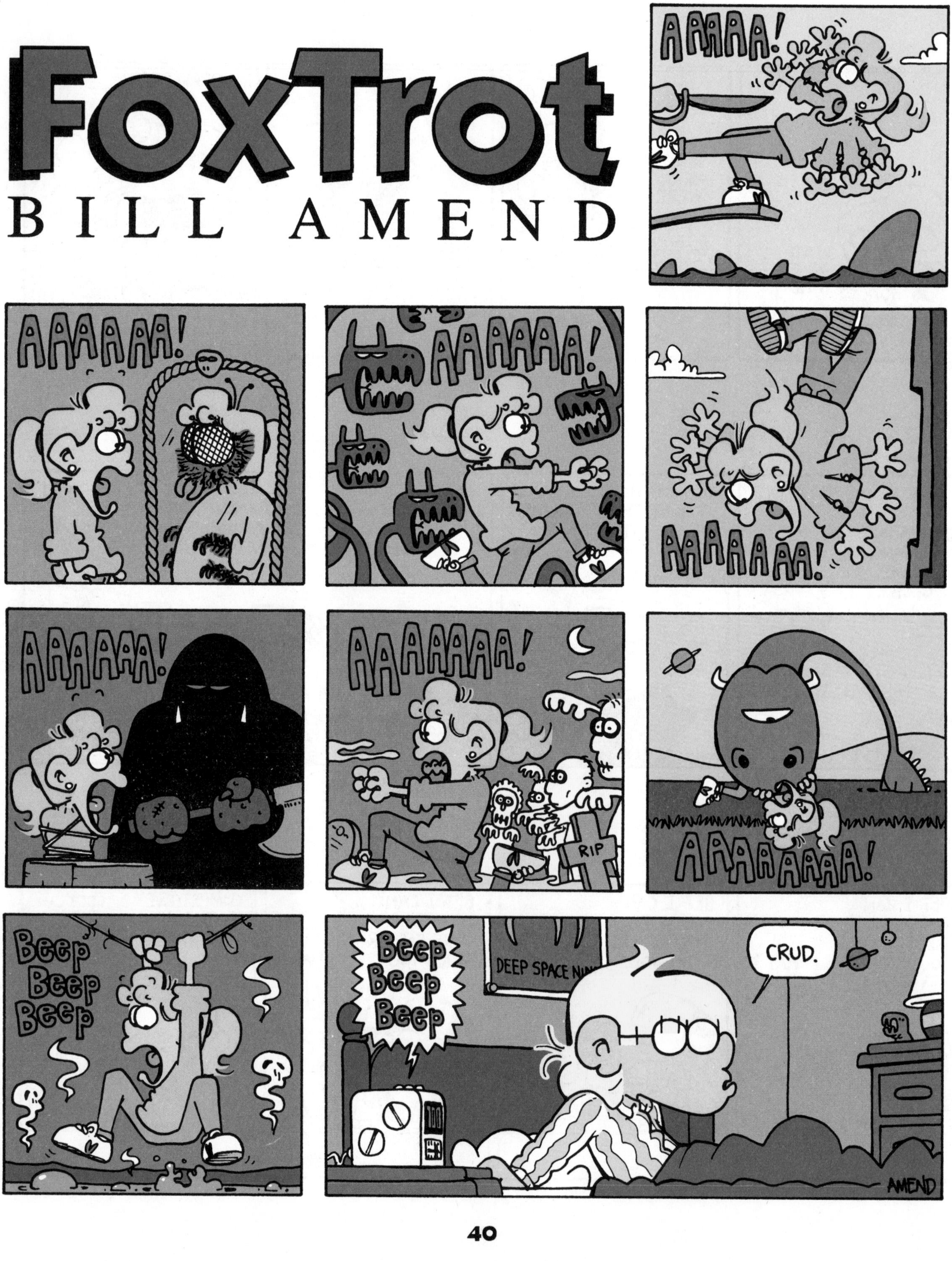

AAAAA!
AAAAAA!
AAAAAA!
AAAAAAA!
AAAAAA!
AAAAAAA!
RIP
AAAAAAAA!
Beep
Beep
Beep
Beep
Beep
Beep
DEEP SPACE NIN
CRUD.
AMEND

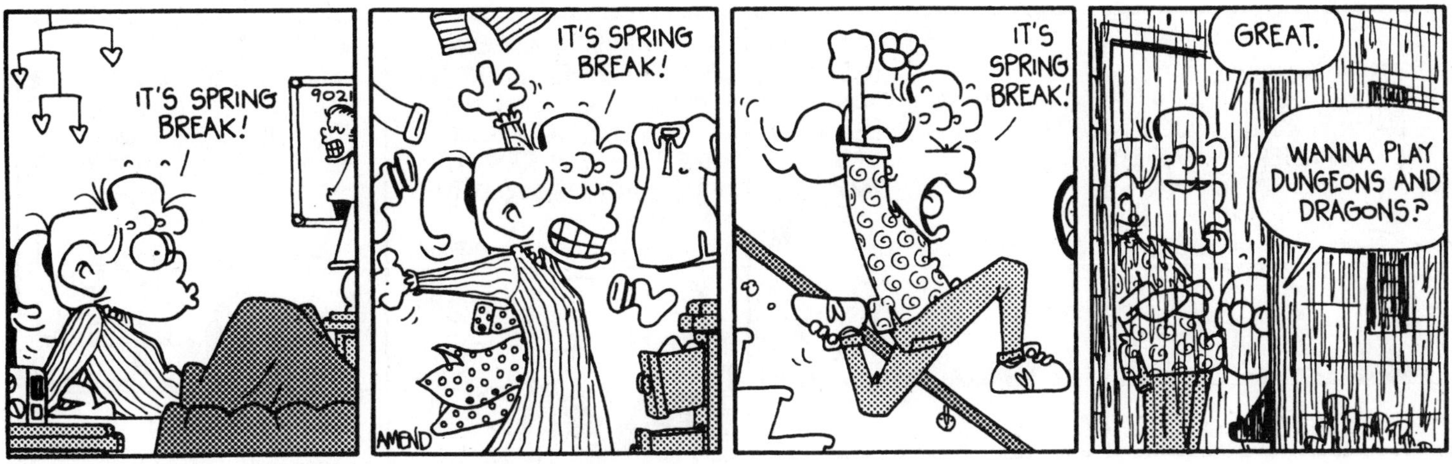
IT'S SPRING BREAK!
9021
IT'S SPRING BREAK!
AMEND
IT'S SPRING BREAK!
GREAT.
WANNA PLAY DUNGEONS AND DRAGONS?

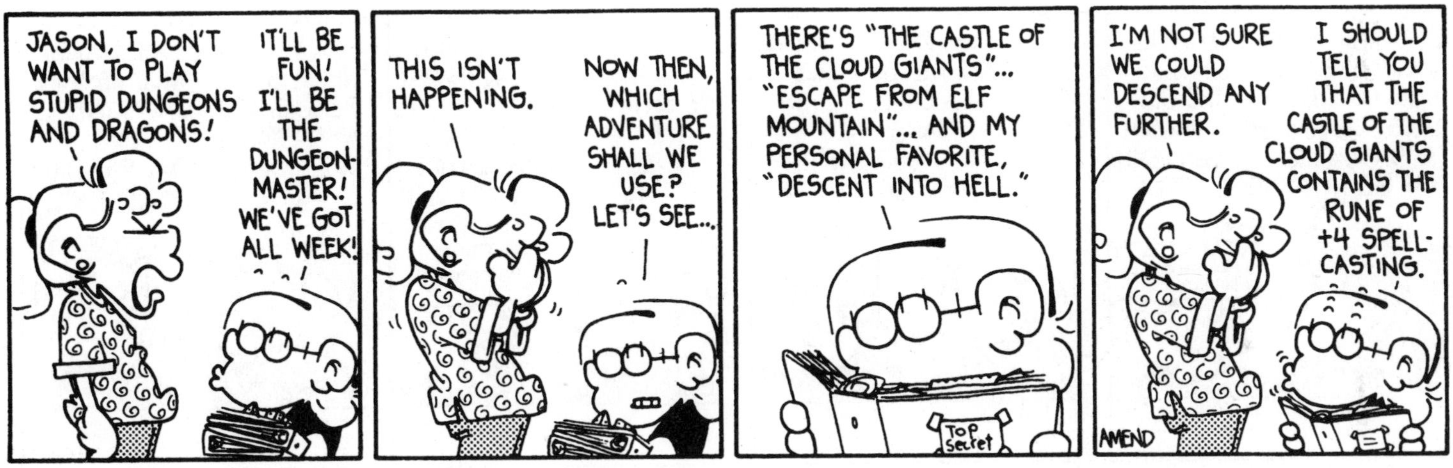
JASON, I DON'T WANT TO PLAY STUPID DUNGEONS AND DRAGONS!
IT'LL BE FUN! I'LL BE THE DUNGEON-MASTER! WE'VE GOT ALL WEEK!
THIS ISN'T HAPPENING.
NOW THEN, WHICH ADVENTURE SHALL WE USE? LET'S SEE...
THERE'S "THE CASTLE OF THE CLOUD GIANTS"... "ESCAPE FROM ELF MOUNTAIN"... AND MY PERSONAL FAVORITE, "DESCENT INTO HELL."
TOP SECRET
I'M NOT SURE WE COULD DESCEND ANY FURTHER.
I SHOULD TELL YOU THAT THE CASTLE OF THE CLOUD GIANTS CONTAINS THE RUNE OF +4 SPELL-CASTING.
AMEND

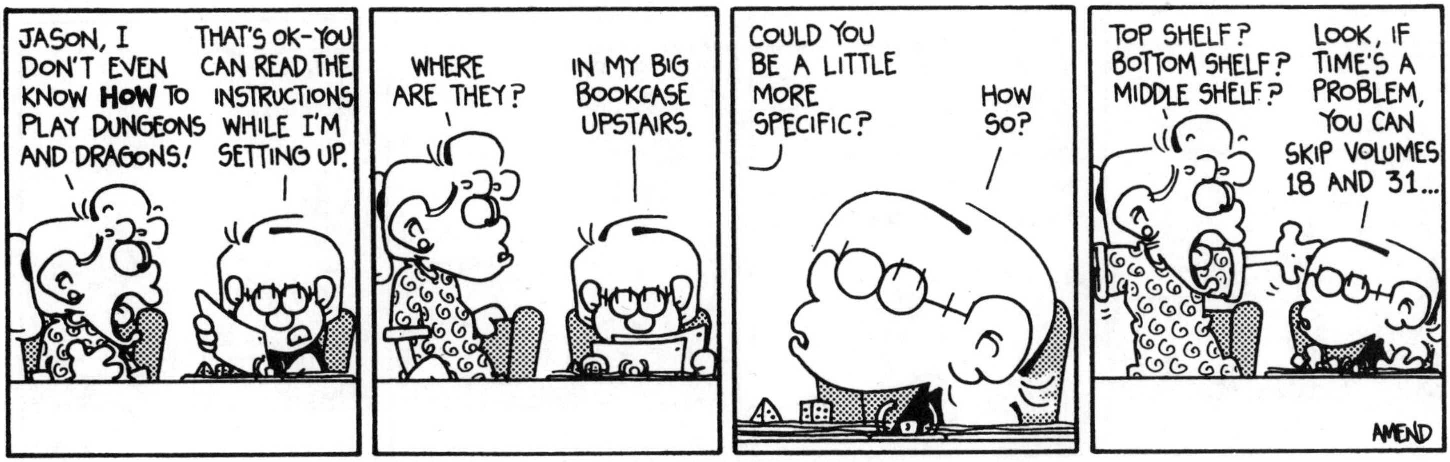
JASON, I DON'T EVEN KNOW HOW TO PLAY DUNGEONS AND DRAGONS!
THAT'S OK-YOU CAN READ THE INSTRUCTIONS WHILE I'M SETTING UP.
WHERE ARE THEY?
IN MY BIG BOOKCASE UPSTAIRS.
COULD YOU BE A LITTLE MORE SPECIFIC?
HOW SO?
TOP SHELF? BOTTOM SHELF? MIDDLE SHELF?
LOOK, IF TIME'S A PROBLEM, YOU CAN SKIP VOLUMES 18 AND 31...
AMEND

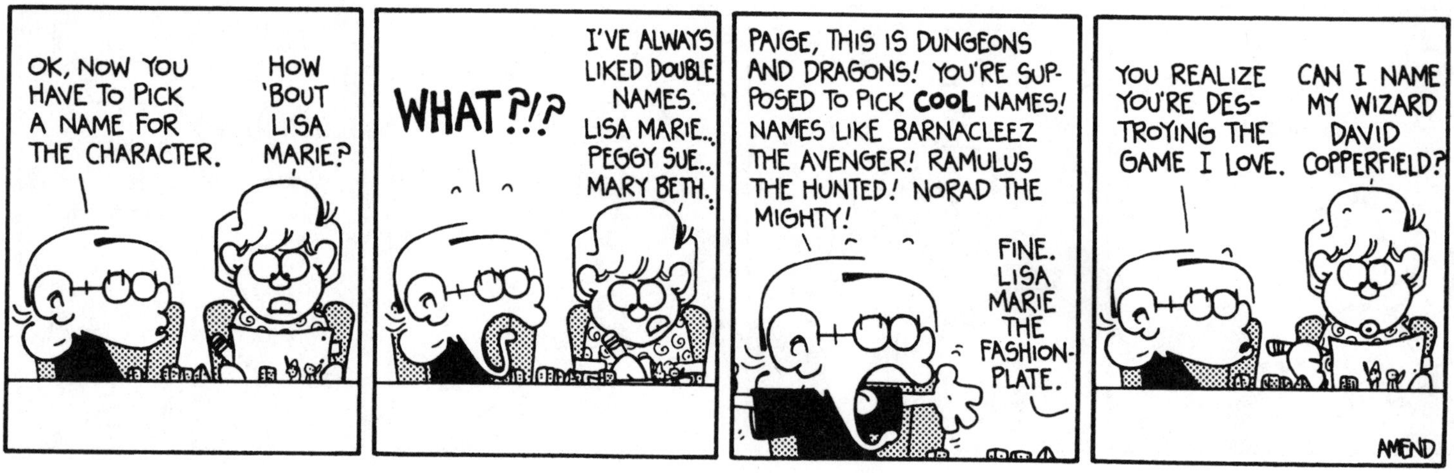
OK, NOW YOU HAVE TO PICK A NAME FOR THE CHARACTER.
HOW 'BOUT LISA MARIE?
WHAT?!?
I'VE ALWAYS LIKED DOUBLE NAMES. LISA MARIE... PEGGY SUE... MARY BETH...
PAIGE, THIS IS DUNGEONS AND DRAGONS! YOU'RE SUPPOSED TO PICK COOL NAMES! NAMES LIKE BARNACLEEZ THE AVENGER! RAMULUS THE HUNTED! NORAD THE MIGHTY!
FINE. LISA MARIE THE FASHION-PLATE.
YOU REALIZE YOU'RE DESTROYING THE GAME I LOVE.
CAN I NAME MY WIZARD DAVID COPPERFIELD?
AMEND

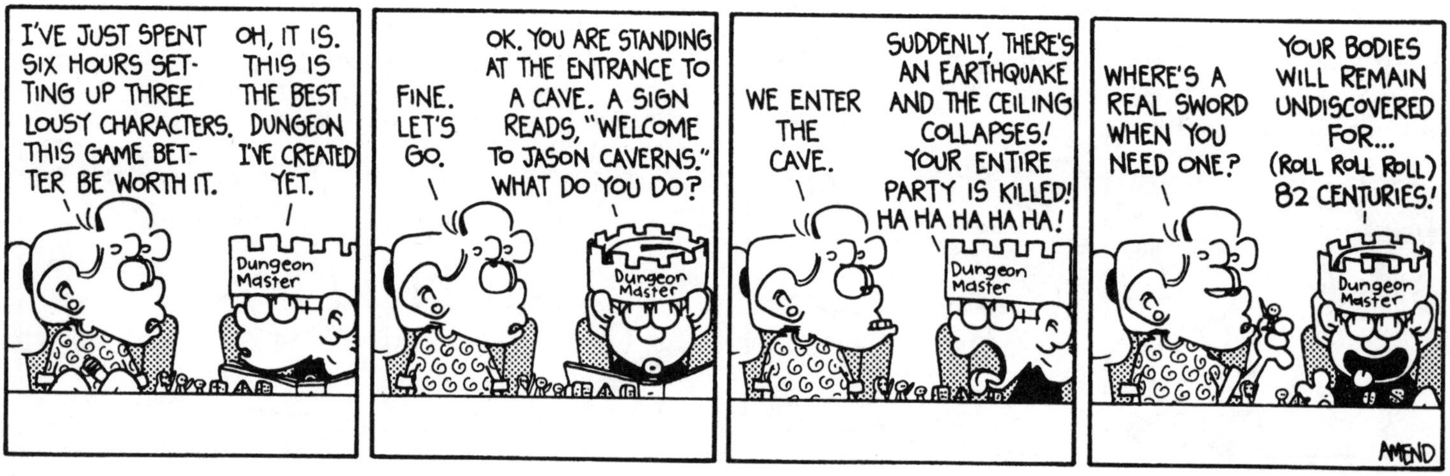
I'VE JUST SPENT SIX HOURS SETTING UP THREE LOUSY CHARACTERS. THIS GAME BETTER BE WORTH IT.
OH, IT IS. THIS IS THE BEST DUNGEON I'VE CREATED YET.
Dungeon Master
FINE. LET'S GO.
OK. YOU ARE STANDING AT THE ENTRANCE TO A CAVE. A SIGN READS, "WELCOME TO JASON CAVERNS." WHAT DO YOU DO?
Dungeon Master
WE ENTER THE CAVE.
SUDDENLY, THERE'S AN EARTHQUAKE AND THE CEILING COLLAPSES! YOUR ENTIRE PARTY IS KILLED! HA HA HA HA HA!
Dungeon Master
WHERE'S A REAL SWORD WHEN YOU NEED ONE?
YOUR BODIES WILL REMAIN UNDISCOVERED FOR... (ROLL ROLL ROLL) 82 CENTURIES!
Dungeon Master
AMEND

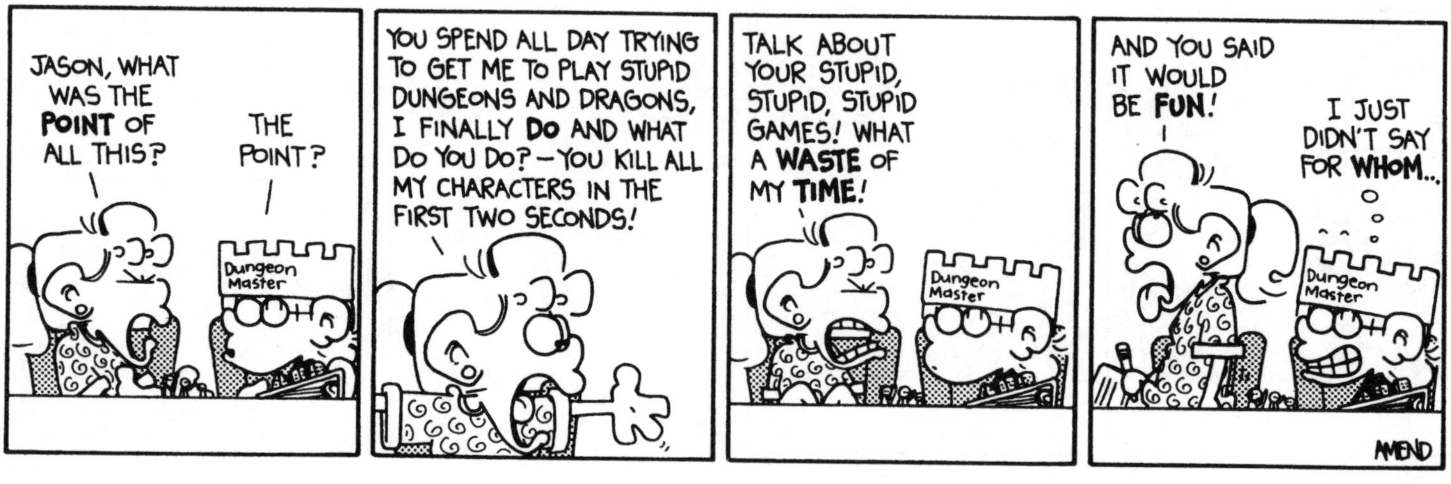
JASON, WHAT WAS THE POINT OF ALL THIS?
THE POINT?
Dungeon Master
YOU SPEND ALL DAY TRYING TO GET ME TO PLAY STUPID DUNGEONS AND DRAGONS, I FINALLY DO AND WHAT DO YOU DO? —YOU KILL ALL MY CHARACTERS IN THE FIRST TWO SECONDS!
TALK ABOUT YOUR STUPID, STUPID, STUPID GAMES! WHAT A WASTE OF MY TIME!
Dungeon Master
AND YOU SAID IT WOULD BE FUN!
I JUST DIDN'T SAY FOR WHOM...
Dungeon Master
AMEND

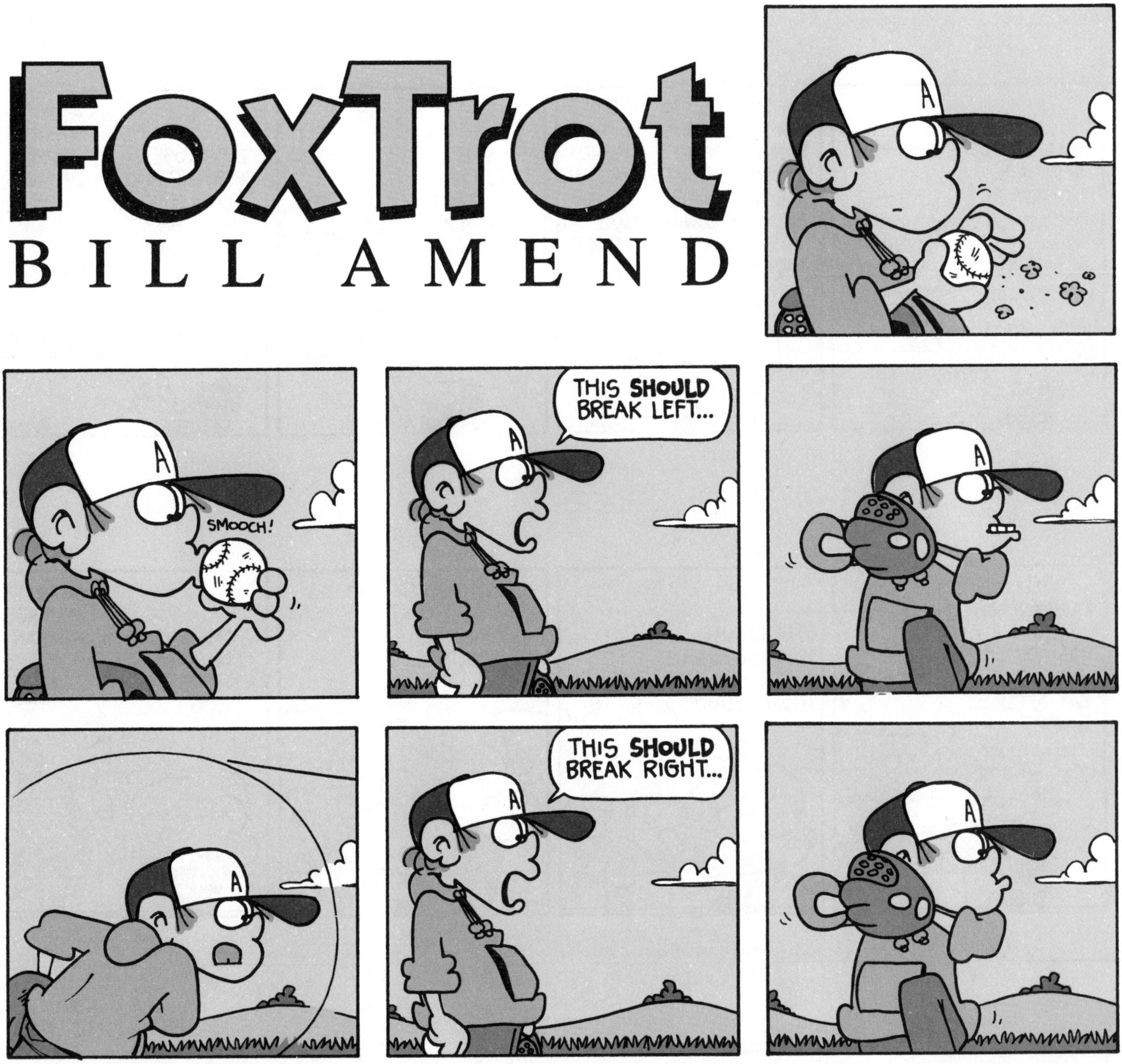
FoxTrot
BILL AMEND
SMOOCH!
THIS SHOULD BREAK LEFT...
THIS SHOULD BREAK RIGHT...
THIS SHOULD BREAK—...
OK, OK, MAYBE I DID TAKE A FEW PHOTOS OF YOU AND DENISE LAST NIGHT...
AMEND

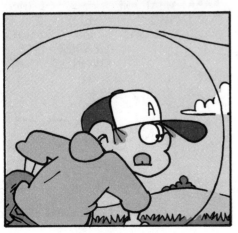

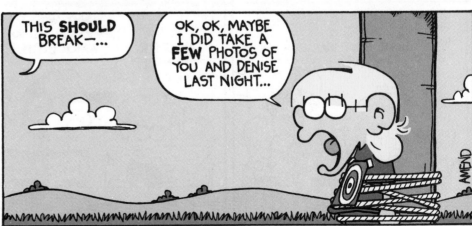

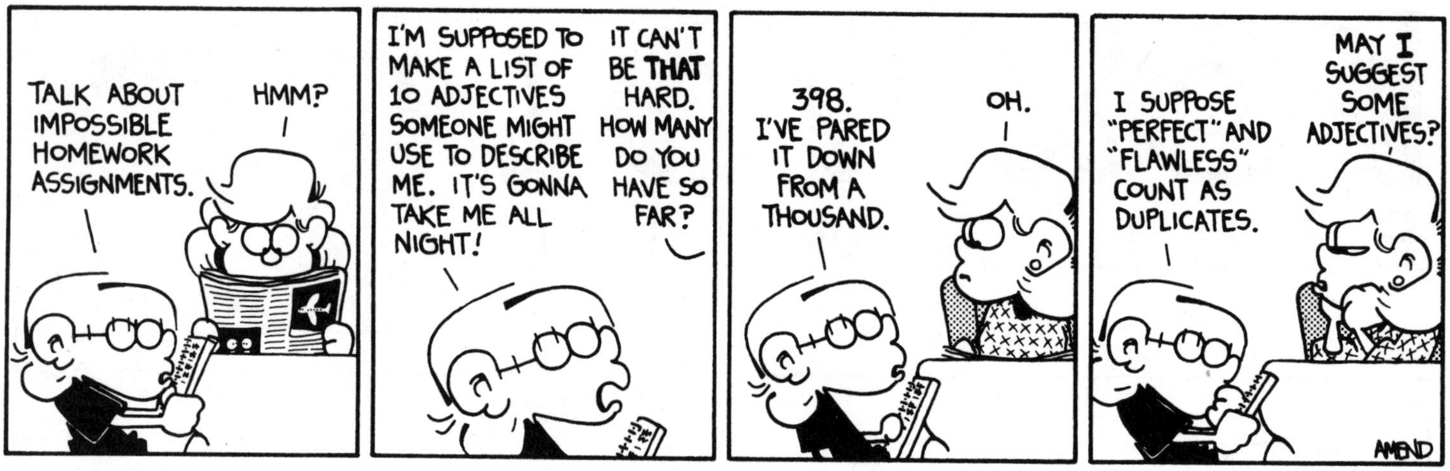
TALK ABOUT IMPOSSIBLE HOMEWORK ASSIGNMENTS.
HMM?
I'M SUPPOSED TO MAKE A LIST OF 10 ADJECTIVES SOMEONE MIGHT USE TO DESCRIBE ME. IT'S GONNA TAKE ME ALL NIGHT!
IT CAN'T BE **THAT** HARD. HOW MANY DO YOU HAVE SO FAR?
398. I'VE PARED IT DOWN FROM A THOUSAND.
OH.
I SUPPOSE "PERFECT" AND "FLAWLESS" COUNT AS DUPLICATES.
MAY **I** SUGGEST SOME ADJECTIVES?
AMEND

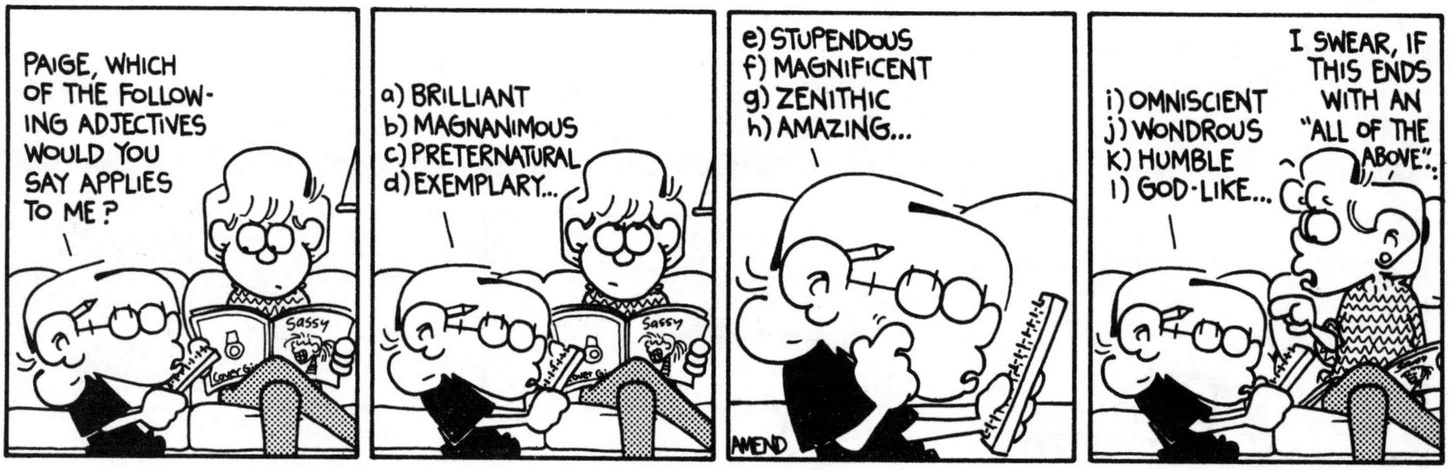
PAIGE, WHICH OF THE FOLLOWING ADJECTIVES WOULD YOU SAY APPLIES TO ME?
a) BRILLIANT
b) MAGNANIMOUS
c) PRETERNATURAL
d) EXEMPLARY...
e) STUPENDOUS
f) MAGNIFICENT
g) ZENITHIC
h) AMAZING...
AMEND
i) OMNISCIENT
j) WONDROUS
K) HUMBLE
l) GOD-LIKE...
I SWEAR, IF THIS ENDS WITH AN "ALL OF THE ABOVE"...

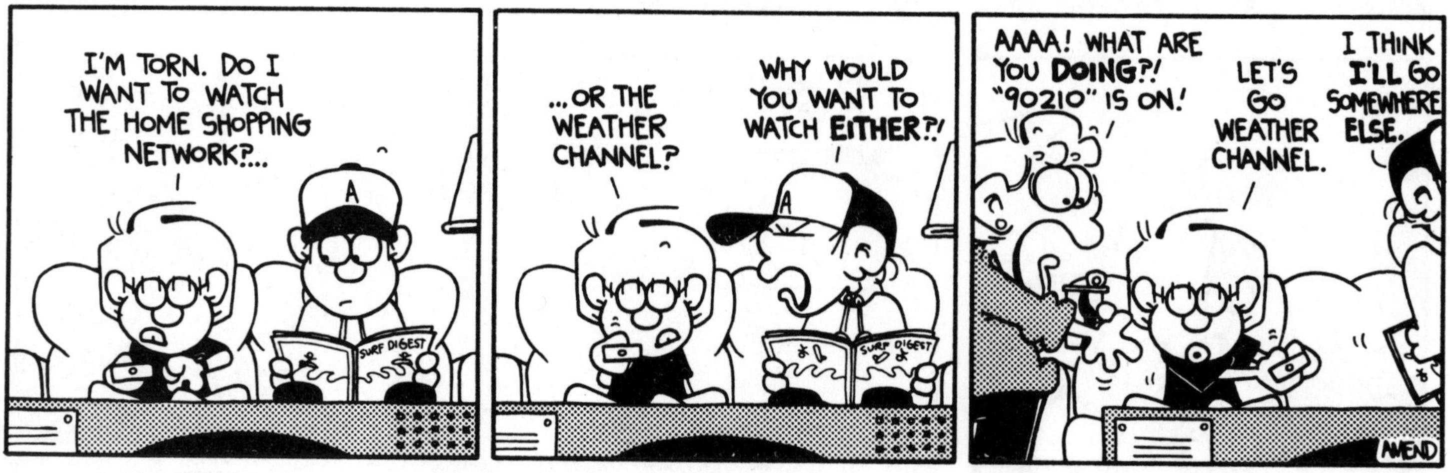
I'M TORN. DO I WANT TO WATCH THE HOME SHOPPING NETWORK?...
...OR THE WEATHER CHANNEL?
WHY WOULD YOU WANT TO WATCH **EITHER**?!
AAAA! WHAT ARE YOU **DOING**?! "90210" IS ON!
LET'S GO WEATHER CHANNEL.
I THINK **I'LL** GO SOMEWHERE **ELSE**.
AMEND

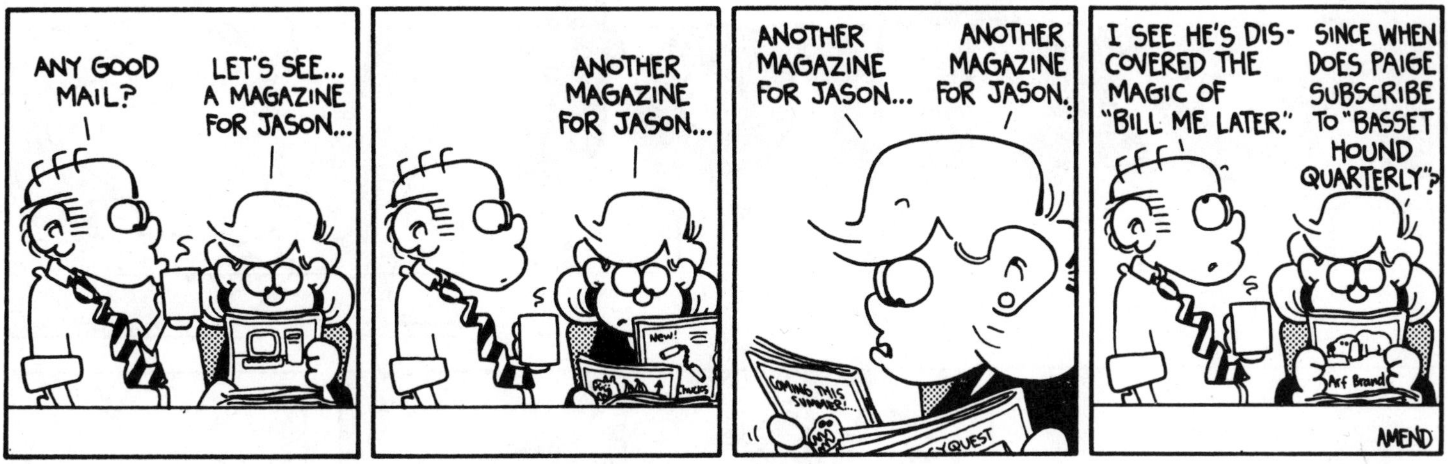
ANY GOOD MAIL?
LET'S SEE... A MAGAZINE FOR JASON...
ANOTHER MAGAZINE FOR JASON...
ANOTHER MAGAZINE FOR JASON...
ANOTHER MAGAZINE FOR JASON.
I SEE HE'S DISCOVERED THE MAGIC OF "BILL ME LATER."
SINCE WHEN DOES PAIGE SUBSCRIBE TO "BASSET HOUND QUARTERLY"?
AMEND

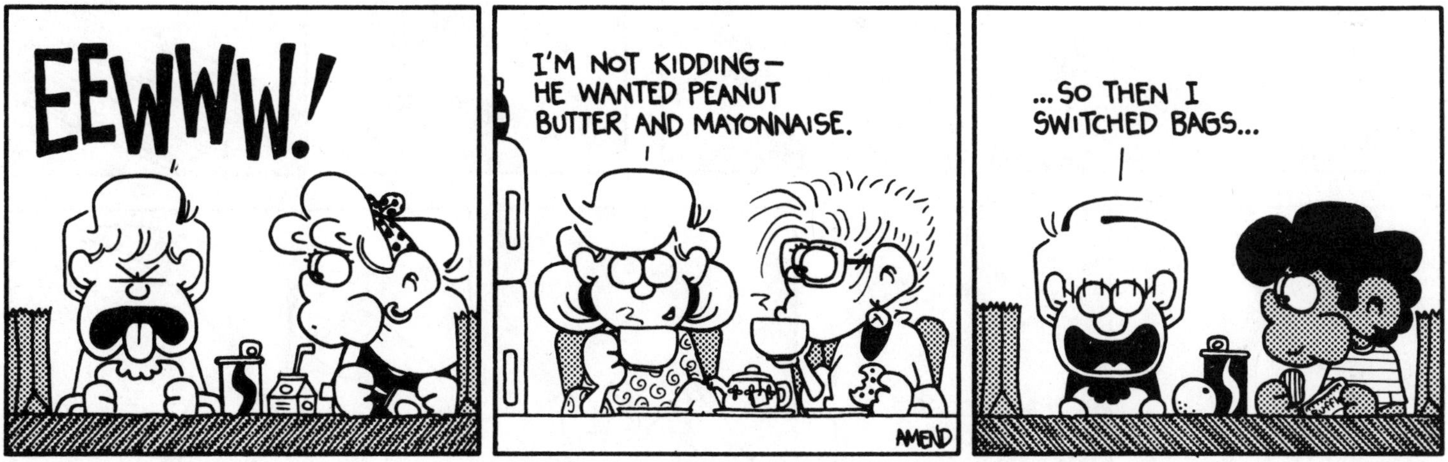
EEWWW!
I'M NOT KIDDING– HE WANTED PEANUT BUTTER AND MAYONNAISE.
AMEND
...SO THEN I SWITCHED BAGS...

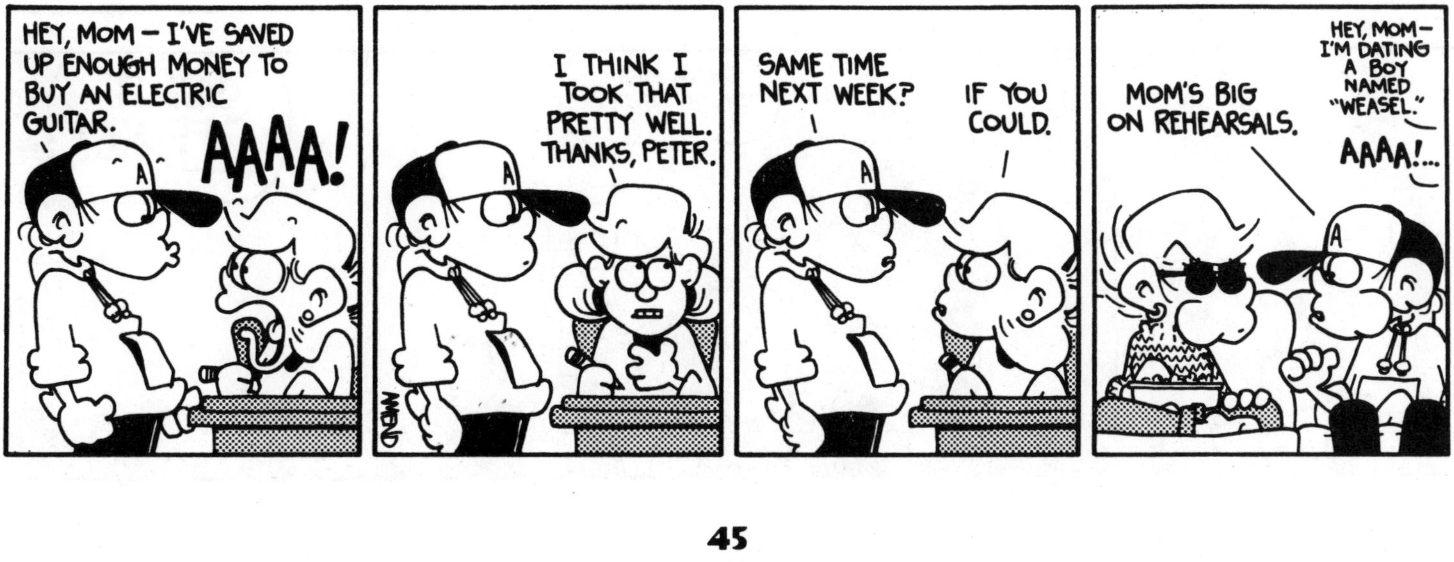
HEY, MOM – I'VE SAVED UP ENOUGH MONEY TO BUY AN ELECTRIC GUITAR.
AAAA!
I THINK I TOOK THAT PRETTY WELL. THANKS, PETER.
SAME TIME NEXT WEEK?
IF YOU COULD.
MOM'S BIG ON REHEARSALS.
HEY, MOM– I'M DATING A BOY NAMED "WEASEL."
AAAA!...

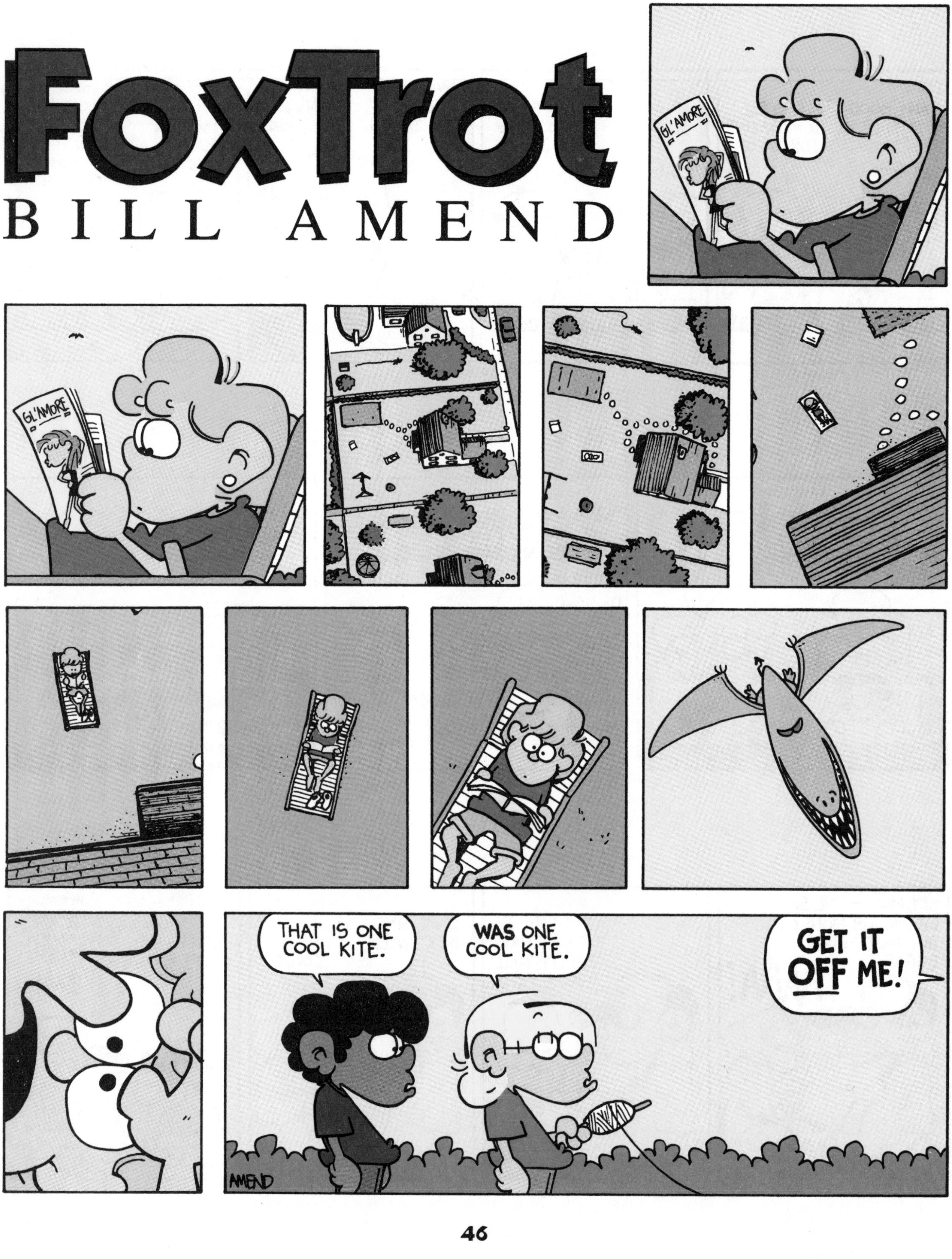
FoxTrot
BILL AMEND
GIL'AMORE
THAT IS ONE COOL KITE.
WAS ONE COOL KITE.
GET IT OFF ME!
AMEND

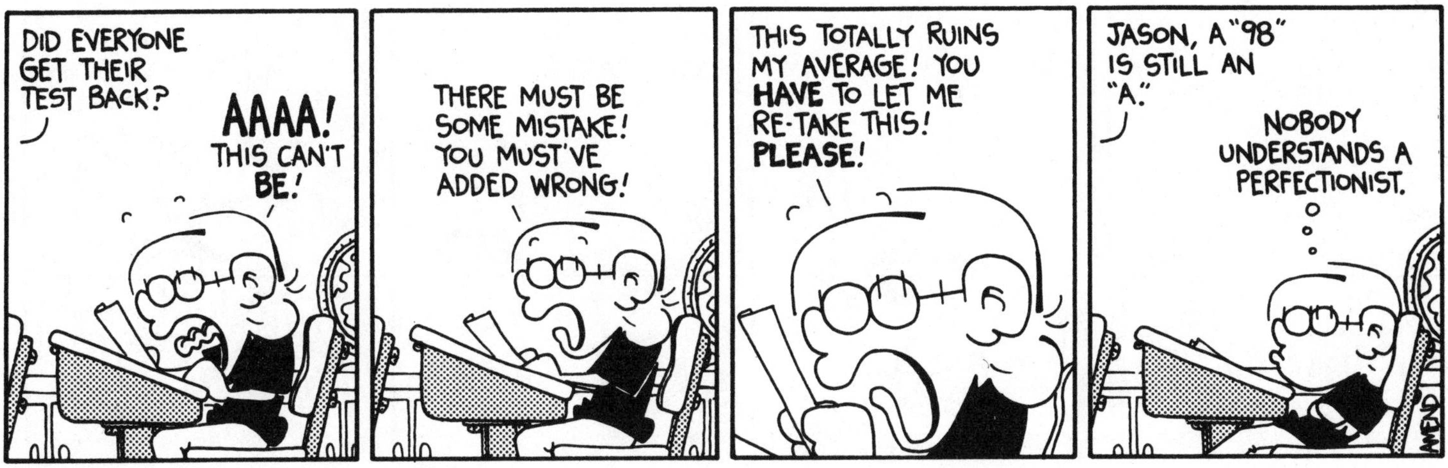
DID EVERYONE GET THEIR TEST BACK?
AAAA! THIS CAN'T BE!
THERE MUST BE SOME MISTAKE! YOU MUST'VE ADDED WRONG!
THIS TOTALLY RUINS MY AVERAGE! YOU HAVE TO LET ME RE-TAKE THIS! PLEASE!
JASON, A "98" IS STILL AN "A."
NOBODY UNDERSTANDS A PERFECTIONIST.
AMEND

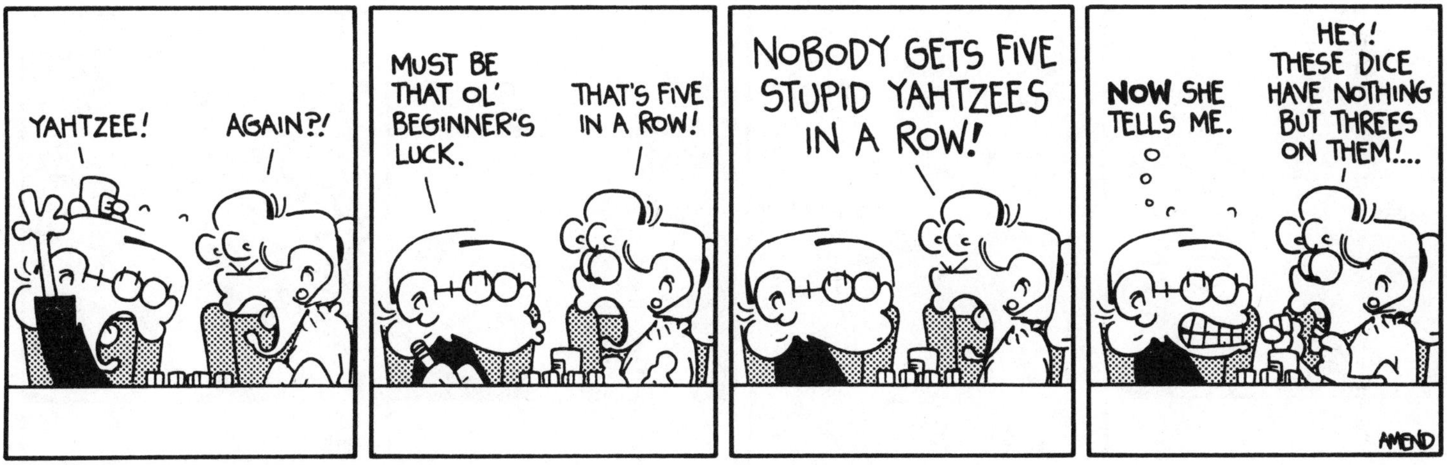
YAHTZEE!
AGAIN?!
MUST BE THAT OL' BEGINNER'S LUCK.
THAT'S FIVE IN A ROW!
NOBODY GETS FIVE STUPID YAHTZEES IN A ROW!
NOW SHE TELLS ME.
HEY! THESE DICE HAVE NOTHING BUT THREES ON THEM!...
AMEND

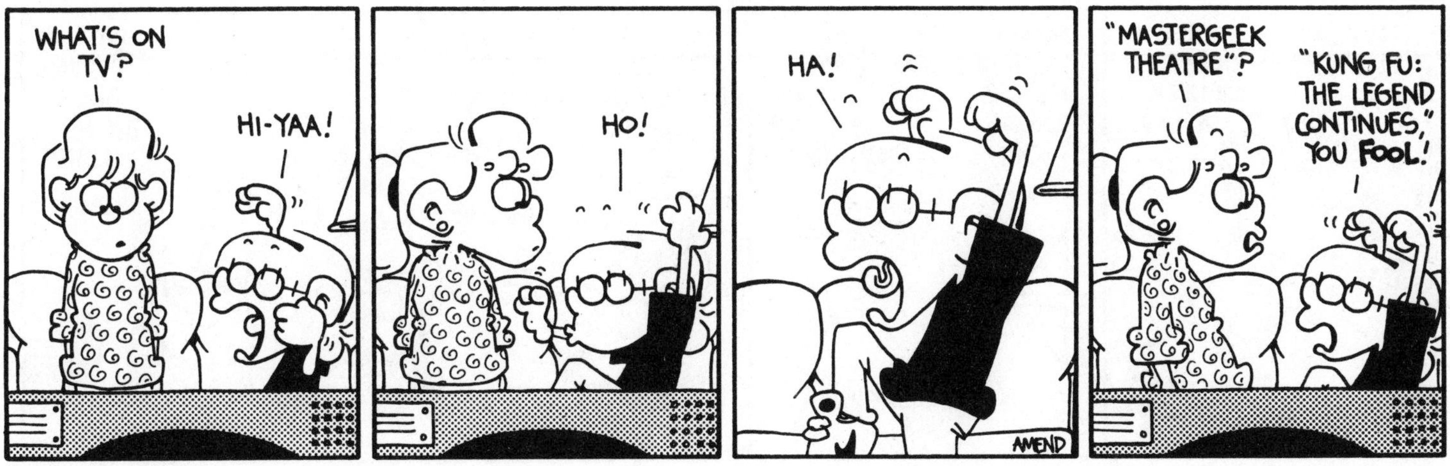
WHAT'S ON TV?
HI-YAA!
HO!
HA!
"MASTERGEEK THEATRE"?
"KUNG FU: THE LEGEND CONTINUES," YOU FOOL!
AMEND

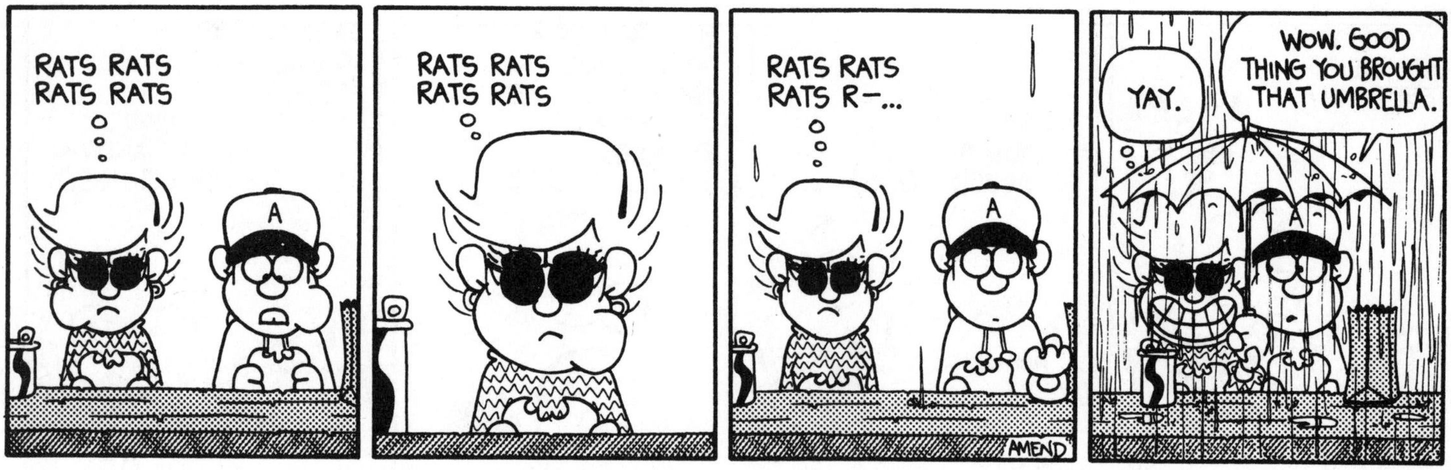
RATS RATS RATS RATS
RATS RATS RATS RATS
RATS RATS RATS R–...
YAY.
WOW. GOOD THING YOU BROUGHT THAT UMBRELLA.
AMEND

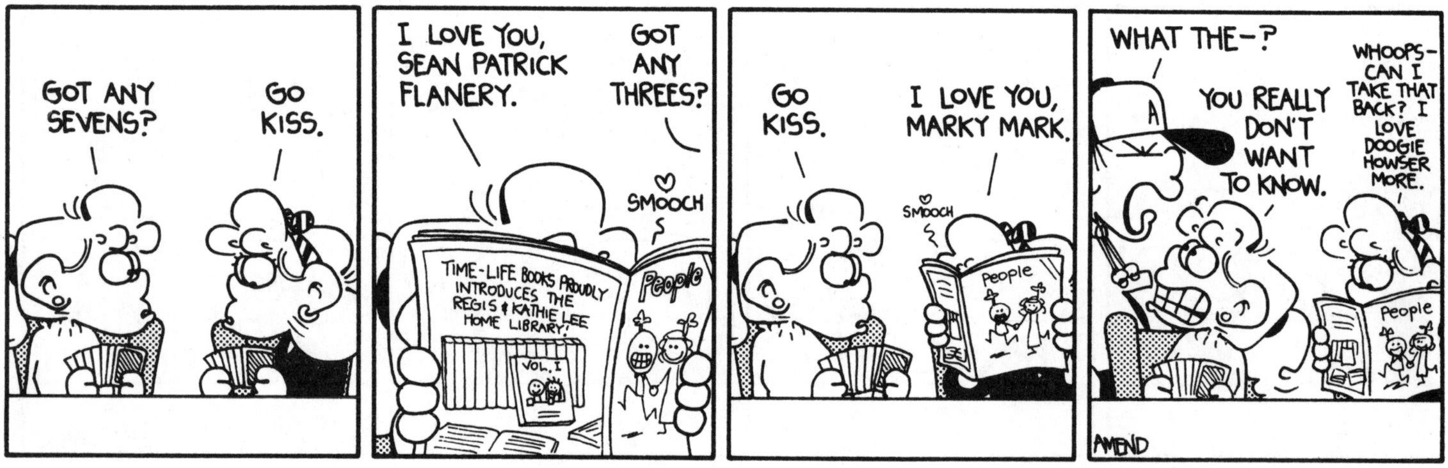
GOT ANY SEVENS?
GO KISS.
I LOVE YOU, SEAN PATRICK FLANERY.
GOT ANY THREES?
SMOOCH
TIME-LIFE BOOKS PROUDLY INTRODUCES THE REGIS & KATHIE LEE HOME LIBRARY!
VOL. I
People
GO KISS.
I LOVE YOU, MARKY MARK.
SMOOCH
People
WHAT THE–?
YOU REALLY DON'T WANT TO KNOW.
WHOOPS– CAN I TAKE THAT BACK? I LOVE DOOGIE HOWSER MORE.
People
AMEND

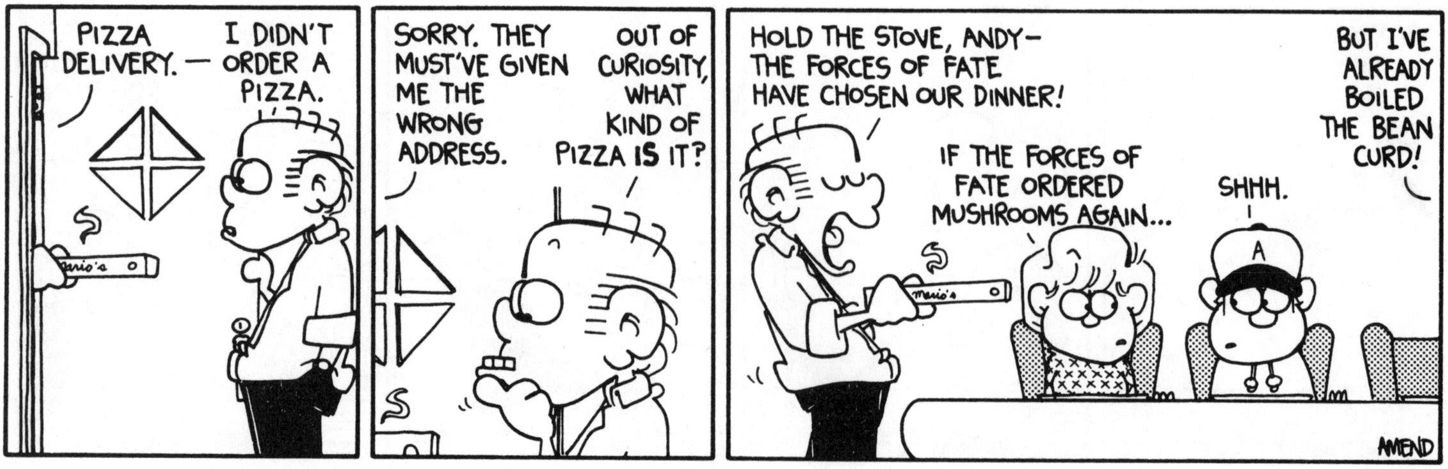
PIZZA DELIVERY.
I DIDN'T ORDER A PIZZA.
SORRY. THEY MUST'VE GIVEN ME THE WRONG ADDRESS.
OUT OF CURIOSITY, WHAT KIND OF PIZZA IS IT?
HOLD THE STOVE, ANDY– THE FORCES OF FATE HAVE CHOSEN OUR DINNER!
BUT I'VE ALREADY BOILED THE BEAN CURD!
IF THE FORCES OF FATE ORDERED MUSHROOMS AGAIN...
SHHH.
AMEND

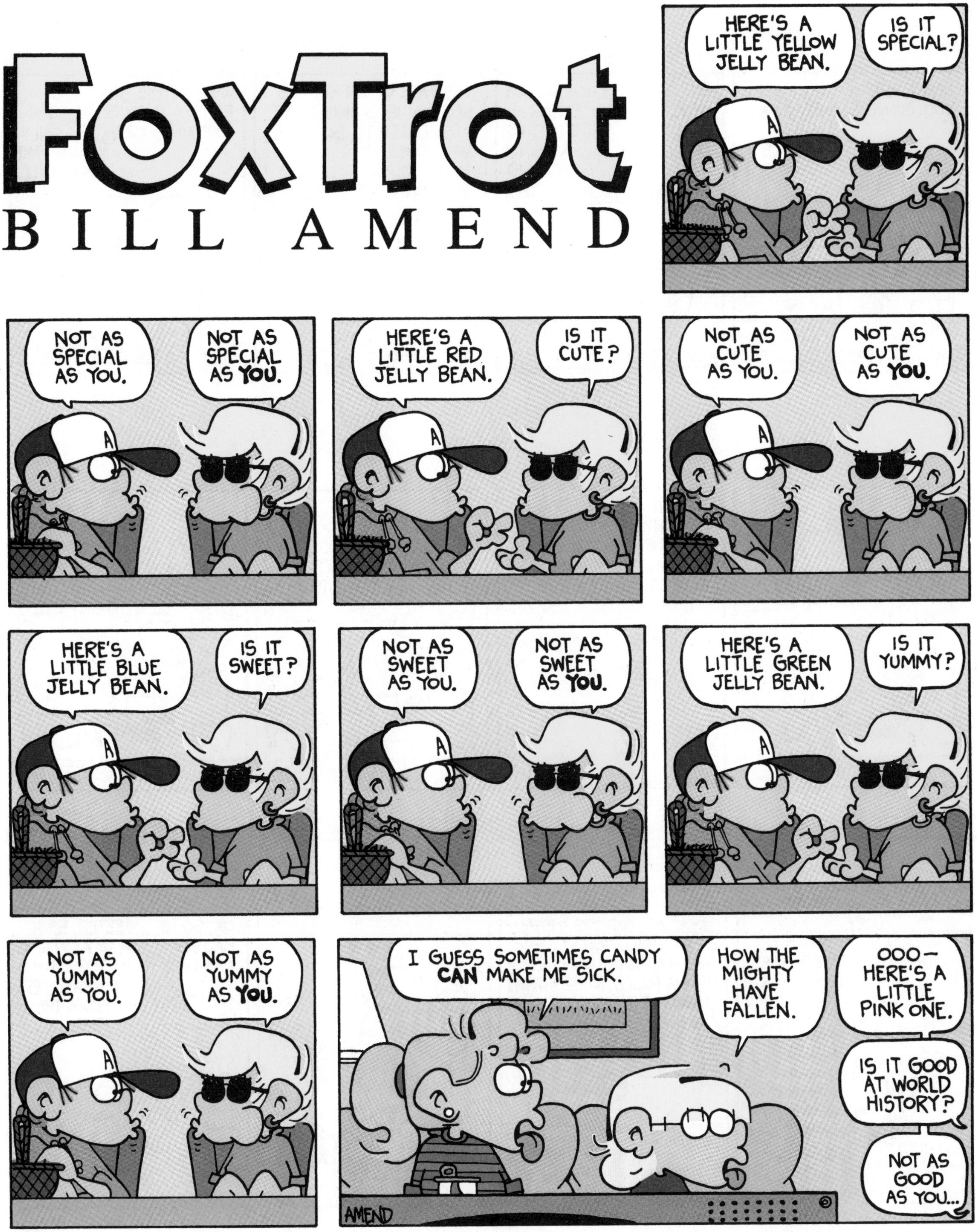
FoxTrot
BILL AMEND
HERE'S A LITTLE YELLOW JELLY BEAN.
IS IT SPECIAL?
NOT AS SPECIAL AS YOU.
NOT AS SPECIAL AS YOU.
HERE'S A LITTLE RED JELLY BEAN.
IS IT CUTE?
NOT AS CUTE AS YOU.
NOT AS CUTE AS YOU.
HERE'S A LITTLE BLUE JELLY BEAN.
IS IT SWEET?
NOT AS SWEET AS YOU.
NOT AS SWEET AS YOU.
HERE'S A LITTLE GREEN JELLY BEAN.
IS IT YUMMY?
NOT AS YUMMY AS YOU.
NOT AS YUMMY AS YOU.
I GUESS SOMETIMES CANDY CAN MAKE ME SICK.
HOW THE MIGHTY HAVE FALLEN.
OOO— HERE'S A LITTLE PINK ONE.
IS IT GOOD AT WORLD HISTORY?
NOT AS GOOD AS YOU...
AMEND

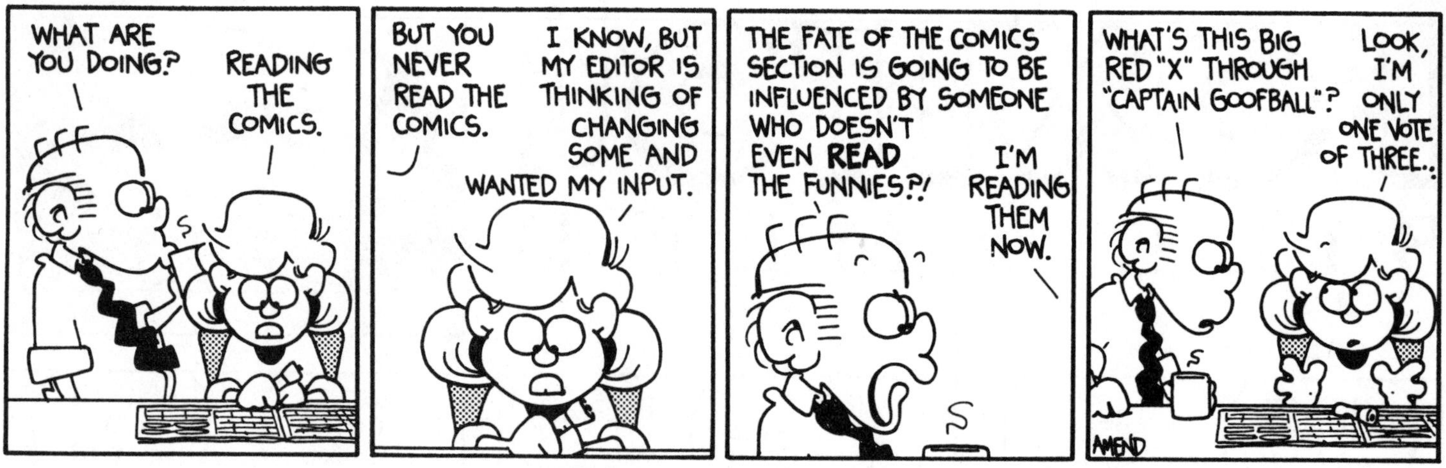
WHAT ARE YOU DOING?
READING THE COMICS.
BUT YOU NEVER READ THE COMICS.
I KNOW, BUT MY EDITOR IS THINKING OF CHANGING SOME AND WANTED MY INPUT.
THE FATE OF THE COMICS SECTION IS GOING TO BE INFLUENCED BY SOMEONE WHO DOESN'T EVEN READ THE FUNNIES?!
I'M READING THEM NOW.
WHAT'S THIS BIG RED "X" THROUGH "CAPTAIN GOOFBALL"?
LOOK, I'M ONLY ONE VOTE OF THREE..
AMEND

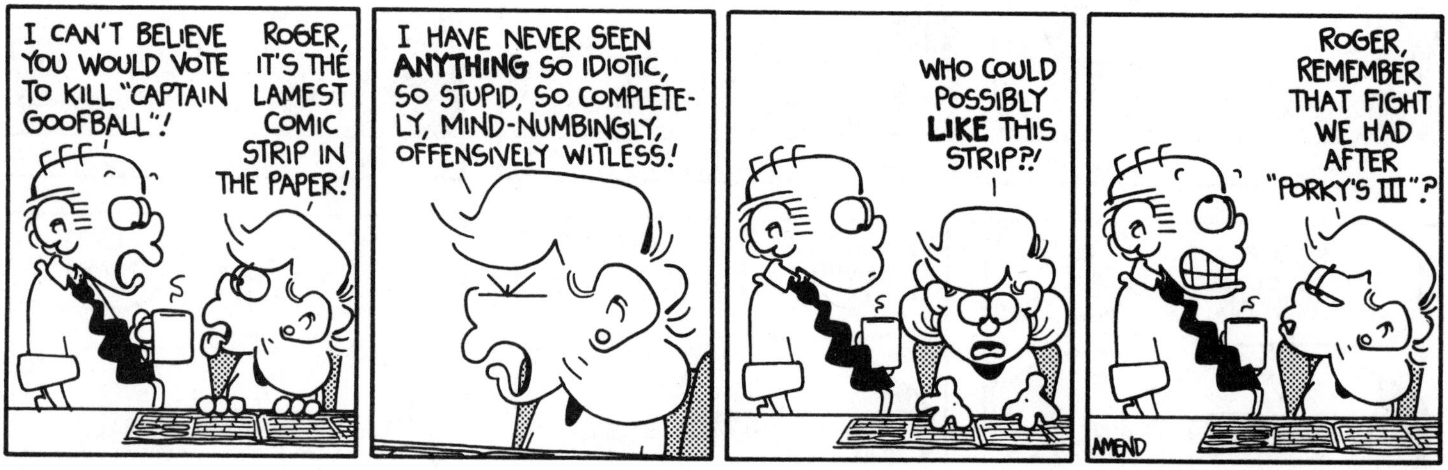
I CAN'T BELIEVE YOU WOULD VOTE TO KILL "CAPTAIN GOOFBALL"!
ROGER, IT'S THE LAMEST COMIC STRIP IN THE PAPER!
I HAVE NEVER SEEN ANYTHING SO IDIOTIC, SO STUPID, SO COMPLETELY, MIND-NUMBINGLY, OFFENSIVELY WITLESS!
WHO COULD POSSIBLY LIKE THIS STRIP?!
ROGER, REMEMBER THAT FIGHT WE HAD AFTER "PORKY'S III"?
AMEND

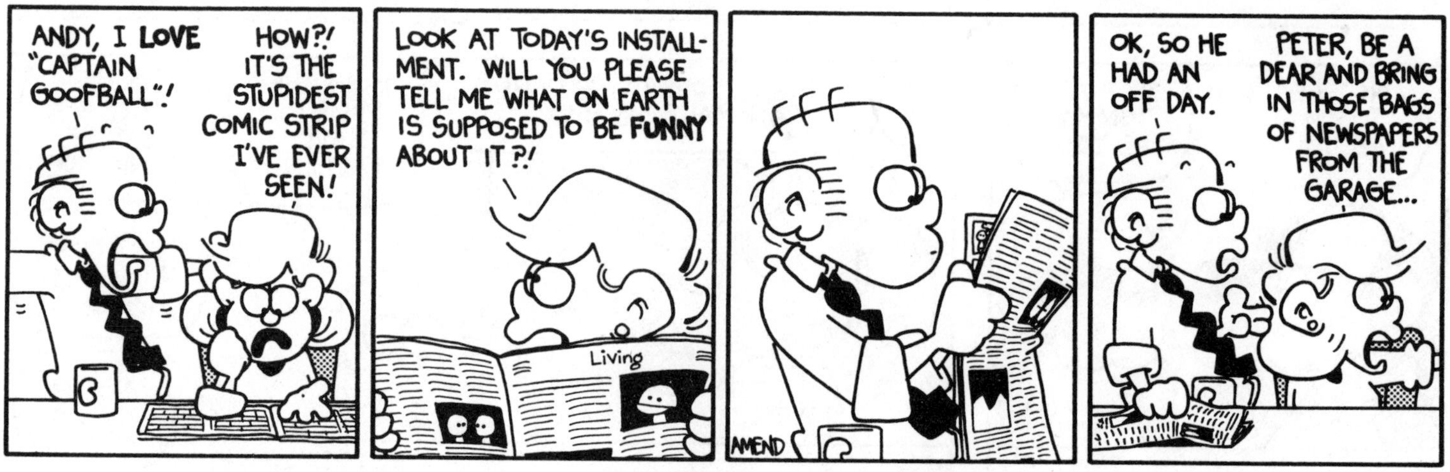
ANDY, I LOVE "CAPTAIN GOOFBALL"!
HOW?! IT'S THE STUPIDEST COMIC STRIP I'VE EVER SEEN!
LOOK AT TODAY'S INSTALLMENT. WILL YOU PLEASE TELL ME WHAT ON EARTH IS SUPPOSED TO BE FUNNY ABOUT IT?!
Living
AMEND
OK, SO HE HAD AN OFF DAY.
PETER, BE A DEAR AND BRING IN THOSE BAGS OF NEWSPAPERS FROM THE GARAGE...

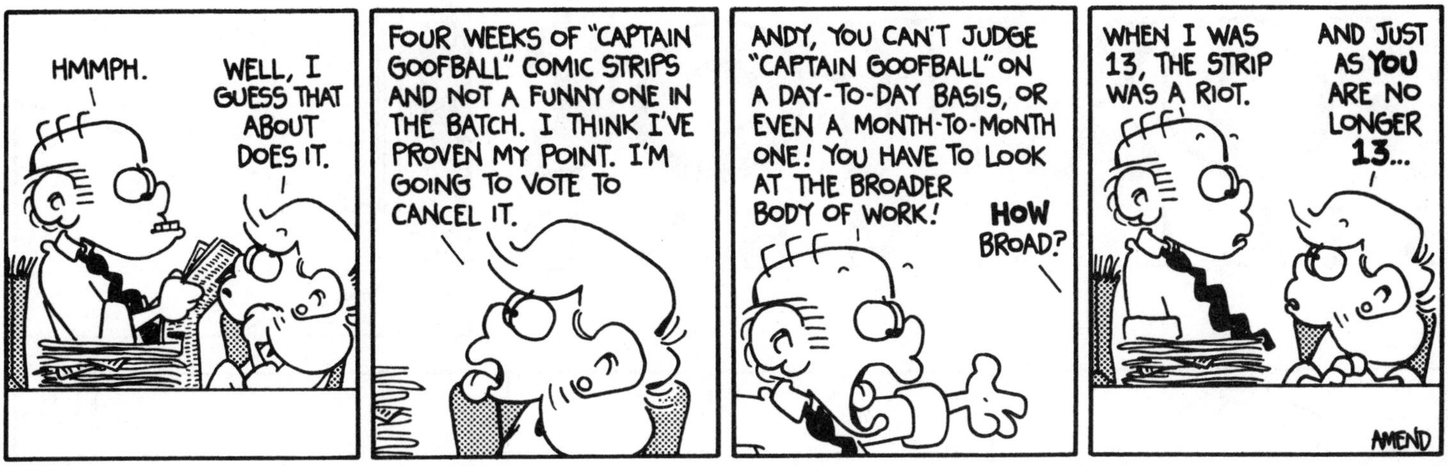
HMMPH.
WELL, I GUESS THAT ABOUT DOES IT.
FOUR WEEKS OF "CAPTAIN GOOFBALL" COMIC STRIPS AND NOT A FUNNY ONE IN THE BATCH. I THINK I'VE PROVEN MY POINT. I'M GOING TO VOTE TO CANCEL IT.
ANDY, YOU CAN'T JUDGE "CAPTAIN GOOFBALL" ON A DAY-TO-DAY BASIS, OR EVEN A MONTH-TO-MONTH ONE! YOU HAVE TO LOOK AT THE BROADER BODY OF WORK!
HOW BROAD?
WHEN I WAS 13, THE STRIP WAS A RIOT.
AND JUST AS YOU ARE NO LONGER 13...
AMEND

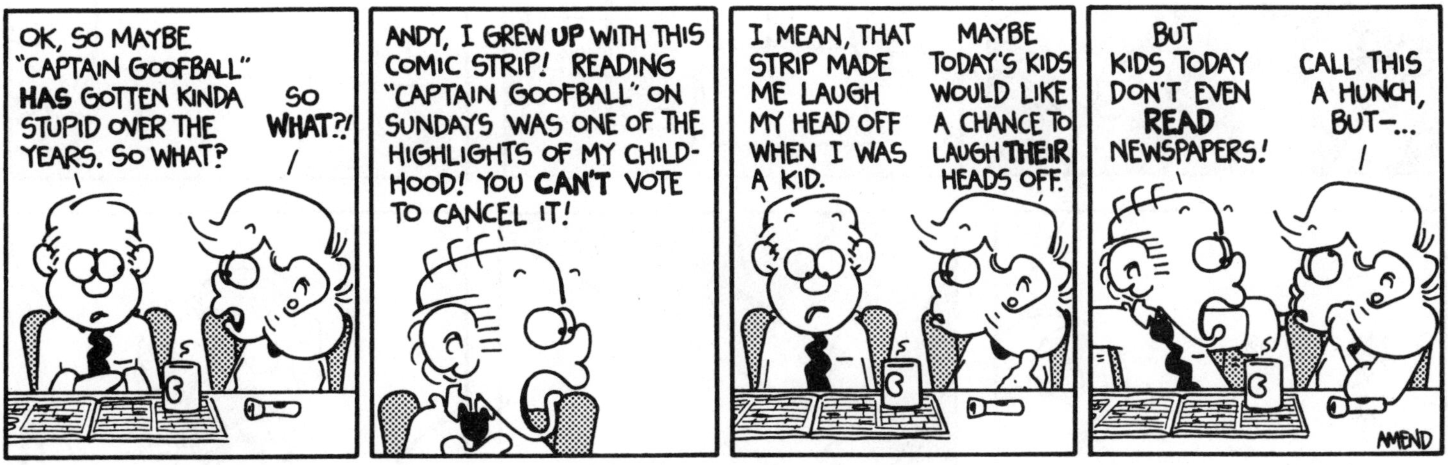
OK, SO MAYBE "CAPTAIN GOOFBALL" HAS GOTTEN KINDA STUPID OVER THE YEARS. SO WHAT?
SO WHAT?!
ANDY, I GREW UP WITH THIS COMIC STRIP! READING "CAPTAIN GOOFBALL" ON SUNDAYS WAS ONE OF THE HIGHLIGHTS OF MY CHILDHOOD! YOU CAN'T VOTE TO CANCEL IT!
I MEAN, THAT STRIP MADE ME LAUGH MY HEAD OFF WHEN I WAS A KID.
MAYBE TODAY'S KIDS WOULD LIKE A CHANCE TO LAUGH THEIR HEADS OFF.
BUT KIDS TODAY DON'T EVEN READ NEWSPAPERS!
CALL THIS A HUNCH, BUT--...
AMEND

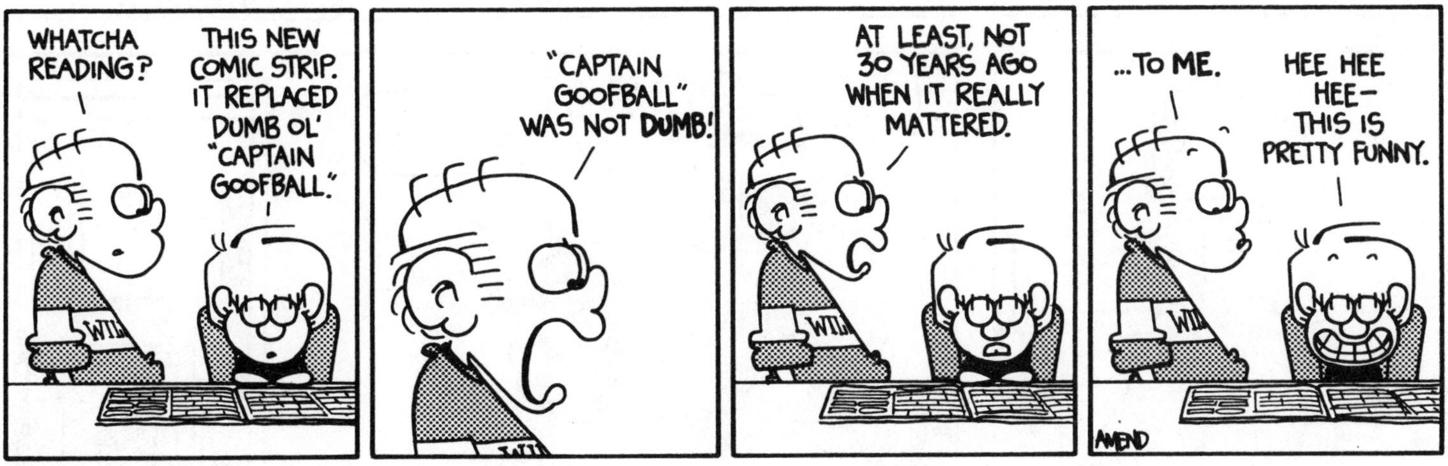
WHATCHA READING?
THIS NEW COMIC STRIP. IT REPLACED DUMB OL' "CAPTAIN GOOFBALL."
"CAPTAIN GOOFBALL" WAS NOT DUMB!
AT LEAST, NOT 30 YEARS AGO WHEN IT REALLY MATTERED.
...TO ME.
HEE HEE HEE– THIS IS PRETTY FUNNY.
AMEND

FoxTrot
BILL AMEND

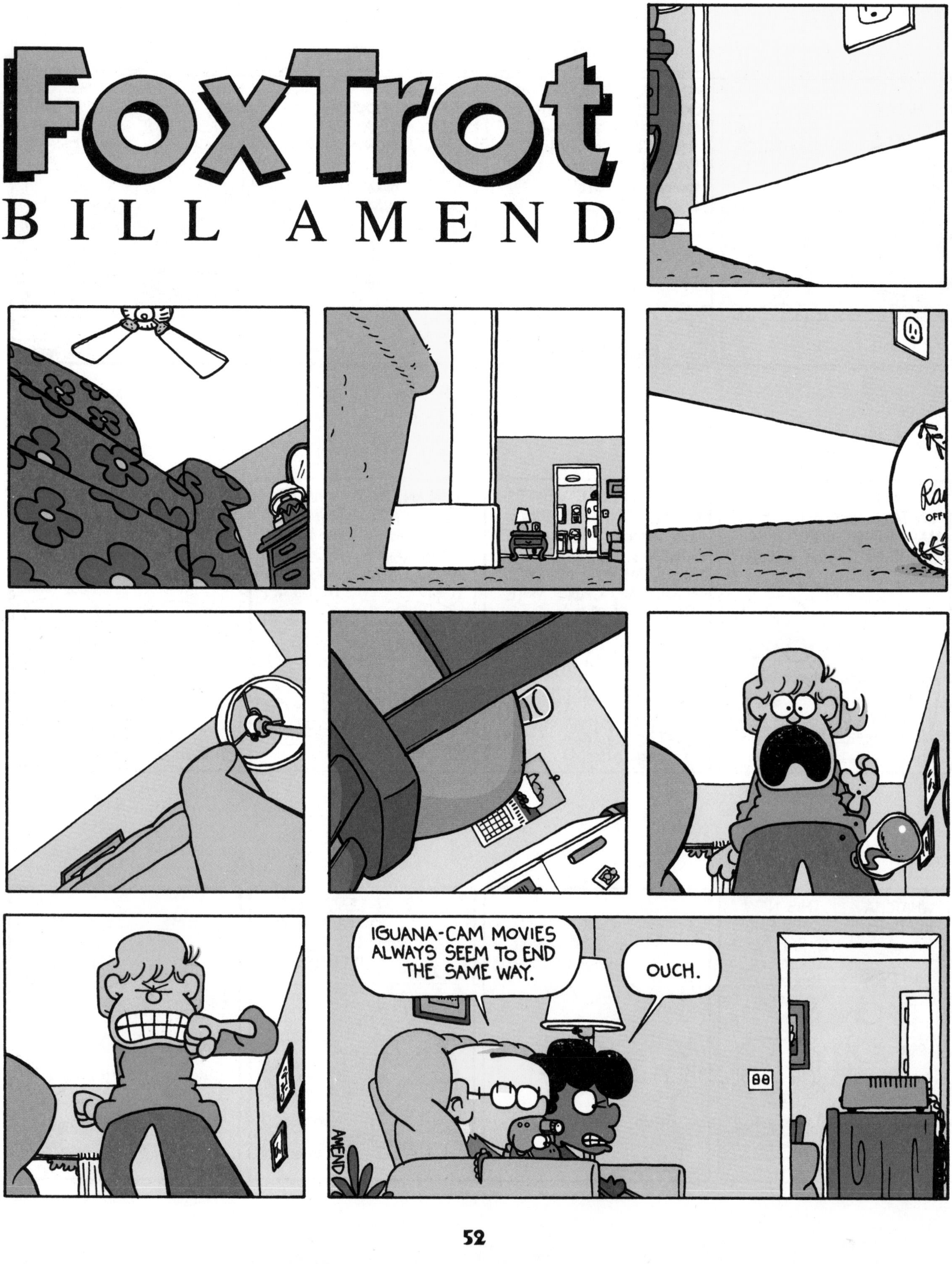

IGUANA-CAM MOVIES ALWAYS SEEM TO END THE SAME WAY.
OUCH.
AMEND

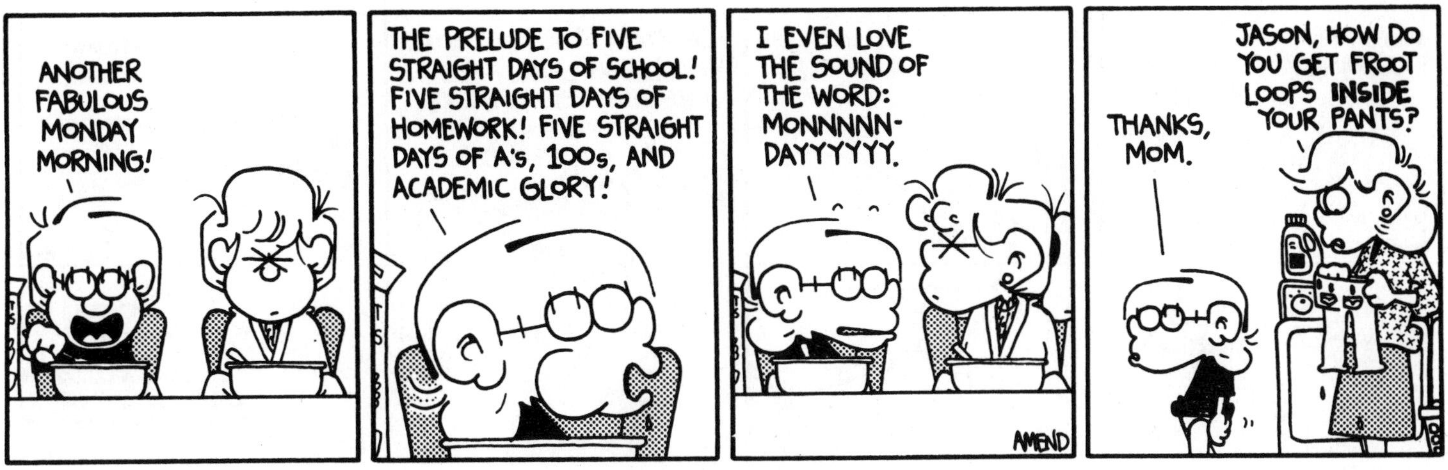
ANOTHER FABULOUS MONDAY MORNING!
THE PRELUDE TO FIVE STRAIGHT DAYS OF SCHOOL! FIVE STRAIGHT DAYS OF HOMEWORK! FIVE STRAIGHT DAYS OF A'S, 100s, AND ACADEMIC GLORY!
I EVEN LOVE THE SOUND OF THE WORD: MONNNNN-DAYYYYYY.
THANKS, MOM.
JASON, HOW DO YOU GET FROOT LOOPS INSIDE YOUR PANTS?
AMEND

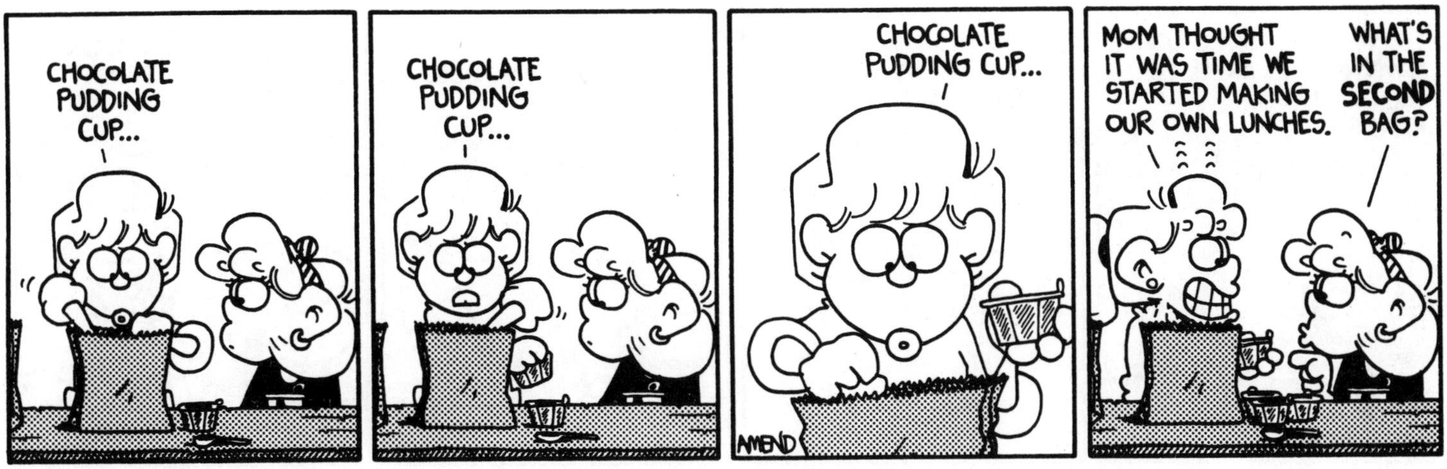
CHOCOLATE PUDDING CUP...
CHOCOLATE PUDDING CUP...
CHOCOLATE PUDDING CUP...
AMEND
MOM THOUGHT IT WAS TIME WE STARTED MAKING OUR OWN LUNCHES.
WHAT'S IN THE SECOND BAG?

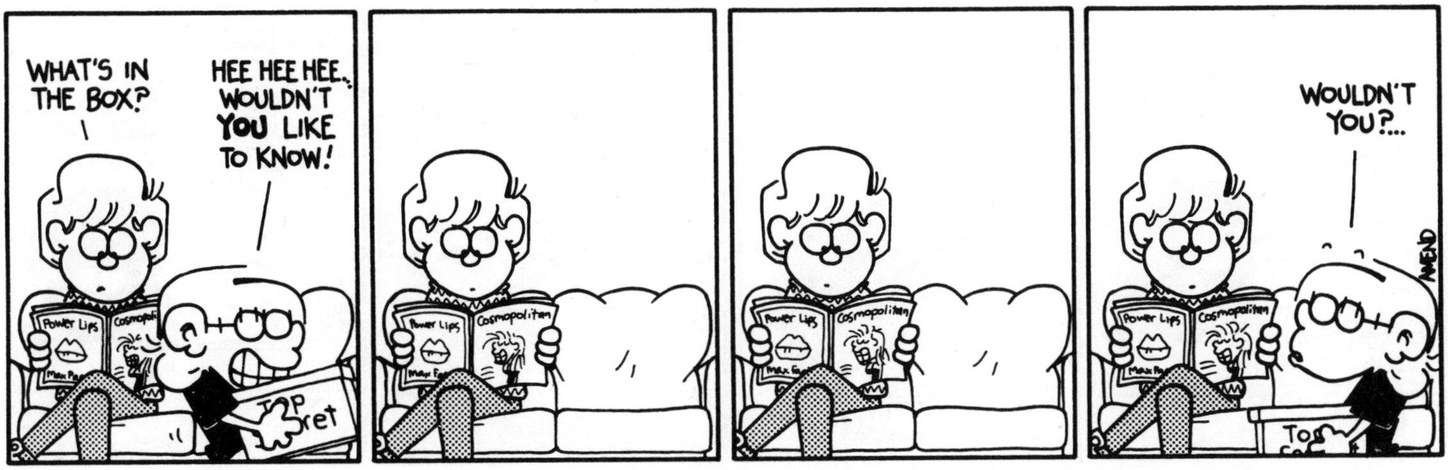
WHAT'S IN THE BOX?
HEE HEE HEE... WOULDN'T YOU LIKE TO KNOW!
WOULDN'T YOU?...
AMEND

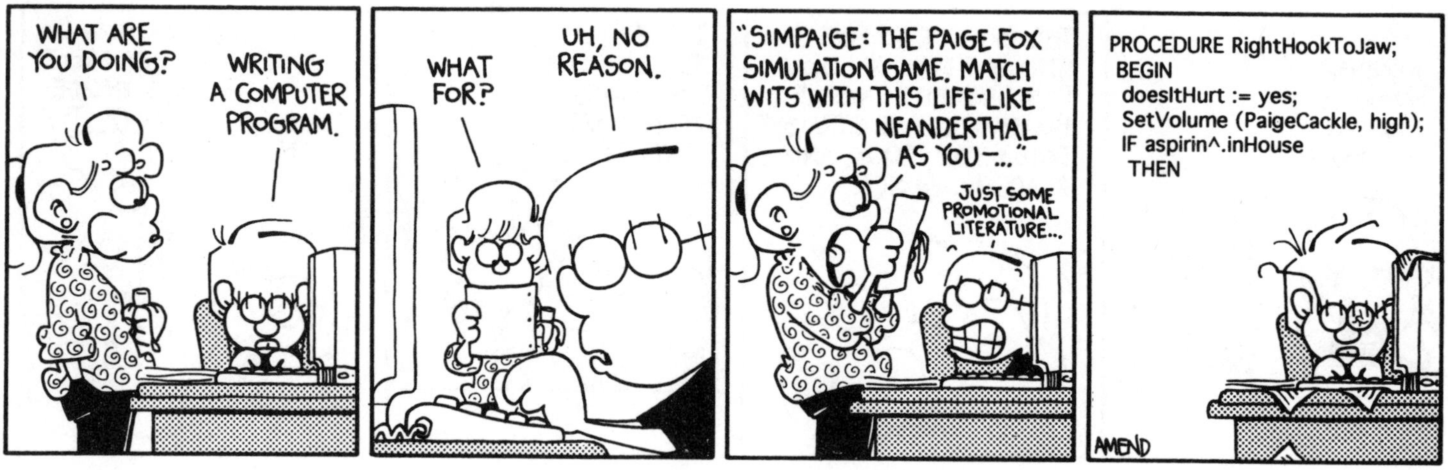
WHAT ARE YOU DOING?
WRITING A COMPUTER PROGRAM.
WHAT FOR?
UH, NO REASON.
"SIMPAIGE: THE PAIGE FOX SIMULATION GAME. MATCH WITS WITH THIS LIFE-LIKE NEANDERTHAL AS YOU-..."
JUST SOME PROMOTIONAL LITERATURE...
PROCEDURE RightHookToJaw;
BEGIN
doesItHurt := yes;
SetVolume (PaigeCackle, high);
IF aspirin^.inHouse
THEN
AMEND

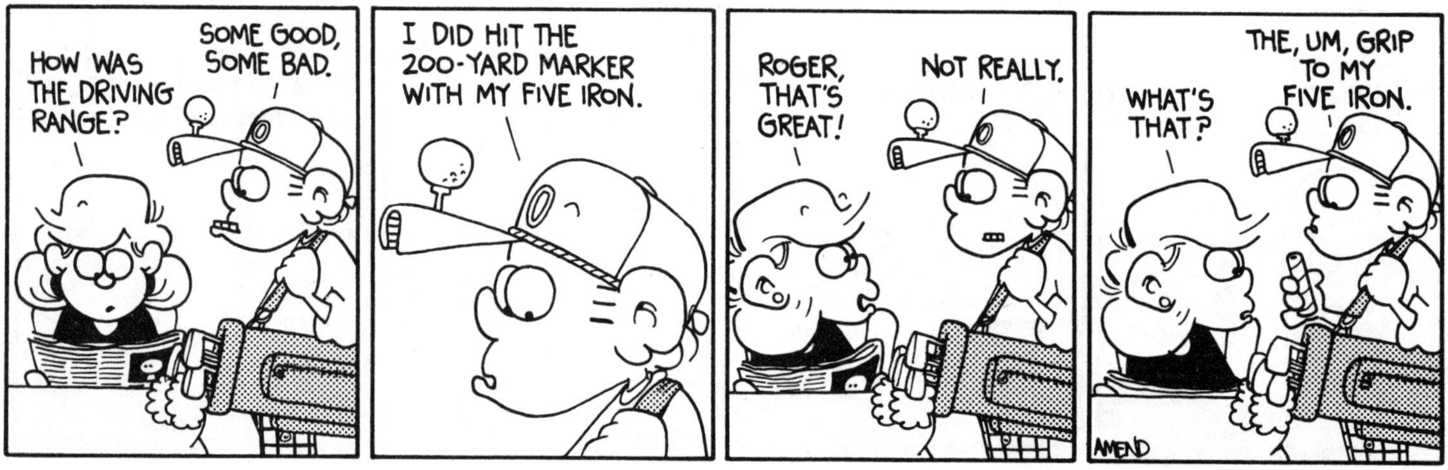
HOW WAS THE DRIVING RANGE?
SOME GOOD, SOME BAD.
I DID HIT THE 200-YARD MARKER WITH MY FIVE IRON.
ROGER, THAT'S GREAT!
NOT REALLY.
WHAT'S THAT?
THE, UM, GRIP TO MY FIVE IRON.
AMEND

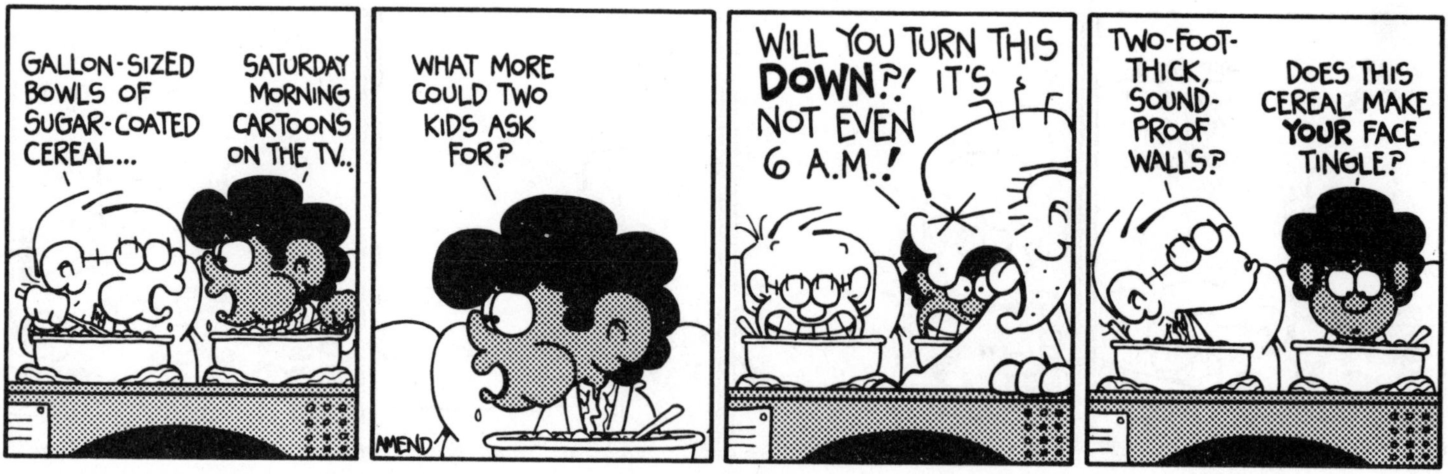
GALLON-SIZED BOWLS OF SUGAR-COATED CEREAL...
SATURDAY MORNING CARTOONS ON THE TV...
WHAT MORE COULD TWO KIDS ASK FOR?
AMEND
WILL YOU TURN THIS DOWN?! IT'S NOT EVEN 6 A.M.!
TWO-FOOT-THICK, SOUND-PROOF WALLS?
DOES THIS CEREAL MAKE YOUR FACE TINGLE?

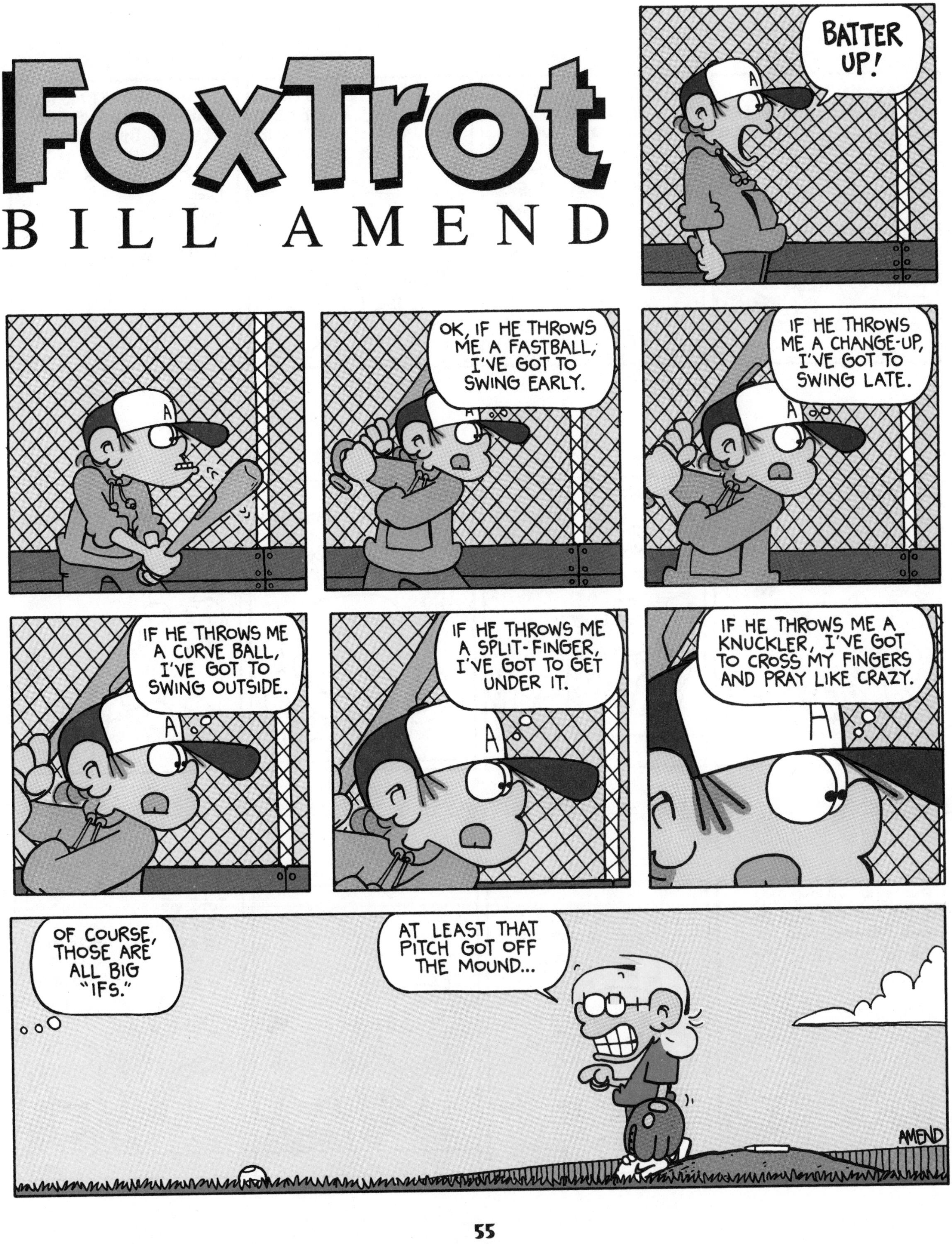
FoxTrot
BILL AMEND
BATTER UP!
OK, IF HE THROWS ME A FASTBALL, I'VE GOT TO SWING EARLY.
IF HE THROWS ME A CHANGE-UP, I'VE GOT TO SWING LATE.
IF HE THROWS ME A CURVE BALL, I'VE GOT TO SWING OUTSIDE.
IF HE THROWS ME A SPLIT-FINGER, I'VE GOT TO GET UNDER IT.
IF HE THROWS ME A KNUCKLER, I'VE GOT TO CROSS MY FINGERS AND PRAY LIKE CRAZY.
OF COURSE, THOSE ARE ALL BIG "IFS."
AT LEAST THAT PITCH GOT OFF THE MOUND...
AMEND

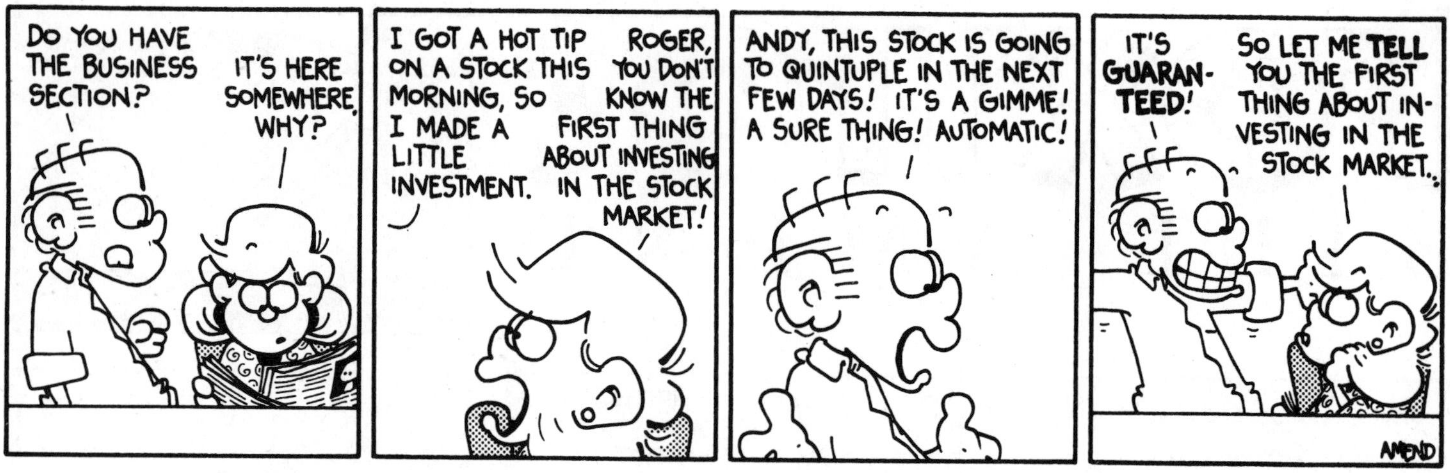
DO YOU HAVE THE BUSINESS SECTION?
IT'S HERE SOMEWHERE. WHY?
I GOT A HOT TIP ON A STOCK THIS MORNING, SO I MADE A LITTLE INVESTMENT.
ROGER, YOU DON'T KNOW THE FIRST THING ABOUT INVESTING IN THE STOCK MARKET!
ANDY, THIS STOCK IS GOING TO QUINTUPLE IN THE NEXT FEW DAYS! IT'S A GIMME! A SURE THING! AUTOMATIC!
IT'S **GUARANTEED**!
SO LET ME **TELL** YOU THE FIRST THING ABOUT INVESTING IN THE STOCK MARKET...
AMEND

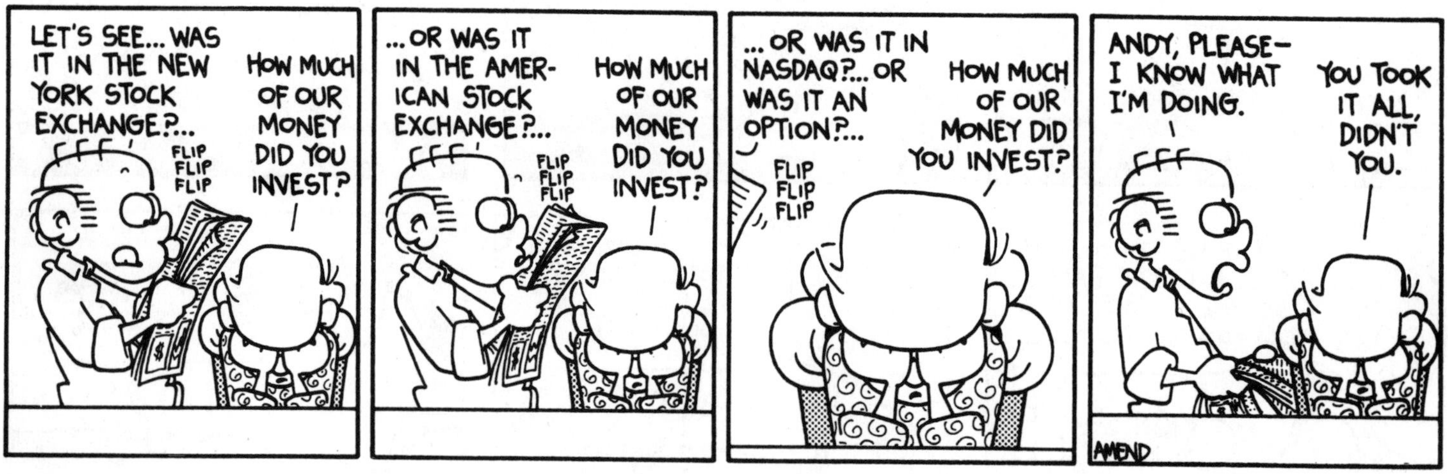
LET'S SEE... WAS IT IN THE NEW YORK STOCK EXCHANGE?...
FLIP FLIP FLIP
HOW MUCH OF OUR MONEY DID YOU INVEST?
...OR WAS IT IN THE AMERICAN STOCK EXCHANGE?...
FLIP FLIP FLIP
HOW MUCH OF OUR MONEY DID YOU INVEST?
...OR WAS IT IN NASDAQ?... OR WAS IT AN OPTION?...
FLIP FLIP FLIP
HOW MUCH OF OUR MONEY DID YOU INVEST?
ANDY, PLEASE- I KNOW WHAT I'M DOING.
YOU TOOK IT ALL, DIDN'T YOU.
AMEND

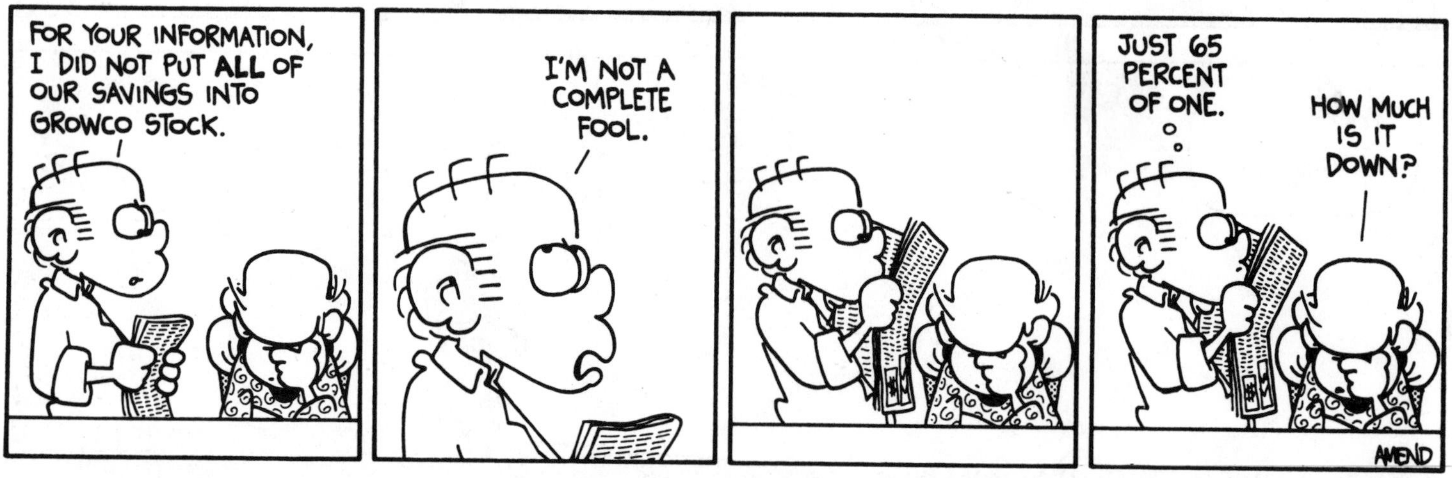
FOR YOUR INFORMATION, I DID NOT PUT **ALL** OF OUR SAVINGS INTO GROWCO STOCK.
I'M NOT A COMPLETE FOOL.
JUST 65 PERCENT OF ONE.
HOW MUCH IS IT DOWN?
AMEND

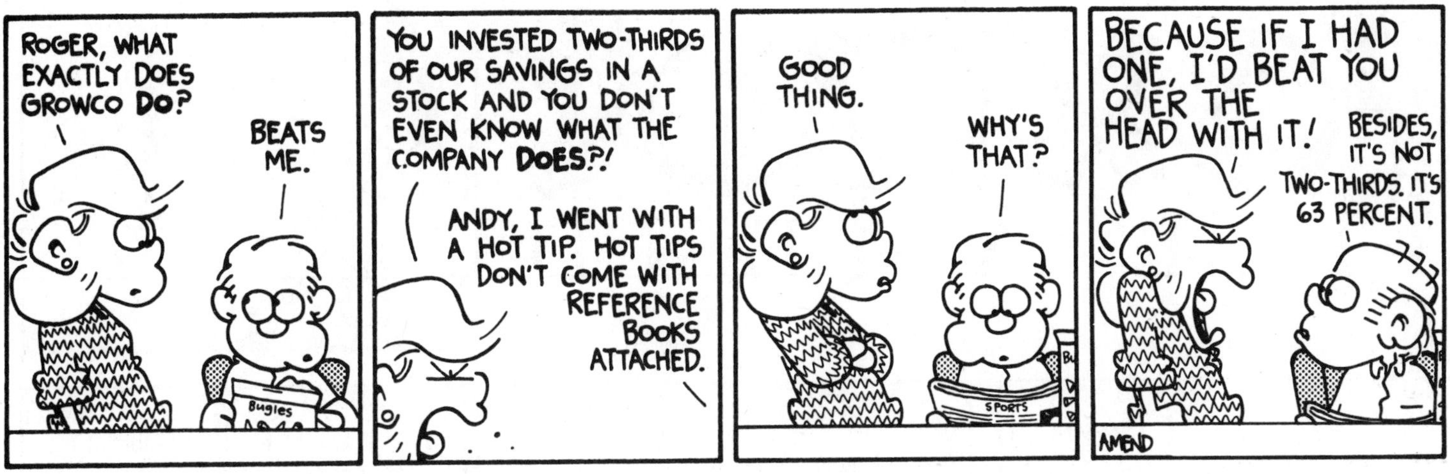
ROGER, WHAT EXACTLY DOES GROWCO DO?
BEATS ME.
Bugles
YOU INVESTED TWO-THIRDS OF OUR SAVINGS IN A STOCK AND YOU DON'T EVEN KNOW WHAT THE COMPANY DOES?!
ANDY, I WENT WITH A HOT TIP. HOT TIPS DON'T COME WITH REFERENCE BOOKS ATTACHED.
GOOD THING.
WHY'S THAT?
SPORTS
BECAUSE IF I HAD ONE, I'D BEAT YOU OVER THE HEAD WITH IT!
BESIDES, IT'S NOT TWO-THIRDS. IT'S 63 PERCENT.
AMEND

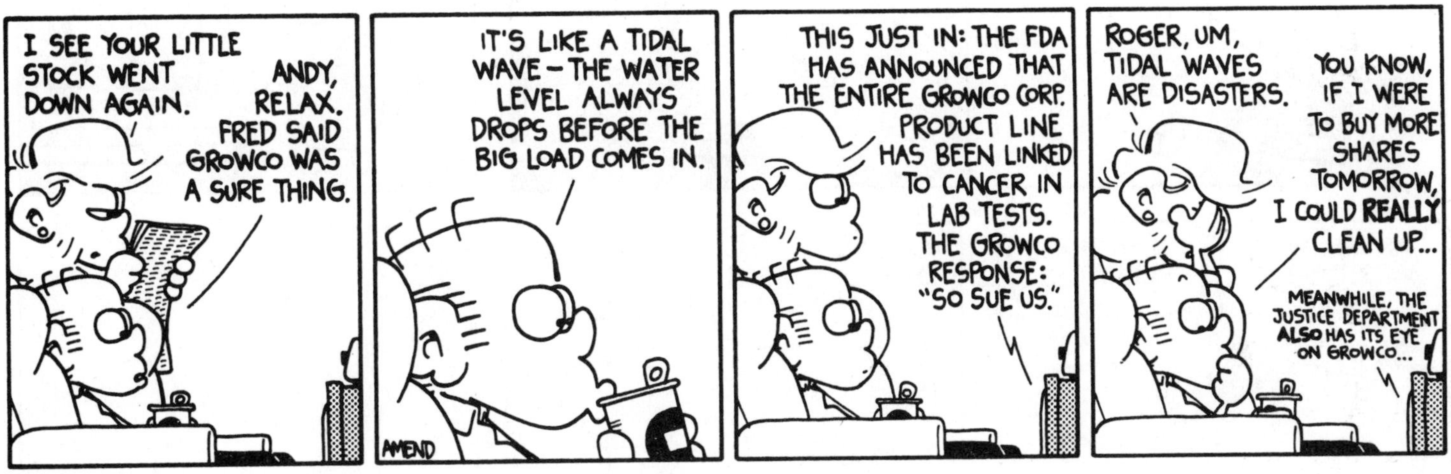
I SEE YOUR LITTLE STOCK WENT DOWN AGAIN.
ANDY, RELAX. FRED SAID GROWCO WAS A SURE THING.
IT'S LIKE A TIDAL WAVE – THE WATER LEVEL ALWAYS DROPS BEFORE THE BIG LOAD COMES IN.
AMEND
THIS JUST IN: THE FDA HAS ANNOUNCED THAT THE ENTIRE GROWCO CORP. PRODUCT LINE HAS BEEN LINKED TO CANCER IN LAB TESTS. THE GROWCO RESPONSE: "SO SUE US."
ROGER, UM, TIDAL WAVES ARE DISASTERS.
YOU KNOW, IF I WERE TO BUY MORE SHARES TOMORROW, I COULD REALLY CLEAN UP...
MEANWHILE, THE JUSTICE DEPARTMENT ALSO HAS ITS EYE ON GROWCO...

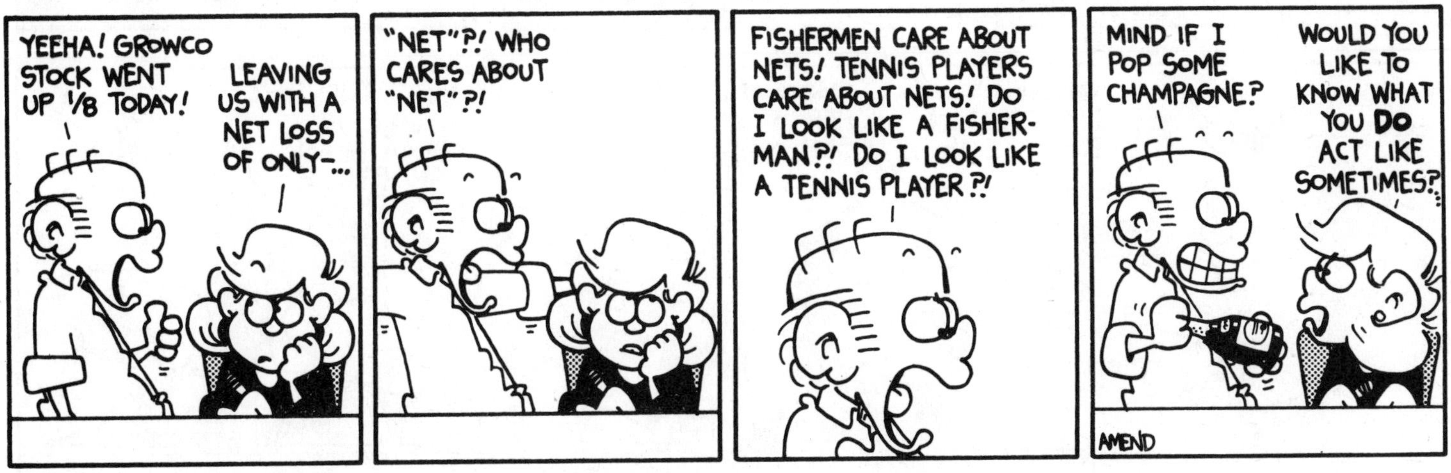
YEEHA! GROWCO STOCK WENT UP 1/8 TODAY!
LEAVING US WITH A NET LOSS OF ONLY–...
"NET"?! WHO CARES ABOUT "NET"?!
FISHERMEN CARE ABOUT NETS! TENNIS PLAYERS CARE ABOUT NETS! DO I LOOK LIKE A FISHERMAN?! DO I LOOK LIKE A TENNIS PLAYER?!
MIND IF I POP SOME CHAMPAGNE?
WOULD YOU LIKE TO KNOW WHAT YOU DO ACT LIKE SOMETIMES?
AMEND

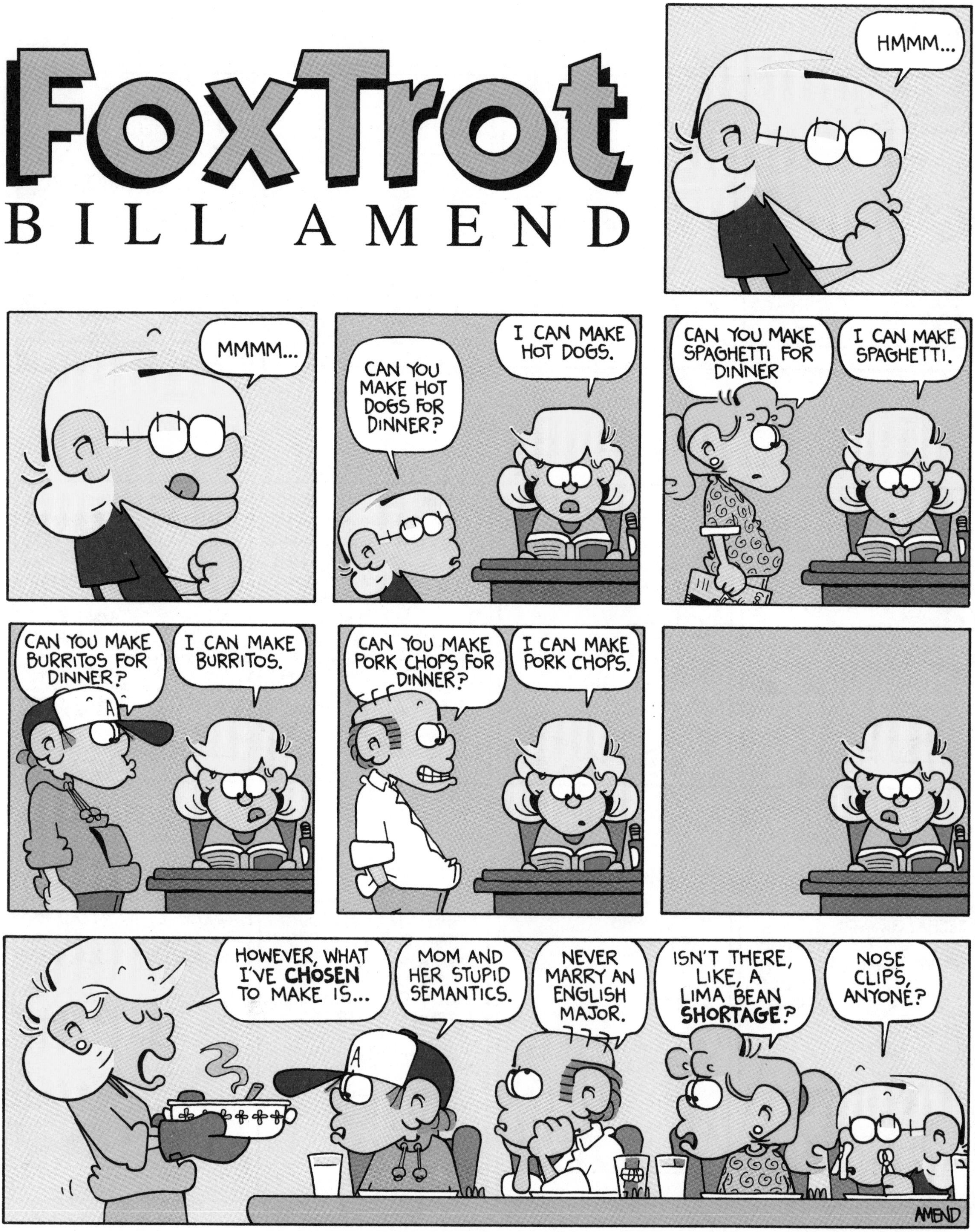
FoxTrot
BILL AMEND
HMMM...
MMMM...
CAN YOU MAKE HOT DOGS FOR DINNER?
I CAN MAKE HOT DOGS.
CAN YOU MAKE SPAGHETTI FOR DINNER
I CAN MAKE SPAGHETTI.
CAN YOU MAKE BURRITOS FOR DINNER?
I CAN MAKE BURRITOS.
CAN YOU MAKE PORK CHOPS FOR DINNER?
I CAN MAKE PORK CHOPS.
HOWEVER, WHAT I'VE **CHOSEN** TO MAKE IS...
MOM AND HER STUPID SEMANTICS.
NEVER MARRY AN ENGLISH MAJOR.
ISN'T THERE, LIKE, A LIMA BEAN **SHORTAGE**?
NOSE CLIPS, ANYONE?
AMEND

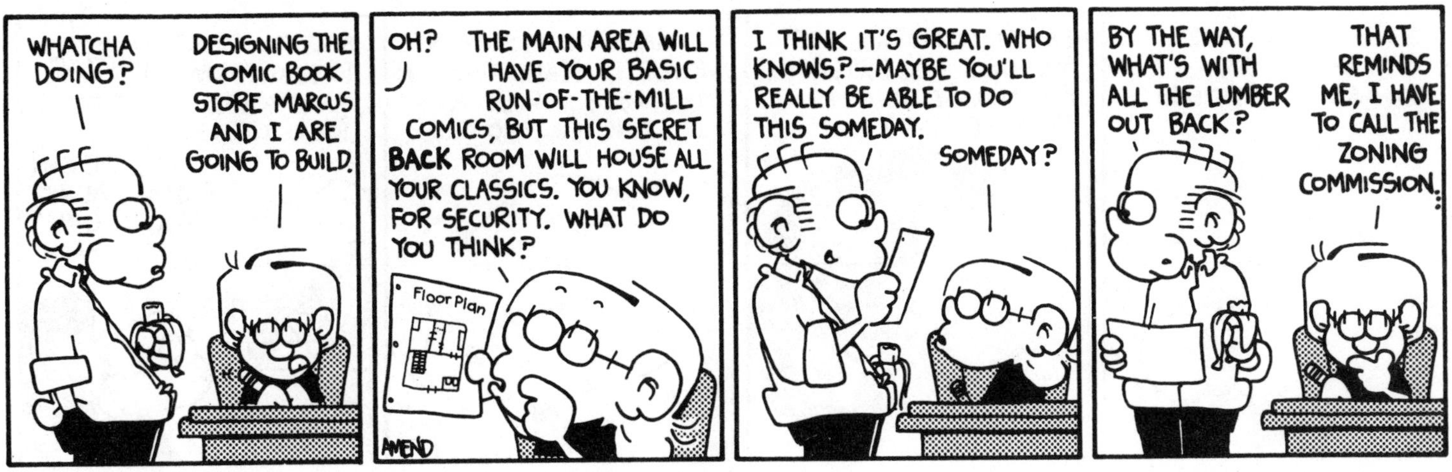
WHATCHA DOING?
DESIGNING THE COMIC BOOK STORE MARCUS AND I ARE GOING TO BUILD.
OH?
THE MAIN AREA WILL HAVE YOUR BASIC RUN-OF-THE-MILL COMICS, BUT THIS SECRET BACK ROOM WILL HOUSE ALL YOUR CLASSICS. YOU KNOW, FOR SECURITY. WHAT DO YOU THINK?
Floor Plan
AMEND
I THINK IT'S GREAT. WHO KNOWS?—MAYBE YOU'LL REALLY BE ABLE TO DO THIS SOMEDAY.
SOMEDAY?
BY THE WAY, WHAT'S WITH ALL THE LUMBER OUT BACK?
THAT REMINDS ME, I HAVE TO CALL THE ZONING COMMISSION.

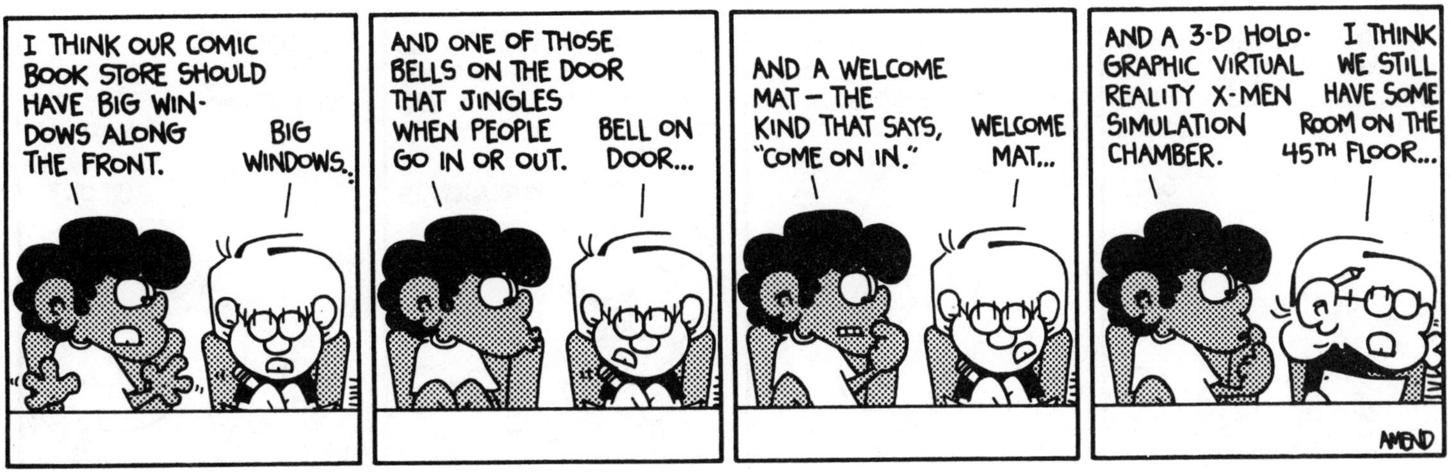
I THINK OUR COMIC BOOK STORE SHOULD HAVE BIG WINDOWS ALONG THE FRONT.
BIG WINDOWS..
AND ONE OF THOSE BELLS ON THE DOOR THAT JINGLES WHEN PEOPLE GO IN OR OUT.
BELL ON DOOR...
AND A WELCOME MAT – THE KIND THAT SAYS, "COME ON IN."
WELCOME MAT...
AND A 3-D HOLOGRAPHIC VIRTUAL REALITY X-MEN SIMULATION CHAMBER.
I THINK WE STILL HAVE SOME ROOM ON THE 45TH FLOOR...
AMEND

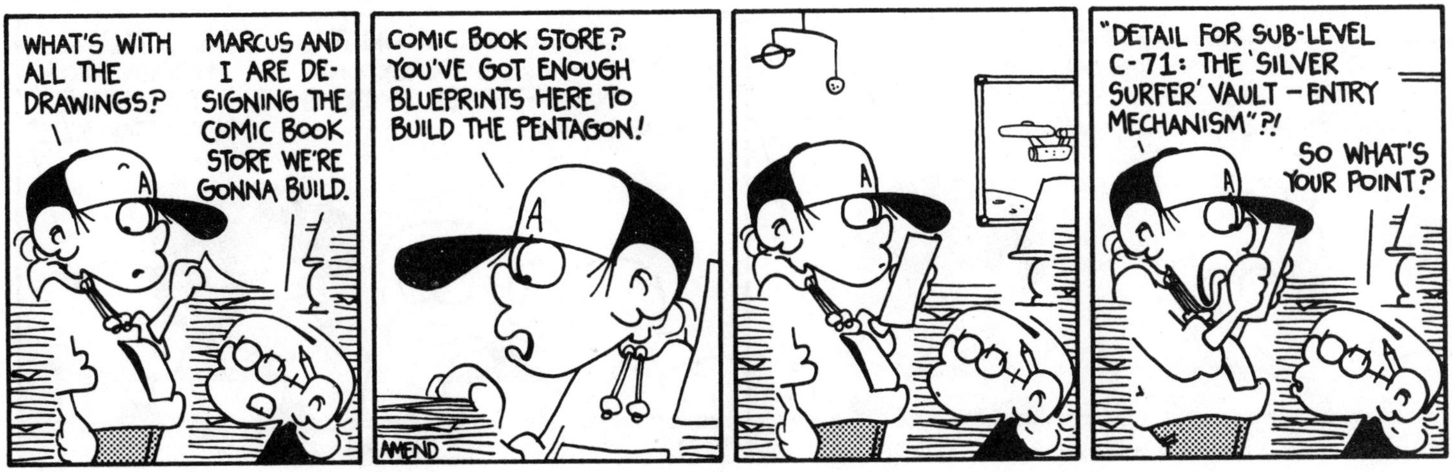
WHAT'S WITH ALL THE DRAWINGS?
MARCUS AND I ARE DESIGNING THE COMIC BOOK STORE WE'RE GONNA BUILD.
COMIC BOOK STORE? YOU'VE GOT ENOUGH BLUEPRINTS HERE TO BUILD THE PENTAGON!
AMEND
"DETAIL FOR SUB-LEVEL C-71: THE 'SILVER SURFER' VAULT – ENTRY MECHANISM"?!
SO WHAT'S YOUR POINT?

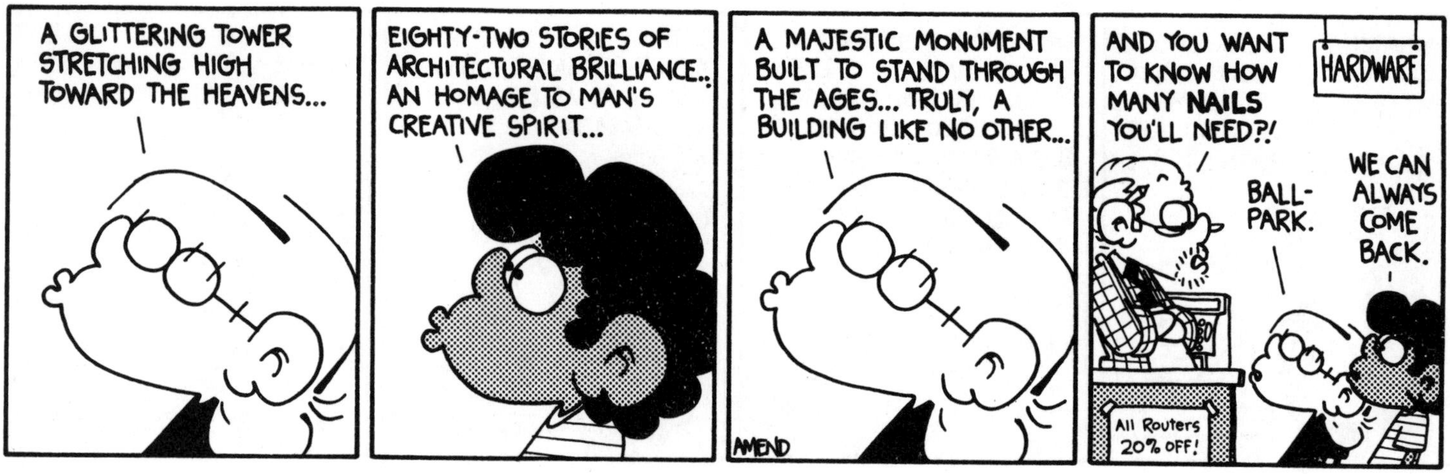
A GLITTERING TOWER STRETCHING HIGH TOWARD THE HEAVENS...
EIGHTY-TWO STORIES OF ARCHITECTURAL BRILLIANCE... AN HOMAGE TO MAN'S CREATIVE SPIRIT...
A MAJESTIC MONUMENT BUILT TO STAND THROUGH THE AGES... TRULY, A BUILDING LIKE NO OTHER...
AMEND
HARDWARE
AND YOU WANT TO KNOW HOW MANY NAILS YOU'LL NEED?!
BALL-PARK.
WE CAN ALWAYS COME BACK.
All Routers 20% OFF!

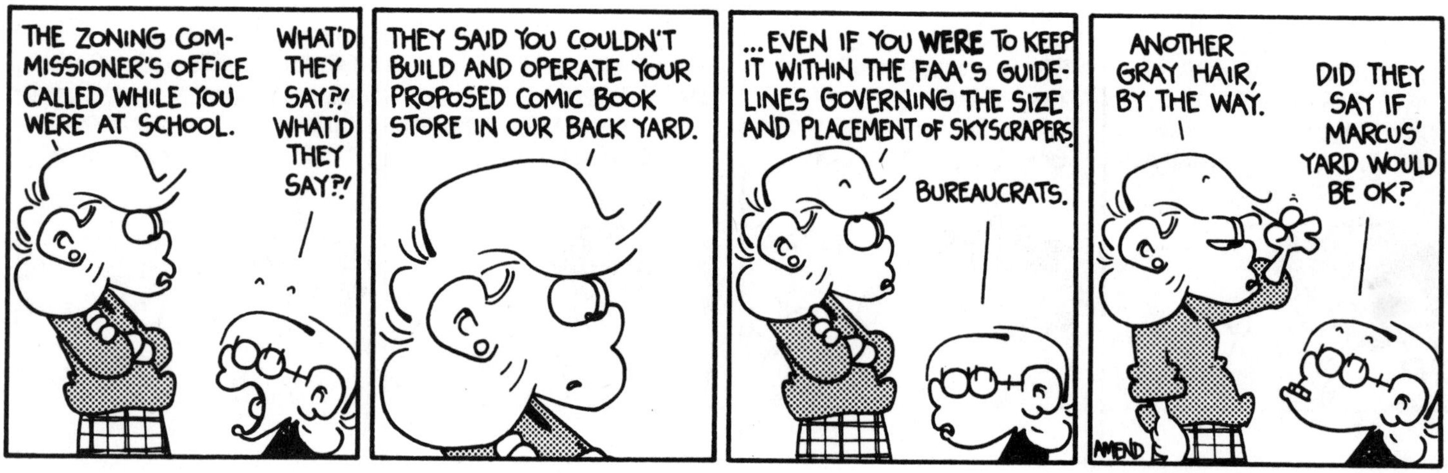
THE ZONING COM-MISSIONER'S OFFICE CALLED WHILE YOU WERE AT SCHOOL.
WHAT'D THEY SAY?! WHAT'D THEY SAY?!
THEY SAID YOU COULDN'T BUILD AND OPERATE YOUR PROPOSED COMIC BOOK STORE IN OUR BACK YARD.
...EVEN IF YOU WERE TO KEEP IT WITHIN THE FAA'S GUIDE-LINES GOVERNING THE SIZE AND PLACEMENT OF SKYSCRAPERS.
BUREAUCRATS.
ANOTHER GRAY HAIR, BY THE WAY.
DID THEY SAY IF MARCUS' YARD WOULD BE OK?
AMEND

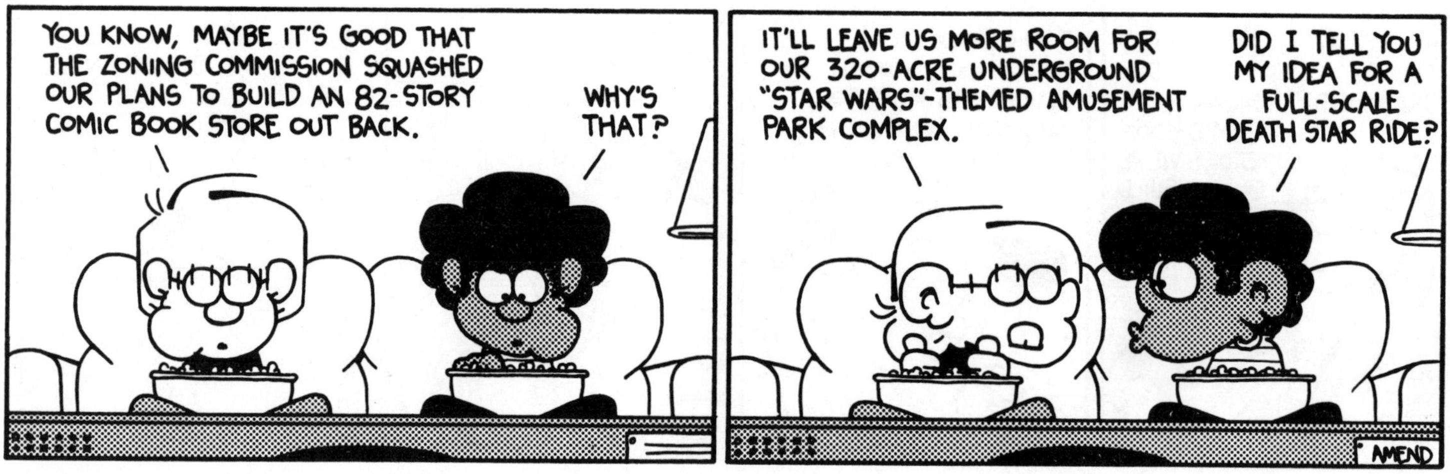
YOU KNOW, MAYBE IT'S GOOD THAT THE ZONING COMMISSION SQUASHED OUR PLANS TO BUILD AN 82-STORY COMIC BOOK STORE OUT BACK.
WHY'S THAT?
IT'LL LEAVE US MORE ROOM FOR OUR 320-ACRE UNDERGROUND "STAR WARS"-THEMED AMUSEMENT PARK COMPLEX.
DID I TELL YOU MY IDEA FOR A FULL-SCALE DEATH STAR RIDE?
AMEND

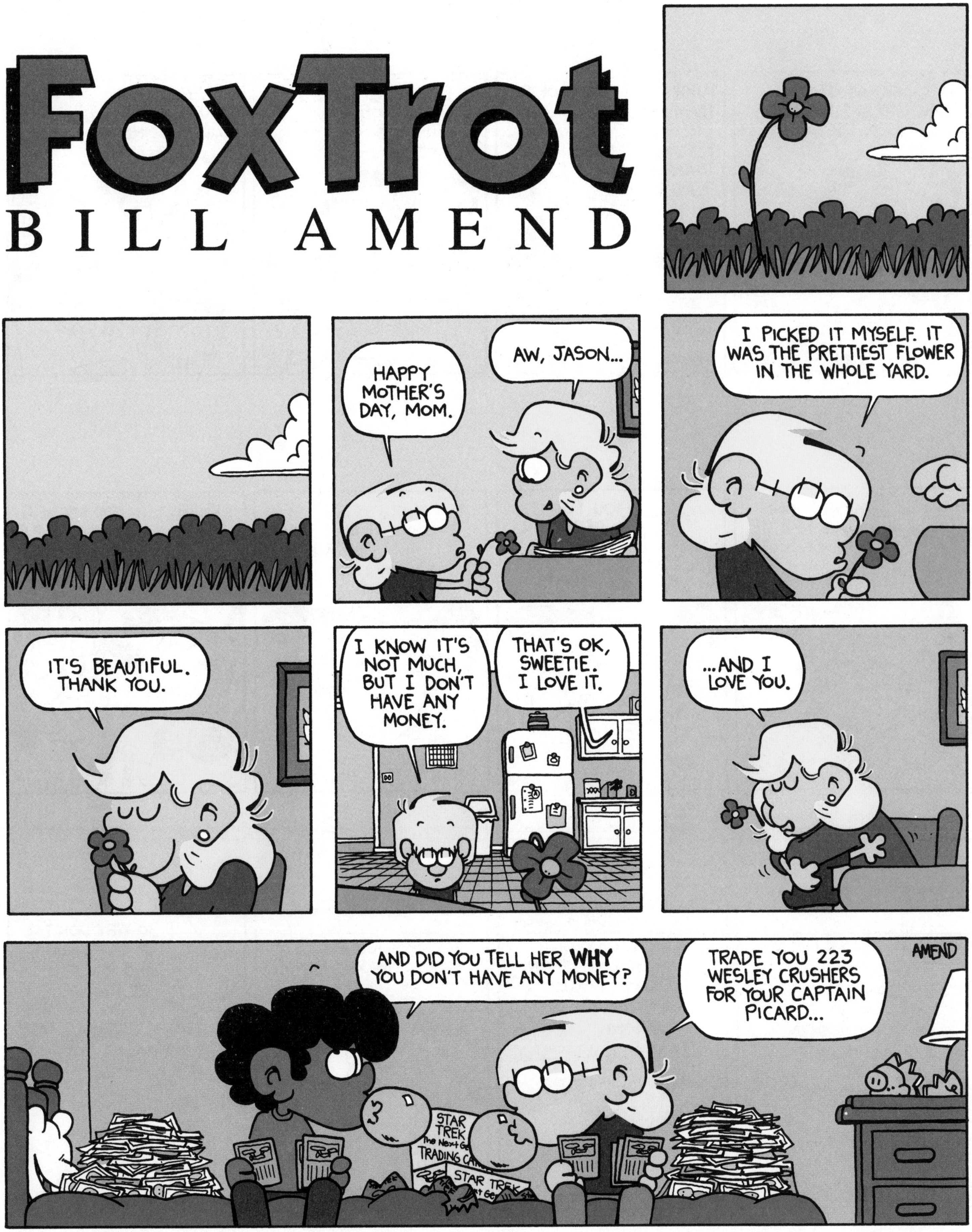
FoxTrot
BILL AMEND
HAPPY MOTHER'S DAY, MOM.
AW, JASON...
I PICKED IT MYSELF. IT WAS THE PRETTIEST FLOWER IN THE WHOLE YARD.
IT'S BEAUTIFUL. THANK YOU.
I KNOW IT'S NOT MUCH, BUT I DON'T HAVE ANY MONEY.
THAT'S OK, SWEETIE. I LOVE IT.
...AND I LOVE YOU.
AND DID YOU TELL HER **WHY** YOU DON'T HAVE ANY MONEY?
TRADE YOU 223 WESLEY CRUSHERS FOR YOUR CAPTAIN PICARD...
AMEND

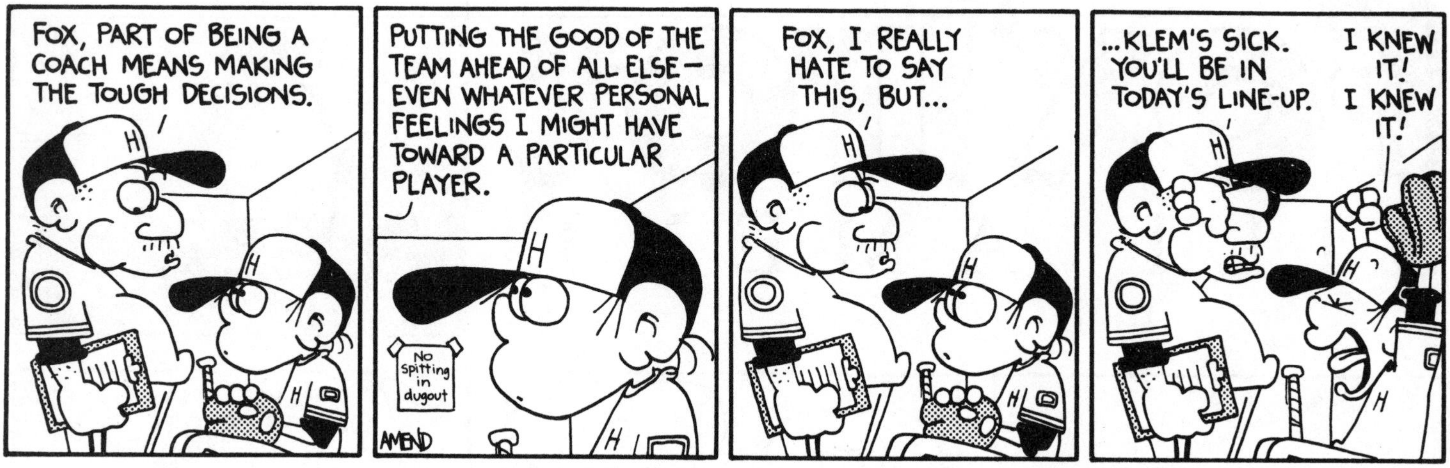
FOX, PART OF BEING A COACH MEANS MAKING THE TOUGH DECISIONS.
PUTTING THE GOOD OF THE TEAM AHEAD OF ALL ELSE— EVEN WHATEVER PERSONAL FEELINGS I MIGHT HAVE TOWARD A PARTICULAR PLAYER.
No spitting in dugout
AMEND
FOX, I REALLY HATE TO SAY THIS, BUT...
...KLEM'S SICK. YOU'LL BE IN TODAY'S LINE-UP.
I KNEW IT! I KNEW IT!

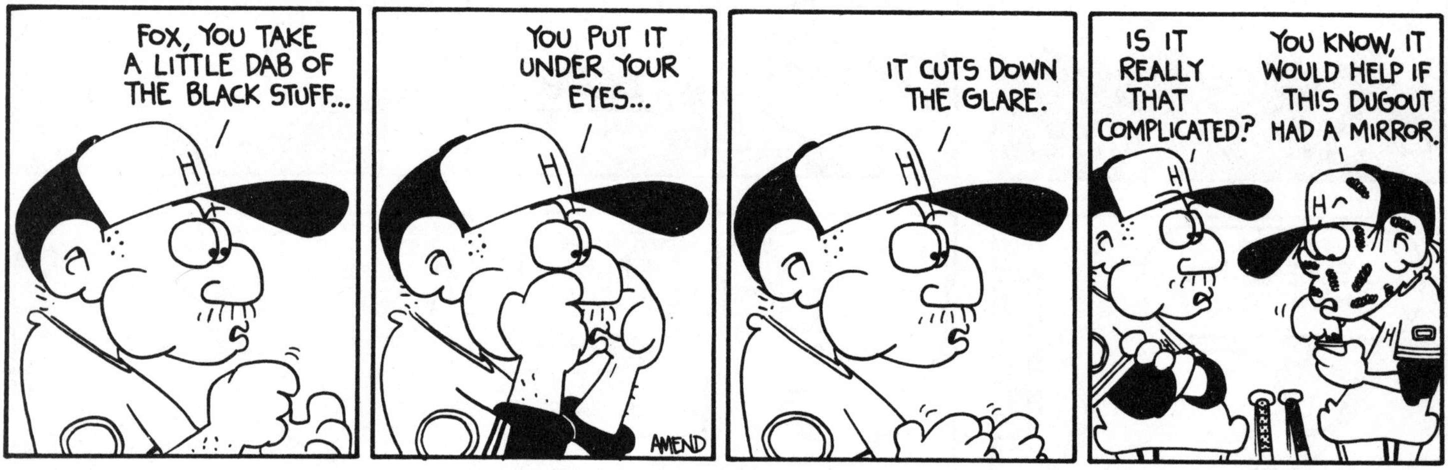
FOX, YOU TAKE A LITTLE DAB OF THE BLACK STUFF...
YOU PUT IT UNDER YOUR EYES...
AMEND
IT CUTS DOWN THE GLARE.
IS IT REALLY THAT COMPLICATED?
YOU KNOW, IT WOULD HELP IF THIS DUGOUT HAD A MIRROR.

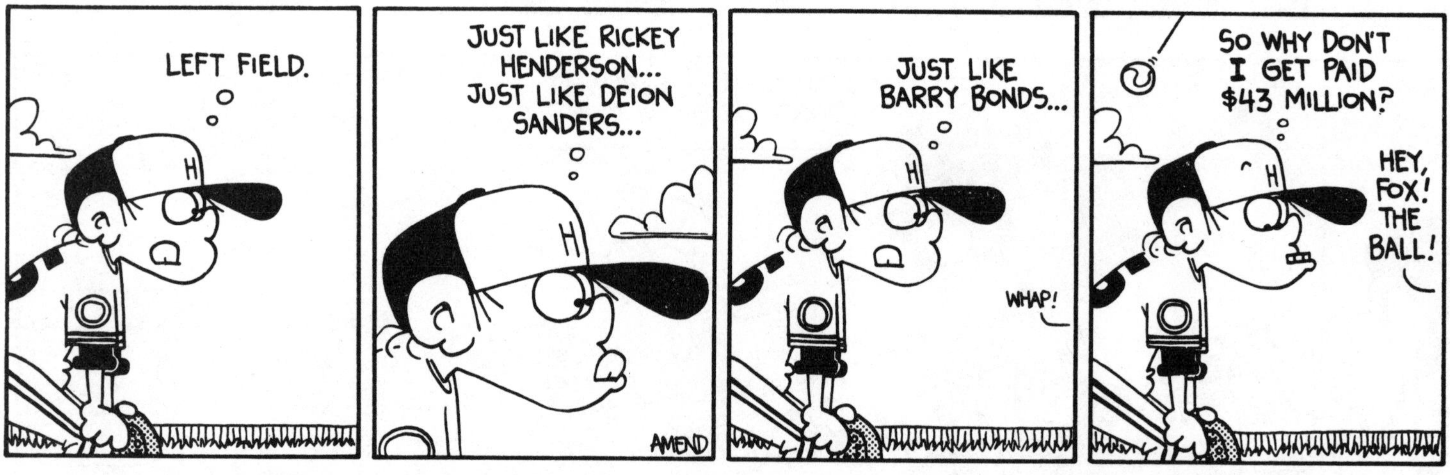
LEFT FIELD.
JUST LIKE RICKEY HENDERSON... JUST LIKE DEION SANDERS...
AMEND
JUST LIKE BARRY BONDS...
WHAP!
SO WHY DON'T I GET PAID $43 MILLION?
HEY, FOX! THE BALL!

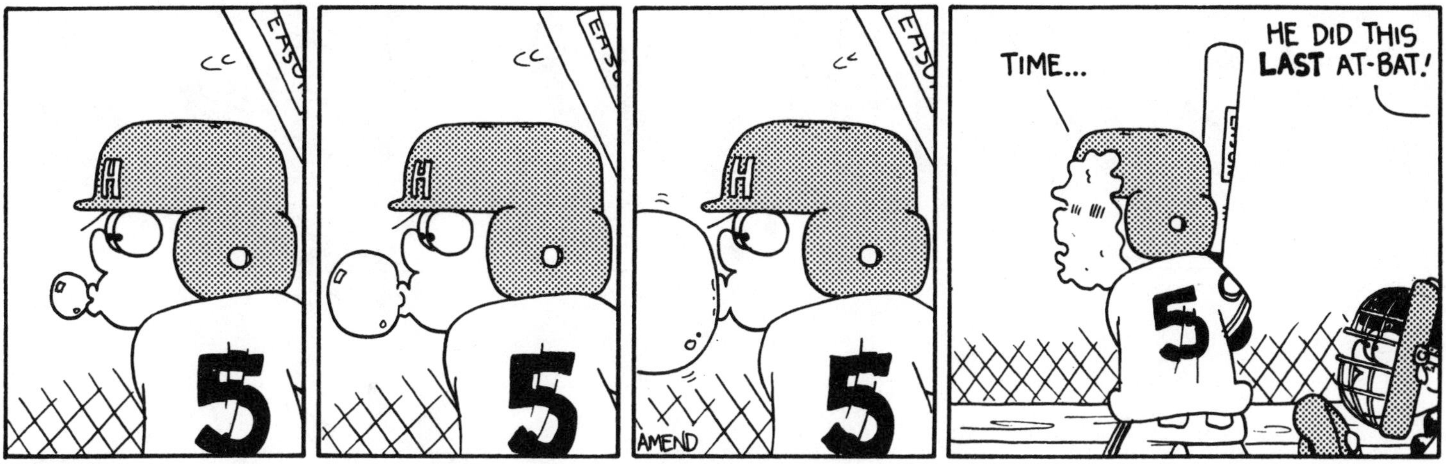
TIME...
HE DID THIS **LAST** AT-BAT!

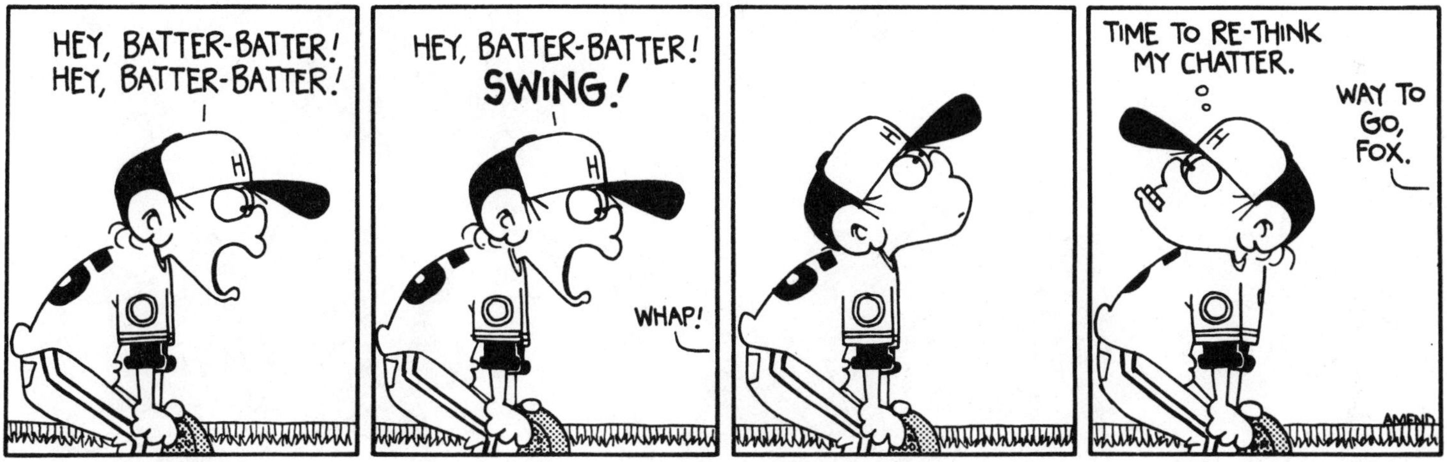
HEY, BATTER-BATTER! HEY, BATTER-BATTER!
HEY, BATTER-BATTER! **SWING!**
WHAP!
TIME TO RE-THINK MY CHATTER.
WAY TO GO, FOX.

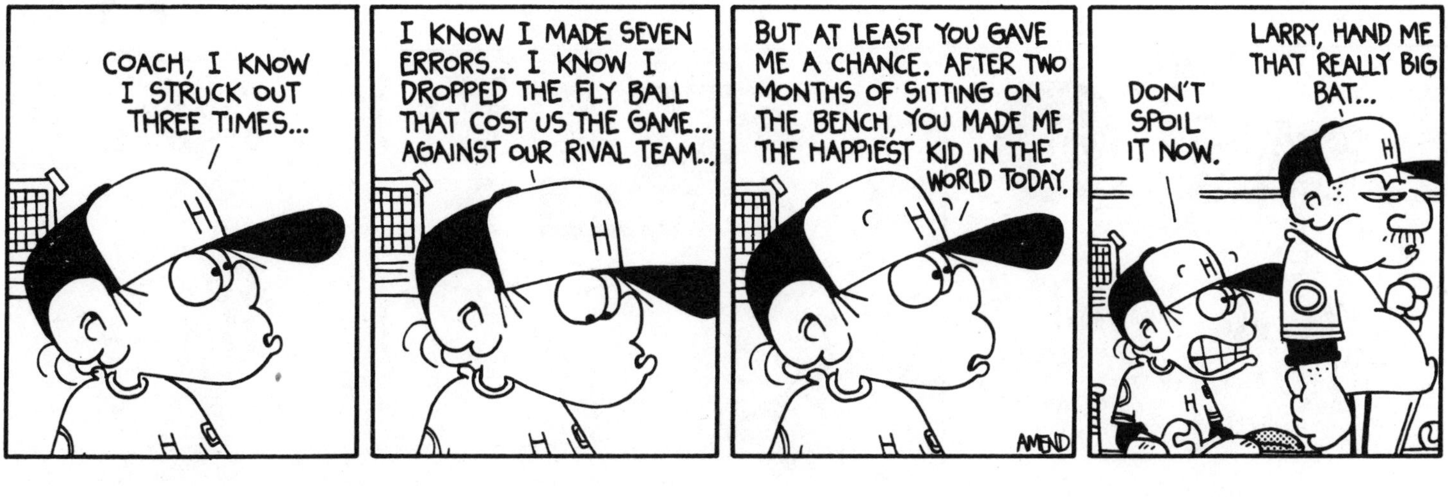
COACH, I KNOW I STRUCK OUT THREE TIMES...
I KNOW I MADE SEVEN ERRORS... I KNOW I DROPPED THE FLY BALL THAT COST US THE GAME... AGAINST OUR RIVAL TEAM...
BUT AT LEAST YOU GAVE ME A CHANCE. AFTER TWO MONTHS OF SITTING ON THE BENCH, YOU MADE ME THE HAPPIEST KID IN THE WORLD TODAY.
DON'T SPOIL IT NOW.
LARRY, HAND ME THAT REALLY BIG BAT...

FoxTrot
BILL AMEND

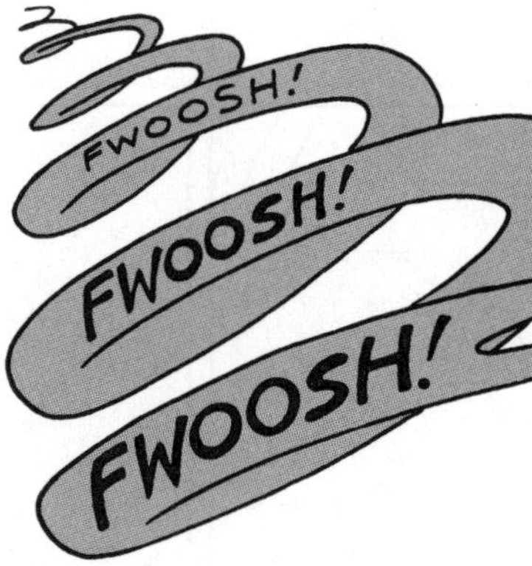
FWOOSH!
FWOOSH!
FWOOSH!
FWOOSH!

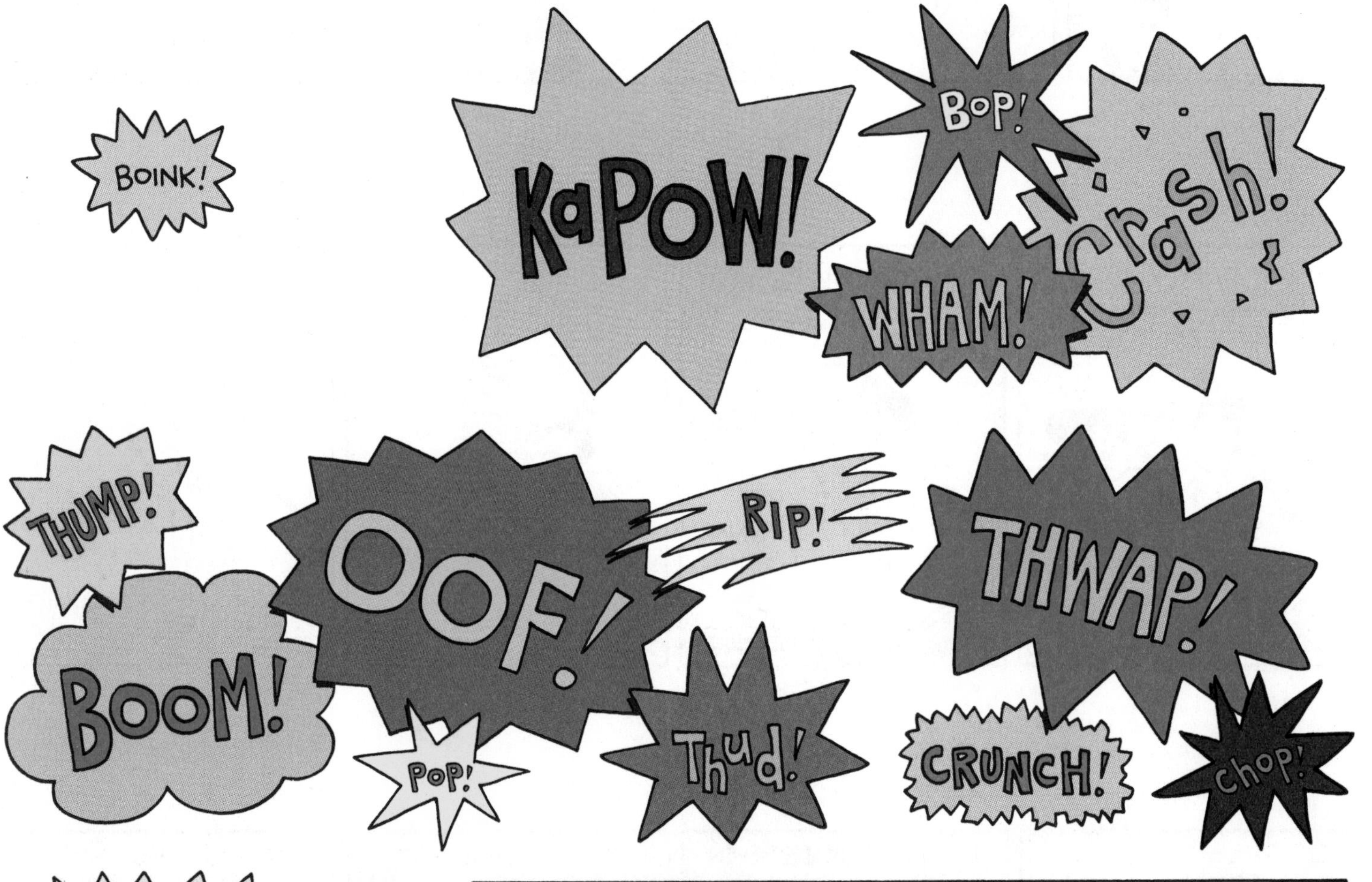
BOINK!
KaPOW!
BOP!
WHAM!
Crash!
THUMP!
OOF!
RIP!
THWAP!
BOOM!
POP!
Thud!
CRUNCH!
chop!

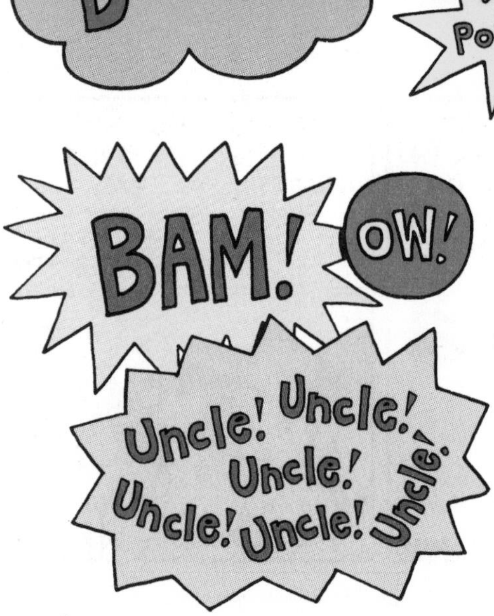
BAM!
OW!
Uncle! Uncle! Uncle! Uncle! Uncle! Uncle!

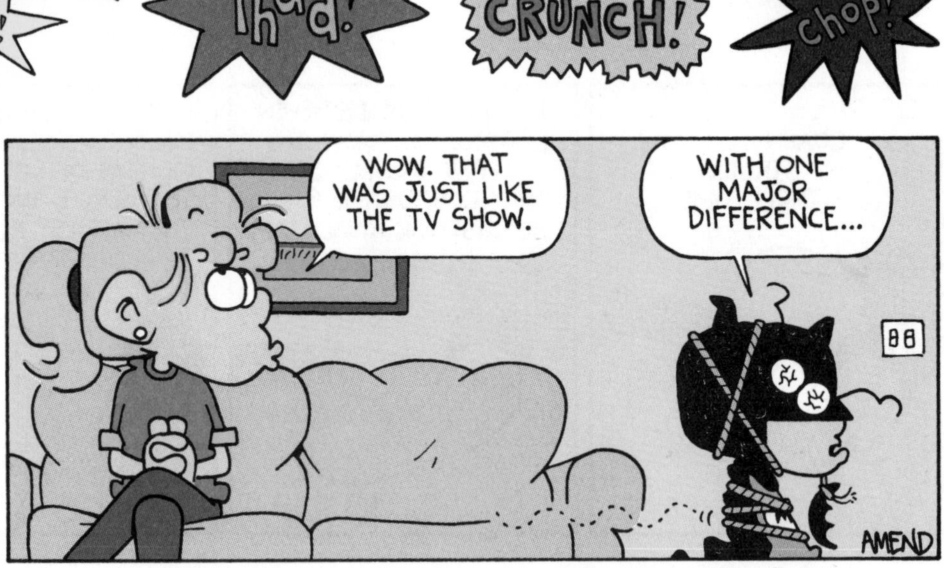
WOW. THAT WAS JUST LIKE THE TV SHOW.
WITH ONE MAJOR DIFFERENCE...
AMEND

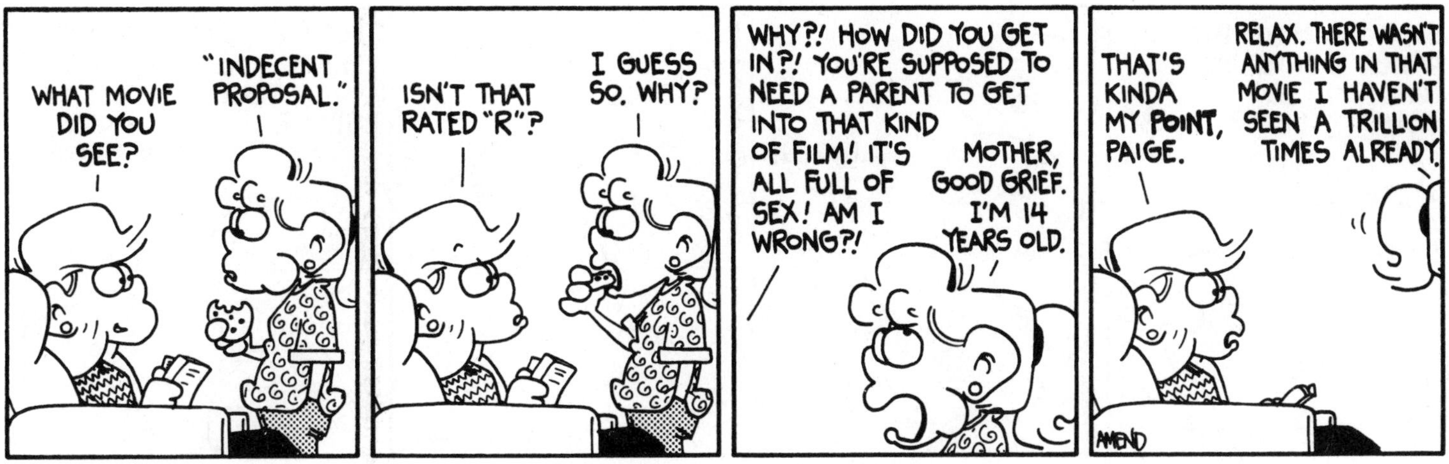
WHAT MOVIE DID YOU SEE?
"INDECENT PROPOSAL."
ISN'T THAT RATED "R"?
I GUESS SO. WHY?
WHY?! HOW DID YOU GET IN?! YOU'RE SUPPOSED TO NEED A PARENT TO GET INTO THAT KIND OF FILM! IT'S ALL FULL OF SEX! AM I WRONG?!
MOTHER, GOOD GRIEF. I'M 14 YEARS OLD.
RELAX. THERE WASN'T ANYTHING IN THAT MOVIE I HAVEN'T SEEN A TRILLION TIMES ALREADY.
THAT'S KINDA MY **POINT**, PAIGE.
AMEND

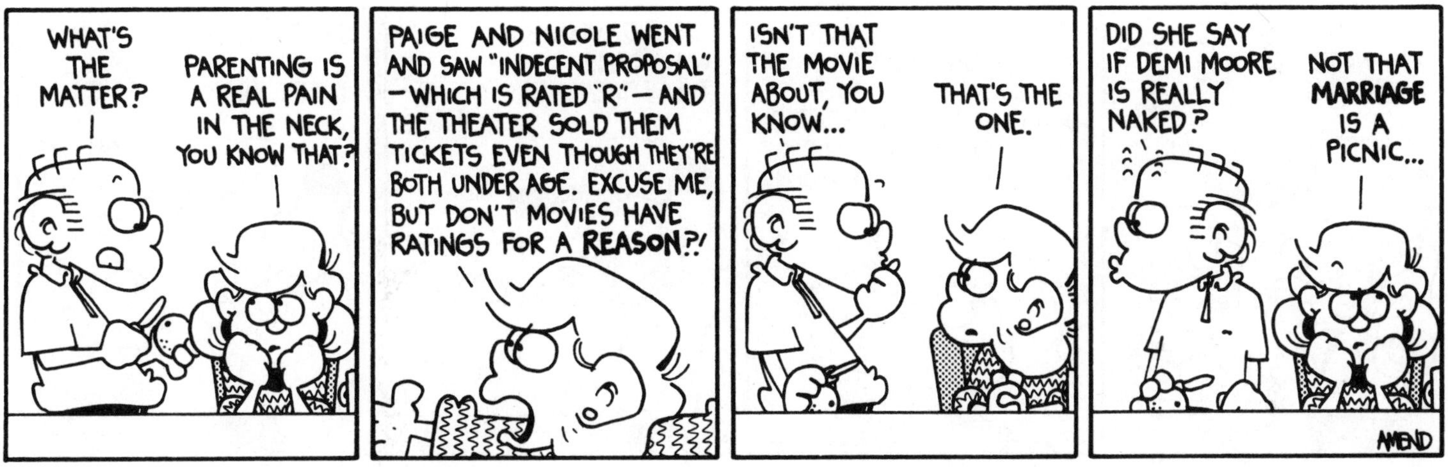
WHAT'S THE MATTER?
PARENTING IS A REAL PAIN IN THE NECK, YOU KNOW THAT?
PAIGE AND NICOLE WENT AND SAW "INDECENT PROPOSAL" —WHICH IS RATED "R"— AND THE THEATER SOLD THEM TICKETS EVEN THOUGH THEY'RE BOTH UNDER AGE. EXCUSE ME, BUT DON'T MOVIES HAVE RATINGS FOR A **REASON**?!
ISN'T THAT THE MOVIE ABOUT, YOU KNOW...
THAT'S THE ONE.
DID SHE SAY IF DEMI MOORE IS REALLY NAKED?
NOT THAT **MARRIAGE** IS A PICNIC...
AMEND

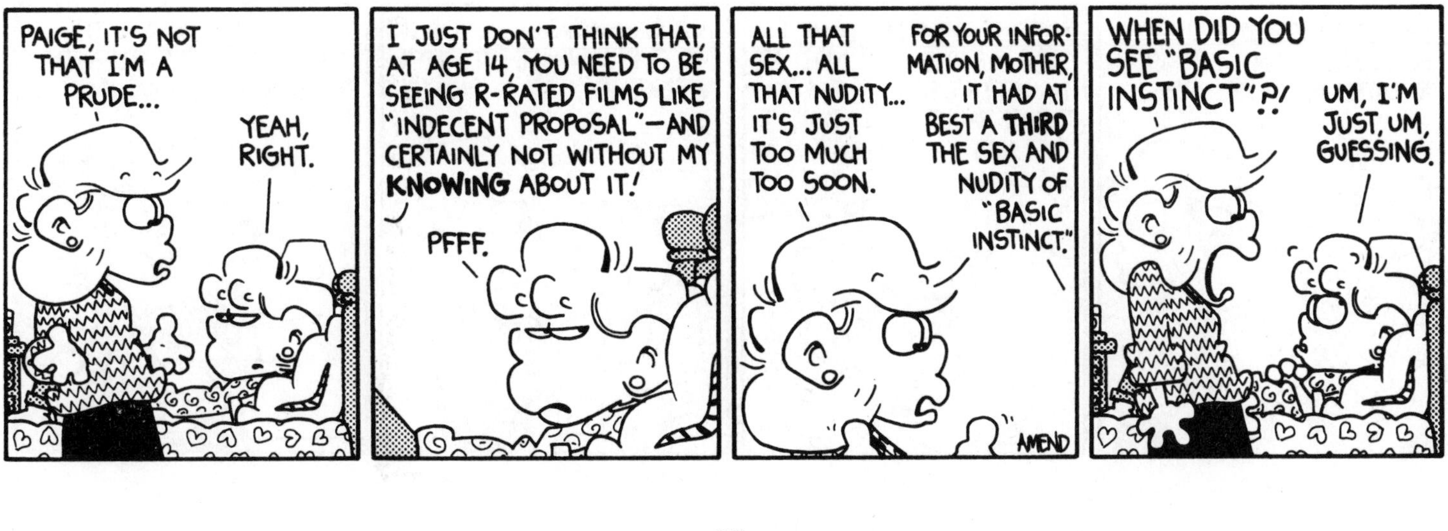
PAIGE, IT'S NOT THAT I'M A PRUDE...
YEAH, RIGHT.
I JUST DON'T THINK THAT, AT AGE 14, YOU NEED TO BE SEEING R-RATED FILMS LIKE "INDECENT PROPOSAL"—AND CERTAINLY NOT WITHOUT MY **KNOWING** ABOUT IT!
PFFF.
ALL THAT SEX... ALL THAT NUDITY... IT'S JUST TOO MUCH TOO SOON.
FOR YOUR INFORMATION, MOTHER, IT HAD AT BEST A **THIRD** THE SEX AND NUDITY OF "BASIC INSTINCT."
AMEND
WHEN DID YOU SEE "BASIC INSTINCT"?!
UM, I'M JUST, UM, GUESSING.

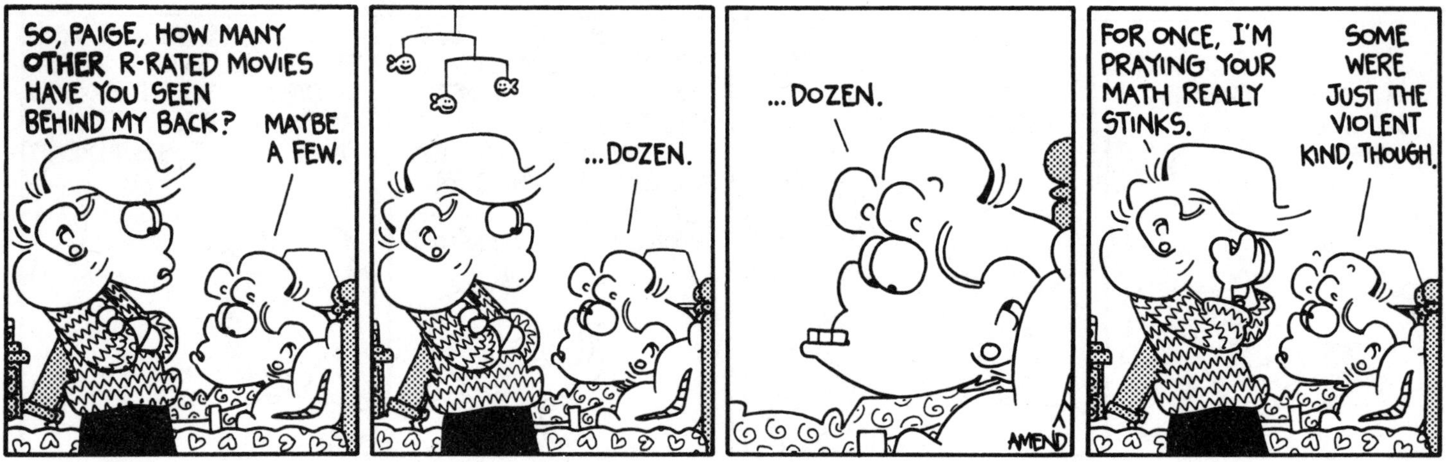
SO, PAIGE, HOW MANY **OTHER** R-RATED MOVIES HAVE YOU SEEN BEHIND MY BACK?
MAYBE A FEW.
...DOZEN.
...DOZEN.
AMEND
FOR ONCE, I'M PRAYING YOUR MATH REALLY STINKS.
SOME WERE JUST THE VIOLENT KIND, THOUGH.

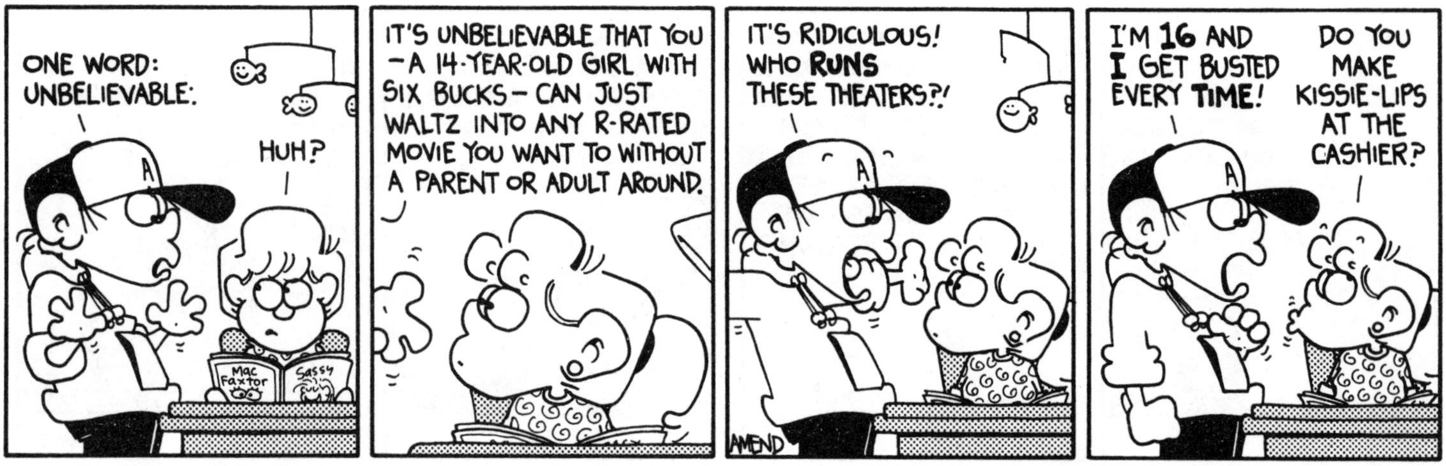
ONE WORD: UNBELIEVABLE.
HUH?
Mac Faxtor
Sassy
IT'S UNBELIEVABLE THAT YOU —A 14-YEAR-OLD GIRL WITH SIX BUCKS— CAN JUST WALTZ INTO ANY R-RATED MOVIE YOU WANT TO WITHOUT A PARENT OR ADULT AROUND.
IT'S RIDICULOUS! WHO **RUNS** THESE THEATERS?!
AMEND
I'M **16** AND **I** GET BUSTED EVERY **TIME**!
DO YOU MAKE KISSIE-LIPS AT THE CASHIER?

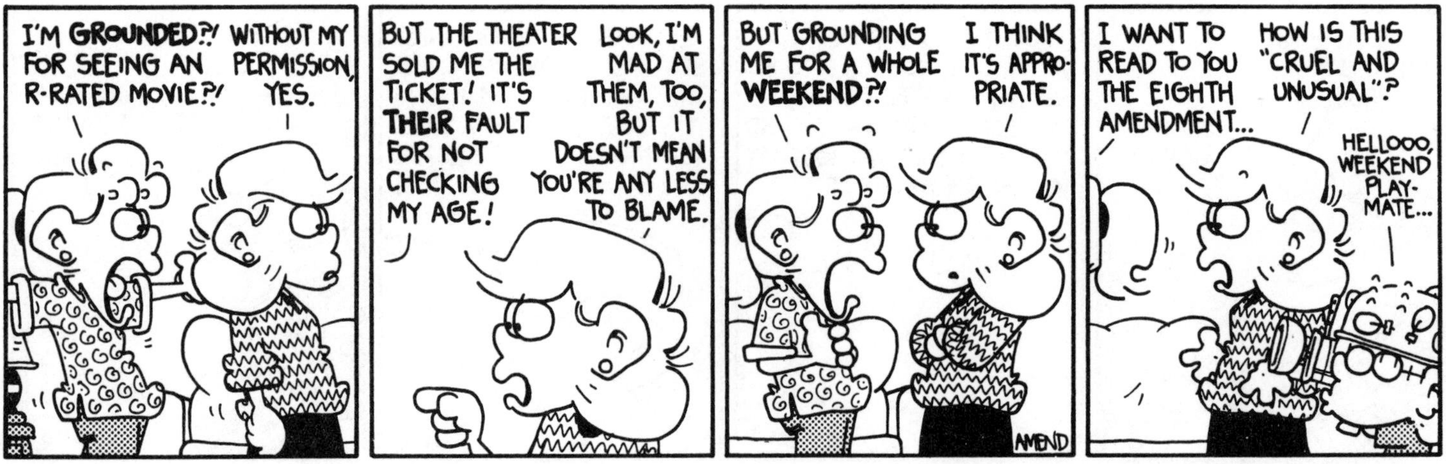
I'M **GROUNDED**?! FOR SEEING AN R-RATED MOVIE?!
WITHOUT MY PERMISSION, YES.
BUT THE THEATER SOLD ME THE TICKET! IT'S **THEIR** FAULT FOR NOT CHECKING MY AGE!
LOOK, I'M MAD AT THEM, TOO, BUT IT DOESN'T MEAN YOU'RE ANY LESS TO BLAME.
BUT GROUNDING ME FOR A WHOLE **WEEKEND**?!
I THINK IT'S APPROPRIATE.
AMEND
I WANT TO READ TO YOU THE EIGHTH AMENDMENT...
HOW IS THIS "CRUEL AND UNUSUAL"?
HELLOOO, WEEKEND PLAYMATE...

FoxTrot

BILL AMEND

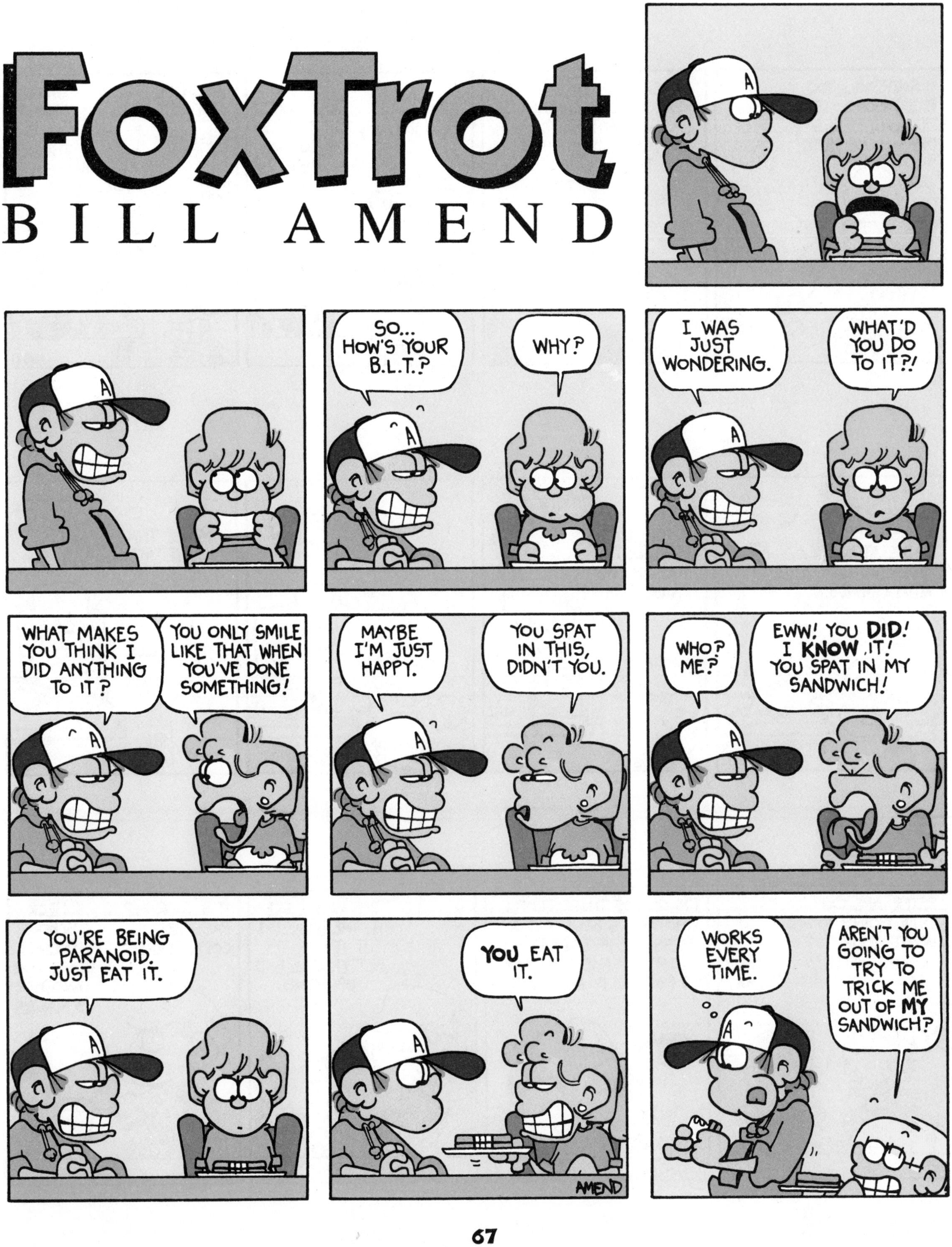
SO... HOW'S YOUR B.L.T.?
WHY?
I WAS JUST WONDERING.
WHAT'D YOU DO TO IT?!
WHAT MAKES YOU THINK I DID ANYTHING TO IT?
YOU ONLY SMILE LIKE THAT WHEN YOU'VE DONE SOMETHING!
MAYBE I'M JUST HAPPY.
YOU SPAT IN THIS, DIDN'T YOU.
WHO? ME?
EWW! YOU DID! I KNOW IT! YOU SPAT IN MY SANDWICH!
YOU'RE BEING PARANOID. JUST EAT IT.
YOU EAT IT.
AMEND
WORKS EVERY TIME.
AREN'T YOU GOING TO TRY TO TRICK ME OUT OF MY SANDWICH?

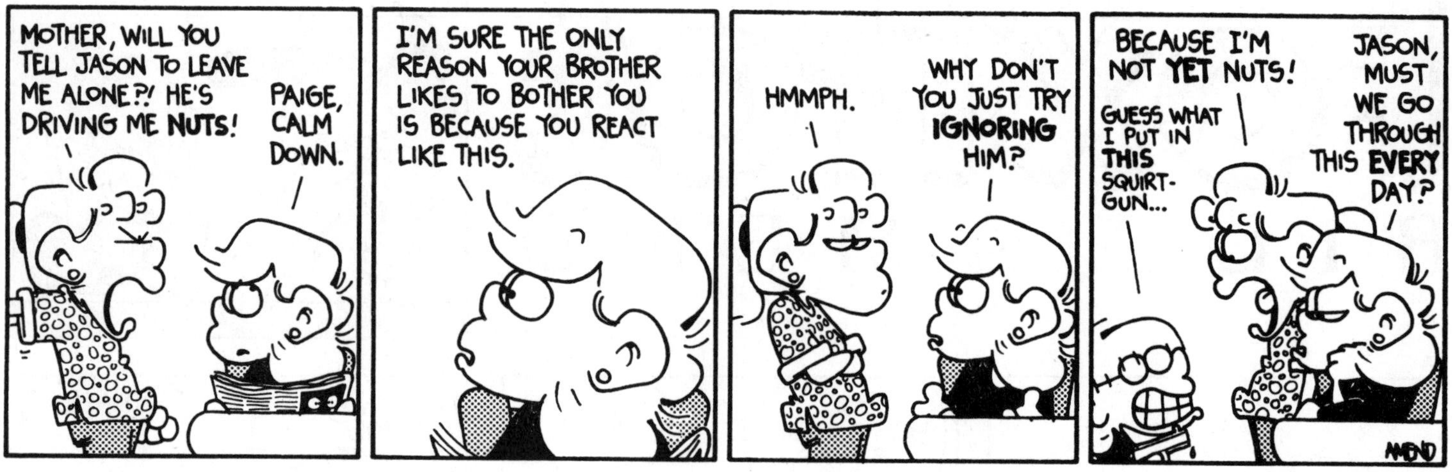
MOTHER, WILL YOU TELL JASON TO LEAVE ME ALONE?! HE'S DRIVING ME **NUTS**!
PAIGE, CALM DOWN.
I'M SURE THE ONLY REASON YOUR BROTHER LIKES TO BOTHER YOU IS BECAUSE YOU REACT LIKE THIS.
HMMPH.
WHY DON'T YOU JUST TRY **IGNORING** HIM?
BECAUSE I'M NOT **YET** NUTS!
GUESS WHAT I PUT IN **THIS** SQUIRT-GUN...
JASON, MUST WE GO THROUGH THIS **EVERY** DAY?
AMEND

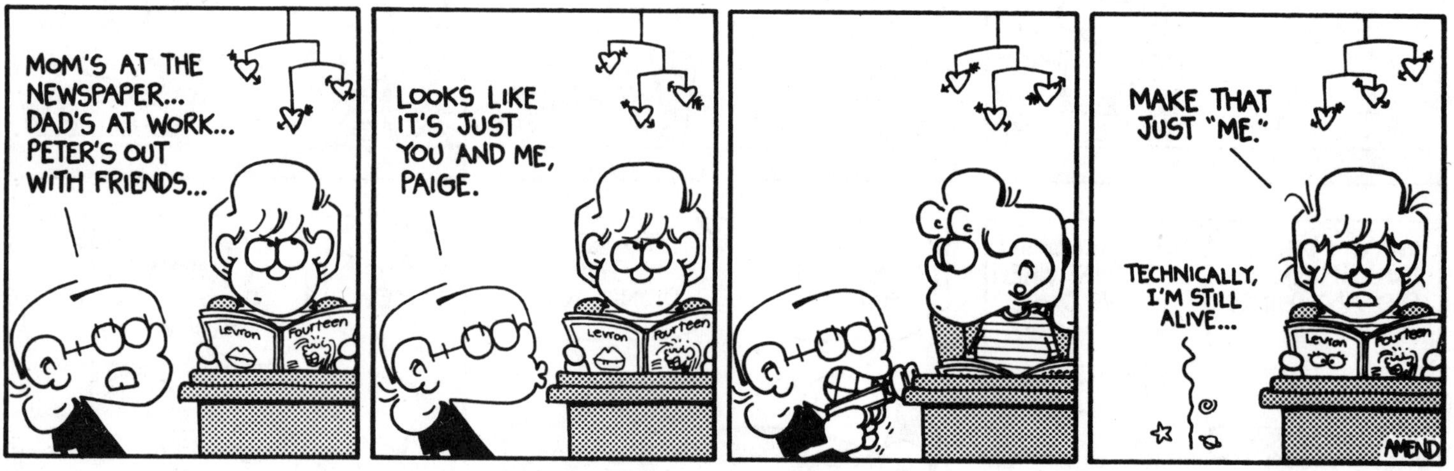
MOM'S AT THE NEWSPAPER... DAD'S AT WORK... PETER'S OUT WITH FRIENDS...
LOOKS LIKE IT'S JUST YOU AND ME, PAIGE.
MAKE THAT JUST "ME."
TECHNICALLY, I'M STILL ALIVE...
AMEND

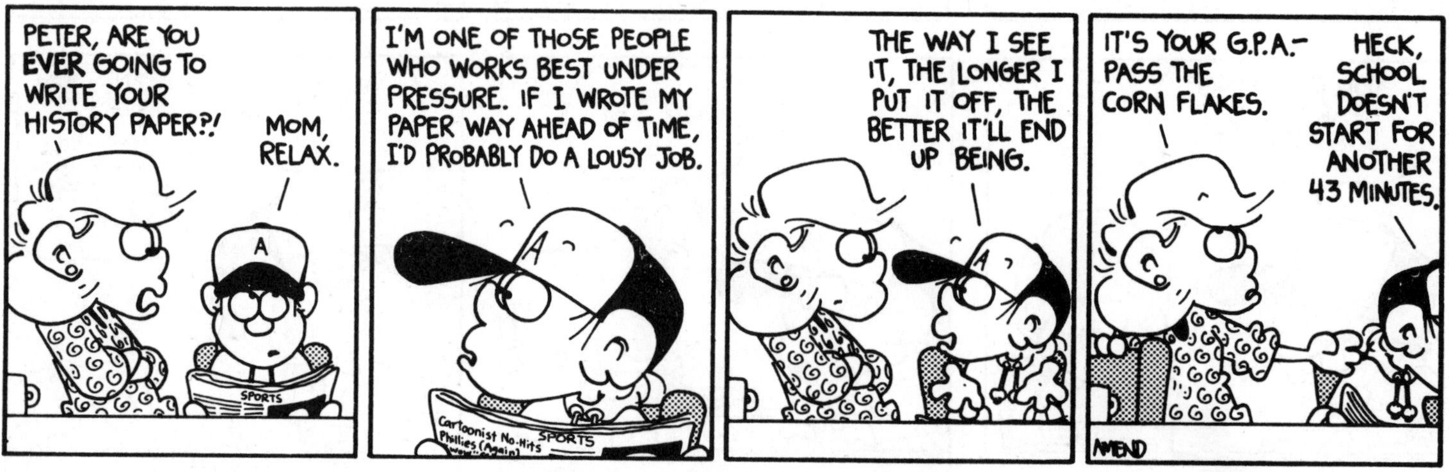
PETER, ARE YOU **EVER** GOING TO WRITE YOUR HISTORY PAPER?!
MOM, RELAX.
I'M ONE OF THOSE PEOPLE WHO WORKS BEST UNDER PRESSURE. IF I WROTE MY PAPER WAY AHEAD OF TIME, I'D PROBABLY DO A LOUSY JOB.
THE WAY I SEE IT, THE LONGER I PUT IT OFF, THE BETTER IT'LL END UP BEING.
IT'S YOUR G.P.A.– PASS THE CORN FLAKES.
HECK, SCHOOL DOESN'T START FOR ANOTHER 43 MINUTES.
AMEND

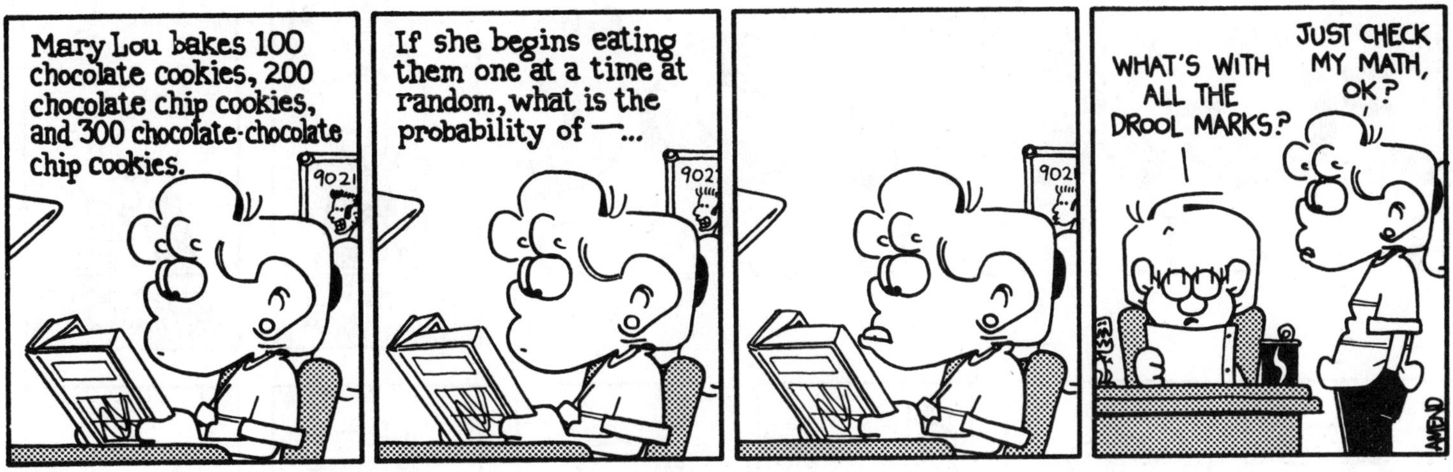
Mary Lou bakes 100 chocolate cookies, 200 chocolate chip cookies, and 300 chocolate-chocolate chip cookies.
If she begins eating them one at a time at random, what is the probability of —...
WHAT'S WITH ALL THE DROOL MARKS?
JUST CHECK MY MATH, OK?
AMEND

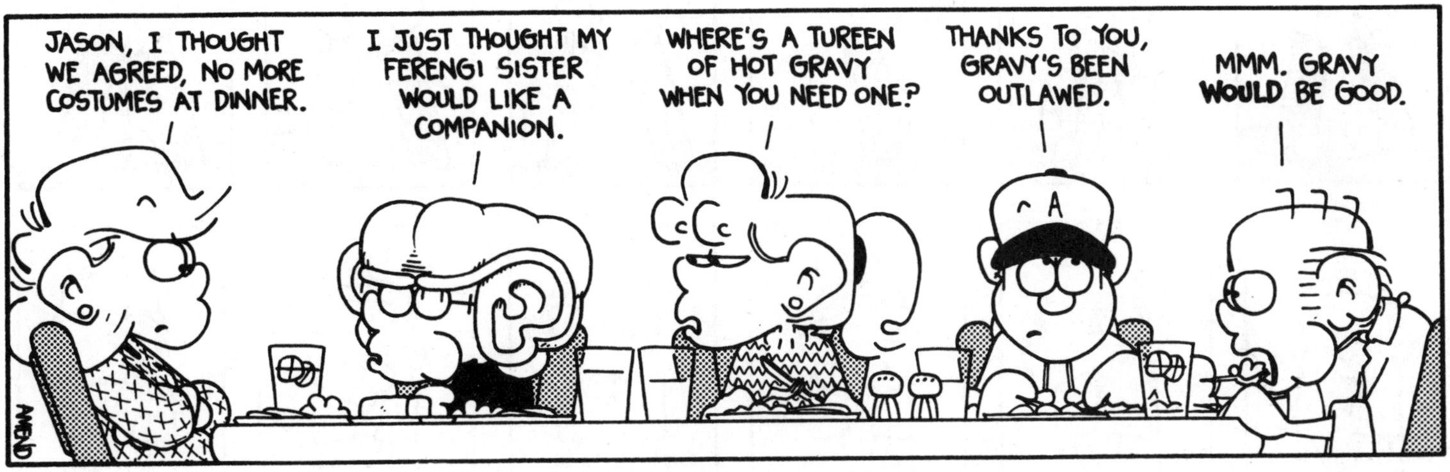
JASON, I THOUGHT WE AGREED, NO MORE COSTUMES AT DINNER.
I JUST THOUGHT MY FERENGI SISTER WOULD LIKE A COMPANION.
WHERE'S A TUREEN OF HOT GRAVY WHEN YOU NEED ONE?
THANKS TO YOU, GRAVY'S BEEN OUTLAWED.
MMM. GRAVY **WOULD** BE GOOD.
AMEND

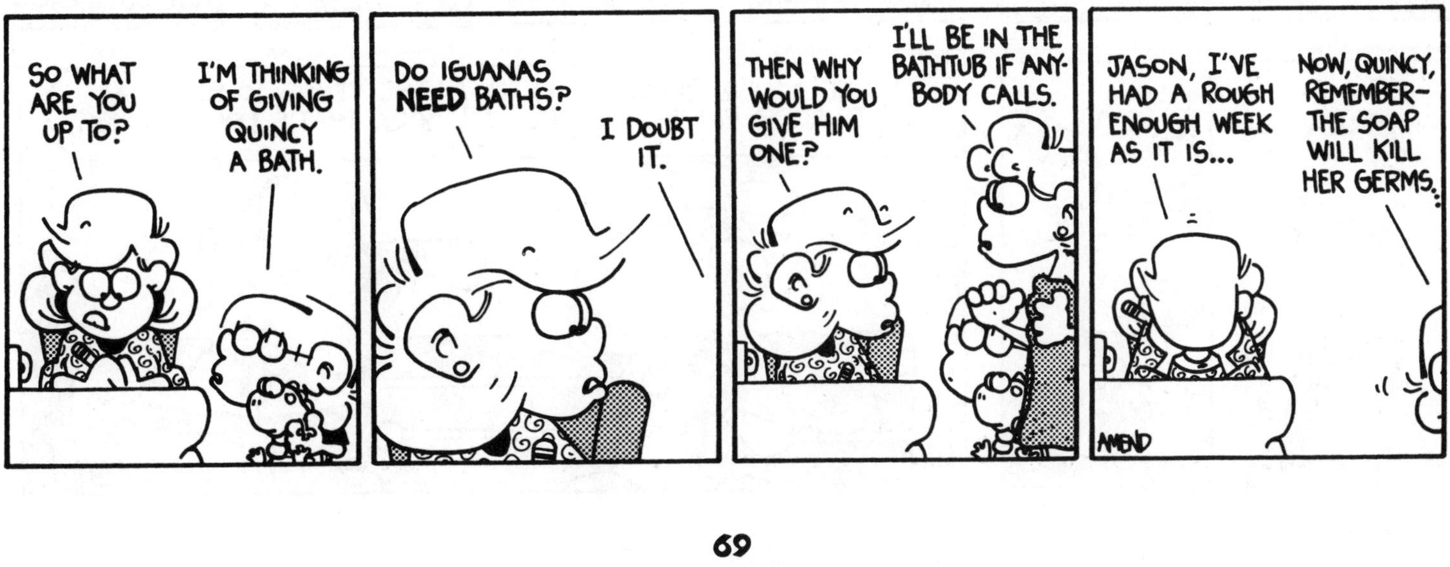
SO WHAT ARE YOU UP TO?
I'M THINKING OF GIVING QUINCY A BATH.
DO IGUANAS **NEED** BATHS?
I DOUBT IT.
THEN WHY WOULD YOU GIVE HIM ONE?
I'LL BE IN THE BATHTUB IF ANYBODY CALLS.
JASON, I'VE HAD A ROUGH ENOUGH WEEK AS IT IS...
NOW, QUINCY, REMEMBER— THE SOAP WILL KILL HER GERMS.
AMEND

FoxTrot
BILL AMEND

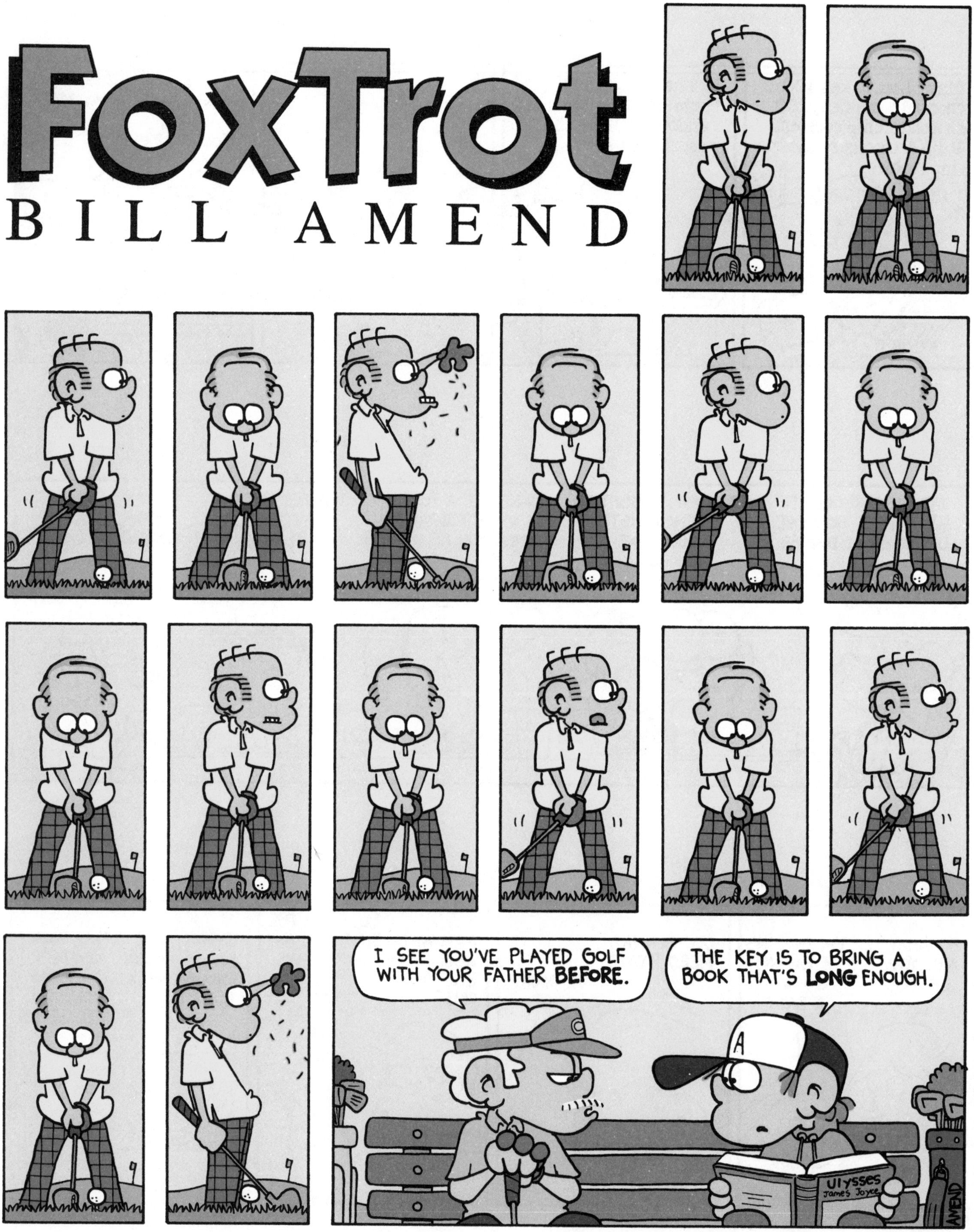
I SEE YOU'VE PLAYED GOLF WITH YOUR FATHER BEFORE.
THE KEY IS TO BRING A BOOK THAT'S LONG ENOUGH.
Ulysses
James Joyce
AMEND

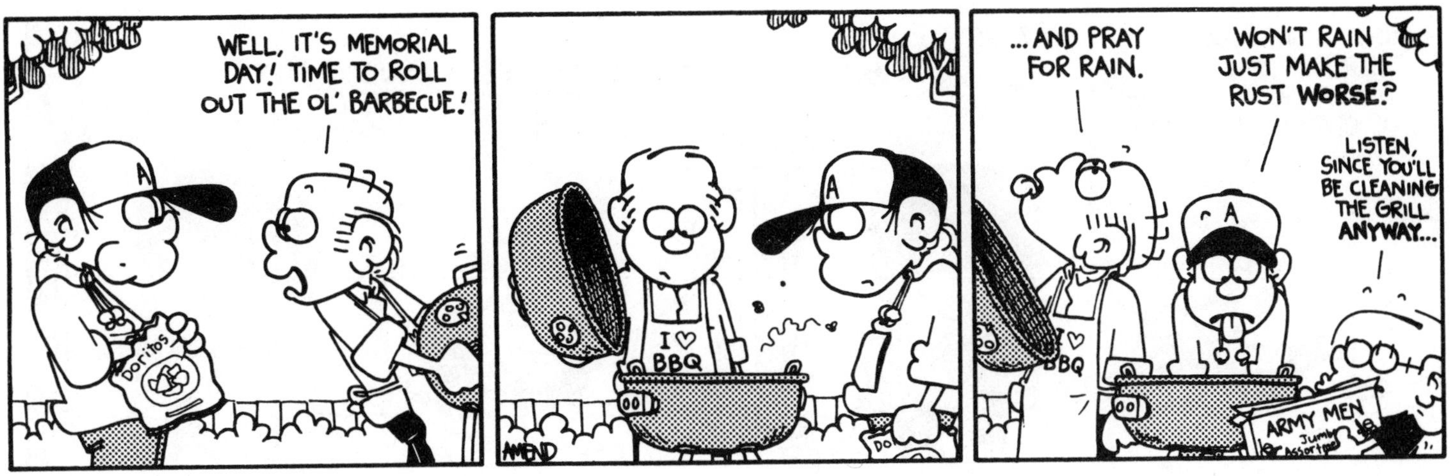
WELL, IT'S MEMORIAL DAY! TIME TO ROLL OUT THE OL' BARBECUE!
Doritos
I ♡ BBQ
AMEND
...AND PRAY FOR RAIN.
WON'T RAIN JUST MAKE THE RUST **WORSE**?
LISTEN, SINCE YOU'LL BE CLEANING THE GRILL **ANYWAY**...
ARMY MEN

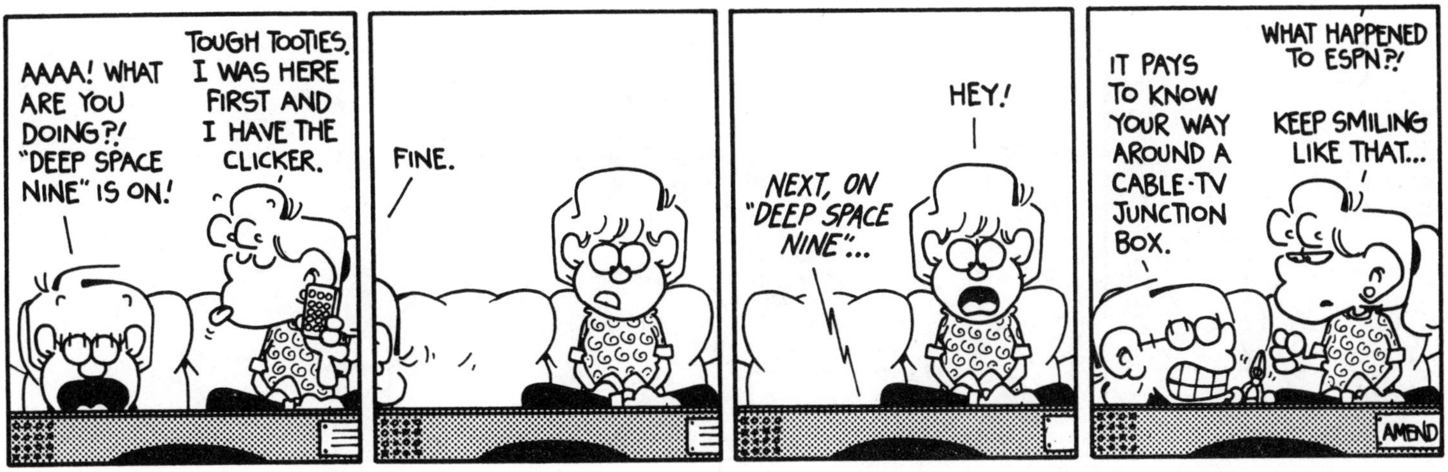
AAAA! WHAT ARE YOU DOING?! "DEEP SPACE NINE" IS ON!
TOUGH TOOTIES. I WAS HERE FIRST AND I HAVE THE CLICKER.
FINE.
NEXT, ON "DEEP SPACE NINE"...
HEY!
IT PAYS TO KNOW YOUR WAY AROUND A CABLE-TV JUNCTION BOX.
WHAT HAPPENED TO ESPN?!
KEEP SMILING LIKE THAT...
AMEND

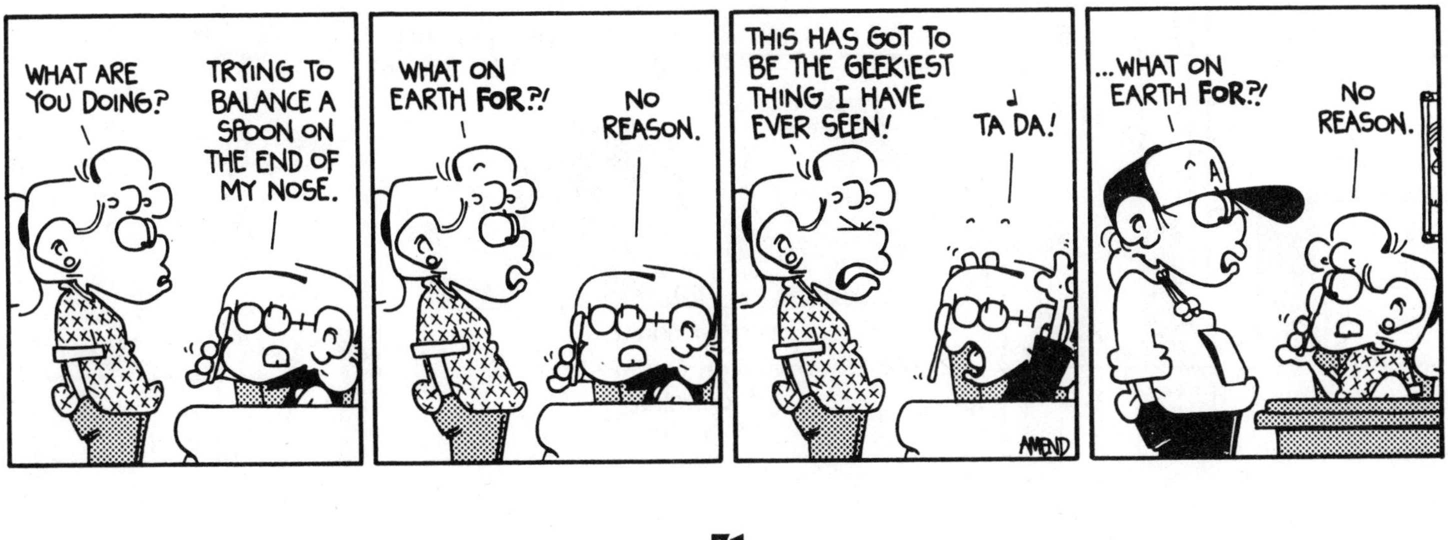
WHAT ARE YOU DOING?
TRYING TO BALANCE A SPOON ON THE END OF MY NOSE.
WHAT ON EARTH **FOR**?!
NO REASON.
THIS HAS GOT TO BE THE GEEKIEST THING I HAVE EVER SEEN!
TA DA!
AMEND
...WHAT ON EARTH **FOR**?!
NO REASON.

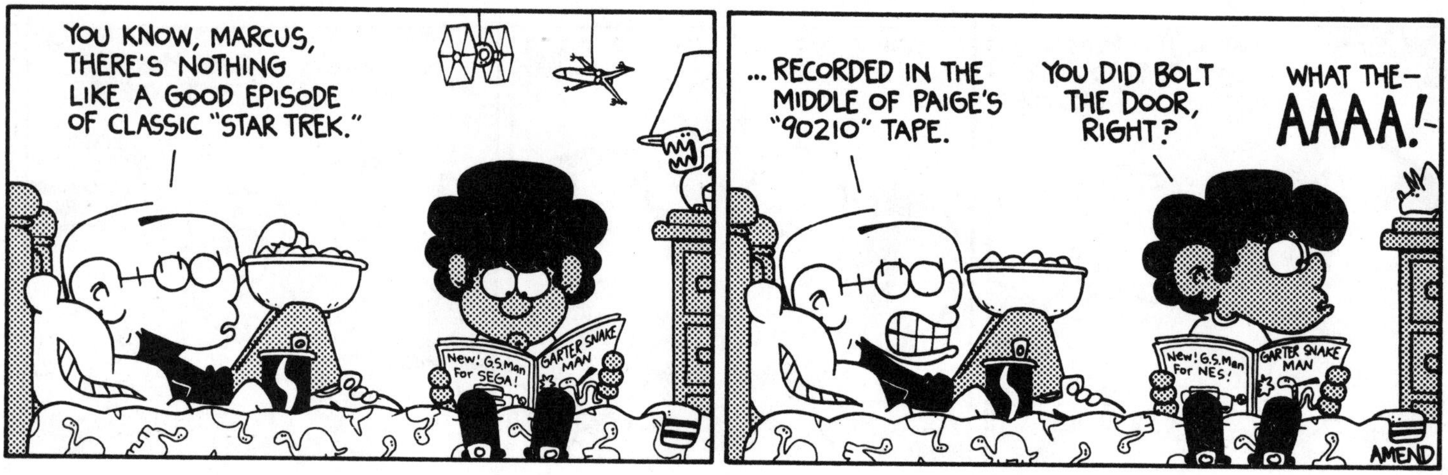
YOU KNOW, MARCUS, THERE'S NOTHING LIKE A GOOD EPISODE OF CLASSIC "STAR TREK."
New! G.S.Man For SEGA!
GARTER SNAKE MAN
... RECORDED IN THE MIDDLE OF PAIGE'S "90210" TAPE.
YOU DID BOLT THE DOOR, RIGHT?
WHAT THE— AAAA!—
New! G.S.Man For NES!
GARTER SNAKE MAN
AMEND

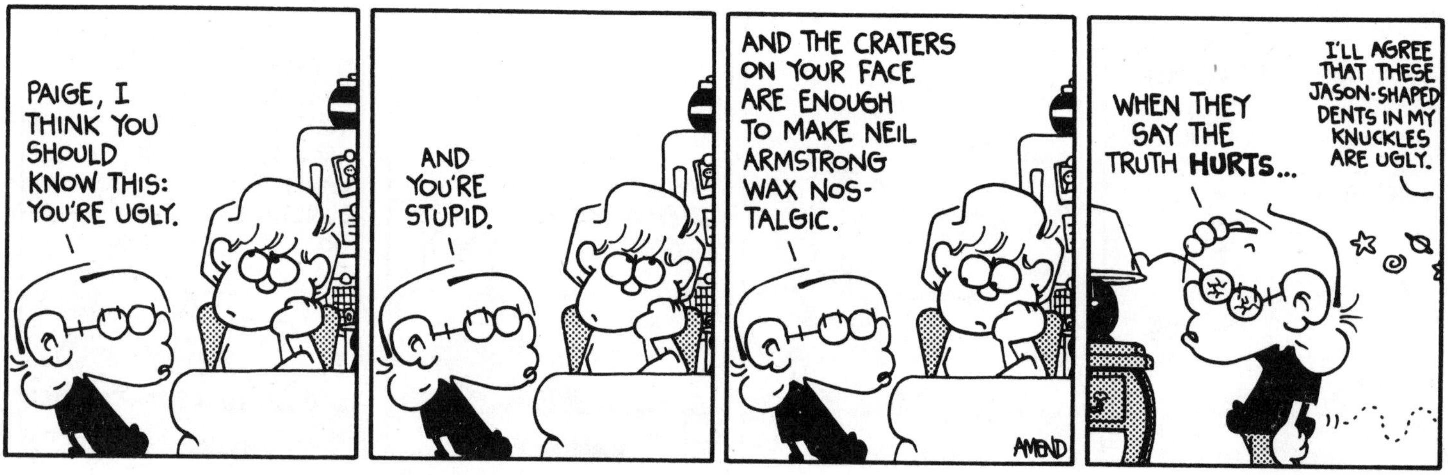
PAIGE, I THINK YOU SHOULD KNOW THIS: YOU'RE UGLY.
AND YOU'RE STUPID.
AND THE CRATERS ON YOUR FACE ARE ENOUGH TO MAKE NEIL ARMSTRONG WAX NOS-TALGIC.
AMEND
WHEN THEY SAY THE TRUTH **HURTS**...
I'LL AGREE THAT THESE JASON-SHAPED DENTS IN MY KNUCKLES ARE UGLY.

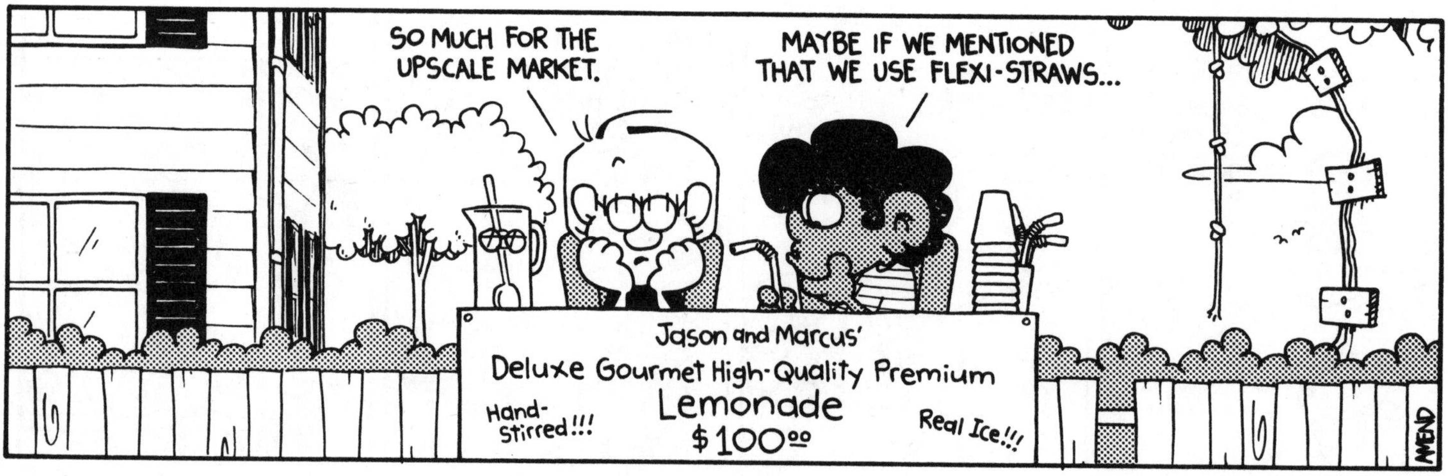
SO MUCH FOR THE UPSCALE MARKET.
MAYBE IF WE MENTIONED THAT WE USE FLEXI-STRAWS...
Jason and Marcus'
Deluxe Gourmet High-Quality Premium
Lemonade
$100.00
Hand-Stirred!!!
Real Ice!!!
AMEND

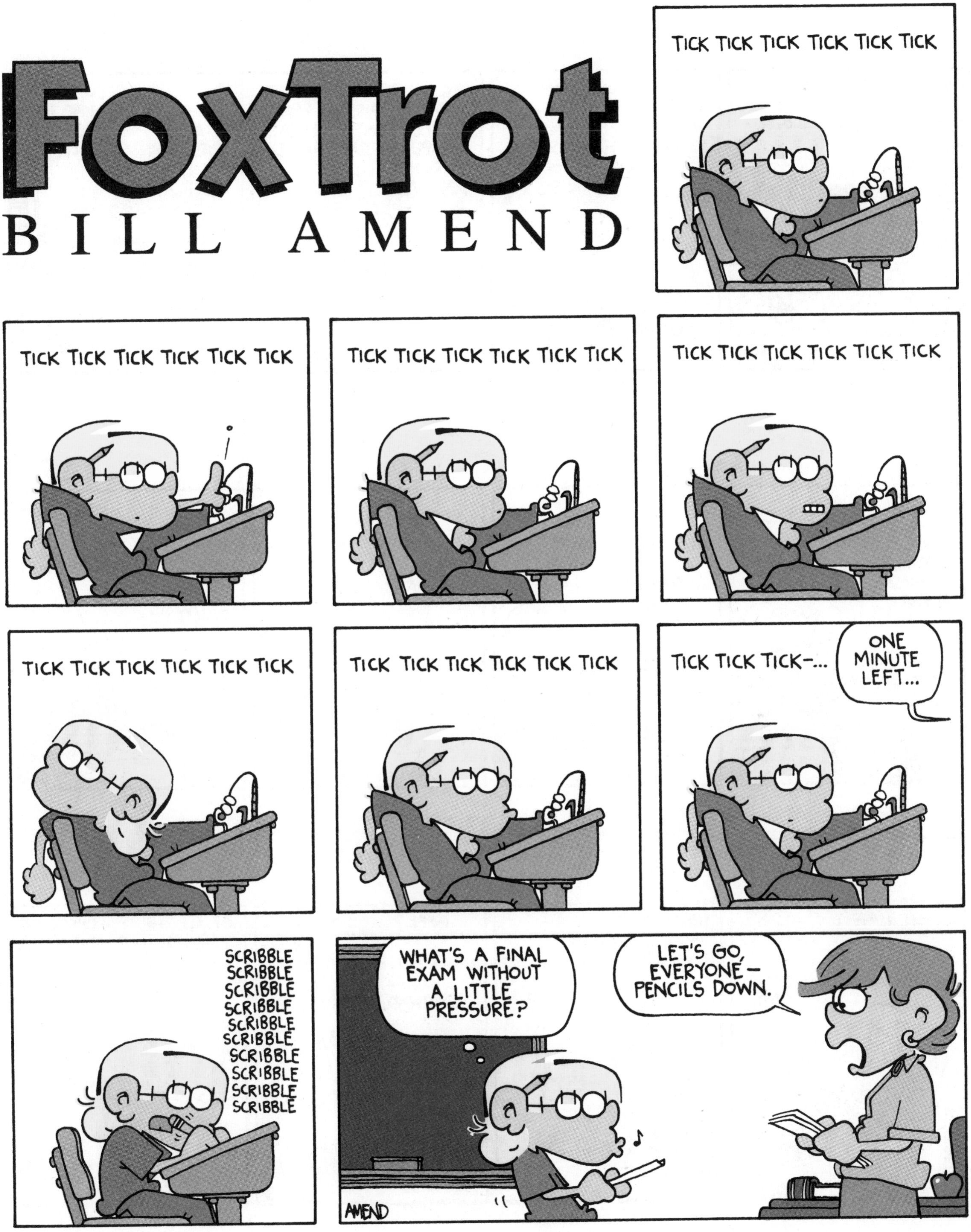
FoxTrot
BILL AMEND
TICK TICK TICK TICK TICK TICK
TICK TICK TICK TICK TICK TICK
TICK TICK TICK TICK TICK TICK
TICK TICK TICK TICK TICK TICK
TICK TICK TICK TICK TICK TICK
TICK TICK TICK TICK TICK TICK
TICK TICK TICK–...
ONE MINUTE LEFT...
SCRIBBLE SCRIBBLE SCRIBBLE SCRIBBLE SCRIBBLE SCRIBBLE SCRIBBLE SCRIBBLE SCRIBBLE SCRIBBLE
WHAT'S A FINAL EXAM WITHOUT A LITTLE PRESSURE?
LET'S GO, EVERYONE– PENCILS DOWN.
AMEND

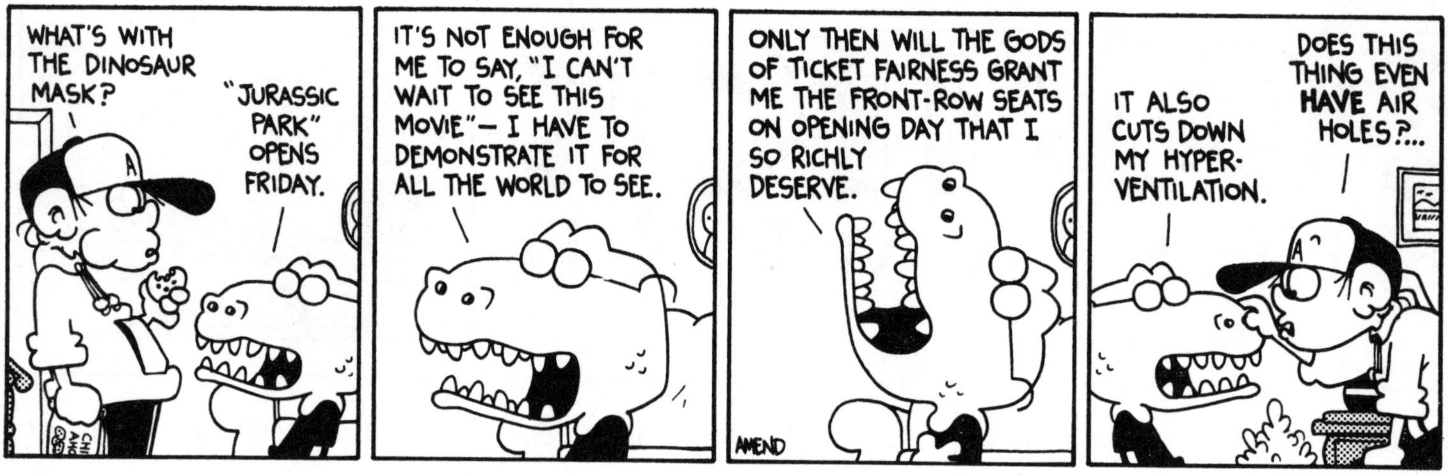
WHAT'S WITH THE DINOSAUR MASK?
"JURASSIC PARK" OPENS FRIDAY.
IT'S NOT ENOUGH FOR ME TO SAY, "I CAN'T WAIT TO SEE THIS MOVIE"— I HAVE TO DEMONSTRATE IT FOR ALL THE WORLD TO SEE.
ONLY THEN WILL THE GODS OF TICKET FAIRNESS GRANT ME THE FRONT-ROW SEATS ON OPENING DAY THAT I SO RICHLY DESERVE.
AMEND
IT ALSO CUTS DOWN MY HYPER-VENTILATION.
DOES THIS THING EVEN HAVE AIR HOLES?...

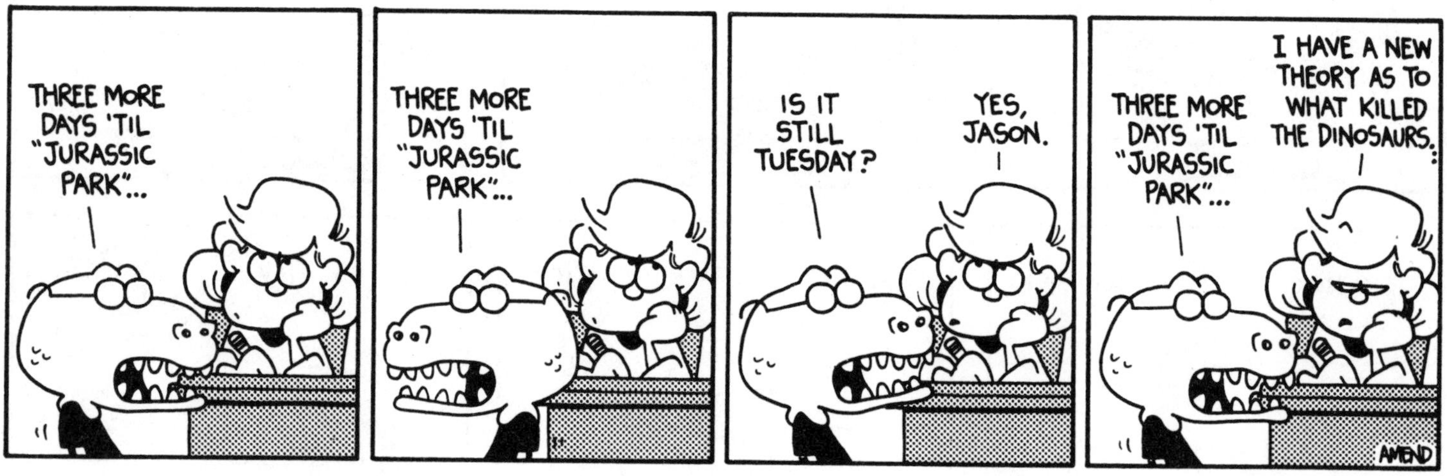
THREE MORE DAYS 'TIL "JURASSIC PARK"...
THREE MORE DAYS 'TIL "JURASSIC PARK"...
IS IT STILL TUESDAY?
YES, JASON.
THREE MORE DAYS 'TIL "JURASSIC PARK"...
I HAVE A NEW THEORY AS TO WHAT KILLED THE DINOSAURS.
AMEND

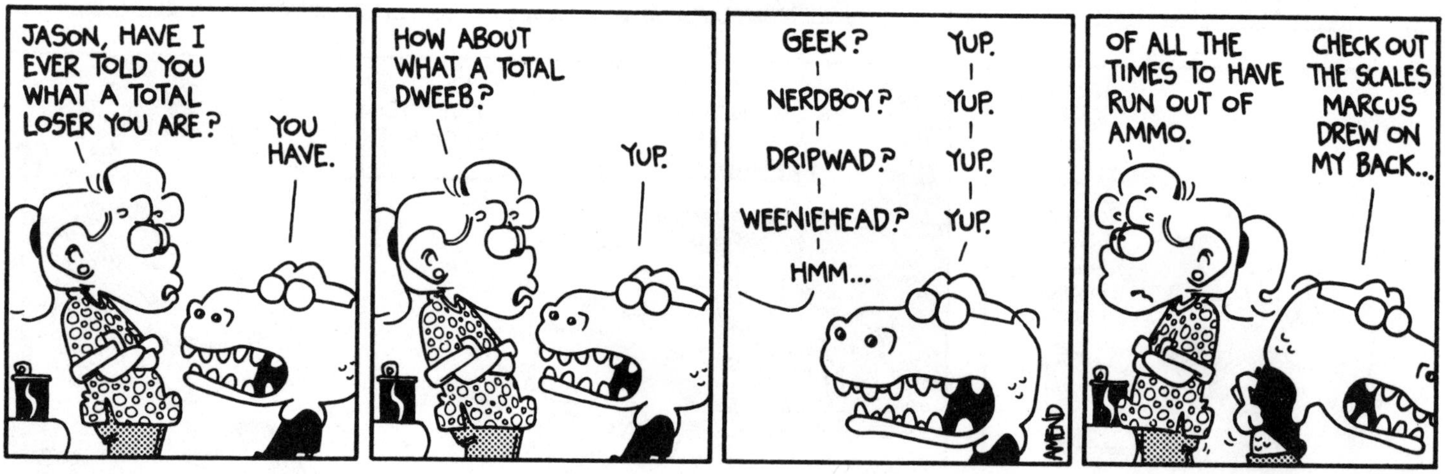
JASON, HAVE I EVER TOLD YOU WHAT A TOTAL LOSER YOU ARE?
YOU HAVE.
HOW ABOUT WHAT A TOTAL DWEEB?
YUP.
GEEK?
YUP.
NERDBOY?
YUP.
DRIPWAD?
YUP.
WEENIEHEAD?
YUP.
HMM...
AMEND
OF ALL THE TIMES TO HAVE RUN OUT OF AMMO.
CHECK OUT THE SCALES MARCUS DREW ON MY BACK...

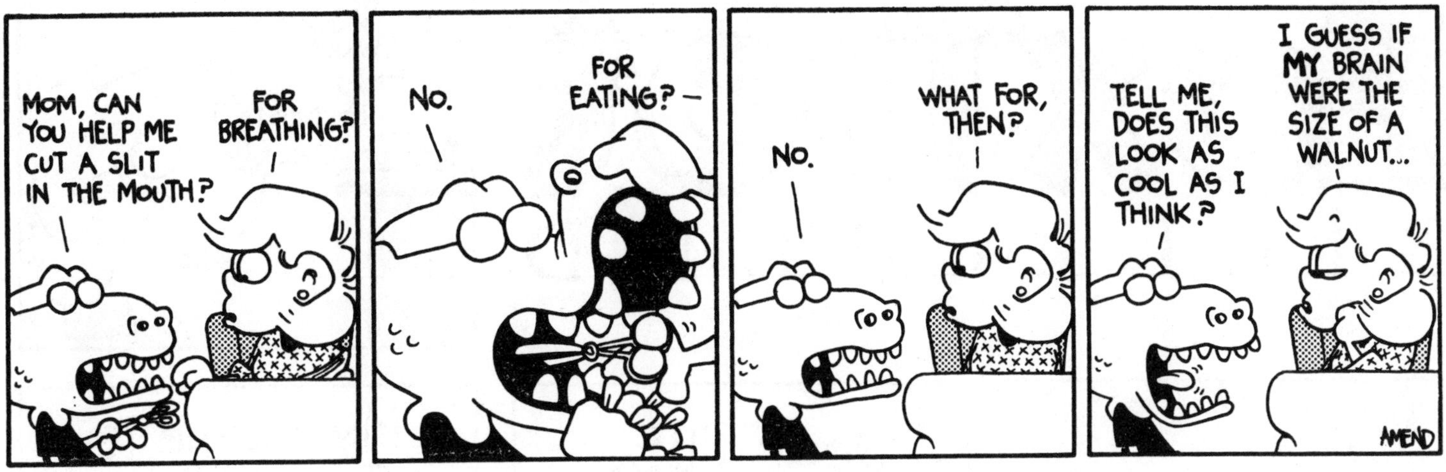
MOM, CAN YOU HELP ME CUT A SLIT IN THE MOUTH?
FOR BREATHING?
NO.
FOR EATING?
NO.
WHAT FOR, THEN?
TELL ME, DOES THIS LOOK AS COOL AS I THINK?
I GUESS IF MY BRAIN WERE THE SIZE OF A WALNUT...
AMEND

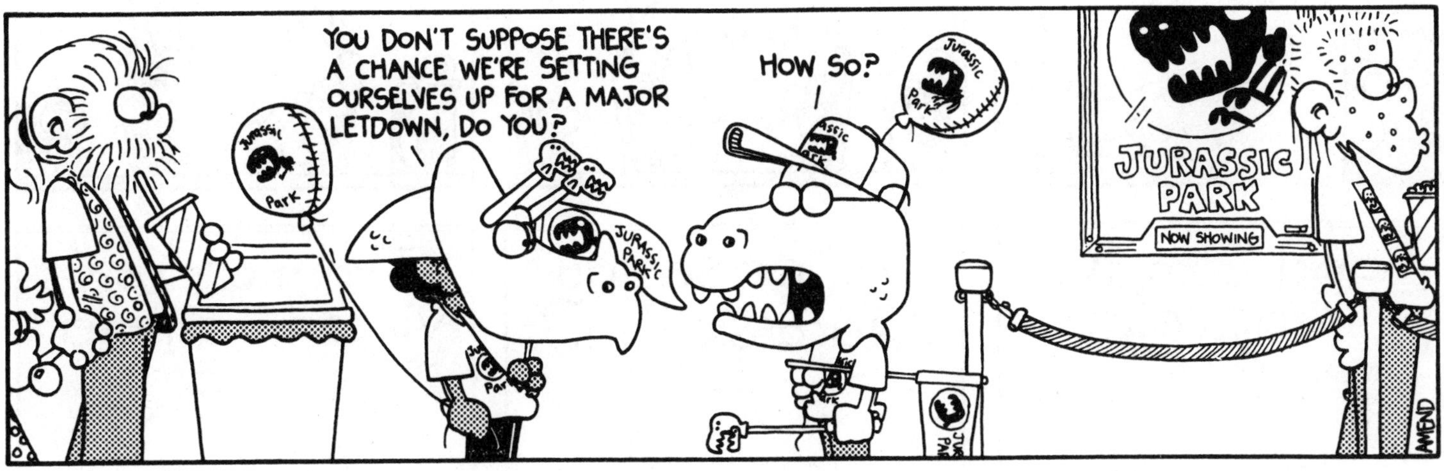
YOU DON'T SUPPOSE THERE'S A CHANCE WE'RE SETTING OURSELVES UP FOR A MAJOR LETDOWN, DO YOU?
HOW SO?
JURASSIC PARK
NOW SHOWING
AMEND

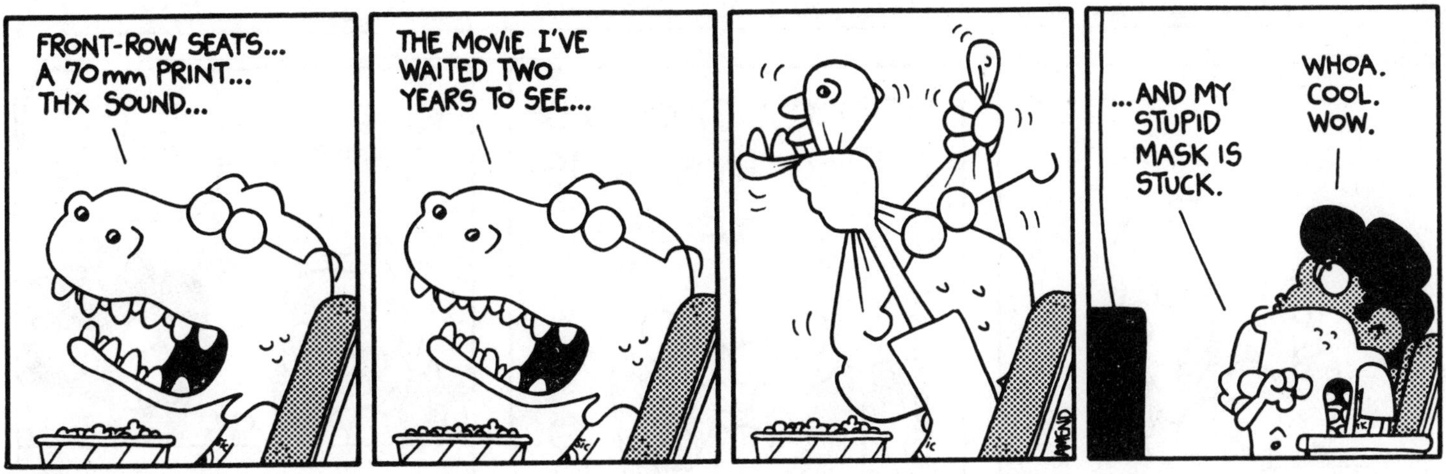
FRONT-ROW SEATS... A 70mm PRINT... THX SOUND...
THE MOVIE I'VE WAITED TWO YEARS TO SEE...
...AND MY STUPID MASK IS STUCK.
WHOA. COOL. WOW.
AMEND

FoxTrot

BILL AMEND

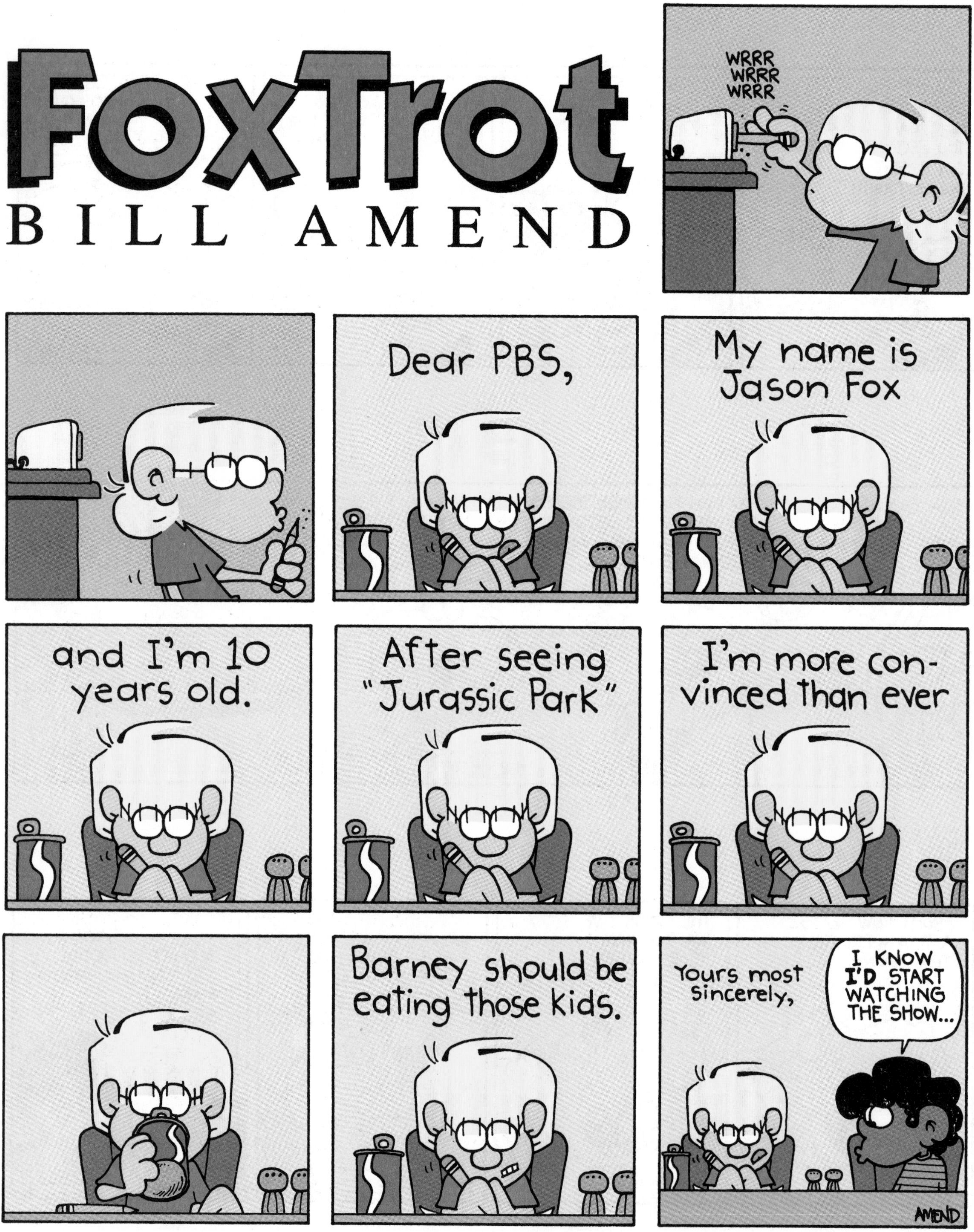

WRRR WRRR WRRR
Dear PBS,
My name is Jason Fox
and I'm 10 years old.
After seeing "Jurassic Park"
I'm more con-vinced than ever
Barney should be eating those kids.
Yours most sincerely,
I KNOW I'D START WATCHING THE SHOW...
AMEND

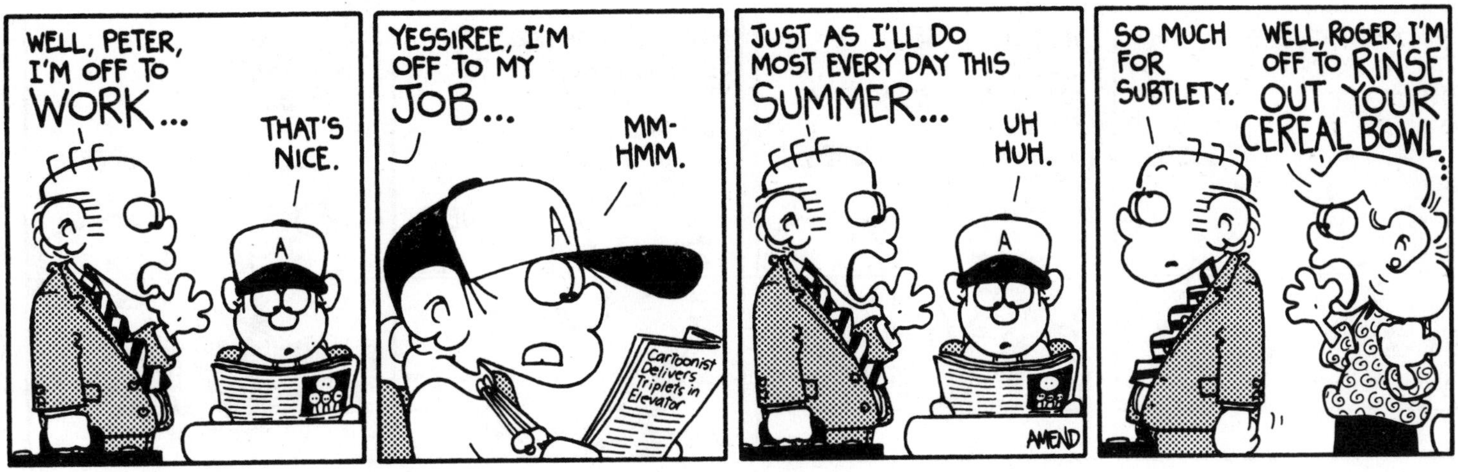
WELL, PETER, I'M OFF TO WORK...
THAT'S NICE.
YESSIREE, I'M OFF TO MY JOB...
MM-HMM.
Cartoonist Delivers Triplets in Elevator
JUST AS I'LL DO MOST EVERY DAY THIS SUMMER...
UH HUH.
AMEND
SO MUCH FOR SUBTLETY.
WELL, ROGER, I'M OFF TO RINSE OUT YOUR CEREAL BOWL...

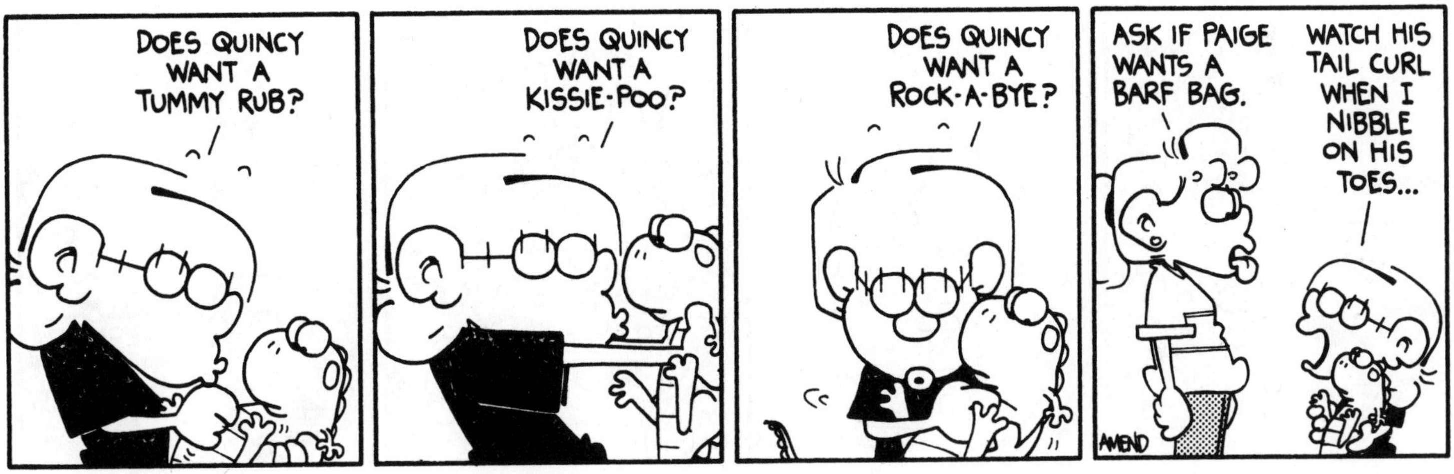
DOES QUINCY WANT A TUMMY RUB?
DOES QUINCY WANT A KISSIE-POO?
DOES QUINCY WANT A ROCK-A-BYE?
ASK IF PAIGE WANTS A BARF BAG.
WATCH HIS TAIL CURL WHEN I NIBBLE ON HIS TOES...
AMEND

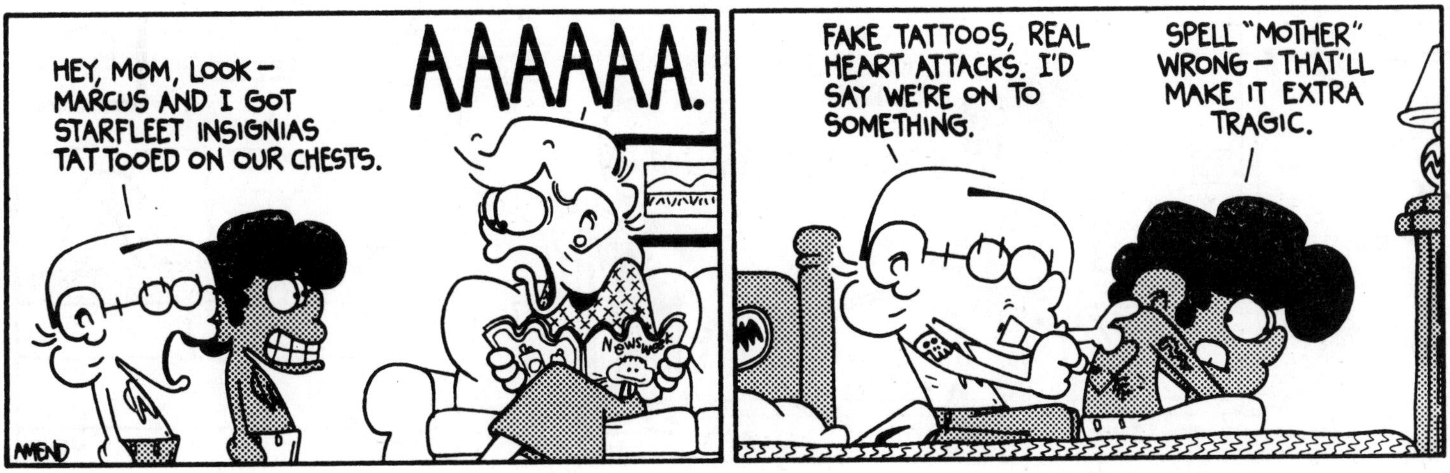
HEY, MOM, LOOK – MARCUS AND I GOT STARFLEET INSIGNIAS TATTOOED ON OUR CHESTS.
AAAAAA!
Newsweek
AMEND
FAKE TATTOOS, REAL HEART ATTACKS. I'D SAY WE'RE ON TO SOMETHING.
SPELL "MOTHER" WRONG – THAT'LL MAKE IT EXTRA TRAGIC.

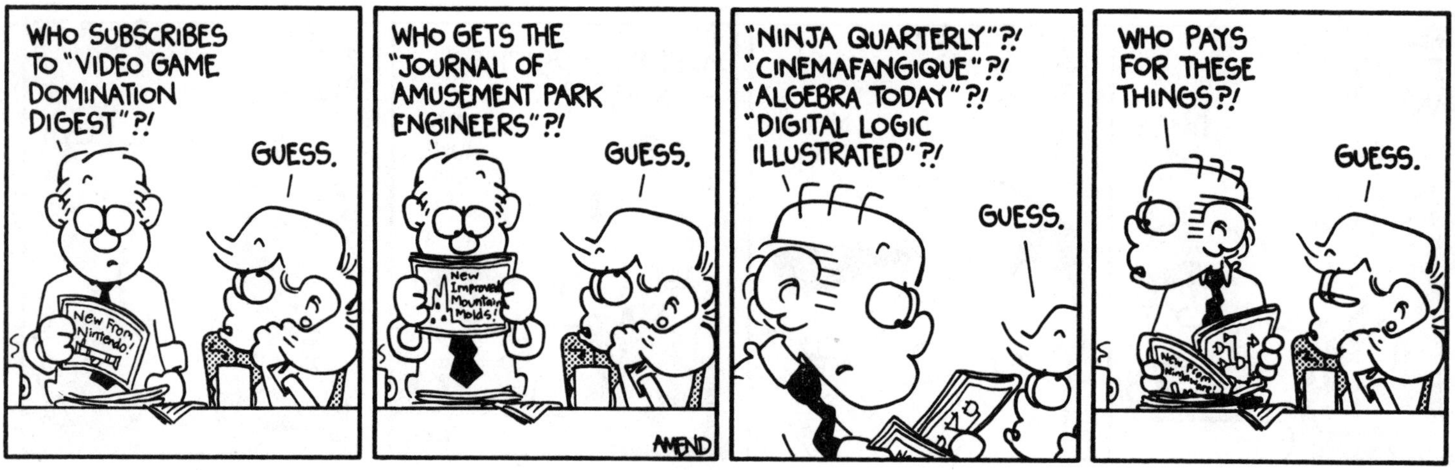
WHO SUBSCRIBES TO "VIDEO GAME DOMINATION DIGEST"?!
GUESS.
New From Nintendo!
WHO GETS THE "JOURNAL OF AMUSEMENT PARK ENGINEERS"?!
GUESS.
New Improved Mountain Molds!
AMEND
"NINJA QUARTERLY"?! "CINEMAFANGIQUE"?! "ALGEBRA TODAY"?! "DIGITAL LOGIC ILLUSTRATED"?!
GUESS.
WHO PAYS FOR THESE THINGS?!
GUESS.

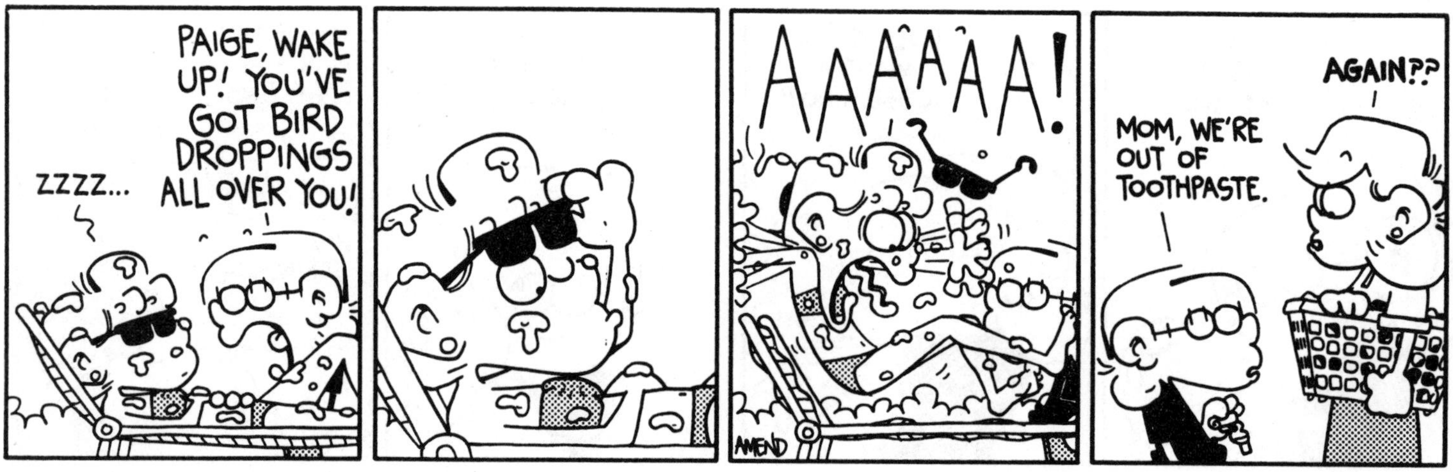
ZZZZ...
PAIGE, WAKE UP! YOU'VE GOT BIRD DROPPINGS ALL OVER YOU!
AAAAAA!
AMEND
MOM, WE'RE OUT OF TOOTHPASTE.
AGAIN??

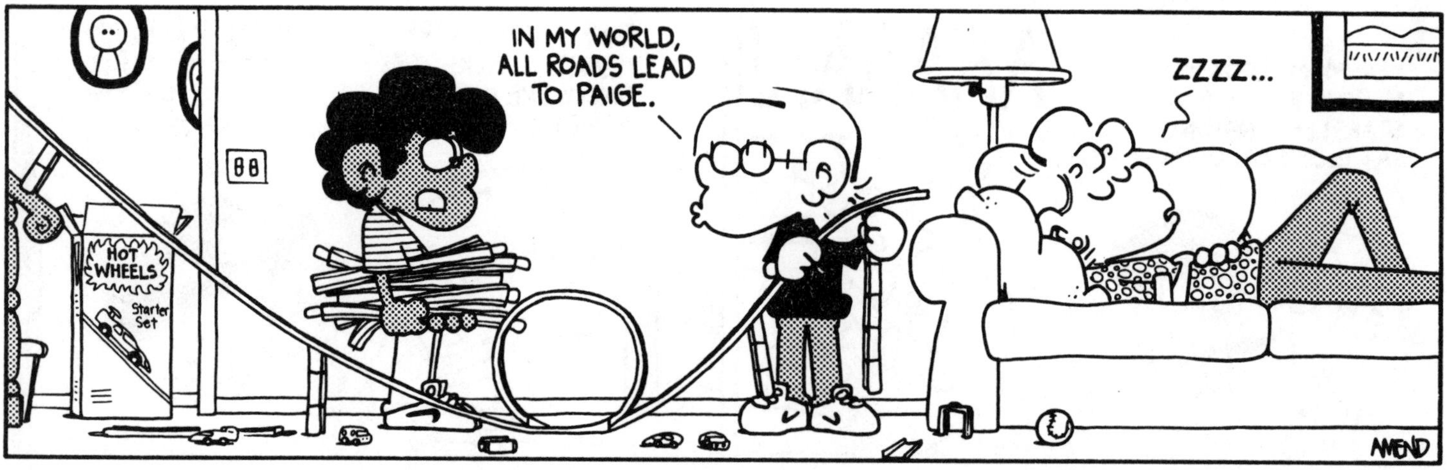
HOT WHEELS
Starter Set
IN MY WORLD, ALL ROADS LEAD TO PAIGE.
ZZZZ...
AMEND

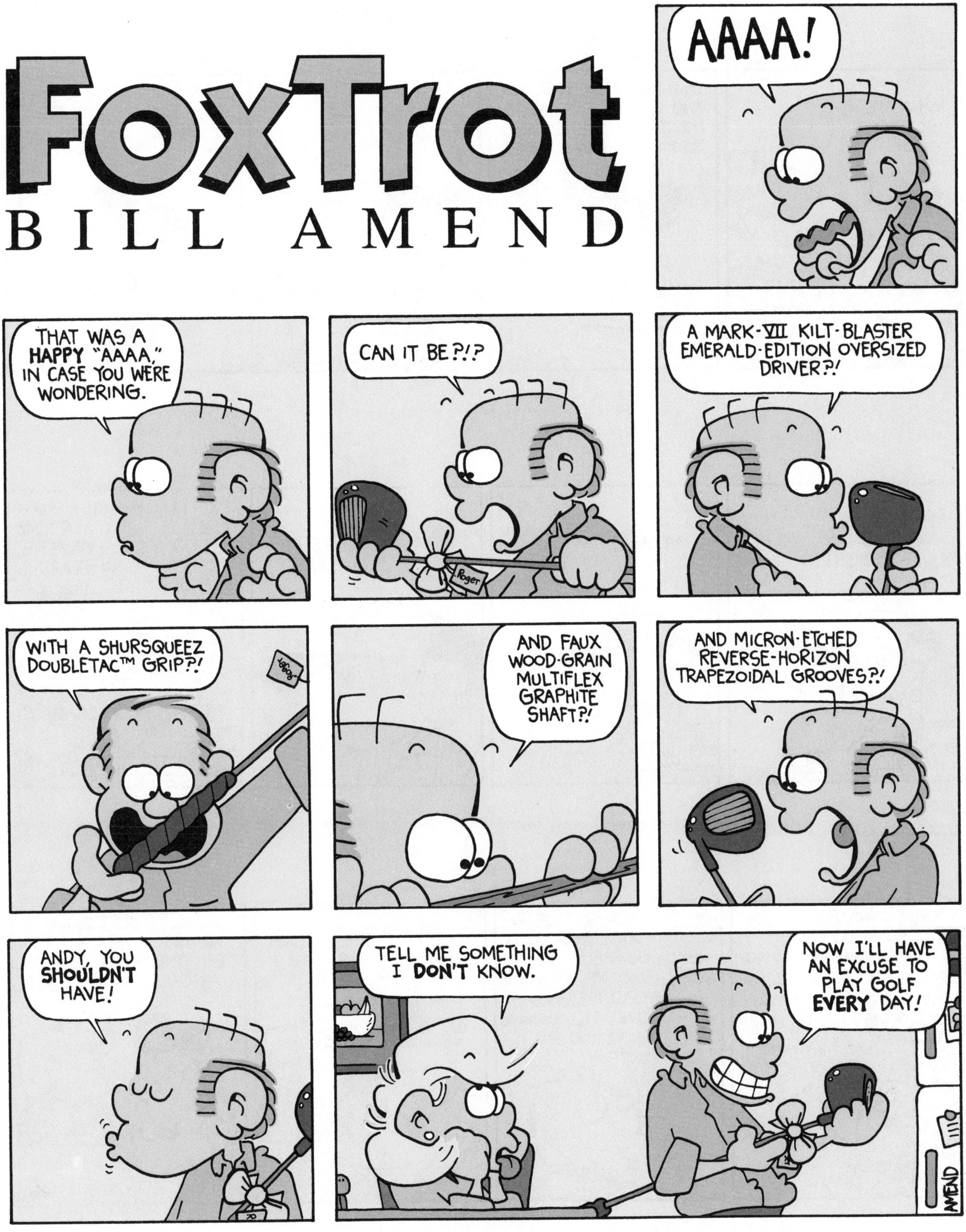
FoxTrot
BILL AMEND
AAAA!
THAT WAS A HAPPY "AAAA," IN CASE YOU WERE WONDERING.
CAN IT BE?!?
A MARK-VII KILT-BLASTER EMERALD-EDITION OVERSIZED DRIVER?!
WITH A SHURSQUEEZ DOUBLETAC™ GRIP?!
AND FAUX WOOD-GRAIN MULTIFLEX GRAPHITE SHAFT?!
AND MICRON-ETCHED REVERSE-HORIZON TRAPEZOIDAL GROOVES?!
ANDY, YOU SHOULDN'T HAVE!
TELL ME SOMETHING I DON'T KNOW.
NOW I'LL HAVE AN EXCUSE TO PLAY GOLF EVERY DAY!
AMEND

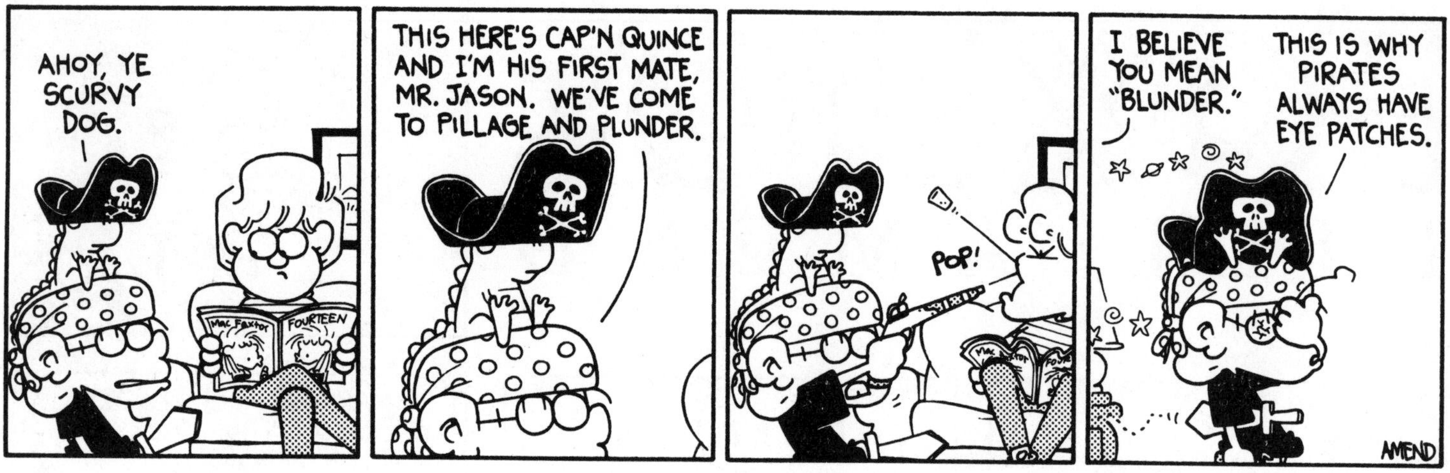
AHOY, YE SCURVY DOG.
FOURTEEN
THIS HERE'S CAP'N QUINCE AND I'M HIS FIRST MATE, MR. JASON. WE'VE COME TO PILLAGE AND PLUNDER.
POP!
I BELIEVE YOU MEAN "BLUNDER."
THIS IS WHY PIRATES ALWAYS HAVE EYE PATCHES.
AMEND

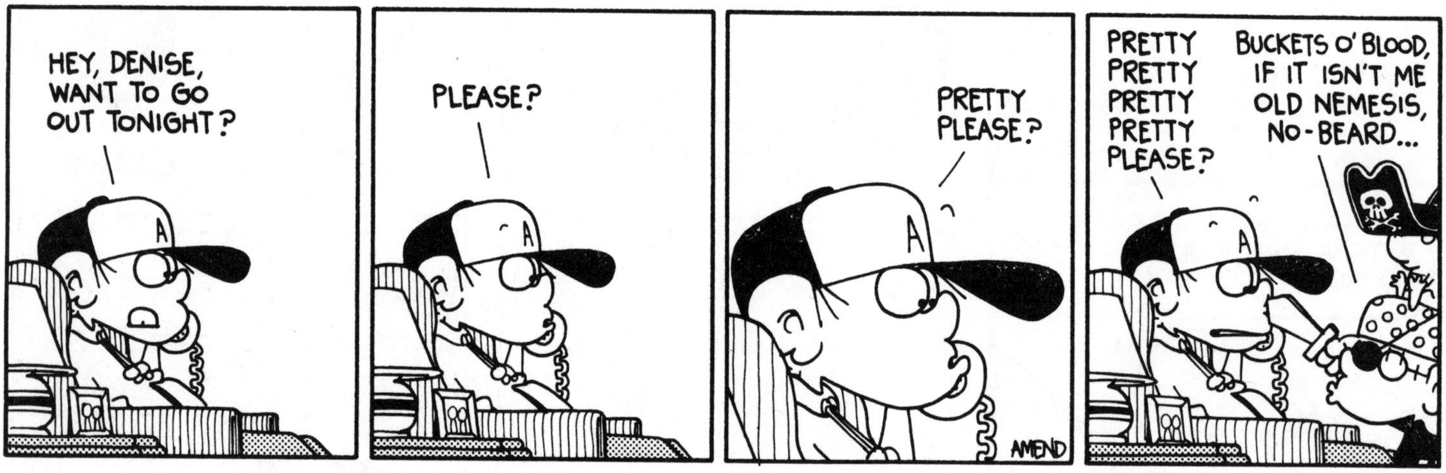
HEY, DENISE, WANT TO GO OUT TONIGHT?
PLEASE?
PRETTY PLEASE?
AMEND
PRETTY PRETTY PRETTY PRETTY PLEASE?
BUCKETS O' BLOOD, IF IT ISN'T ME OLD NEMESIS, NO-BEARD...

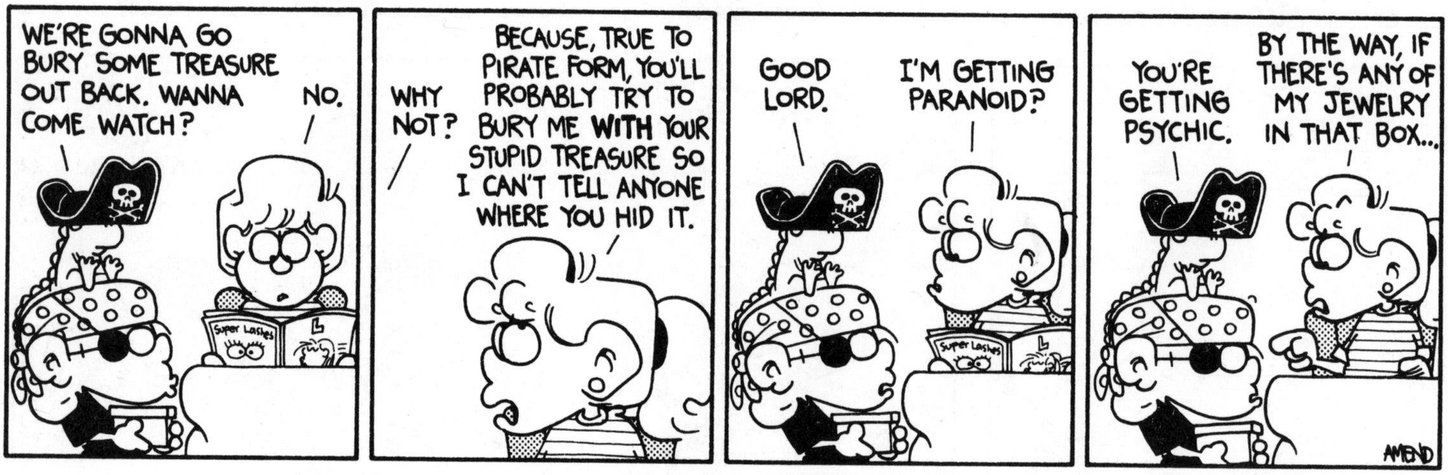
WE'RE GONNA GO BURY SOME TREASURE OUT BACK. WANNA COME WATCH?
NO.
WHY NOT?
BECAUSE, TRUE TO PIRATE FORM, YOU'LL PROBABLY TRY TO BURY ME WITH YOUR STUPID TREASURE SO I CAN'T TELL ANYONE WHERE YOU HID IT.
GOOD LORD.
I'M GETTING PARANOID?
YOU'RE GETTING PSYCHIC.
BY THE WAY, IF THERE'S ANY OF MY JEWELRY IN THAT BOX...
AMEND

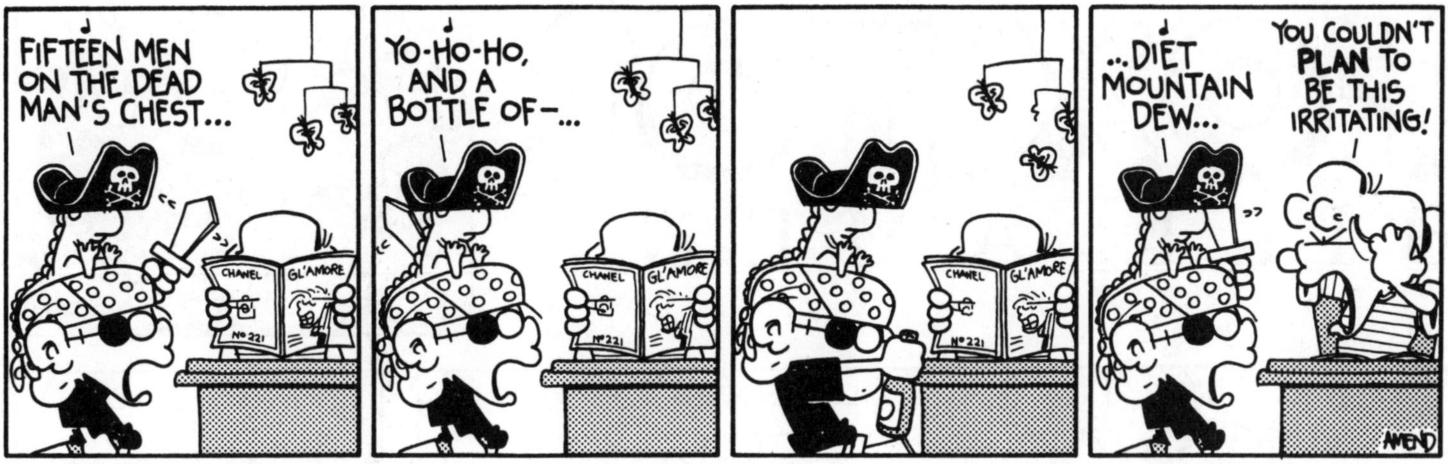
FIFTEEN MEN ON THE DEAD MAN'S CHEST...
CHANEL
GL'AMORE
Nº221
YO-HO-HO, AND A BOTTLE OF–...
...DIET MOUNTAIN DEW...
YOU COULDN'T **PLAN** TO BE THIS IRRITATING!
AMEND

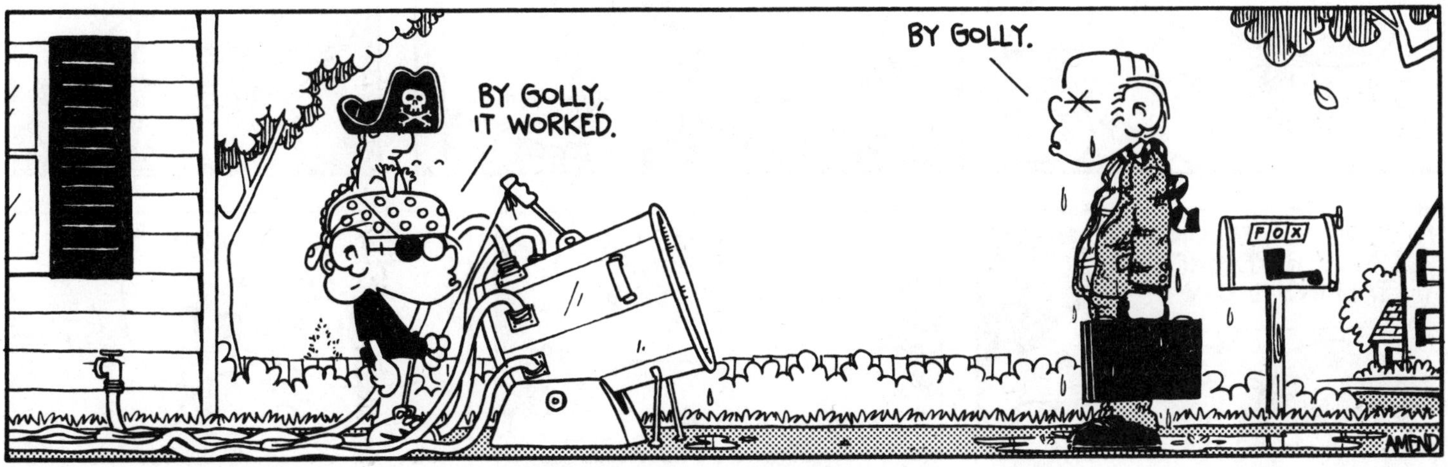
BY GOLLY, IT WORKED.
BY GOLLY.
FOX
AMEND

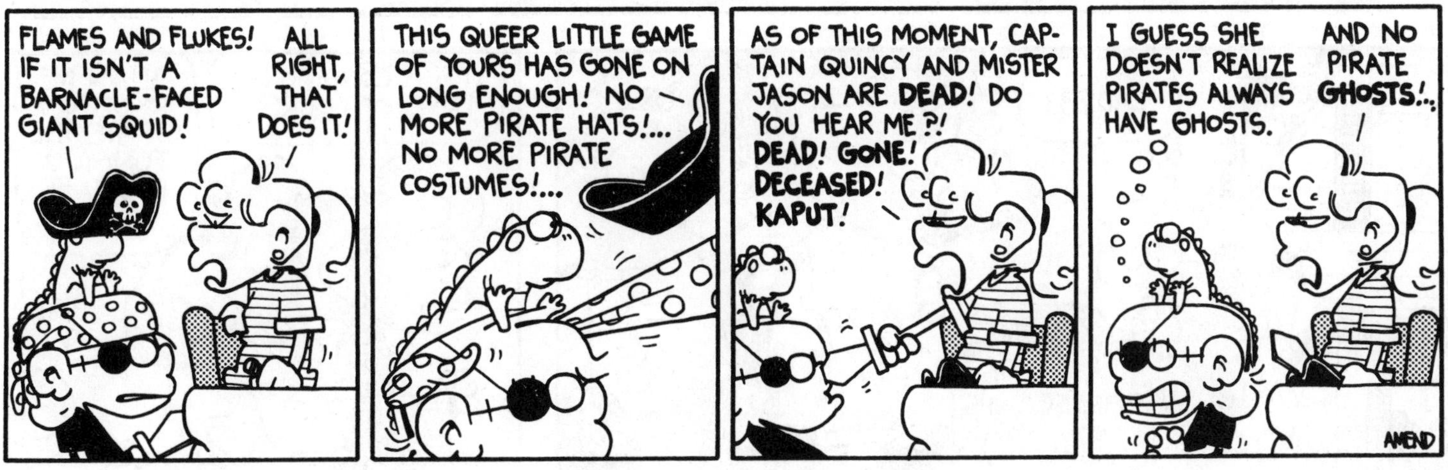
FLAMES AND FLUKES! IF IT ISN'T A BARNACLE-FACED GIANT SQUID!
ALL RIGHT, THAT DOES IT!
THIS QUEER LITTLE GAME OF YOURS HAS GONE ON LONG ENOUGH! NO MORE PIRATE HATS!... NO MORE PIRATE COSTUMES!...
AS OF THIS MOMENT, CAPTAIN QUINCY AND MISTER JASON ARE **DEAD**! DO YOU HEAR ME?! **DEAD! GONE! DECEASED! KAPUT**!
I GUESS SHE DOESN'T REALIZE PIRATES ALWAYS HAVE GHOSTS.
AND NO PIRATE **GHOSTS**!...
AMEND

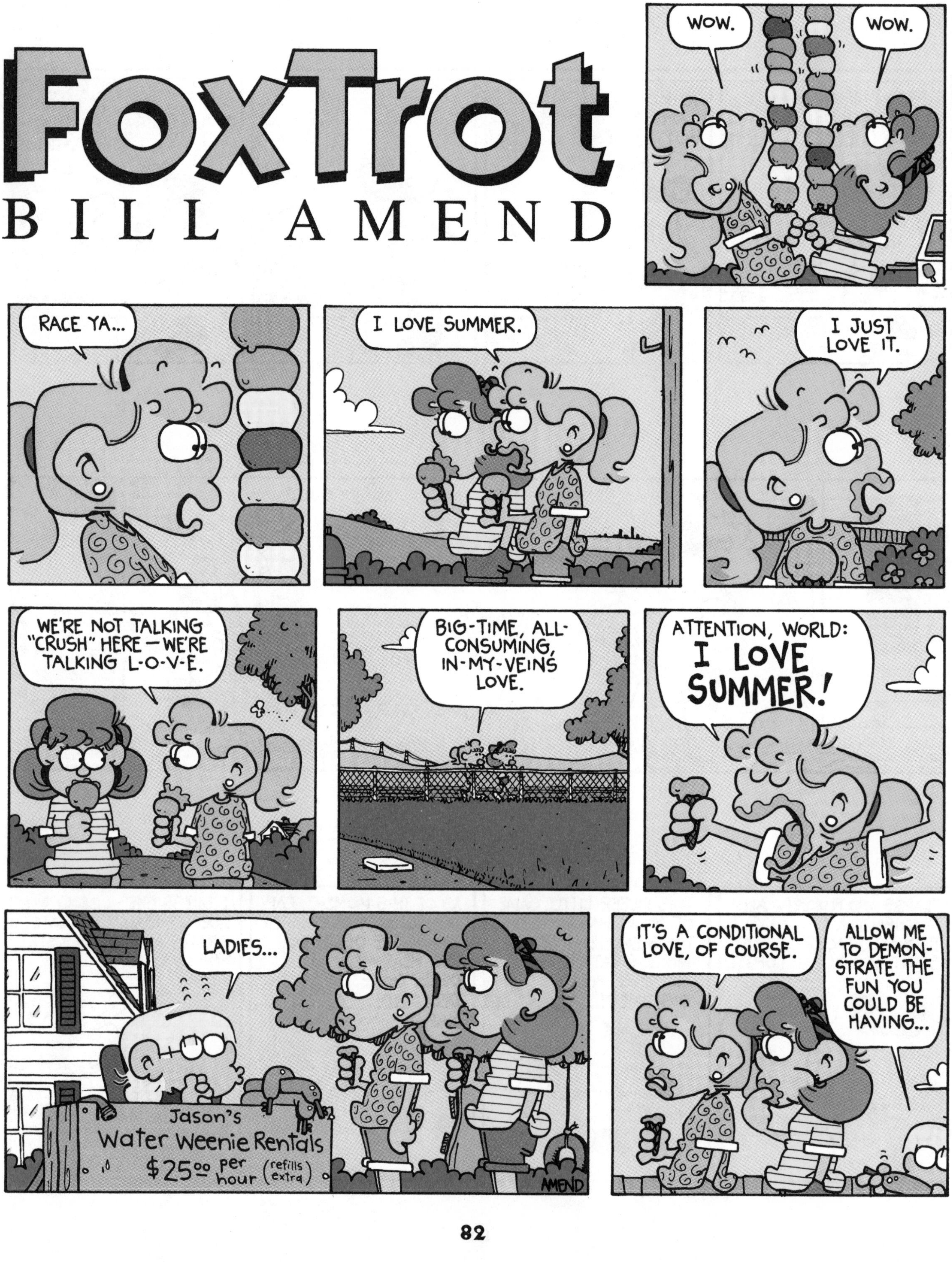
FoxTrot
BILL AMEND
WOW.
WOW.
RACE YA...
I LOVE SUMMER.
I JUST LOVE IT.
WE'RE NOT TALKING "CRUSH" HERE — WE'RE TALKING L-O-V-E.
BIG-TIME, ALL-CONSUMING, IN-MY-VEINS LOVE.
ATTENTION, WORLD: I LOVE SUMMER!
LADIES...
Jason's Water Weenie Rentals $25.00 per hour (refills extra)
AMEND
IT'S A CONDITIONAL LOVE, OF COURSE.
ALLOW ME TO DEMONSTRATE THE FUN YOU COULD BE HAVING...

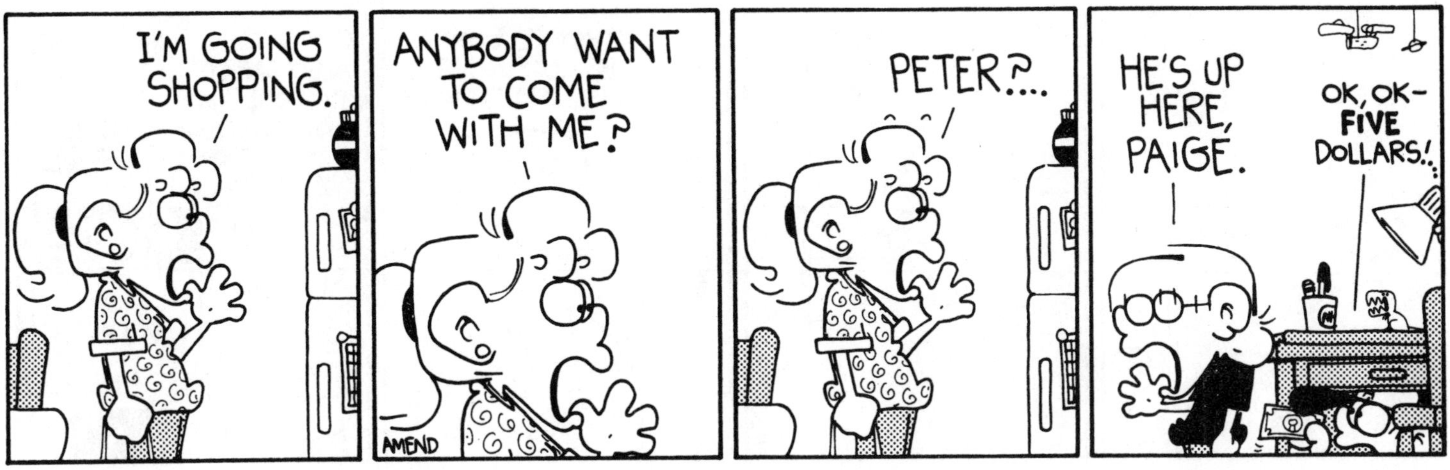
I'M GOING SHOPPING.
ANYBODY WANT TO COME WITH ME?
AMEND
PETER?...
HE'S UP HERE, PAIGE.
OK, OK- **FIVE** DOLLARS!

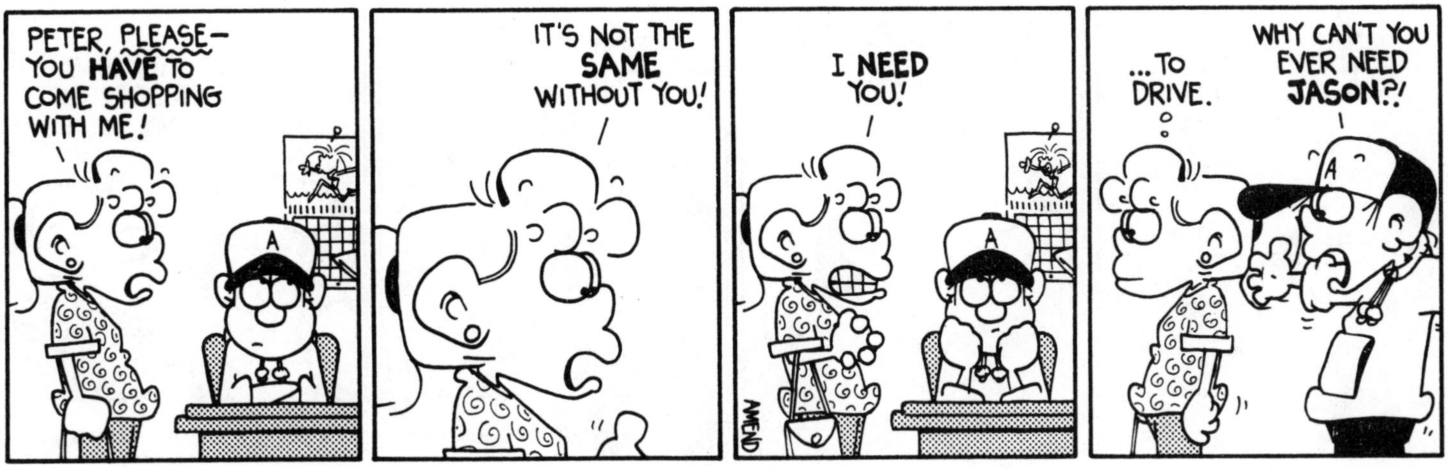
PETER, PLEASE- YOU **HAVE** TO COME SHOPPING WITH ME!
IT'S NOT THE **SAME** WITHOUT YOU!
I **NEED** YOU!
AMEND
...TO DRIVE.
WHY CAN'T YOU EVER NEED **JASON**?!

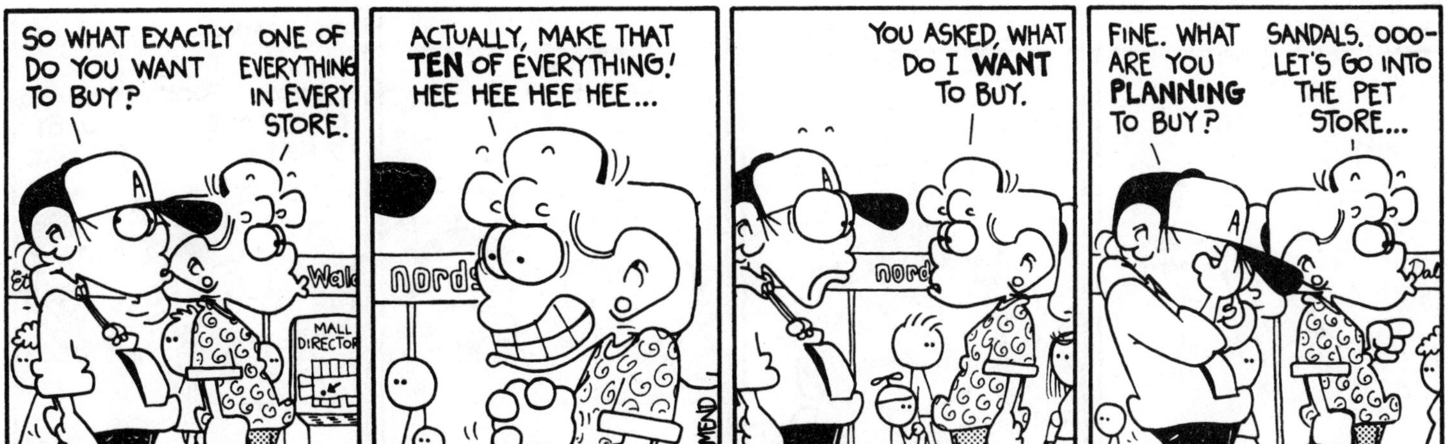
SO WHAT EXACTLY DO YOU WANT TO BUY?
ONE OF EVERYTHING IN EVERY STORE.
MALL DIRECTOR
ACTUALLY, MAKE THAT **TEN** OF EVERYTHING! HEE HEE HEE HEE...
AMEND
YOU ASKED, WHAT DO I **WANT** TO BUY.
FINE. WHAT ARE YOU **PLANNING** TO BUY?
SANDALS. OOO- LET'S GO INTO THE PET STORE...

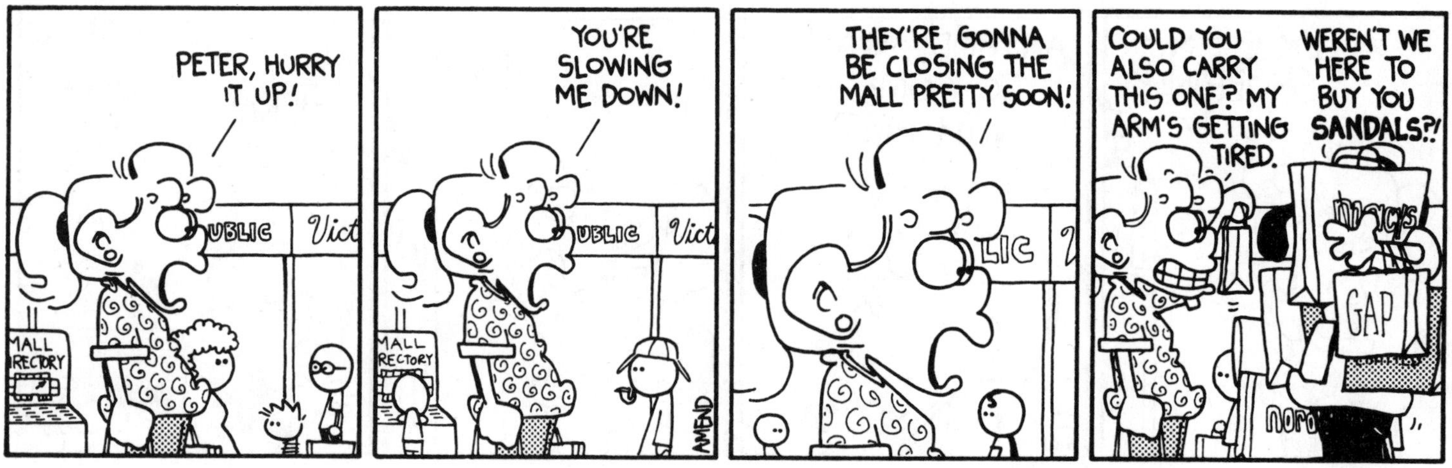
PETER, HURRY IT UP!
YOU'RE SLOWING ME DOWN!
AMEND
THEY'RE GONNA BE CLOSING THE MALL PRETTY SOON!
COULD YOU ALSO CARRY THIS ONE? MY ARM'S GETTING TIRED.
WEREN'T WE HERE TO BUY YOU SANDALS?!
GAP

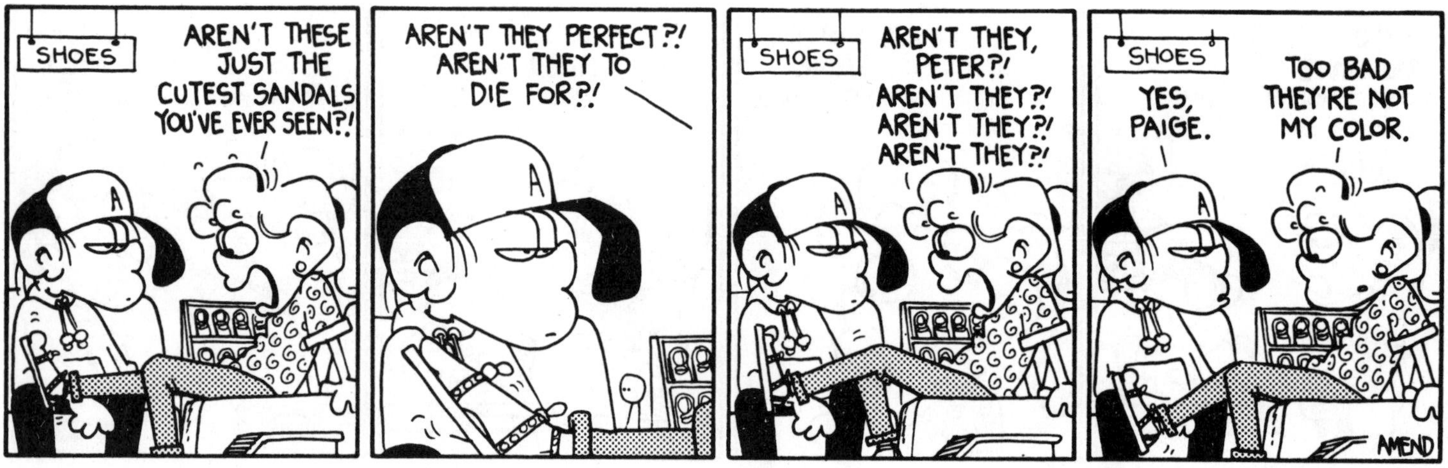
SHOES
AREN'T THESE JUST THE CUTEST SANDALS YOU'VE EVER SEEN?!
AREN'T THEY PERFECT?! AREN'T THEY TO DIE FOR?!
SHOES
AREN'T THEY, PETER?! AREN'T THEY?! AREN'T THEY?! AREN'T THEY?!
SHOES
YES, PAIGE.
TOO BAD THEY'RE NOT MY COLOR.
AMEND

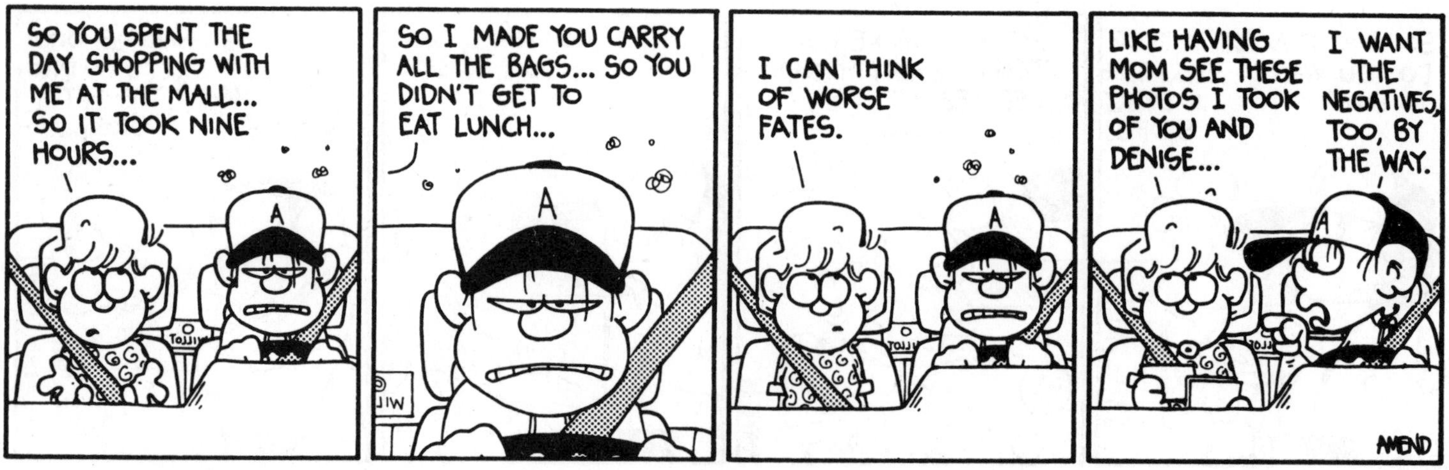
SO YOU SPENT THE DAY SHOPPING WITH ME AT THE MALL... SO IT TOOK NINE HOURS...
SO I MADE YOU CARRY ALL THE BAGS... SO YOU DIDN'T GET TO EAT LUNCH...
I CAN THINK OF WORSE FATES.
LIKE HAVING MOM SEE THESE PHOTOS I TOOK OF YOU AND DENISE...
I WANT THE NEGATIVES, TOO, BY THE WAY.
AMEND

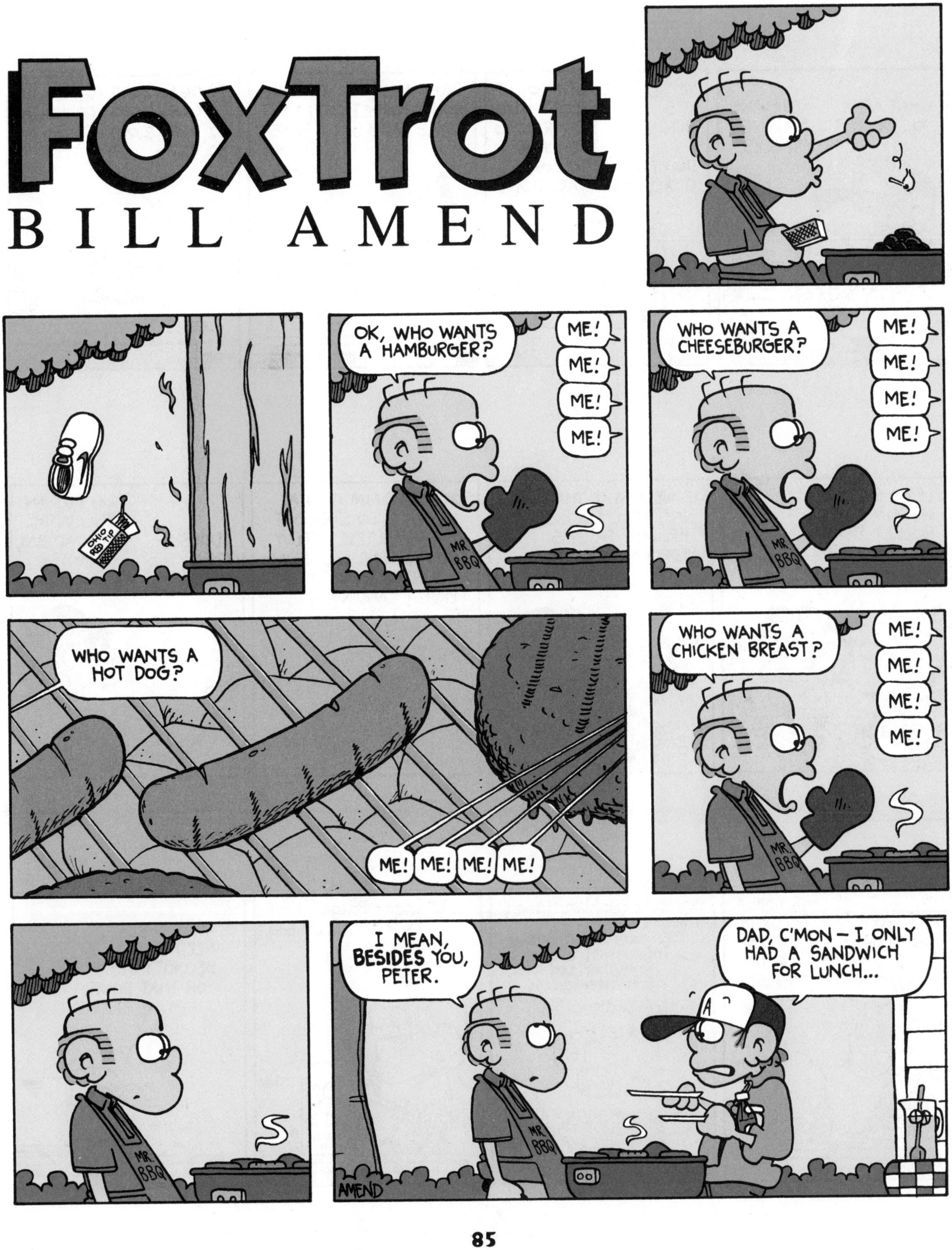
FoxTrot
BILL AMEND
OHIO RED TIP
OK, WHO WANTS A HAMBURGER?
ME!
ME!
ME!
ME!
MR BBQ
WHO WANTS A CHEESEBURGER?
ME!
ME!
ME!
ME!
WHO WANTS A HOT DOG?
ME!
ME!
ME!
ME!
WHO WANTS A CHICKEN BREAST?
ME!
ME!
ME!
ME!
I MEAN, **BESIDES** YOU, PETER.
DAD, C'MON – I ONLY HAD A SANDWICH FOR LUNCH...
AMEND

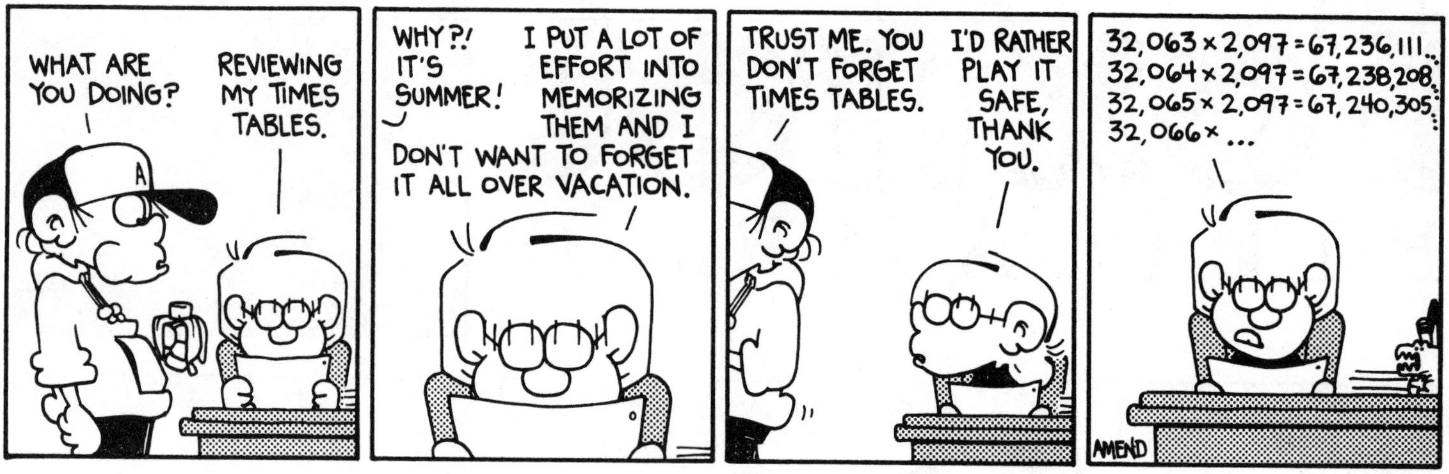
WHAT ARE YOU DOING?
REVIEWING MY TIMES TABLES.
WHY?! IT'S SUMMER!
I PUT A LOT OF EFFORT INTO MEMORIZING THEM AND I DON'T WANT TO FORGET IT ALL OVER VACATION.
TRUST ME. YOU DON'T FORGET TIMES TABLES.
I'D RATHER PLAY IT SAFE, THANK YOU.
32,063 × 2,097 = 67,236,111...
32,064 × 2,097 = 67,238,208
32,065 × 2,097 = 67,240,305
32,066 × ...
AMEND

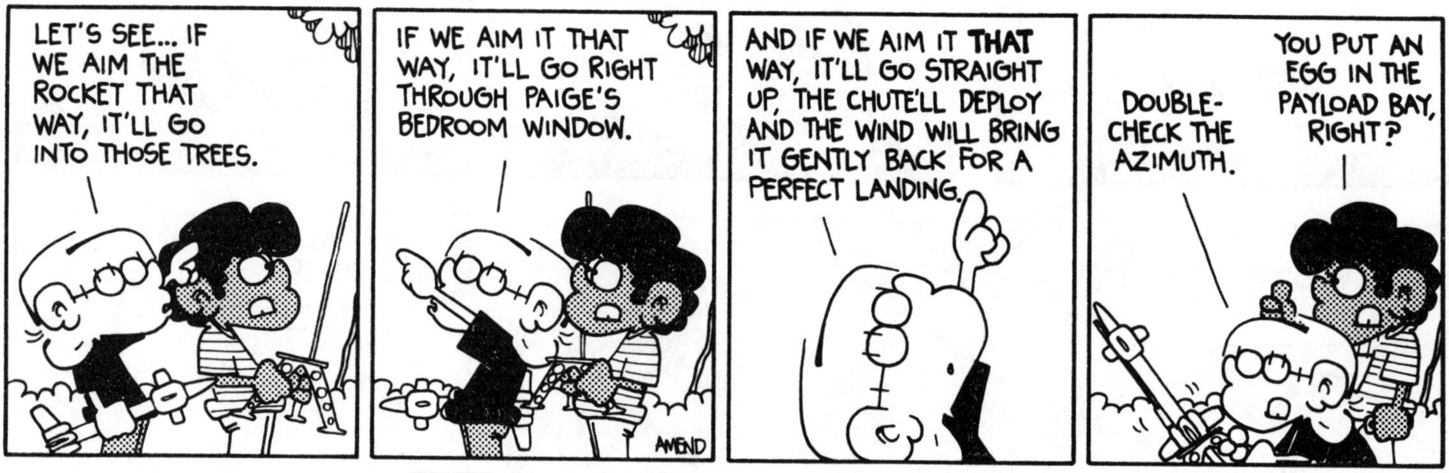
LET'S SEE... IF WE AIM THE ROCKET THAT WAY, IT'LL GO INTO THOSE TREES.
IF WE AIM IT THAT WAY, IT'LL GO RIGHT THROUGH PAIGE'S BEDROOM WINDOW.
AMEND
AND IF WE AIM IT **THAT** WAY, IT'LL GO STRAIGHT UP, THE CHUTE'LL DEPLOY AND THE WIND WILL BRING IT GENTLY BACK FOR A PERFECT LANDING.
DOUBLE-CHECK THE AZIMUTH.
YOU PUT AN EGG IN THE PAYLOAD BAY, RIGHT?

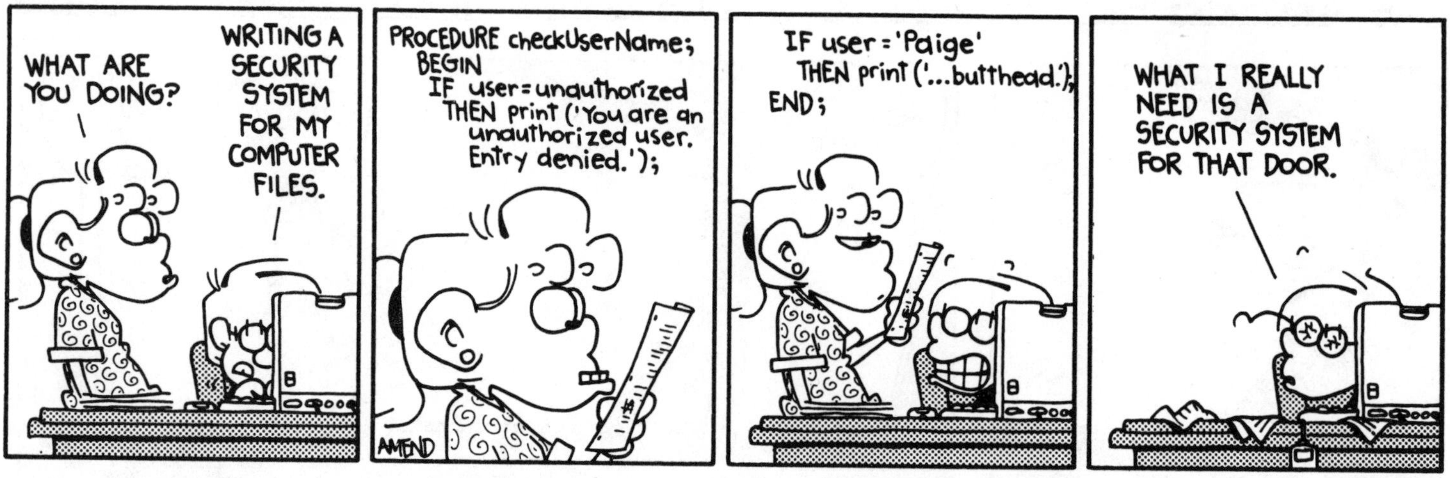
WHAT ARE YOU DOING?
WRITING A SECURITY SYSTEM FOR MY COMPUTER FILES.
PROCEDURE checkUserName;
BEGIN
IF user=unauthorized
THEN print ('You are an unauthorized user. Entry denied.');
AMEND
IF user='Paige'
THEN print ('...butthead.');
END;
WHAT I REALLY NEED IS A SECURITY SYSTEM FOR THAT DOOR.

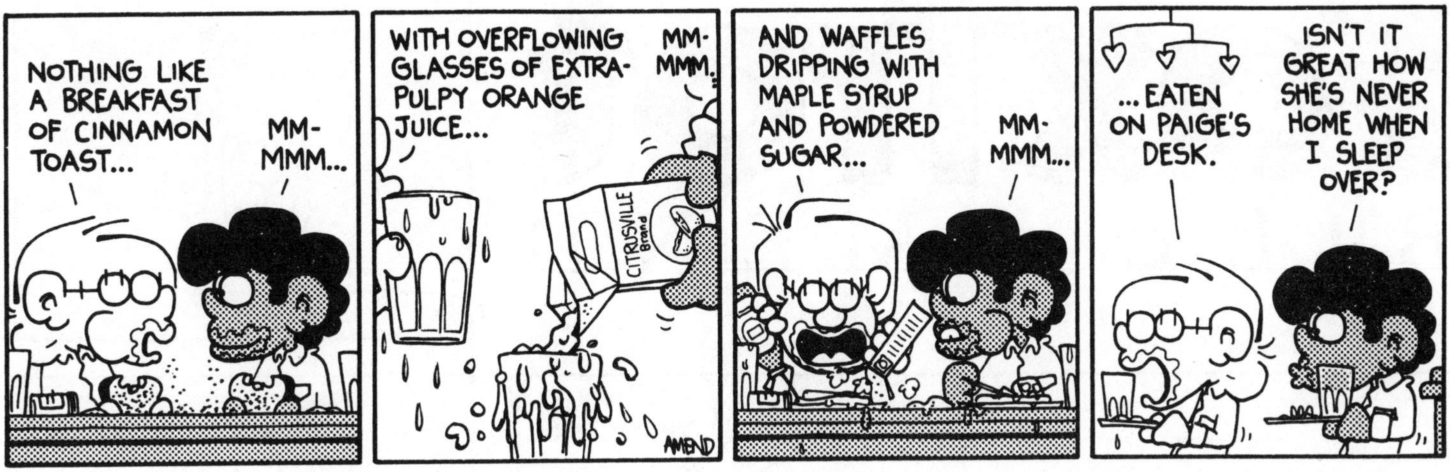
NOTHING LIKE A BREAKFAST OF CINNAMON TOAST...
MM-MMM...
WITH OVERFLOWING GLASSES OF EXTRA-PULPY ORANGE JUICE...
MM-MMM.
CITRUSVILLE Brand
AMEND
AND WAFFLES DRIPPING WITH MAPLE SYRUP AND POWDERED SUGAR...
MM-MMM...
...EATEN ON PAIGE'S DESK.
ISN'T IT GREAT HOW SHE'S NEVER HOME WHEN I SLEEP OVER?

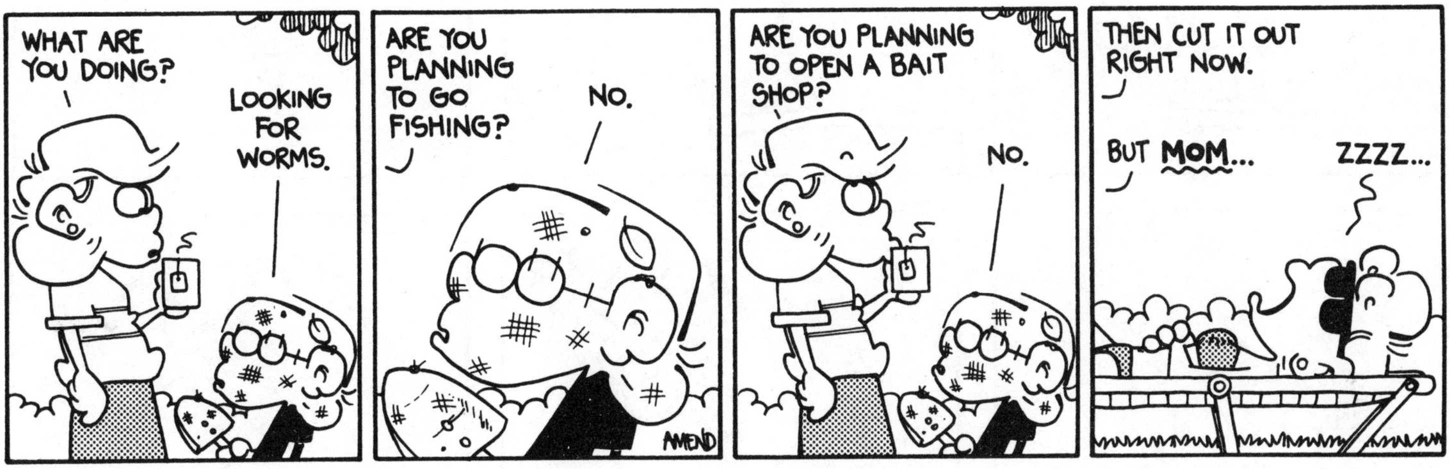
WHAT ARE YOU DOING?
LOOKING FOR WORMS.
ARE YOU PLANNING TO GO FISHING?
NO.
AMEND
ARE YOU PLANNING TO OPEN A BAIT SHOP?
NO.
THEN CUT IT OUT RIGHT NOW.
BUT MOM...
ZZZZ...

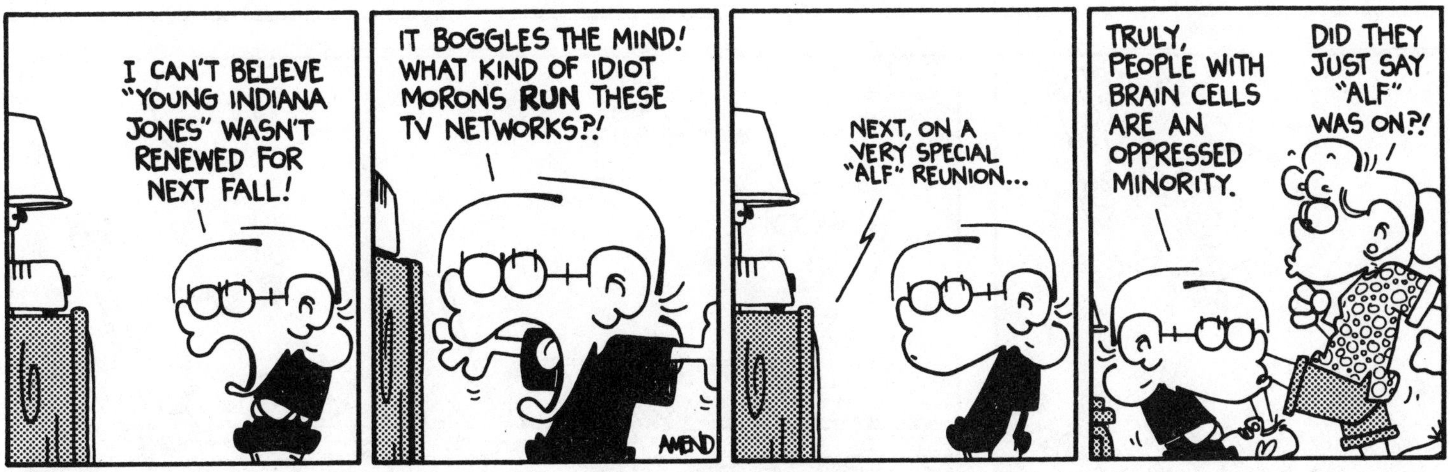
I CAN'T BELIEVE "YOUNG INDIANA JONES" WASN'T RENEWED FOR NEXT FALL!
IT BOGGLES THE MIND! WHAT KIND OF IDIOT MORONS RUN THESE TV NETWORKS?!
AMEND
NEXT, ON A VERY SPECIAL "ALF" REUNION...
TRULY, PEOPLE WITH BRAIN CELLS ARE AN OPPRESSED MINORITY.
DID THEY JUST SAY "ALF" WAS ON?!

FoxTrot
BILL AMEND

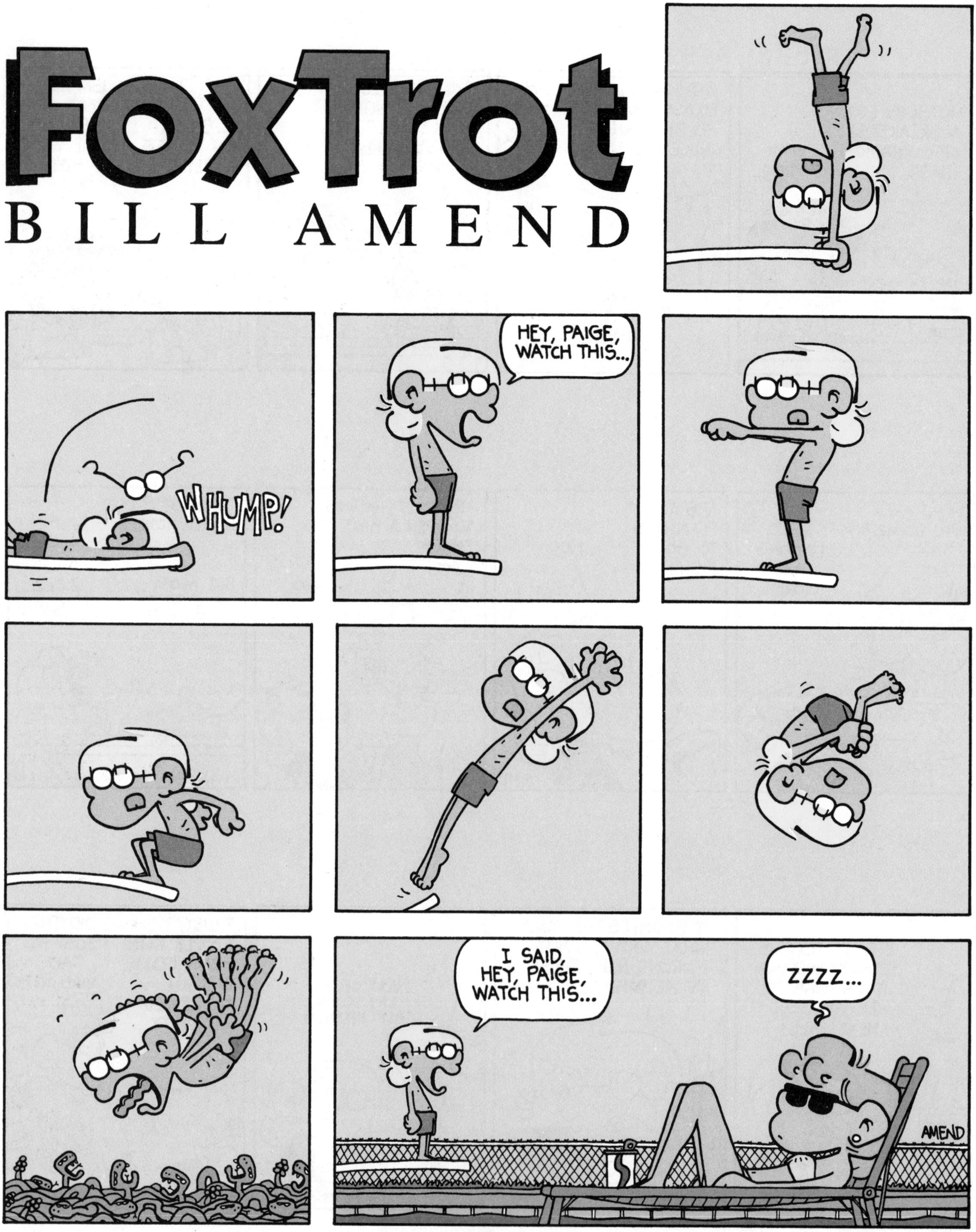

WHUMP!
HEY, PAIGE, WATCH THIS...
I SAID, HEY, PAIGE, WATCH THIS...
ZZZZ...
AMEND

WOW. LISTEN TO THIS...

THE LOCAL CHAPTER OF THE CHECKHEAD SOCIETY IS SPONSORING A FATHER-SON CHESS TOURNAMENT NEXT WEEKEND.

Cartoonist to Be Letterman's First Guest

PETER, WE COULD CLEAN UP!

WE COULD?

JASON AND ME? ABSOLUTELY.

ANY NEWS OF A FATHER-SON KICK-BOXING TOURNAMENT?

AMEND

JASON, DO YOU WANT TO PLAY CHESS?...

NO.

MRI Specs *Manatee Man*

WITH ME?...

NO.

AT A FATHER-SON TOURNAMENT THIS WEEKEND?...

NO.

MRI Specs *Manatee Man*

FOR A $50 CASH PRIZE?...

KEEP TALKING...

MRI Specs *Manatee Man*

AMEND

JASON, IT'S BEEN A WHILE SINCE WE'VE PLAYED A GAME OF CHESS.

SEVERAL YEARS, I THINK.

WHY DON'T I REVIEW THE PIECES WITH YOU. NOW THIS IS A PAWN. I'LL MOVE IT TO HERE.

NOW YOU MOVE.

CHECK-MATE.

MAYBE I SHOULD EXPLAIN **WHY** IT'S BEEN A WHILE SINCE WE'VE PLAYED...

WHAT'S THAT DANCE YOU DO WHEN YOU WIN?

AMEND

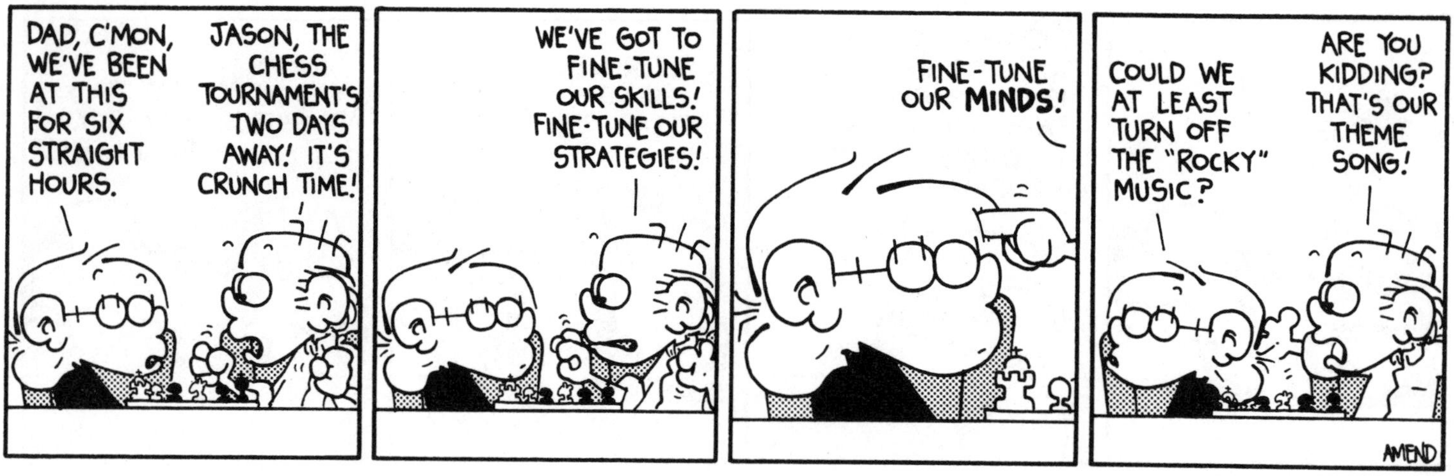
DAD, C'MON, WE'VE BEEN AT THIS FOR SIX STRAIGHT HOURS.
JASON, THE CHESS TOURNAMENT'S TWO DAYS AWAY! IT'S CRUNCH TIME!
WE'VE GOT TO FINE-TUNE OUR SKILLS! FINE-TUNE OUR STRATEGIES!
FINE-TUNE OUR **MINDS**!
COULD WE AT LEAST TURN OFF THE "ROCKY" MUSIC?
ARE YOU KIDDING? THAT'S OUR THEME SONG!
AMEND

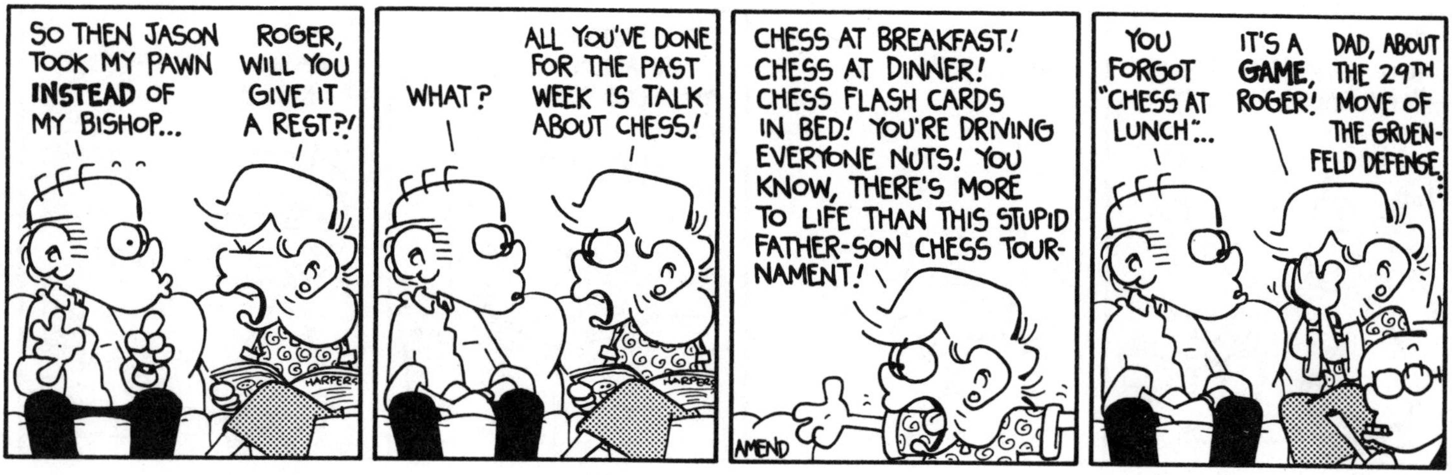
SO THEN JASON TOOK MY PAWN **INSTEAD** OF MY BISHOP...
ROGER, WILL YOU GIVE IT A REST?!
WHAT?
ALL YOU'VE DONE FOR THE PAST WEEK IS TALK ABOUT CHESS!
CHESS AT BREAKFAST! CHESS AT DINNER! CHESS FLASH CARDS IN BED! YOU'RE DRIVING EVERYONE NUTS! YOU KNOW, THERE'S MORE TO LIFE THAN THIS STUPID FATHER-SON CHESS TOURNAMENT!
AMEND
YOU FORGOT "CHESS AT LUNCH"...
IT'S A **GAME**, ROGER!
DAD, ABOUT THE 29TH MOVE OF THE GRUENFELD DEFENSE...

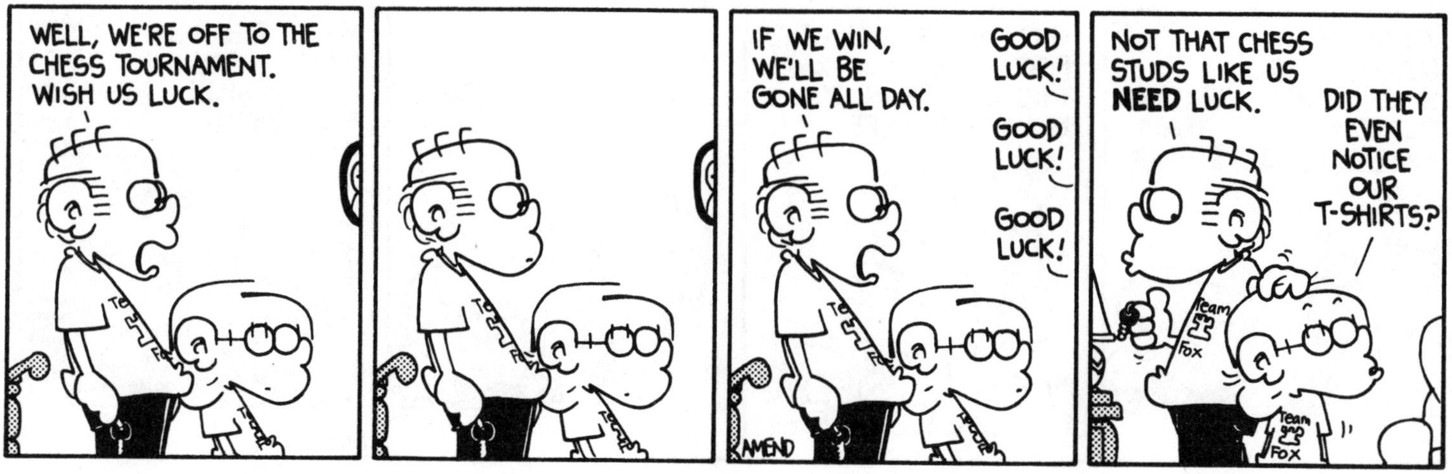
WELL, WE'RE OFF TO THE CHESS TOURNAMENT. WISH US LUCK.
IF WE WIN, WE'LL BE GONE ALL DAY.
GOOD LUCK!
GOOD LUCK!
GOOD LUCK!
AMEND
NOT THAT CHESS STUDS LIKE US **NEED** LUCK.
DID THEY EVEN NOTICE OUR T-SHIRTS?

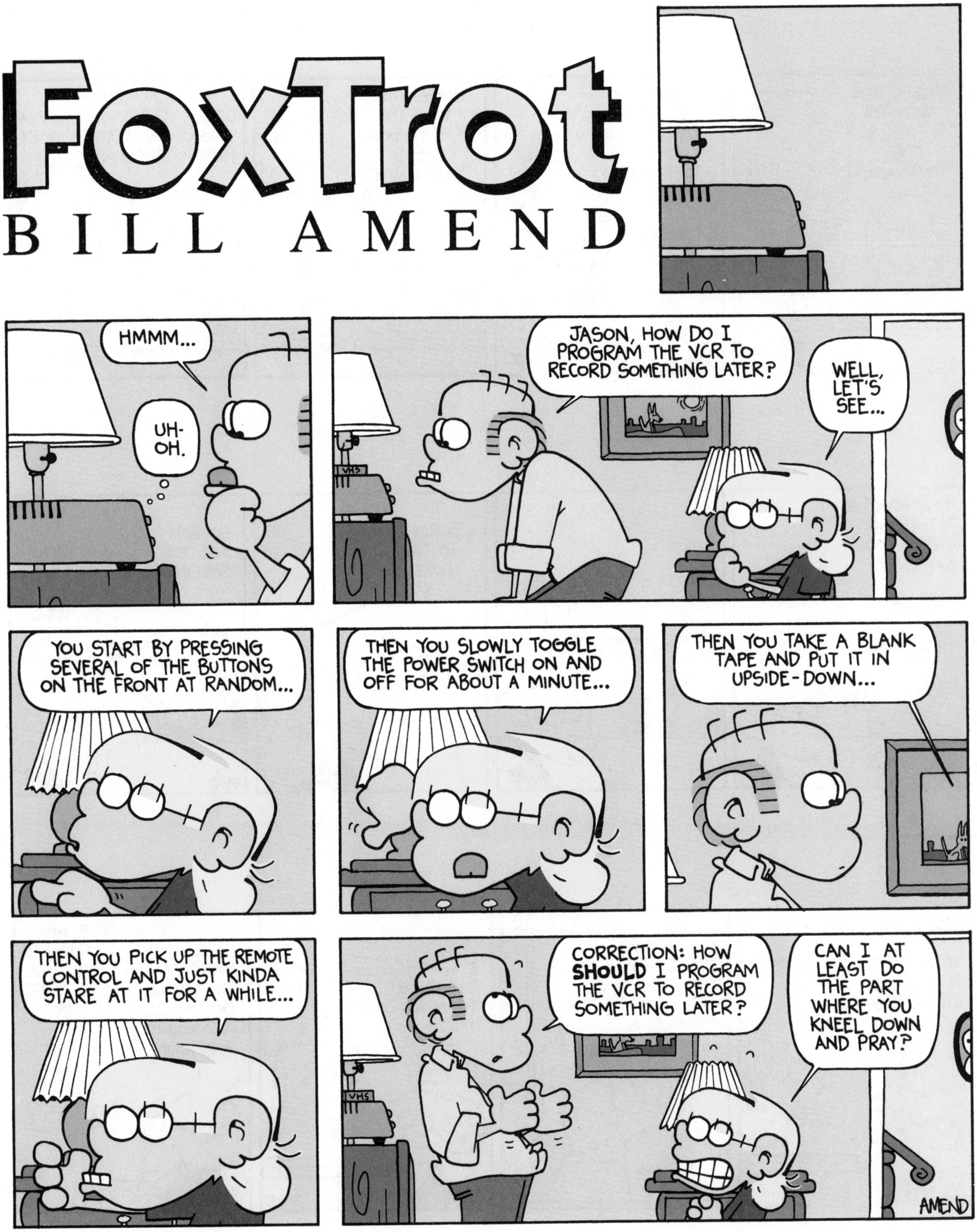
FoxTrot
BILL AMEND
HMMM...
UH-OH.
JASON, HOW DO I PROGRAM THE VCR TO RECORD SOMETHING LATER?
WELL, LET'S SEE...
VHS
YOU START BY PRESSING SEVERAL OF THE BUTTONS ON THE FRONT AT RANDOM...
THEN YOU SLOWLY TOGGLE THE POWER SWITCH ON AND OFF FOR ABOUT A MINUTE...
THEN YOU TAKE A BLANK TAPE AND PUT IT IN UPSIDE-DOWN...
THEN YOU PICK UP THE REMOTE CONTROL AND JUST KINDA STARE AT IT FOR A WHILE...
CORRECTION: HOW **SHOULD** I PROGRAM THE VCR TO RECORD SOMETHING LATER?
CAN I AT LEAST DO THE PART WHERE YOU KNEEL DOWN AND PRAY?
VHS
AMEND

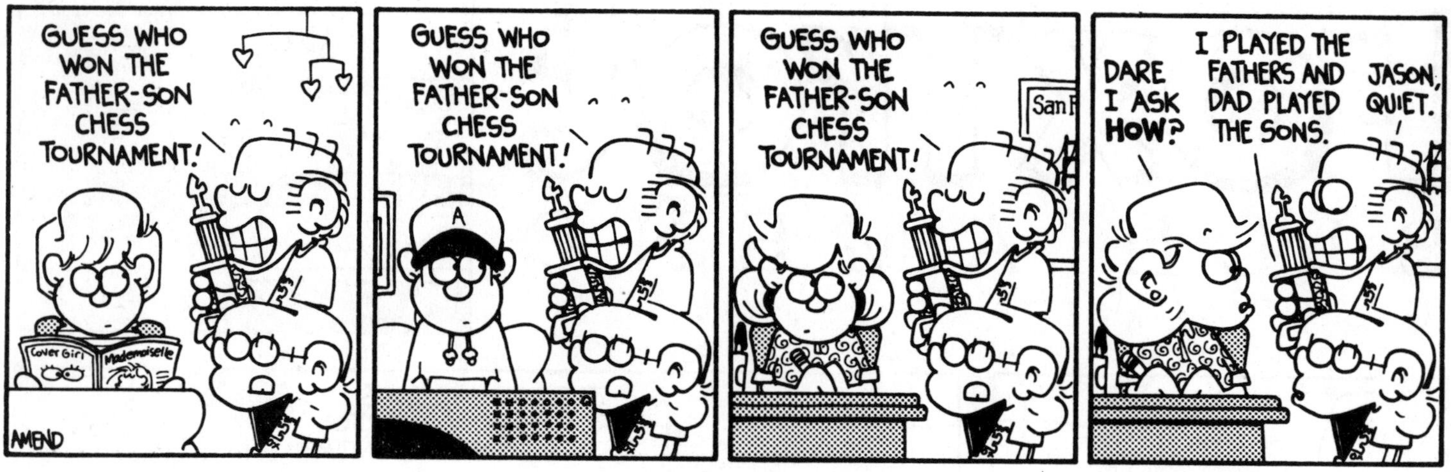
GUESS WHO WON THE FATHER-SON CHESS TOURNAMENT!
AMEND
GUESS WHO WON THE FATHER-SON CHESS TOURNAMENT!
GUESS WHO WON THE FATHER-SON CHESS TOURNAMENT!
DARE I ASK **HOW**?
I PLAYED THE FATHERS AND DAD PLAYED THE SONS.
JASON, QUIET.

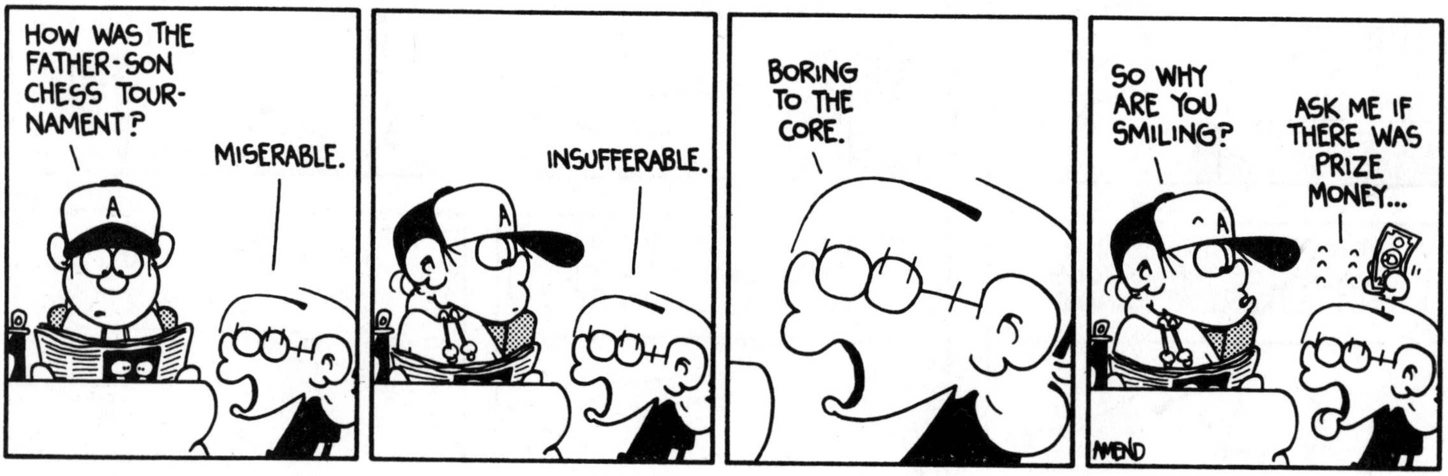
HOW WAS THE FATHER-SON CHESS TOURNAMENT?
MISERABLE.
INSUFFERABLE.
BORING TO THE CORE.
SO WHY ARE YOU SMILING?
ASK ME IF THERE WAS PRIZE MONEY...
AMEND

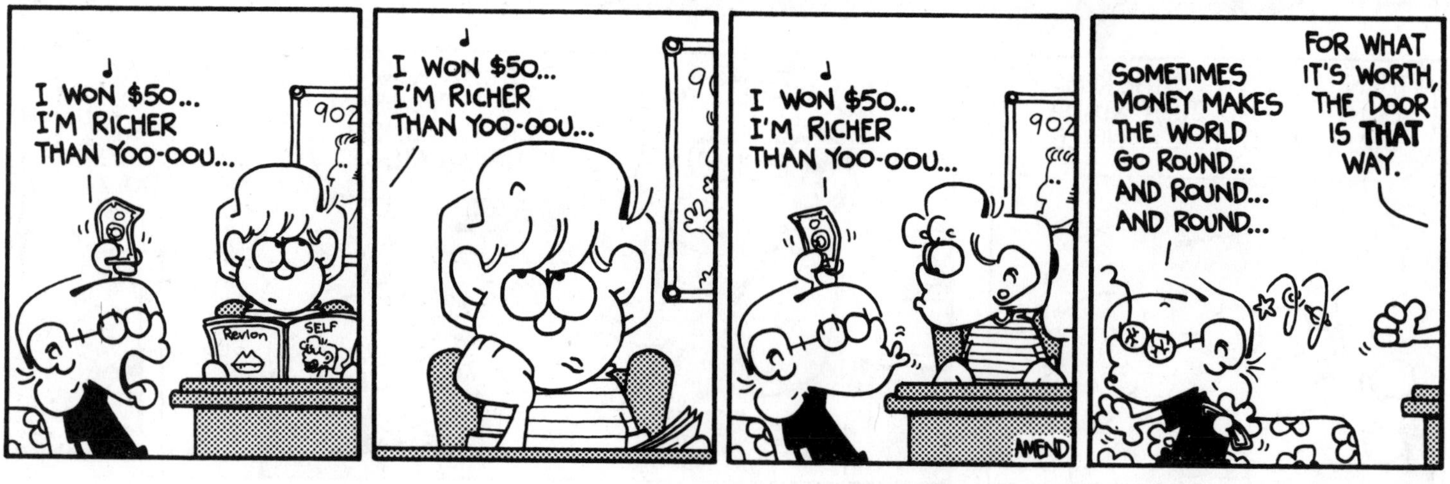
I WON $50... I'M RICHER THAN YOO-OOU...
I WON $50... I'M RICHER THAN YOO-OOU...
I WON $50... I'M RICHER THAN YOO-OOU...
AMEND
SOMETIMES MONEY MAKES THE WORLD GO ROUND... AND ROUND... AND ROUND...
FOR WHAT IT'S WORTH, THE DOOR IS **THAT** WAY.

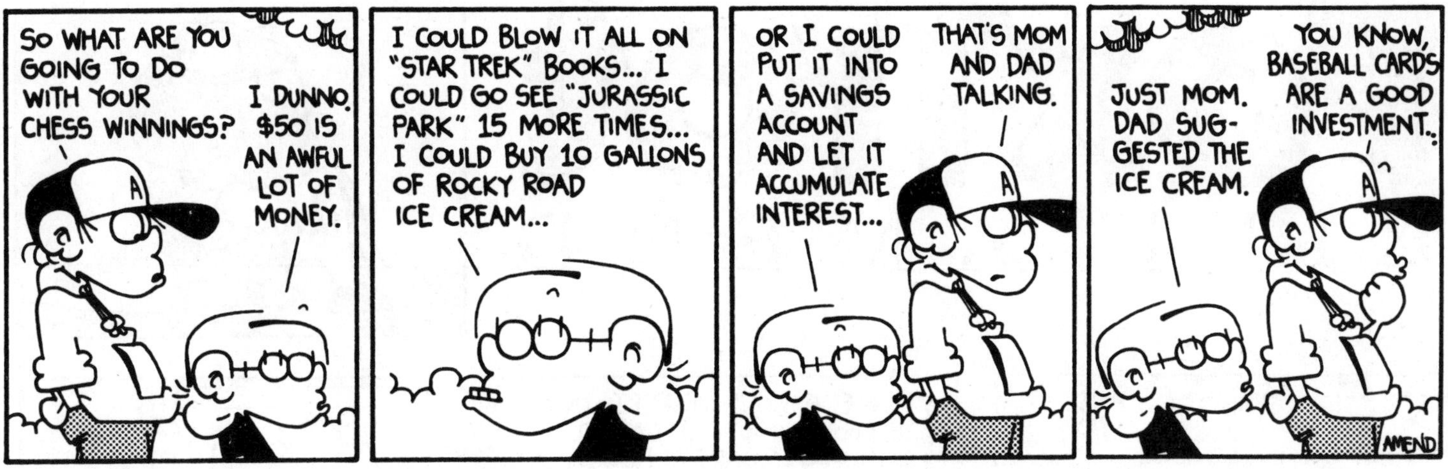
SO WHAT ARE YOU GOING TO DO WITH YOUR CHESS WINNINGS?
I DUNNO. $50 IS AN AWFUL LOT OF MONEY.
I COULD BLOW IT ALL ON "STAR TREK" BOOKS... I COULD GO SEE "JURASSIC PARK" 15 MORE TIMES... I COULD BUY 10 GALLONS OF ROCKY ROAD ICE CREAM...
OR I COULD PUT IT INTO A SAVINGS ACCOUNT AND LET IT ACCUMULATE INTEREST...
THAT'S MOM AND DAD TALKING.
YOU KNOW, BASEBALL CARDS ARE A GOOD INVESTMENT..
JUST MOM. DAD SUGGESTED THE ICE CREAM.
AMEND

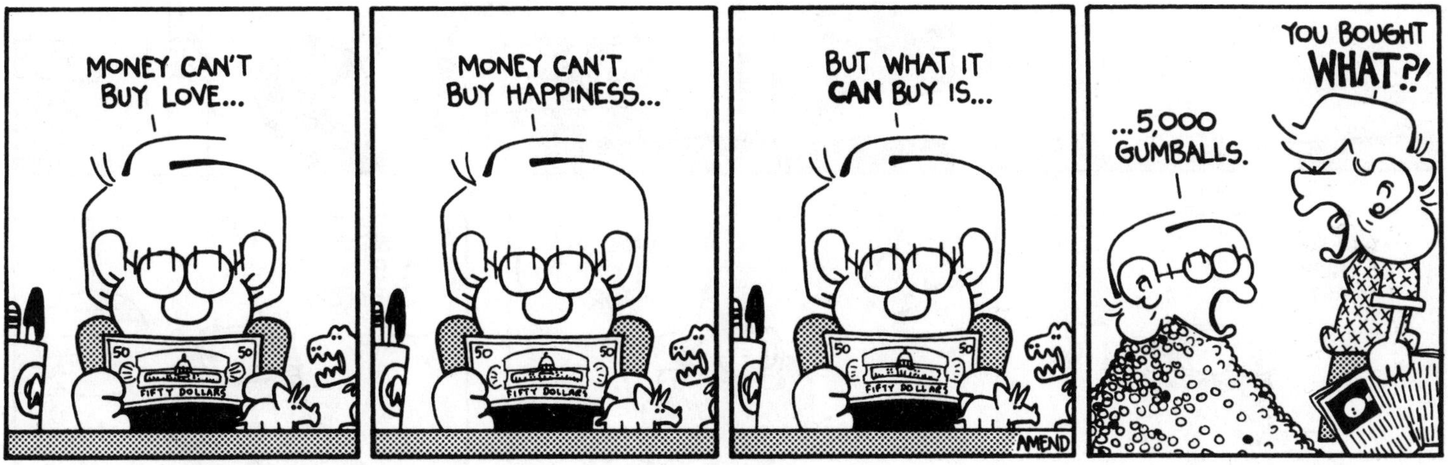
MONEY CAN'T BUY LOVE...
MONEY CAN'T BUY HAPPINESS...
BUT WHAT IT **CAN** BUY IS...
AMEND
...5,000 GUMBALLS.
YOU BOUGHT **WHAT?!**

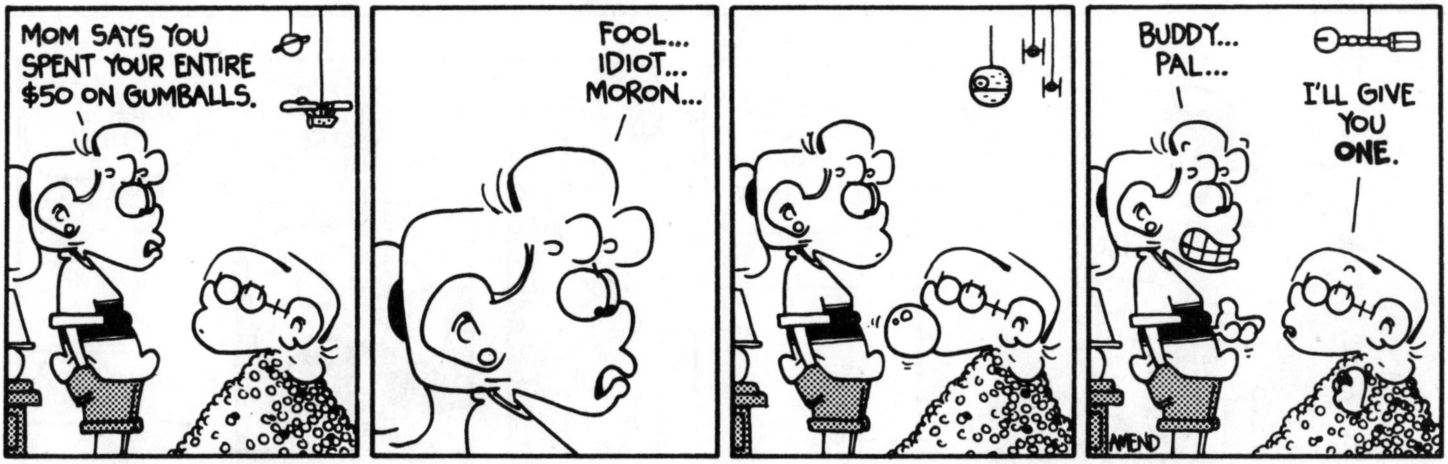
MOM SAYS YOU SPENT YOUR ENTIRE $50 ON GUMBALLS.
FOOL... IDIOT... MORON...
BUDDY... PAL...
I'LL GIVE YOU **ONE**.
AMEND

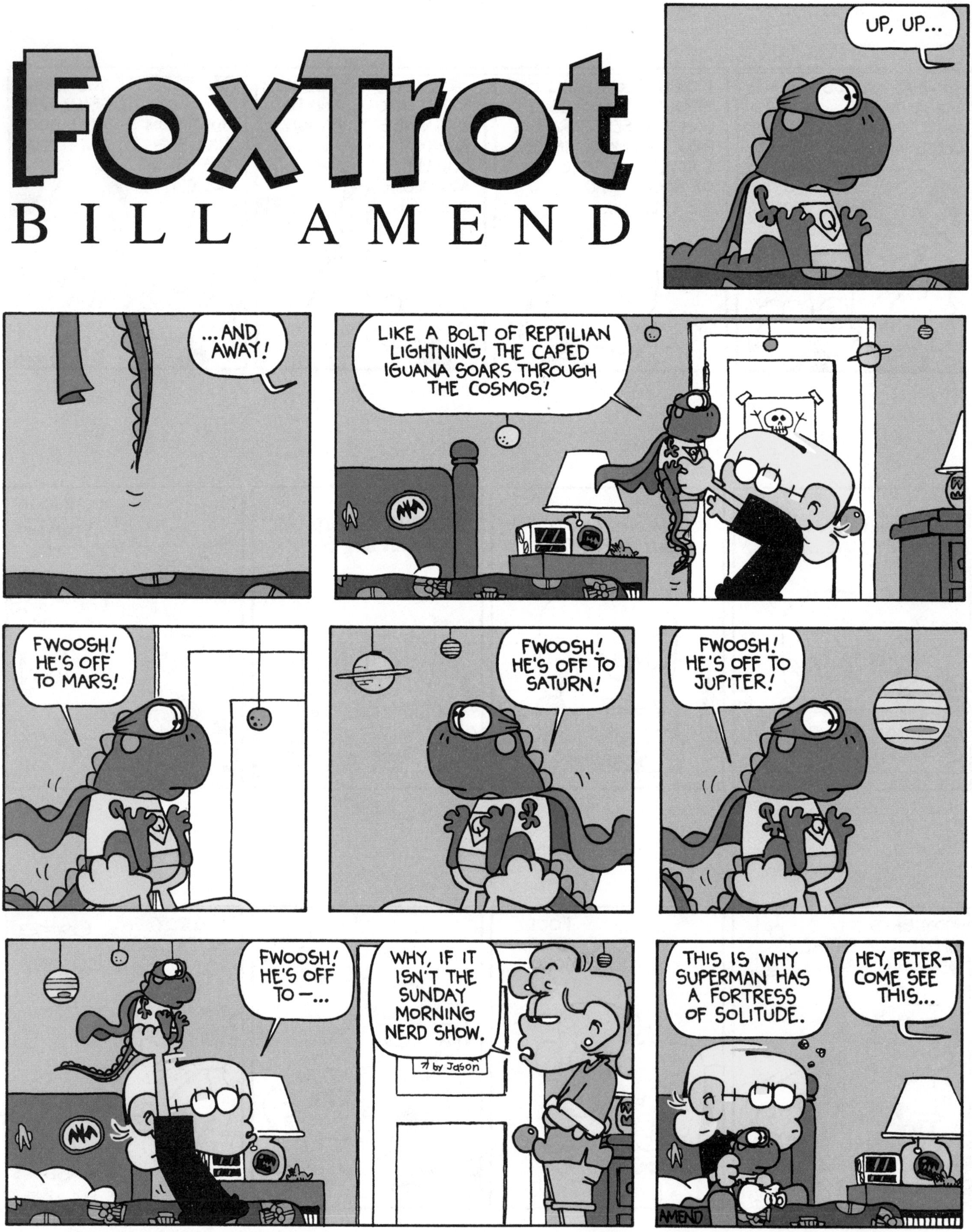
FoxTrot
BILL AMEND
UP, UP...
...AND AWAY!
LIKE A BOLT OF REPTILIAN LIGHTNING, THE CAPED IGUANA SOARS THROUGH THE COSMOS!
FWOOSH! HE'S OFF TO MARS!
FWOOSH! HE'S OFF TO SATURN!
FWOOSH! HE'S OFF TO JUPITER!
FWOOSH! HE'S OFF TO —...
WHY, IF IT ISN'T THE SUNDAY MORNING NERD SHOW.
by Jason
THIS IS WHY SUPERMAN HAS A FORTRESS OF SOLITUDE.
HEY, PETER— COME SEE THIS...
AMEND

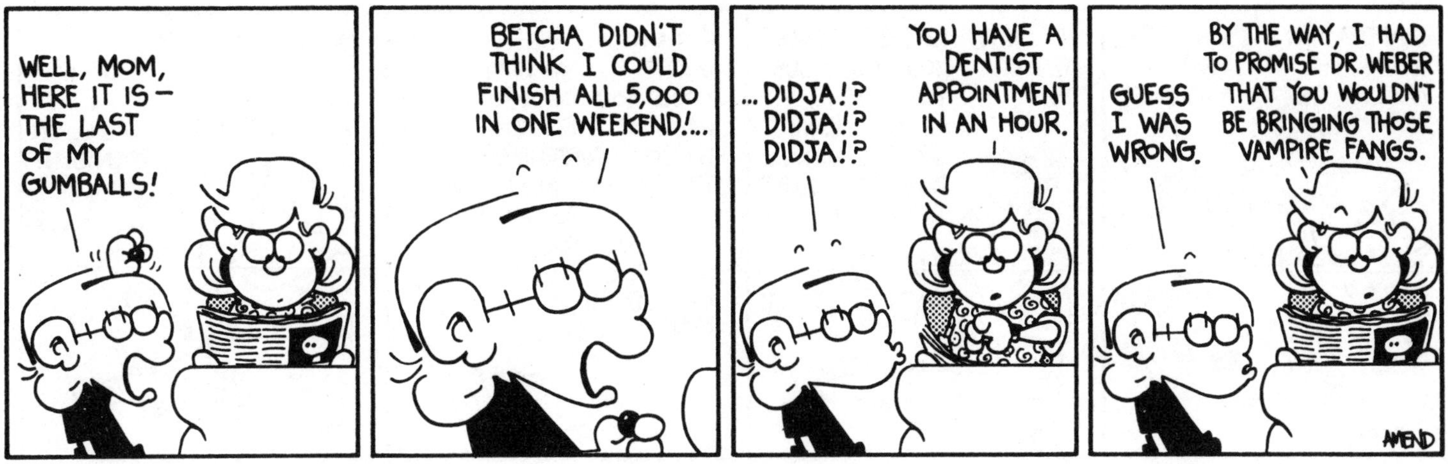
WELL, MOM, HERE IT IS — THE LAST OF MY GUMBALLS!
BETCHA DIDN'T THINK I COULD FINISH ALL 5,000 IN ONE WEEKEND!...
...DIDJA!? DIDJA!? DIDJA!?
YOU HAVE A DENTIST APPOINTMENT IN AN HOUR.
GUESS I WAS WRONG.
BY THE WAY, I HAD TO PROMISE DR. WEBER THAT YOU WOULDN'T BE BRINGING THOSE VAMPIRE FANGS.
AMEND

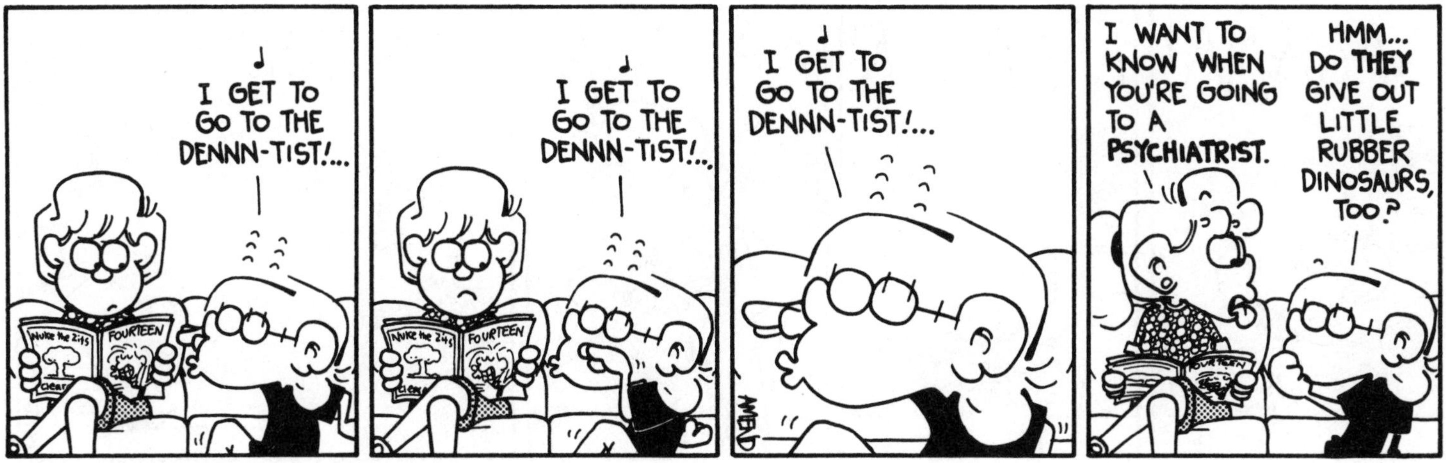
Nuke the Zits
FOURTEEN
I GET TO GO TO THE DENNN-TIST!...
I GET TO GO TO THE DENNN-TIST!...
I GET TO GO TO THE DENNN-TIST!...
AMEND
I WANT TO KNOW WHEN YOU'RE GOING TO A **PSYCHIATRIST**.
HMM... DO **THEY** GIVE OUT LITTLE RUBBER DINOSAURS, TOO?

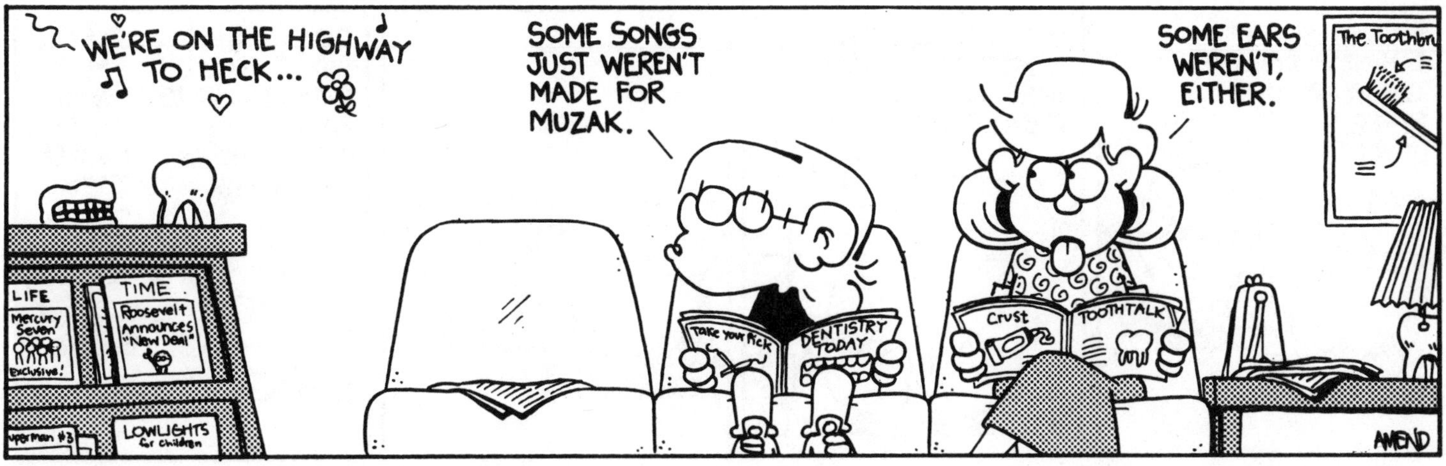
WE'RE ON THE HIGHWAY TO HECK...
SOME SONGS JUST WEREN'T MADE FOR MUZAK.
SOME EARS WEREN'T, EITHER.
LIFE
Mercury Seven
Exclusive!
TIME
Roosevelt Announces "New Deal"
LOWLIGHTS for children
Take your Pick
DENTISTRY TODAY
Crust
TOOTHTALK
AMEND

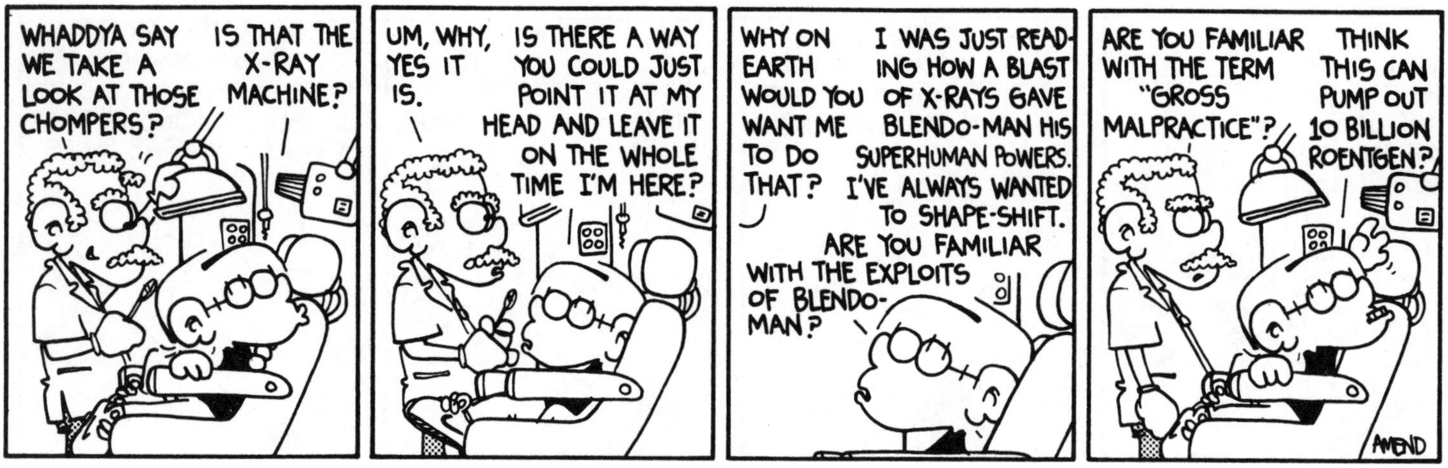
WHADDYA SAY WE TAKE A LOOK AT THOSE CHOMPERS?
IS THAT THE X-RAY MACHINE?
UM, WHY, YES IT IS.
IS THERE A WAY YOU COULD JUST POINT IT AT MY HEAD AND LEAVE IT ON THE WHOLE TIME I'M HERE?
WHY ON EARTH WOULD YOU WANT ME TO DO THAT?
I WAS JUST READING HOW A BLAST OF X-RAYS GAVE BLENDO-MAN HIS SUPERHUMAN POWERS. I'VE ALWAYS WANTED TO SHAPE-SHIFT.
ARE YOU FAMILIAR WITH THE EXPLOITS OF BLENDO-MAN?
ARE YOU FAMILIAR WITH THE TERM "GROSS MALPRACTICE"?
THINK THIS CAN PUMP OUT 10 BILLION ROENTGEN?
AMEND

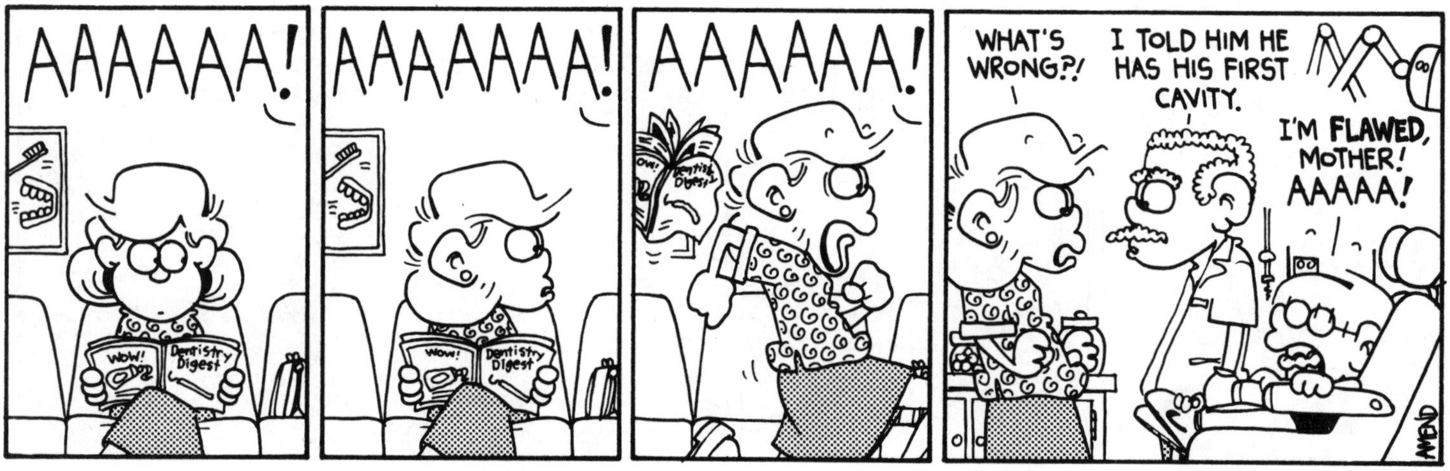
AAAAAA!
AAAAAAAA!
AAAAAA!
WHAT'S WRONG?!
I TOLD HIM HE HAS HIS FIRST CAVITY.
I'M FLAWED, MOTHER! AAAAA!
AMEND

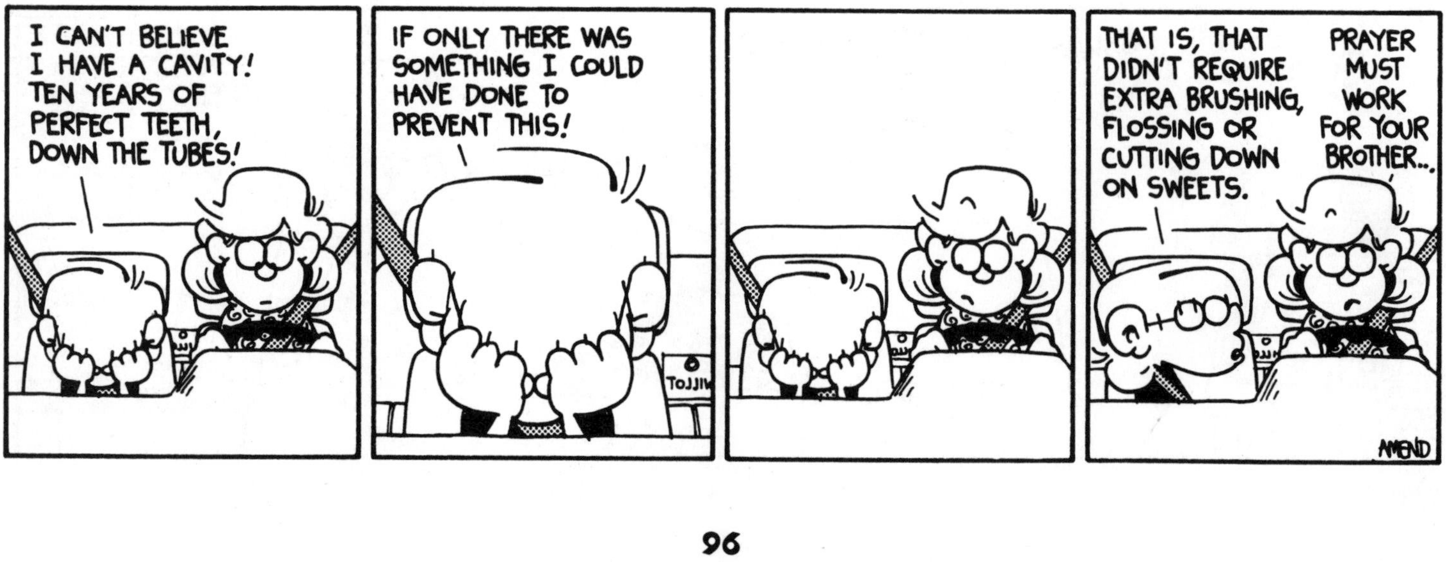
I CAN'T BELIEVE I HAVE A CAVITY! TEN YEARS OF PERFECT TEETH, DOWN THE TUBES!
IF ONLY THERE WAS SOMETHING I COULD HAVE DONE TO PREVENT THIS!
THAT IS, THAT DIDN'T REQUIRE EXTRA BRUSHING, FLOSSING OR CUTTING DOWN ON SWEETS.
PRAYER MUST WORK FOR YOUR BROTHER...
AMEND

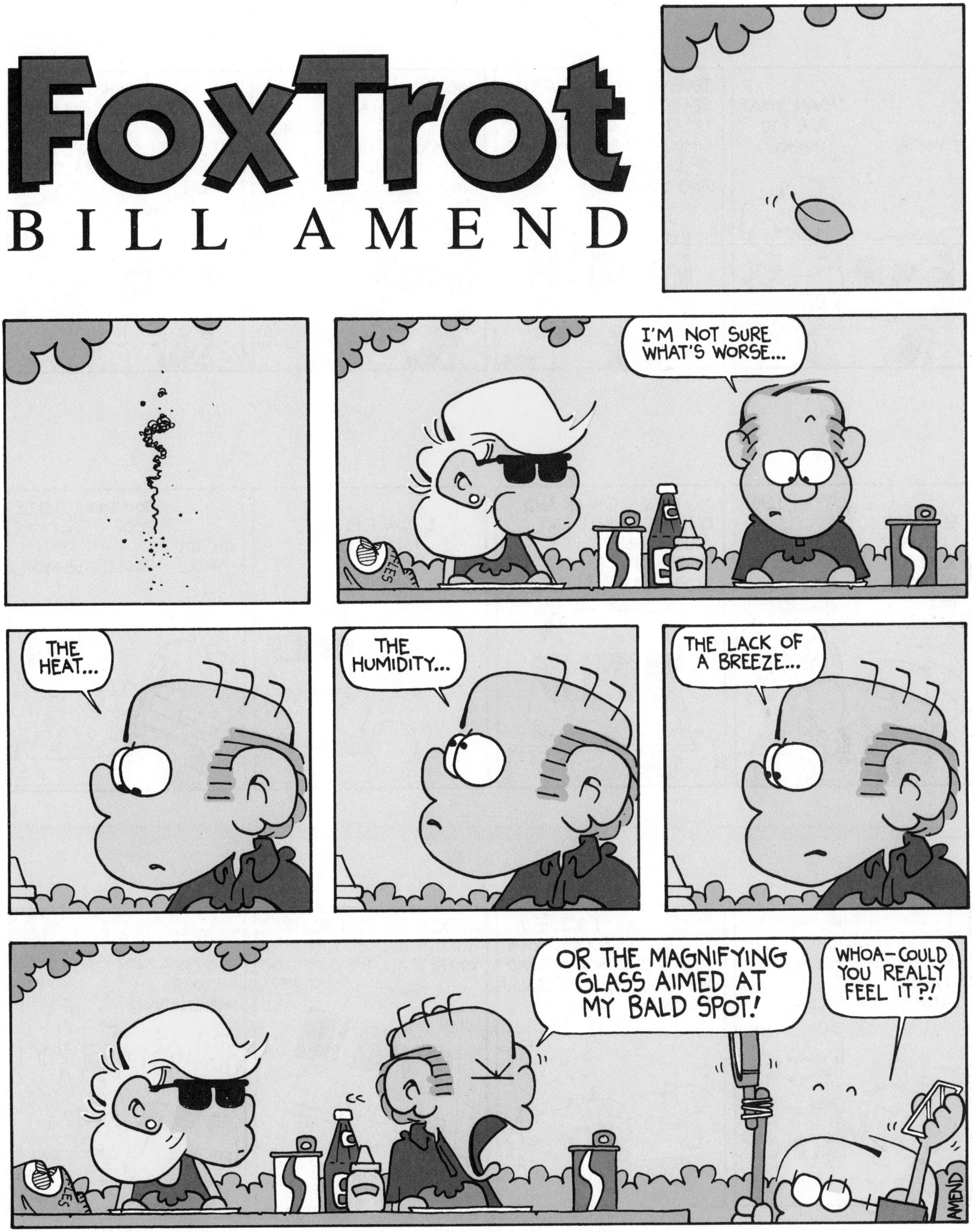
FoxTrot
BILL AMEND
I'M NOT SURE WHAT'S WORSE...
THE HEAT...
THE HUMIDITY...
THE LACK OF A BREEZE...
OR THE MAGNIFYING GLASS AIMED AT MY BALD SPOT!
WHOA—COULD YOU REALLY FEEL IT?!
AMEND

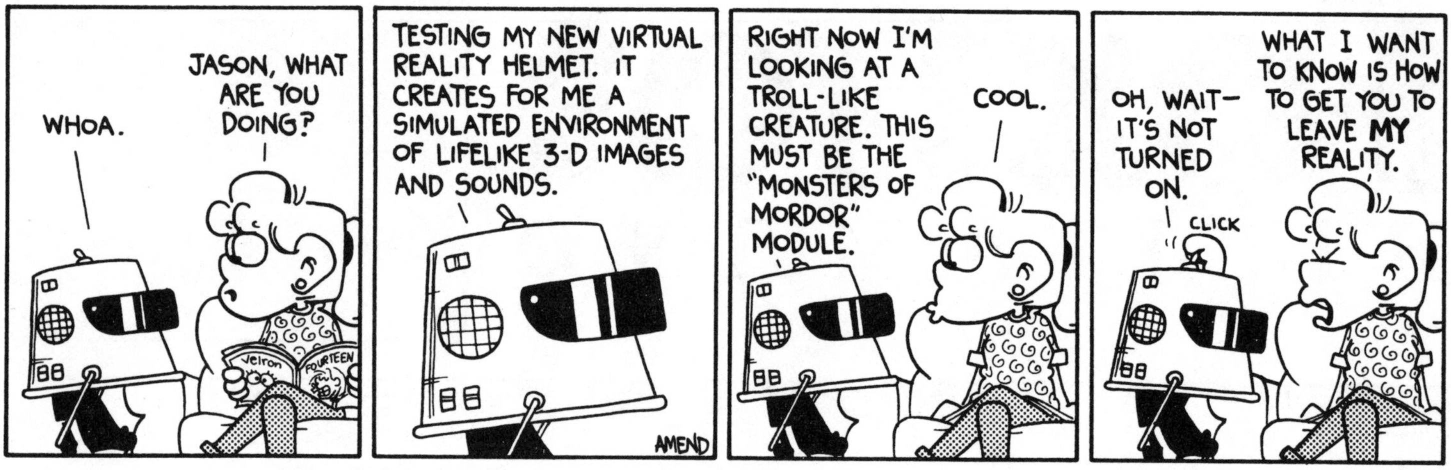
JASON, WHAT ARE YOU DOING?
WHOA.
TESTING MY NEW VIRTUAL REALITY HELMET. IT CREATES FOR ME A SIMULATED ENVIRONMENT OF LIFELIKE 3-D IMAGES AND SOUNDS.
AMEND
RIGHT NOW I'M LOOKING AT A TROLL-LIKE CREATURE. THIS MUST BE THE "MONSTERS OF MORDOR" MODULE.
COOL.
OH, WAIT— IT'S NOT TURNED ON.
CLICK
WHAT I WANT TO KNOW IS HOW TO GET YOU TO LEAVE MY REALITY.

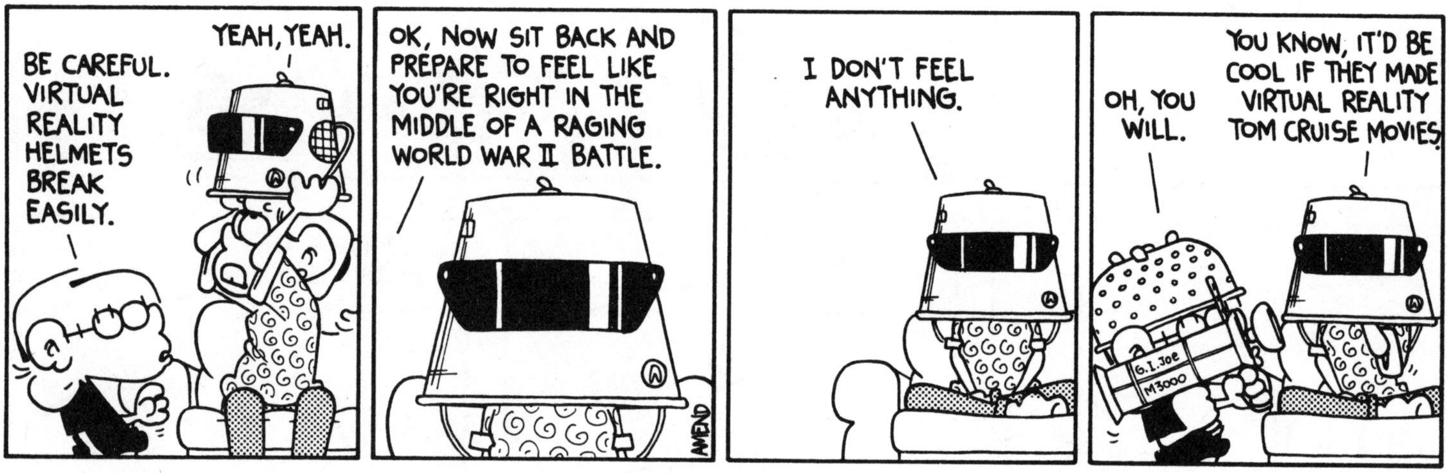
BE CAREFUL. VIRTUAL REALITY HELMETS BREAK EASILY.
YEAH, YEAH.
OK, NOW SIT BACK AND PREPARE TO FEEL LIKE YOU'RE RIGHT IN THE MIDDLE OF A RAGING WORLD WAR II BATTLE.
AMEND
I DON'T FEEL ANYTHING.
OH, YOU WILL.
YOU KNOW, IT'D BE COOL IF THEY MADE VIRTUAL REALITY TOM CRUISE MOVIES.

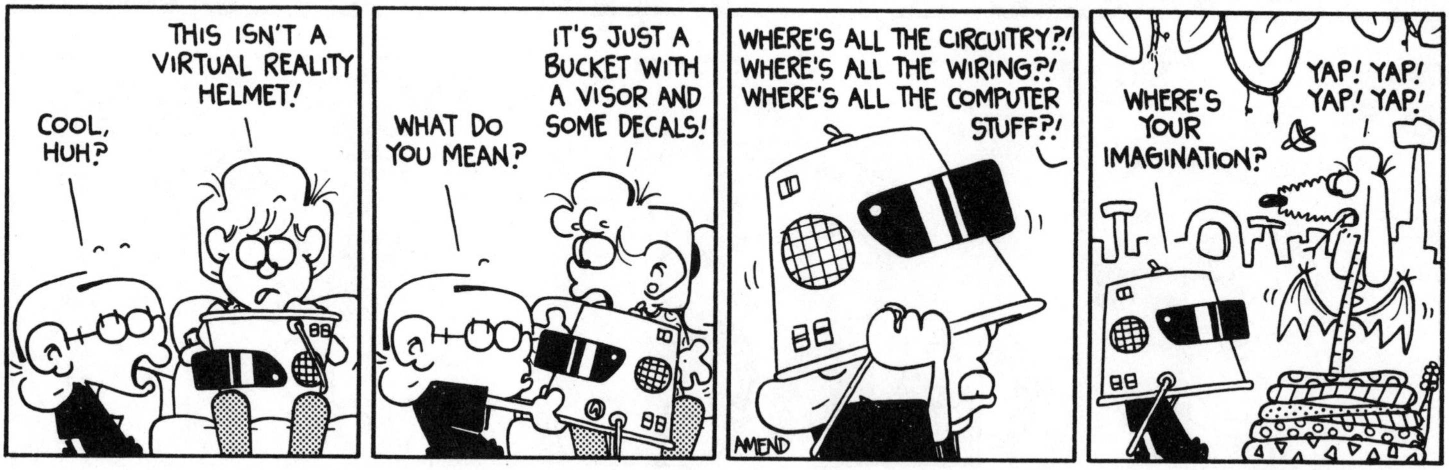
COOL, HUH?
THIS ISN'T A VIRTUAL REALITY HELMET!
WHAT DO YOU MEAN?
IT'S JUST A BUCKET WITH A VISOR AND SOME DECALS!
WHERE'S ALL THE CIRCUITRY?! WHERE'S ALL THE WIRING?! WHERE'S ALL THE COMPUTER STUFF?!
AMEND
WHERE'S YOUR IMAGINATION?
YAP! YAP! YAP! YAP!

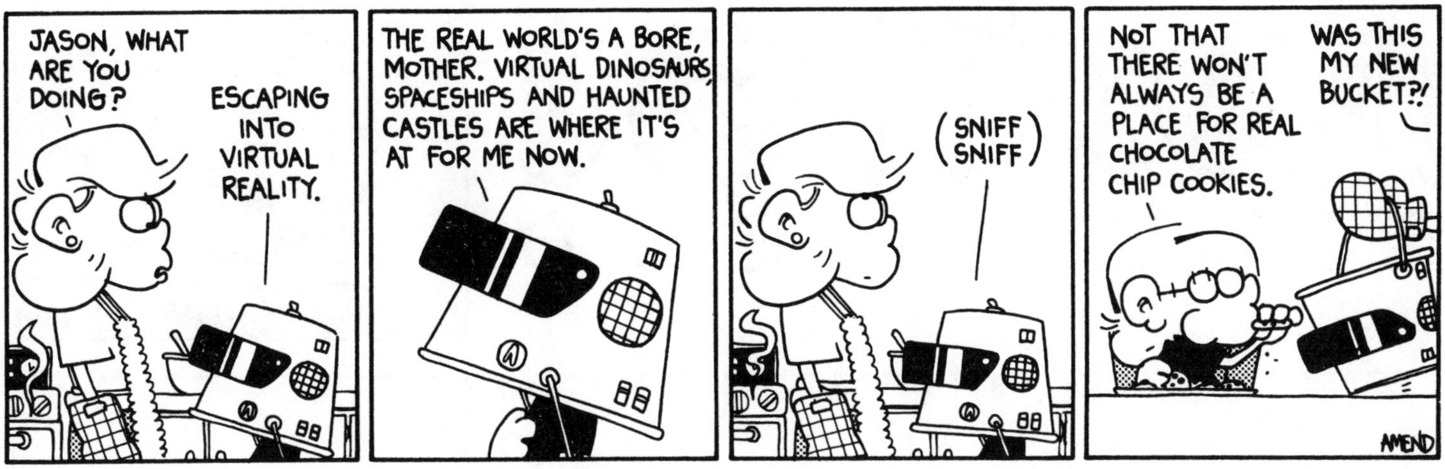
JASON, WHAT ARE YOU DOING?
ESCAPING INTO VIRTUAL REALITY.
THE REAL WORLD'S A BORE, MOTHER. VIRTUAL DINOSAURS, SPACESHIPS AND HAUNTED CASTLES ARE WHERE IT'S AT FOR ME NOW.
(SNIFF SNIFF)
NOT THAT THERE WON'T ALWAYS BE A PLACE FOR REAL CHOCOLATE CHIP COOKIES.
WAS THIS MY NEW BUCKET?!
AMEND

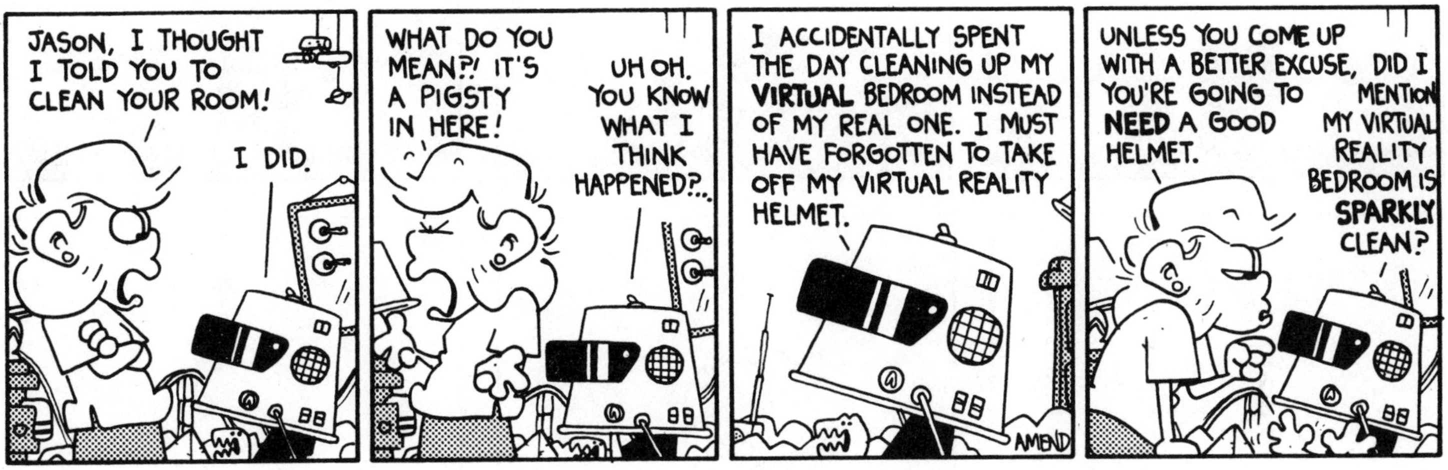
JASON, I THOUGHT I TOLD YOU TO CLEAN YOUR ROOM!
I DID.
WHAT DO YOU MEAN?! IT'S A PIGSTY IN HERE!
UH OH. YOU KNOW WHAT I THINK HAPPENED?..
I ACCIDENTALLY SPENT THE DAY CLEANING UP MY VIRTUAL BEDROOM INSTEAD OF MY REAL ONE. I MUST HAVE FORGOTTEN TO TAKE OFF MY VIRTUAL REALITY HELMET.
AMEND
UNLESS YOU COME UP WITH A BETTER EXCUSE, YOU'RE GOING TO NEED A GOOD HELMET.
DID I MENTION MY VIRTUAL REALITY BEDROOM IS SPARKLY CLEAN?

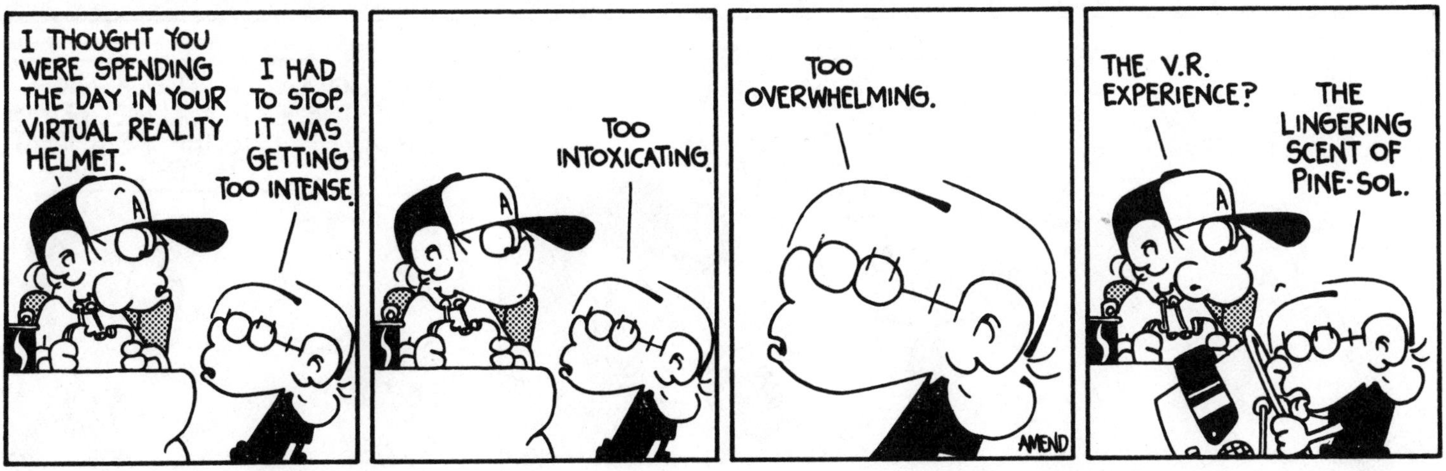
I THOUGHT YOU WERE SPENDING THE DAY IN YOUR VIRTUAL REALITY HELMET.
I HAD TO STOP. IT WAS GETTING TOO INTENSE.
TOO INTOXICATING.
TOO OVERWHELMING.
AMEND
THE V.R. EXPERIENCE?
THE LINGERING SCENT OF PINE-SOL.

FoxTrot
BILL AMEND

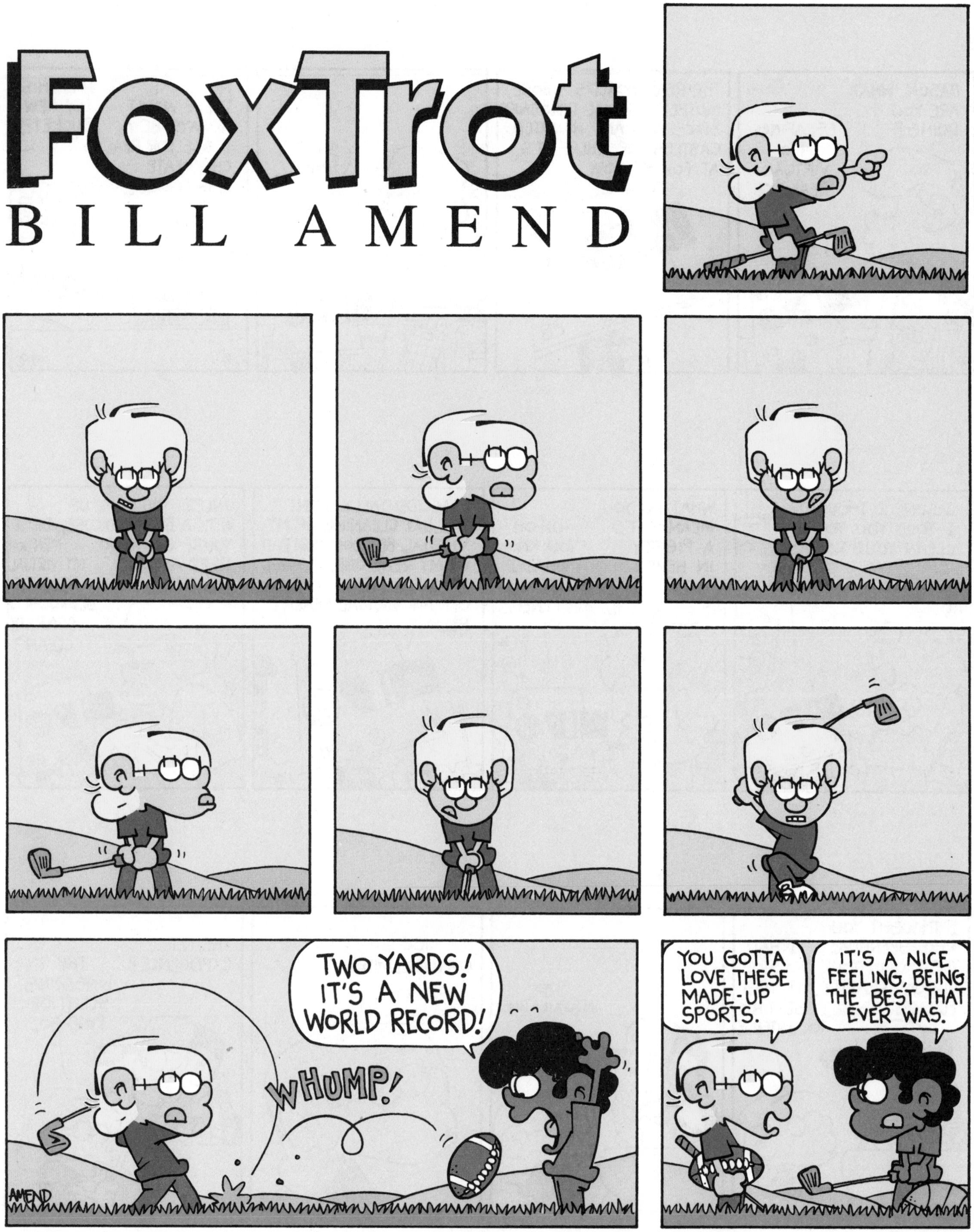

TWO YARDS! IT'S A NEW WORLD RECORD!
WHUMP!
AMEND
YOU GOTTA LOVE THESE MADE-UP SPORTS.
IT'S A NICE FEELING, BEING THE BEST THAT EVER WAS.

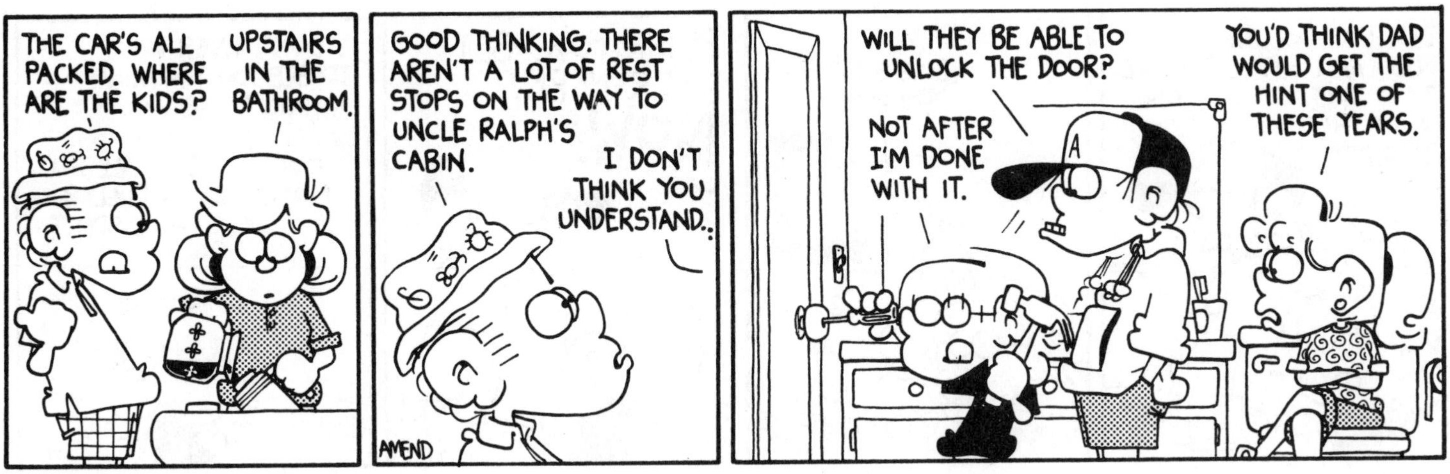
THE CAR'S ALL PACKED. WHERE ARE THE KIDS?
UPSTAIRS IN THE BATHROOM.
GOOD THINKING. THERE AREN'T A LOT OF REST STOPS ON THE WAY TO UNCLE RALPH'S CABIN.
I DON'T THINK YOU UNDERSTAND.
AMEND
WILL THEY BE ABLE TO UNLOCK THE DOOR?
NOT AFTER I'M DONE WITH IT.
YOU'D THINK DAD WOULD GET THE HINT ONE OF THESE YEARS.

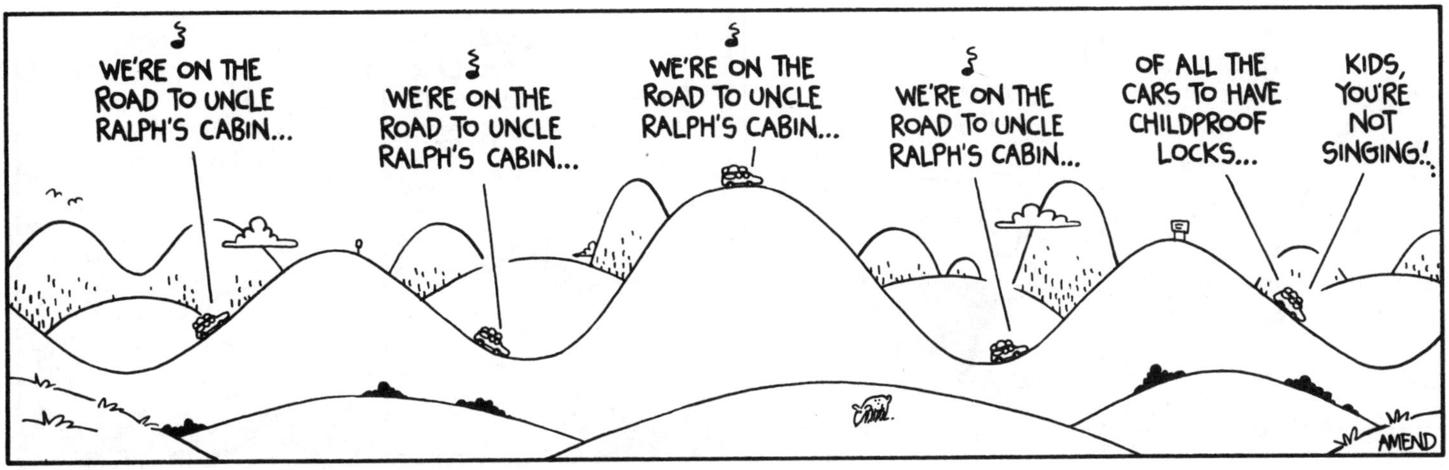
WE'RE ON THE ROAD TO UNCLE RALPH'S CABIN...
WE'RE ON THE ROAD TO UNCLE RALPH'S CABIN...
WE'RE ON THE ROAD TO UNCLE RALPH'S CABIN...
WE'RE ON THE ROAD TO UNCLE RALPH'S CABIN...
OF ALL THE CARS TO HAVE CHILDPROOF LOCKS...
KIDS, YOU'RE NOT SINGING!
AMEND

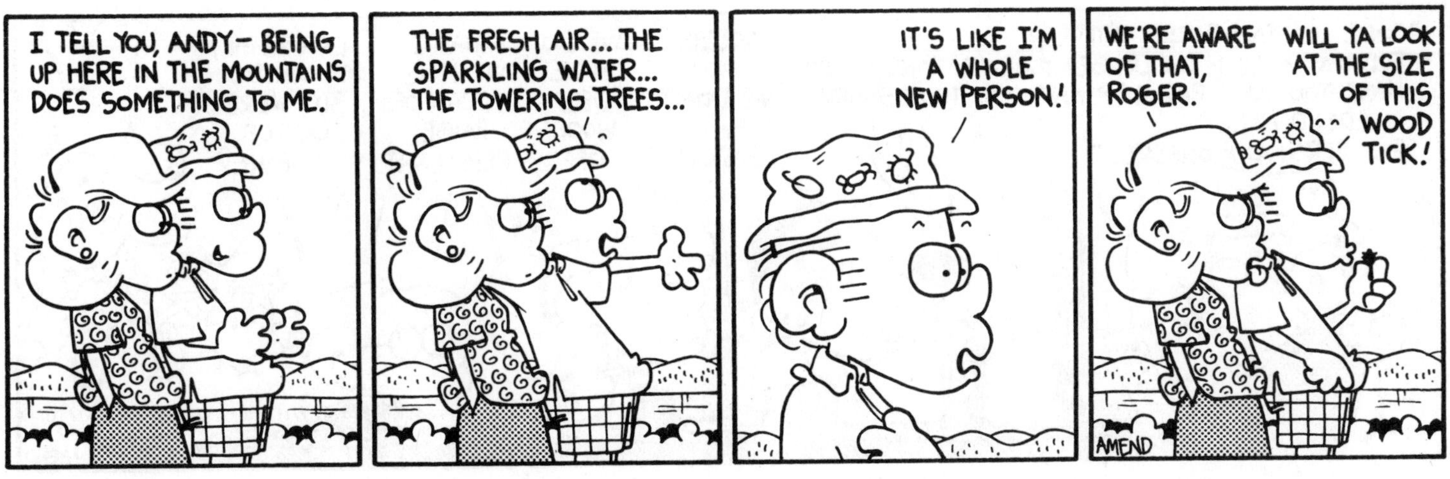
I TELL YOU, ANDY– BEING UP HERE IN THE MOUNTAINS DOES SOMETHING TO ME.
THE FRESH AIR... THE SPARKLING WATER... THE TOWERING TREES...
IT'S LIKE I'M A WHOLE NEW PERSON!
WE'RE AWARE OF THAT, ROGER.
WILL YA LOOK AT THE SIZE OF THIS WOOD TICK!
AMEND

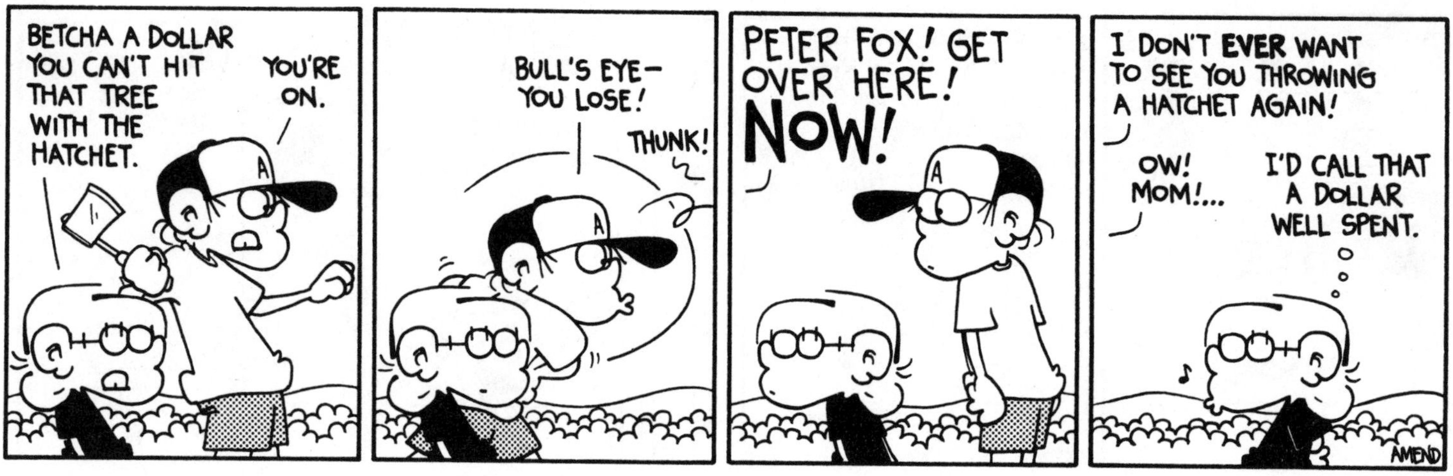
BETCHA A DOLLAR YOU CAN'T HIT THAT TREE WITH THE HATCHET.
YOU'RE ON.
BULL'S EYE— YOU LOSE!
THUNK!
PETER FOX! GET OVER HERE! NOW!
I DON'T EVER WANT TO SEE YOU THROWING A HATCHET AGAIN!
OW! MOM!...
I'D CALL THAT A DOLLAR WELL SPENT.
AMEND

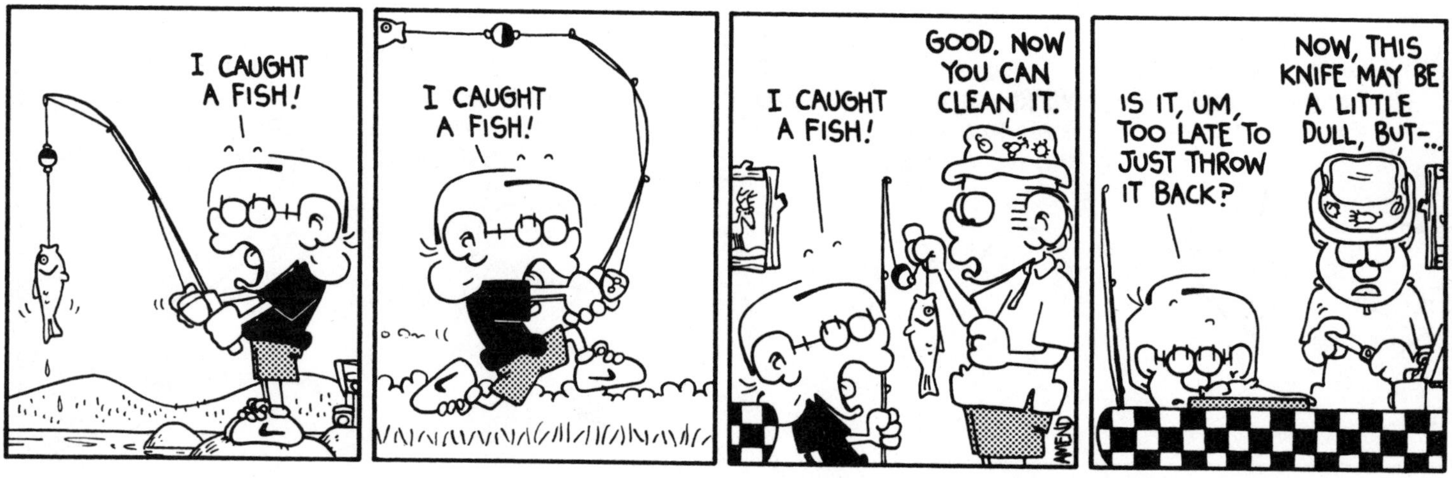
I CAUGHT A FISH!
I CAUGHT A FISH!
I CAUGHT A FISH!
GOOD. NOW YOU CAN CLEAN IT.
IS IT, UM, TOO LATE TO JUST THROW IT BACK?
NOW, THIS KNIFE MAY BE A LITTLE DULL, BUT-...
AMEND

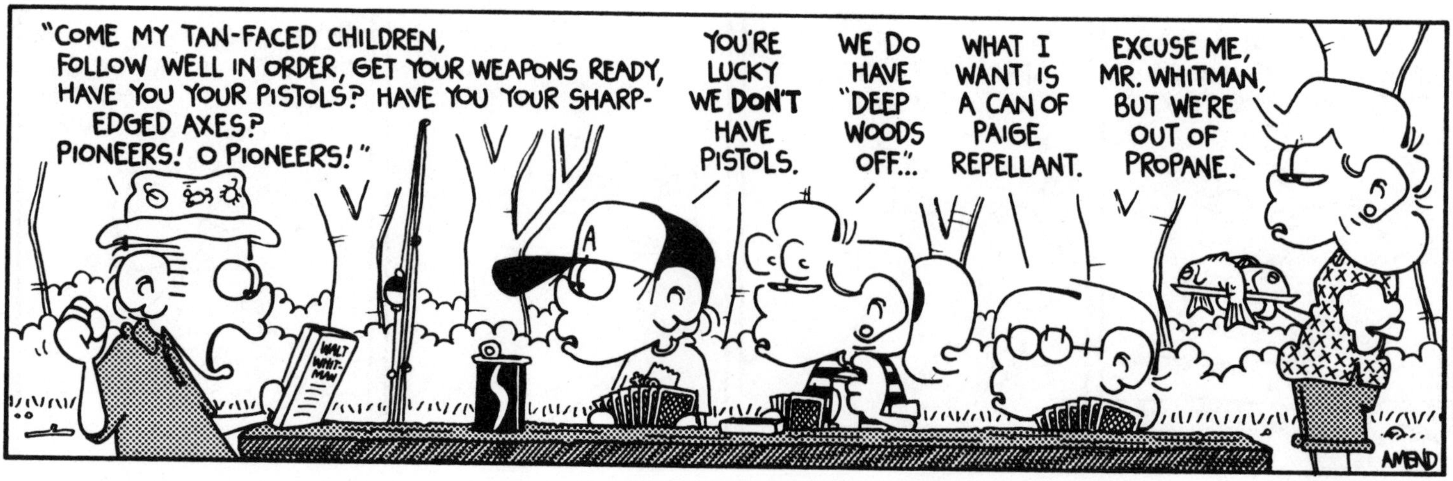
"COME MY TAN-FACED CHILDREN, FOLLOW WELL IN ORDER, GET YOUR WEAPONS READY, HAVE YOU YOUR PISTOLS? HAVE YOU YOUR SHARP-EDGED AXES? PIONEERS! O PIONEERS!"
YOU'RE LUCKY WE DON'T HAVE PISTOLS.
WE DO HAVE "DEEP WOODS OFF."...
WHAT I WANT IS A CAN OF PAIGE REPELLANT.
EXCUSE ME, MR. WHITMAN, BUT WE'RE OUT OF PROPANE.
WALT WHITMAN
AMEND

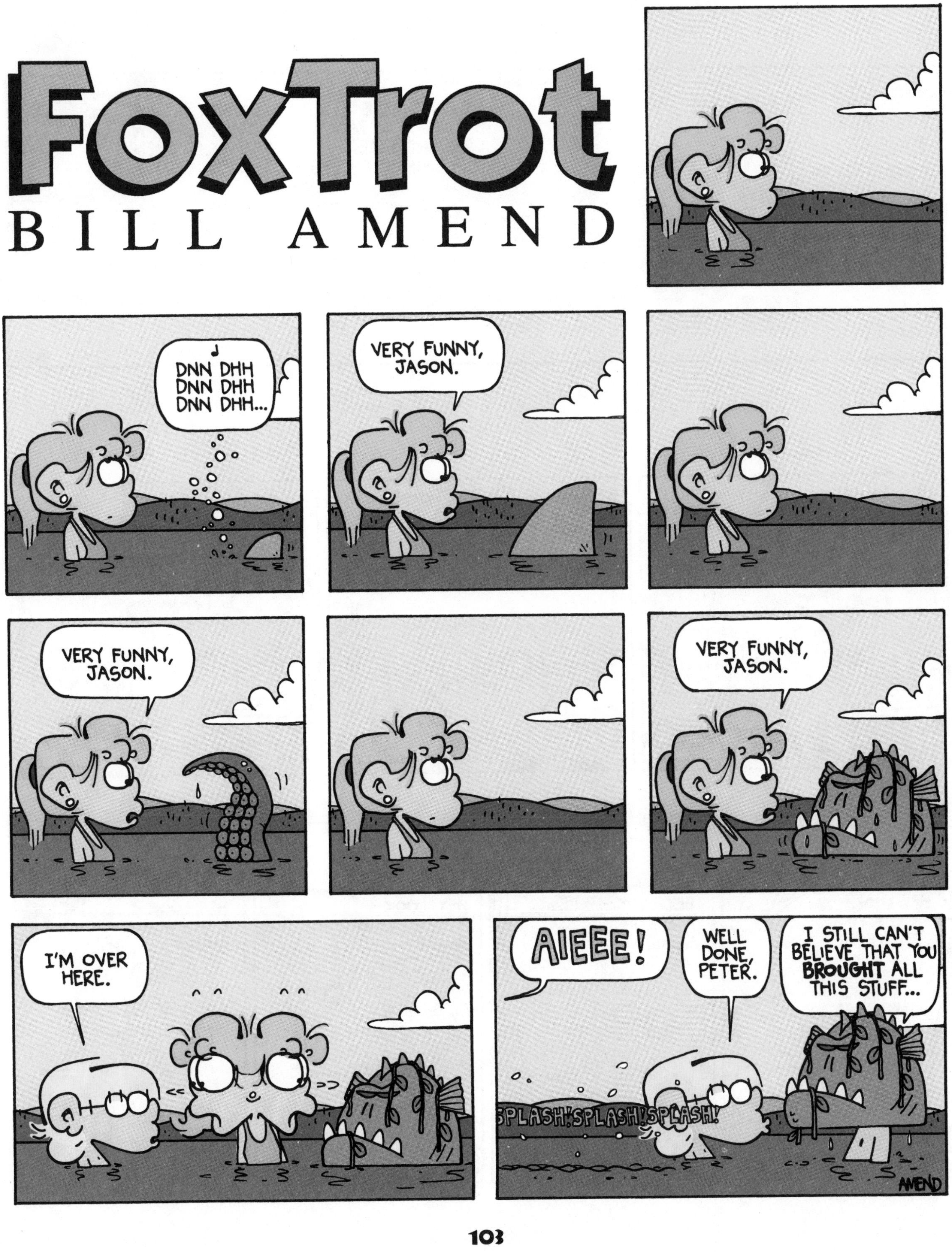
FoxTrot
BILL AMEND
DNN DHH DNN DHH DNN DHH...
VERY FUNNY, JASON.
VERY FUNNY, JASON.
VERY FUNNY, JASON.
I'M OVER HERE.
AIEEE!
SPLASH! SPLASH! SPLASH!
WELL DONE, PETER.
I STILL CAN'T BELIEVE THAT YOU **BROUGHT** ALL THIS STUFF...
AMEND

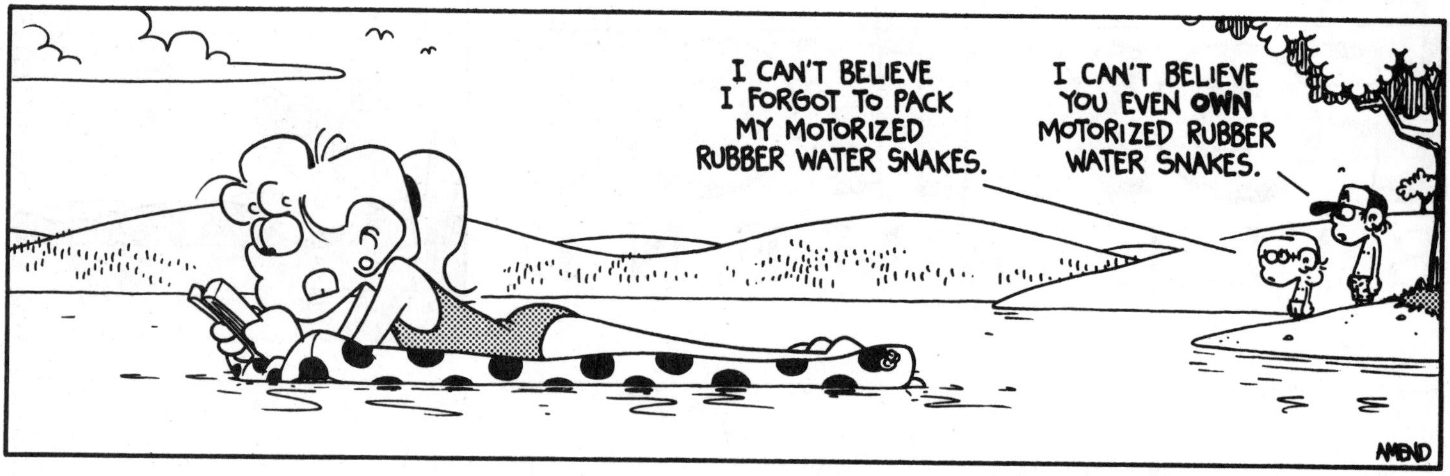
I CAN'T BELIEVE I FORGOT TO PACK MY MOTORIZED RUBBER WATER SNAKES.
I CAN'T BELIEVE YOU EVEN OWN MOTORIZED RUBBER WATER SNAKES.
AMEND

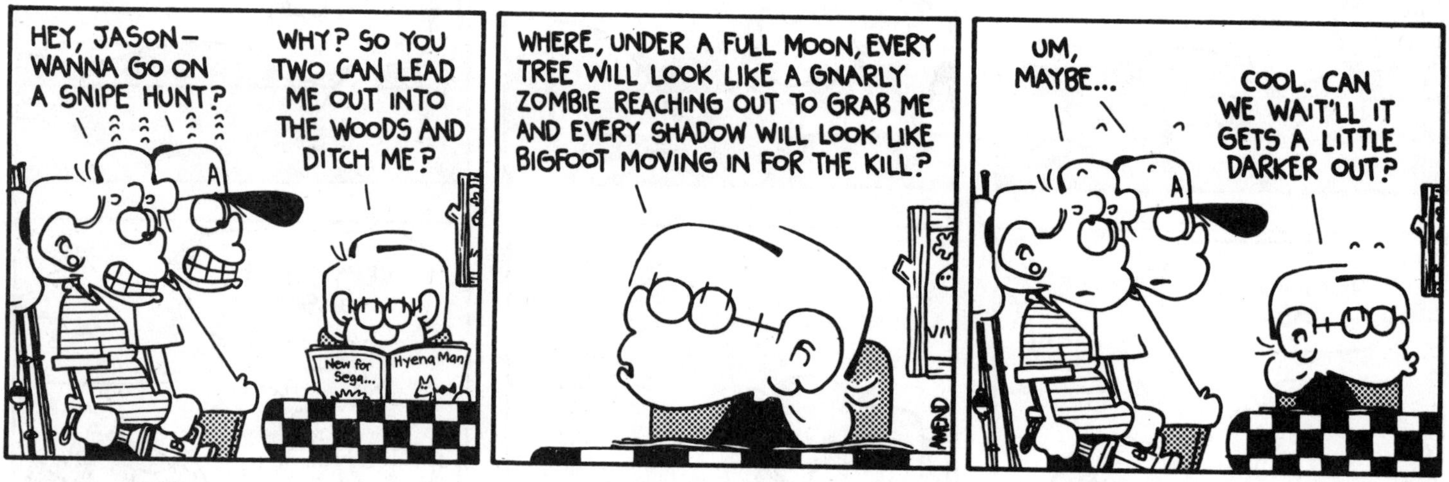
HEY, JASON– WANNA GO ON A SNIPE HUNT?
WHY? SO YOU TWO CAN LEAD ME OUT INTO THE WOODS AND DITCH ME?
New for Sega...
Hyena Man
WHERE, UNDER A FULL MOON, EVERY TREE WILL LOOK LIKE A GNARLY ZOMBIE REACHING OUT TO GRAB ME AND EVERY SHADOW WILL LOOK LIKE BIGFOOT MOVING IN FOR THE KILL?
AMEND
UM, MAYBE...
COOL. CAN WE WAIT'LL IT GETS A LITTLE DARKER OUT?

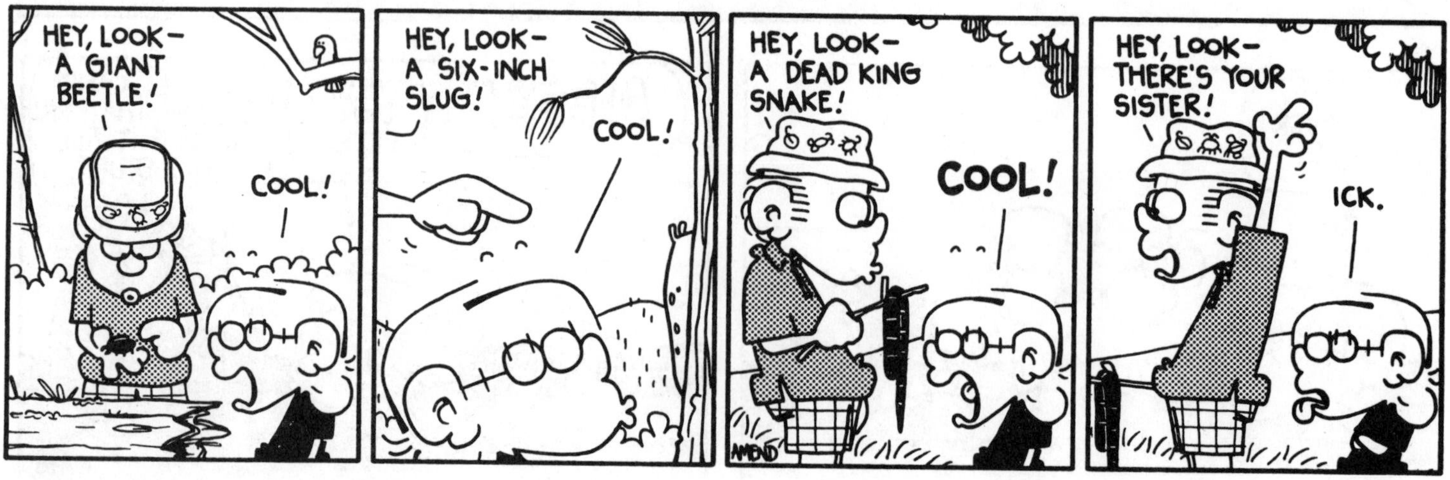
HEY, LOOK– A GIANT BEETLE!
COOL!
HEY, LOOK– A SIX-INCH SLUG!
COOL!
HEY, LOOK– A DEAD KING SNAKE!
COOL!
AMEND
HEY, LOOK– THERE'S YOUR SISTER!
ICK.

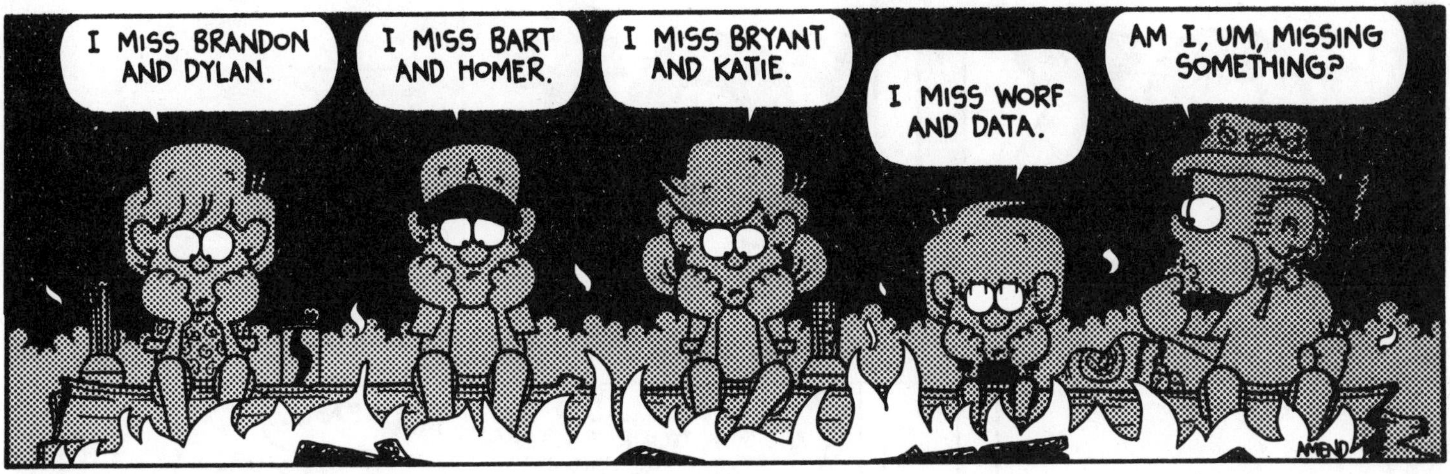
I MISS BRANDON AND DYLAN.
I MISS BART AND HOMER.
I MISS BRYANT AND KATIE.
I MISS WORF AND DATA.
AM I, UM, MISSING SOMETHING?
AMEND

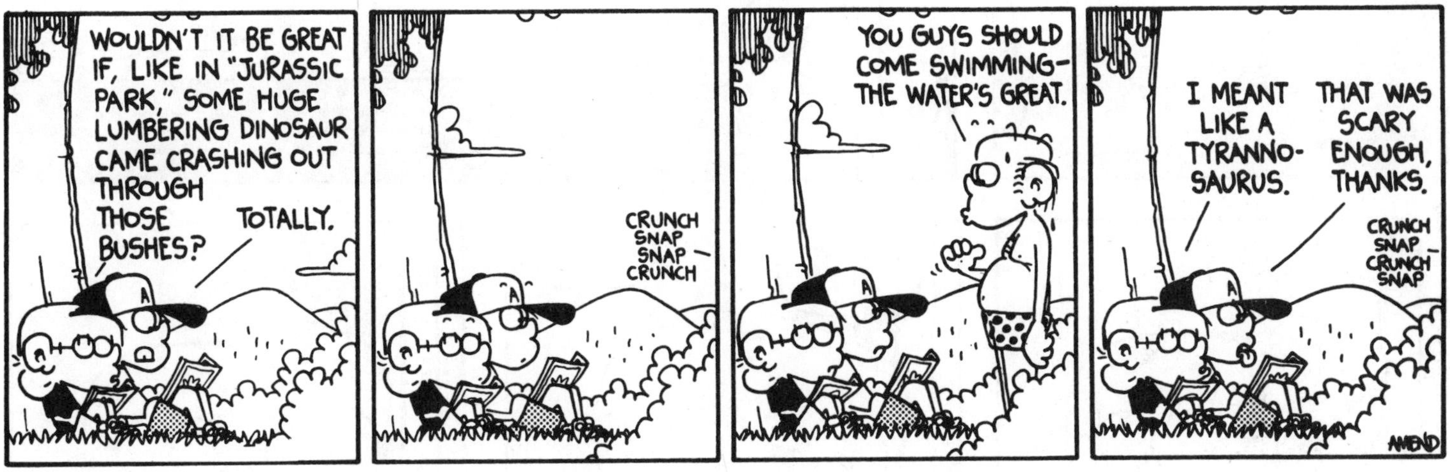
WOULDN'T IT BE GREAT IF, LIKE IN "JURASSIC PARK," SOME HUGE LUMBERING DINOSAUR CAME CRASHING OUT THROUGH THOSE BUSHES?
TOTALLY.
CRUNCH SNAP SNAP CRUNCH
YOU GUYS SHOULD COME SWIMMING- THE WATER'S GREAT.
I MEANT LIKE A TYRANNO-SAURUS.
THAT WAS SCARY ENOUGH, THANKS.
CRUNCH SNAP CRUNCH SNAP
AMEND

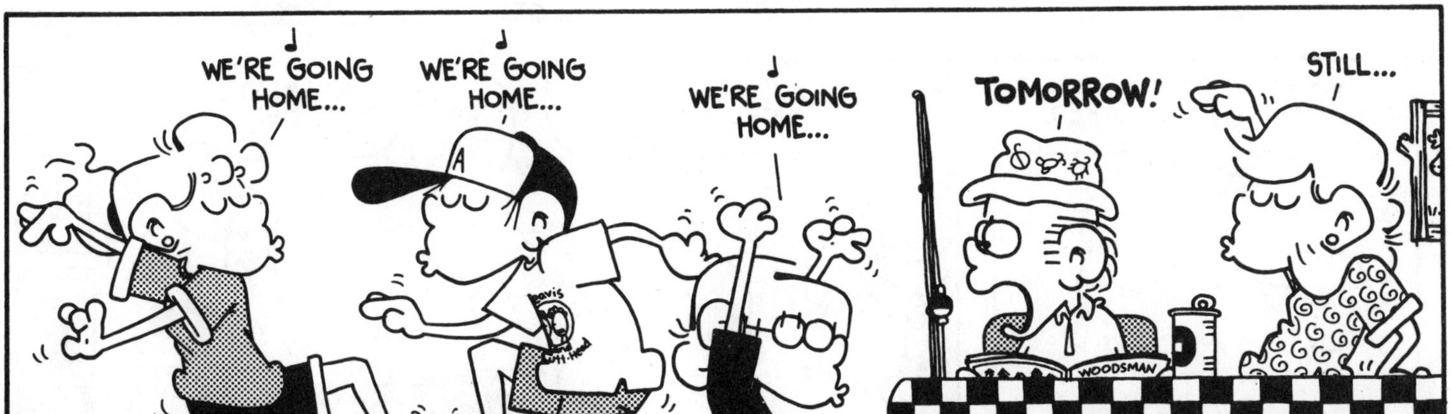
WE'RE GOING HOME...
WE'RE GOING HOME...
WE'RE GOING HOME...
TOMORROW!
STILL...
WOODSMAN
AMEND

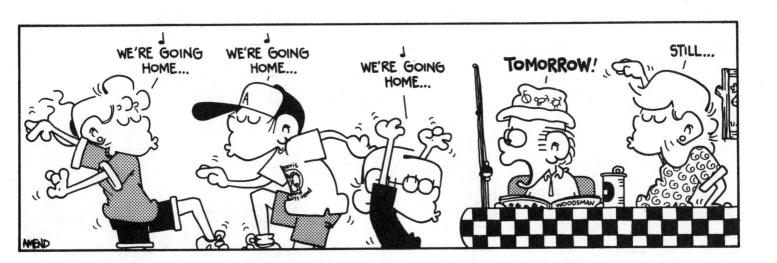

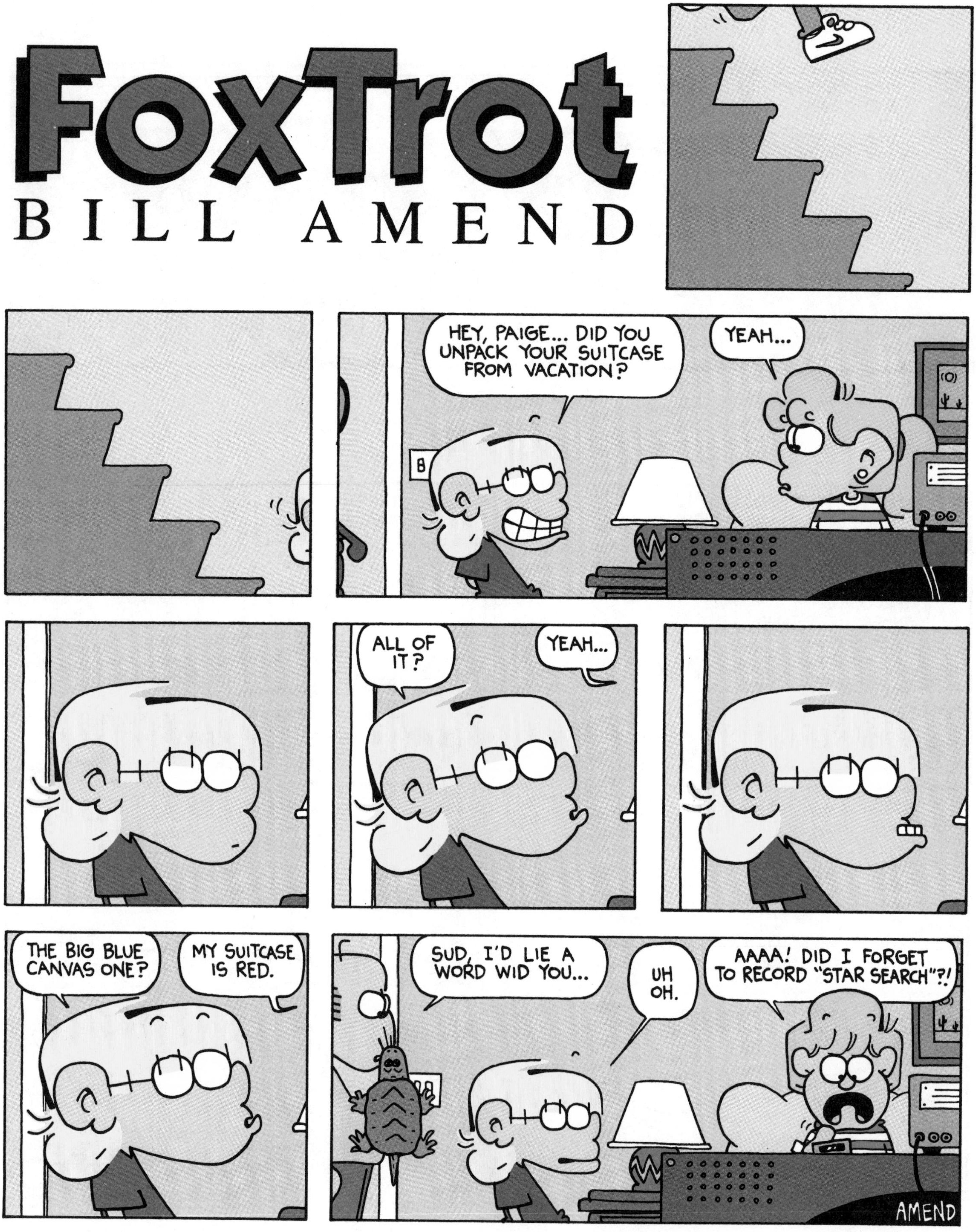
FoxTrot
BILL AMEND
HEY, PAIGE... DID YOU UNPACK YOUR SUITCASE FROM VACATION?
YEAH...
ALL OF IT?
YEAH...
THE BIG BLUE CANVAS ONE?
MY SUITCASE IS RED.
SUD, I'D LIE A WORD WID YOU...
UH OH.
AAAA! DID I FORGET TO RECORD "STAR SEARCH"?!
AMEND

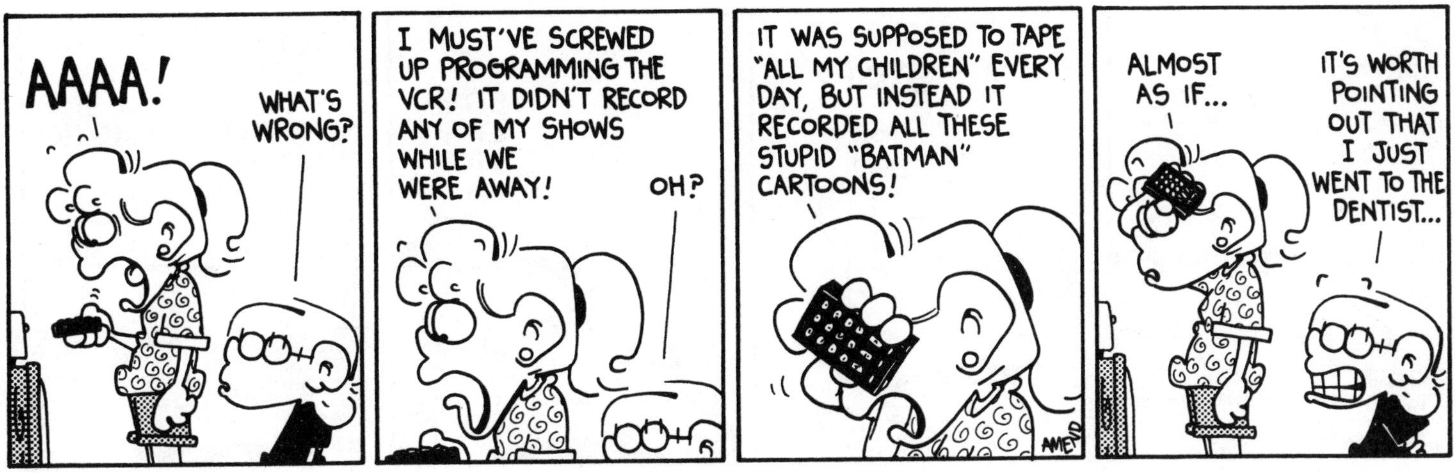
AAAA!
WHAT'S WRONG?
I MUST'VE SCREWED UP PROGRAMMING THE VCR! IT DIDN'T RECORD ANY OF MY SHOWS WHILE WE WERE AWAY!
OH?
IT WAS SUPPOSED TO TAPE "ALL MY CHILDREN" EVERY DAY, BUT INSTEAD IT RECORDED ALL THESE STUPID "BATMAN" CARTOONS!
ALMOST AS IF...
IT'S WORTH POINTING OUT THAT I JUST WENT TO THE DENTIST...

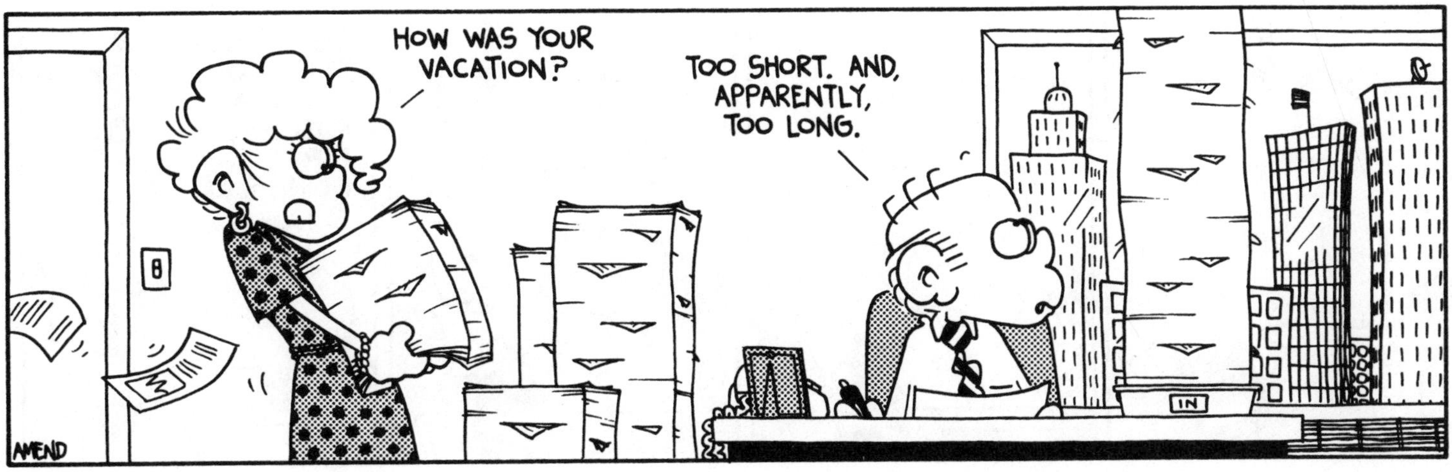
HOW WAS YOUR VACATION?
TOO SHORT. AND, APPARENTLY, TOO LONG.
IN
AMEND

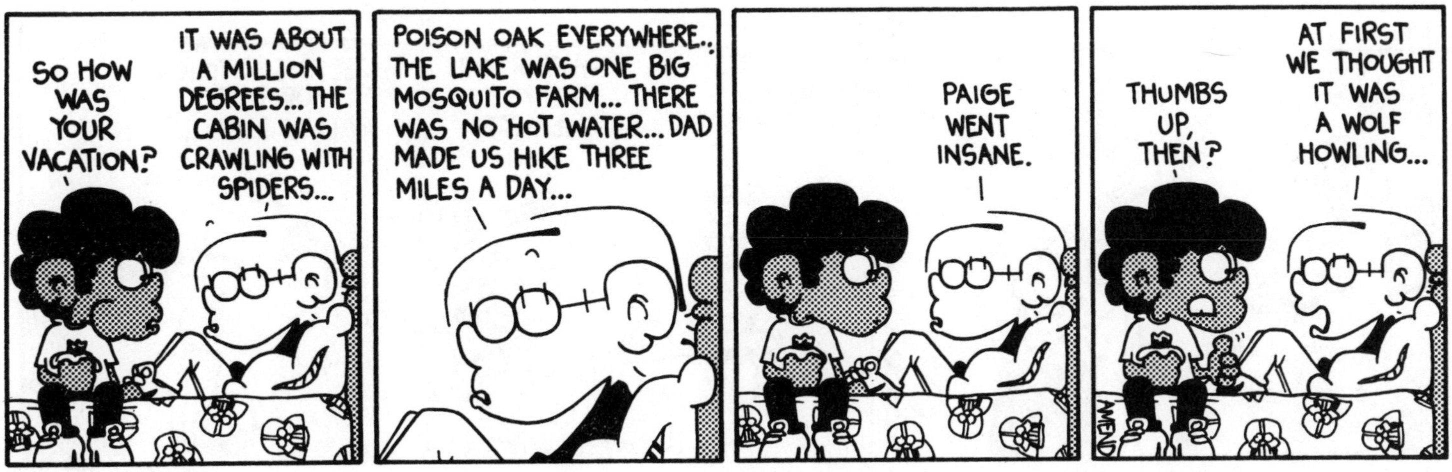
SO HOW WAS YOUR VACATION?
IT WAS ABOUT A MILLION DEGREES... THE CABIN WAS CRAWLING WITH SPIDERS...
POISON OAK EVERYWHERE... THE LAKE WAS ONE BIG MOSQUITO FARM... THERE WAS NO HOT WATER... DAD MADE US HIKE THREE MILES A DAY...
PAIGE WENT INSANE.
THUMBS UP, THEN?
AT FIRST WE THOUGHT IT WAS A WOLF HOWLING...

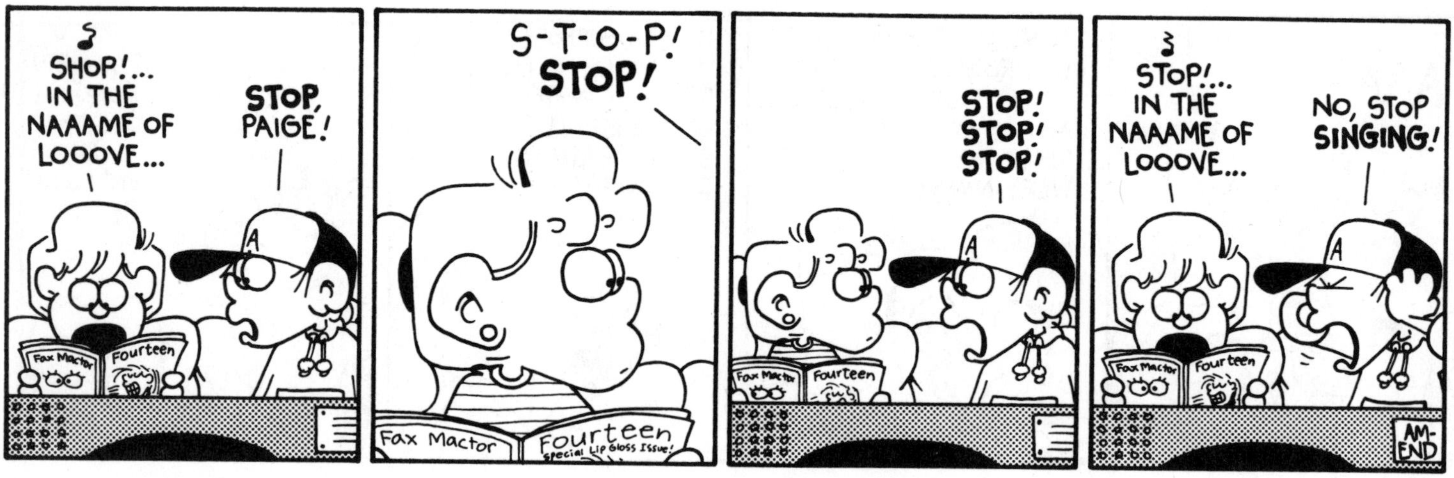
SHOP!... IN THE NAAAME OF LOOOVE...
STOP, PAIGE!
Fax Mactor
Fourteen
S-T-O-P! STOP!
Fourteen
Special Lip Gloss Issue!
STOP! STOP! STOP!
STOP!... IN THE NAAAME OF LOOOVE...
NO, STOP SINGING!
AMEND

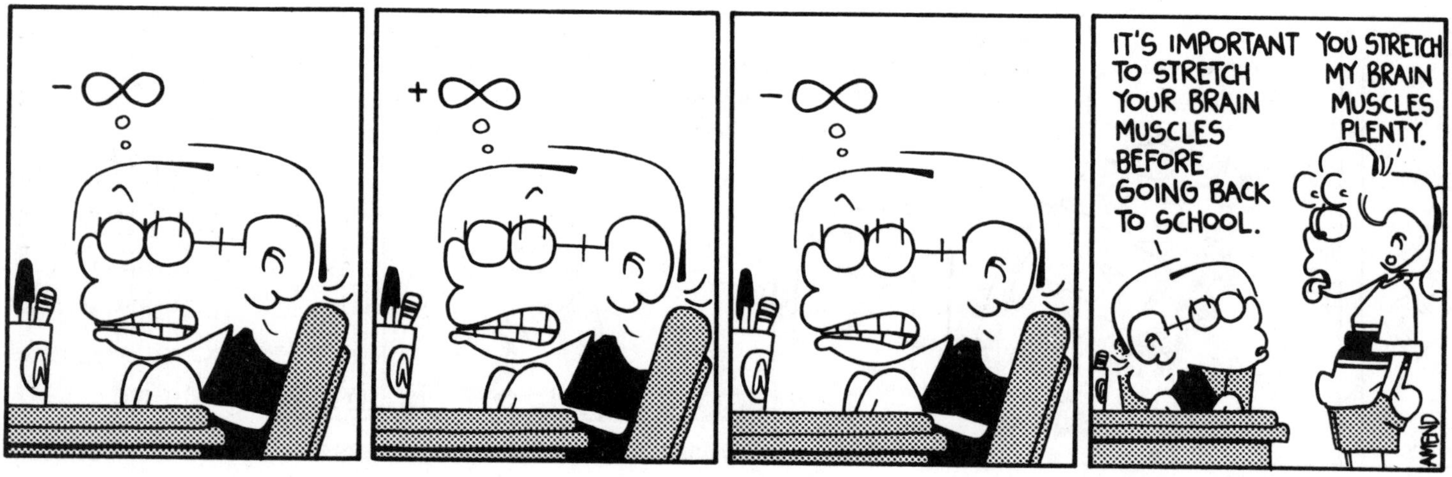
-∞
+∞
-∞
IT'S IMPORTANT TO STRETCH YOUR BRAIN MUSCLES BEFORE GOING BACK TO SCHOOL.
YOU STRETCH MY BRAIN MUSCLES PLENTY.
AMEND

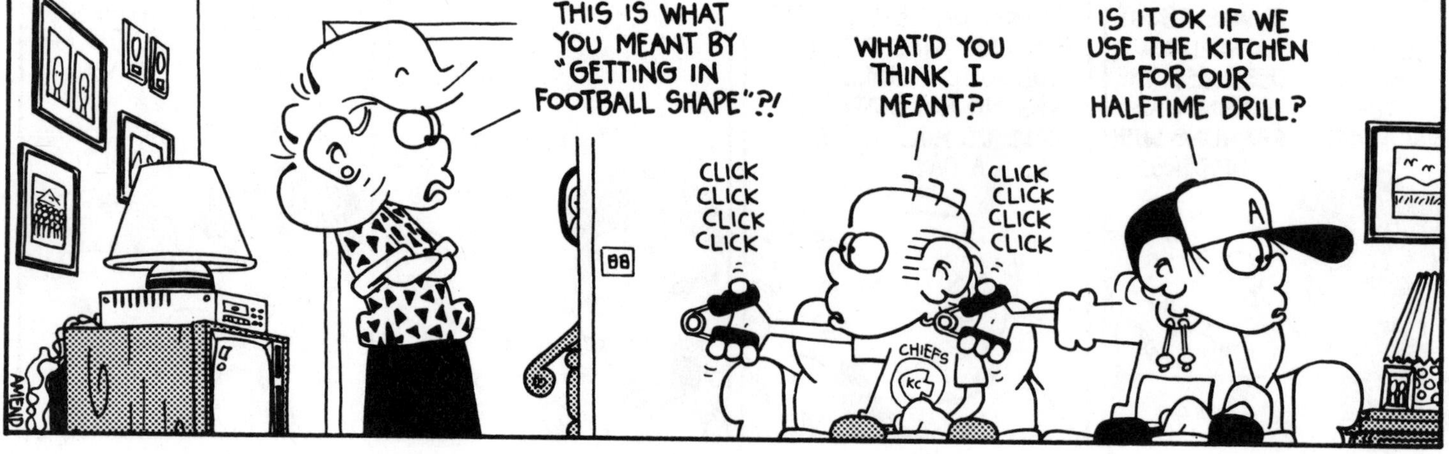
THIS IS WHAT YOU MEANT BY "GETTING IN FOOTBALL SHAPE"?!
WHAT'D YOU THINK I MEANT?
IS IT OK IF WE USE THE KITCHEN FOR OUR HALFTIME DRILL?
CLICK CLICK CLICK CLICK
CLICK CLICK CLICK CLICK
CHIEFS
KC
AMEND

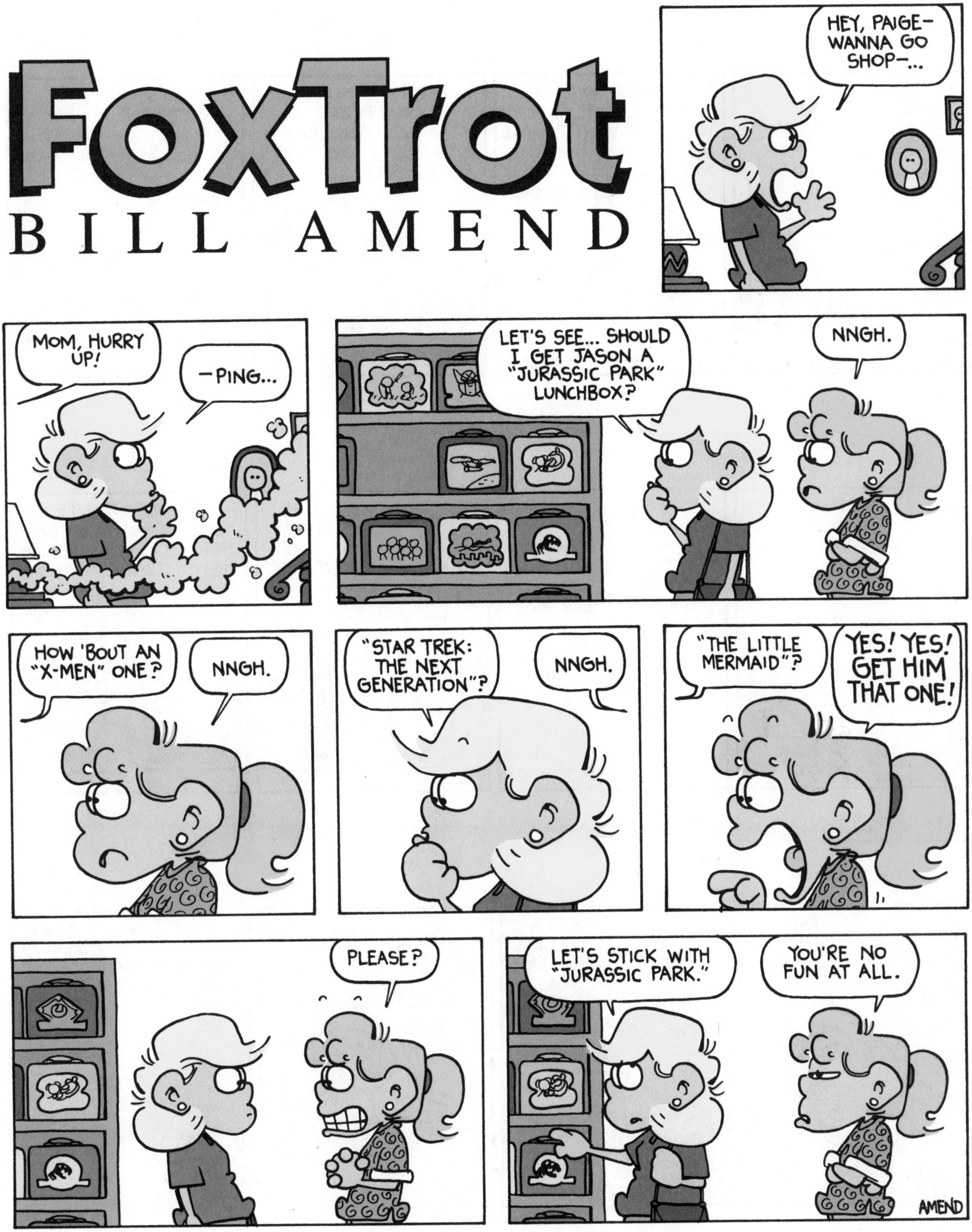
FoxTrot
BILL AMEND
HEY, PAIGE— WANNA GO SHOP—...
MOM, HURRY UP!
—PING...
LET'S SEE... SHOULD I GET JASON A "JURASSIC PARK" LUNCHBOX?
NNGH.
HOW 'BOUT AN "X-MEN" ONE?
NNGH.
"STAR TREK: THE NEXT GENERATION"?
NNGH.
"THE LITTLE MERMAID"?
YES! YES! GET HIM THAT ONE!
PLEASE?
LET'S STICK WITH "JURASSIC PARK."
YOU'RE NO FUN AT ALL.
AMEND

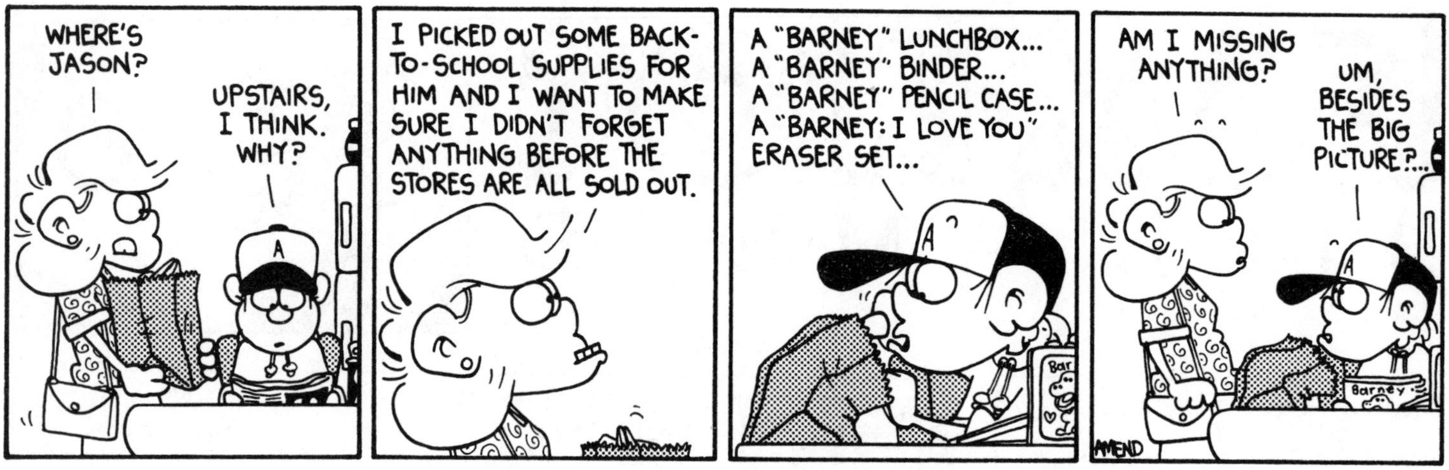
WHERE'S JASON?
UPSTAIRS, I THINK. WHY?
I PICKED OUT SOME BACK-TO-SCHOOL SUPPLIES FOR HIM AND I WANT TO MAKE SURE I DIDN'T FORGET ANYTHING BEFORE THE STORES ARE ALL SOLD OUT.
A "BARNEY" LUNCHBOX... A "BARNEY" BINDER... A "BARNEY" PENCIL CASE... A "BARNEY: I LOVE YOU" ERASER SET...
AM I MISSING ANYTHING?
UM, BESIDES THE BIG PICTURE?...
AMEND

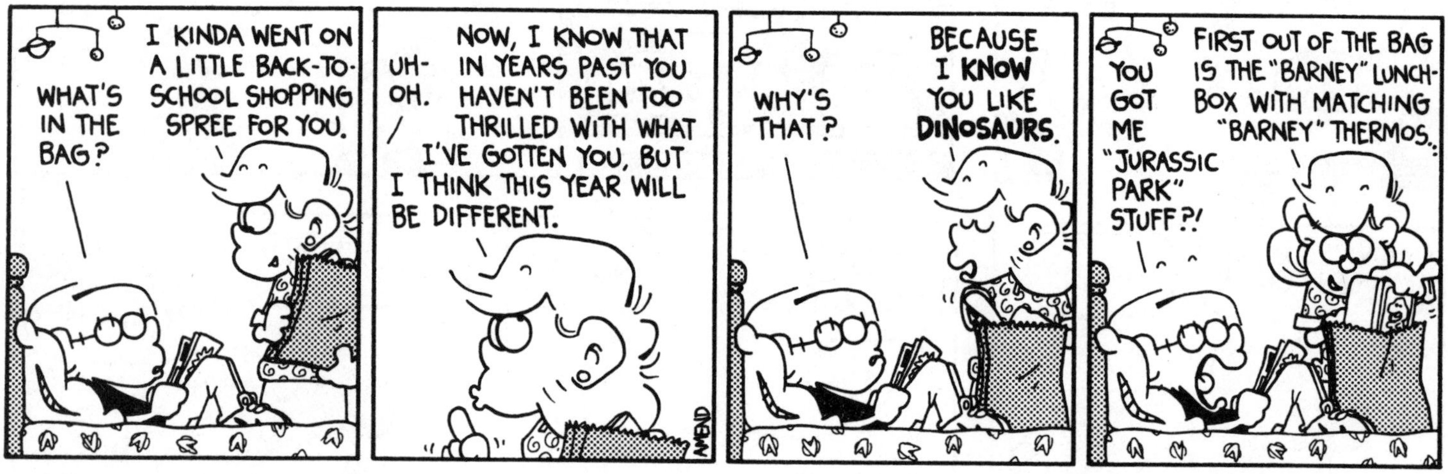
WHAT'S IN THE BAG?
I KINDA WENT ON A LITTLE BACK-TO-SCHOOL SHOPPING SPREE FOR YOU.
UH-OH.
NOW, I KNOW THAT IN YEARS PAST YOU HAVEN'T BEEN TOO THRILLED WITH WHAT I'VE GOTTEN YOU, BUT I THINK THIS YEAR WILL BE DIFFERENT.
AMEND
WHY'S THAT?
BECAUSE I **KNOW** YOU LIKE **DINOSAURS**.
YOU GOT ME "JURASSIC PARK" STUFF?!
FIRST OUT OF THE BAG IS THE "BARNEY" LUNCHBOX WITH MATCHING "BARNEY" THERMOS...

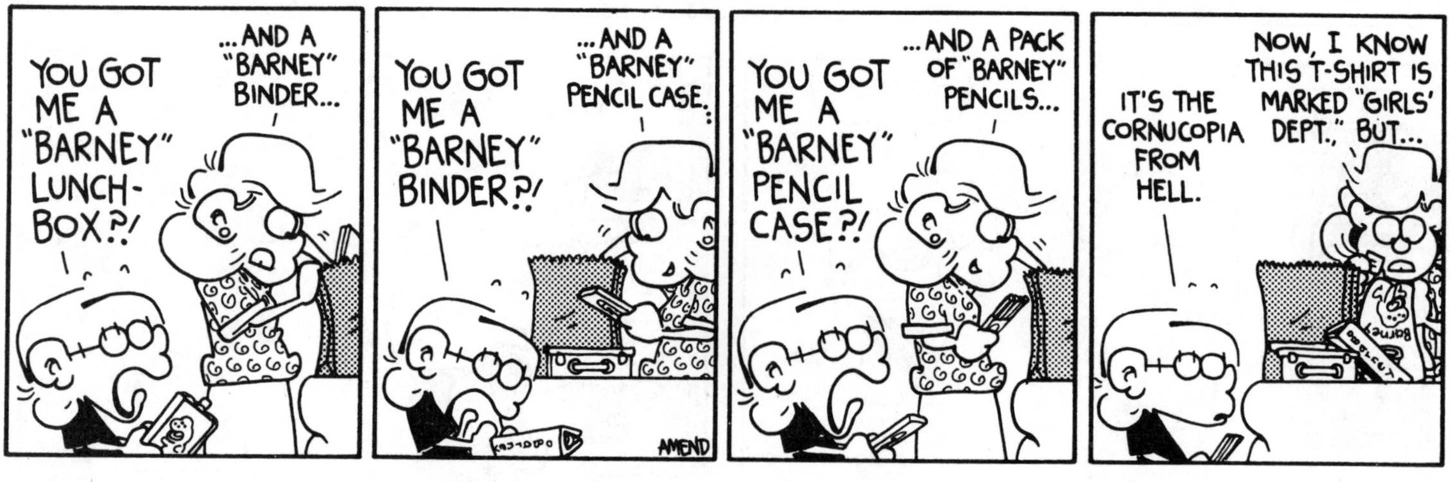
YOU GOT ME A "BARNEY" LUNCH-BOX?!
...AND A "BARNEY" BINDER...
YOU GOT ME A "BARNEY" BINDER?!
...AND A "BARNEY" PENCIL CASE...
AMEND
YOU GOT ME A "BARNEY" PENCIL CASE?!
...AND A PACK OF "BARNEY" PENCILS...
IT'S THE CORNUCOPIA FROM HELL.
NOW, I KNOW THIS T-SHIRT IS MARKED "GIRLS' DEPT.," BUT...

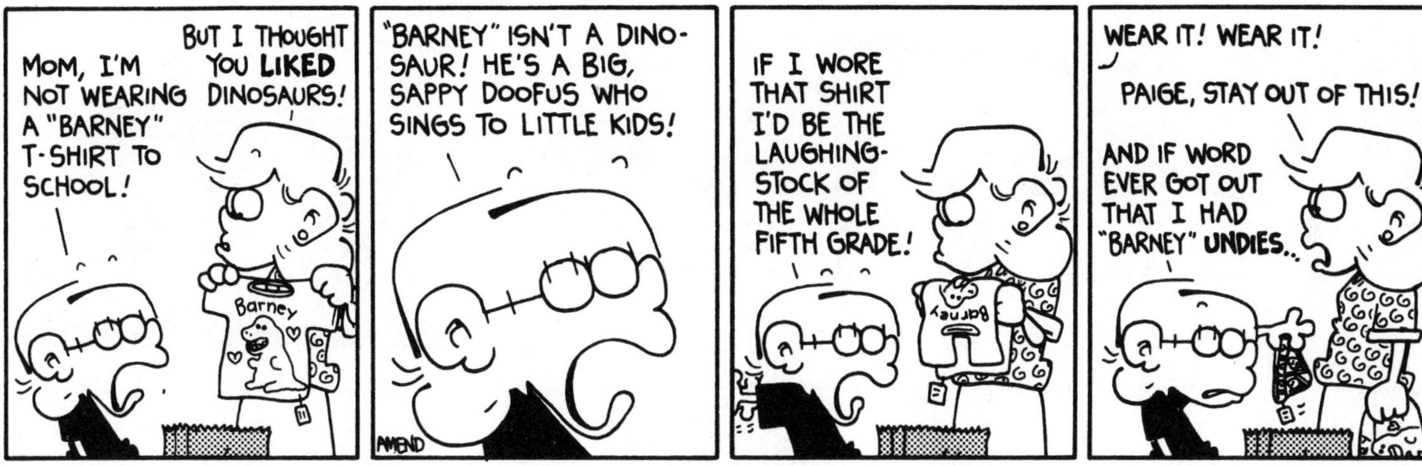
MOM, I'M NOT WEARING A "BARNEY" T-SHIRT TO SCHOOL!
BUT I THOUGHT YOU **LIKED** DINOSAURS!
Barney
"BARNEY" ISN'T A DINOSAUR! HE'S A BIG, SAPPY DOOFUS WHO SINGS TO LITTLE KIDS!
AMEND
IF I WORE THAT SHIRT I'D BE THE LAUGHING-STOCK OF THE WHOLE FIFTH GRADE!
WEAR IT! WEAR IT!
PAIGE, STAY OUT OF THIS!
AND IF WORD EVER GOT OUT THAT I HAD "BARNEY" **UNDIES**...

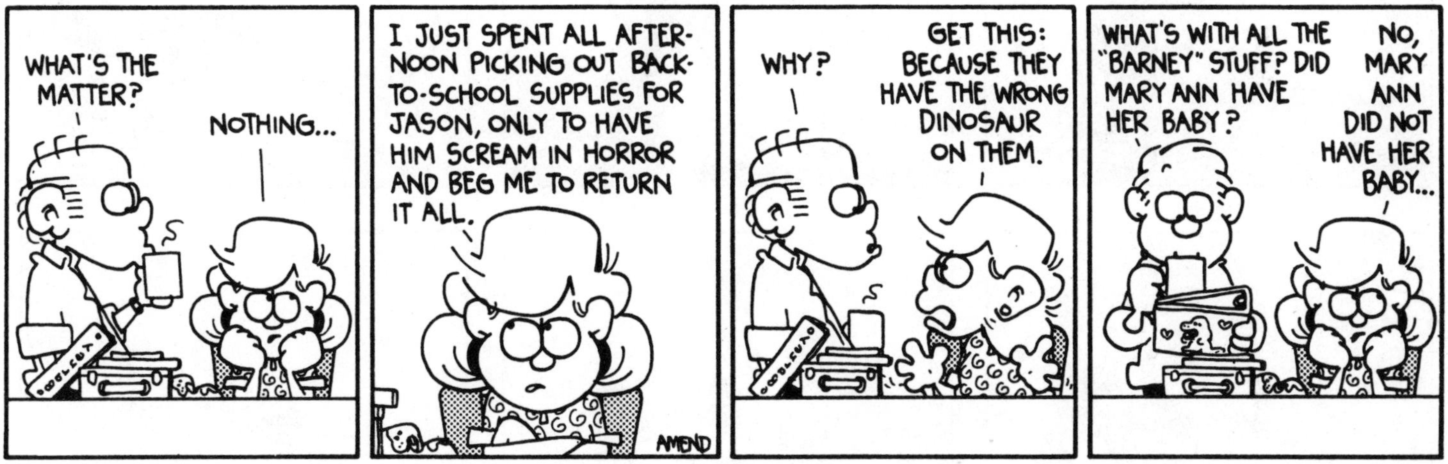
WHAT'S THE MATTER?
NOTHING...
I JUST SPENT ALL AFTERNOON PICKING OUT BACK-TO-SCHOOL SUPPLIES FOR JASON, ONLY TO HAVE HIM SCREAM IN HORROR AND BEG ME TO RETURN IT ALL.
AMEND
WHY?
GET THIS: BECAUSE THEY HAVE THE WRONG DINOSAUR ON THEM.
WHAT'S WITH ALL THE "BARNEY" STUFF? DID MARY ANN HAVE HER BABY?
NO, MARY ANN DID NOT HAVE HER BABY...

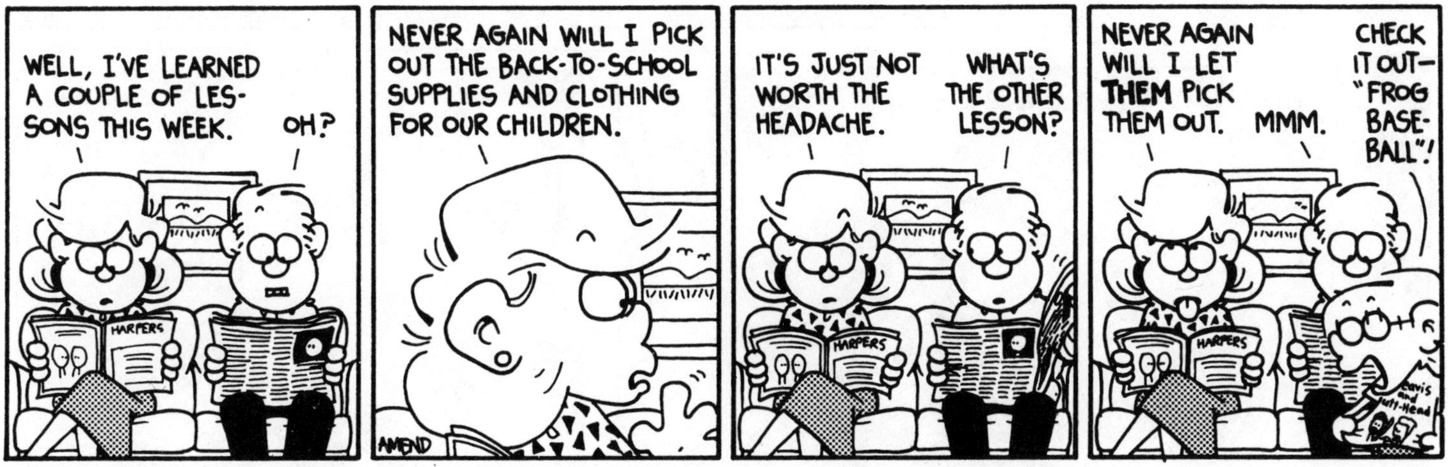
WELL, I'VE LEARNED A COUPLE OF LESSONS THIS WEEK.
OH?
HARPERS
NEVER AGAIN WILL I PICK OUT THE BACK-TO-SCHOOL SUPPLIES AND CLOTHING FOR OUR CHILDREN.
AMEND
IT'S JUST NOT WORTH THE HEADACHE.
WHAT'S THE OTHER LESSON?
NEVER AGAIN WILL I LET **THEM** PICK THEM OUT.
MMM.
CHECK IT OUT— "FROG BASEBALL"!

FoxTrot
BILL AMEND

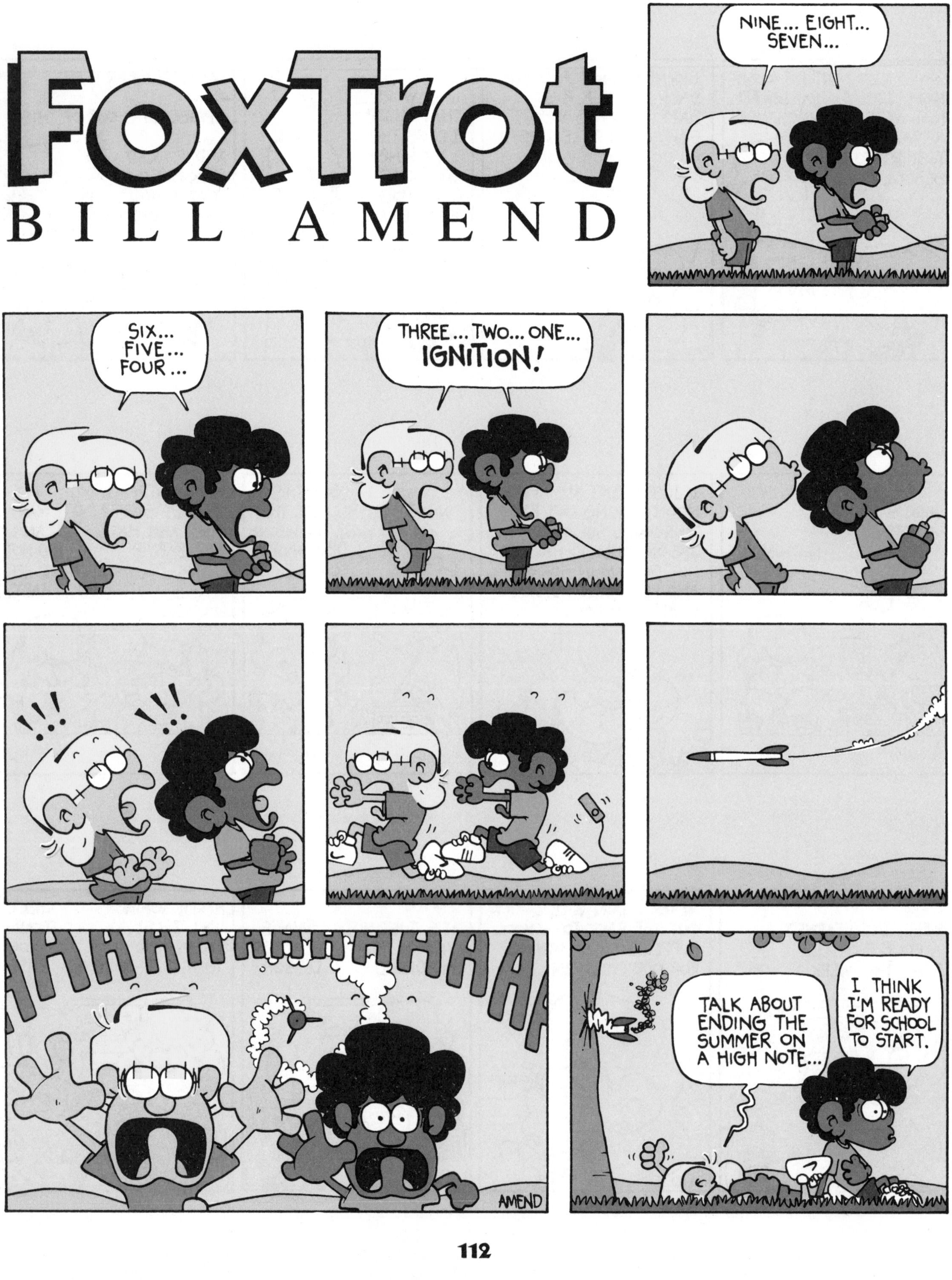
NINE... EIGHT... SEVEN...
SIX... FIVE... FOUR...
THREE... TWO... ONE... IGNITION!
AAAAAAAAAAAAAAA
AMEND
TALK ABOUT ENDING THE SUMMER ON A HIGH NOTE...
I THINK I'M READY FOR SCHOOL TO START.

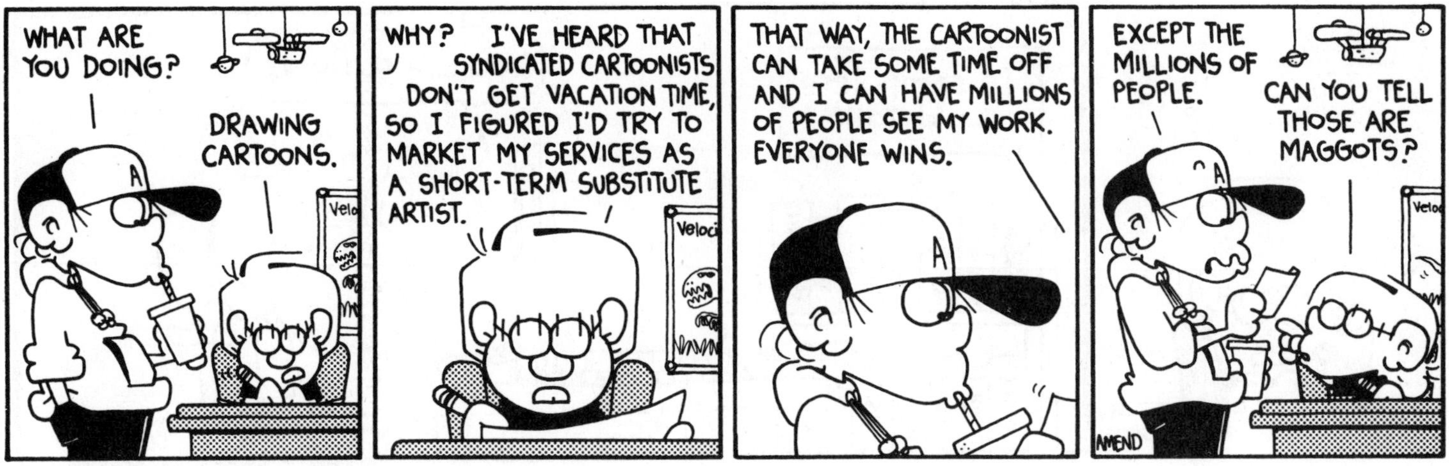
WHAT ARE YOU DOING?
DRAWING CARTOONS.
WHY? I'VE HEARD THAT SYNDICATED CARTOONISTS DON'T GET VACATION TIME, SO I FIGURED I'D TRY TO MARKET MY SERVICES AS A SHORT-TERM SUBSTITUTE ARTIST.
THAT WAY, THE CARTOONIST CAN TAKE SOME TIME OFF AND I CAN HAVE MILLIONS OF PEOPLE SEE MY WORK. EVERYONE WINS.
EXCEPT THE MILLIONS OF PEOPLE.
CAN YOU TELL THOSE ARE MAGGOTS?
AMEND

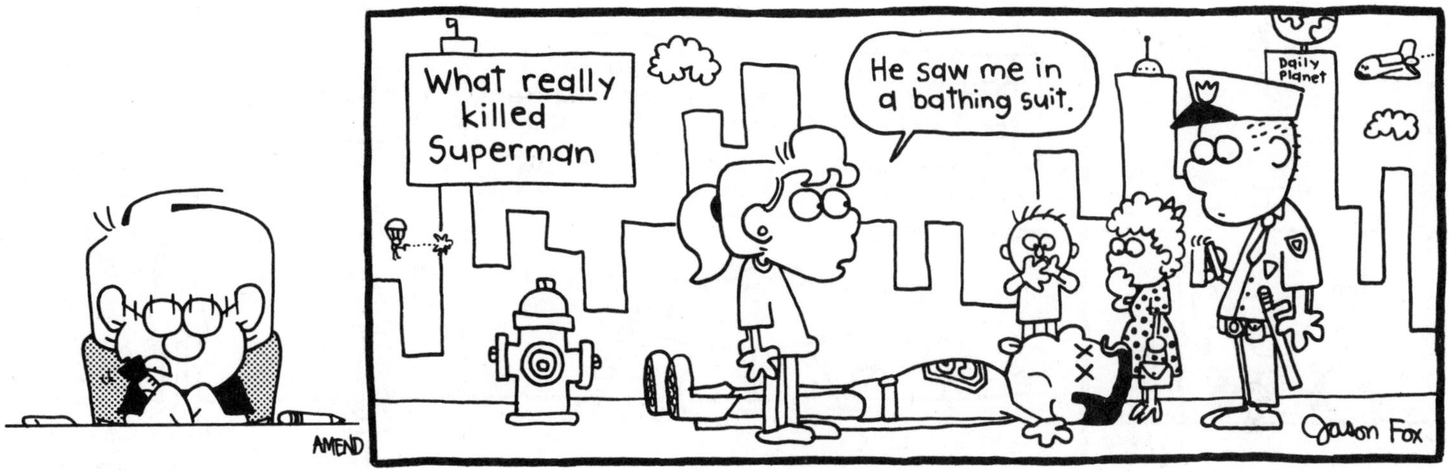
AMEND
What really killed Superman
He saw me in a bathing suit.
Daily Planet
Jason Fox

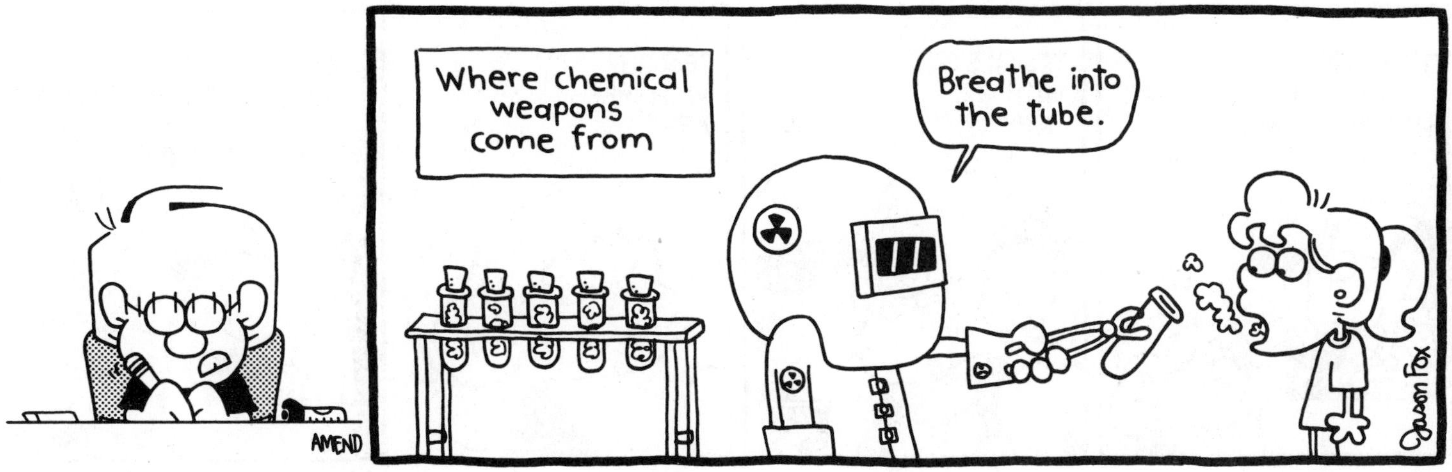
AMEND
Where chemical weapons come from
Breathe into the tube.
Jason Fox

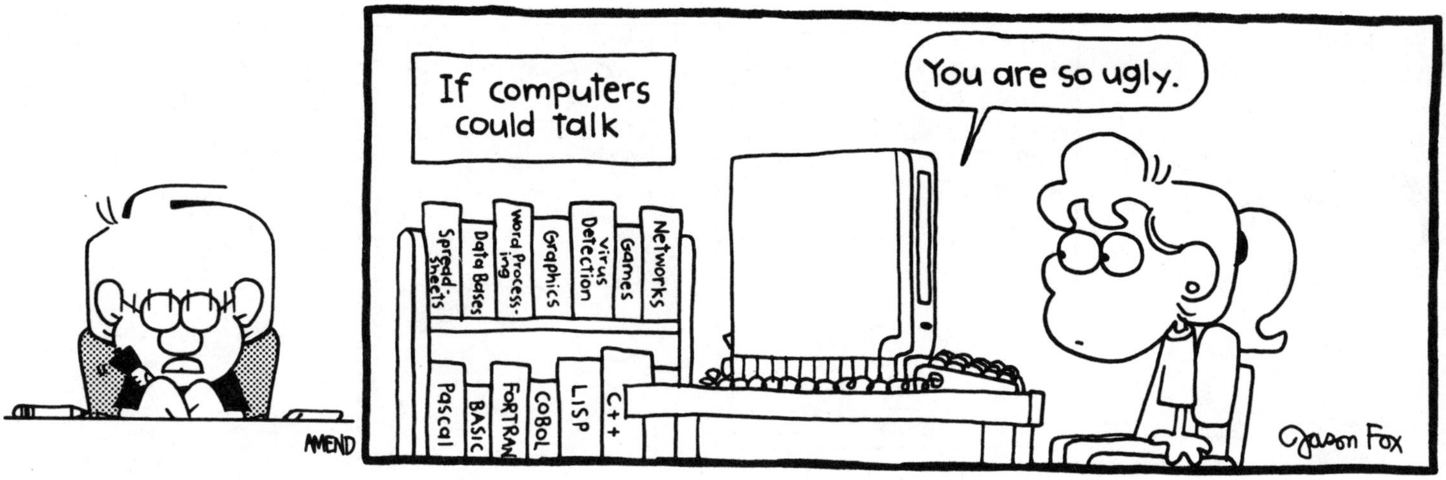
AMEND
If computers could talk
You are so ugly.
Spread-sheets
Data Bases
Word Process-ing
Graphics
Virus Detection
Games
Networks
Pascal
BASIC
FORTRAN
COBOL
LISP
C++
Jason Fox

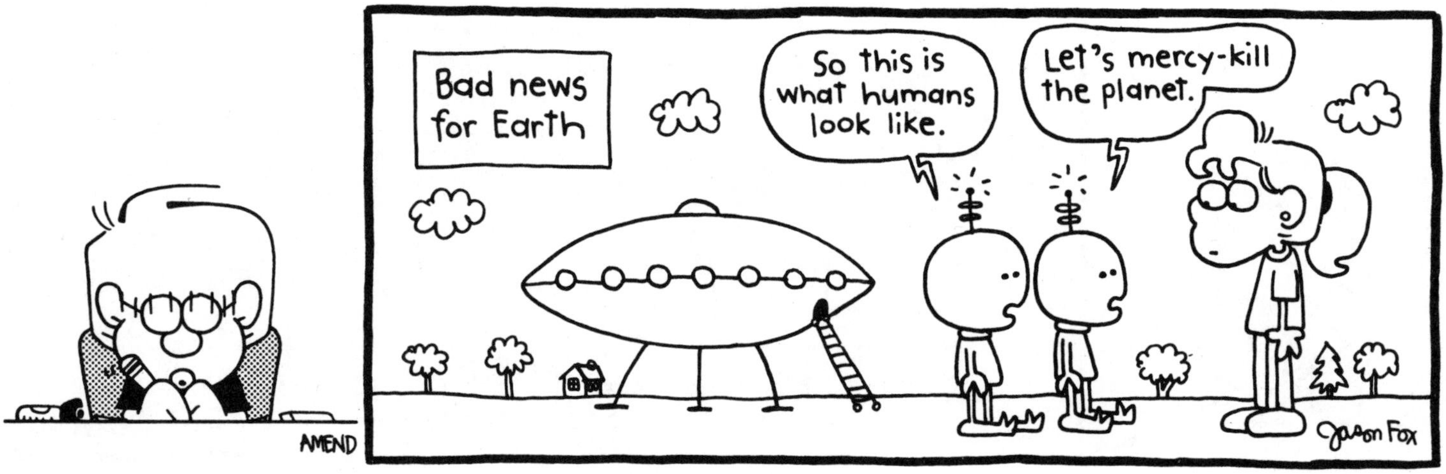
AMEND
Bad news for Earth
So this is what humans look like.
Let's mercy-kill the planet.
Jason Fox

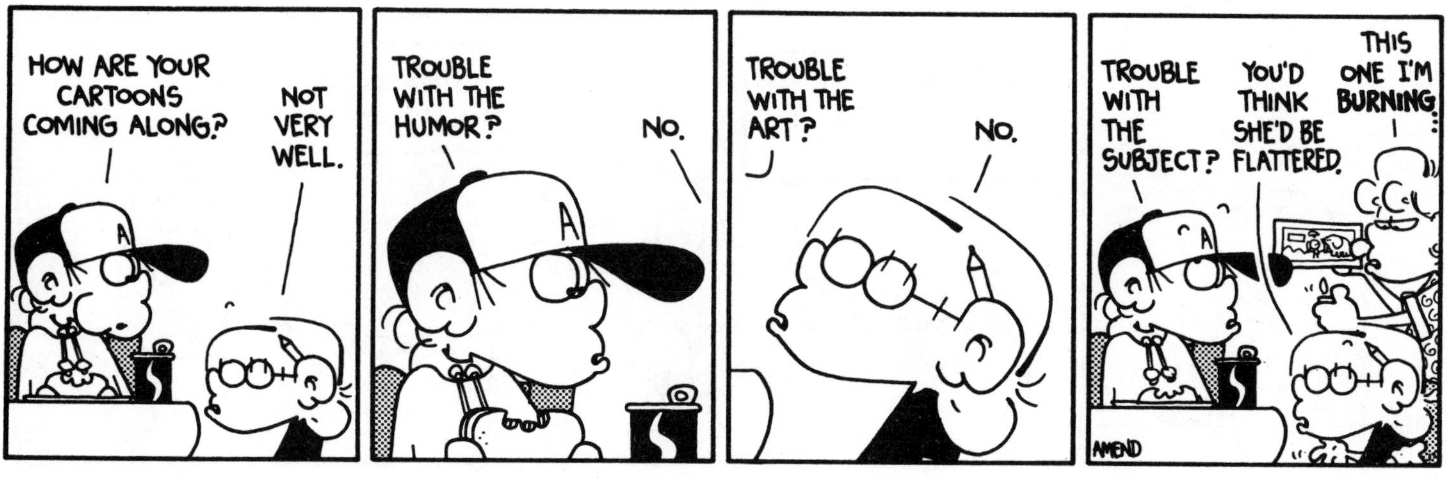
HOW ARE YOUR CARTOONS COMING ALONG?
NOT VERY WELL.
TROUBLE WITH THE HUMOR?
NO.
TROUBLE WITH THE ART?
NO.
TROUBLE WITH THE SUBJECT?
YOU'D THINK SHE'D BE FLATTERED.
THIS ONE I'M BURNING.
AMEND

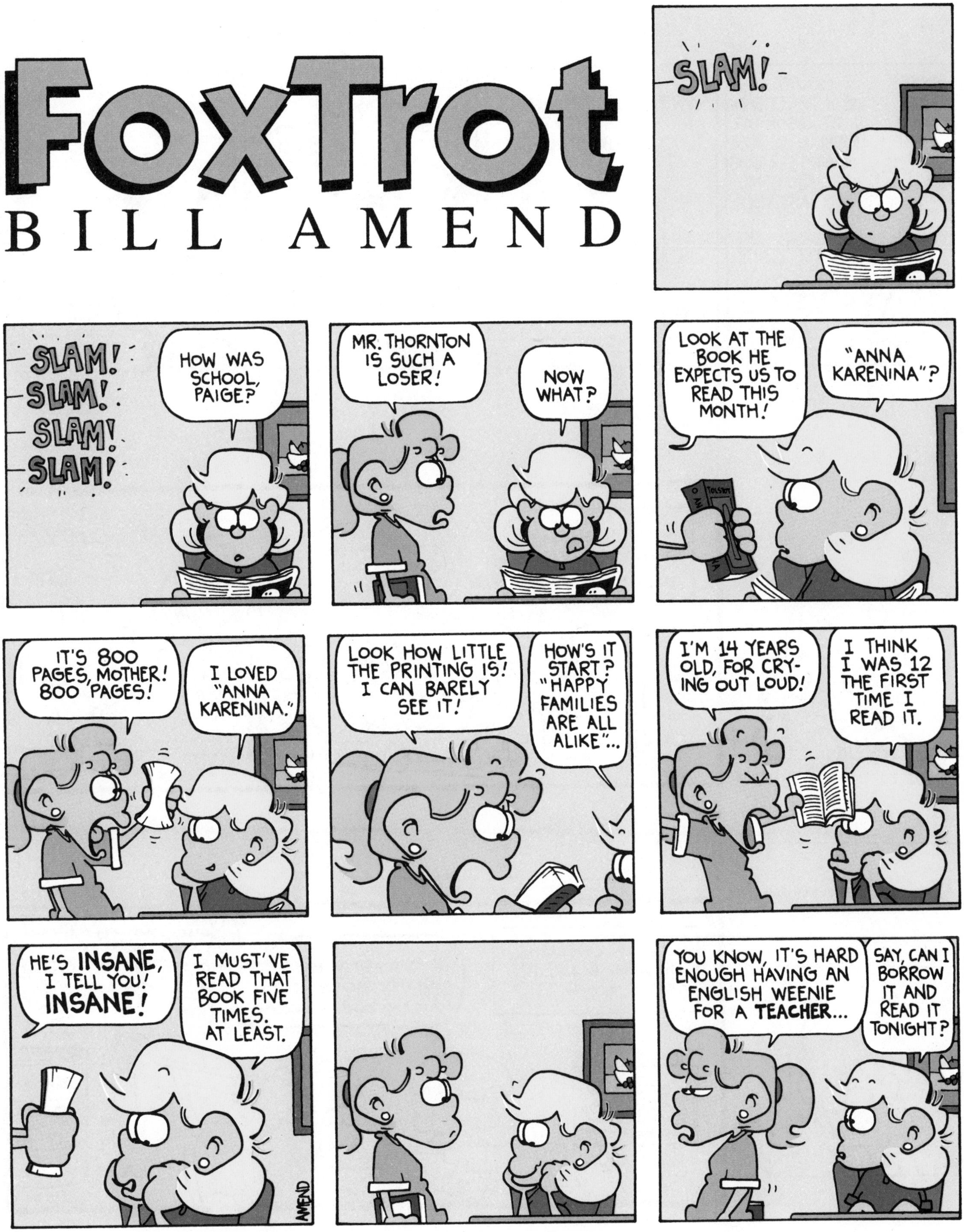
FoxTrot
BILL AMEND
SLAM!
SLAM!
SLAM!
SLAM!
SLAM!
HOW WAS SCHOOL, PAIGE?
MR. THORNTON IS SUCH A LOSER!
NOW WHAT?
LOOK AT THE BOOK HE EXPECTS US TO READ THIS MONTH!
"ANNA KARENINA"?
IT'S 800 PAGES, MOTHER! 800 PAGES!
I LOVED "ANNA KARENINA."
LOOK HOW LITTLE THE PRINTING IS! I CAN BARELY SEE IT!
HOW'S IT START? "HAPPY FAMILIES ARE ALL ALIKE"...
I'M 14 YEARS OLD, FOR CRYING OUT LOUD!
I THINK I WAS 12 THE FIRST TIME I READ IT.
HE'S **INSANE**, I TELL YOU! **INSANE**!
I MUST'VE READ THAT BOOK FIVE TIMES. AT LEAST.
AMEND
YOU KNOW, IT'S HARD ENOUGH HAVING AN ENGLISH WEENIE FOR A **TEACHER**...
SAY, CAN I BORROW IT AND READ IT TONIGHT?

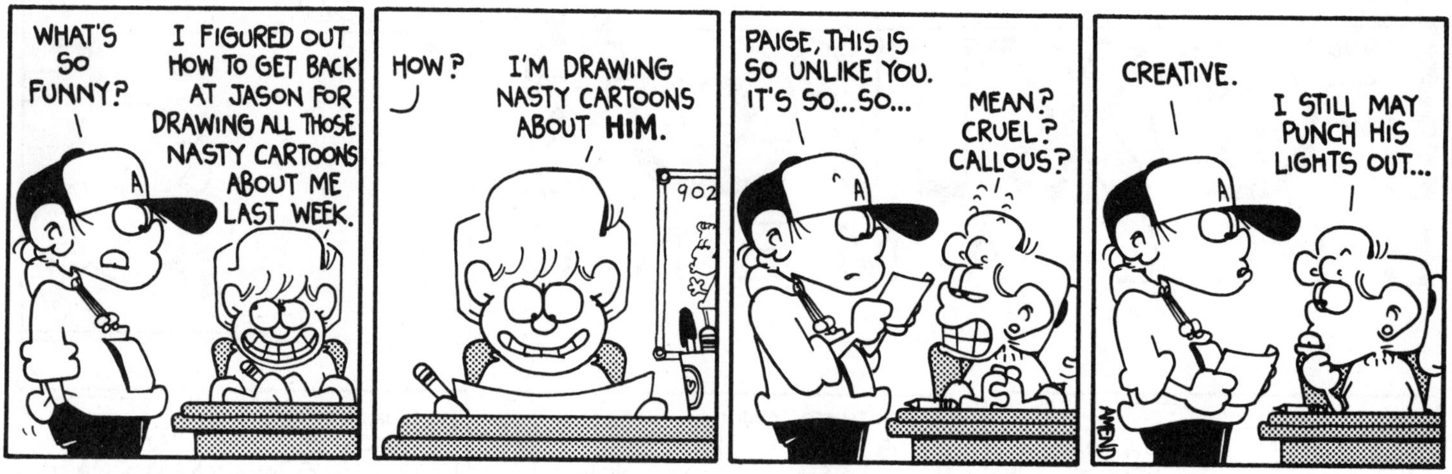
WHAT'S SO FUNNY?
I FIGURED OUT HOW TO GET BACK AT JASON FOR DRAWING ALL THOSE NASTY CARTOONS ABOUT ME LAST WEEK.
HOW?
I'M DRAWING NASTY CARTOONS ABOUT HIM.
PAIGE, THIS IS SO UNLIKE YOU. IT'S SO...SO...
MEAN? CRUEL? CALLOUS?
CREATIVE.
I STILL MAY PUNCH HIS LIGHTS OUT...
AMEND

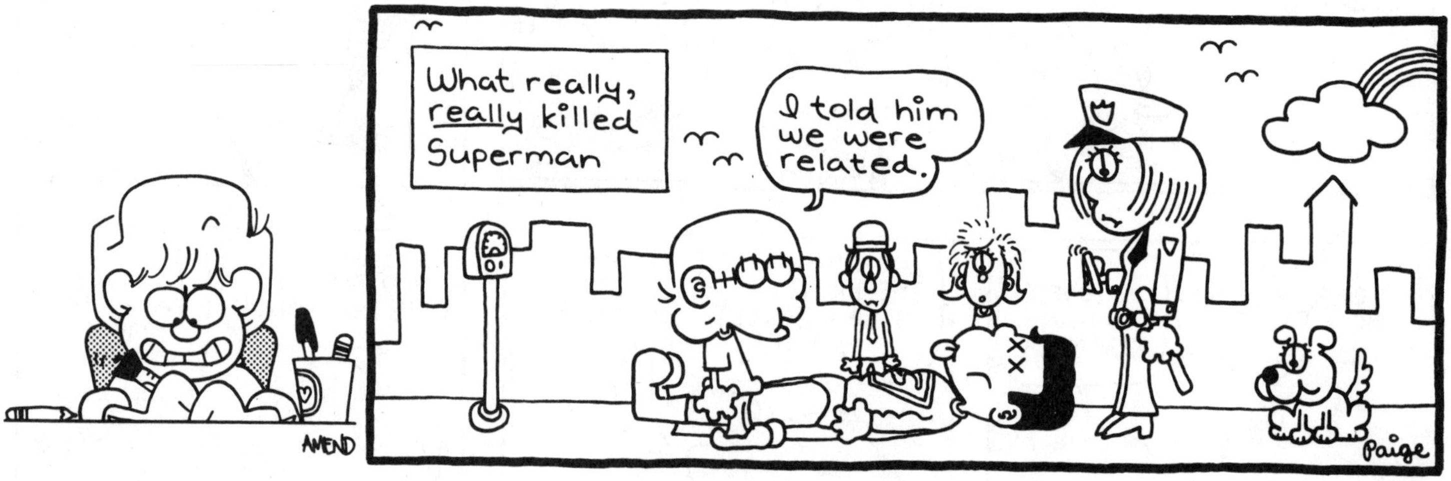
What really, really killed Superman
I told him we were related.
Paige
AMEND

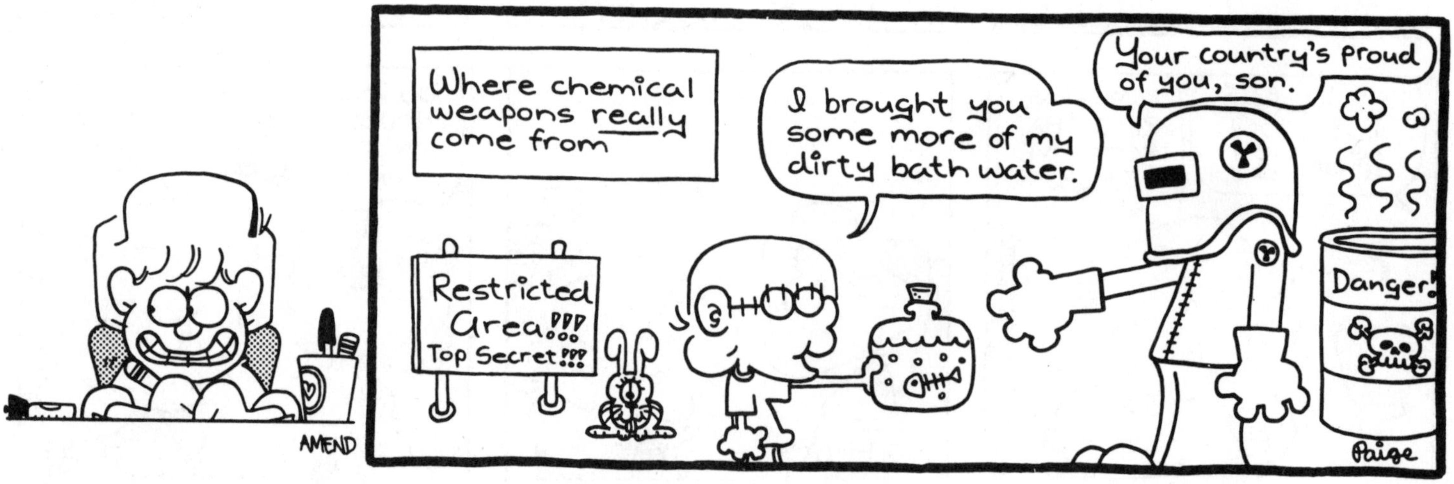
Where chemical weapons really come from
I brought you some more of my dirty bath water.
Your country's proud of you, son.
Restricted Area!!!
Top Secret!!!
Danger!
Paige
AMEND

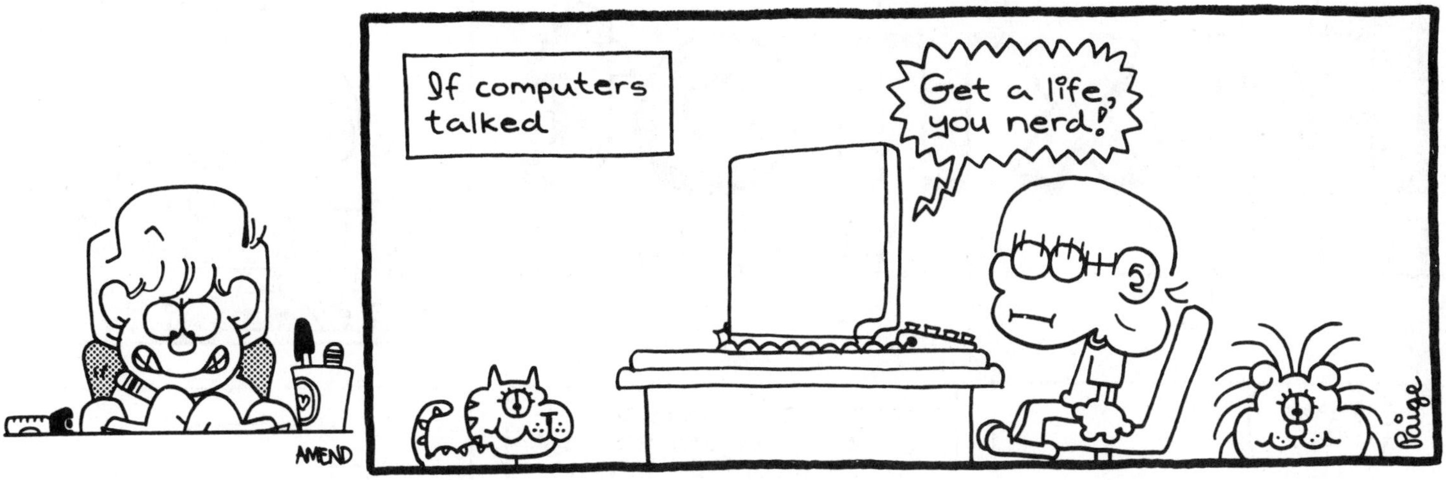
If computers talked
Get a life, you nerd!
AMEND
Paige

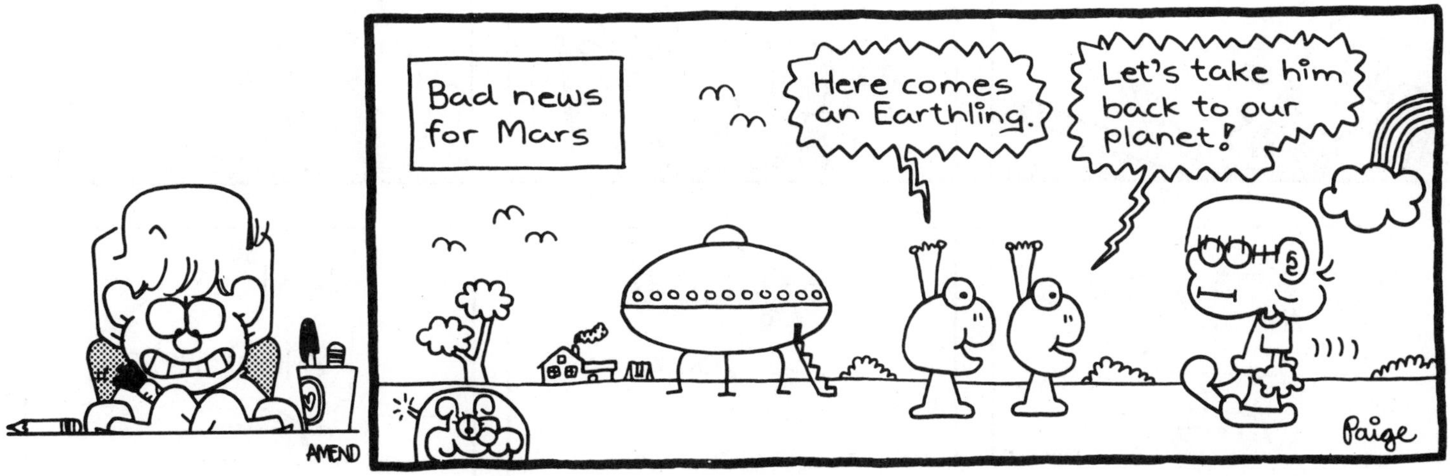
Bad news for Mars
Here comes an Earthling.
Let's take him back to our planet!
AMEND
Paige

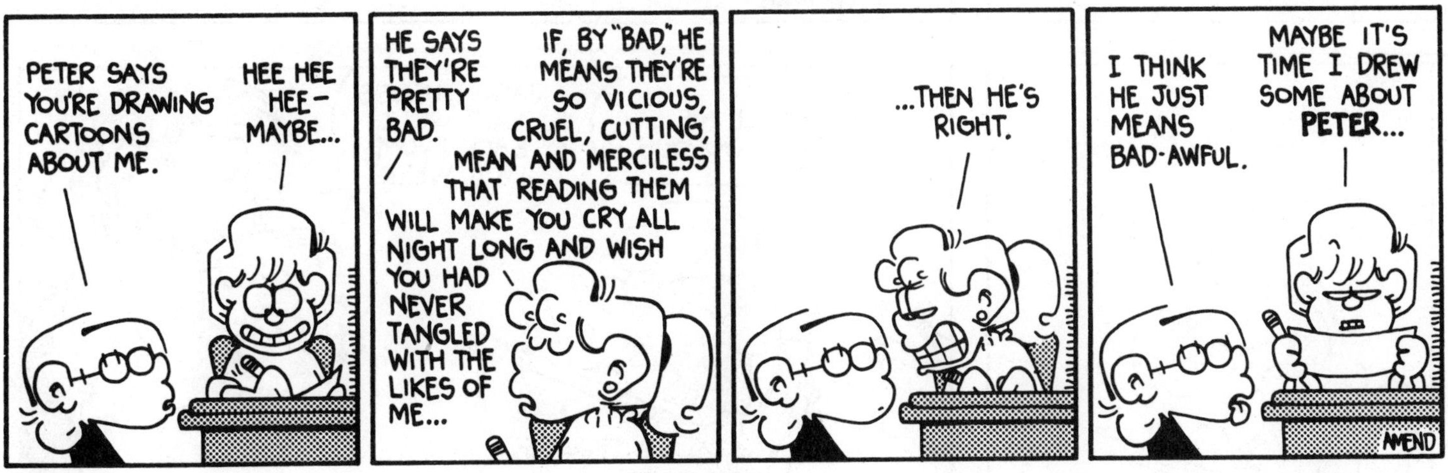
PETER SAYS YOU'RE DRAWING CARTOONS ABOUT ME.
HEE HEE HEE– MAYBE...
HE SAYS THEY'RE PRETTY BAD.
IF, BY "BAD," HE MEANS THEY'RE SO VICIOUS, CRUEL, CUTTING, MEAN AND MERCILESS THAT READING THEM WILL MAKE YOU CRY ALL NIGHT LONG AND WISH YOU HAD NEVER TANGLED WITH THE LIKES OF ME...
...THEN HE'S RIGHT.
I THINK HE JUST MEANS BAD-AWFUL.
MAYBE IT'S TIME I DREW SOME ABOUT PETER...
AMEND

FoxTrot
BILL AMEND
WORD PROBLEMS. NOTHING BUT WORD PROBLEMS.
THANK YOU.
Farmer Bob's vegetable garden is 20 feet wide by 30 feet long. Calculate its area in square footage.
20
A
30
y
20
A
y=f(x)=20
0
30
x
A = ∫_0^30 f(x) dx
= ∫_0^30 20 dx
= 20x |_0^30
= [(20)(30) - (20)(0)]
= 600 ft²
CALL ME MR. RIGOROUS.
JASON, HERE'S YOUR QUIZ BACK FROM LAST WEEK.
AMEND

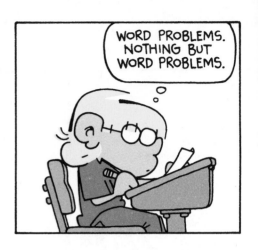

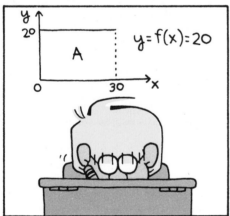

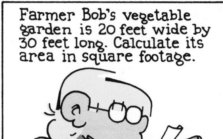

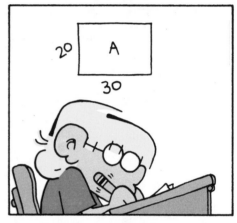

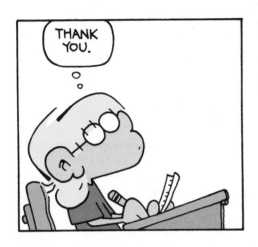

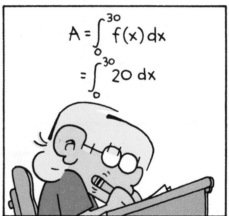

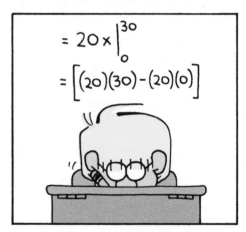

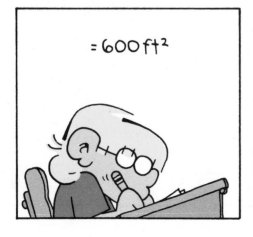

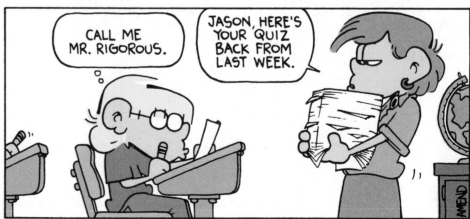

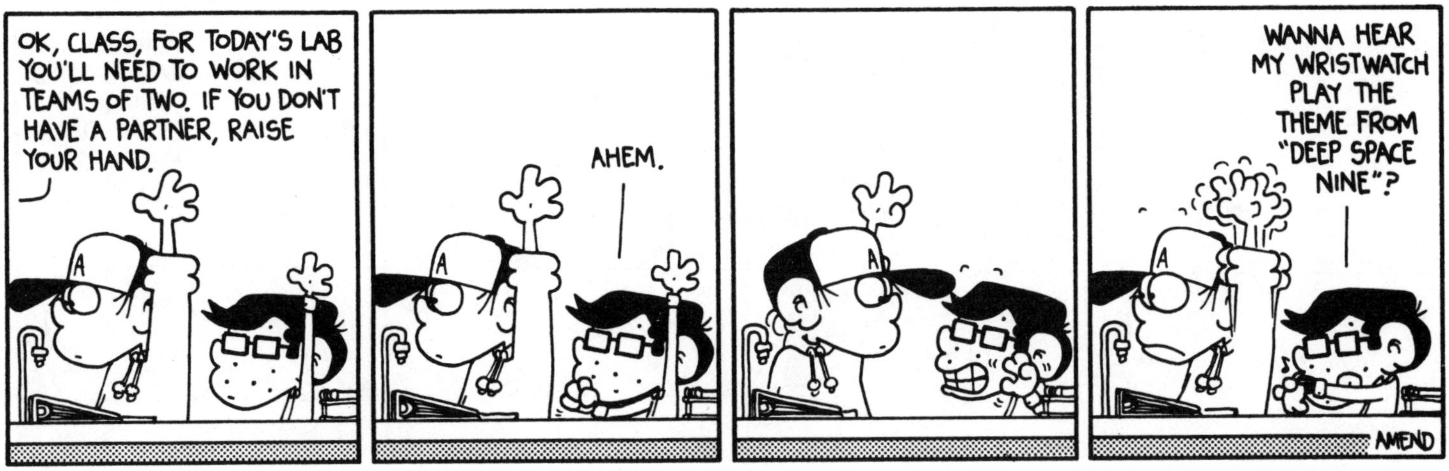
OK, CLASS, FOR TODAY'S LAB YOU'LL NEED TO WORK IN TEAMS OF TWO. IF YOU DON'T HAVE A PARTNER, RAISE YOUR HAND.
AHEM.
WANNA HEAR MY WRISTWATCH PLAY THE THEME FROM "DEEP SPACE NINE"?
AMEND

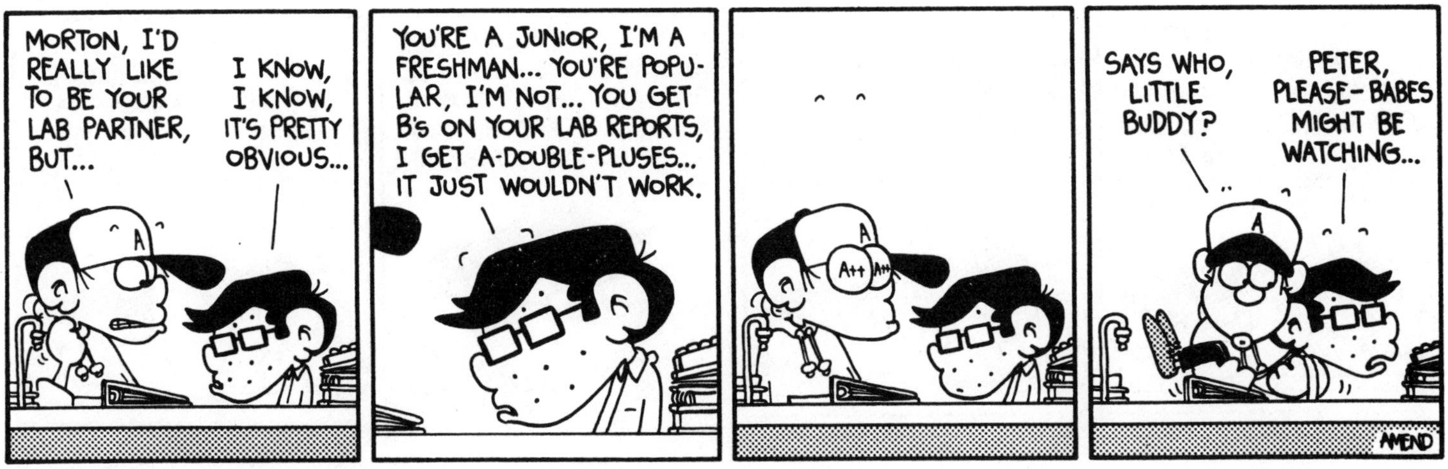
MORTON, I'D REALLY LIKE TO BE YOUR LAB PARTNER, BUT...
I KNOW, I KNOW, IT'S PRETTY OBVIOUS...
YOU'RE A JUNIOR, I'M A FRESHMAN... YOU'RE POPULAR, I'M NOT... YOU GET B'S ON YOUR LAB REPORTS, I GET A-DOUBLE-PLUSES... IT JUST WOULDN'T WORK.
A++ A++
SAYS WHO, LITTLE BUDDY?
PETER, PLEASE-BABES MIGHT BE WATCHING...
AMEND

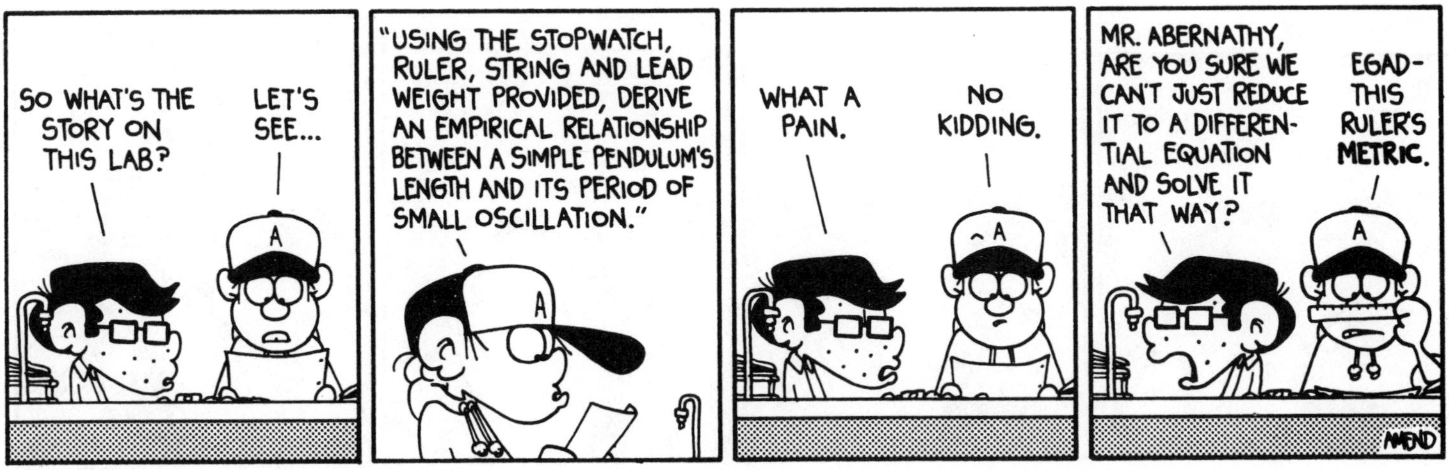
SO WHAT'S THE STORY ON THIS LAB?
LET'S SEE...
"USING THE STOPWATCH, RULER, STRING AND LEAD WEIGHT PROVIDED, DERIVE AN EMPIRICAL RELATIONSHIP BETWEEN A SIMPLE PENDULUM'S LENGTH AND ITS PERIOD OF SMALL OSCILLATION."
WHAT A PAIN.
NO KIDDING.
MR. ABERNATHY, ARE YOU SURE WE CAN'T JUST REDUCE IT TO A DIFFERENTIAL EQUATION AND SOLVE IT THAT WAY?
EGAD- THIS RULER'S **METRIC**.
AMEND

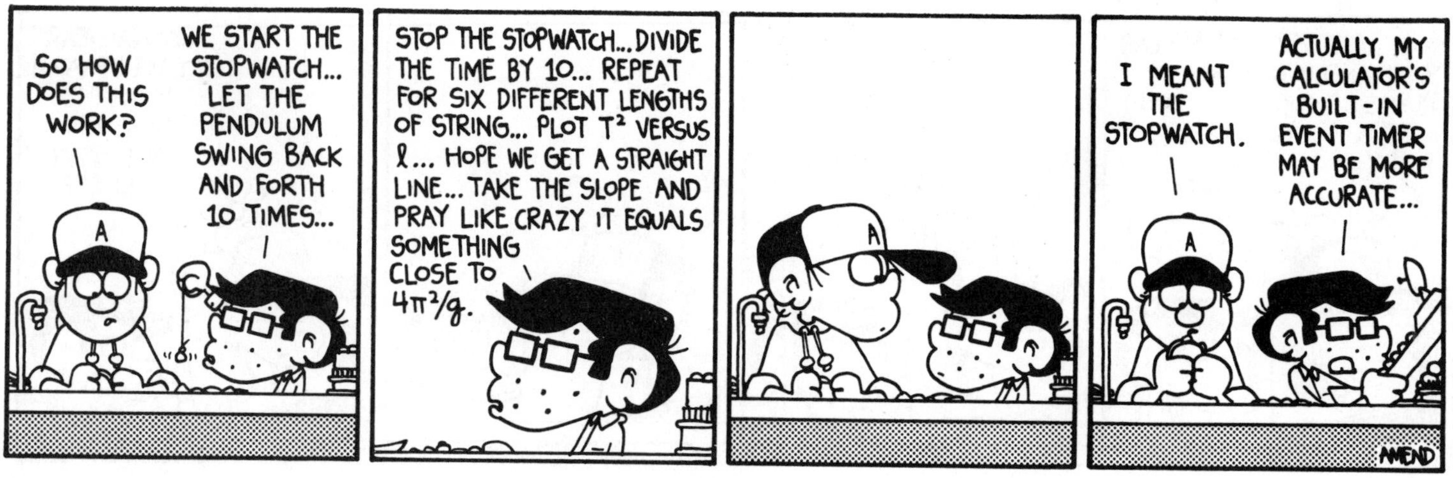
SO HOW DOES THIS WORK?
WE START THE STOPWATCH... LET THE PENDULUM SWING BACK AND FORTH 10 TIMES...
STOP THE STOPWATCH... DIVIDE THE TIME BY 10... REPEAT FOR SIX DIFFERENT LENGTHS OF STRING... PLOT T^2 VERSUS ℓ... HOPE WE GET A STRAIGHT LINE... TAKE THE SLOPE AND PRAY LIKE CRAZY IT EQUALS SOMETHING CLOSE TO $4\pi^2/g$.
I MEANT THE STOPWATCH.
ACTUALLY, MY CALCULATOR'S BUILT-IN EVENT TIMER MAY BE MORE ACCURATE...

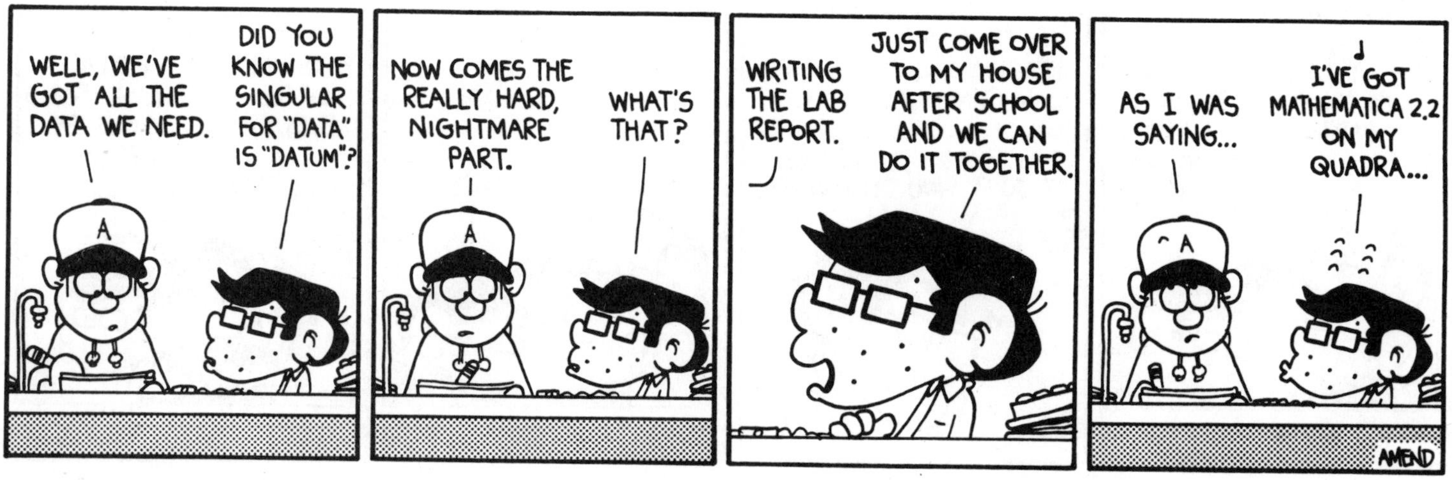
WELL, WE'VE GOT ALL THE DATA WE NEED.
DID YOU KNOW THE SINGULAR FOR "DATA" IS "DATUM"?
NOW COMES THE REALLY HARD, NIGHTMARE PART.
WHAT'S THAT?
WRITING THE LAB REPORT.
JUST COME OVER TO MY HOUSE AFTER SCHOOL AND WE CAN DO IT TOGETHER.
AS I WAS SAYING...
I'VE GOT MATHEMATICA 2.2 ON MY QUADRA...

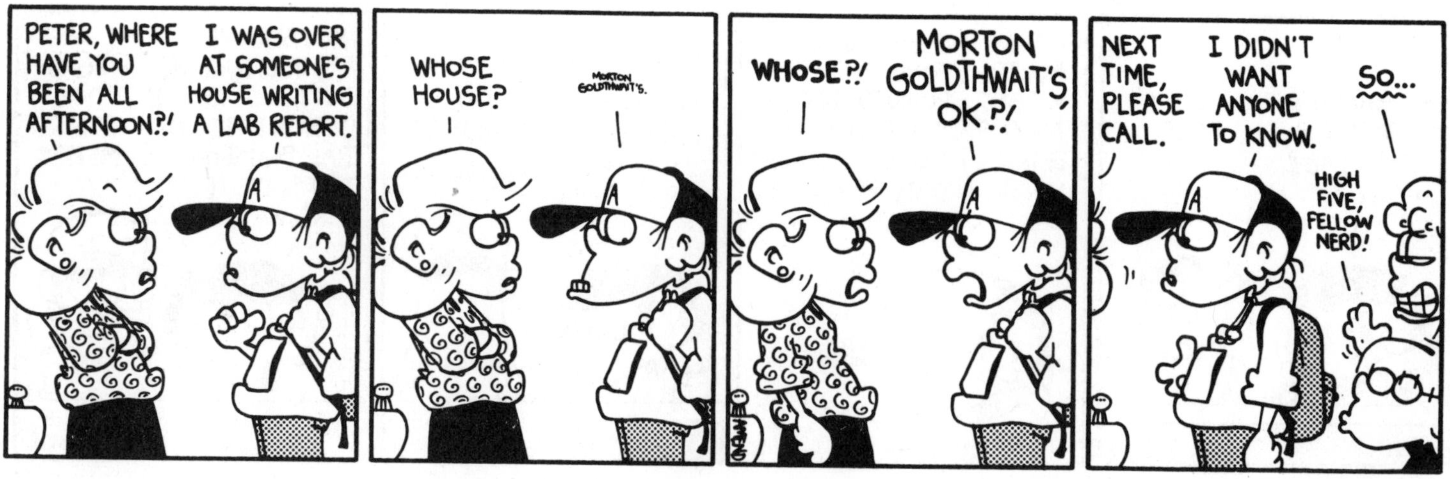
PETER, WHERE HAVE YOU BEEN ALL AFTERNOON?!
I WAS OVER AT SOMEONE'S HOUSE WRITING A LAB REPORT.
WHOSE HOUSE?
MORTON GOLDTHWAIT'S.
WHOSE?!
MORTON GOLDTHWAIT'S, OK?!
NEXT TIME, PLEASE CALL.
I DIDN'T WANT ANYONE TO KNOW.
SO...
HIGH FIVE, FELLOW NERD!

FoxTrot

BILL AMEND

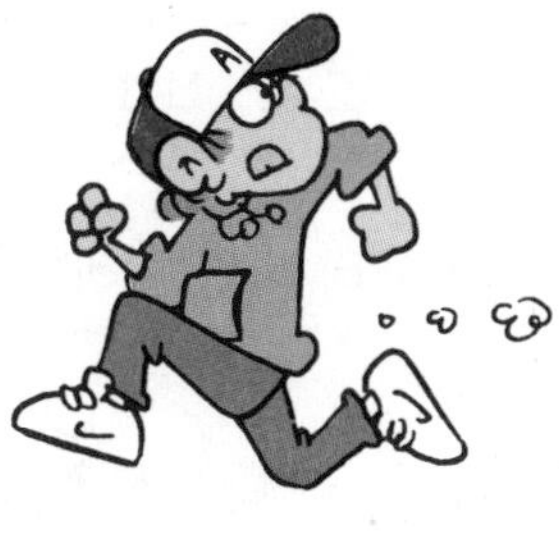

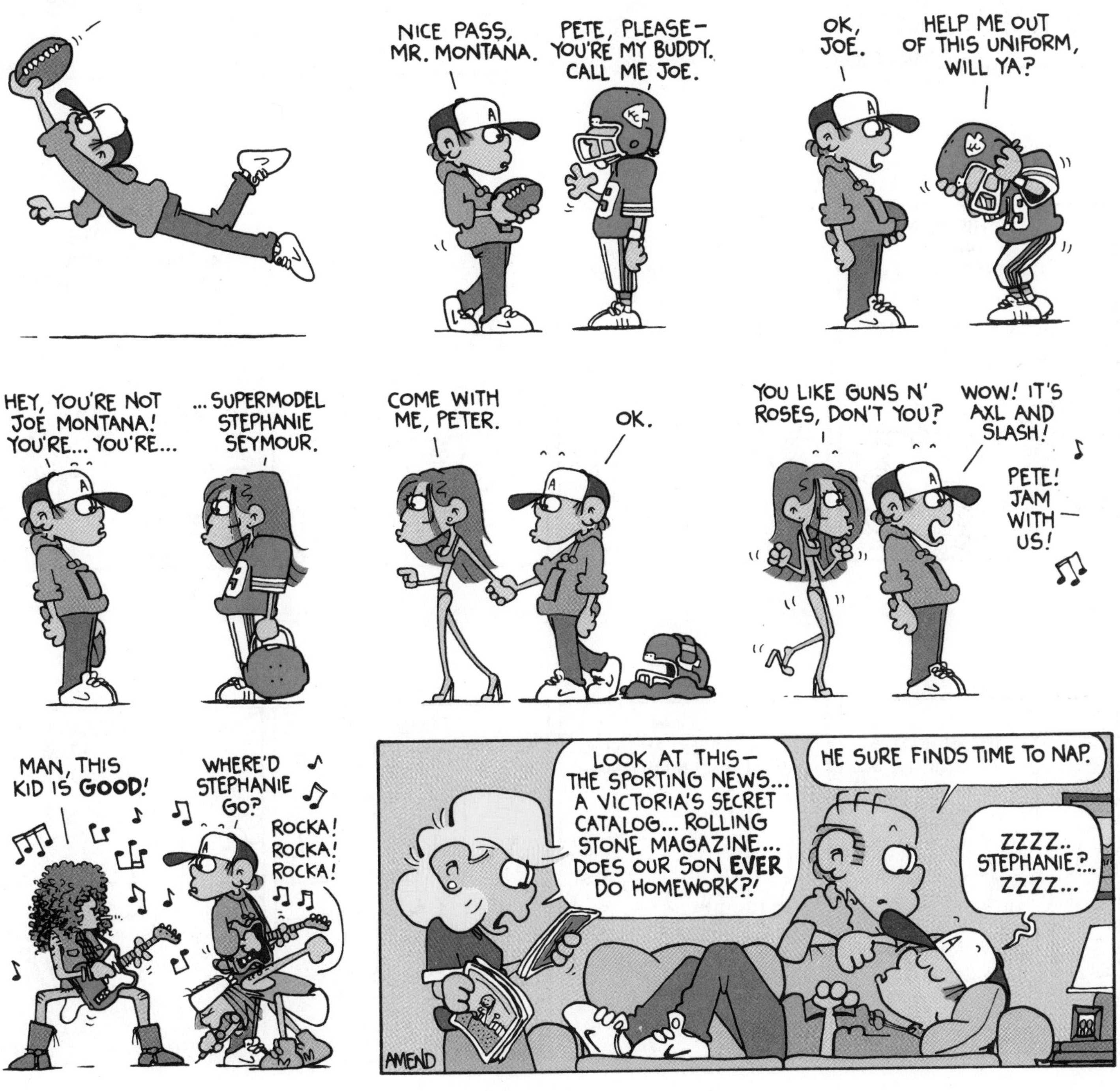

NICE PASS, MR. MONTANA.
PETE, PLEASE— YOU'RE MY BUDDY. CALL ME JOE.
OK, JOE.
HELP ME OUT OF THIS UNIFORM, WILL YA?
HEY, YOU'RE NOT JOE MONTANA! YOU'RE... YOU'RE...
...SUPERMODEL STEPHANIE SEYMOUR.
COME WITH ME, PETER.
OK.
YOU LIKE GUNS N' ROSES, DON'T YOU?
WOW! IT'S AXL AND SLASH!
PETE! JAM WITH US!
MAN, THIS KID IS **GOOD**!
WHERE'D STEPHANIE GO?
ROCKA! ROCKA! ROCKA!
LOOK AT THIS— THE SPORTING NEWS... A VICTORIA'S SECRET CATALOG... ROLLING STONE MAGAZINE... DOES OUR SON **EVER** DO HOMEWORK?!
HE SURE FINDS TIME TO NAP.
ZZZZ.. STEPHANIE?... ZZZZ...
AMEND

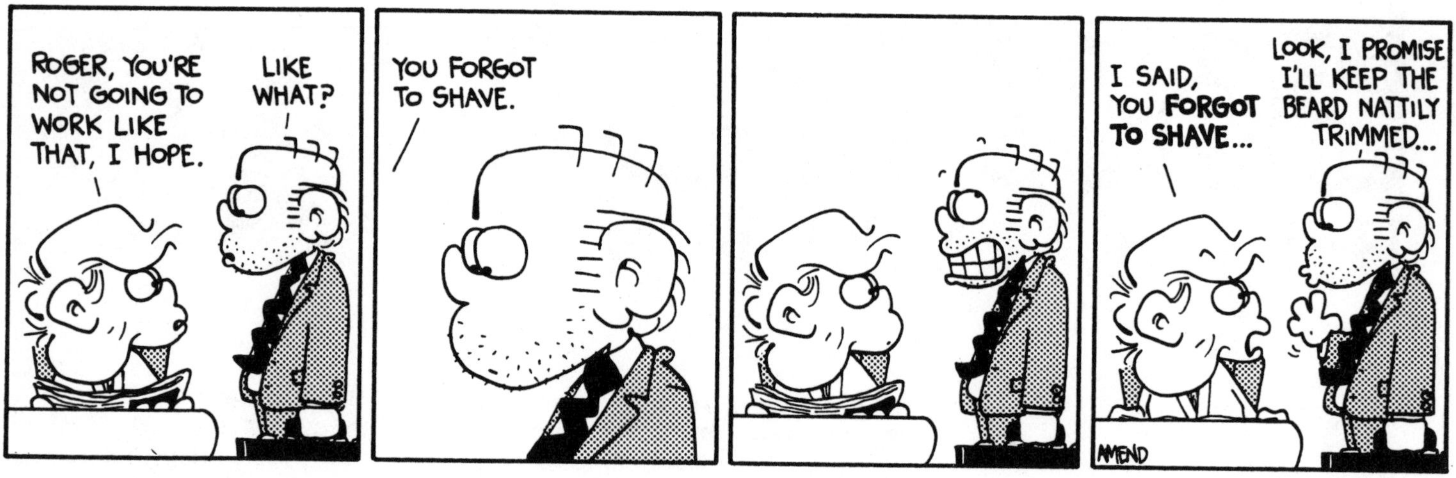
ROGER, YOU'RE NOT GOING TO WORK LIKE THAT, I HOPE.
LIKE WHAT?
YOU FORGOT TO SHAVE.
I SAID, YOU **FORGOT TO SHAVE**...
LOOK, I PROMISE I'LL KEEP THE BEARD NATTILY TRIMMED...
AMEND

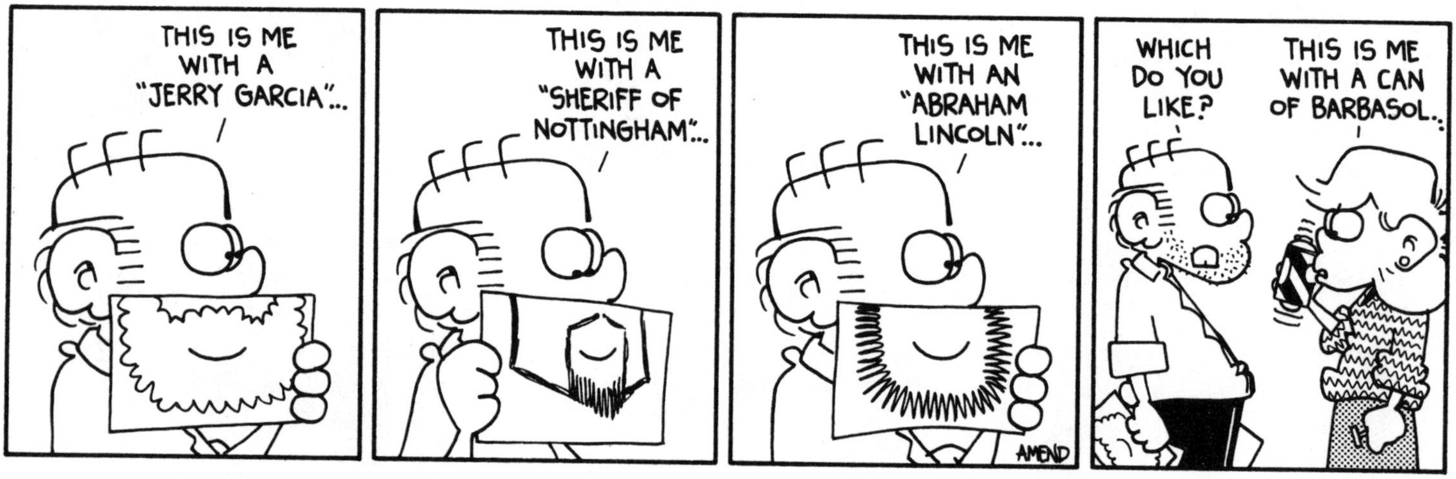
THIS IS ME WITH A "JERRY GARCIA"...
THIS IS ME WITH A "SHERIFF OF NOTTINGHAM"...
THIS IS ME WITH AN "ABRAHAM LINCOLN"...
AMEND
WHICH DO YOU LIKE?
THIS IS ME WITH A CAN OF BARBASOL.

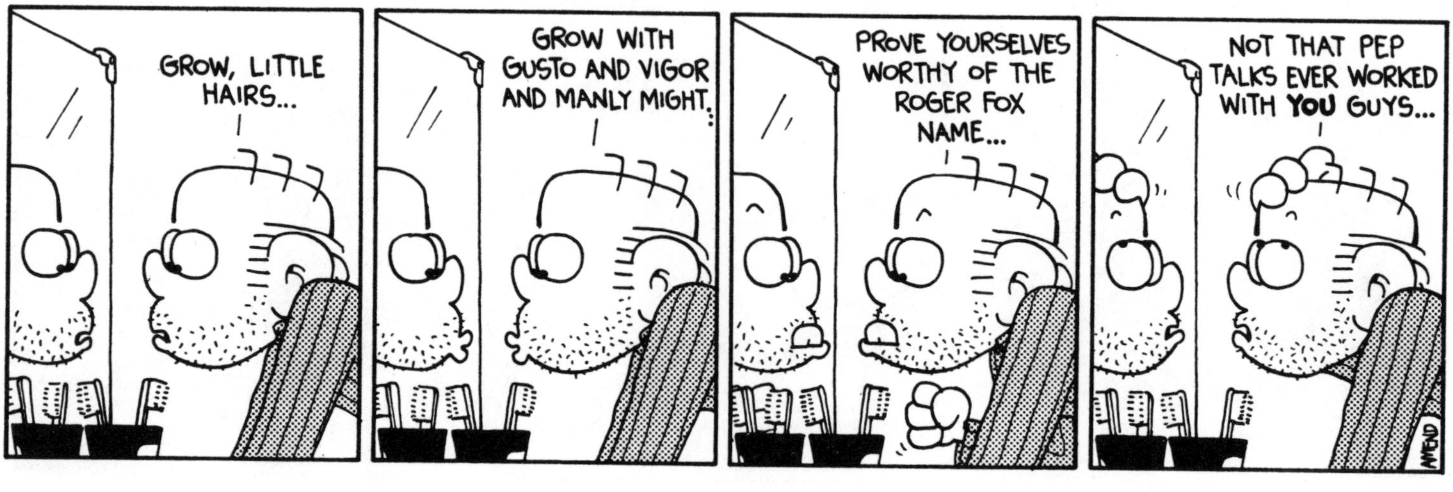
GROW, LITTLE HAIRS...
GROW WITH GUSTO AND VIGOR AND MANLY MIGHT.
PROVE YOURSELVES WORTHY OF THE ROGER FOX NAME...
NOT THAT PEP TALKS EVER WORKED WITH **YOU** GUYS...
AMEND

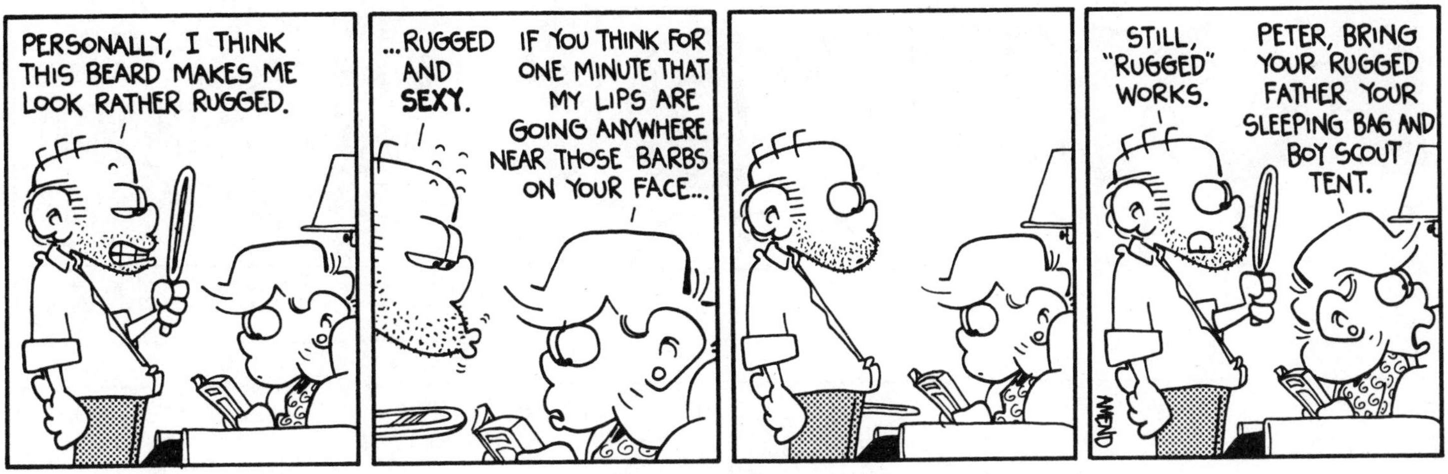
PERSONALLY, I THINK THIS BEARD MAKES ME LOOK RATHER RUGGED.
...RUGGED AND **SEXY**.
IF YOU THINK FOR ONE MINUTE THAT MY LIPS ARE GOING ANYWHERE NEAR THOSE BARBS ON YOUR FACE...
STILL, "RUGGED" WORKS.
PETER, BRING YOUR RUGGED FATHER YOUR SLEEPING BAG AND BOY SCOUT TENT.
AMEND

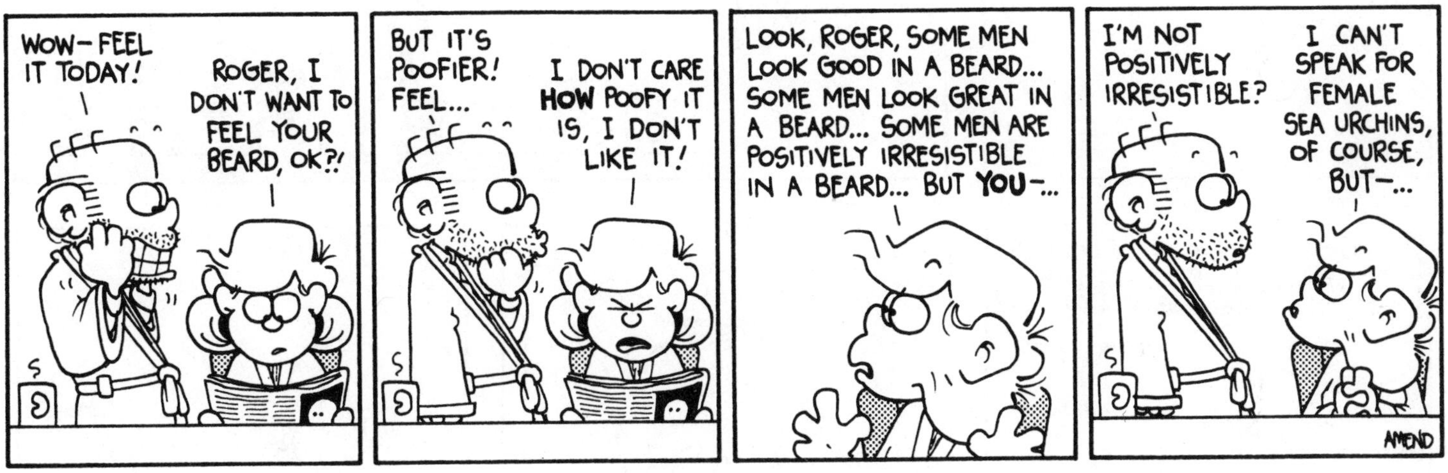
WOW- FEEL IT TODAY!
ROGER, I DON'T WANT TO FEEL YOUR BEARD, OK?!
BUT IT'S POOFIER! FEEL...
I DON'T CARE **HOW** POOFY IT IS, I DON'T LIKE IT!
LOOK, ROGER, SOME MEN LOOK GOOD IN A BEARD... SOME MEN LOOK GREAT IN A BEARD... SOME MEN ARE POSITIVELY IRRESISTIBLE IN A BEARD... BUT **YOU**-...
I'M NOT POSITIVELY IRRESISTIBLE?
I CAN'T SPEAK FOR FEMALE SEA URCHINS, OF COURSE, BUT-...
AMEND

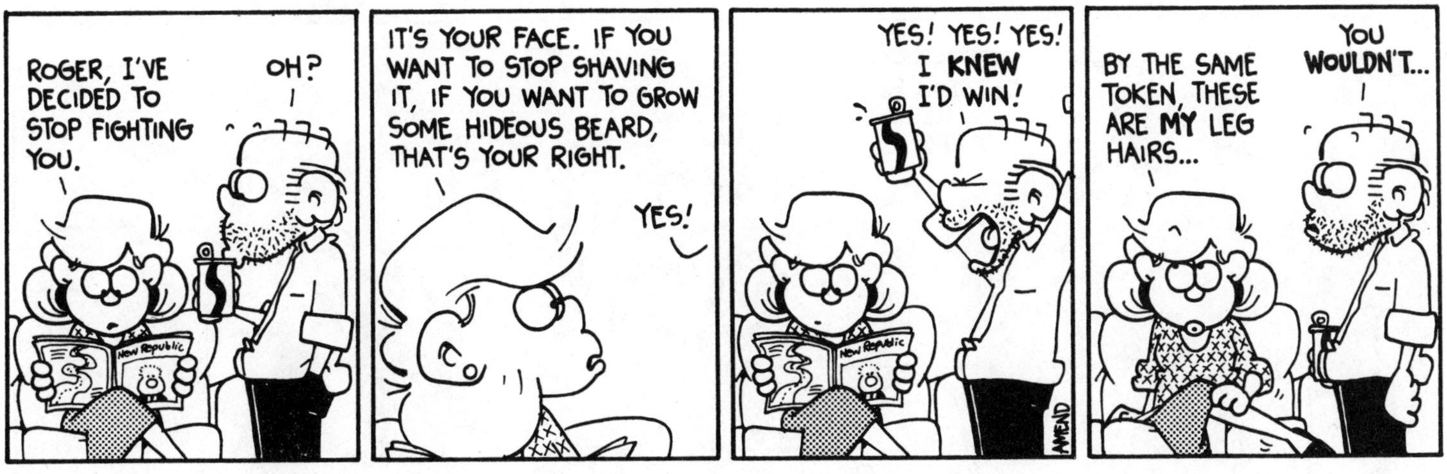
ROGER, I'VE DECIDED TO STOP FIGHTING YOU.
OH?
IT'S YOUR FACE. IF YOU WANT TO STOP SHAVING IT, IF YOU WANT TO GROW SOME HIDEOUS BEARD, THAT'S YOUR RIGHT.
YES!
YES! YES! YES! I **KNEW** I'D WIN!
AMEND
BY THE SAME TOKEN, THESE ARE **MY** LEG HAIRS...
YOU **WOULDN'T**...

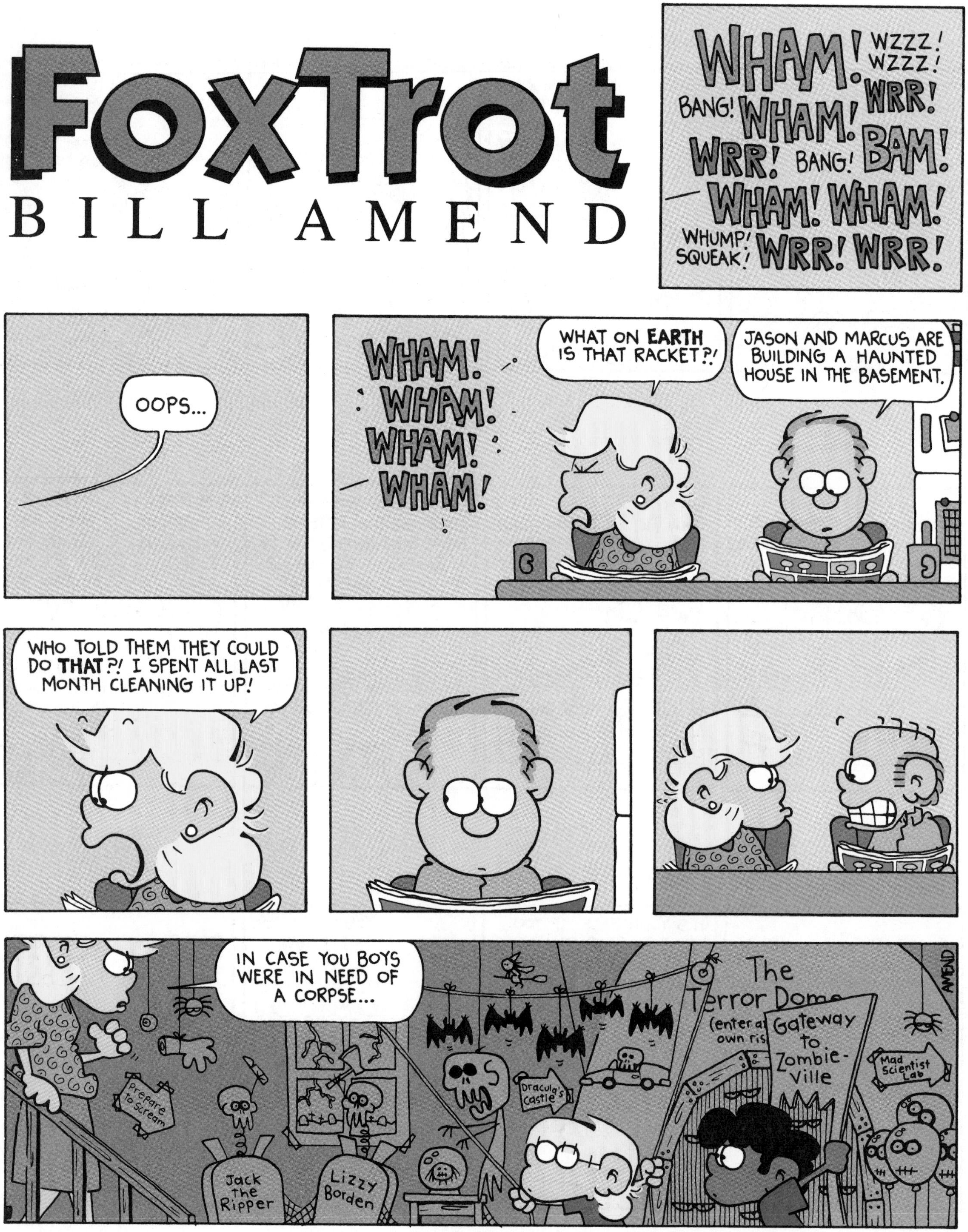
FoxTrot
BILL AMEND
WHAM! WZZZ! WZZZ! BANG! WHAM! WRR! WRR! BANG! BAM! WHAM! WHAM! WHUMP! SQUEAK! WRR! WRR!
OOPS...
WHAM! WHAM! WHAM! WHAM!
WHAT ON **EARTH** IS THAT RACKET?!
JASON AND MARCUS ARE BUILDING A HAUNTED HOUSE IN THE BASEMENT.
WHO TOLD THEM THEY COULD DO **THAT**?! I SPENT ALL LAST MONTH CLEANING IT UP!
IN CASE YOU BOYS WERE IN NEED OF A CORPSE...
Prepare to Scream
Dracula's Castle
Gateway to Zombie-ville
Mad Scientist Lab
Jack the Ripper
Lizzy Borden
AMEND

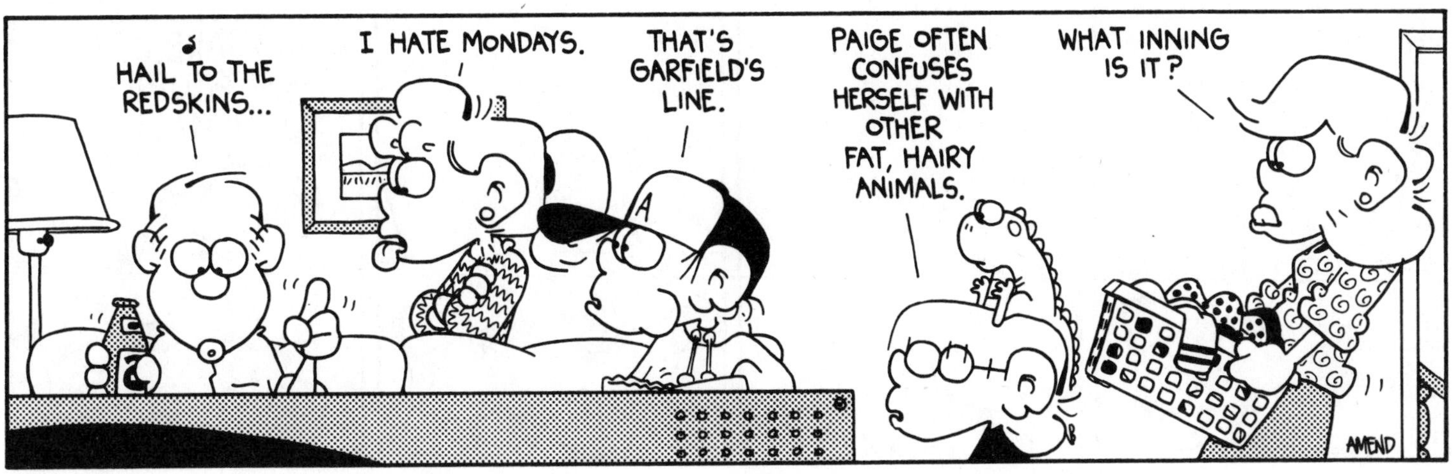
HAIL TO THE REDSKINS...
I HATE MONDAYS.
THAT'S GARFIELD'S LINE.
PAIGE OFTEN CONFUSES HERSELF WITH OTHER FAT, HAIRY ANIMALS.
WHAT INNING IS IT?
AMEND

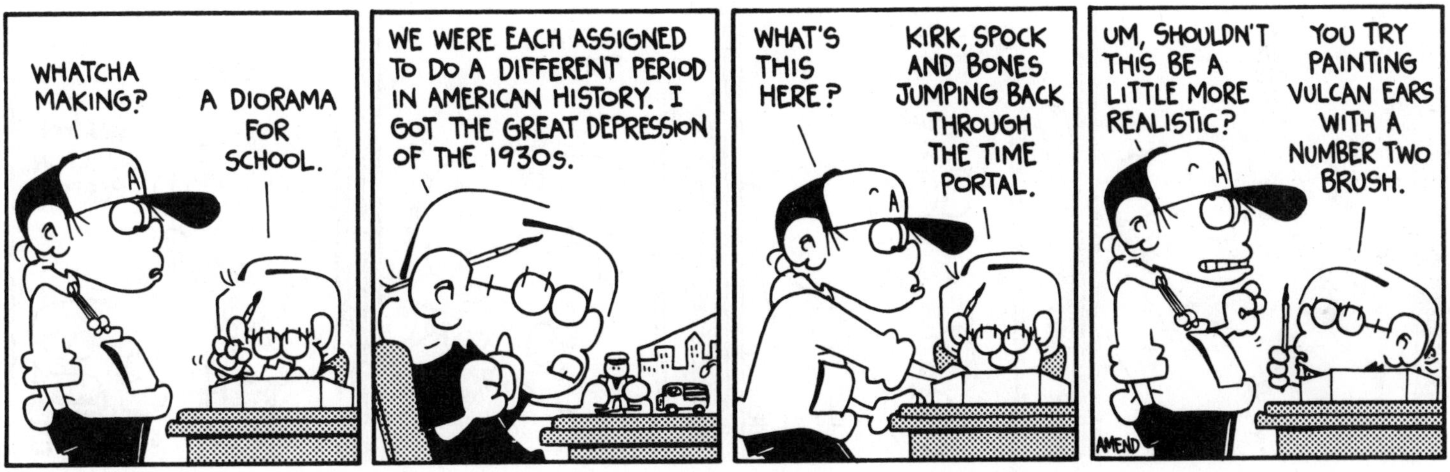
WHATCHA MAKING?
A DIORAMA FOR SCHOOL.
WE WERE EACH ASSIGNED TO DO A DIFFERENT PERIOD IN AMERICAN HISTORY. I GOT THE GREAT DEPRESSION OF THE 1930s.
WHAT'S THIS HERE?
KIRK, SPOCK AND BONES JUMPING BACK THROUGH THE TIME PORTAL.
UM, SHOULDN'T THIS BE A LITTLE MORE REALISTIC?
YOU TRY PAINTING VULCAN EARS WITH A NUMBER TWO BRUSH.
AMEND

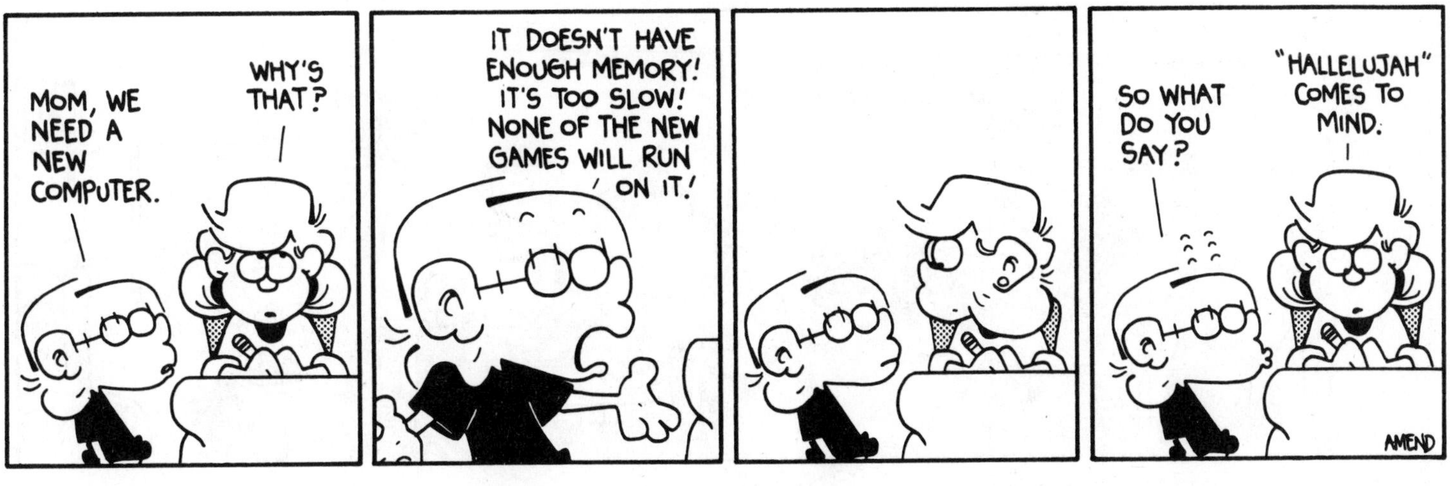
MOM, WE NEED A NEW COMPUTER.
WHY'S THAT?
IT DOESN'T HAVE ENOUGH MEMORY! IT'S TOO SLOW! NONE OF THE NEW GAMES WILL RUN ON IT!
SO WHAT DO YOU SAY?
"HALLELUJAH" COMES TO MIND.
AMEND

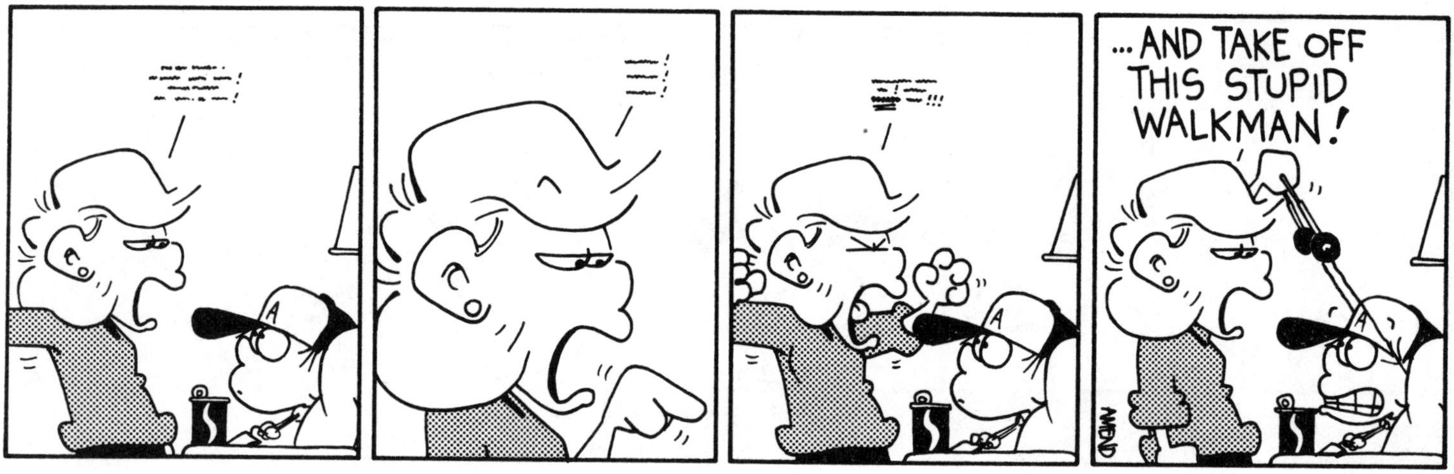
...AND TAKE OFF THIS STUPID WALKMAN!
AMEND

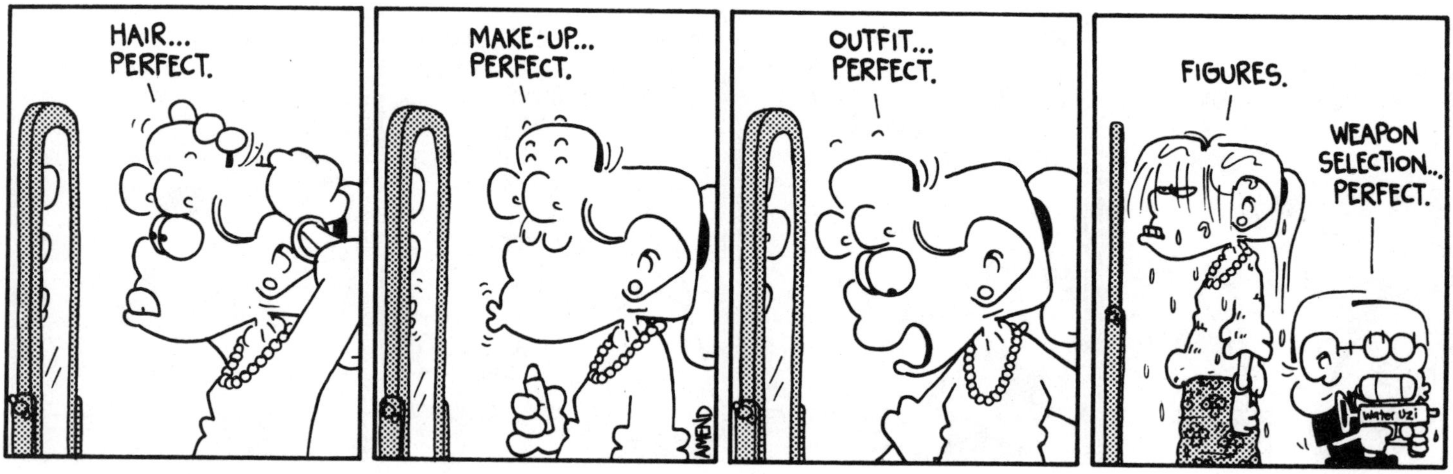
HAIR... PERFECT.
MAKE-UP... PERFECT.
OUTFIT... PERFECT.
FIGURES.
WEAPON SELECTION... PERFECT.
Water Uzi
AMEND

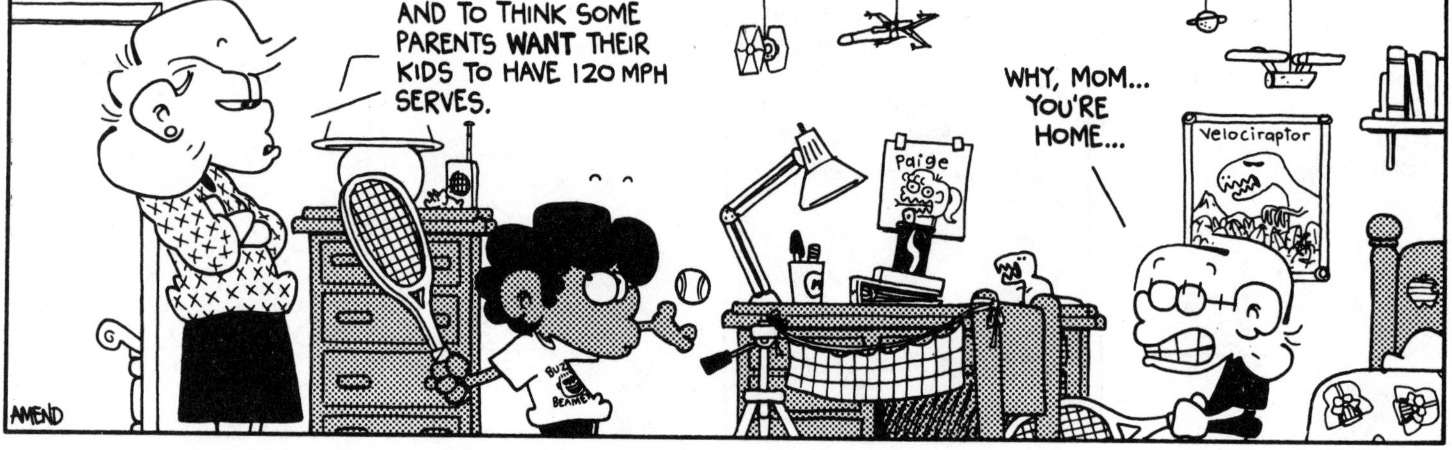
AND TO THINK SOME PARENTS **WANT** THEIR KIDS TO HAVE 120 MPH SERVES.
WHY, MOM... YOU'RE HOME...
Paige
Velociraptor
AMEND

FoxTrot
BILL AMEND

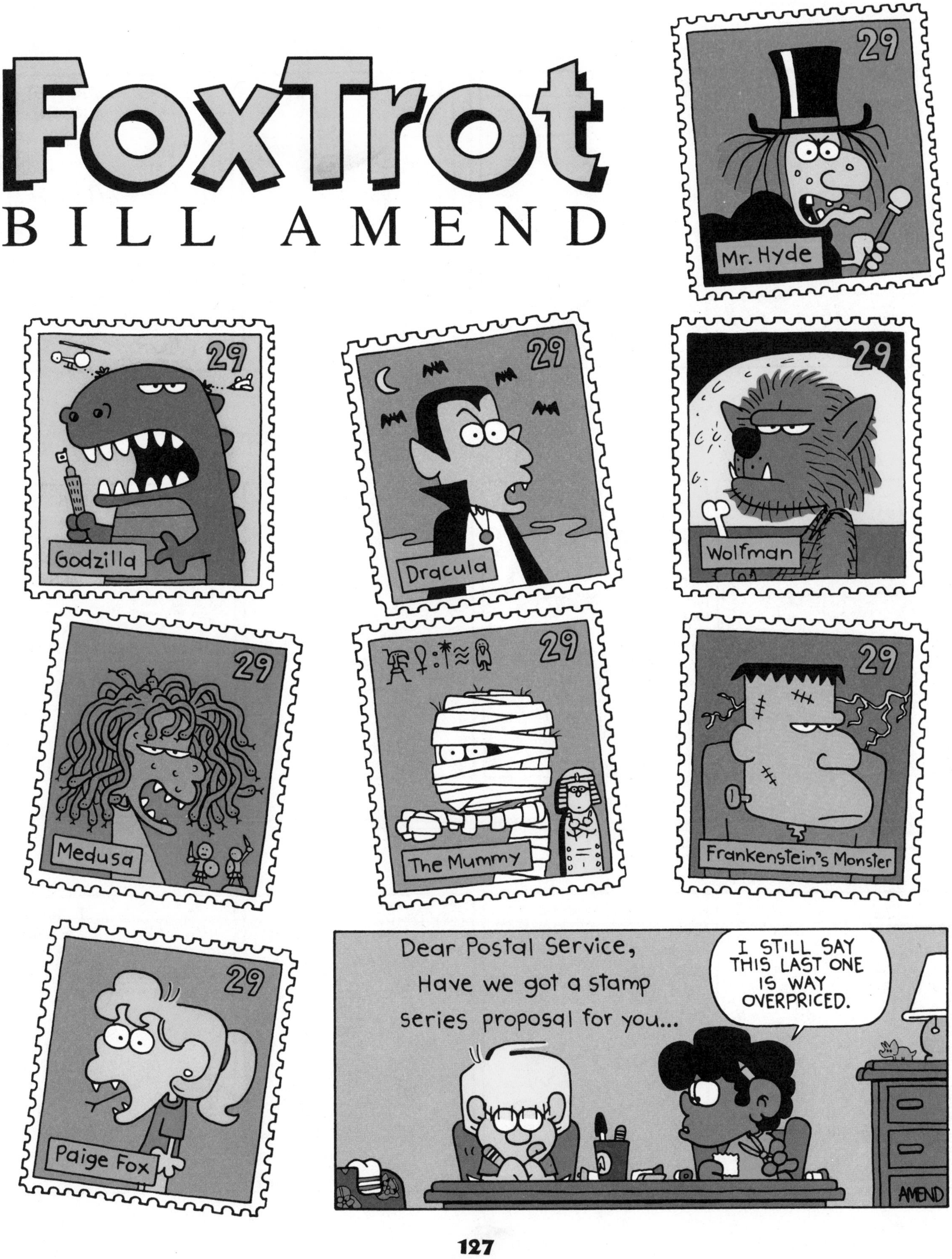
29
Mr. Hyde
29
Godzilla
29
Dracula
29
Wolfman
29
Medusa
29
The Mummy
29
Frankenstein's Monster
29
Paige Fox
Dear Postal Service,
Have we got a stamp series proposal for you...
I STILL SAY THIS LAST ONE IS WAY OVERPRICED.
AMEND

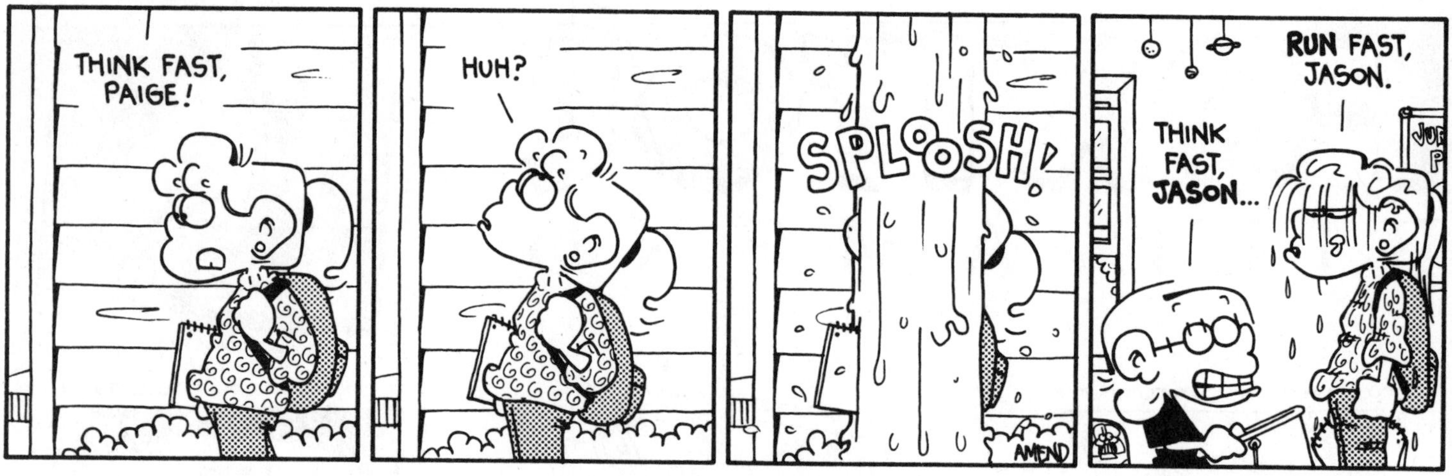
THINK FAST, PAIGE!
HUH?
SPLOOSH!
THINK FAST, JASON...
RUN FAST, JASON.
AMEND

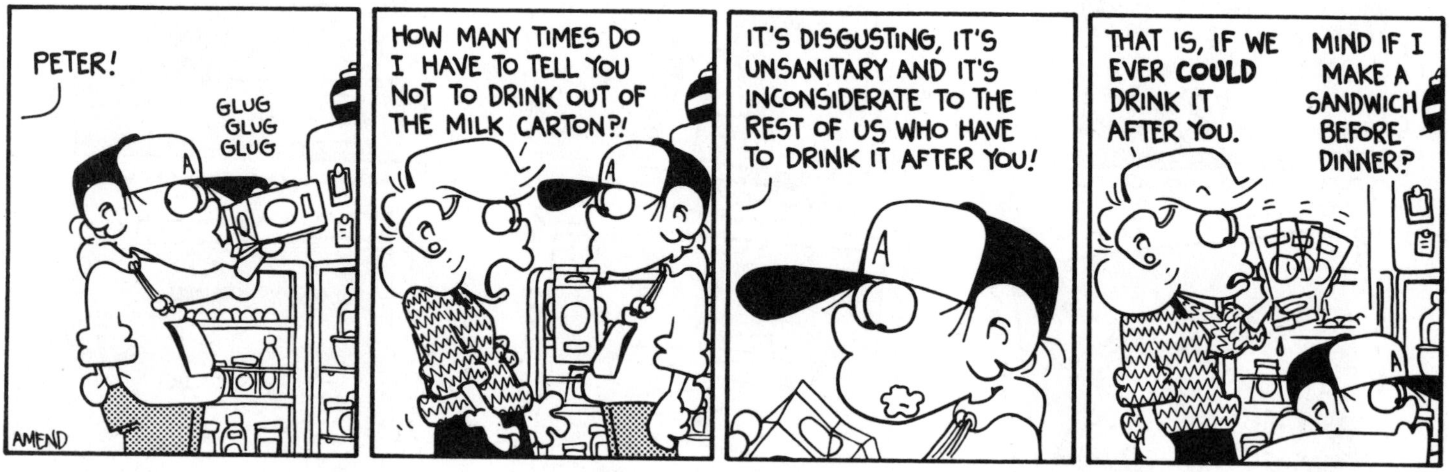
PETER!
GLUG GLUG GLUG
AMEND
HOW MANY TIMES DO I HAVE TO TELL YOU NOT TO DRINK OUT OF THE MILK CARTON?!
IT'S DISGUSTING, IT'S UNSANITARY AND IT'S INCONSIDERATE TO THE REST OF US WHO HAVE TO DRINK IT AFTER YOU!
THAT IS, IF WE EVER COULD DRINK IT AFTER YOU.
MIND IF I MAKE A SANDWICH BEFORE DINNER?

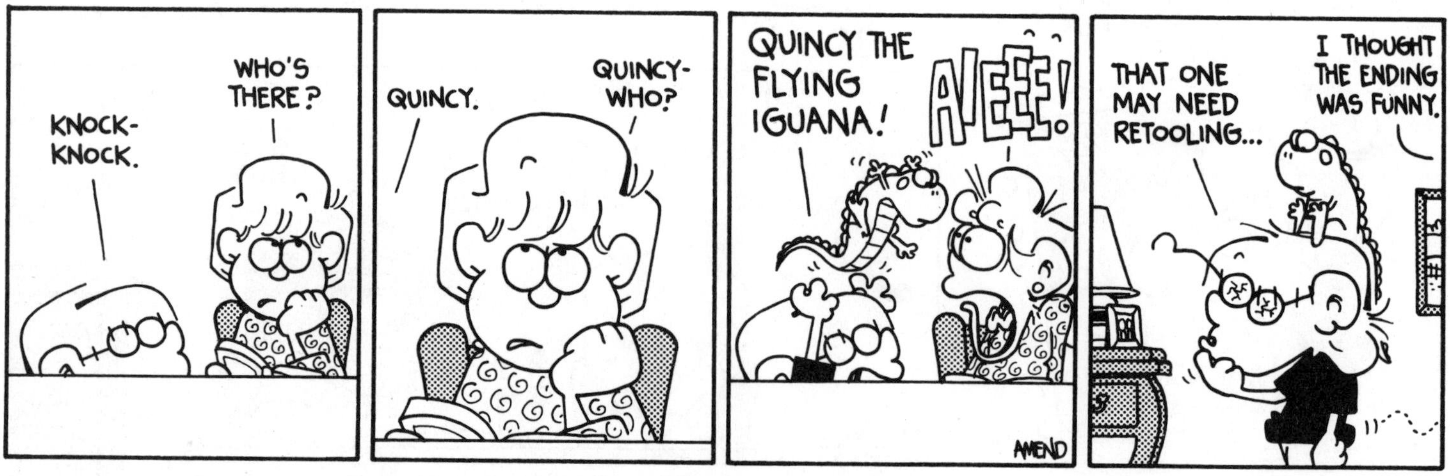
KNOCK-KNOCK.
WHO'S THERE?
QUINCY.
QUINCY-WHO?
QUINCY THE FLYING IGUANA!
AIEEE!
AMEND
THAT ONE MAY NEED RETOOLING...
I THOUGHT THE ENDING WAS FUNNY.

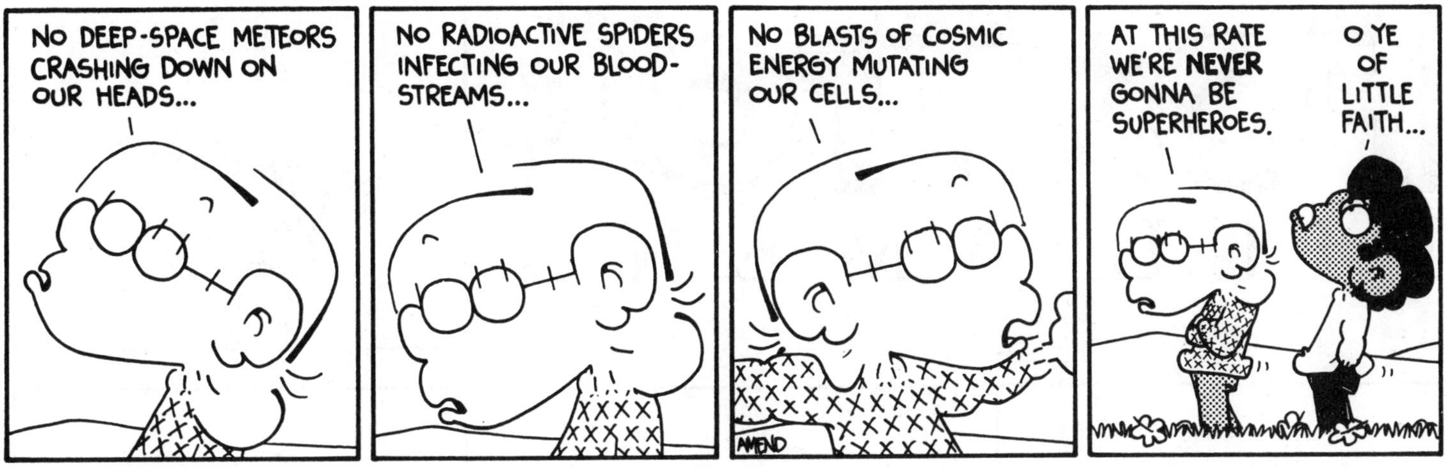
NO DEEP-SPACE METEORS CRASHING DOWN ON OUR HEADS...
NO RADIOACTIVE SPIDERS INFECTING OUR BLOOD-STREAMS...
NO BLASTS OF COSMIC ENERGY MUTATING OUR CELLS...
AT THIS RATE WE'RE **NEVER** GONNA BE SUPERHEROES.
O YE OF LITTLE FAITH...
AMEND

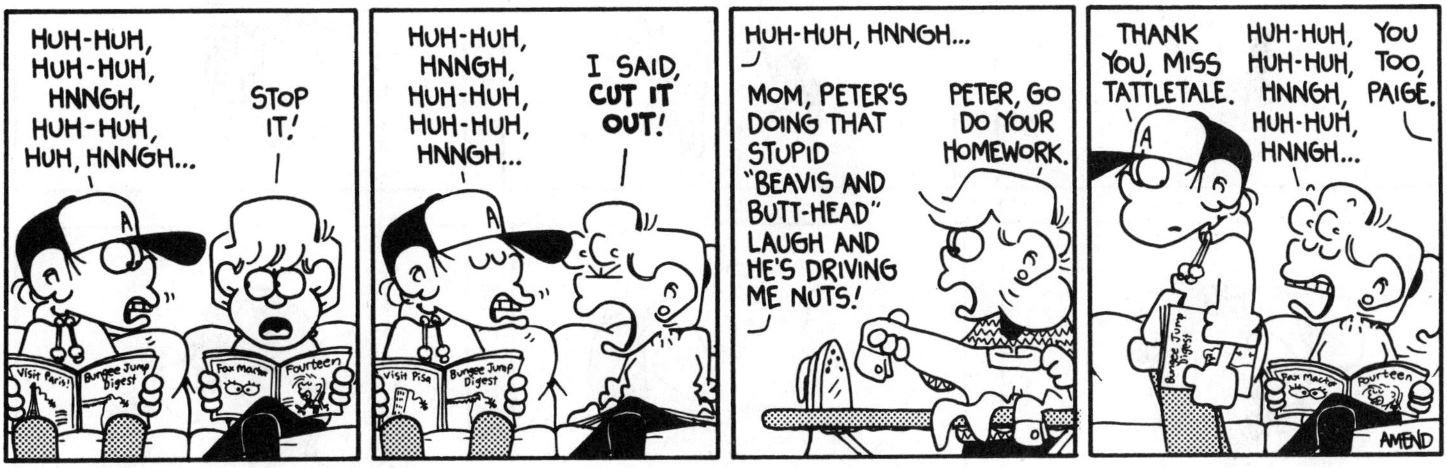
HUH-HUH, HUH-HUH, HNNGH, HUH-HUH, HUH, HNNGH...
STOP IT!
HUH-HUH, HNNGH, HUH-HUH, HUH-HUH, HNNGH...
I SAID, **CUT IT OUT!**
HUH-HUH, HNNGH...
MOM, PETER'S DOING THAT STUPID "BEAVIS AND BUTT-HEAD" LAUGH AND HE'S DRIVING ME NUTS!
PETER, GO DO YOUR HOMEWORK.
THANK YOU, MISS TATTLETALE.
HUH-HUH, HUH-HUH, HNNGH, HUH-HUH, HNNGH...
YOU TOO, PAIGE.
Bungee Jump Digest
Fourteen
AMEND

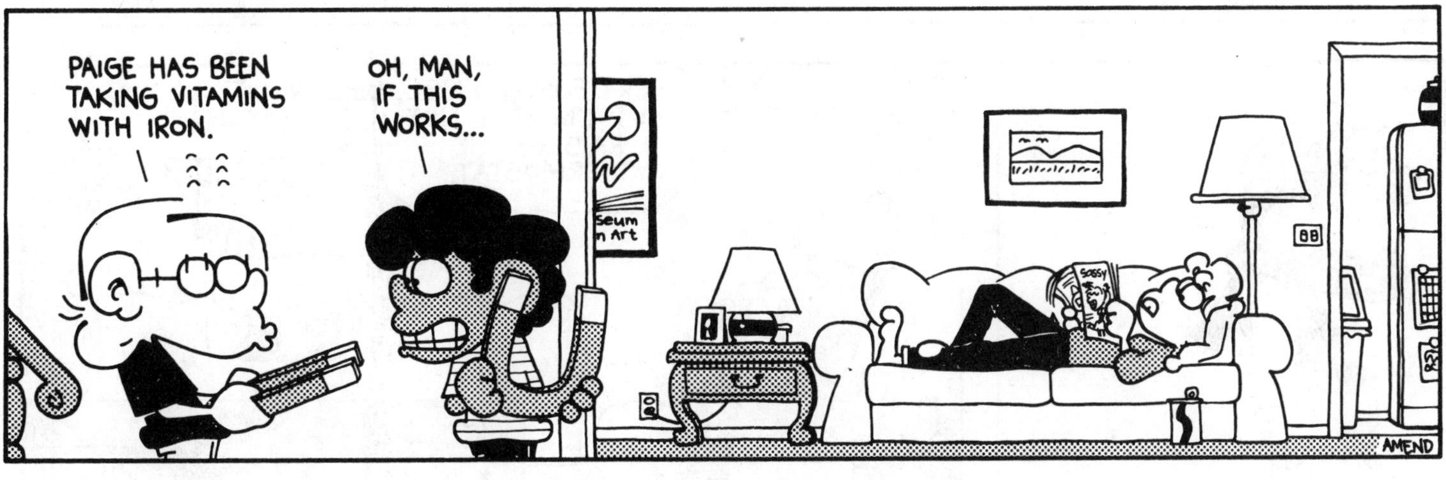
PAIGE HAS BEEN TAKING VITAMINS WITH IRON.
OH, MAN, IF THIS WORKS...
AMEND

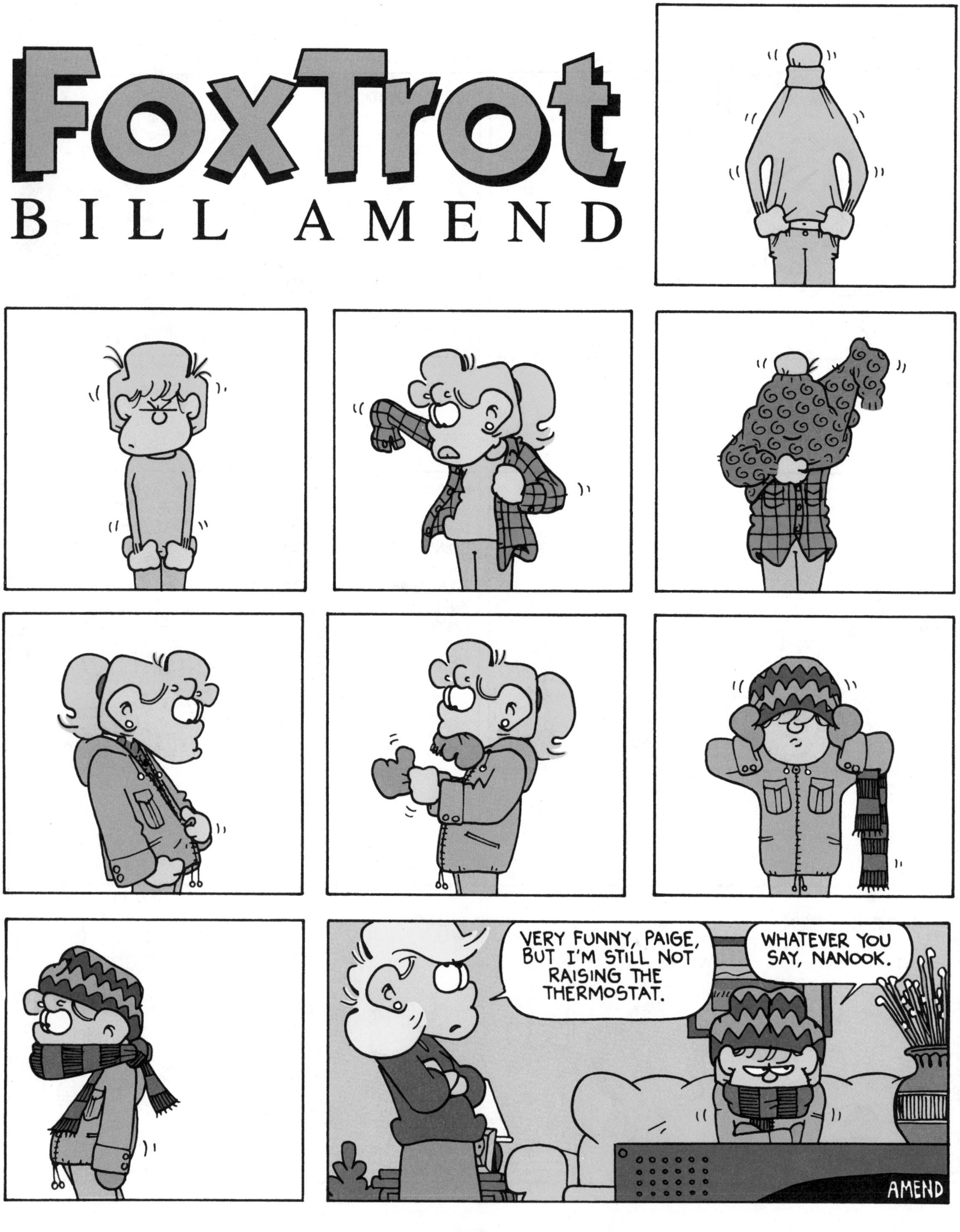
FoxTrot
BILL AMEND
VERY FUNNY, PAIGE, BUT I'M STILL NOT RAISING THE THERMOSTAT.
WHATEVER YOU SAY, NANOOK.
AMEND

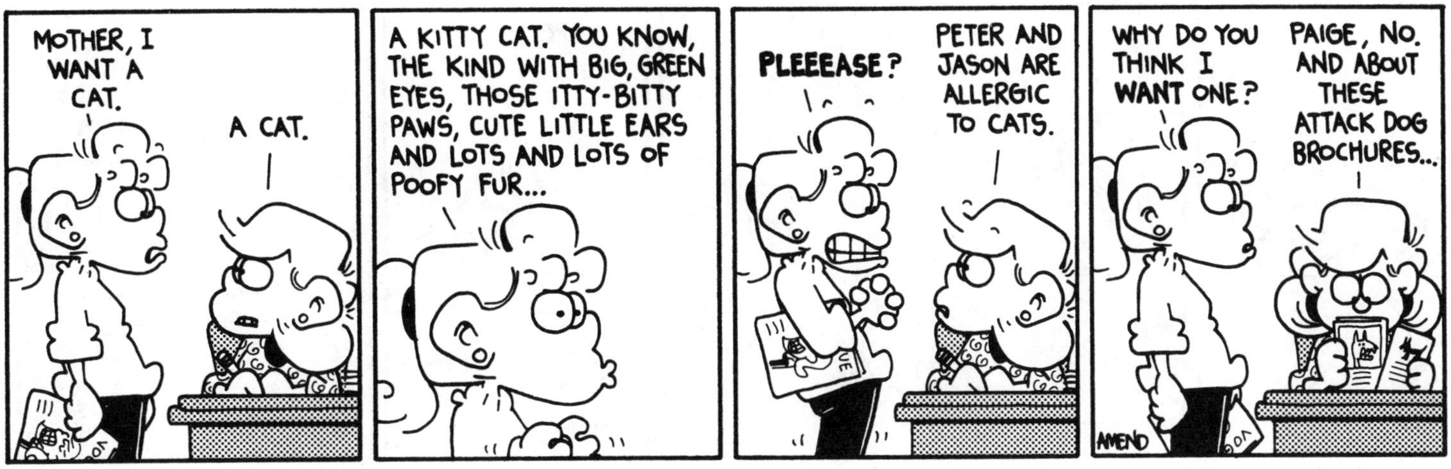

MOTHER, I WANT A CAT.
A CAT.
A KITTY CAT. YOU KNOW, THE KIND WITH BIG, GREEN EYES, THOSE ITTY-BITTY PAWS, CUTE LITTLE EARS AND LOTS AND LOTS OF POOFY FUR...
PLEEEASE?
PETER AND JASON ARE ALLERGIC TO CATS.
WHY DO YOU THINK I **WANT** ONE?
PAIGE, NO. AND ABOUT THESE ATTACK DOG BROCHURES...
AMEND

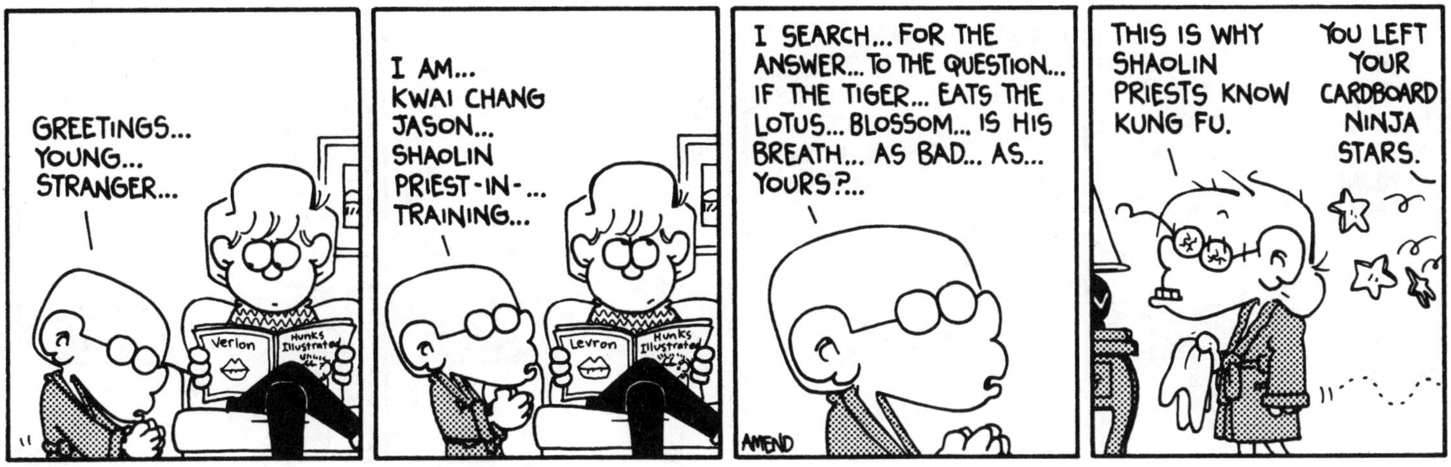

GREETINGS... YOUNG... STRANGER...
Verlon
Hunks Illustrated
I AM... KWAI CHANG JASON... SHAOLIN PRIEST-IN-... TRAINING...
Levron
Hunks Illustrated
I SEARCH... FOR THE ANSWER... TO THE QUESTION... IF THE TIGER... EATS THE LOTUS... BLOSSOM... IS HIS BREATH... AS BAD... AS... YOURS?...
AMEND
THIS IS WHY SHAOLIN PRIESTS KNOW KUNG FU.
YOU LEFT YOUR CARDBOARD NINJA STARS.

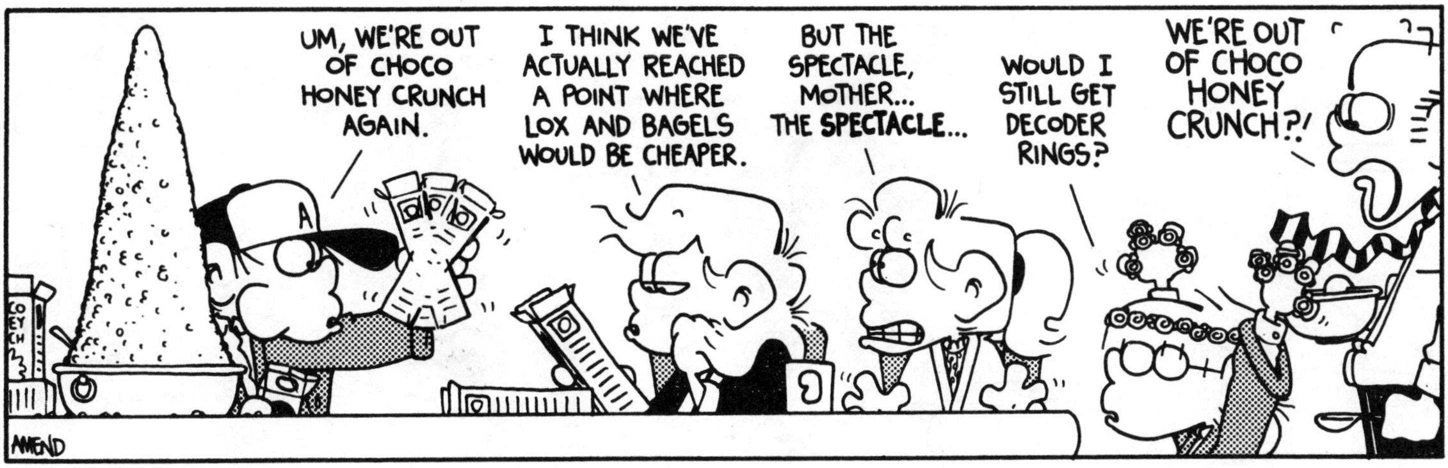

UM, WE'RE OUT OF CHOCO HONEY CRUNCH AGAIN.
I THINK WE'VE ACTUALLY REACHED A POINT WHERE LOX AND BAGELS WOULD BE CHEAPER.
BUT THE SPECTACLE, MOTHER... THE **SPECTACLE**...
WOULD I STILL GET DECODER RINGS?
WE'RE OUT OF CHOCO HONEY CRUNCH?!
AMEND

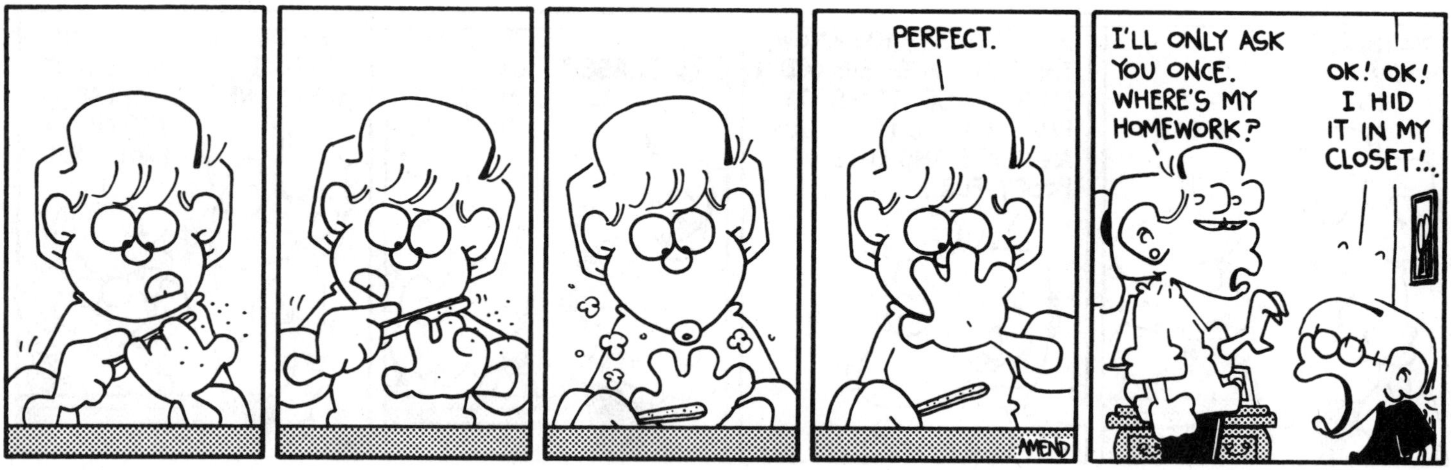
PERFECT.
I'LL ONLY ASK YOU ONCE. WHERE'S MY HOMEWORK?
OK! OK! I HID IT IN MY CLOSET!..
AMEND

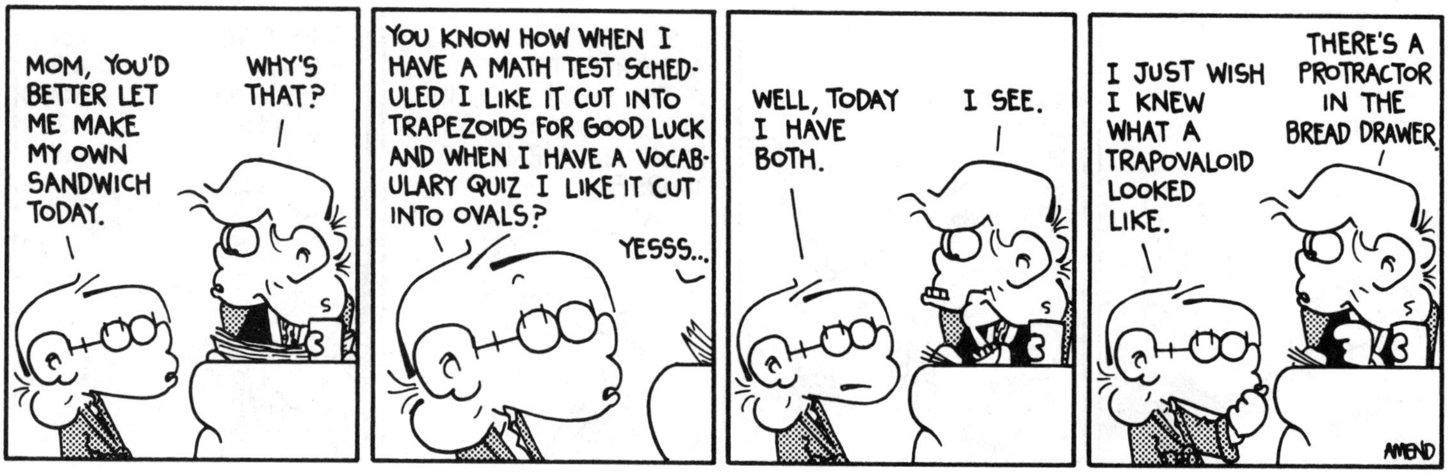
MOM, YOU'D BETTER LET ME MAKE MY OWN SANDWICH TODAY.
WHY'S THAT?
YOU KNOW HOW WHEN I HAVE A MATH TEST SCHEDULED I LIKE IT CUT INTO TRAPEZOIDS FOR GOOD LUCK AND WHEN I HAVE A VOCABULARY QUIZ I LIKE IT CUT INTO OVALS?
YESSS...
WELL, TODAY I HAVE BOTH.
I SEE.
I JUST WISH I KNEW WHAT A TRAPOVALOID LOOKED LIKE.
THERE'S A PROTRACTOR IN THE BREAD DRAWER.
AMEND

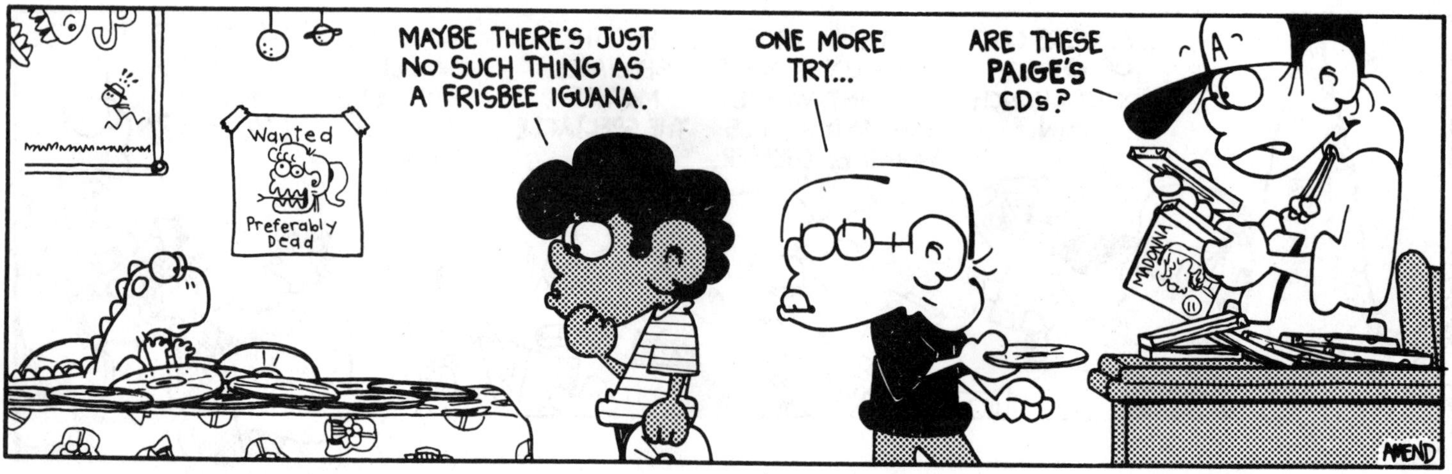
Wanted
Preferably Dead
MAYBE THERE'S JUST NO SUCH THING AS A FRISBEE IGUANA.
ONE MORE TRY...
ARE THESE PAIGE'S CDs?
MADONNA
AMEND

FoxTrot

BILL AMEND

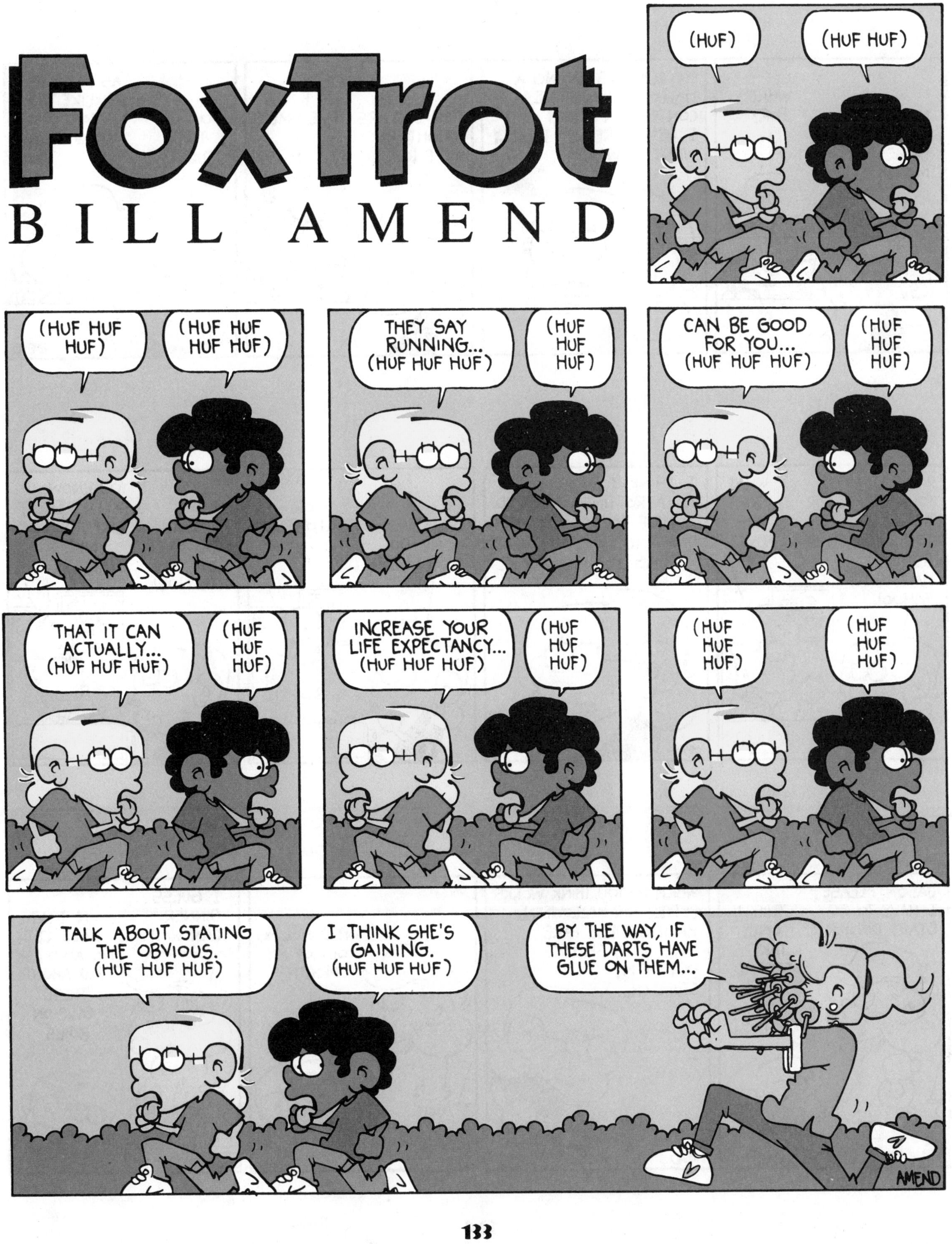

(HUF)
(HUF HUF)
(HUF HUF HUF)
(HUF HUF HUF HUF)
THEY SAY RUNNING... (HUF HUF HUF)
(HUF HUF HUF)
CAN BE GOOD FOR YOU... (HUF HUF HUF)
(HUF HUF HUF)
THAT IT CAN ACTUALLY... (HUF HUF HUF)
(HUF HUF HUF)
INCREASE YOUR LIFE EXPECTANCY... (HUF HUF HUF)
(HUF HUF HUF)
(HUF HUF HUF)
(HUF HUF HUF)
TALK ABOUT STATING THE OBVIOUS. (HUF HUF HUF)
I THINK SHE'S GAINING. (HUF HUF HUF)
BY THE WAY, IF THESE DARTS HAVE GLUE ON THEM...
AMEND

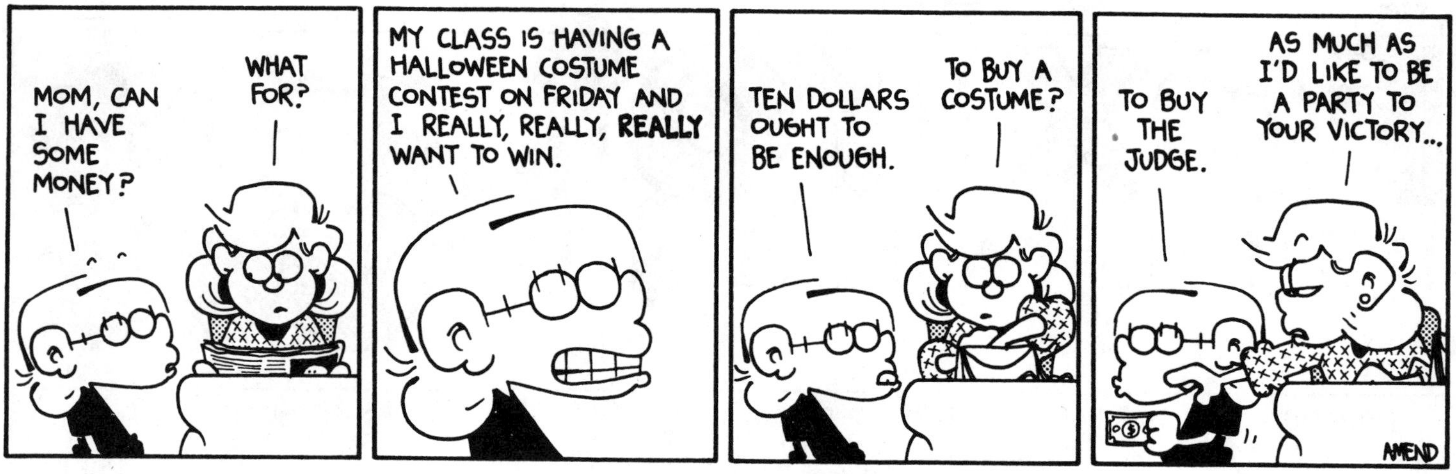
MOM, CAN I HAVE SOME MONEY?
WHAT FOR?
MY CLASS IS HAVING A HALLOWEEN COSTUME CONTEST ON FRIDAY AND I REALLY, REALLY, **REALLY** WANT TO WIN.
TEN DOLLARS OUGHT TO BE ENOUGH.
TO BUY A COSTUME?
TO BUY THE JUDGE.
AS MUCH AS I'D LIKE TO BE A PARTY TO YOUR VICTORY...
AMEND

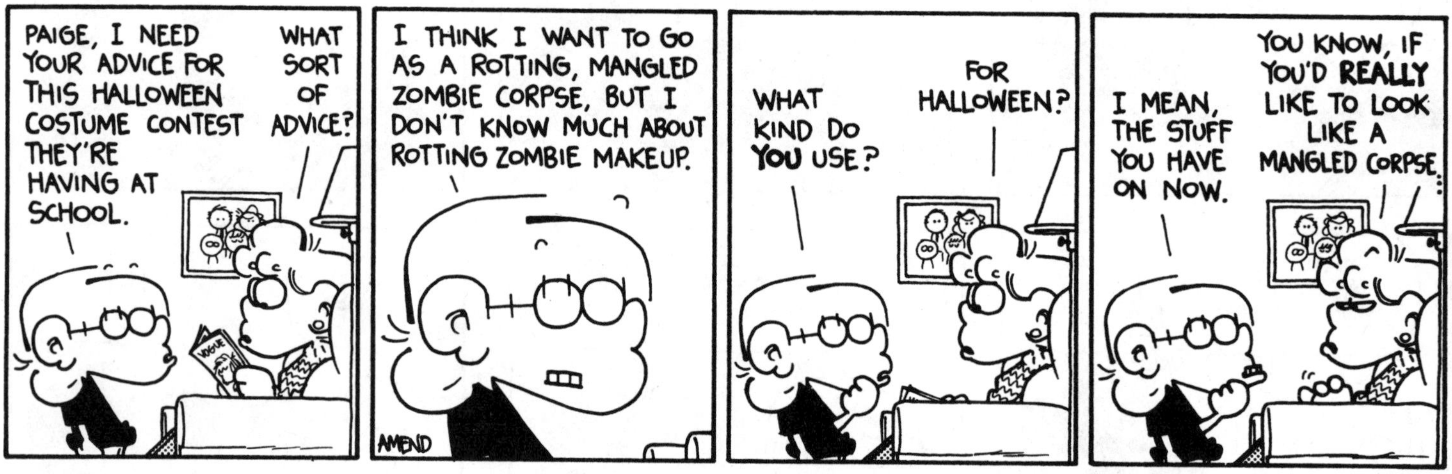
PAIGE, I NEED YOUR ADVICE FOR THIS HALLOWEEN COSTUME CONTEST THEY'RE HAVING AT SCHOOL.
WHAT SORT OF ADVICE?
VOGUE
I THINK I WANT TO GO AS A ROTTING, MANGLED ZOMBIE CORPSE, BUT I DON'T KNOW MUCH ABOUT ROTTING ZOMBIE MAKEUP.
AMEND
WHAT KIND DO **YOU** USE?
FOR HALLOWEEN?
I MEAN, THE STUFF YOU HAVE ON NOW.
YOU KNOW, IF YOU'D **REALLY** LIKE TO LOOK LIKE A MANGLED CORPSE...

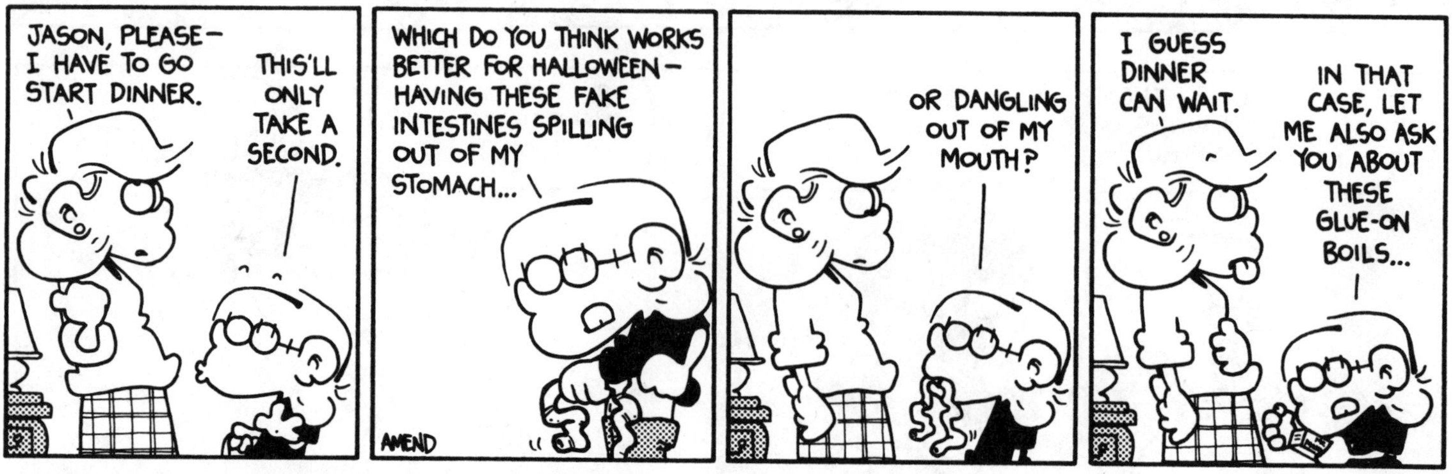
JASON, PLEASE– I HAVE TO GO START DINNER.
THIS'LL ONLY TAKE A SECOND.
WHICH DO YOU THINK WORKS BETTER FOR HALLOWEEN– HAVING THESE FAKE INTESTINES SPILLING OUT OF MY STOMACH...
AMEND
OR DANGLING OUT OF MY MOUTH?
I GUESS DINNER CAN WAIT.
IN THAT CASE, LET ME ALSO ASK YOU ABOUT THESE GLUE-ON BOILS...

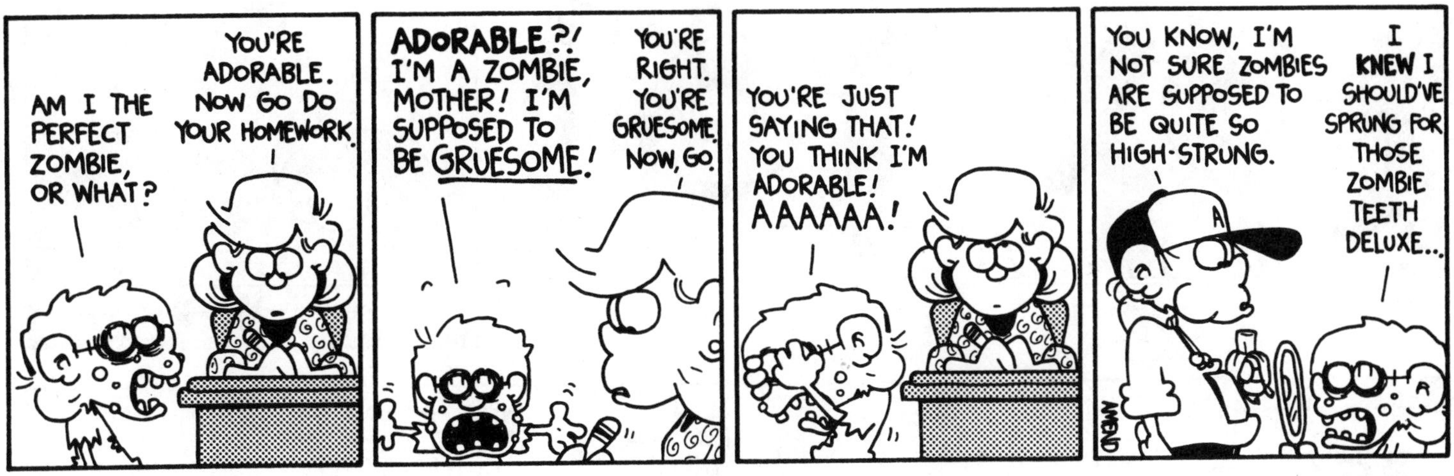

AM I THE PERFECT ZOMBIE, OR WHAT?
YOU'RE ADORABLE. NOW GO DO YOUR HOMEWORK.
ADORABLE?! I'M A ZOMBIE, MOTHER! I'M SUPPOSED TO BE GRUESOME!
YOU'RE RIGHT. YOU'RE GRUESOME. NOW, GO.
YOU'RE JUST SAYING THAT! YOU THINK I'M ADORABLE! AAAAAA!
YOU KNOW, I'M NOT SURE ZOMBIES ARE SUPPOSED TO BE QUITE SO HIGH-STRUNG.
I KNEW I SHOULD'VE SPRUNG FOR THOSE ZOMBIE TEETH DELUXE...
AMEND

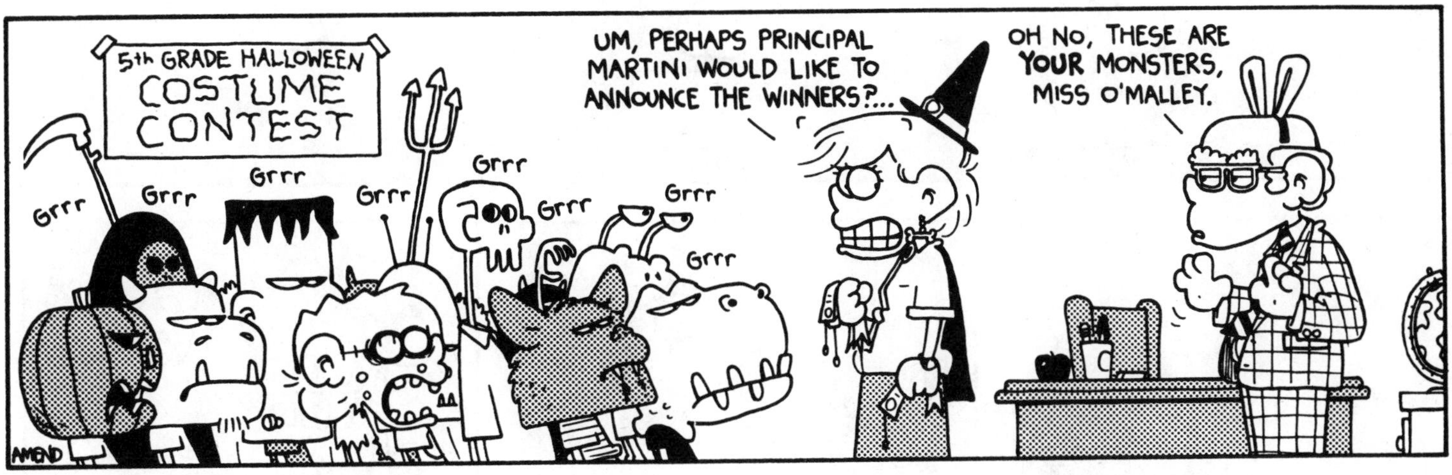

5th GRADE HALLOWEEN COSTUME CONTEST
Grrr
Grrr
Grrr
Grrr
Grrr
Grrr
Grrr
Grrr
UM, PERHAPS PRINCIPAL MARTINI WOULD LIKE TO ANNOUNCE THE WINNERS?...
OH NO, THESE ARE YOUR MONSTERS, MISS O'MALLEY.
AMEND

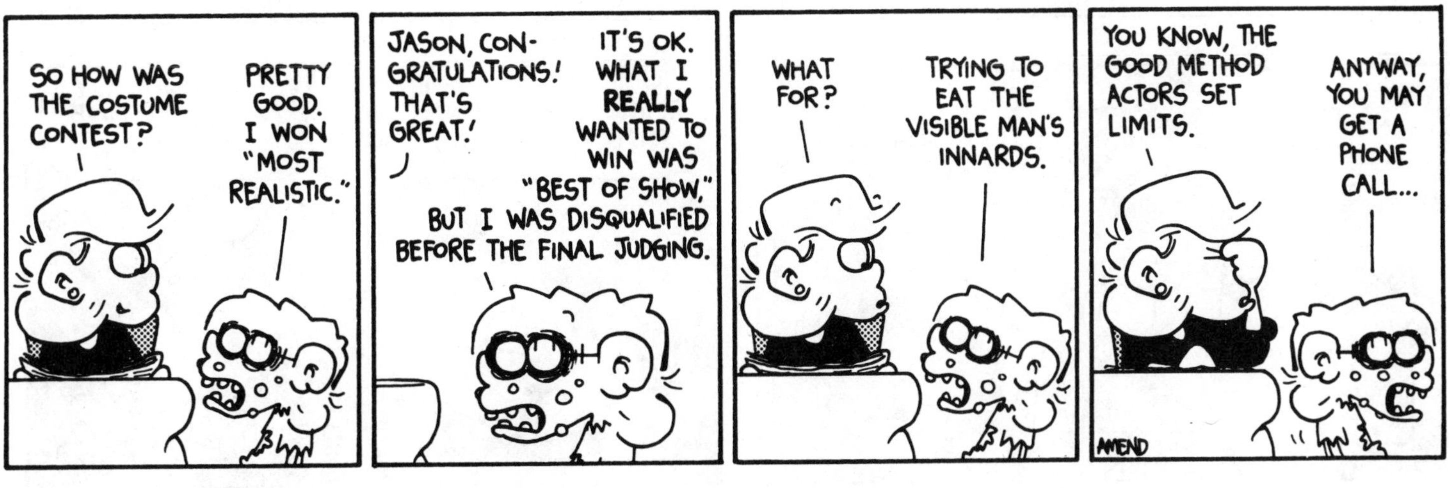

SO HOW WAS THE COSTUME CONTEST?
PRETTY GOOD. I WON "MOST REALISTIC."
JASON, CONGRATULATIONS! THAT'S GREAT!
IT'S OK. WHAT I REALLY WANTED TO WIN WAS "BEST OF SHOW," BUT I WAS DISQUALIFIED BEFORE THE FINAL JUDGING.
WHAT FOR?
TRYING TO EAT THE VISIBLE MAN'S INNARDS.
YOU KNOW, THE GOOD METHOD ACTORS SET LIMITS.
ANYWAY, YOU MAY GET A PHONE CALL...
AMEND

FoxTrot
BILL AMEND
BOO...
TRY IT DEEPER.
BOO...
SOMETHING'S STILL NOT RIGHT...
TRICK OR TREAT.
WELL, IF YOU TWO AREN'T JUST THE CUTEST LITTLE—...
RIP!
RIP!
HISS! HISS! HISS! HISS! HISS! HISS! HISS!
AAAA!
AMEND
IS IT ME, OR ARE PEOPLE BEING EXTRA STINGY WITH THEIR CANDY THIS YEAR?
THAT ONE LADY WOULDN'T GIVE US **ANY**...

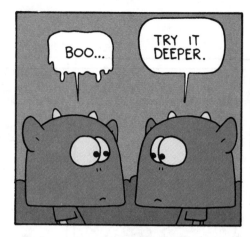

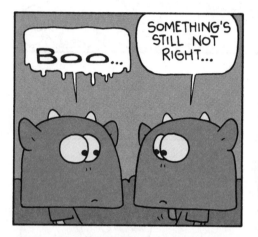

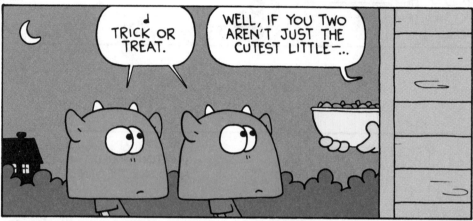

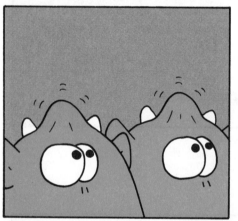

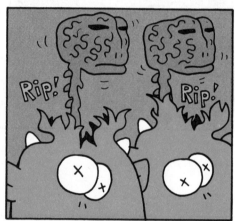

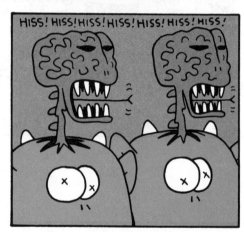

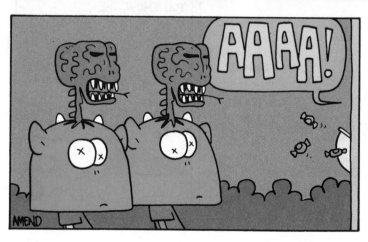

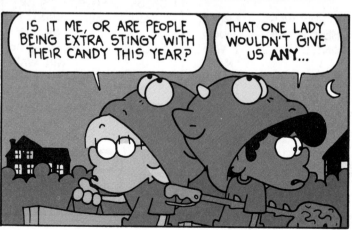

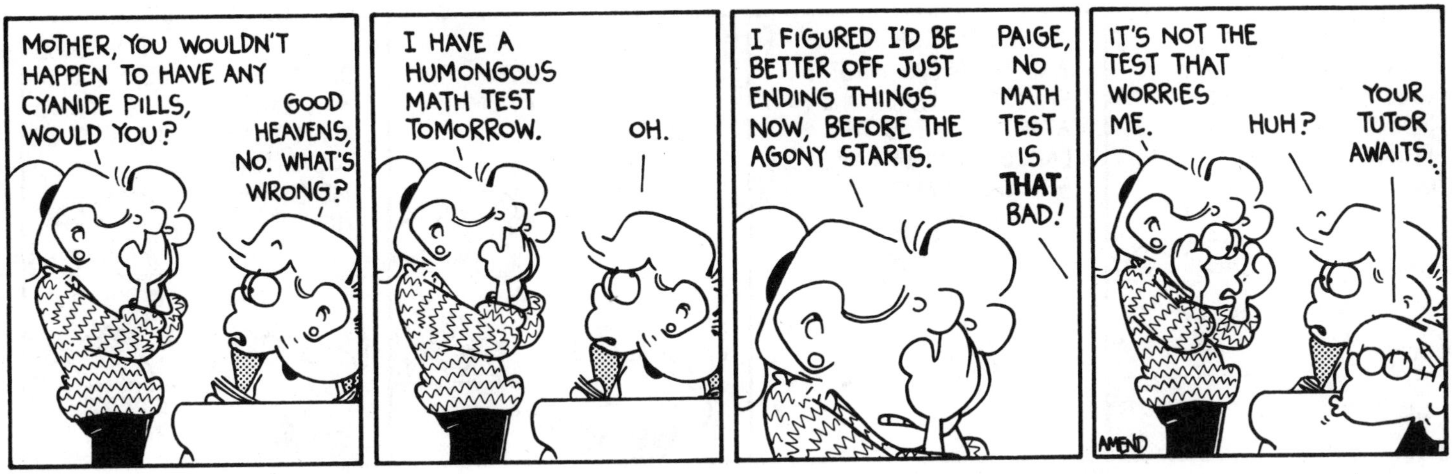
MOTHER, YOU WOULDN'T HAPPEN TO HAVE ANY CYANIDE PILLS, WOULD YOU?
GOOD HEAVENS, NO. WHAT'S WRONG?
I HAVE A HUMONGOUS MATH TEST TOMORROW.
OH.
I FIGURED I'D BE BETTER OFF JUST ENDING THINGS NOW, BEFORE THE AGONY STARTS.
PAIGE, NO MATH TEST IS **THAT** BAD!
IT'S NOT THE TEST THAT WORRIES ME.
HUH?
YOUR TUTOR AWAITS...
AMEND

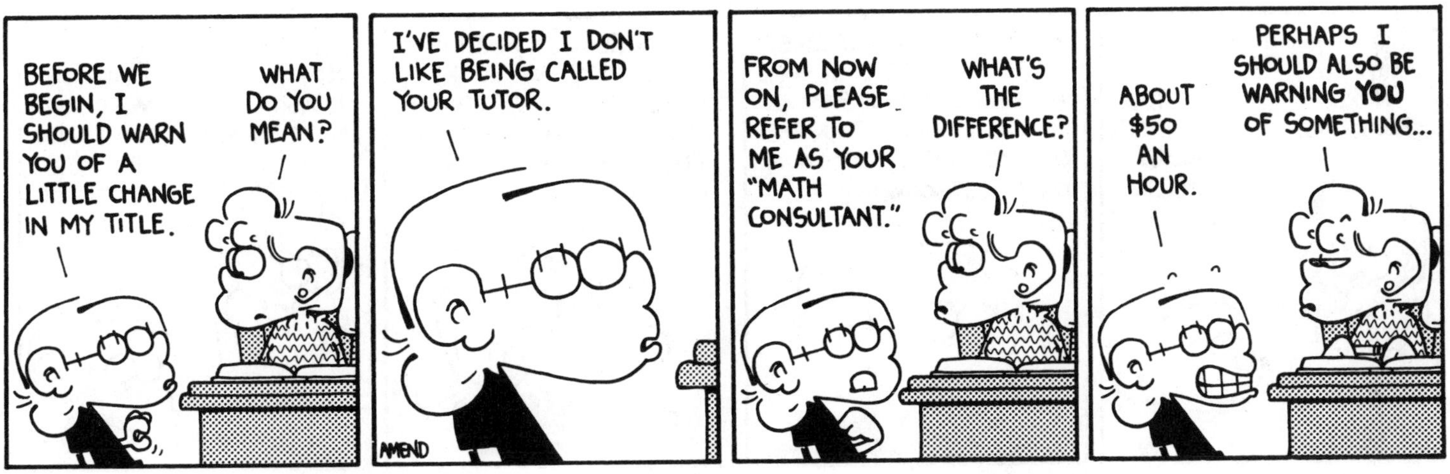
BEFORE WE BEGIN, I SHOULD WARN YOU OF A LITTLE CHANGE IN MY TITLE.
WHAT DO YOU MEAN?
I'VE DECIDED I DON'T LIKE BEING CALLED YOUR TUTOR.
AMEND
FROM NOW ON, PLEASE REFER TO ME AS YOUR "MATH CONSULTANT."
WHAT'S THE DIFFERENCE?
ABOUT $50 AN HOUR.
PERHAPS I SHOULD ALSO BE WARNING **YOU** OF SOMETHING...

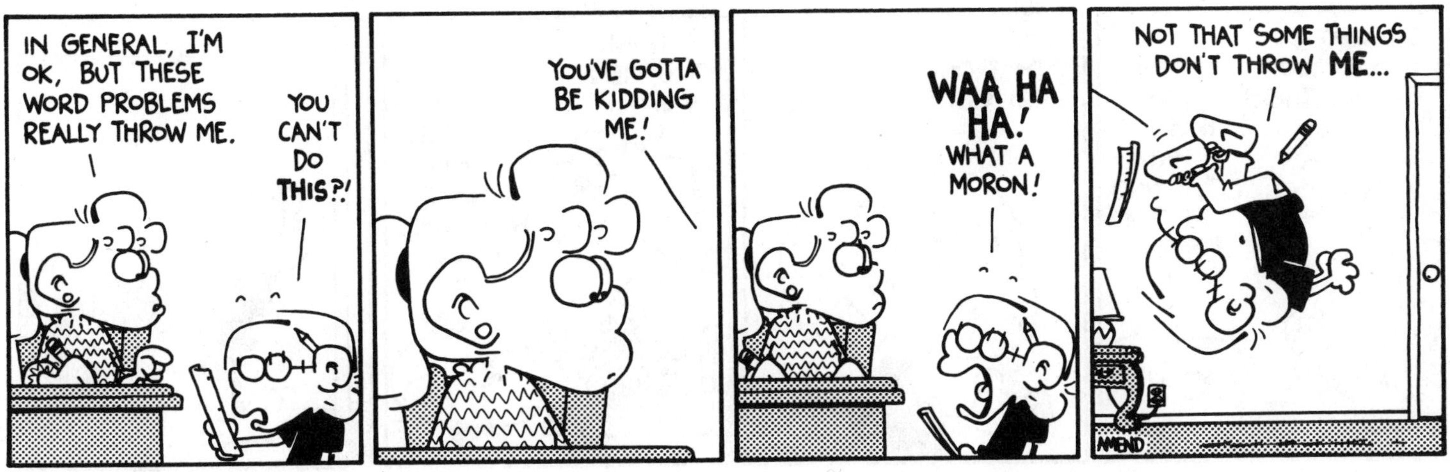
IN GENERAL, I'M OK, BUT THESE WORD PROBLEMS REALLY THROW ME.
YOU CAN'T DO **THIS**?!
YOU'VE GOTTA BE KIDDING ME!
WAA HA HA!
WHAT A MORON!
NOT THAT SOME THINGS DON'T THROW **ME**...
AMEND

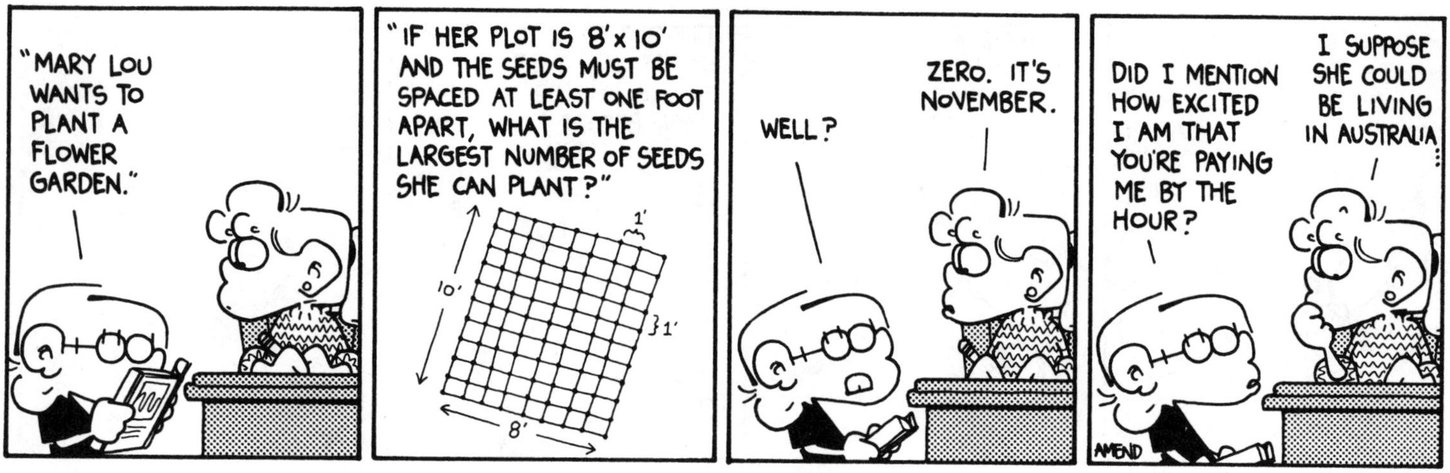
"MARY LOU WANTS TO PLANT A FLOWER GARDEN."
"IF HER PLOT IS 8' x 10' AND THE SEEDS MUST BE SPACED AT LEAST ONE FOOT APART, WHAT IS THE LARGEST NUMBER OF SEEDS SHE CAN PLANT?"
1'
10'
1'
8'
WELL?
ZERO. IT'S NOVEMBER.
DID I MENTION HOW EXCITED I AM THAT YOU'RE PAYING ME BY THE HOUR?
I SUPPOSE SHE COULD BE LIVING IN AUSTRALIA...
AMEND

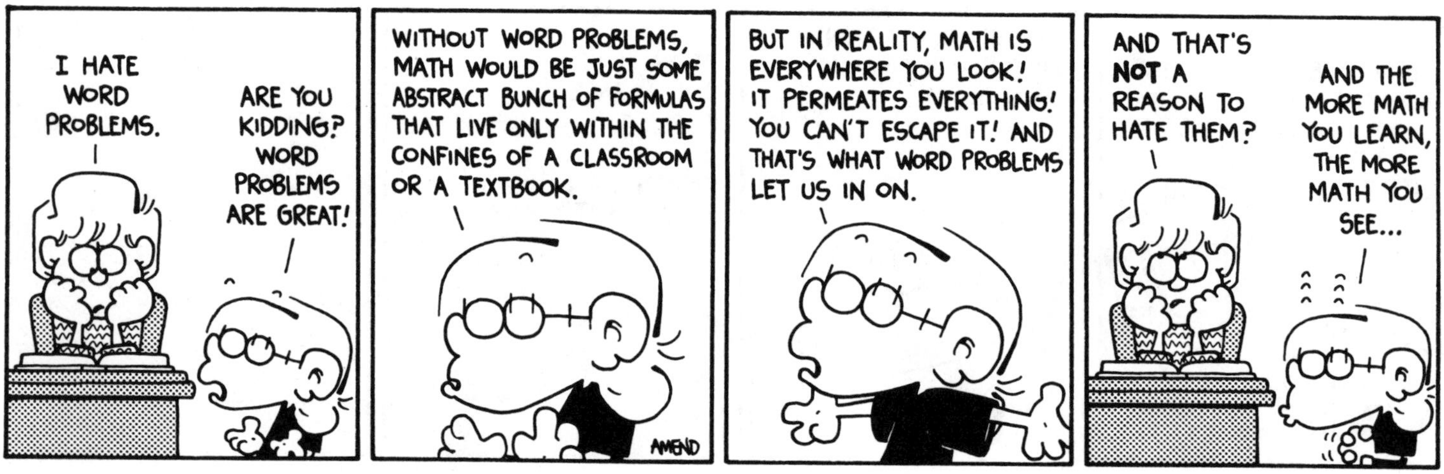
I HATE WORD PROBLEMS.
ARE YOU KIDDING? WORD PROBLEMS ARE GREAT!
WITHOUT WORD PROBLEMS, MATH WOULD BE JUST SOME ABSTRACT BUNCH OF FORMULAS THAT LIVE ONLY WITHIN THE CONFINES OF A CLASSROOM OR A TEXTBOOK.
AMEND
BUT IN REALITY, MATH IS EVERYWHERE YOU LOOK! IT PERMEATES EVERYTHING! YOU CAN'T ESCAPE IT! AND THAT'S WHAT WORD PROBLEMS LET US IN ON.
AND THAT'S **NOT** A REASON TO HATE THEM?
AND THE MORE MATH YOU LEARN, THE MORE MATH YOU SEE...

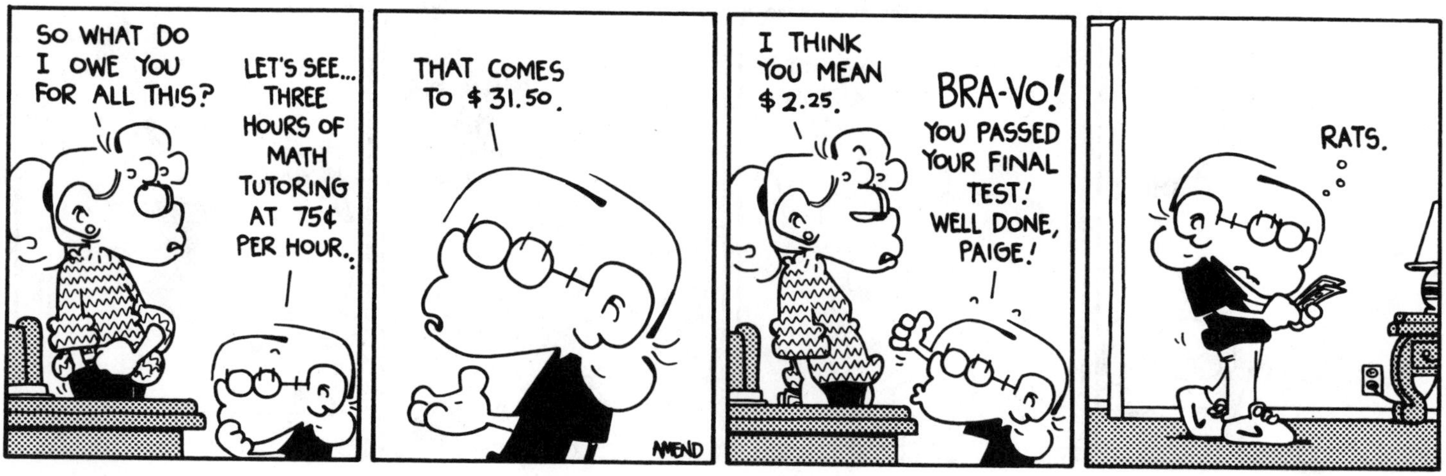
SO WHAT DO I OWE YOU FOR ALL THIS?
LET'S SEE... THREE HOURS OF MATH TUTORING AT 75¢ PER HOUR...
THAT COMES TO $31.50.
AMEND
I THINK YOU MEAN $2.25.
BRA-VO! YOU PASSED YOUR FINAL TEST! WELL DONE, PAIGE!
RATS.

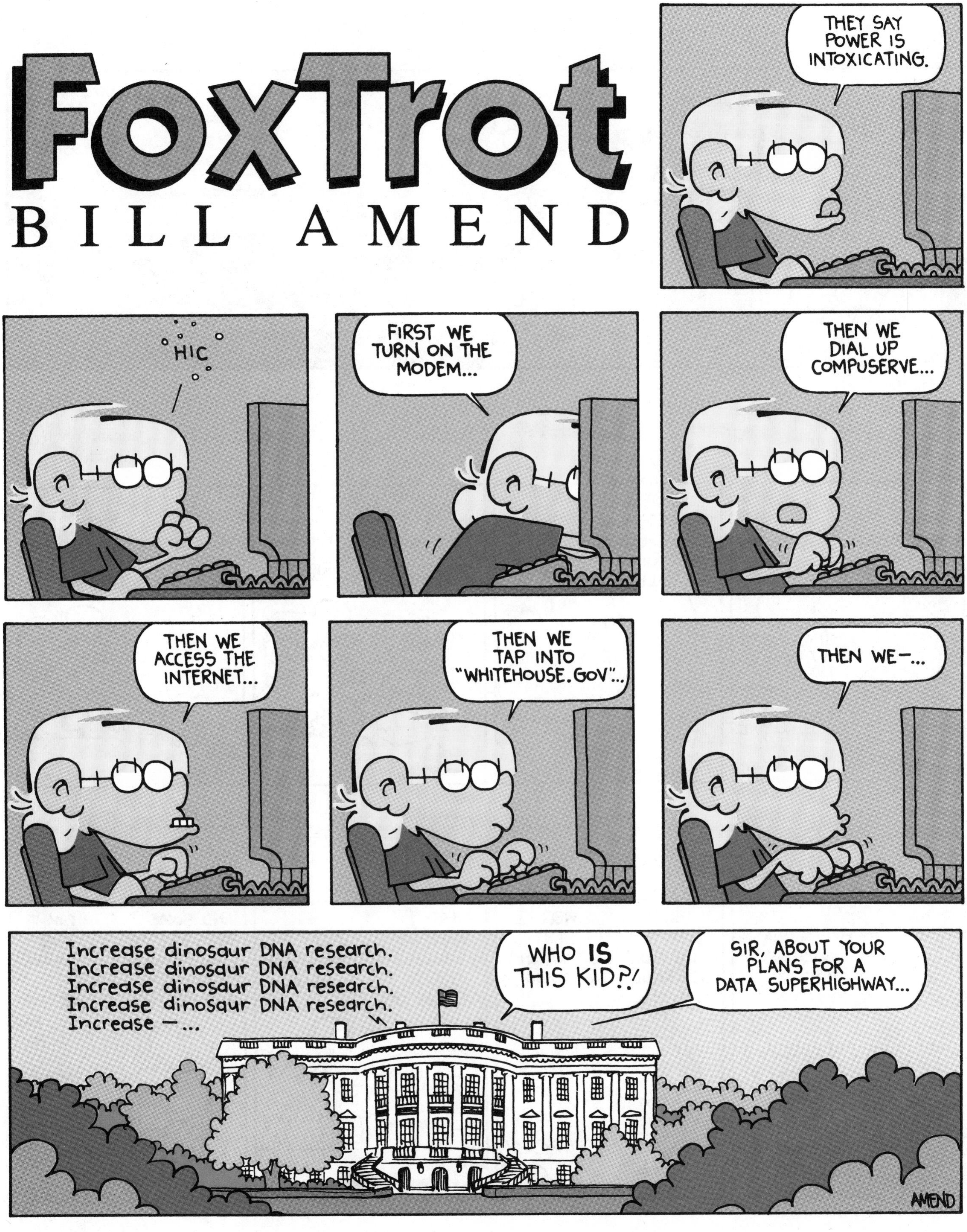
FoxTrot
BILL AMEND
THEY SAY POWER IS INTOXICATING.
HIC
FIRST WE TURN ON THE MODEM...
THEN WE DIAL UP COMPUSERVE...
THEN WE ACCESS THE INTERNET...
THEN WE TAP INTO "WHITEHOUSE.GOV"...
THEN WE—...
Increase dinosaur DNA research.
Increase dinosaur DNA research.
Increase dinosaur DNA research.
Increase dinosaur DNA research.
Increase —...
WHO **IS** THIS KID?!
SIR, ABOUT YOUR PLANS FOR A DATA SUPERHIGHWAY...
AMEND

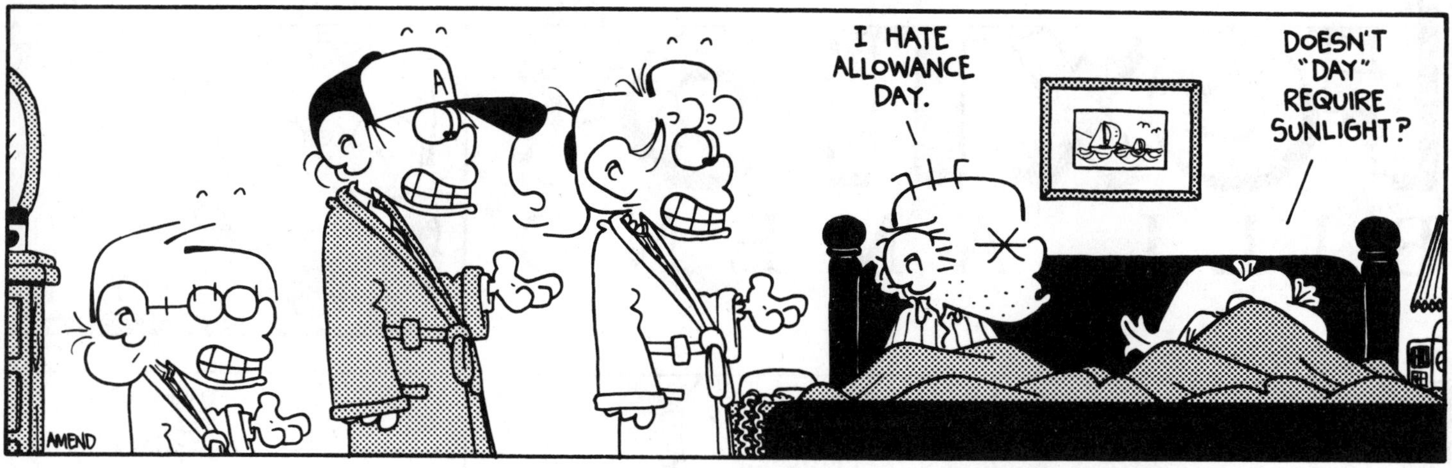
I HATE ALLOWANCE DAY.
DOESN'T "DAY" REQUIRE SUNLIGHT?
AMEND

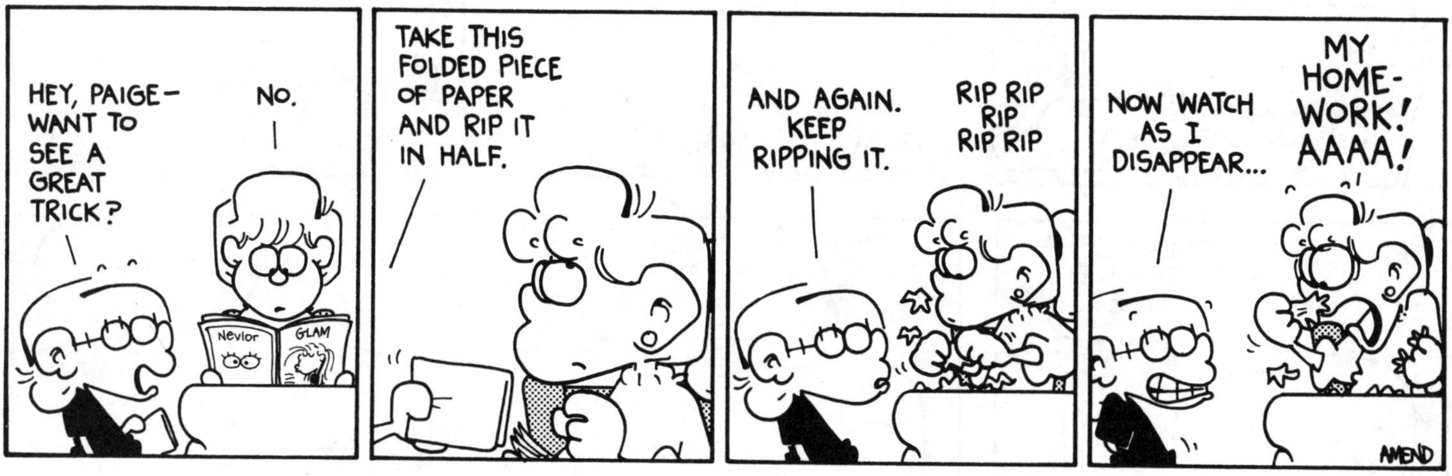
HEY, PAIGE- WANT TO SEE A GREAT TRICK?
NO.
Nevlor
GLAM
TAKE THIS FOLDED PIECE OF PAPER AND RIP IT IN HALF.
AND AGAIN. KEEP RIPPING IT.
RIP RIP RIP RIP RIP
NOW WATCH AS I DISAPPEAR...
MY HOME-WORK! AAAA!
AMEND

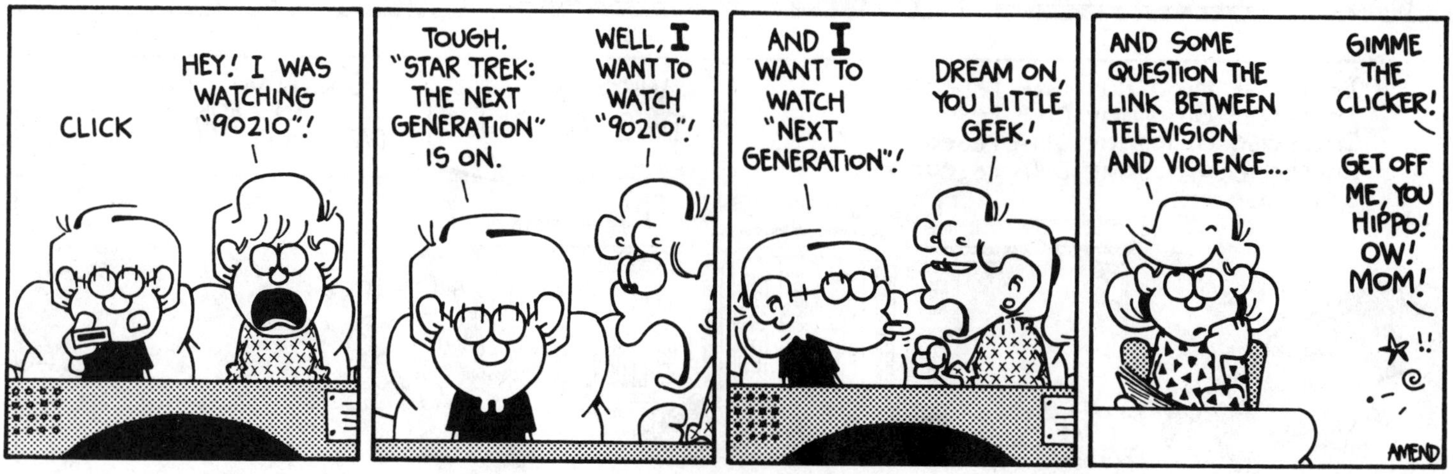
CLICK
HEY! I WAS WATCHING "90210"!
TOUGH. "STAR TREK: THE NEXT GENERATION" IS ON.
WELL, I WANT TO WATCH "90210"!
AND I WANT TO WATCH "NEXT GENERATION"!
DREAM ON, YOU LITTLE GEEK!
AND SOME QUESTION THE LINK BETWEEN TELEVISION AND VIOLENCE...
GIMME THE CLICKER!
GET OFF ME, YOU HIPPO! OW! MOM!
AMEND

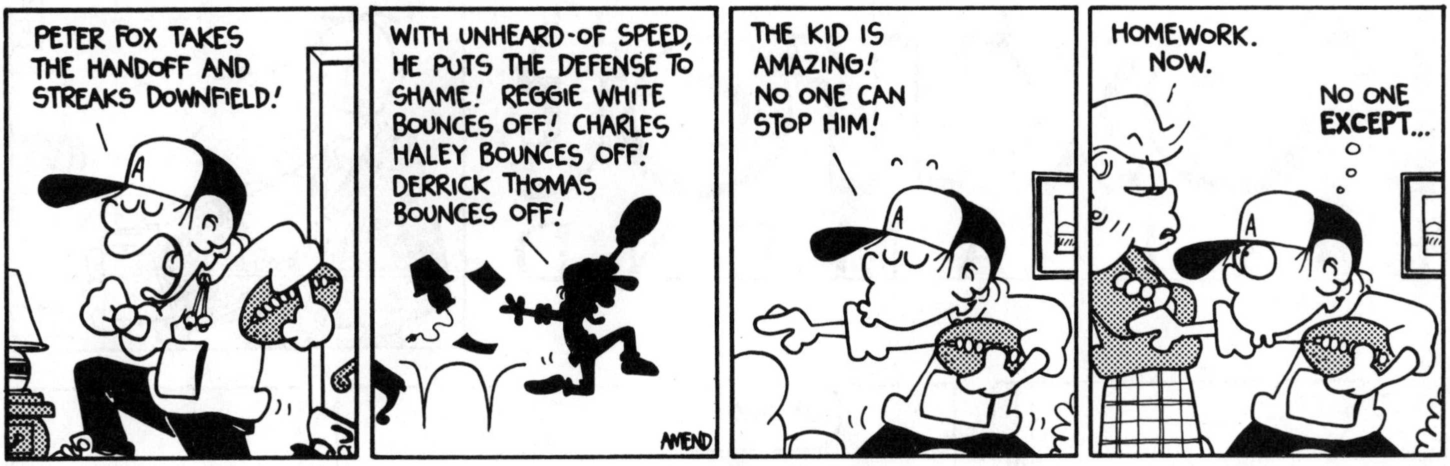
PETER FOX TAKES THE HANDOFF AND STREAKS DOWNFIELD!
WITH UNHEARD-OF SPEED, HE PUTS THE DEFENSE TO SHAME! REGGIE WHITE BOUNCES OFF! CHARLES HALEY BOUNCES OFF! DERRICK THOMAS BOUNCES OFF!
AMEND
THE KID IS AMAZING! NO ONE CAN STOP HIM!
HOMEWORK. NOW.
NO ONE EXCEPT...

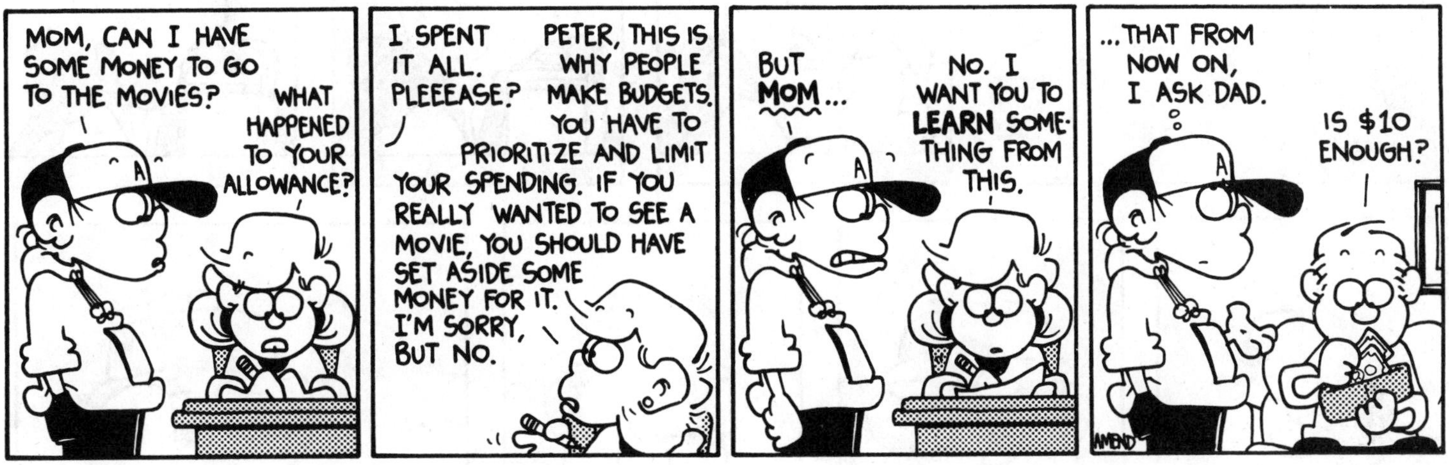
MOM, CAN I HAVE SOME MONEY TO GO TO THE MOVIES?
WHAT HAPPENED TO YOUR ALLOWANCE?
I SPENT IT ALL. PLEEEASE?
PETER, THIS IS WHY PEOPLE MAKE BUDGETS. YOU HAVE TO PRIORITIZE AND LIMIT YOUR SPENDING. IF YOU REALLY WANTED TO SEE A MOVIE, YOU SHOULD HAVE SET ASIDE SOME MONEY FOR IT. I'M SORRY, BUT NO.
BUT MOM...
NO. I WANT YOU TO LEARN SOMETHING FROM THIS.
...THAT FROM NOW ON, I ASK DAD.
IS $10 ENOUGH?
AMEND

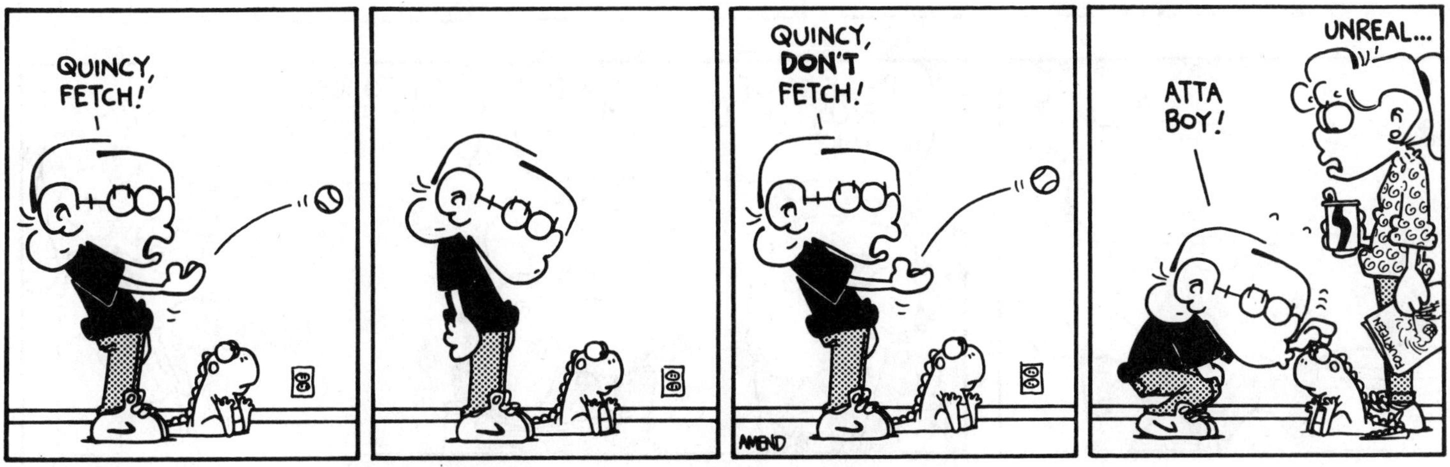
QUINCY, FETCH!
QUINCY, DON'T FETCH!
AMEND
UNREAL...
ATTA BOY!

FoxTrot
BILL AMEND

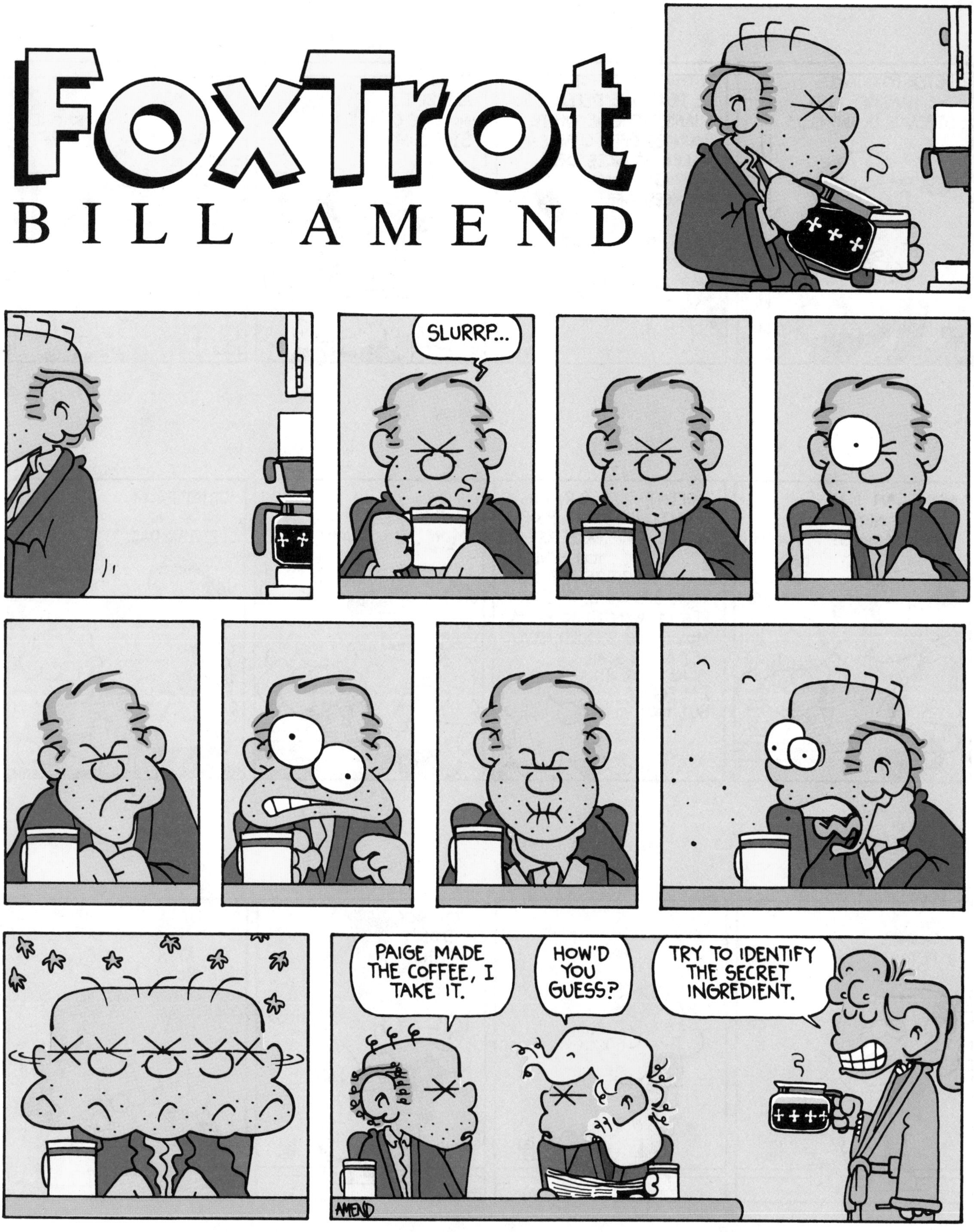
SLURRP...
PAIGE MADE THE COFFEE, I TAKE IT.
HOW'D YOU GUESS?
TRY TO IDENTIFY THE SECRET INGREDIENT.
AMEND

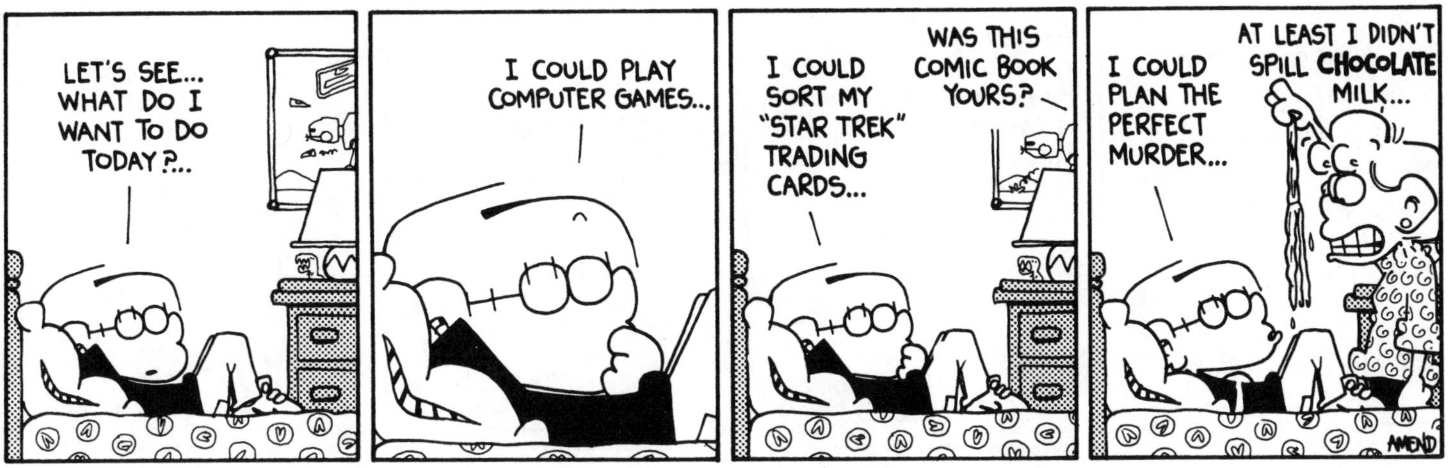
LET'S SEE... WHAT DO I WANT TO DO TODAY?...
I COULD PLAY COMPUTER GAMES...
I COULD SORT MY "STAR TREK" TRADING CARDS...
WAS THIS COMIC BOOK YOURS?
I COULD PLAN THE PERFECT MURDER...
AT LEAST I DIDN'T SPILL **CHOCOLATE** MILK...
AMEND

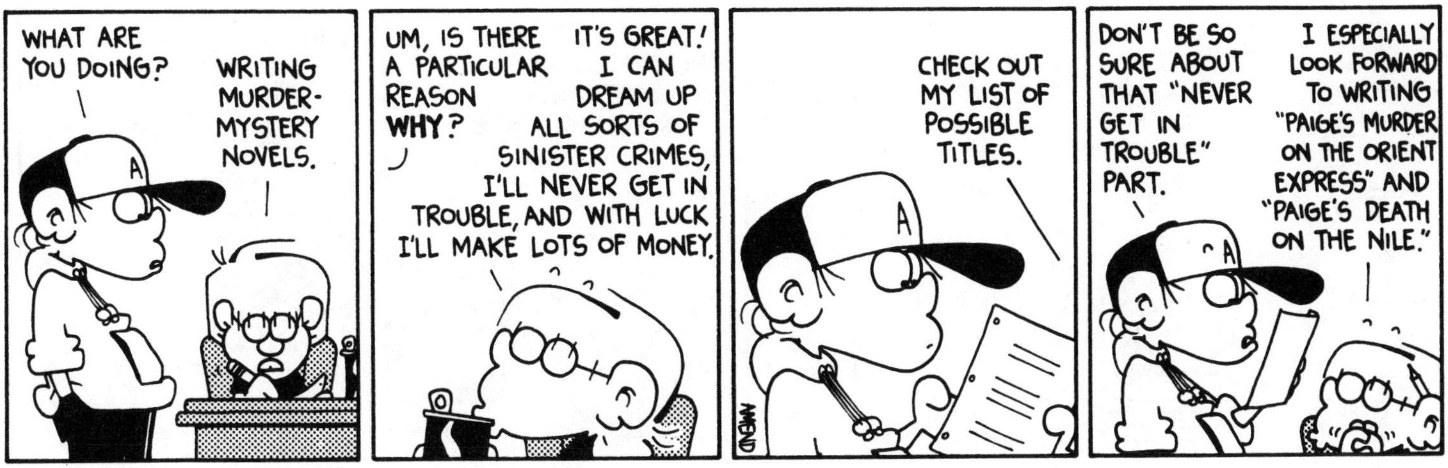
WHAT ARE YOU DOING?
WRITING MURDER-MYSTERY NOVELS.
UM, IS THERE A PARTICULAR REASON **WHY**?
IT'S GREAT! I CAN DREAM UP ALL SORTS OF SINISTER CRIMES, I'LL NEVER GET IN TROUBLE, AND WITH LUCK I'LL MAKE LOTS OF MONEY.
AMEND
CHECK OUT MY LIST OF POSSIBLE TITLES.
DON'T BE SO SURE ABOUT THAT "NEVER GET IN TROUBLE" PART.
I ESPECIALLY LOOK FORWARD TO WRITING "PAIGE'S MURDER ON THE ORIENT EXPRESS" AND "PAIGE'S DEATH ON THE NILE."

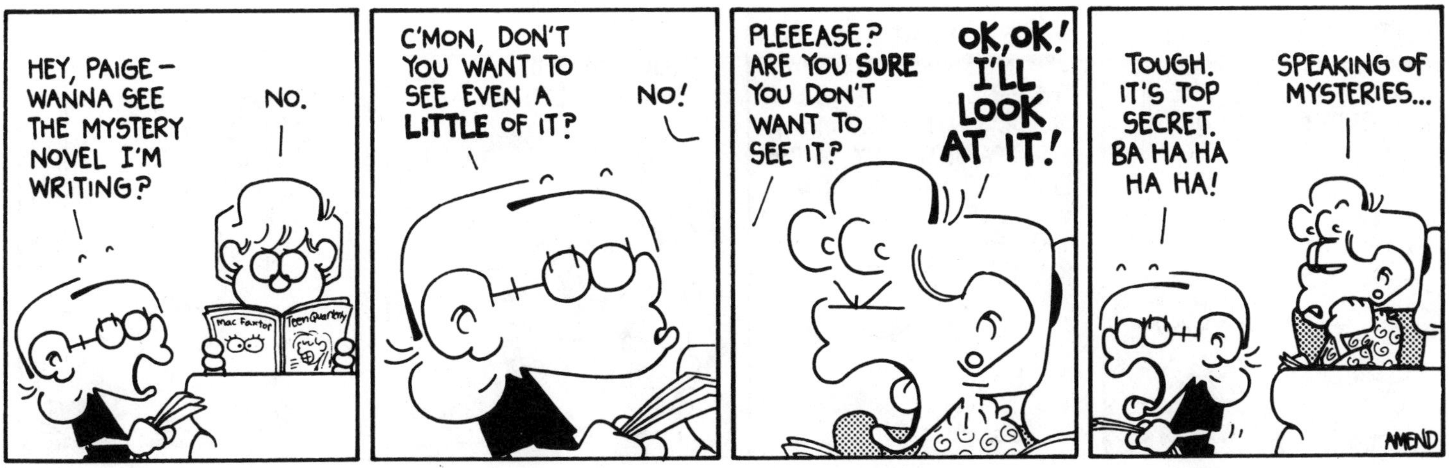
HEY, PAIGE – WANNA SEE THE MYSTERY NOVEL I'M WRITING?
NO.
C'MON, DON'T YOU WANT TO SEE EVEN A **LITTLE** OF IT?
NO!
PLEEEASE? ARE YOU **SURE** YOU DON'T WANT TO SEE IT?
OK, OK! I'LL LOOK AT IT!
TOUGH. IT'S TOP SECRET. BA HA HA HA HA!
SPEAKING OF MYSTERIES...
AMEND

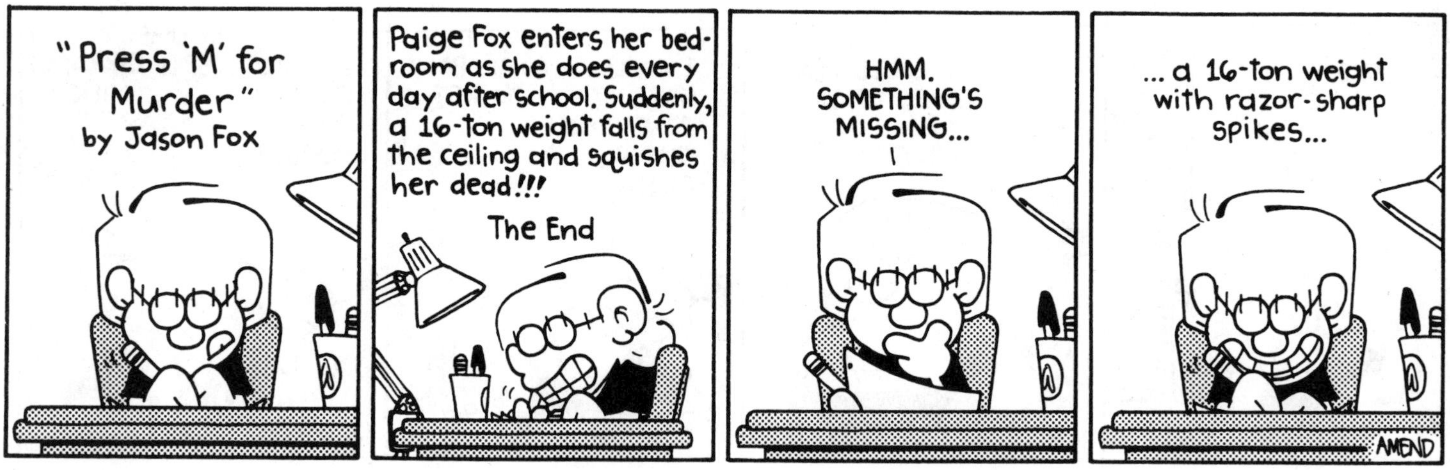
"Press 'M' for Murder" by Jason Fox
Paige Fox enters her bedroom as she does every day after school. Suddenly, a 16-ton weight falls from the ceiling and squishes her dead!!!
The End
HMM. SOMETHING'S MISSING...
... a 16-ton weight with razor-sharp spikes...
AMEND

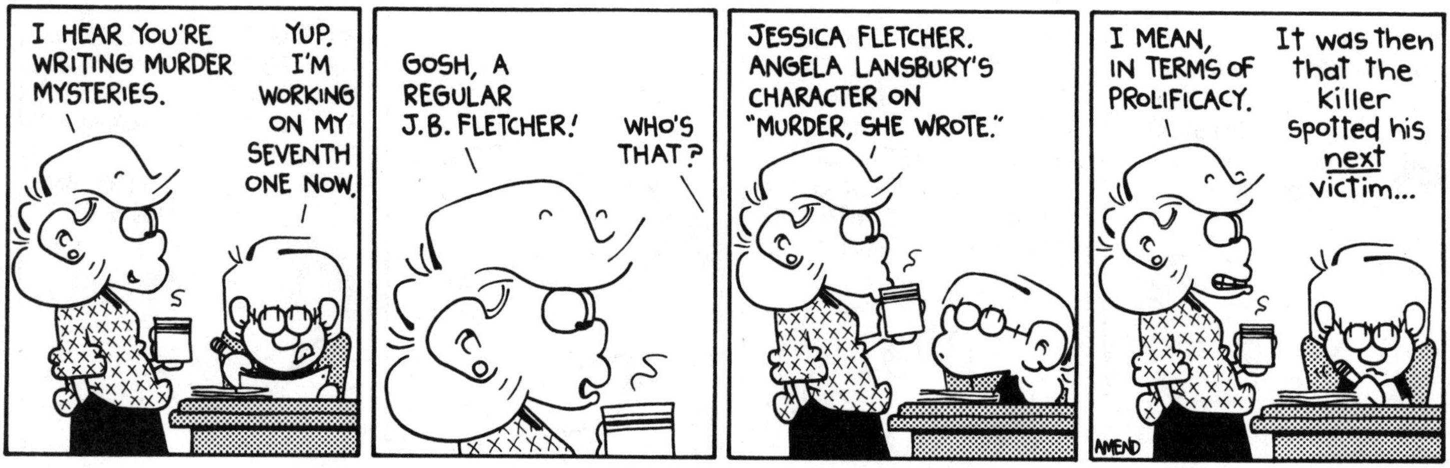
I HEAR YOU'RE WRITING MURDER MYSTERIES.
YUP. I'M WORKING ON MY SEVENTH ONE NOW.
GOSH, A REGULAR J.B. FLETCHER!
WHO'S THAT?
JESSICA FLETCHER. ANGELA LANSBURY'S CHARACTER ON "MURDER, SHE WROTE."
I MEAN, IN TERMS OF PROLIFICACY.
It was then that the killer spotted his next victim...
AMEND

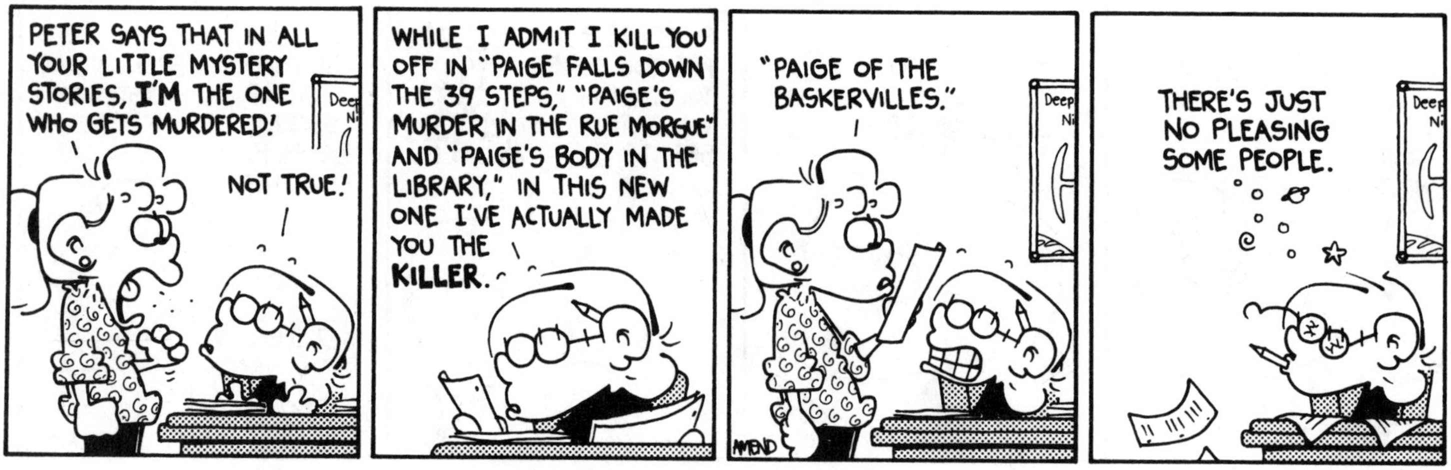
PETER SAYS THAT IN ALL YOUR LITTLE MYSTERY STORIES, I'M THE ONE WHO GETS MURDERED!
NOT TRUE!
WHILE I ADMIT I KILL YOU OFF IN "PAIGE FALLS DOWN THE 39 STEPS," "PAIGE'S MURDER IN THE RUE MORGUE" AND "PAIGE'S BODY IN THE LIBRARY," IN THIS NEW ONE I'VE ACTUALLY MADE YOU THE KILLER.
"PAIGE OF THE BASKERVILLES."
THERE'S JUST NO PLEASING SOME PEOPLE.
AMEND

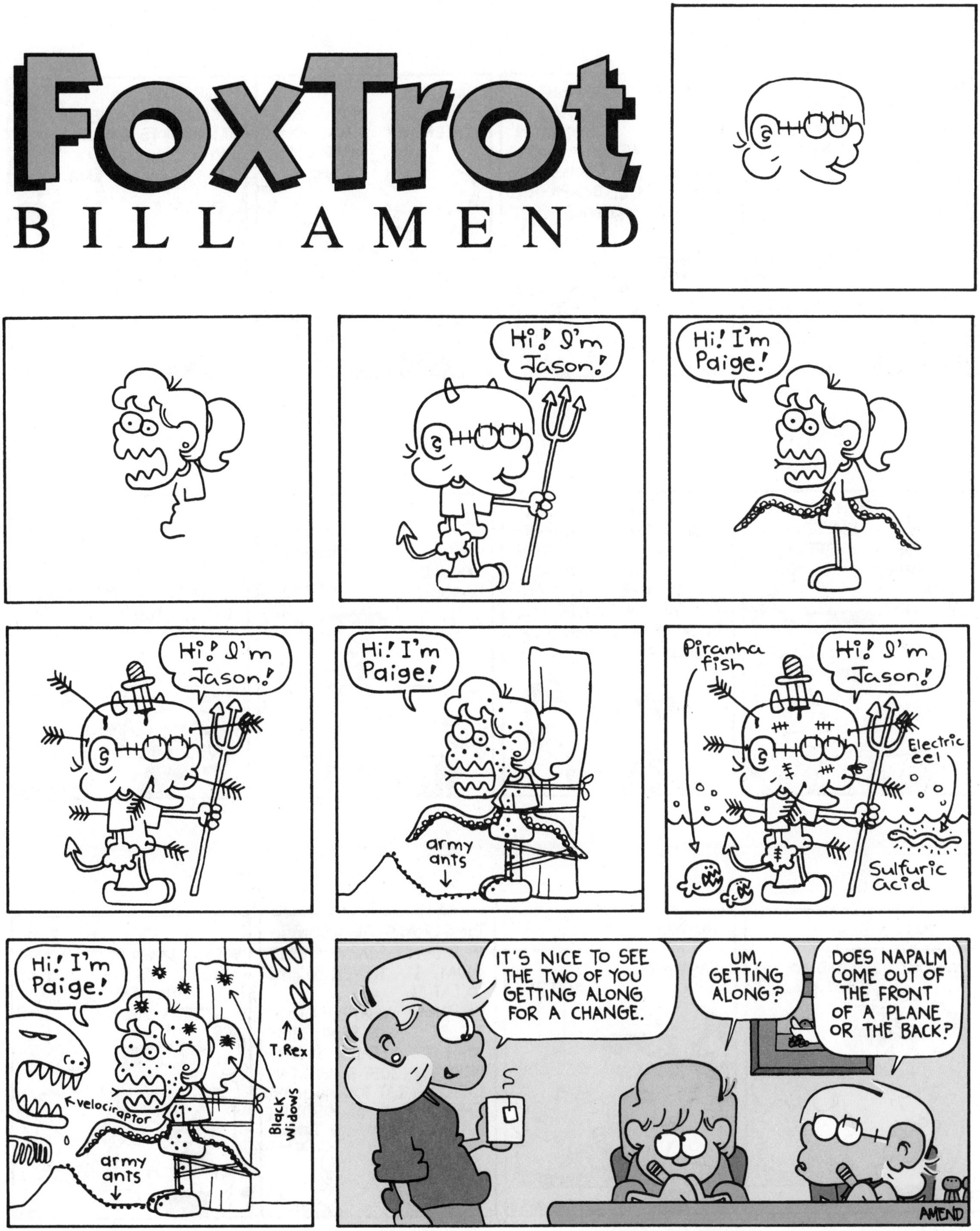
FoxTrot
BILL AMEND
Hi! I'm Jason!
Hi! I'm Paige!
Hi! I'm Jason!
Hi! I'm Paige!
army ants
Piranha fish
Hi! I'm Jason!
Electric eel
Sulfuric acid
Hi! I'm Paige!
T. Rex
velociraptor
Black Widows
army ants
IT'S NICE TO SEE THE TWO OF YOU GETTING ALONG FOR A CHANGE.
UM, GETTING ALONG?
DOES NAPALM COME OUT OF THE FRONT OF A PLANE OR THE BACK?
AMEND

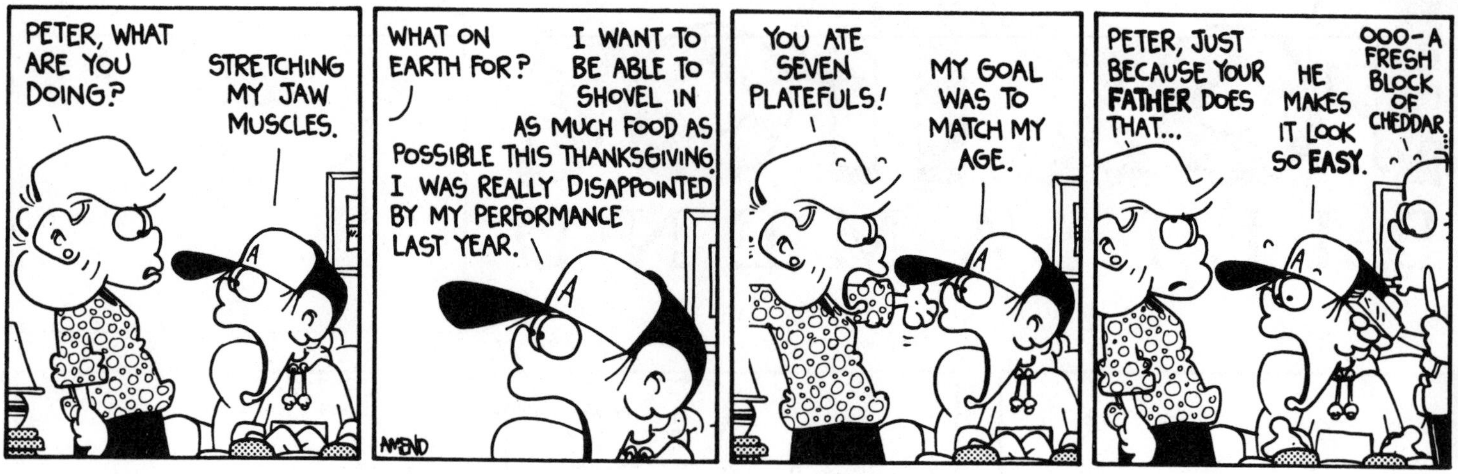
PETER, WHAT ARE YOU DOING?
STRETCHING MY JAW MUSCLES.
WHAT ON EARTH FOR?
I WANT TO BE ABLE TO SHOVEL IN AS MUCH FOOD AS POSSIBLE THIS THANKSGIVING. I WAS REALLY DISAPPOINTED BY MY PERFORMANCE LAST YEAR.
AMEND
YOU ATE SEVEN PLATEFULS!
MY GOAL WAS TO MATCH MY AGE.
PETER, JUST BECAUSE YOUR FATHER DOES THAT...
HE MAKES IT LOOK SO EASY.
OOO-A FRESH BLOCK OF CHEDDAR.

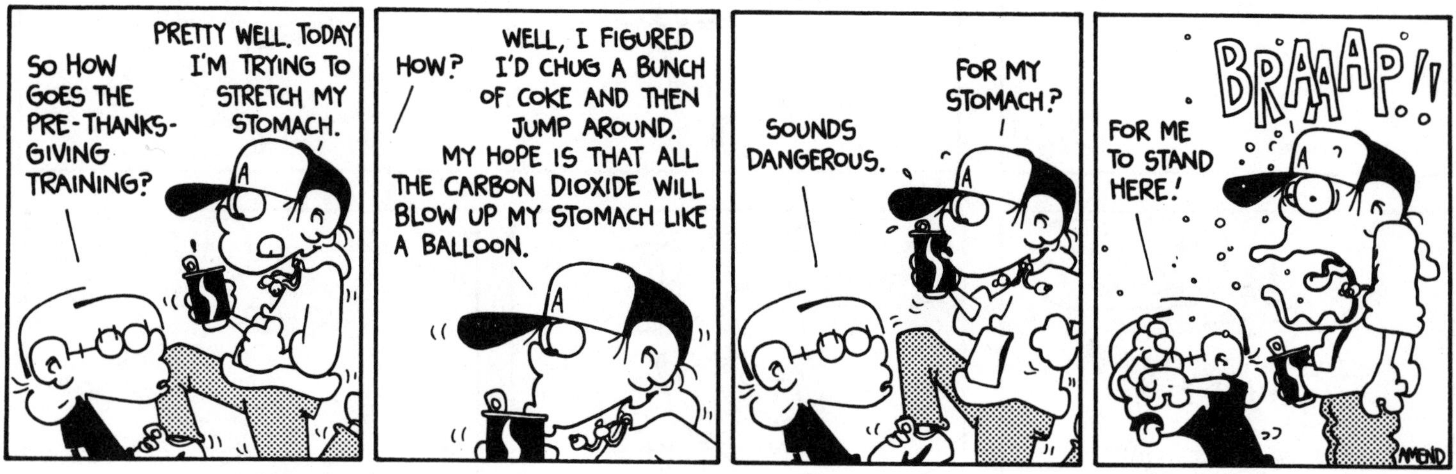
SO HOW GOES THE PRE-THANKS-GIVING TRAINING?
PRETTY WELL. TODAY I'M TRYING TO STRETCH MY STOMACH.
HOW?
WELL, I FIGURED I'D CHUG A BUNCH OF COKE AND THEN JUMP AROUND.
MY HOPE IS THAT ALL THE CARBON DIOXIDE WILL BLOW UP MY STOMACH LIKE A BALLOON.
SOUNDS DANGEROUS.
FOR MY STOMACH?
FOR ME TO STAND HERE!
BRAAAP!!
AMEND

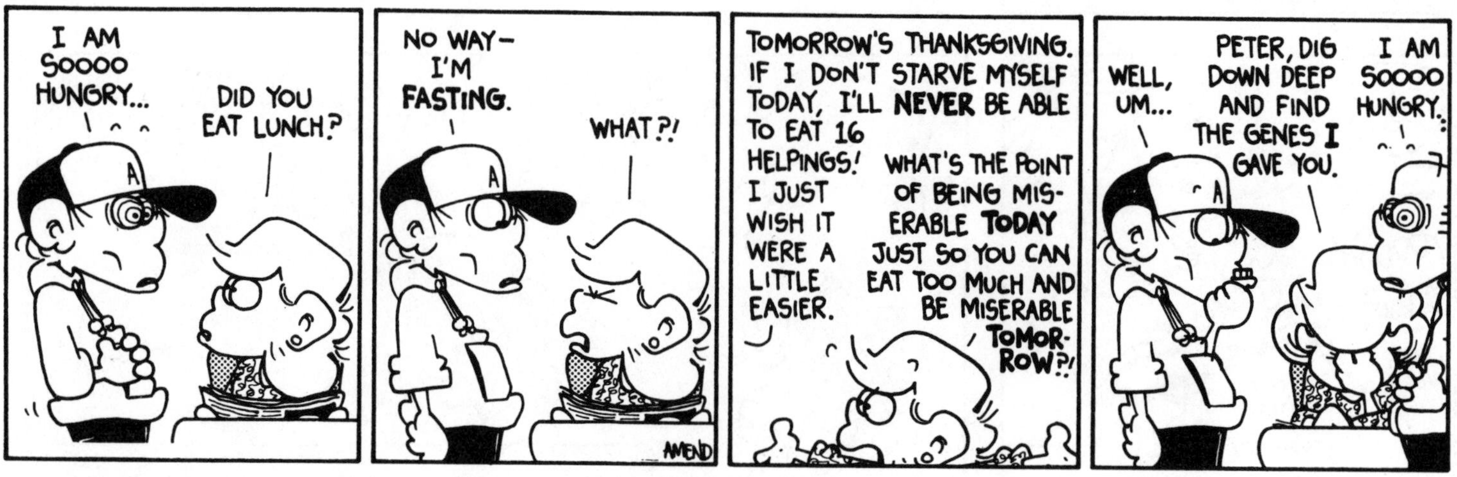
I AM SOOOO HUNGRY...
DID YOU EAT LUNCH?
NO WAY- I'M FASTING.
WHAT?!
AMEND
TOMORROW'S THANKSGIVING. IF I DON'T STARVE MYSELF TODAY, I'LL NEVER BE ABLE TO EAT 16 HELPINGS! I JUST WISH IT WERE A LITTLE EASIER.
WHAT'S THE POINT OF BEING MIS-ERABLE TODAY JUST SO YOU CAN EAT TOO MUCH AND BE MISERABLE TOMOR-ROW?!
WELL, UM...
PETER, DIG DOWN DEEP AND FIND THE GENES I GAVE YOU.
I AM SOOOO HUNGRY.

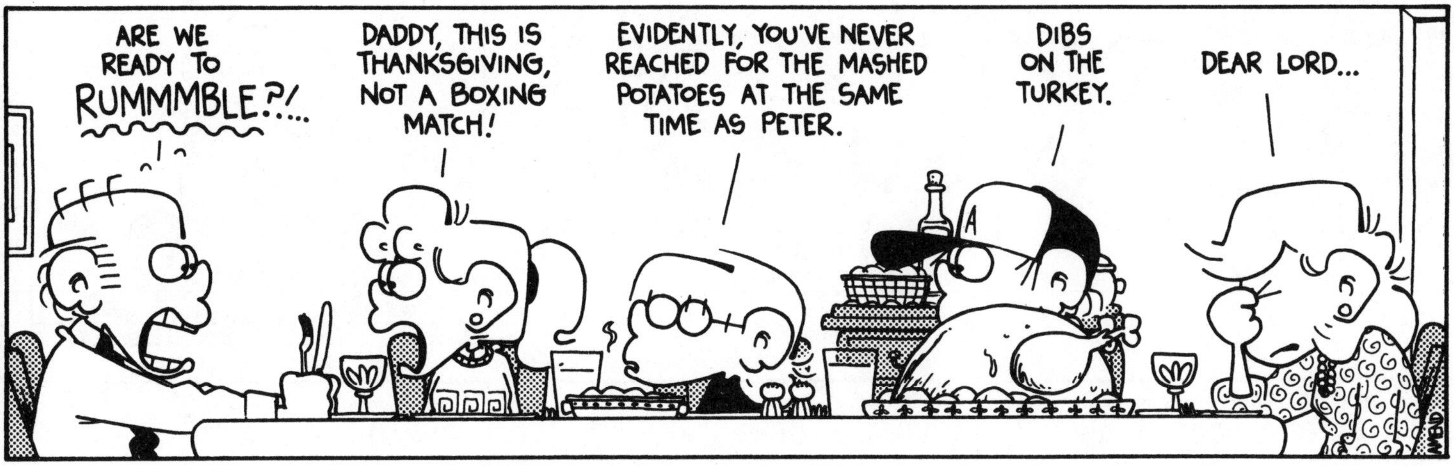
ARE WE READY TO RUMMMBLE?!...
DADDY, THIS IS THANKSGIVING, NOT A BOXING MATCH!
EVIDENTLY, YOU'VE NEVER REACHED FOR THE MASHED POTATOES AT THE SAME TIME AS PETER.
DIBS ON THE TURKEY.
DEAR LORD...

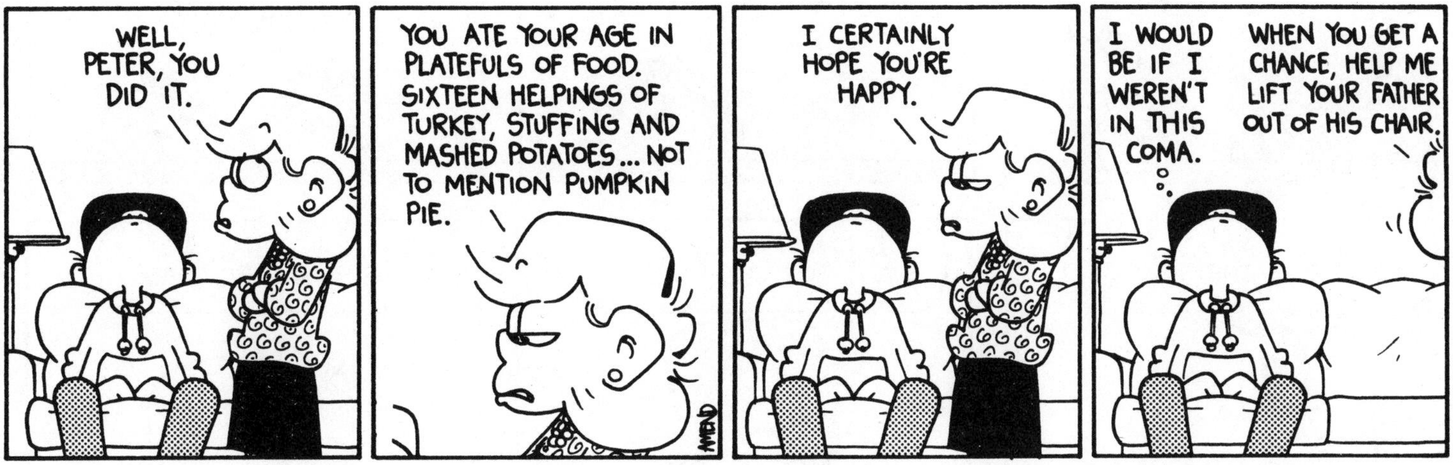
WELL, PETER, YOU DID IT.
YOU ATE YOUR AGE IN PLATEFULS OF FOOD. SIXTEEN HELPINGS OF TURKEY, STUFFING AND MASHED POTATOES... NOT TO MENTION PUMPKIN PIE.
I CERTAINLY HOPE YOU'RE HAPPY.
I WOULD BE IF I WEREN'T IN THIS COMA.
WHEN YOU GET A CHANCE, HELP ME LIFT YOUR FATHER OUT OF HIS CHAIR.

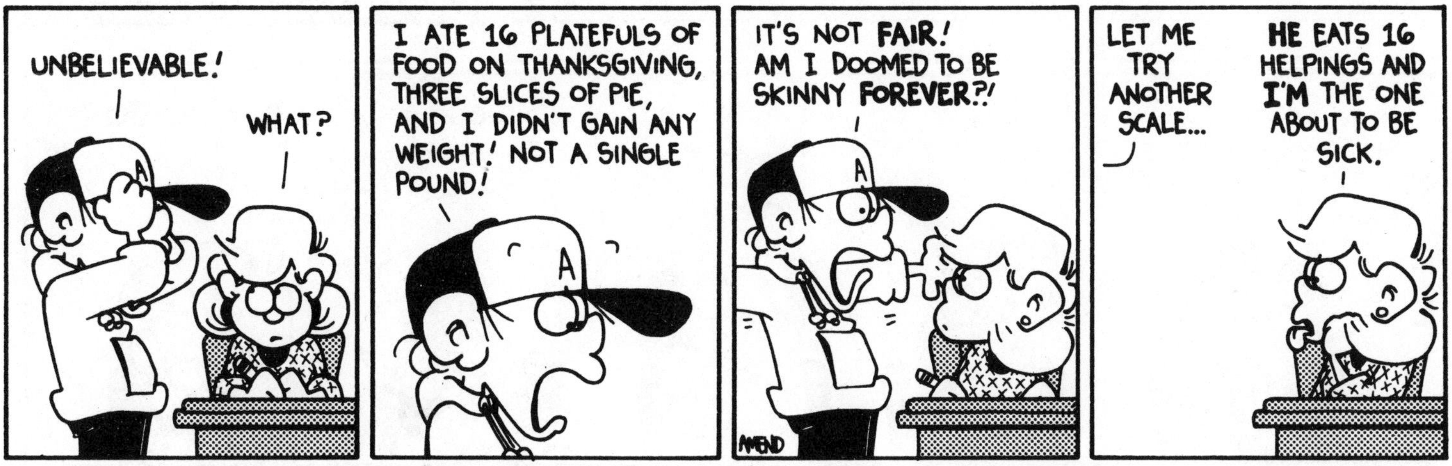
UNBELIEVABLE!
WHAT?
I ATE 16 PLATEFULS OF FOOD ON THANKSGIVING, THREE SLICES OF PIE, AND I DIDN'T GAIN ANY WEIGHT! NOT A SINGLE POUND!
IT'S NOT FAIR! AM I DOOMED TO BE SKINNY FOREVER?!
LET ME TRY ANOTHER SCALE...
HE EATS 16 HELPINGS AND I'M THE ONE ABOUT TO BE SICK.

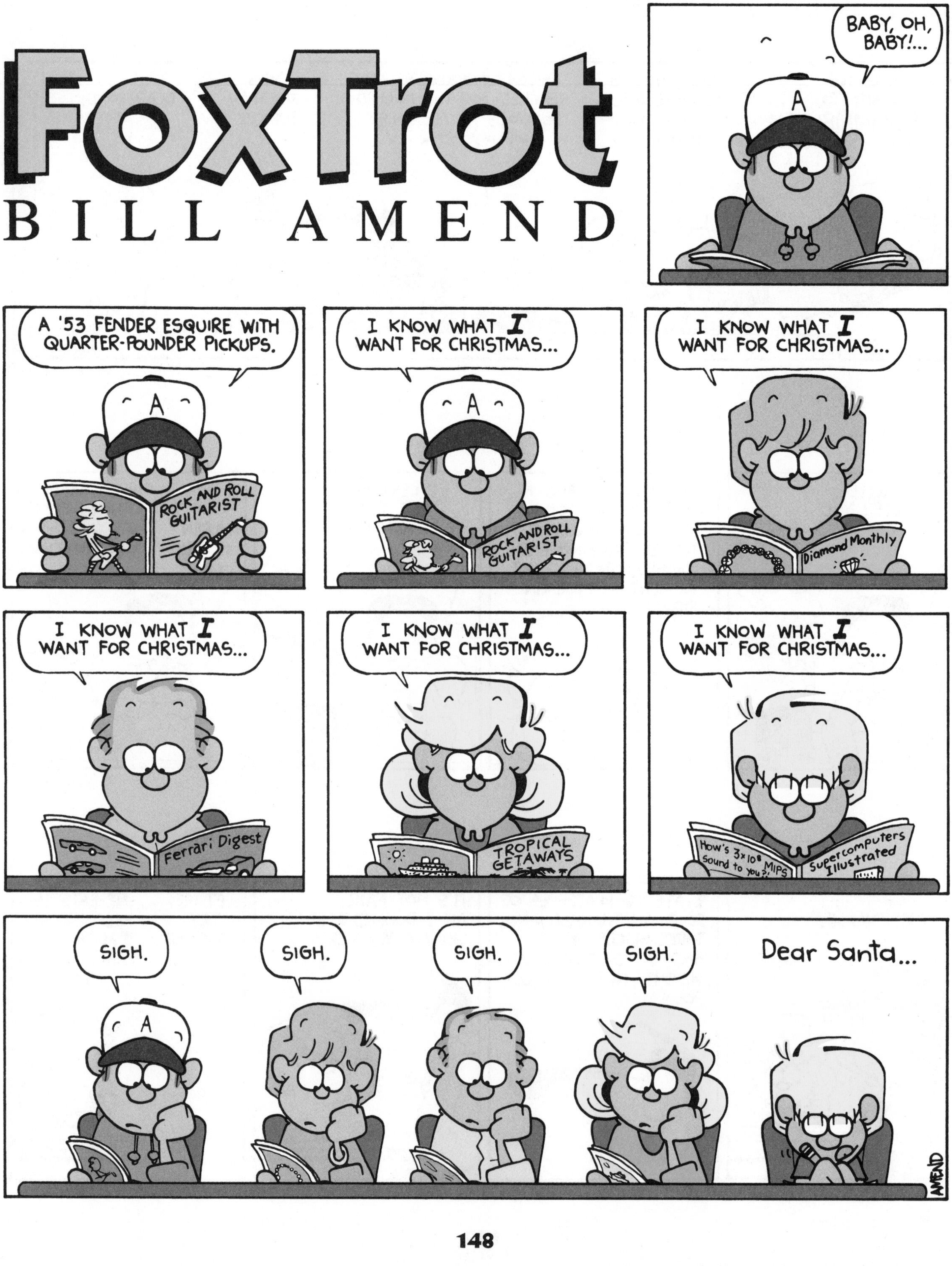
FoxTrot
BILL AMEND
BABY, OH, BABY!...
A '53 FENDER ESQUIRE WITH QUARTER-POUNDER PICKUPS.
ROCK AND ROLL GUITARIST
I KNOW WHAT I WANT FOR CHRISTMAS...
ROCK AND ROLL GUITARIST
I KNOW WHAT I WANT FOR CHRISTMAS...
Diamond Monthly
I KNOW WHAT I WANT FOR CHRISTMAS...
Ferrari Digest
I KNOW WHAT I WANT FOR CHRISTMAS...
TROPICAL GETAWAYS
I KNOW WHAT I WANT FOR CHRISTMAS...
How's 3×10⁸ MIPS sound to you?!
Supercomputers Illustrated
SIGH.
SIGH.
SIGH.
SIGH.
Dear Santa...
AMEND

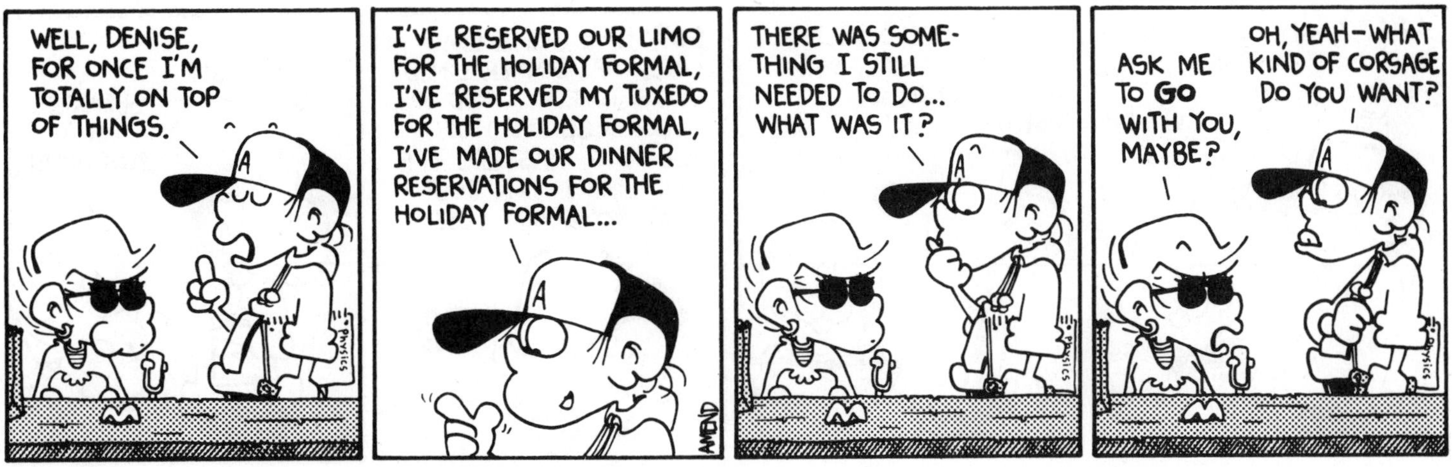
WELL, DENISE, FOR ONCE I'M TOTALLY ON TOP OF THINGS.
I'VE RESERVED OUR LIMO FOR THE HOLIDAY FORMAL, I'VE RESERVED MY TUXEDO FOR THE HOLIDAY FORMAL, I'VE MADE OUR DINNER RESERVATIONS FOR THE HOLIDAY FORMAL...
AMEND
THERE WAS SOME-THING I STILL NEEDED TO DO... WHAT WAS IT?
ASK ME TO **GO** WITH YOU, MAYBE?
OH, YEAH–WHAT KIND OF CORSAGE DO YOU WANT?

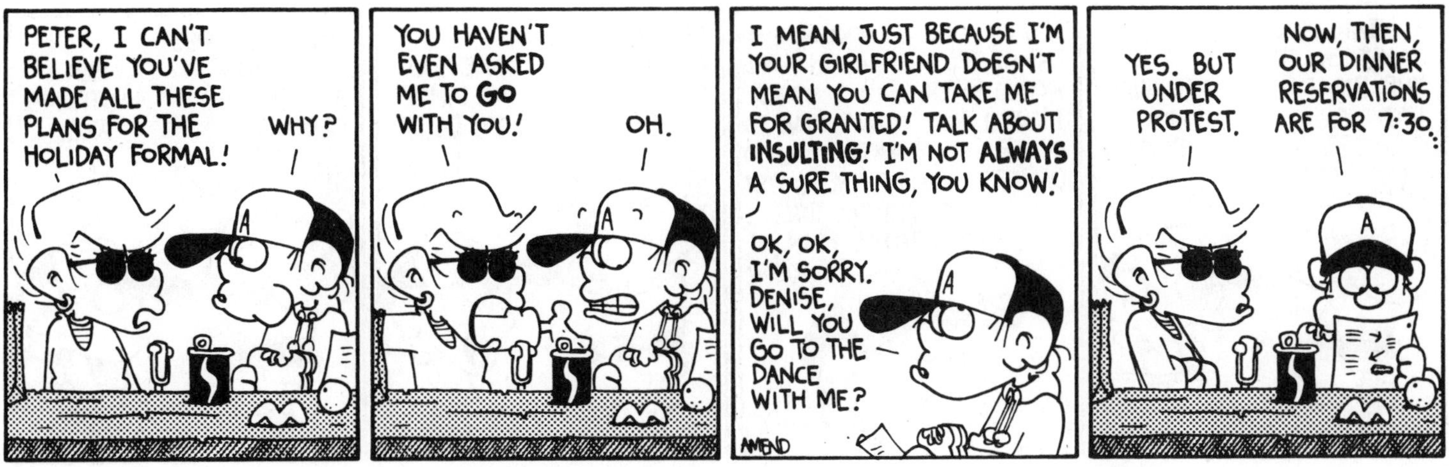
PETER, I CAN'T BELIEVE YOU'VE MADE ALL THESE PLANS FOR THE HOLIDAY FORMAL!
WHY?
YOU HAVEN'T EVEN ASKED ME TO **GO** WITH YOU!
OH.
I MEAN, JUST BECAUSE I'M YOUR GIRLFRIEND DOESN'T MEAN YOU CAN TAKE ME FOR GRANTED! TALK ABOUT **INSULTING**! I'M NOT **ALWAYS** A SURE THING, YOU KNOW!
OK, OK, I'M SORRY. DENISE, WILL YOU GO TO THE DANCE WITH ME?
AMEND
YES. BUT UNDER PROTEST.
NOW, THEN, OUR DINNER RESERVATIONS ARE FOR 7:30...

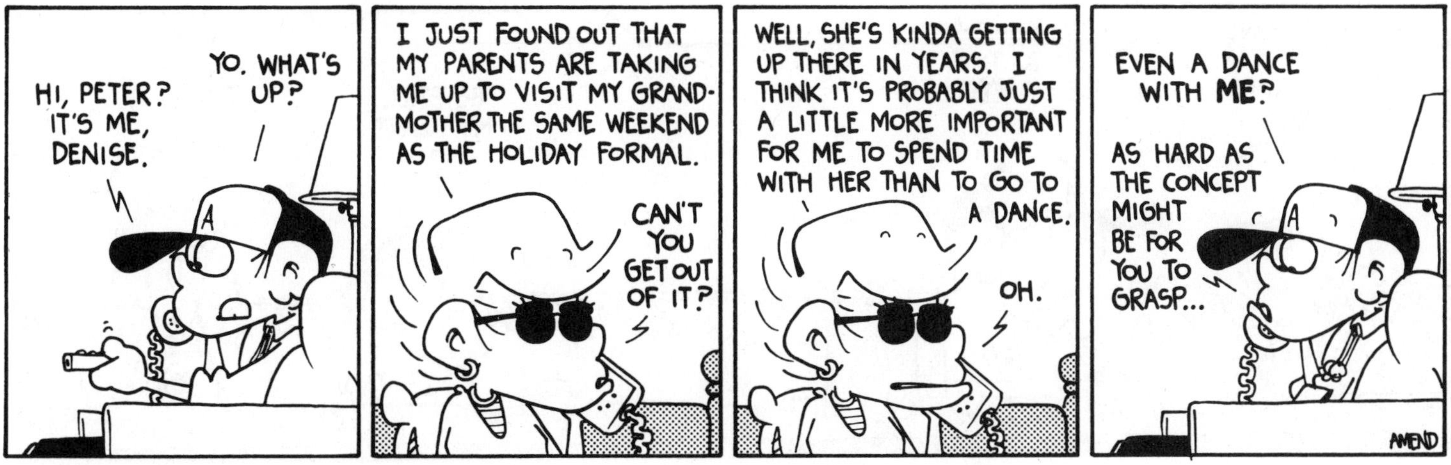
HI, PETER? IT'S ME, DENISE.
YO. WHAT'S UP?
I JUST FOUND OUT THAT MY PARENTS ARE TAKING ME UP TO VISIT MY GRAND-MOTHER THE SAME WEEKEND AS THE HOLIDAY FORMAL.
CAN'T YOU GET OUT OF IT?
WELL, SHE'S KINDA GETTING UP THERE IN YEARS. I THINK IT'S PROBABLY JUST A LITTLE MORE IMPORTANT FOR ME TO SPEND TIME WITH HER THAN TO GO TO A DANCE.
OH.
EVEN A DANCE WITH **ME**?
AS HARD AS THE CONCEPT MIGHT BE FOR YOU TO GRASP...
AMEND

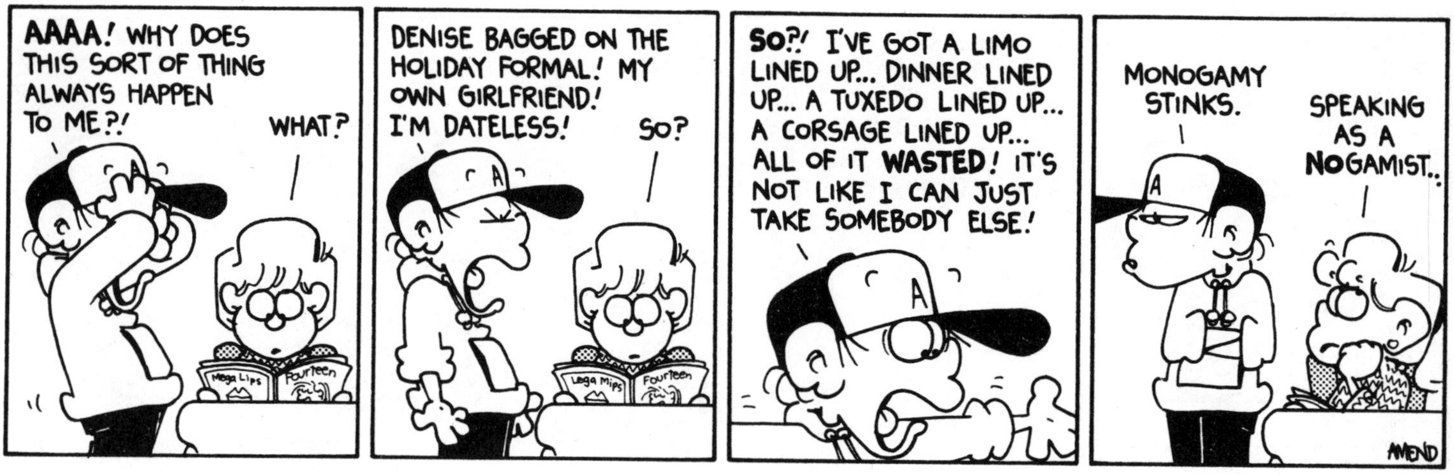
AAAA! WHY DOES THIS SORT OF THING ALWAYS HAPPEN TO ME?!
WHAT?
Mega Lips
Fourteen
DENISE BAGGED ON THE HOLIDAY FORMAL! MY OWN GIRLFRIEND! I'M DATELESS!
SO?
SO?! I'VE GOT A LIMO LINED UP... DINNER LINED UP... A TUXEDO LINED UP... A CORSAGE LINED UP... ALL OF IT WASTED! IT'S NOT LIKE I CAN JUST TAKE SOMEBODY ELSE!
MONOGAMY STINKS.
SPEAKING AS A NOGAMIST...
AMEND

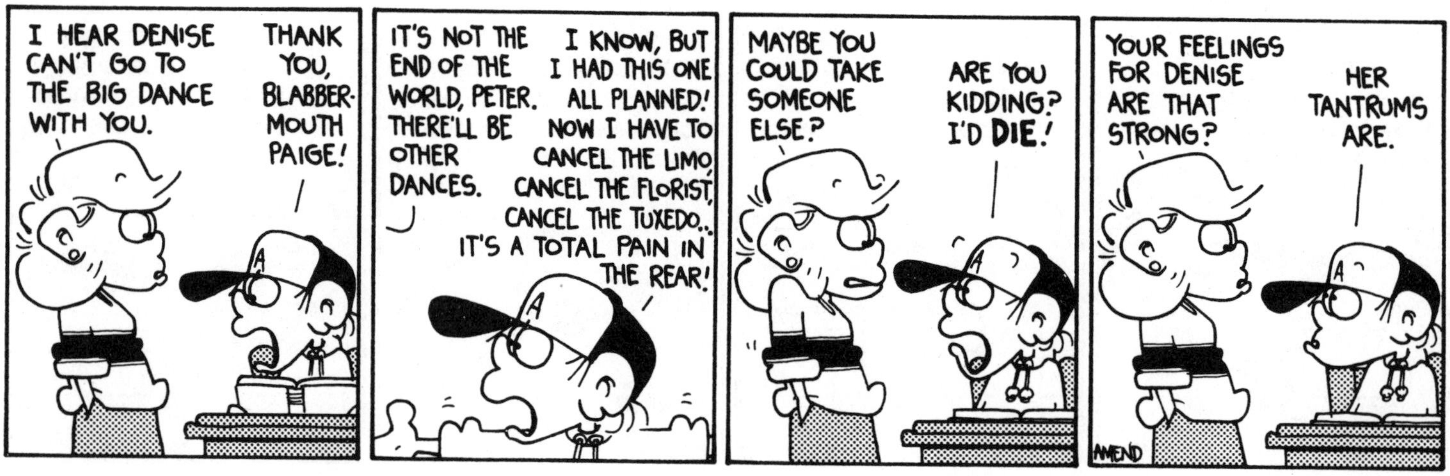
I HEAR DENISE CAN'T GO TO THE BIG DANCE WITH YOU.
THANK YOU, BLABBER-MOUTH PAIGE!
IT'S NOT THE END OF THE WORLD, PETER. THERE'LL BE OTHER DANCES.
I KNOW, BUT I HAD THIS ONE ALL PLANNED! NOW I HAVE TO CANCEL THE LIMO, CANCEL THE FLORIST, CANCEL THE TUXEDO... IT'S A TOTAL PAIN IN THE REAR!
MAYBE YOU COULD TAKE SOMEONE ELSE?
ARE YOU KIDDING? I'D DIE!
YOUR FEELINGS FOR DENISE ARE THAT STRONG?
HER TANTRUMS ARE.
AMEND

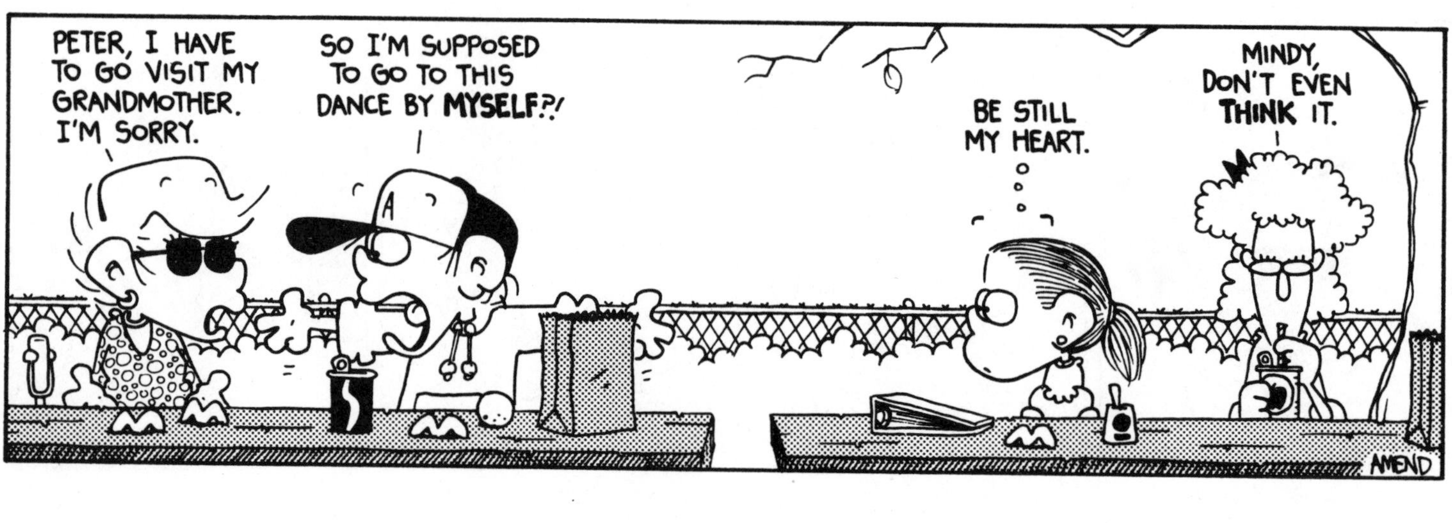
PETER, I HAVE TO GO VISIT MY GRANDMOTHER. I'M SORRY.
SO I'M SUPPOSED TO GO TO THIS DANCE BY MYSELF?!
BE STILL MY HEART.
MINDY, DON'T EVEN THINK IT.
AMEND

FoxTrot
BILL AMEND

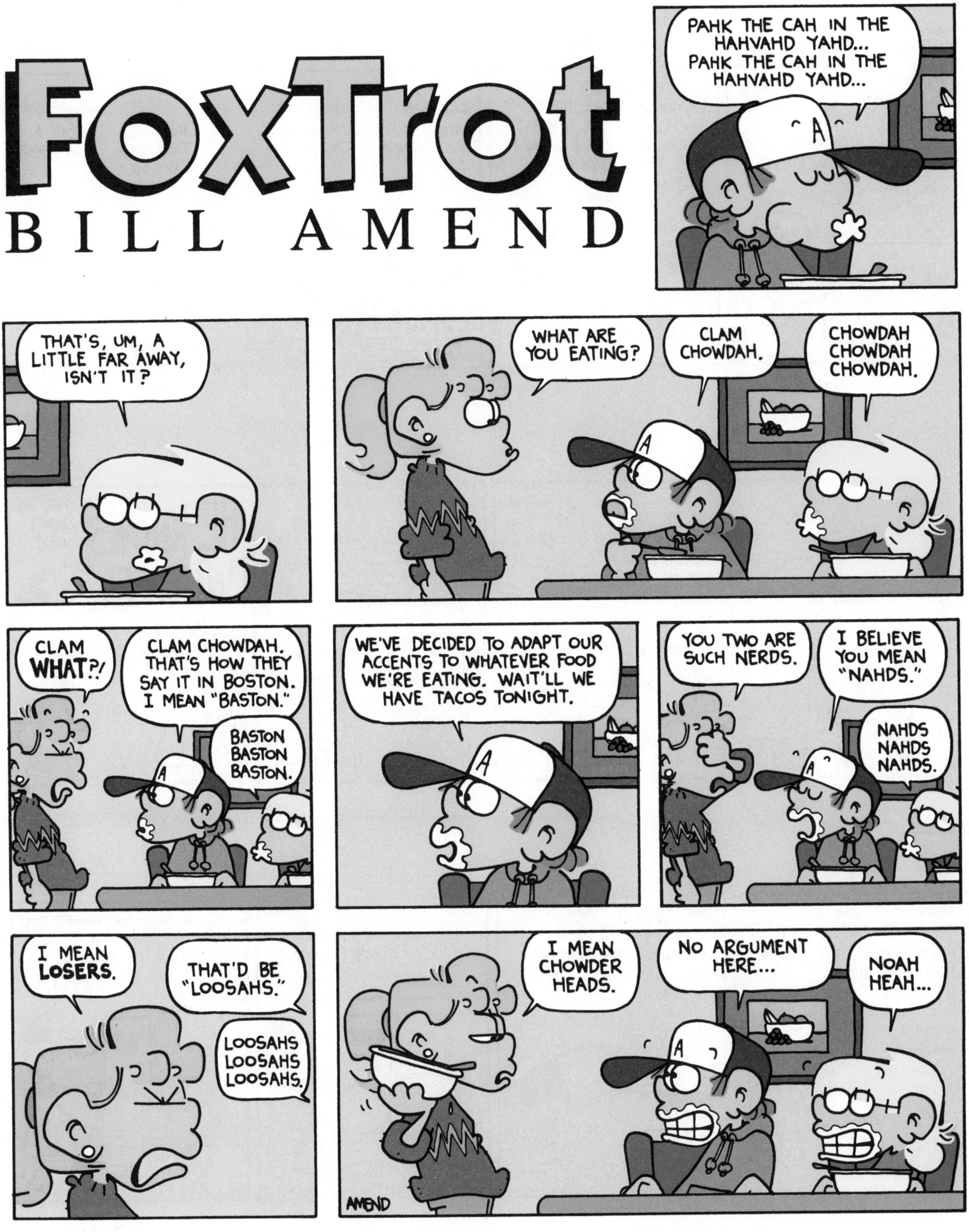
PAHK THE CAH IN THE HAHVAHD YAHD... PAHK THE CAH IN THE HAHVAHD YAHD...
THAT'S, UM, A LITTLE FAR AWAY, ISN'T IT?
WHAT ARE YOU EATING?
CLAM CHOWDAH.
CHOWDAH CHOWDAH CHOWDAH.
CLAM **WHAT**?!
CLAM CHOWDAH. THAT'S HOW THEY SAY IT IN BOSTON. I MEAN "BASTON."
BASTON BASTON BASTON.
WE'VE DECIDED TO ADAPT OUR ACCENTS TO WHATEVER FOOD WE'RE EATING. WAIT'LL WE HAVE TACOS TONIGHT.
YOU TWO ARE SUCH NERDS.
I BELIEVE YOU MEAN "NAHDS."
NAHDS NAHDS NAHDS.
I MEAN **LOSERS**.
THAT'D BE "LOOSAHS."
LOOSAHS LOOSAHS LOOSAHS.
I MEAN CHOWDER HEADS.
NO ARGUMENT HERE...
NOAH HEAH...
AMEND

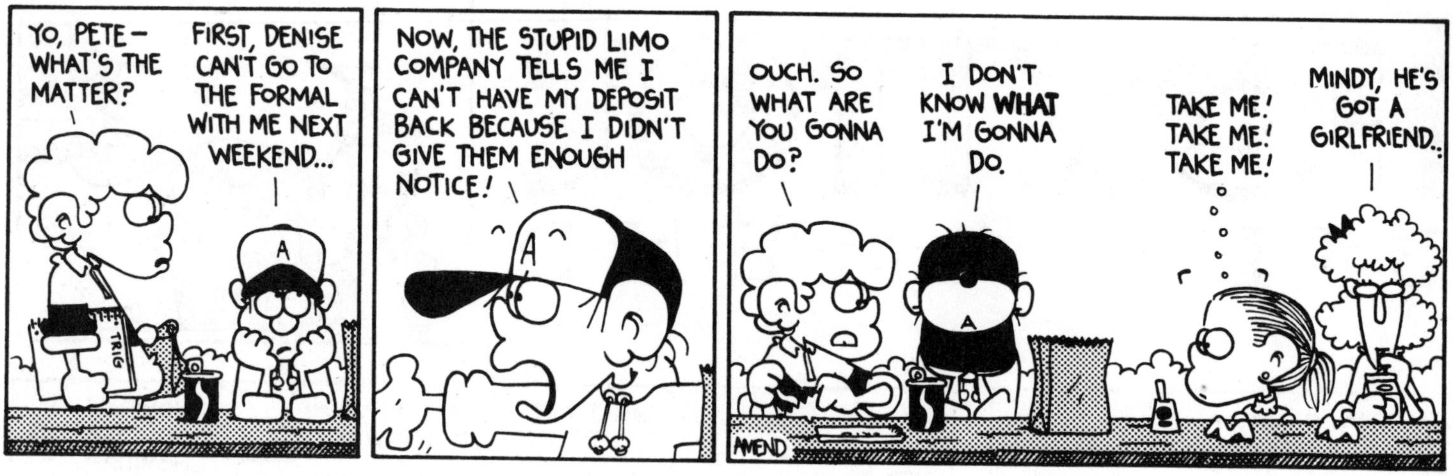
YO, PETE— WHAT'S THE MATTER?
FIRST, DENISE CAN'T GO TO THE FORMAL WITH ME NEXT WEEKEND...
NOW, THE STUPID LIMO COMPANY TELLS ME I CAN'T HAVE MY DEPOSIT BACK BECAUSE I DIDN'T GIVE THEM ENOUGH NOTICE!
OUCH. SO WHAT ARE YOU GONNA DO?
I DON'T KNOW **WHAT** I'M GONNA DO.
TAKE ME! TAKE ME! TAKE ME!
MINDY, HE'S GOT A GIRLFRIEND.

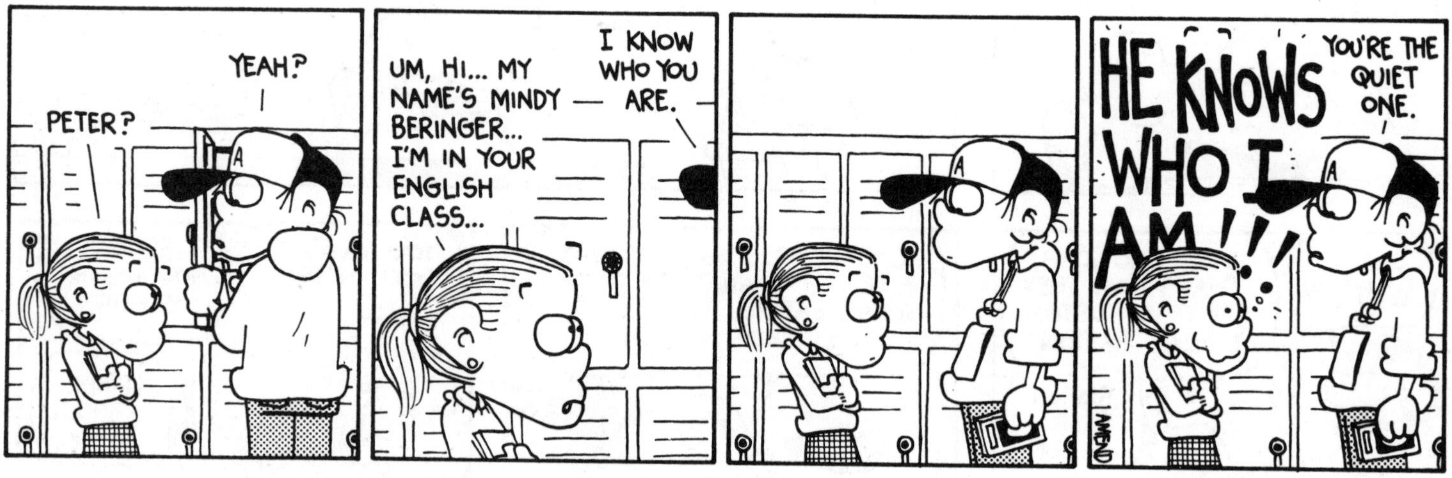
PETER?
YEAH?
UM, HI... MY NAME'S MINDY BERINGER... I'M IN YOUR ENGLISH CLASS...
I KNOW WHO YOU ARE.
HE KNOWS WHO I AM!!!
YOU'RE THE QUIET ONE.

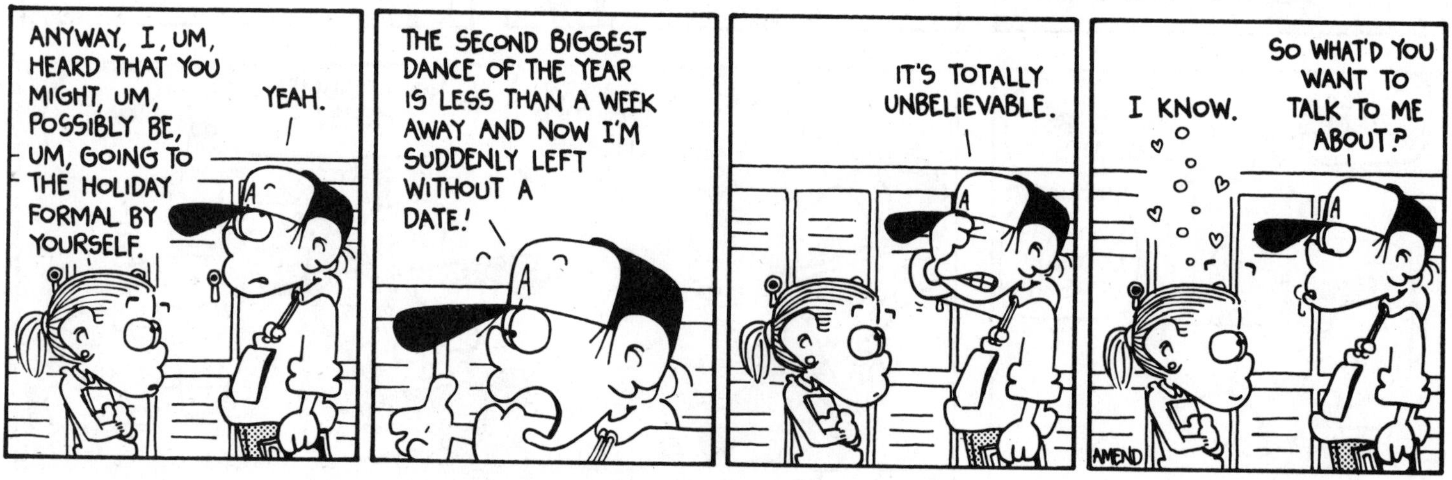
ANYWAY, I, UM, HEARD THAT YOU MIGHT, UM, POSSIBLY BE, UM, GOING TO THE HOLIDAY FORMAL BY YOURSELF.
YEAH.
THE SECOND BIGGEST DANCE OF THE YEAR IS LESS THAN A WEEK AWAY AND NOW I'M SUDDENLY LEFT WITHOUT A DATE!
IT'S TOTALLY UNBELIEVABLE.
I KNOW.
SO WHAT'D YOU WANT TO TALK TO ME ABOUT?

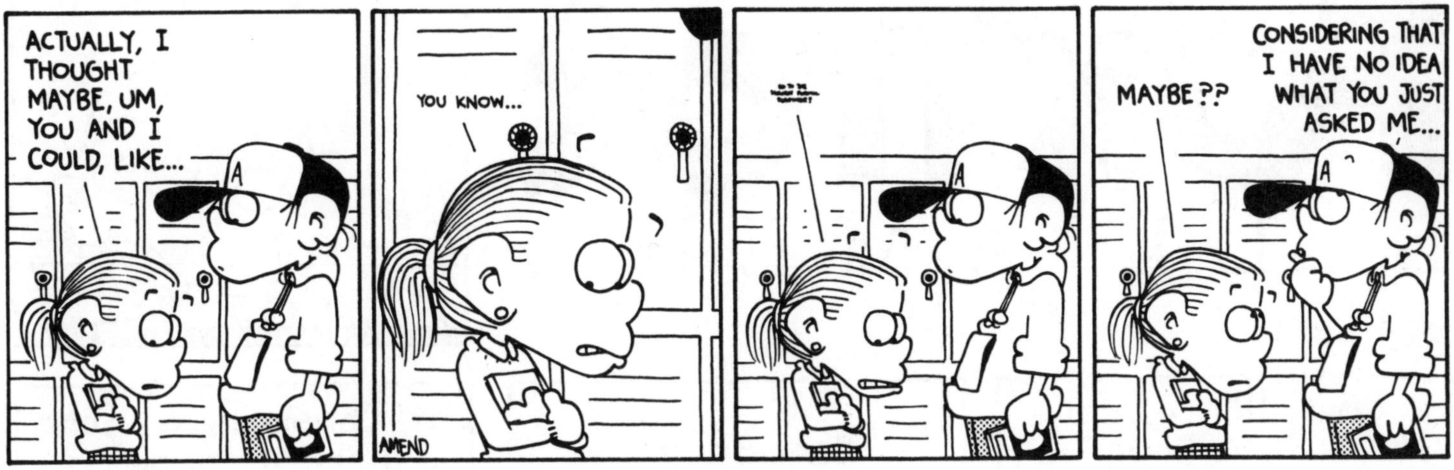
ACTUALLY, I THOUGHT MAYBE, UM, YOU AND I COULD, LIKE...
YOU KNOW...
MAYBE ??
CONSIDERING THAT I HAVE NO IDEA WHAT YOU JUST ASKED ME...
AMEND

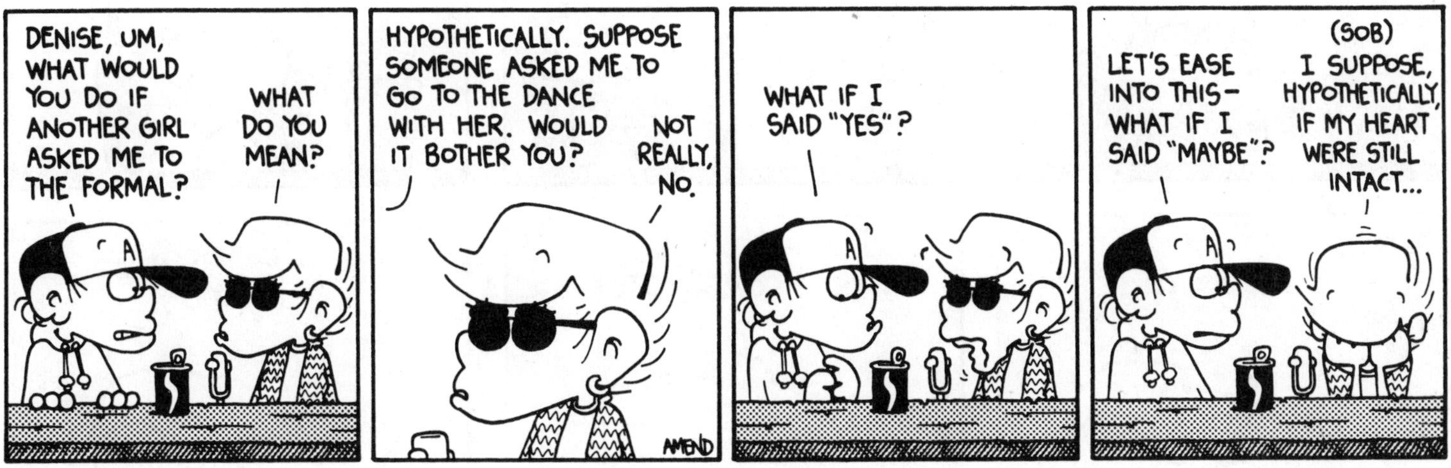
DENISE, UM, WHAT WOULD YOU DO IF ANOTHER GIRL ASKED ME TO THE FORMAL?
WHAT DO YOU MEAN?
HYPOTHETICALLY. SUPPOSE SOMEONE ASKED ME TO GO TO THE DANCE WITH HER. WOULD IT BOTHER YOU?
NOT REALLY, NO.
WHAT IF I SAID "YES"?
LET'S EASE INTO THIS– WHAT IF I SAID "MAYBE"?
(SOB)
I SUPPOSE, HYPOTHETICALLY, IF MY HEART WERE STILL INTACT...
AMEND

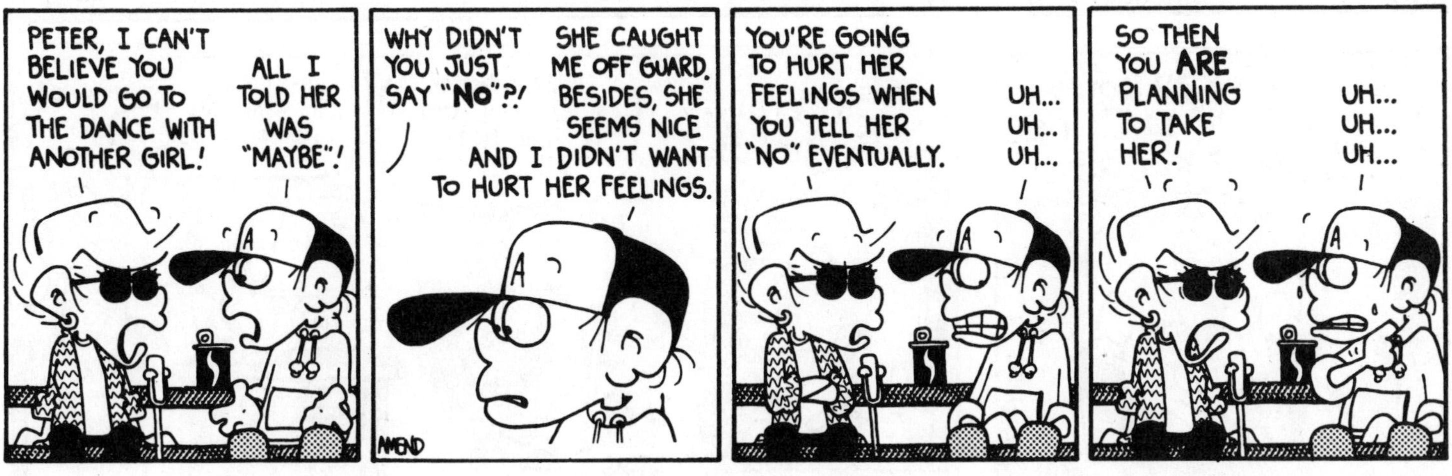
PETER, I CAN'T BELIEVE YOU WOULD GO TO THE DANCE WITH ANOTHER GIRL!
ALL I TOLD HER WAS "MAYBE"!
WHY DIDN'T YOU JUST SAY "NO"?!
SHE CAUGHT ME OFF GUARD. BESIDES, SHE SEEMS NICE
AND I DIDN'T WANT TO HURT HER FEELINGS.
YOU'RE GOING TO HURT HER FEELINGS WHEN YOU TELL HER "NO" EVENTUALLY.
UH... UH... UH...
SO THEN YOU **ARE** PLANNING TO TAKE HER!
UH... UH... UH...
AMEND

FoxTrot

BILL AMEND

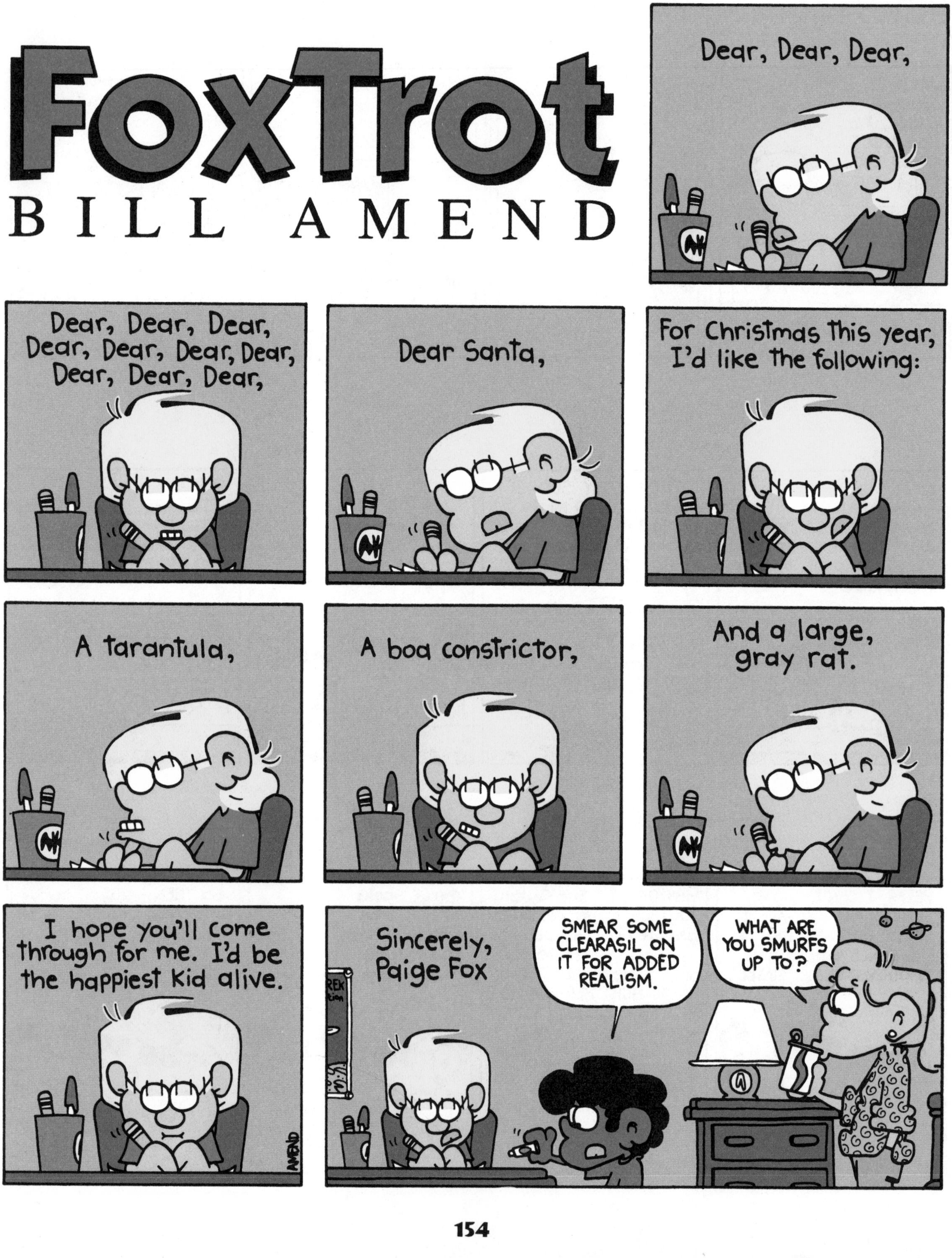

Dear, Dear, Dear,
Dear, Dear, Dear, Dear, Dear, Dear, Dear, Dear, Dear, Dear,
Dear Santa,
For Christmas this year, I'd like the following:
A tarantula,
A boa constrictor,
And a large, gray rat.
I hope you'll come through for me. I'd be the happiest kid alive.
AMEND
Sincerely, Paige Fox
SMEAR SOME CLEARASIL ON IT FOR ADDED REALISM.
WHAT ARE YOU SMURFS UP TO?

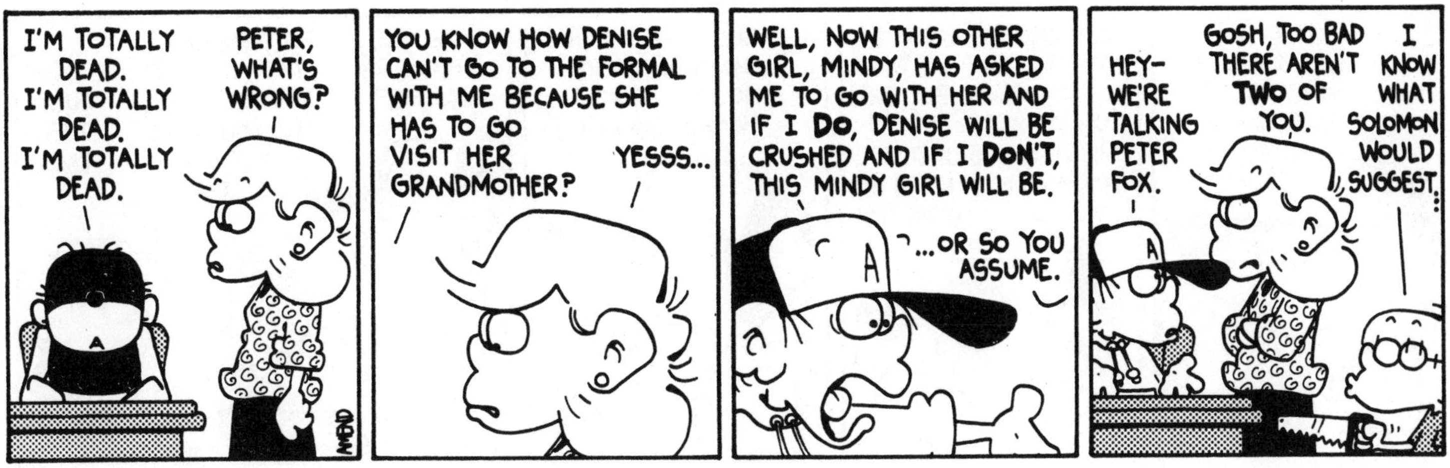
I'M TOTALLY DEAD. I'M TOTALLY DEAD. I'M TOTALLY DEAD.
PETER, WHAT'S WRONG?
YOU KNOW HOW DENISE CAN'T GO TO THE FORMAL WITH ME BECAUSE SHE HAS TO GO VISIT HER GRANDMOTHER?
YESSS...
WELL, NOW THIS OTHER GIRL, MINDY, HAS ASKED ME TO GO WITH HER AND IF I DO, DENISE WILL BE CRUSHED AND IF I DON'T, THIS MINDY GIRL WILL BE.
...OR SO YOU ASSUME.
HEY— WE'RE TALKING PETER FOX.
GOSH, TOO BAD THERE AREN'T TWO OF YOU.
I KNOW WHAT SOLOMON WOULD SUGGEST.
AMEND

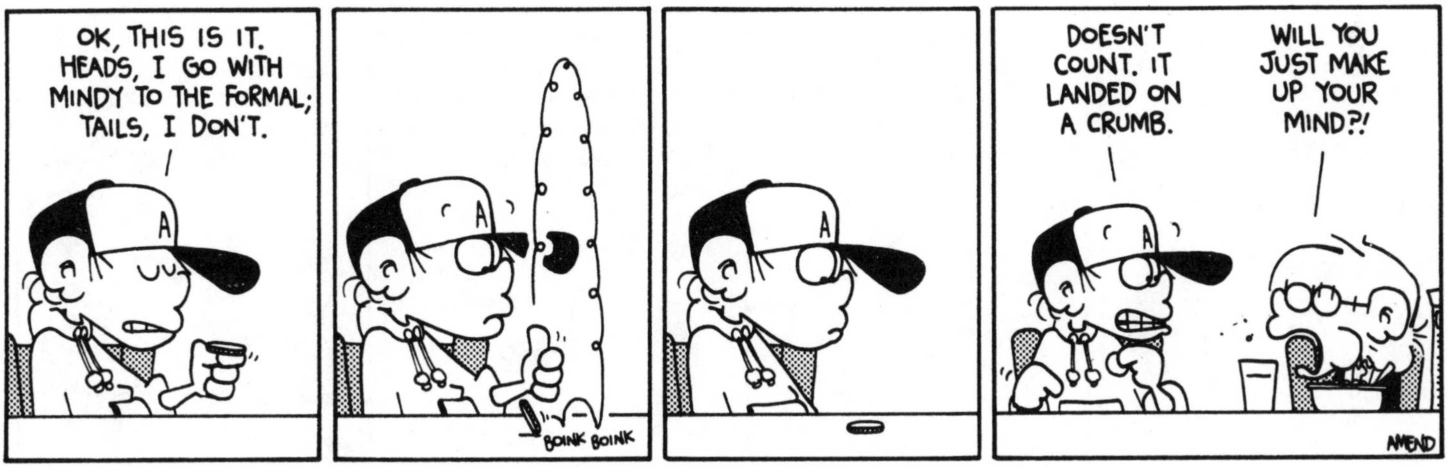
OK, THIS IS IT. HEADS, I GO WITH MINDY TO THE FORMAL; TAILS, I DON'T.
BOINK BOINK
DOESN'T COUNT. IT LANDED ON A CRUMB.
WILL YOU JUST MAKE UP YOUR MIND?!
AMEND

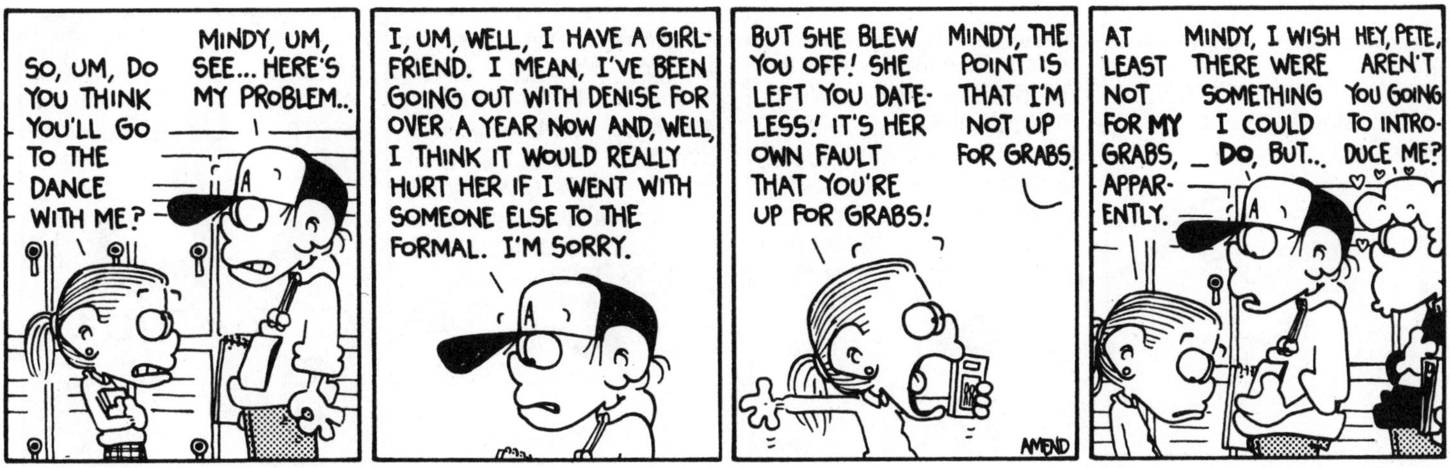
SO, UM, DO YOU THINK YOU'LL GO TO THE DANCE WITH ME?
MINDY, UM, SEE... HERE'S MY PROBLEM...
I, UM, WELL, I HAVE A GIRLFRIEND. I MEAN, I'VE BEEN GOING OUT WITH DENISE FOR OVER A YEAR NOW AND, WELL, I THINK IT WOULD REALLY HURT HER IF I WENT WITH SOMEONE ELSE TO THE FORMAL. I'M SORRY.
BUT SHE BLEW YOU OFF! SHE LEFT YOU DATELESS! IT'S HER OWN FAULT THAT YOU'RE UP FOR GRABS!
MINDY, THE POINT IS THAT I'M NOT UP FOR GRABS.
AMEND
AT LEAST NOT FOR MY GRABS, APPARENTLY.
MINDY, I WISH THERE WERE SOMETHING I COULD DO, BUT...
HEY, PETE, AREN'T YOU GOING TO INTRODUCE ME?

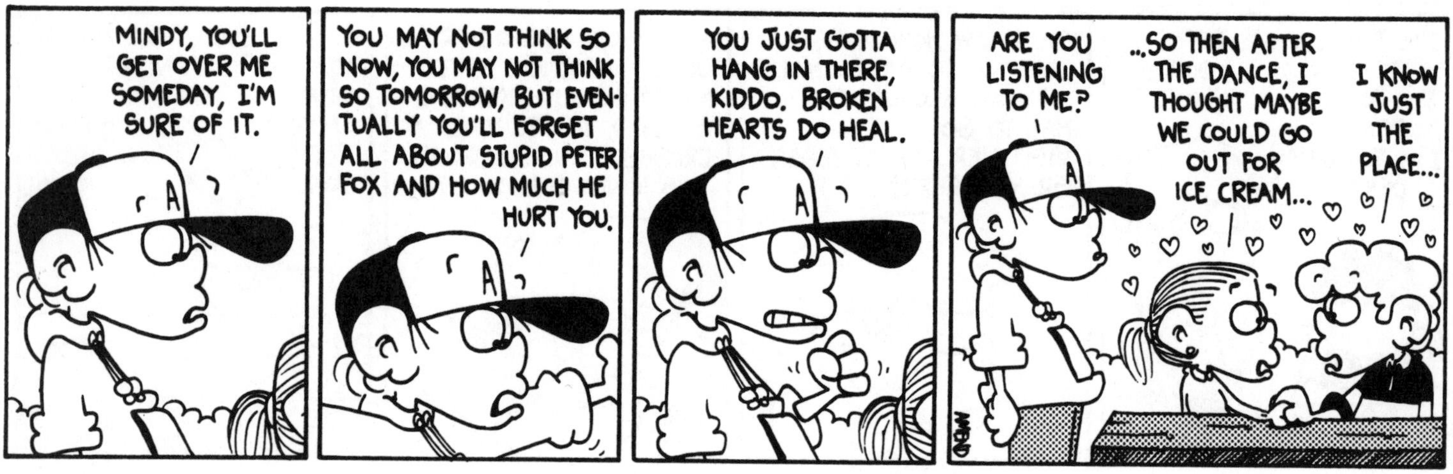
MINDY, YOU'LL GET OVER ME SOMEDAY, I'M SURE OF IT.
YOU MAY NOT THINK SO NOW, YOU MAY NOT THINK SO TOMORROW, BUT EVENTUALLY YOU'LL FORGET ALL ABOUT STUPID PETER FOX AND HOW MUCH HE HURT YOU.
YOU JUST GOTTA HANG IN THERE, KIDDO. BROKEN HEARTS DO HEAL.
ARE YOU LISTENING TO ME?
...SO THEN AFTER THE DANCE, I THOUGHT MAYBE WE COULD GO OUT FOR ICE CREAM...
I KNOW JUST THE PLACE...
AMEND

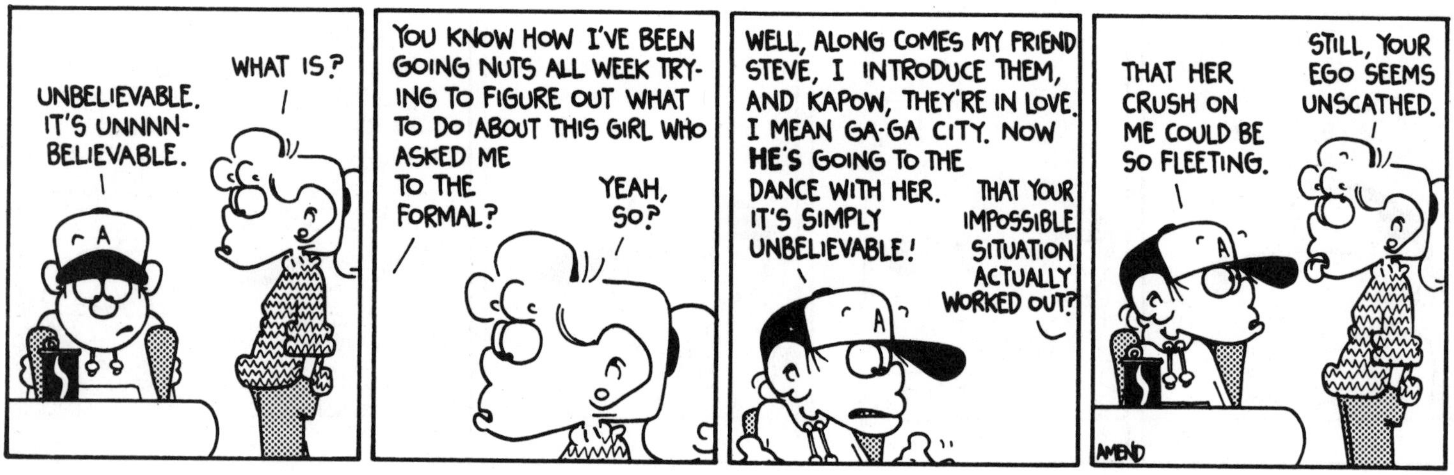
UNBELIEVABLE. IT'S UNNNN-BELIEVABLE.
WHAT IS?
YOU KNOW HOW I'VE BEEN GOING NUTS ALL WEEK TRYING TO FIGURE OUT WHAT TO DO ABOUT THIS GIRL WHO ASKED ME TO THE FORMAL?
YEAH, SO?
WELL, ALONG COMES MY FRIEND STEVE, I INTRODUCE THEM, AND KAPOW, THEY'RE IN LOVE. I MEAN GA-GA CITY. NOW HE'S GOING TO THE DANCE WITH HER. IT'S SIMPLY UNBELIEVABLE!
THAT YOUR IMPOSSIBLE SITUATION ACTUALLY WORKED OUT?
THAT HER CRUSH ON ME COULD BE SO FLEETING.
STILL, YOUR EGO SEEMS UNSCATHED.
AMEND

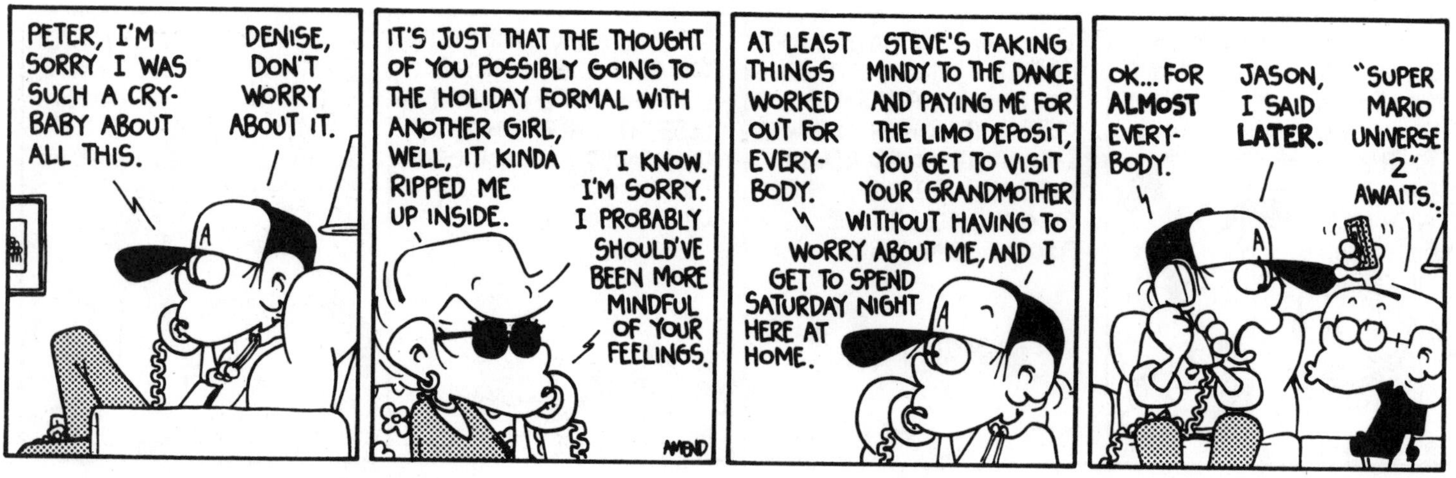
PETER, I'M SORRY I WAS SUCH A CRY-BABY ABOUT ALL THIS.
DENISE, DON'T WORRY ABOUT IT.
IT'S JUST THAT THE THOUGHT OF YOU POSSIBLY GOING TO THE HOLIDAY FORMAL WITH ANOTHER GIRL, WELL, IT KINDA RIPPED ME UP INSIDE.
I KNOW. I'M SORRY. I PROBABLY SHOULD'VE BEEN MORE MINDFUL OF YOUR FEELINGS.
AMEND
AT LEAST THINGS WORKED OUT FOR EVERYBODY.
STEVE'S TAKING MINDY TO THE DANCE AND PAYING ME FOR THE LIMO DEPOSIT, YOU GET TO VISIT YOUR GRANDMOTHER WITHOUT HAVING TO WORRY ABOUT ME, AND I GET TO SPEND SATURDAY NIGHT HERE AT HOME.
OK... FOR ALMOST EVERYBODY.
JASON, I SAID LATER.
"SUPER MARIO UNIVERSE 2" AWAITS..

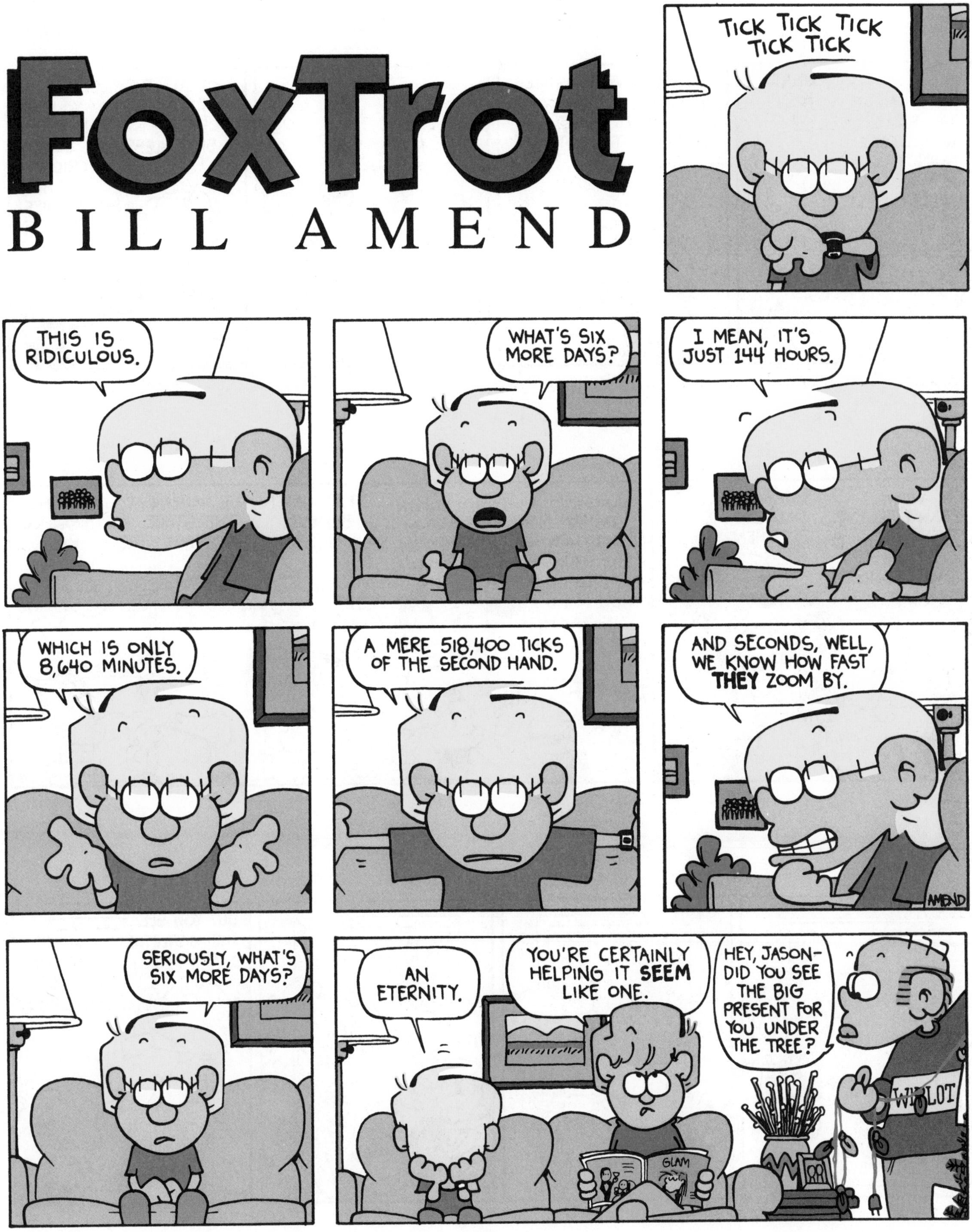
FoxTrot
BILL AMEND
TICK TICK TICK TICK TICK
THIS IS RIDICULOUS.
WHAT'S SIX MORE DAYS?
I MEAN, IT'S JUST 144 HOURS.
WHICH IS ONLY 8,640 MINUTES.
A MERE 518,400 TICKS OF THE SECOND HAND.
AND SECONDS, WELL, WE KNOW HOW FAST **THEY** ZOOM BY.
AMEND
SERIOUSLY, WHAT'S SIX MORE DAYS?
AN ETERNITY.
YOU'RE CERTAINLY HELPING IT **SEEM** LIKE ONE.
HEY, JASON- DID YOU SEE THE BIG PRESENT FOR YOU UNDER THE TREE?
GLAM
WIBLOT

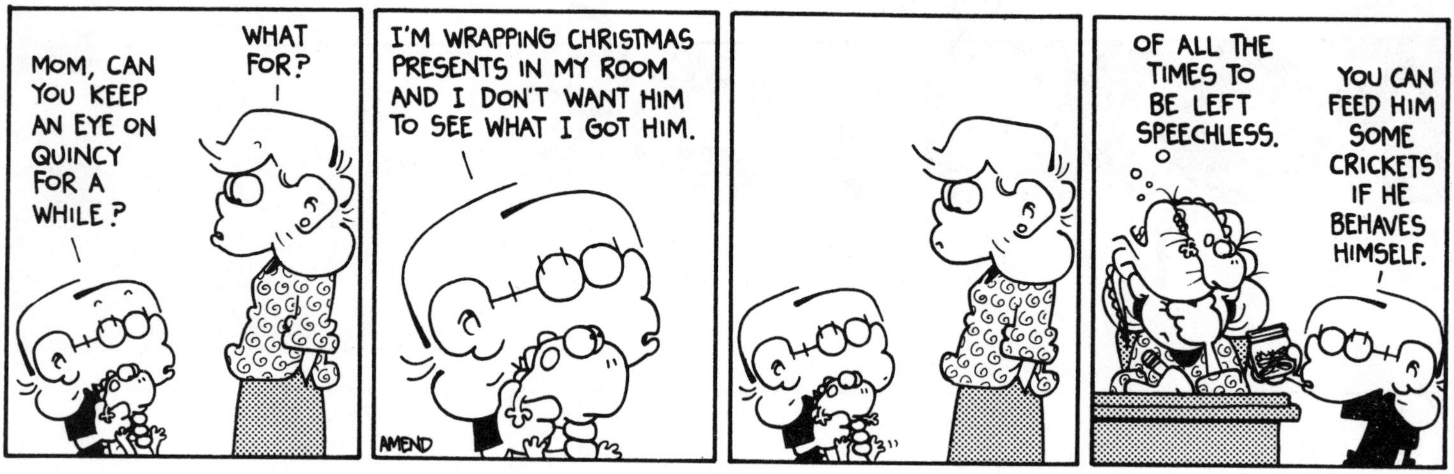
MOM, CAN YOU KEEP AN EYE ON QUINCY FOR A WHILE?
WHAT FOR?
I'M WRAPPING CHRISTMAS PRESENTS IN MY ROOM AND I DON'T WANT HIM TO SEE WHAT I GOT HIM.
AMEND
OF ALL THE TIMES TO BE LEFT SPEECHLESS.
YOU CAN FEED HIM SOME CRICKETS IF HE BEHAVES HIMSELF.

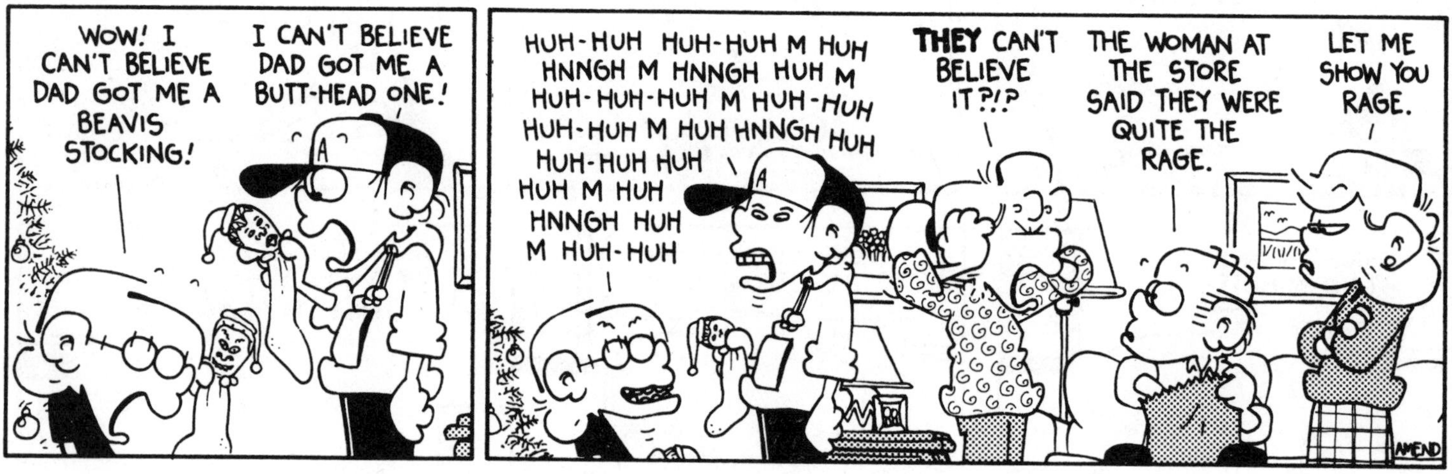
WOW! I CAN'T BELIEVE DAD GOT ME A BEAVIS STOCKING!
I CAN'T BELIEVE DAD GOT ME A BUTT-HEAD ONE!
HUH-HUH HUH-HUH M HUH HNNGH M HNNGH HUH M HUH-HUH-HUH M HUH-HUH HUH-HUH M HUH HNNGH HUH HUH-HUH HUH HUH M HUH HNNGH HUH M HUH-HUH
THEY CAN'T BELIEVE IT?!?
THE WOMAN AT THE STORE SAID THEY WERE QUITE THE RAGE.
LET ME SHOW YOU RAGE.
AMEND

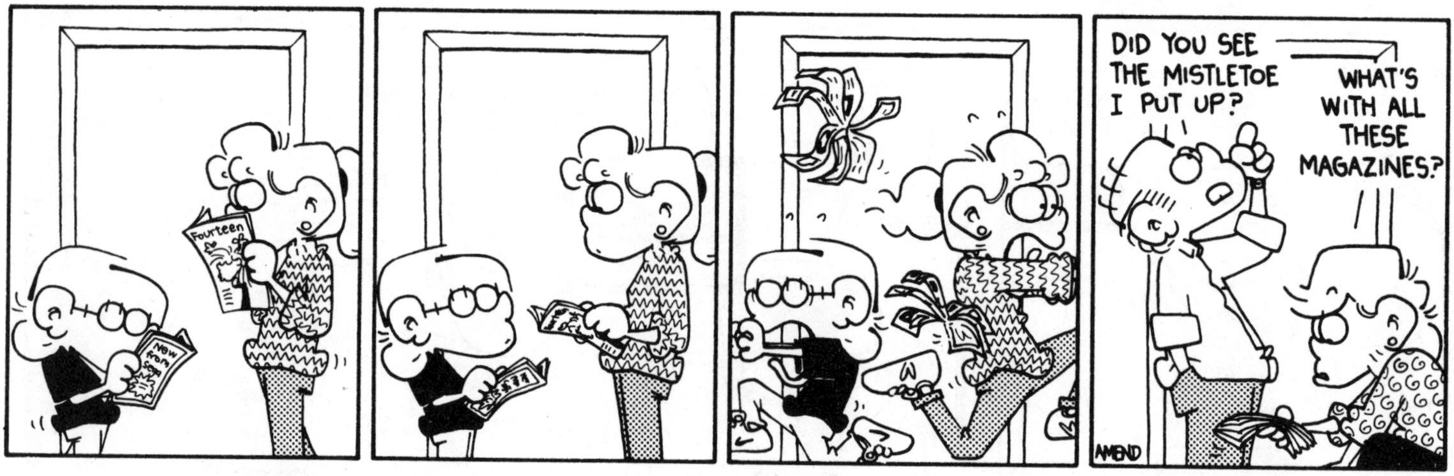
Fourteen
DID YOU SEE THE MISTLETOE I PUT UP?
WHAT'S WITH ALL THESE MAGAZINES?
AMEND

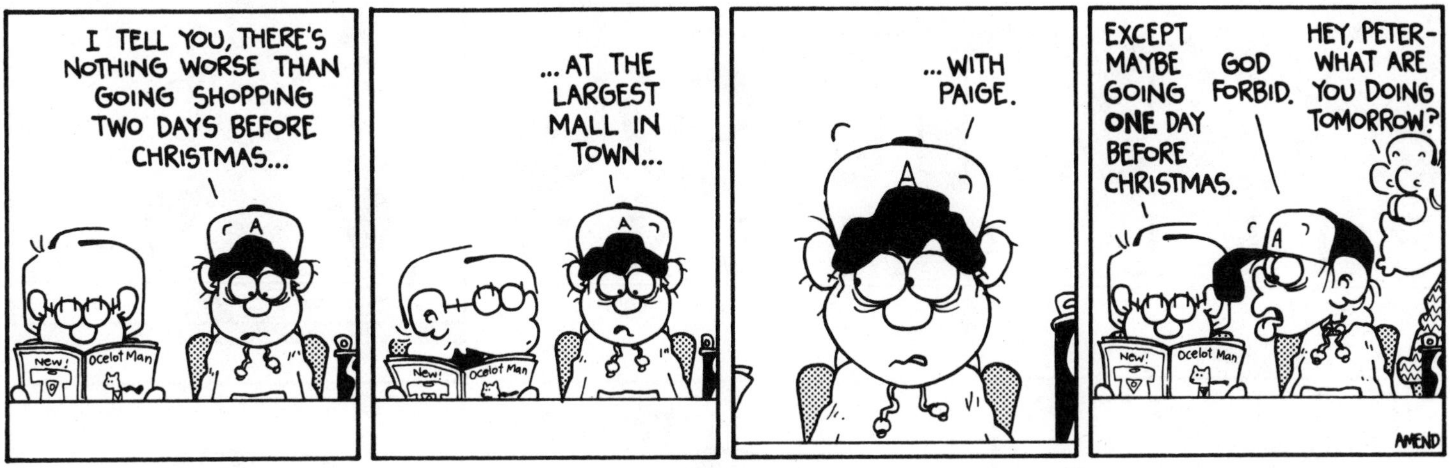
I TELL YOU, THERE'S NOTHING WORSE THAN GOING SHOPPING TWO DAYS BEFORE CHRISTMAS...
...AT THE LARGEST MALL IN TOWN...
...WITH PAIGE.
EXCEPT MAYBE GOING **ONE** DAY BEFORE CHRISTMAS.
GOD FORBID.
HEY, PETER- WHAT ARE YOU DOING TOMORROW?
AMEND

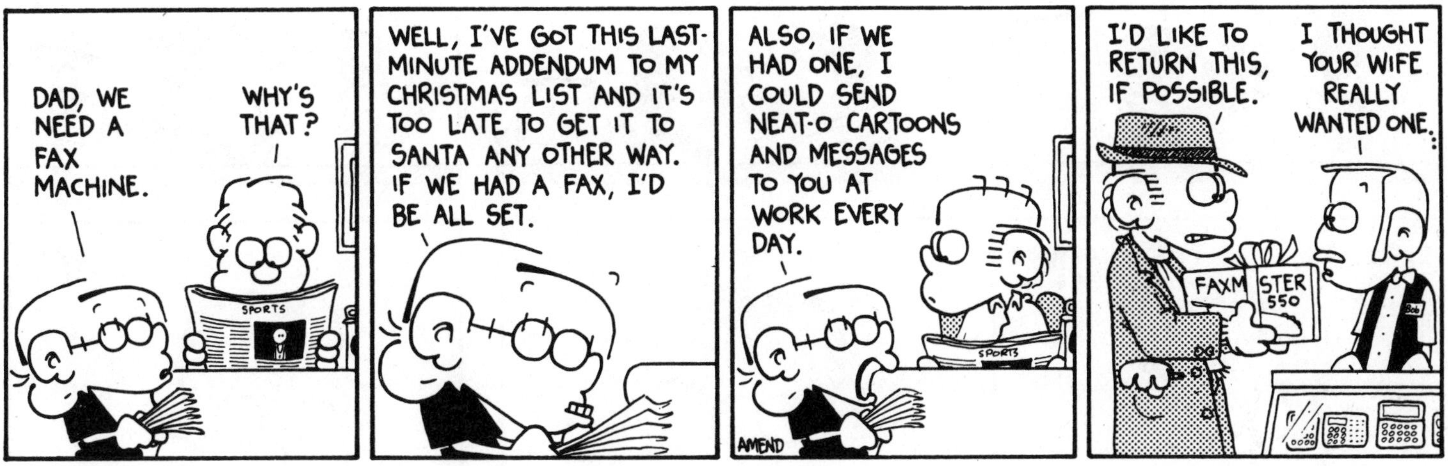
DAD, WE NEED A FAX MACHINE.
WHY'S THAT?
WELL, I'VE GOT THIS LAST-MINUTE ADDENDUM TO MY CHRISTMAS LIST AND IT'S TOO LATE TO GET IT TO SANTA ANY OTHER WAY. IF WE HAD A FAX, I'D BE ALL SET.
ALSO, IF WE HAD ONE, I COULD SEND NEAT-O CARTOONS AND MESSAGES TO YOU AT WORK EVERY DAY.
AMEND
I'D LIKE TO RETURN THIS, IF POSSIBLE.
I THOUGHT YOUR WIFE REALLY WANTED ONE...

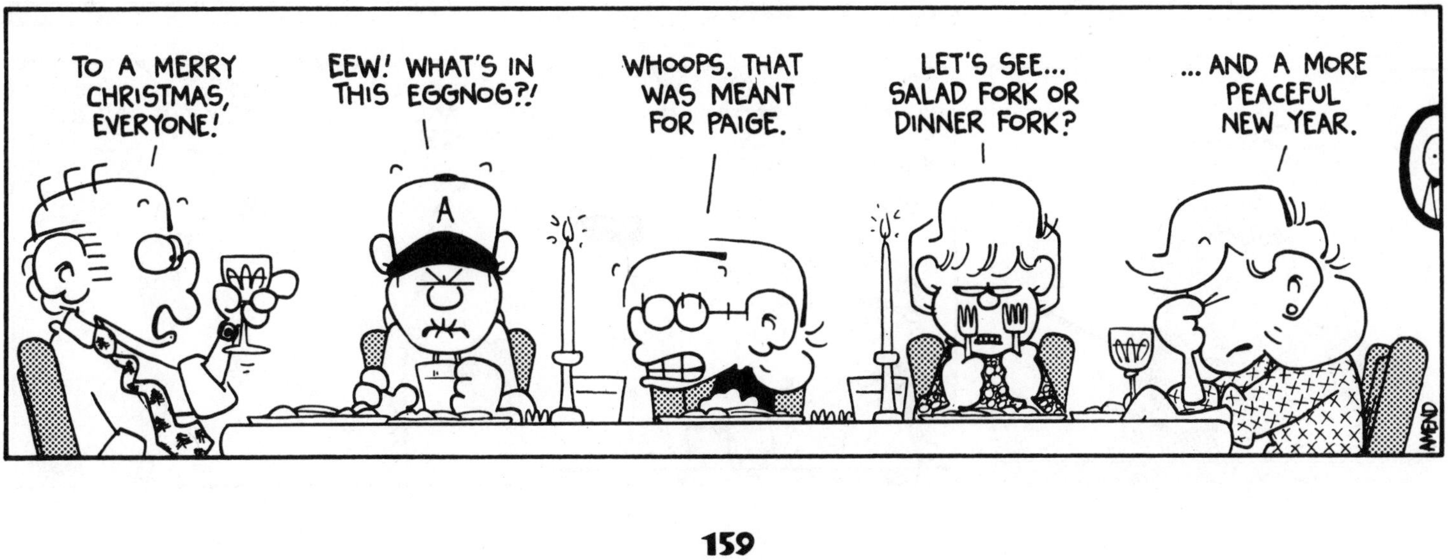
TO A MERRY CHRISTMAS, EVERYONE!
EEW! WHAT'S IN THIS EGGNOG?!
WHOOPS. THAT WAS MEANT FOR PAIGE.
LET'S SEE... SALAD FORK OR DINNER FORK?
...AND A MORE PEACEFUL NEW YEAR.
AMEND

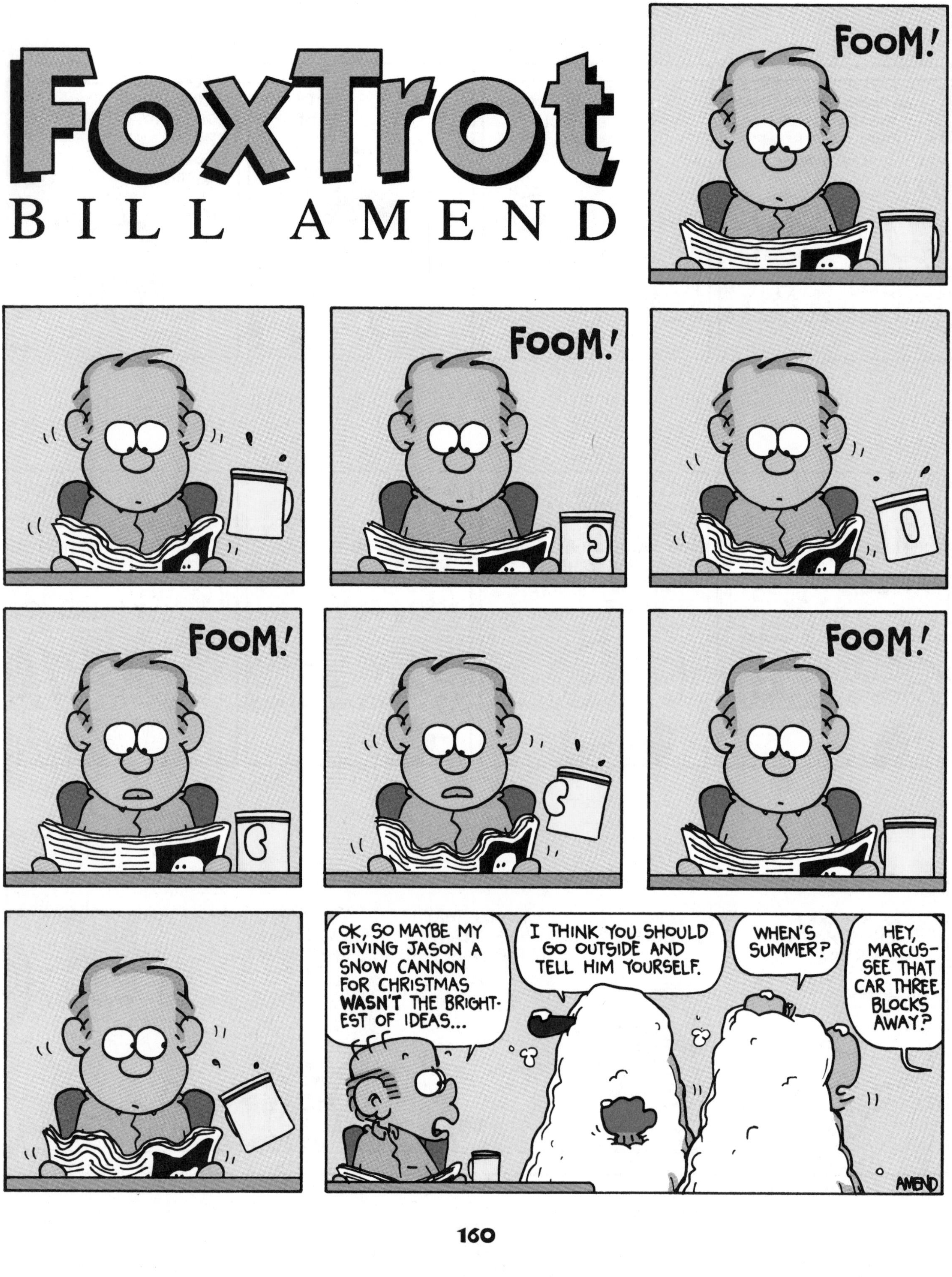
FoxTrot
BILL AMEND
FOOM!
FOOM!
FOOM!
FOOM!
OK, SO MAYBE MY GIVING JASON A SNOW CANNON FOR CHRISTMAS WASN'T THE BRIGHT-EST OF IDEAS...
I THINK YOU SHOULD GO OUTSIDE AND TELL HIM YOURSELF.
WHEN'S SUMMER?
HEY, MARCUS- SEE THAT CAR THREE BLOCKS AWAY?
AMEND

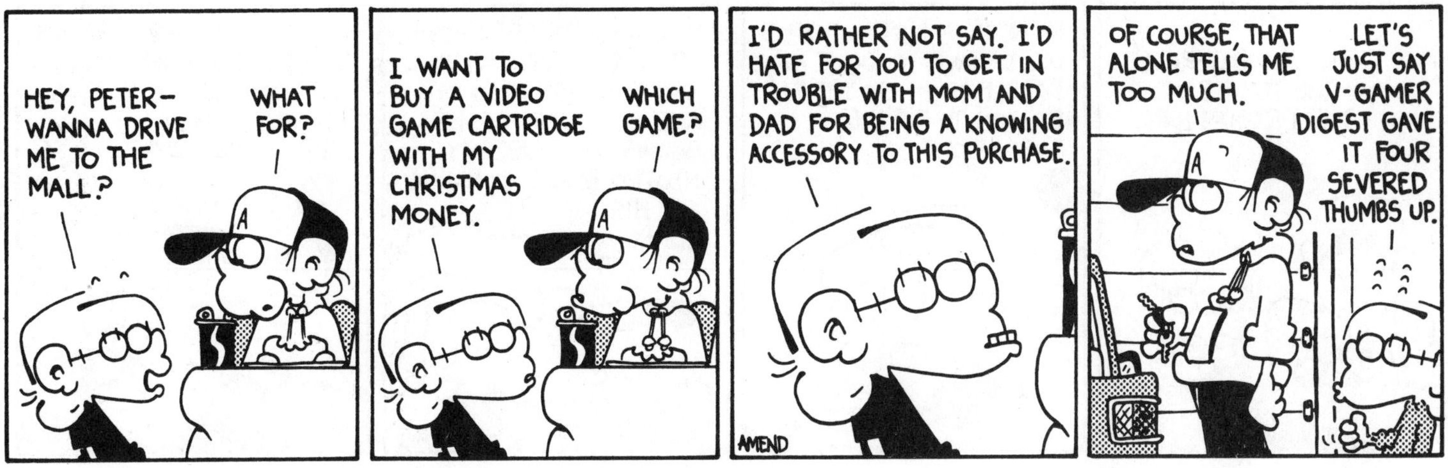
HEY, PETER- WANNA DRIVE ME TO THE MALL?
WHAT FOR?
I WANT TO BUY A VIDEO GAME CARTRIDGE WITH MY CHRISTMAS MONEY.
WHICH GAME?
I'D RATHER NOT SAY. I'D HATE FOR YOU TO GET IN TROUBLE WITH MOM AND DAD FOR BEING A KNOWING ACCESSORY TO THIS PURCHASE.
AMEND
OF COURSE, THAT ALONE TELLS ME TOO MUCH.
LET'S JUST SAY V-GAMER DIGEST GAVE IT FOUR SEVERED THUMBS UP.

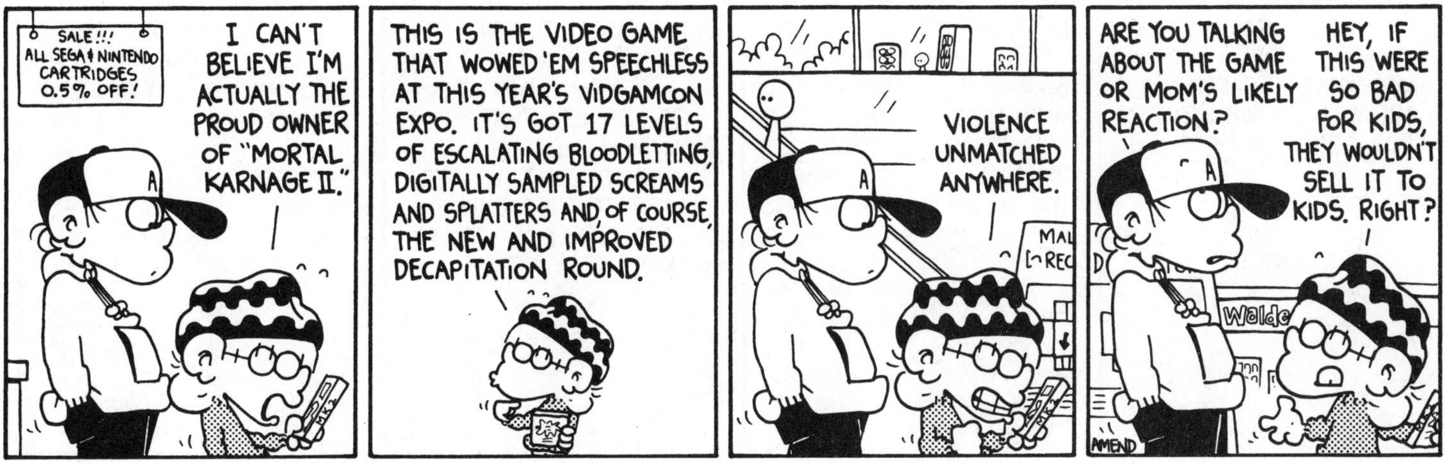
SALE!!! ALL SEGA & NINTENDO CARTRIDGES 0.5% OFF!
I CAN'T BELIEVE I'M ACTUALLY THE PROUD OWNER OF "MORTAL KARNAGE II."
THIS IS THE VIDEO GAME THAT WOWED 'EM SPEECHLESS AT THIS YEAR'S VIDGAMCON EXPO. IT'S GOT 17 LEVELS OF ESCALATING BLOODLETTING, DIGITALLY SAMPLED SCREAMS AND SPLATTERS AND, OF COURSE, THE NEW AND IMPROVED DECAPITATION ROUND.
VIOLENCE UNMATCHED ANYWHERE.
ARE YOU TALKING ABOUT THE GAME OR MOM'S LIKELY REACTION?
HEY, IF THIS WERE SO BAD FOR KIDS, THEY WOULDN'T SELL IT TO KIDS. RIGHT?
AMEND

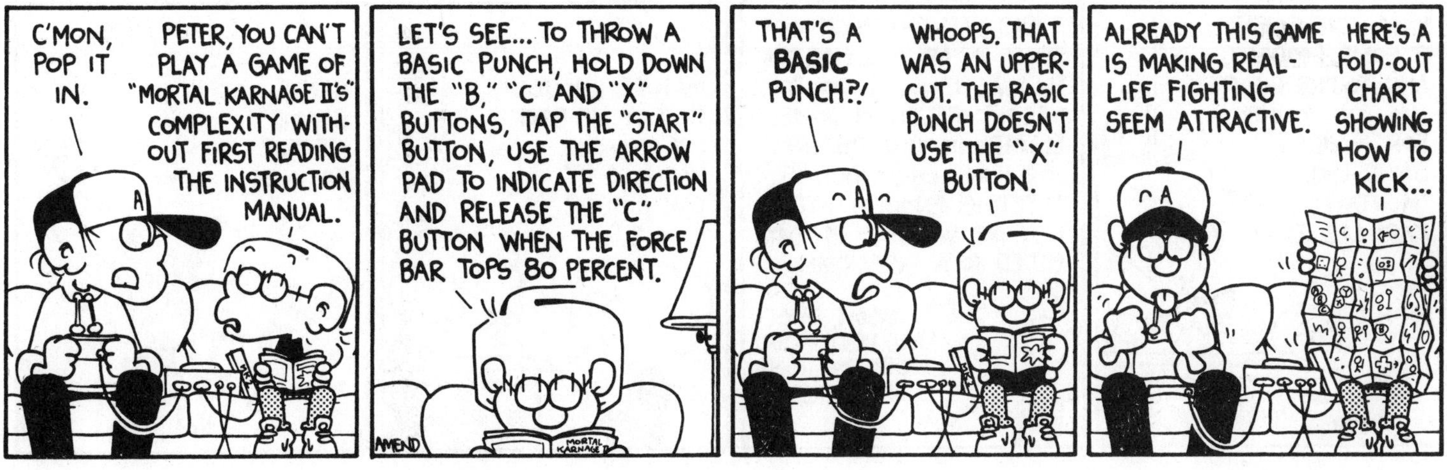
C'MON, POP IT IN.
PETER, YOU CAN'T PLAY A GAME OF "MORTAL KARNAGE II's" COMPLEXITY WITHOUT FIRST READING THE INSTRUCTION MANUAL.
LET'S SEE... TO THROW A BASIC PUNCH, HOLD DOWN THE "B," "C" AND "X" BUTTONS, TAP THE "START" BUTTON, USE THE ARROW PAD TO INDICATE DIRECTION AND RELEASE THE "C" BUTTON WHEN THE FORCE BAR TOPS 80 PERCENT.
AMEND
MORTAL KARNAGE II
THAT'S A **BASIC** PUNCH?!
WHOOPS. THAT WAS AN UPPERCUT. THE BASIC PUNCH DOESN'T USE THE "X" BUTTON.
ALREADY THIS GAME IS MAKING REAL-LIFE FIGHTING SEEM ATTRACTIVE.
HERE'S A FOLD-OUT CHART SHOWING HOW TO KICK...

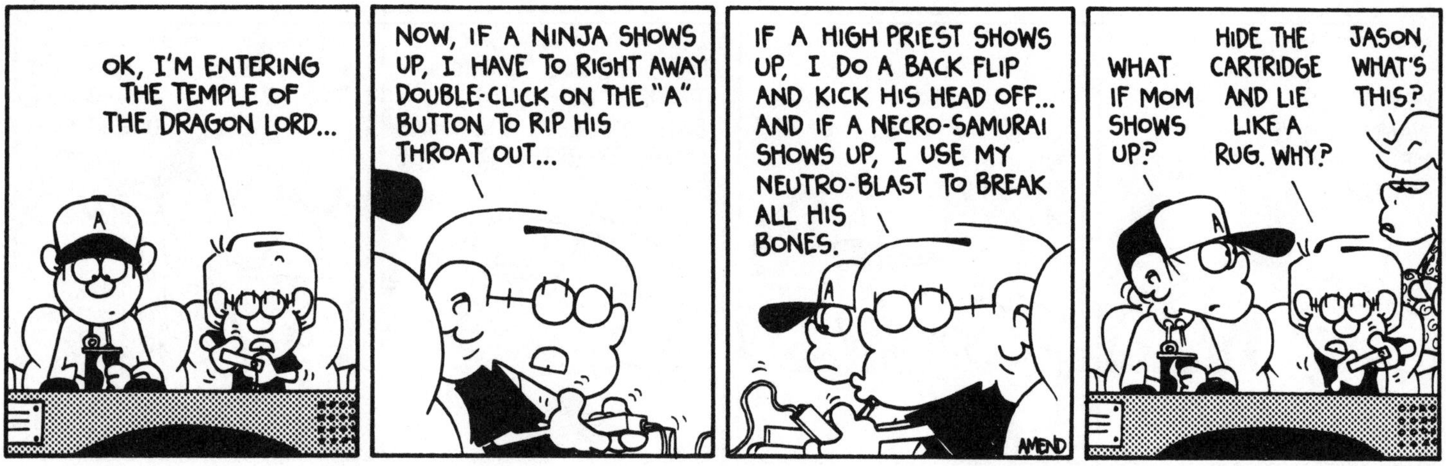
OK, I'M ENTERING THE TEMPLE OF THE DRAGON LORD...
NOW, IF A NINJA SHOWS UP, I HAVE TO RIGHT AWAY DOUBLE-CLICK ON THE "A" BUTTON TO RIP HIS THROAT OUT...
IF A HIGH PRIEST SHOWS UP, I DO A BACK FLIP AND KICK HIS HEAD OFF... AND IF A NECRO-SAMURAI SHOWS UP, I USE MY NEUTRO-BLAST TO BREAK ALL HIS BONES.
AMEND
WHAT IF MOM SHOWS UP?
HIDE THE CARTRIDGE AND LIE LIKE A RUG. WHY?
JASON, WHAT'S THIS?

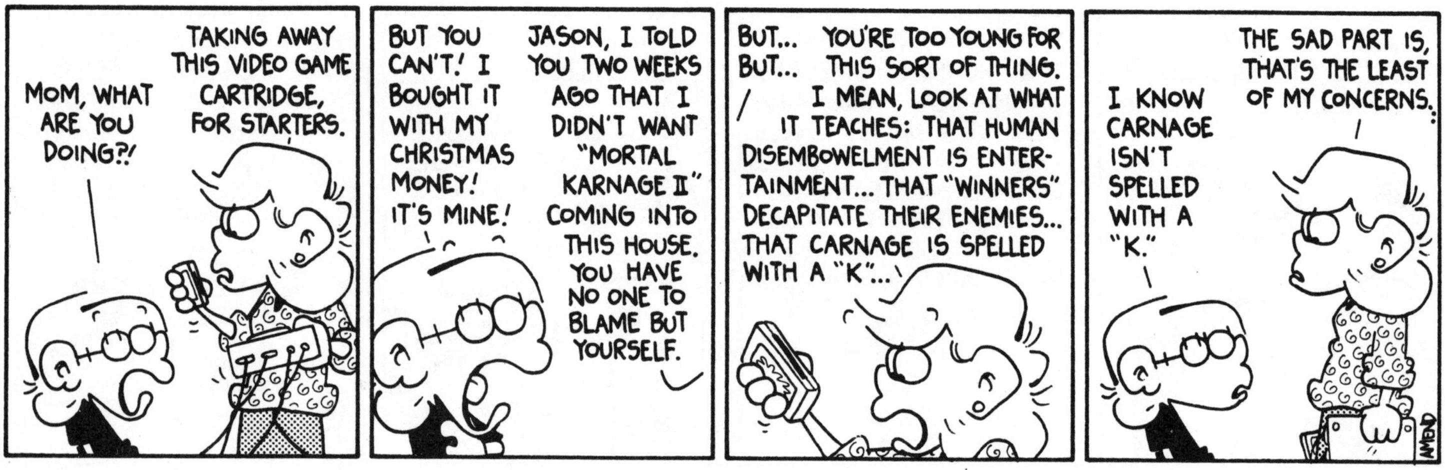
MOM, WHAT ARE YOU DOING?!
TAKING AWAY THIS VIDEO GAME CARTRIDGE, FOR STARTERS.
BUT YOU CAN'T! I BOUGHT IT WITH MY CHRISTMAS MONEY! IT'S MINE!
JASON, I TOLD YOU TWO WEEKS AGO THAT I DIDN'T WANT "MORTAL KARNAGE II" COMING INTO THIS HOUSE. YOU HAVE NO ONE TO BLAME BUT YOURSELF.
BUT... BUT...
YOU'RE TOO YOUNG FOR THIS SORT OF THING. I MEAN, LOOK AT WHAT IT TEACHES: THAT HUMAN DISEMBOWELMENT IS ENTERTAINMENT... THAT "WINNERS" DECAPITATE THEIR ENEMIES... THAT CARNAGE IS SPELLED WITH A "K"...
I KNOW CARNAGE ISN'T SPELLED WITH A "K."
THE SAD PART IS, THAT'S THE LEAST OF MY CONCERNS.
AMEND

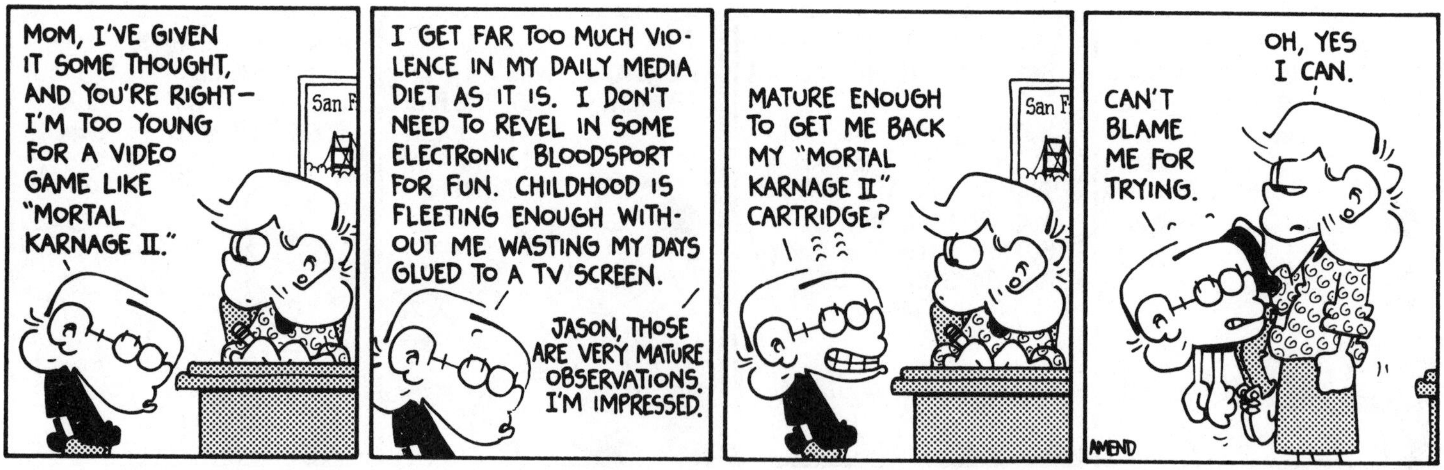
MOM, I'VE GIVEN IT SOME THOUGHT, AND YOU'RE RIGHT— I'M TOO YOUNG FOR A VIDEO GAME LIKE "MORTAL KARNAGE II."
San F
I GET FAR TOO MUCH VIOLENCE IN MY DAILY MEDIA DIET AS IT IS. I DON'T NEED TO REVEL IN SOME ELECTRONIC BLOODSPORT FOR FUN. CHILDHOOD IS FLEETING ENOUGH WITHOUT ME WASTING MY DAYS GLUED TO A TV SCREEN.
JASON, THOSE ARE VERY MATURE OBSERVATIONS. I'M IMPRESSED.
MATURE ENOUGH TO GET ME BACK MY "MORTAL KARNAGE II" CARTRIDGE?
San F
CAN'T BLAME ME FOR TRYING.
OH, YES I CAN.
AMEND

FoxTrot
BILL AMEND

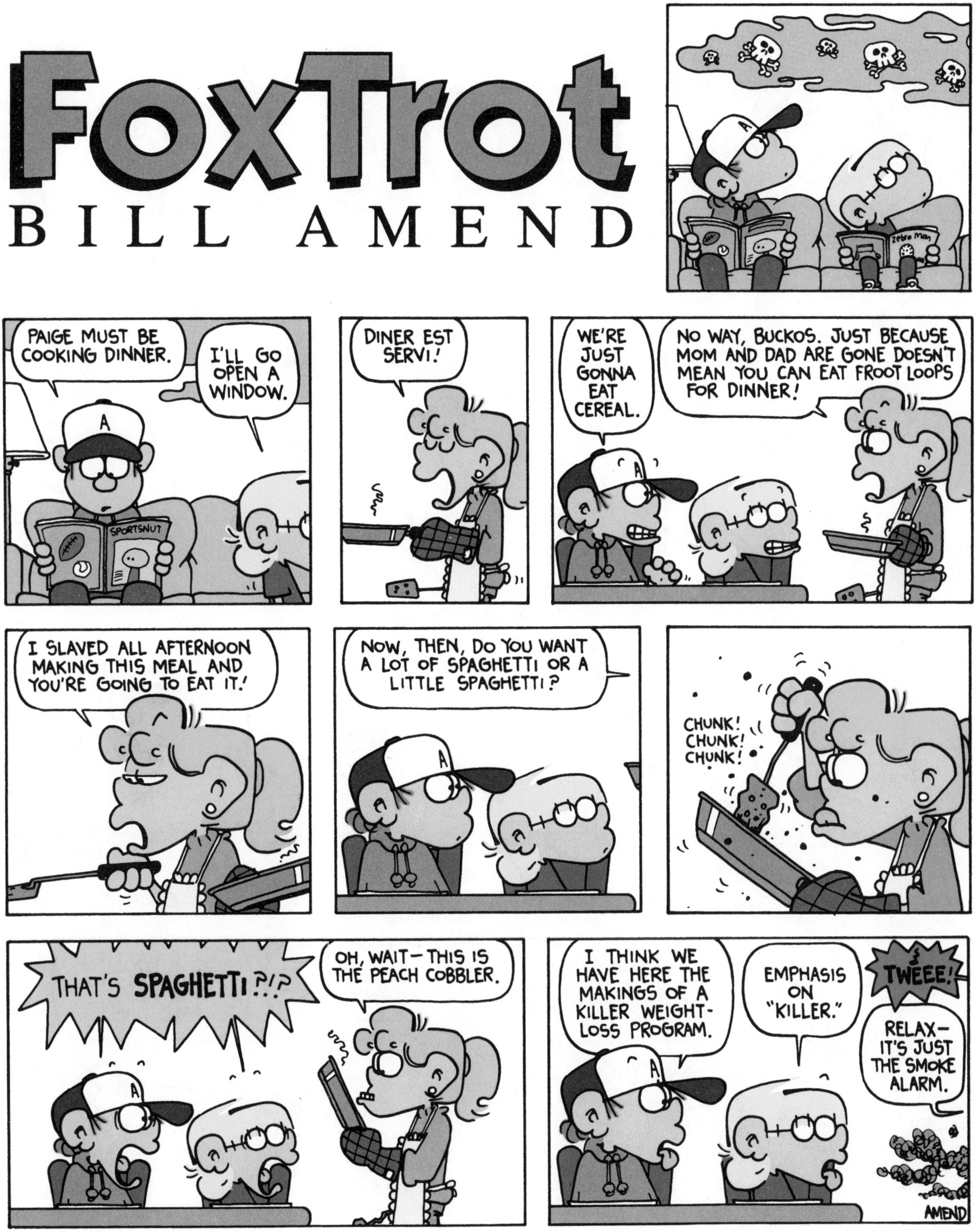

SPORTSNUT
Zebra Man
PAIGE MUST BE COOKING DINNER.
I'LL GO OPEN A WINDOW.
DINER EST SERVI!
WE'RE JUST GONNA EAT CEREAL.
NO WAY, BUCKOS. JUST BECAUSE MOM AND DAD ARE GONE DOESN'T MEAN YOU CAN EAT FROOT LOOPS FOR DINNER!
I SLAVED ALL AFTERNOON MAKING THIS MEAL AND YOU'RE GOING TO EAT IT!
NOW, THEN, DO YOU WANT A LOT OF SPAGHETTI OR A LITTLE SPAGHETTI?
CHUNK! CHUNK! CHUNK!
THAT'S SPAGHETTI?!?
OH, WAIT—THIS IS THE PEACH COBBLER.
I THINK WE HAVE HERE THE MAKINGS OF A KILLER WEIGHT-LOSS PROGRAM.
EMPHASIS ON "KILLER."
TWEEE!
RELAX—IT'S JUST THE SMOKE ALARM.
AMEND

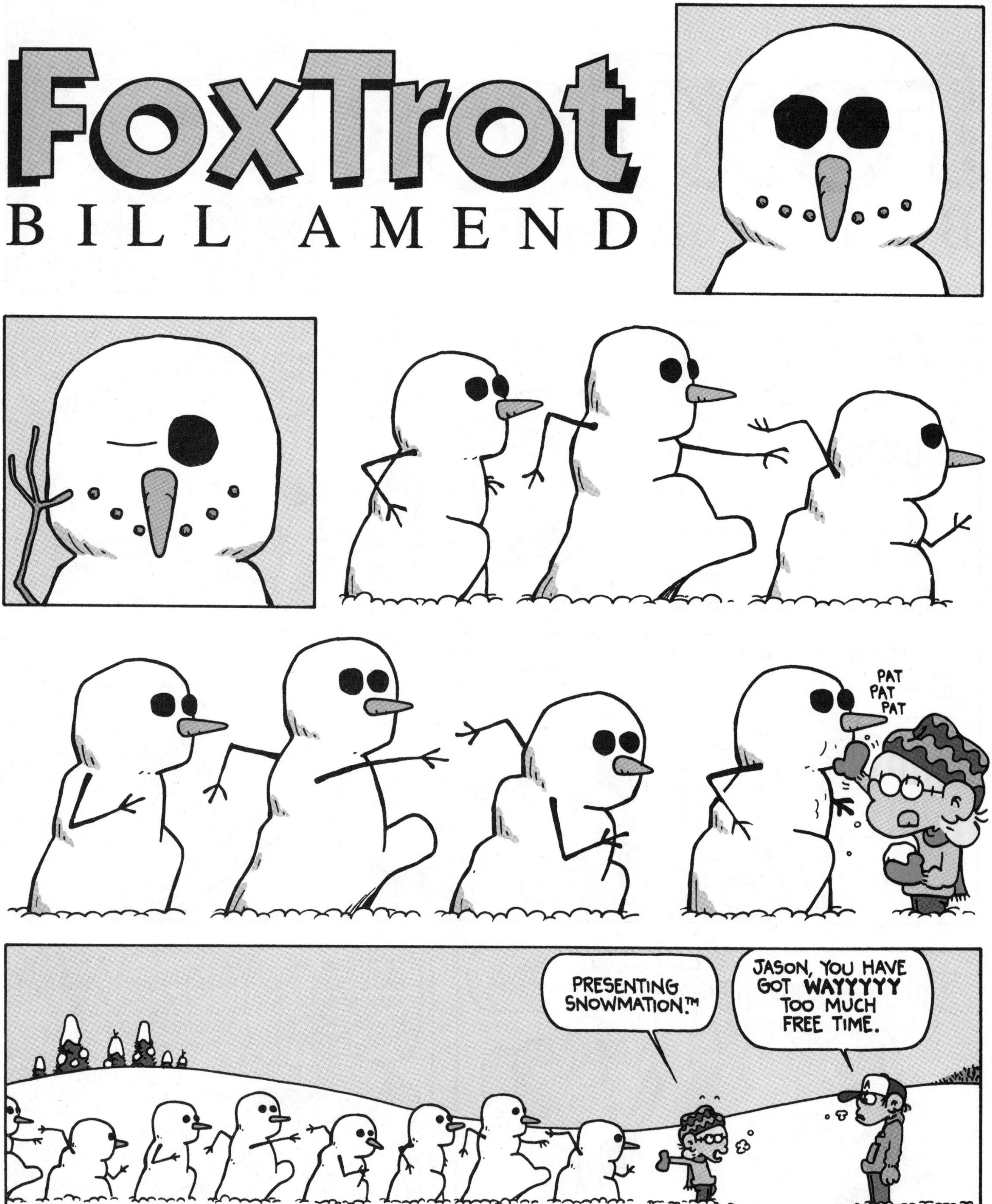
FoxTrot
BILL AMEND
PAT
PAT
PAT
PRESENTING SNOWMATION.™
JASON, YOU HAVE GOT WAYYYYYY TOO MUCH FREE TIME.
AMEND

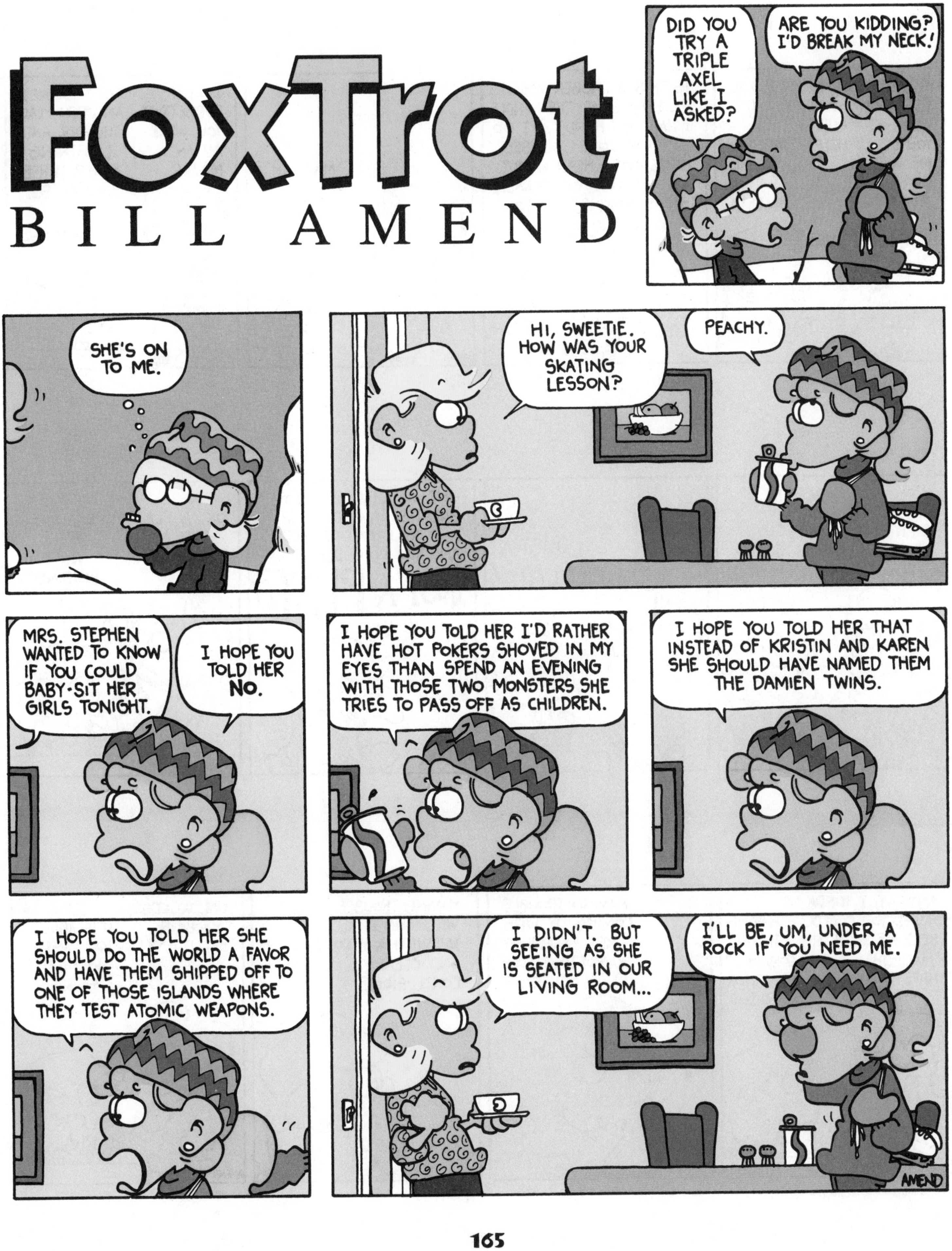
FoxTrot
BILL AMEND
DID YOU TRY A TRIPLE AXEL LIKE I ASKED?
ARE YOU KIDDING? I'D BREAK MY NECK!
SHE'S ON TO ME.
HI, SWEETIE. HOW WAS YOUR SKATING LESSON?
PEACHY.
MRS. STEPHEN WANTED TO KNOW IF YOU COULD BABY-SIT HER GIRLS TONIGHT.
I HOPE YOU TOLD HER NO.
I HOPE YOU TOLD HER I'D RATHER HAVE HOT POKERS SHOVED IN MY EYES THAN SPEND AN EVENING WITH THOSE TWO MONSTERS SHE TRIES TO PASS OFF AS CHILDREN.
I HOPE YOU TOLD HER THAT INSTEAD OF KRISTIN AND KAREN SHE SHOULD HAVE NAMED THEM THE DAMIEN TWINS.
I HOPE YOU TOLD HER SHE SHOULD DO THE WORLD A FAVOR AND HAVE THEM SHIPPED OFF TO ONE OF THOSE ISLANDS WHERE THEY TEST ATOMIC WEAPONS.
I DIDN'T. BUT SEEING AS SHE IS SEATED IN OUR LIVING ROOM...
I'LL BE, UM, UNDER A ROCK IF YOU NEED ME.
AMEND

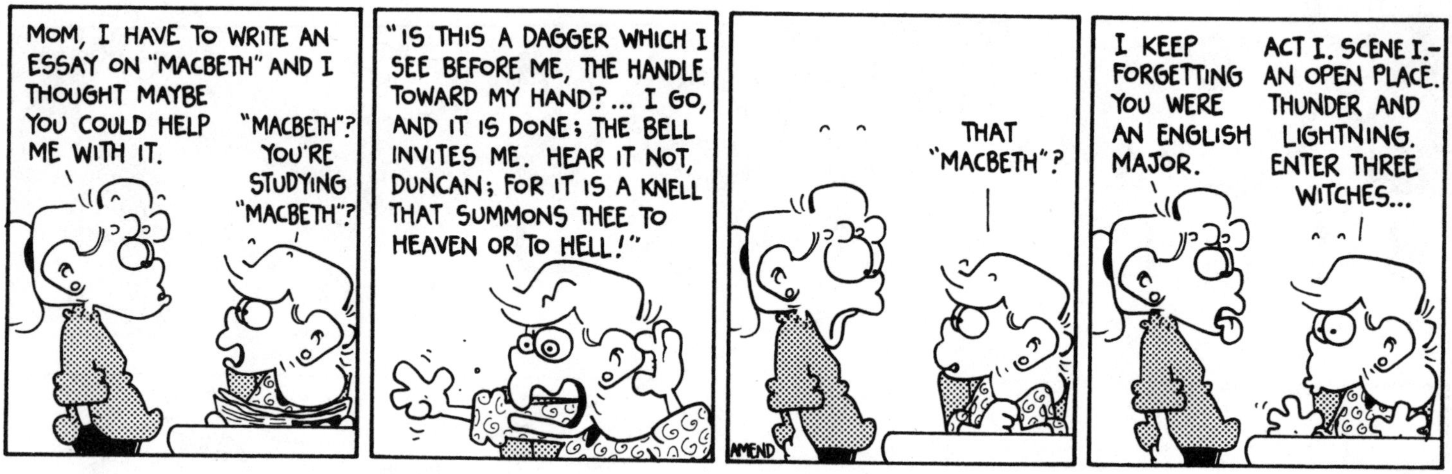
MOM, I HAVE TO WRITE AN ESSAY ON "MACBETH" AND I THOUGHT MAYBE YOU COULD HELP ME WITH IT.
"MACBETH"? YOU'RE STUDYING "MACBETH"?
"IS THIS A DAGGER WHICH I SEE BEFORE ME, THE HANDLE TOWARD MY HAND?... I GO, AND IT IS DONE; THE BELL INVITES ME. HEAR IT NOT, DUNCAN; FOR IT IS A KNELL THAT SUMMONS THEE TO HEAVEN OR TO HELL!"
THAT "MACBETH"?
AMEND
I KEEP FORGETTING YOU WERE AN ENGLISH MAJOR.
ACT I. SCENE I.- AN OPEN PLACE. THUNDER AND LIGHTNING. ENTER THREE WITCHES...

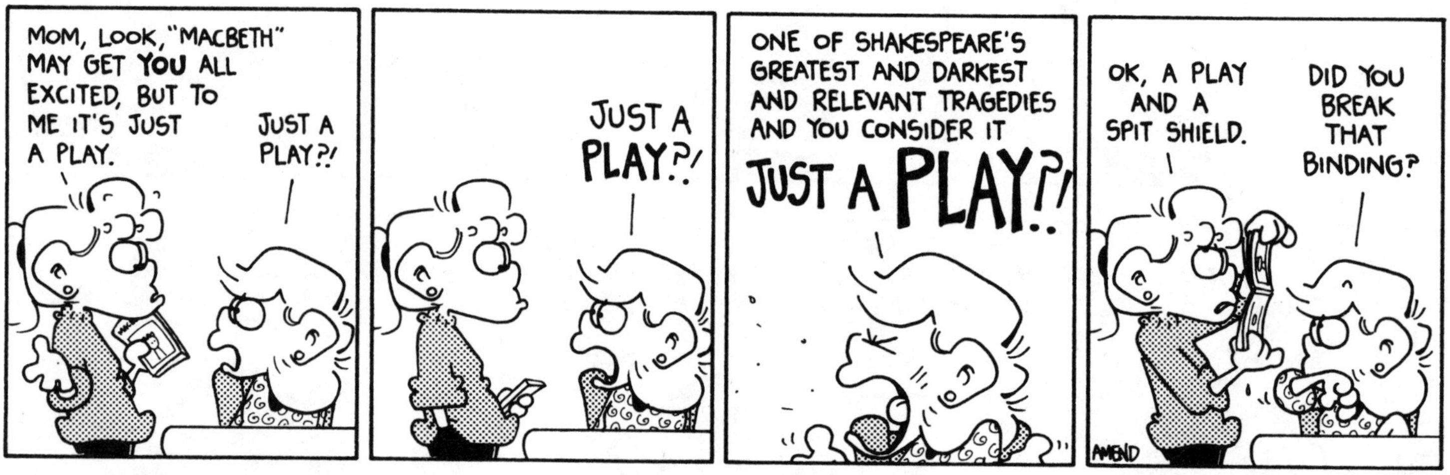
MOM, LOOK, "MACBETH" MAY GET YOU ALL EXCITED, BUT TO ME IT'S JUST A PLAY.
JUST A PLAY?!
JUST A PLAY?!
ONE OF SHAKESPEARE'S GREATEST AND DARKEST AND RELEVANT TRAGEDIES AND YOU CONSIDER IT
JUST A PLAY?!!
OK, A PLAY AND A SPIT SHIELD.
DID YOU BREAK THAT BINDING?
AMEND

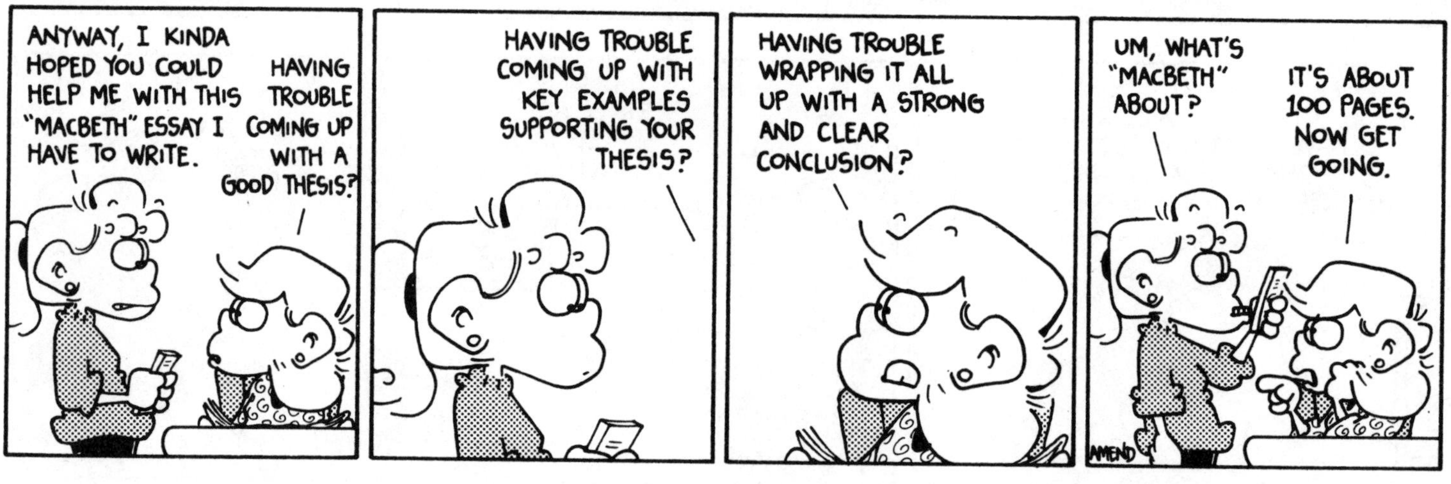
ANYWAY, I KINDA HOPED YOU COULD HELP ME WITH THIS "MACBETH" ESSAY I HAVE TO WRITE.
HAVING TROUBLE COMING UP WITH A GOOD THESIS?
HAVING TROUBLE COMING UP WITH KEY EXAMPLES SUPPORTING YOUR THESIS?
HAVING TROUBLE WRAPPING IT ALL UP WITH A STRONG AND CLEAR CONCLUSION?
UM, WHAT'S "MACBETH" ABOUT?
IT'S ABOUT 100 PAGES. NOW GET GOING.
AMEND

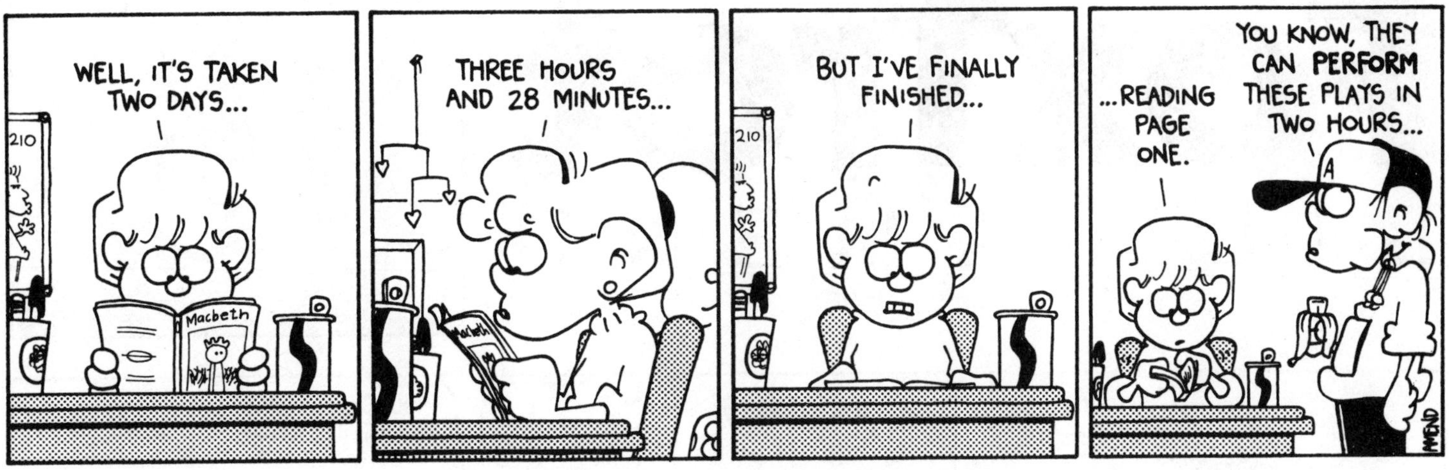
WELL, IT'S TAKEN TWO DAYS...
Macbeth
THREE HOURS AND 28 MINUTES...
BUT I'VE FINALLY FINISHED...
...READING PAGE ONE.
YOU KNOW, THEY CAN **PERFORM** THESE PLAYS IN TWO HOURS...
AMEND

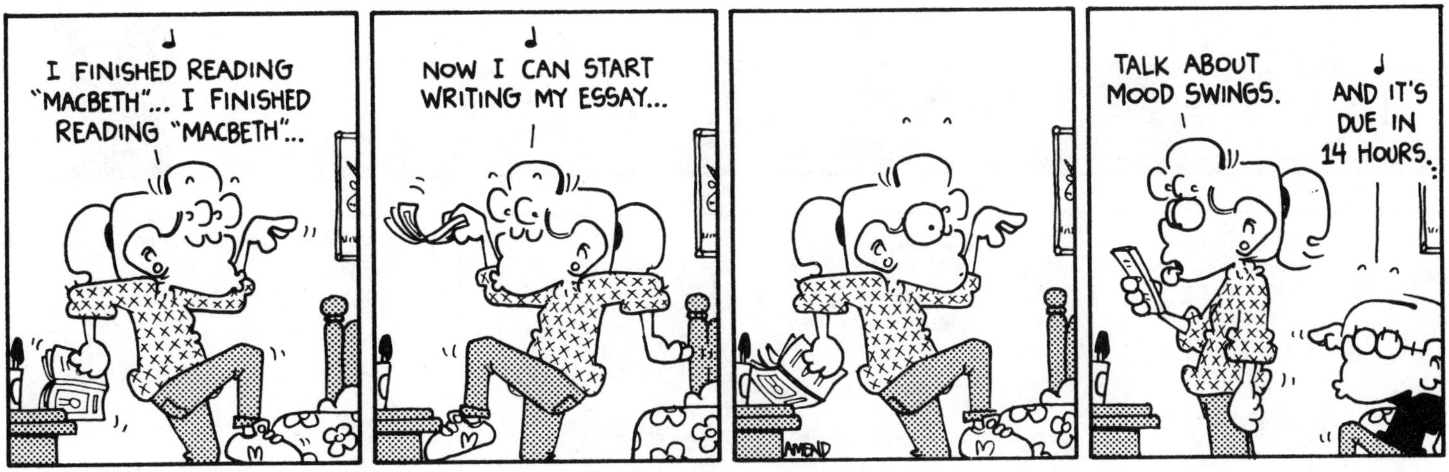
I FINISHED READING "MACBETH"... I FINISHED READING "MACBETH"...
NOW I CAN START WRITING MY ESSAY...
AMEND
TALK ABOUT MOOD SWINGS.
AND IT'S DUE IN 14 HOURS.

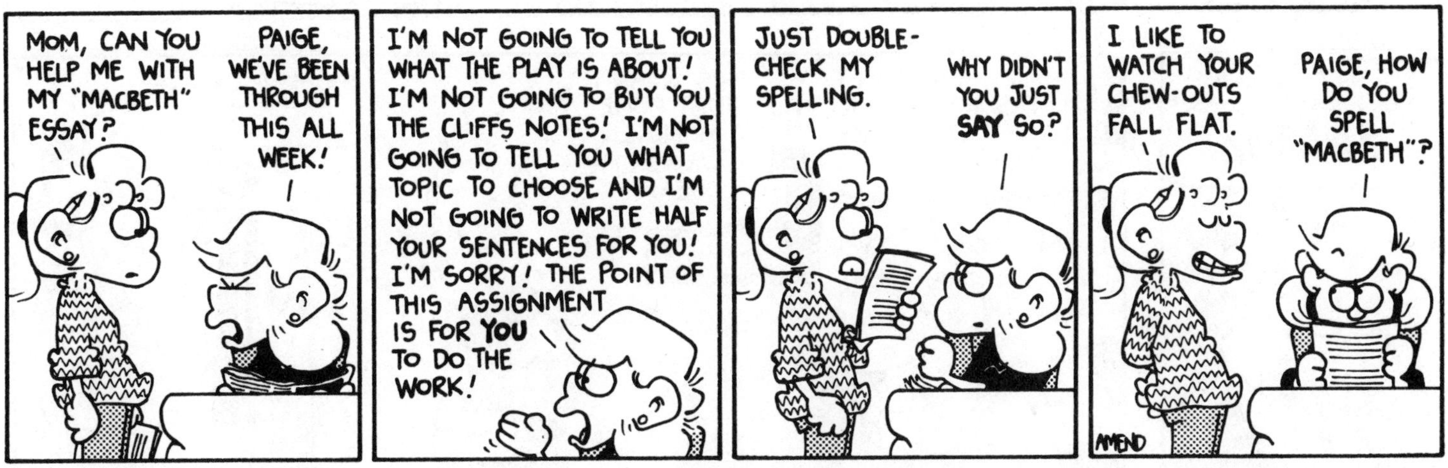
MOM, CAN YOU HELP ME WITH MY "MACBETH" ESSAY?
PAIGE, WE'VE BEEN THROUGH THIS ALL WEEK!
I'M NOT GOING TO TELL YOU WHAT THE PLAY IS ABOUT! I'M NOT GOING TO BUY YOU THE CLIFFS NOTES! I'M NOT GOING TO TELL YOU WHAT TOPIC TO CHOOSE AND I'M NOT GOING TO WRITE HALF YOUR SENTENCES FOR YOU! I'M SORRY! THE POINT OF THIS ASSIGNMENT IS FOR **YOU** TO DO THE WORK!
JUST DOUBLE-CHECK MY SPELLING.
WHY DIDN'T YOU JUST **SAY** SO?
I LIKE TO WATCH YOUR CHEW-OUTS FALL FLAT.
PAIGE, HOW DO YOU SPELL "MACBETH"?
AMEND

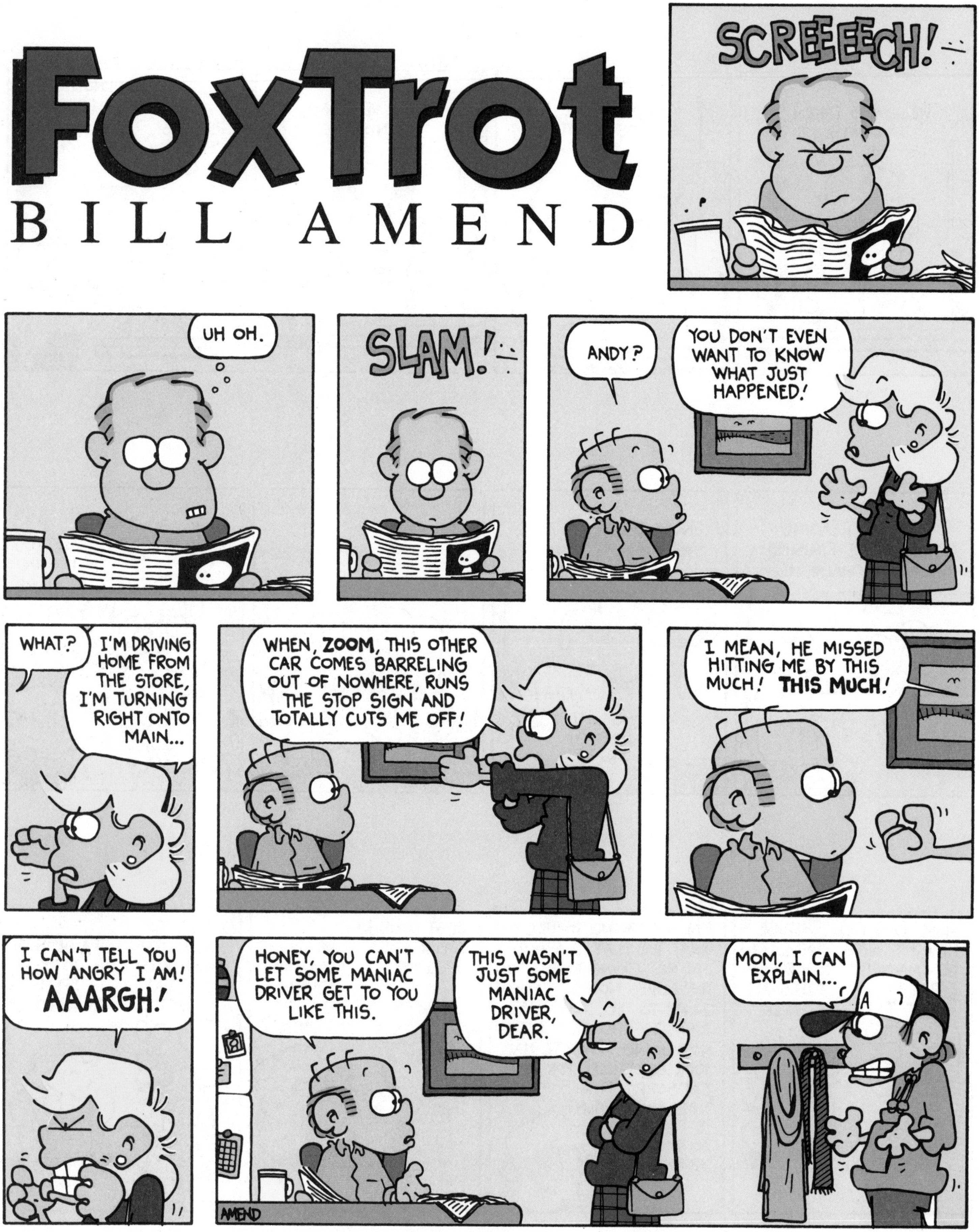
FoxTrot
BILL AMEND
SCREEEECH!
UH OH.
SLAM!
ANDY?
YOU DON'T EVEN WANT TO KNOW WHAT JUST HAPPENED!
WHAT?
I'M DRIVING HOME FROM THE STORE, I'M TURNING RIGHT ONTO MAIN...
WHEN, ZOOM, THIS OTHER CAR COMES BARRELING OUT OF NOWHERE, RUNS THE STOP SIGN AND TOTALLY CUTS ME OFF!
I MEAN, HE MISSED HITTING ME BY THIS MUCH! THIS MUCH!
I CAN'T TELL YOU HOW ANGRY I AM! AAARGH!
HONEY, YOU CAN'T LET SOME MANIAC DRIVER GET TO YOU LIKE THIS.
THIS WASN'T JUST SOME MANIAC DRIVER, DEAR.
MOM, I CAN EXPLAIN...
AMEND

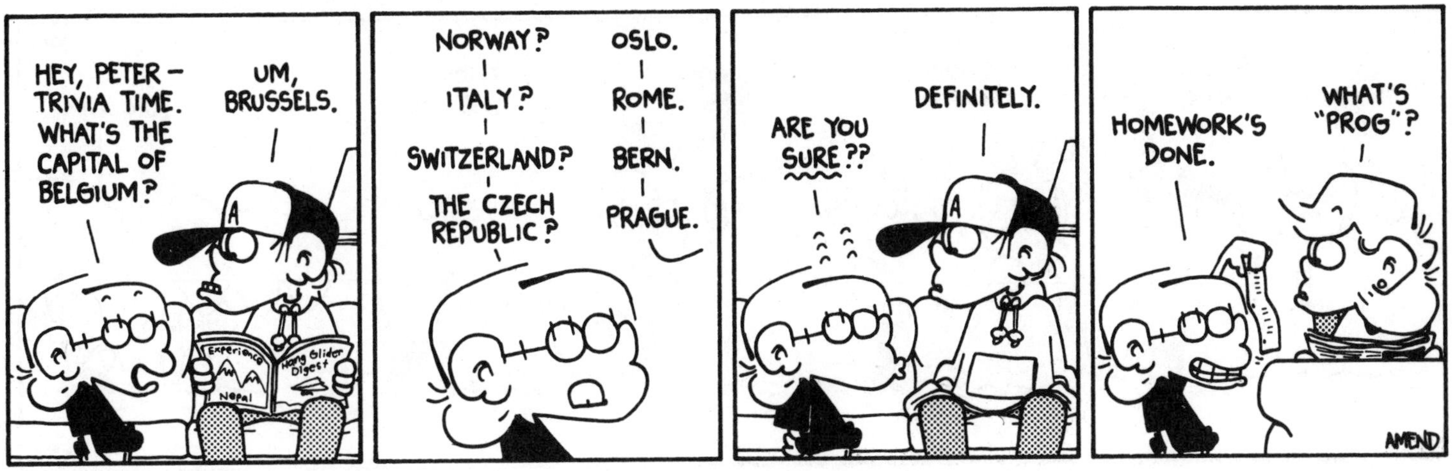
HEY, PETER — TRIVIA TIME. WHAT'S THE CAPITAL OF BELGIUM?
UM, BRUSSELS.
Experience Nepal
Hang Glider Digest
NORWAY?
OSLO.
ITALY?
ROME.
SWITZERLAND?
BERN.
THE CZECH REPUBLIC?
PRAGUE.
ARE YOU SURE??
DEFINITELY.
HOMEWORK'S DONE.
WHAT'S "PROG"?
AMEND

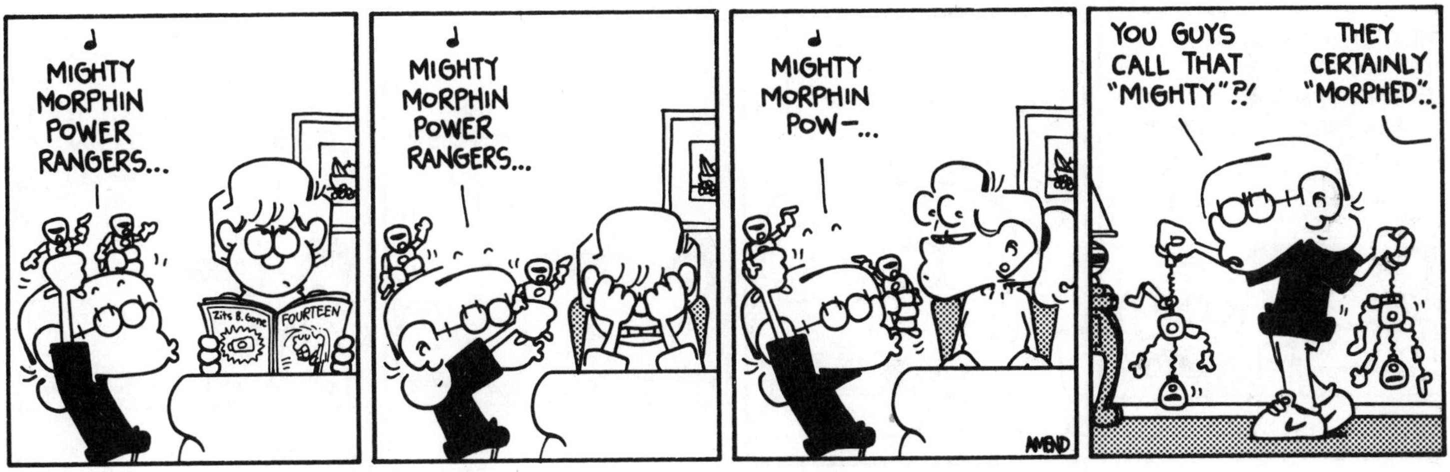
MIGHTY MORPHIN POWER RANGERS...
Zits B. Gone
FOURTEEN
MIGHTY MORPHIN POWER RANGERS...
MIGHTY MORPHIN POW—...
AMEND
YOU GUYS CALL THAT "MIGHTY"?!
THEY CERTAINLY "MORPHED"...

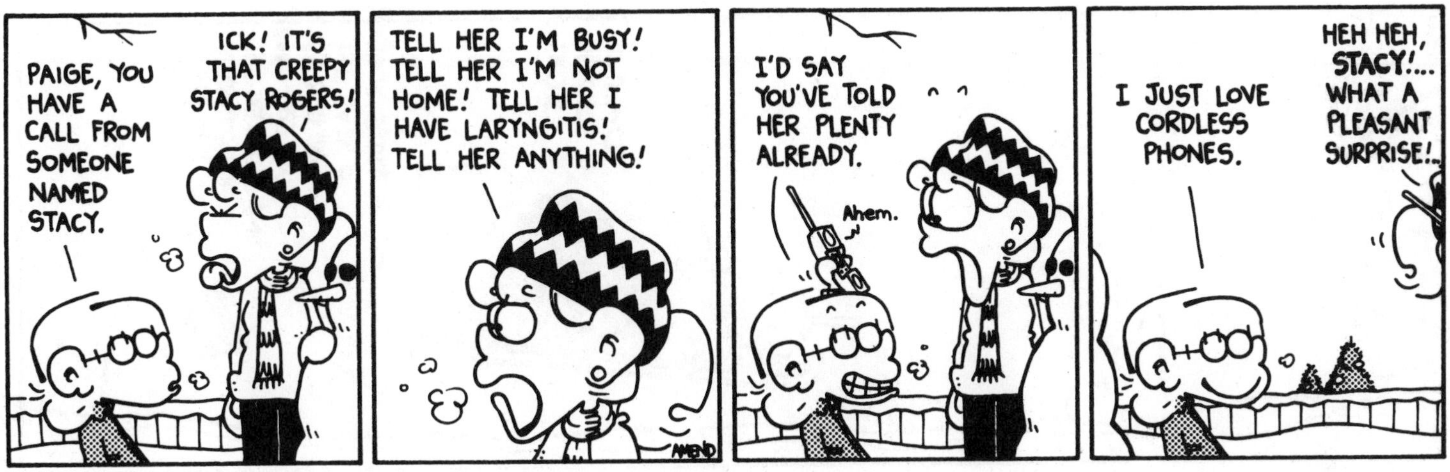
PAIGE, YOU HAVE A CALL FROM SOMEONE NAMED STACY.
ICK! IT'S THAT CREEPY STACY ROGERS!
TELL HER I'M BUSY! TELL HER I'M NOT HOME! TELL HER I HAVE LARYNGITIS! TELL HER ANYTHING!
AMEND
I'D SAY YOU'VE TOLD HER PLENTY ALREADY.
Ahem.
I JUST LOVE CORDLESS PHONES.
HEH HEH, STACY!... WHAT A PLEASANT SURPRISE!...

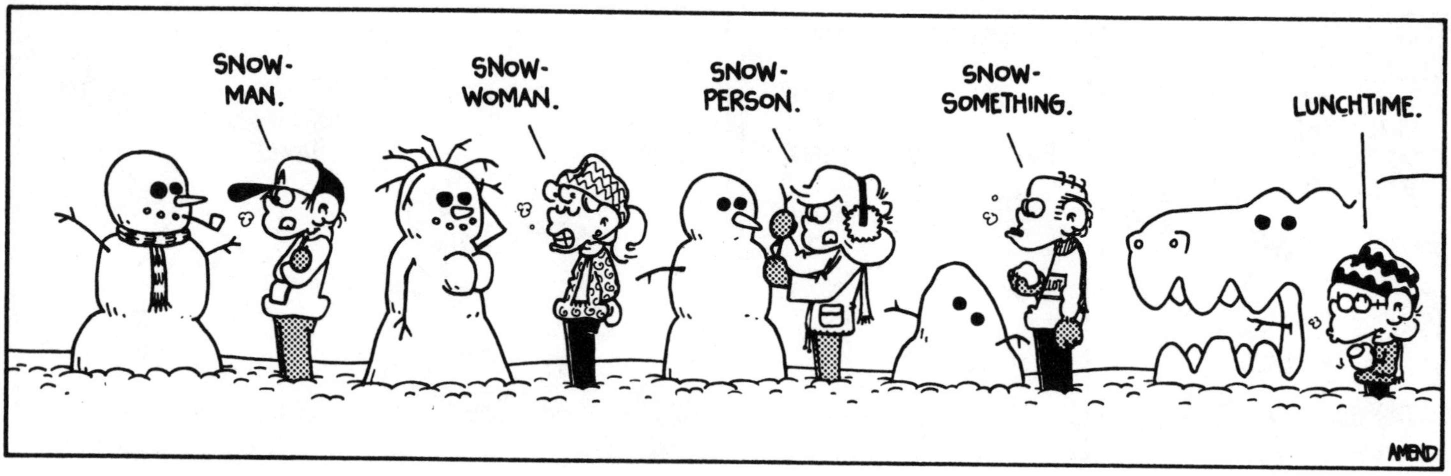
SNOW-MAN.
SNOW-WOMAN.
SNOW-PERSON.
SNOW-SOMETHING.
LUNCHTIME.
AMEND

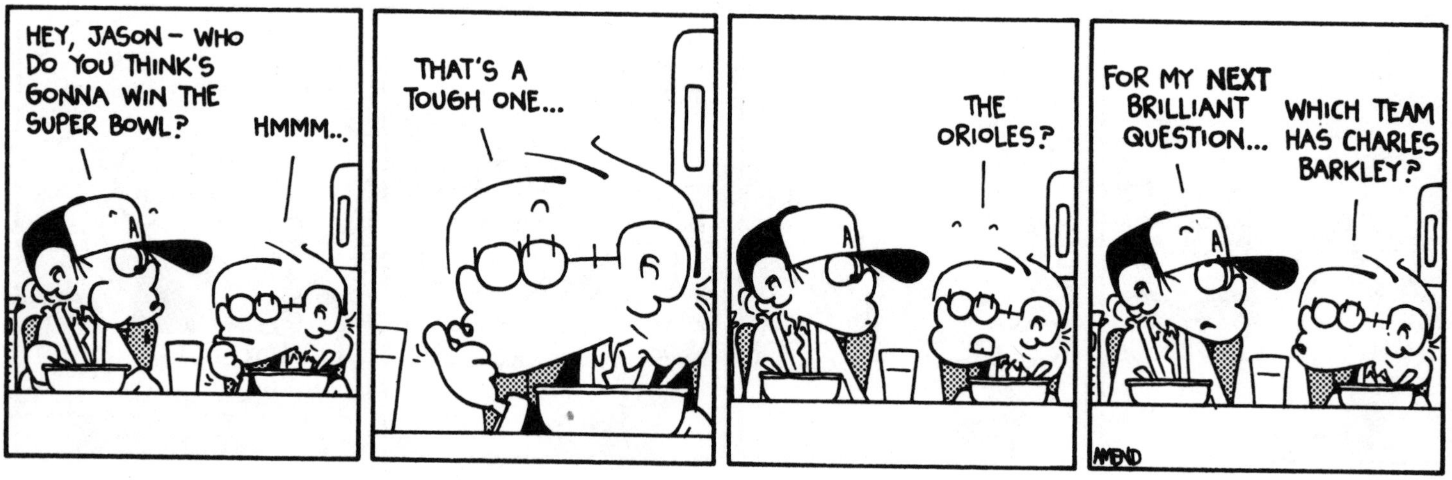
HEY, JASON – WHO DO YOU THINK'S GONNA WIN THE SUPER BOWL?
HMMM...
THAT'S A TOUGH ONE...
THE ORIOLES?
FOR MY NEXT BRILLIANT QUESTION...
WHICH TEAM HAS CHARLES BARKLEY?
AMEND

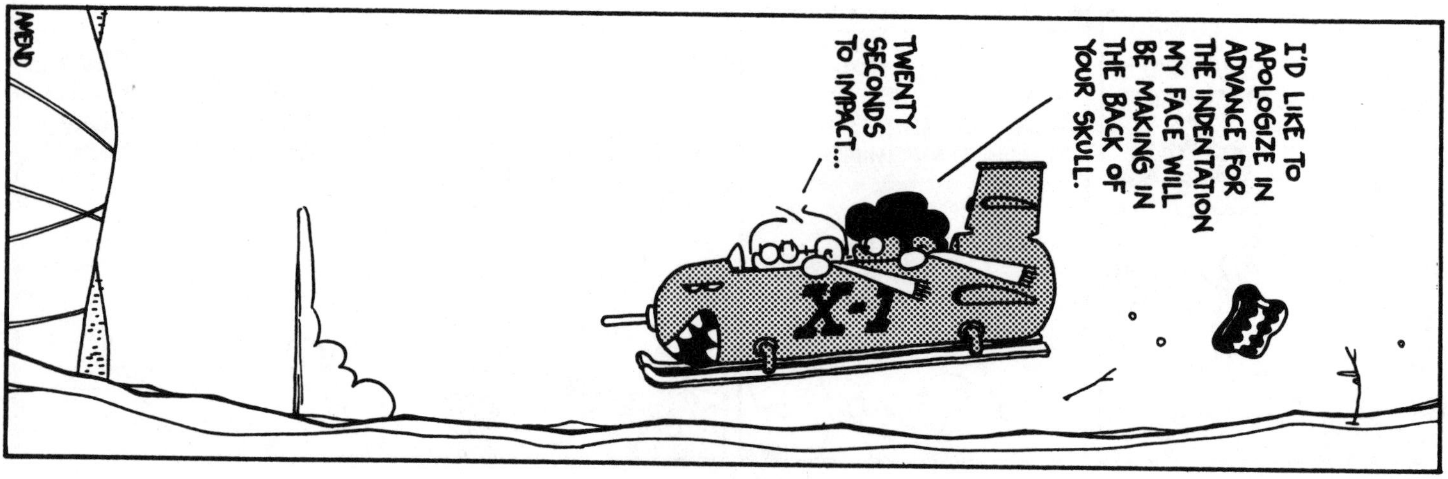
I'D LIKE TO APOLOGIZE IN ADVANCE FOR THE INDENTATION MY FACE WILL BE MAKING IN THE BACK OF YOUR SKULL.
TWENTY SECONDS TO IMPACT...
X-1
AMEND

FoxTrot
BILL AMEND

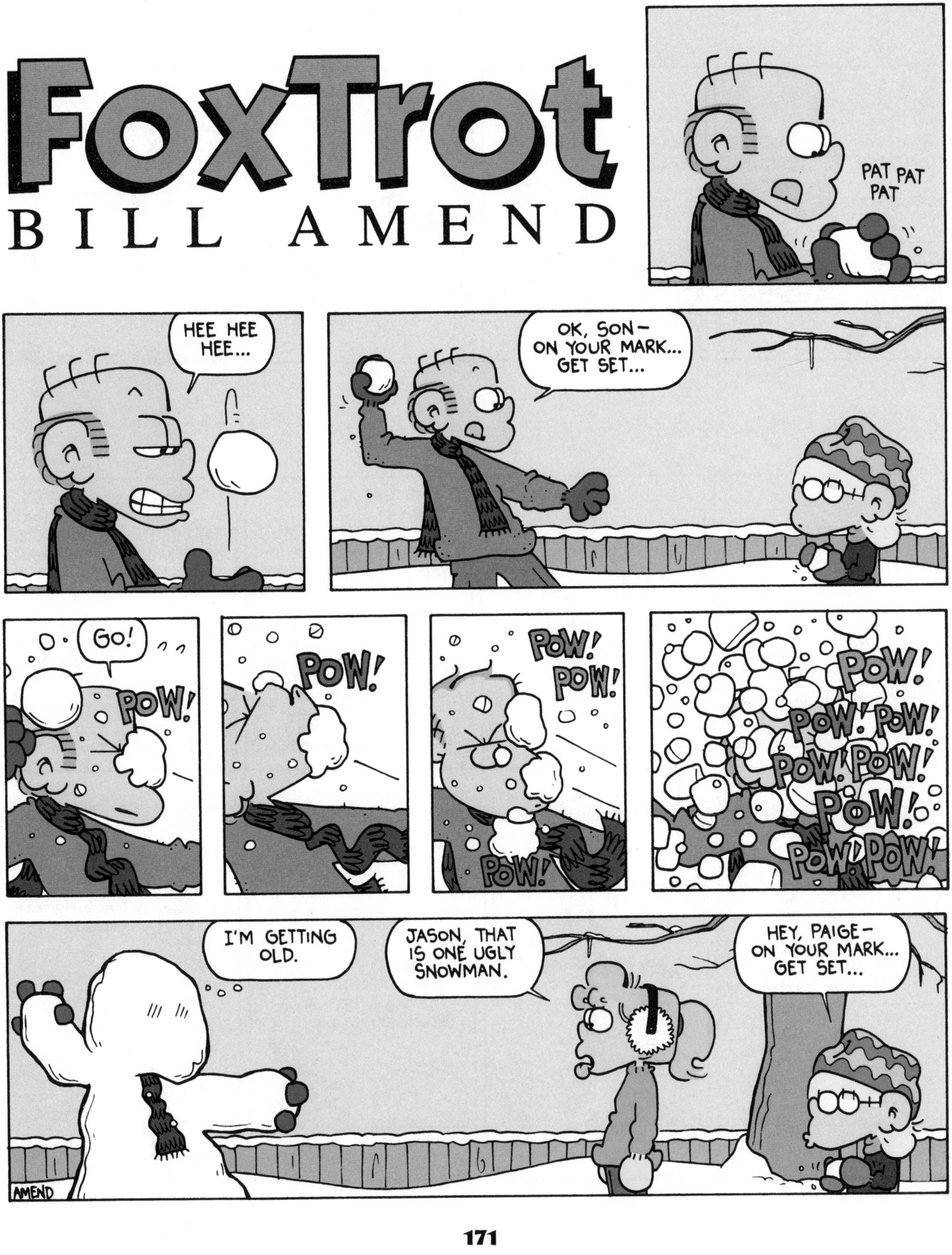

PAT PAT
PAT
HEE HEE
HEE...
OK, SON—
ON YOUR MARK...
GET SET...
GO!
POW!
POW!
POW!
POW!
POW!
POW! POW!
POW! POW!
POW!
POW! POW!
I'M GETTING
OLD.
JASON, THAT
IS ONE UGLY
SNOWMAN.
HEY, PAIGE—
ON YOUR MARK...
GET SET...
AMEND

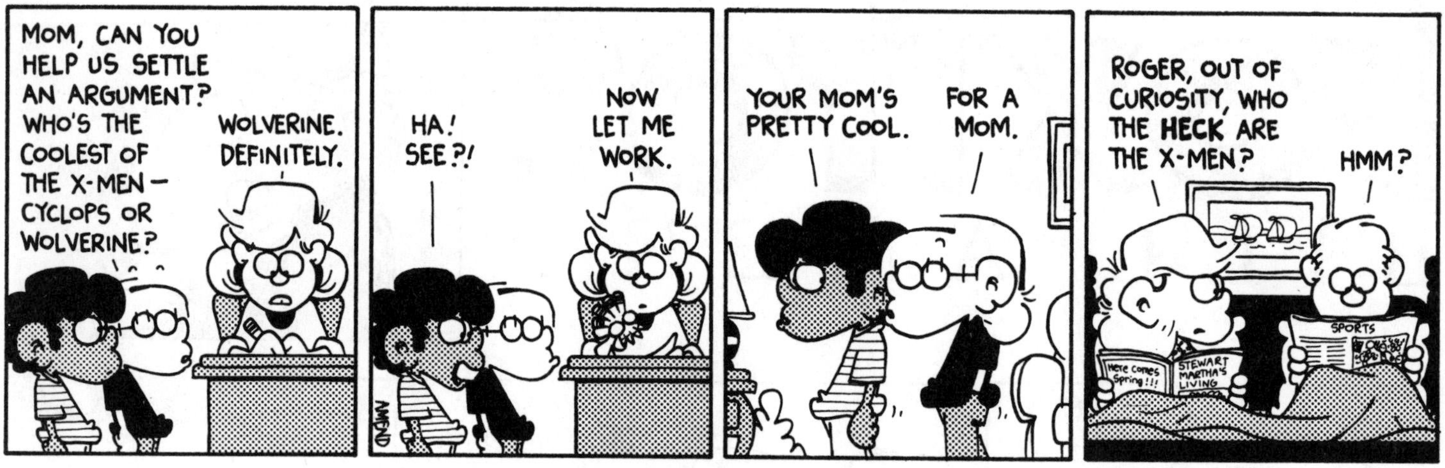
MOM, CAN YOU HELP US SETTLE AN ARGUMENT? WHO'S THE COOLEST OF THE X-MEN — CYCLOPS OR WOLVERINE?
WOLVERINE. DEFINITELY.
HA! SEE?!
NOW LET ME WORK.
AMEND
YOUR MOM'S PRETTY COOL.
FOR A MOM.
ROGER, OUT OF CURIOSITY, WHO THE **HECK** ARE THE X-MEN?
HMM?
Here Comes Spring!!!
STEWART MARTHA'S LIVING
SPORTS

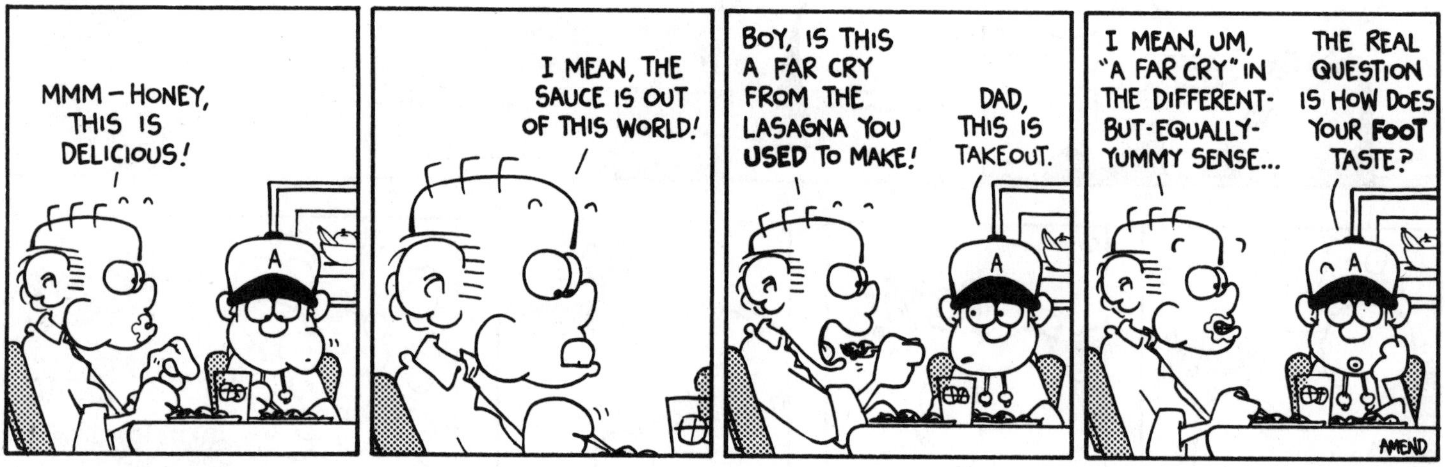
MMM — HONEY, THIS IS DELICIOUS!
I MEAN, THE SAUCE IS OUT OF THIS WORLD!
BOY, IS THIS A FAR CRY FROM THE LASAGNA YOU **USED** TO MAKE!
DAD, THIS IS TAKEOUT.
I MEAN, UM, "A FAR CRY" IN THE DIFFERENT-BUT-EQUALLY-YUMMY SENSE...
THE REAL QUESTION IS HOW DOES YOUR **FOOT** TASTE?
AMEND

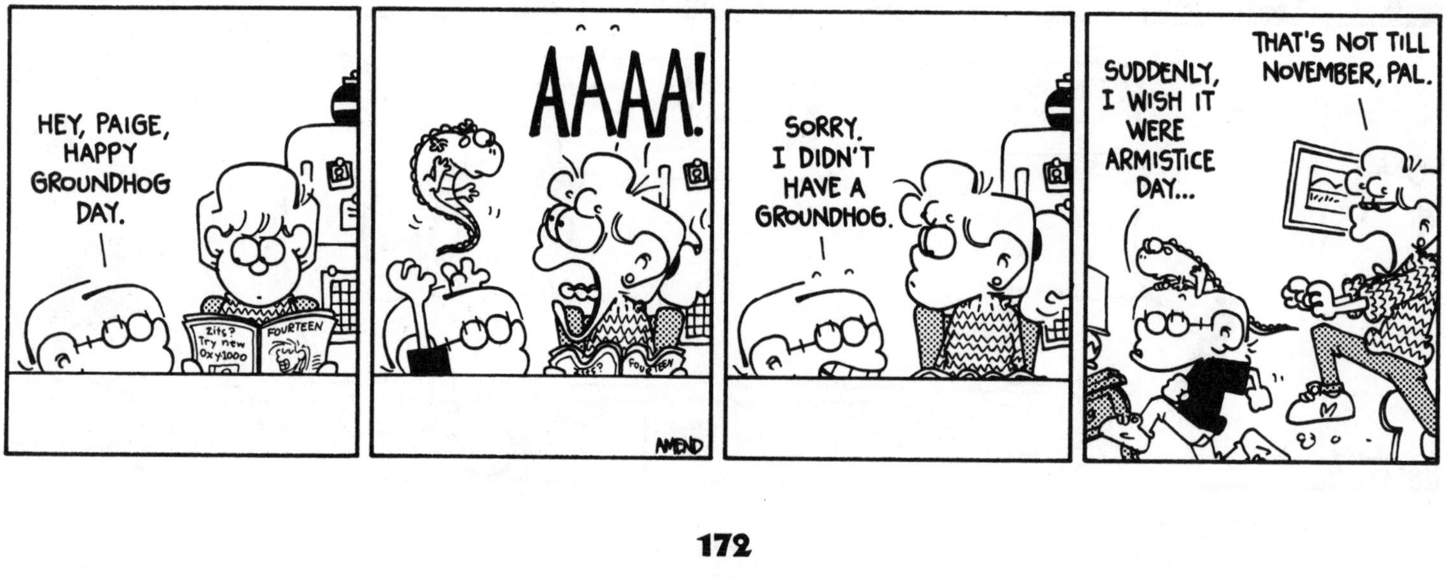
HEY, PAIGE, HAPPY GROUNDHOG DAY.
Zits? Try new Oxy1000
FOURTEEN
AAAA!
AMEND
SORRY. I DIDN'T HAVE A GROUNDHOG.
SUDDENLY, I WISH IT WERE ARMISTICE DAY...
THAT'S NOT TILL NOVEMBER, PAL.

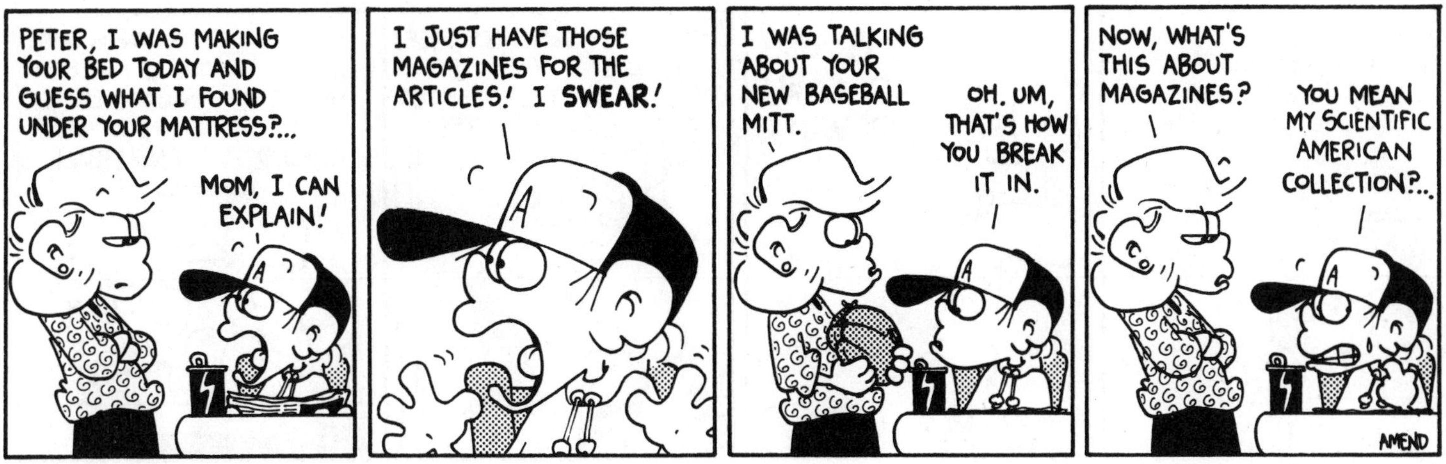
PETER, I WAS MAKING YOUR BED TODAY AND GUESS WHAT I FOUND UNDER YOUR MATTRESS?...
MOM, I CAN EXPLAIN!
I JUST HAVE THOSE MAGAZINES FOR THE ARTICLES! I SWEAR!
I WAS TALKING ABOUT YOUR NEW BASEBALL MITT.
OH. UM, THAT'S HOW YOU BREAK IT IN.
NOW, WHAT'S THIS ABOUT MAGAZINES?
YOU MEAN MY SCIENTIFIC AMERICAN COLLECTION?..
AMEND

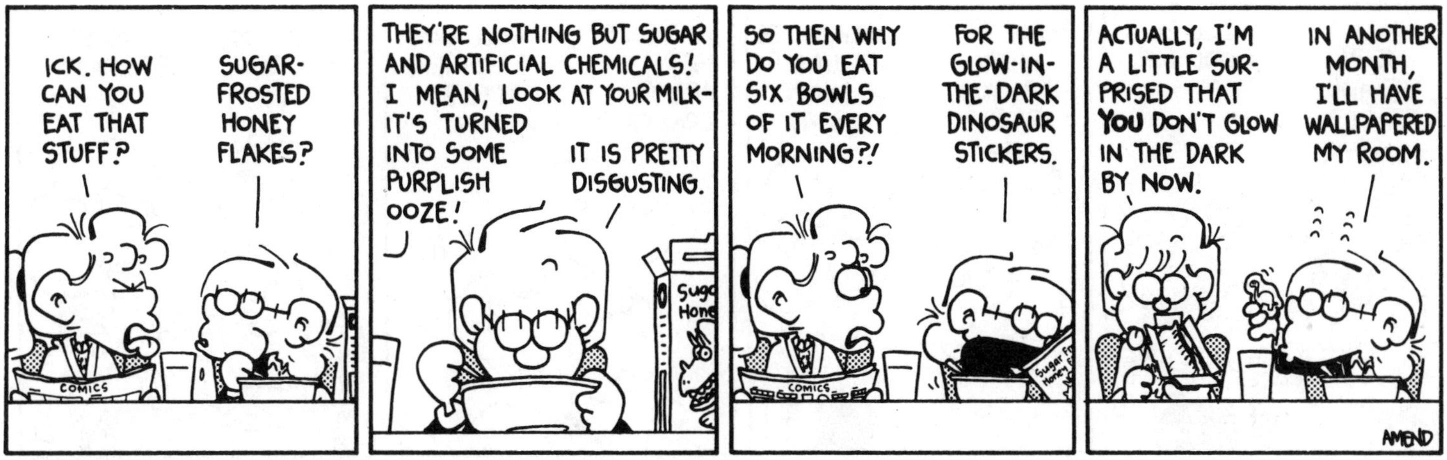
ICK. HOW CAN YOU EAT THAT STUFF?
SUGAR-FROSTED HONEY FLAKES?
THEY'RE NOTHING BUT SUGAR AND ARTIFICIAL CHEMICALS! I MEAN, LOOK AT YOUR MILK-IT'S TURNED INTO SOME PURPLISH OOZE!
IT IS PRETTY DISGUSTING.
COMICS
SO THEN WHY DO YOU EAT SIX BOWLS OF IT EVERY MORNING?!
FOR THE GLOW-IN-THE-DARK DINOSAUR STICKERS.
ACTUALLY, I'M A LITTLE SURPRISED THAT YOU DON'T GLOW IN THE DARK BY NOW.
IN ANOTHER MONTH, I'LL HAVE WALLPAPERED MY ROOM.
AMEND

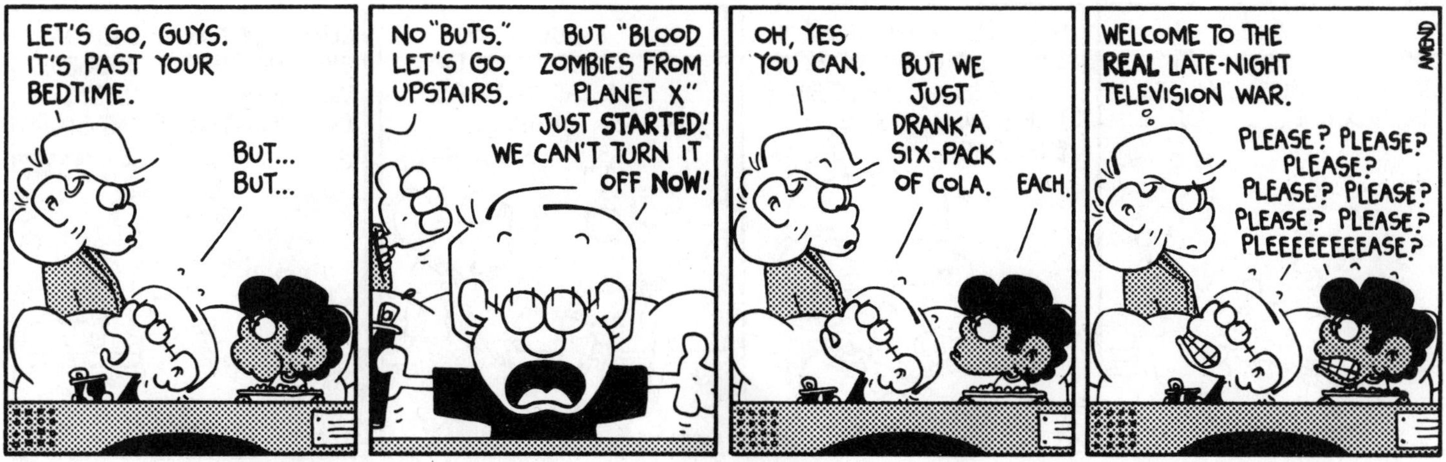
LET'S GO, GUYS. IT'S PAST YOUR BEDTIME.
BUT... BUT...
NO "BUTS." LET'S GO. UPSTAIRS.
BUT "BLOOD ZOMBIES FROM PLANET X" JUST STARTED! WE CAN'T TURN IT OFF NOW!
OH, YES YOU CAN.
BUT WE JUST DRANK A SIX-PACK OF COLA.
EACH.
WELCOME TO THE REAL LATE-NIGHT TELEVISION WAR.
PLEASE? PLEASE? PLEASE? PLEASE? PLEASE? PLEASE? PLEASE? PLEEEEEEEEASE?
AMEND

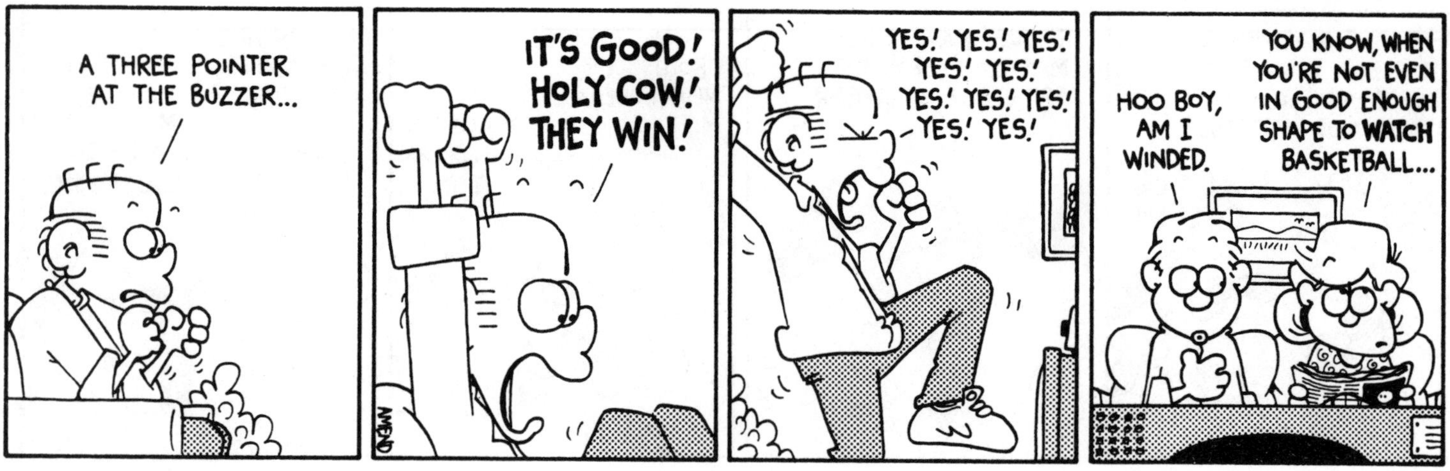
A THREE POINTER AT THE BUZZER...
IT'S GOOD! HOLY COW! THEY WIN!
YES! YES! YES! YES! YES! YES! YES! YES! YES! YES!
HOO BOY, AM I WINDED.
YOU KNOW, WHEN YOU'RE NOT EVEN IN GOOD ENOUGH SHAPE TO WATCH BASKETBALL...
AMEND

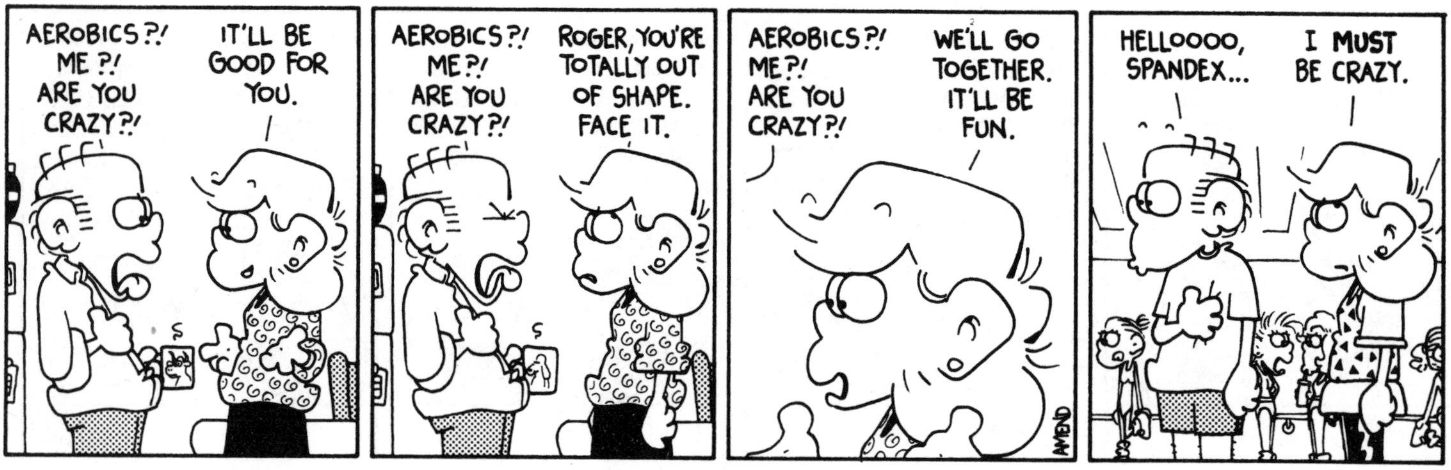
AEROBICS?! ME?! ARE YOU CRAZY?!
IT'LL BE GOOD FOR YOU.
AEROBICS?! ME?! ARE YOU CRAZY?!
ROGER, YOU'RE TOTALLY OUT OF SHAPE. FACE IT.
AEROBICS?! ME?! ARE YOU CRAZY?!
WE'LL GO TOGETHER. IT'LL BE FUN.
AMEND
HELLOOOO, SPANDEX...
I MUST BE CRAZY.

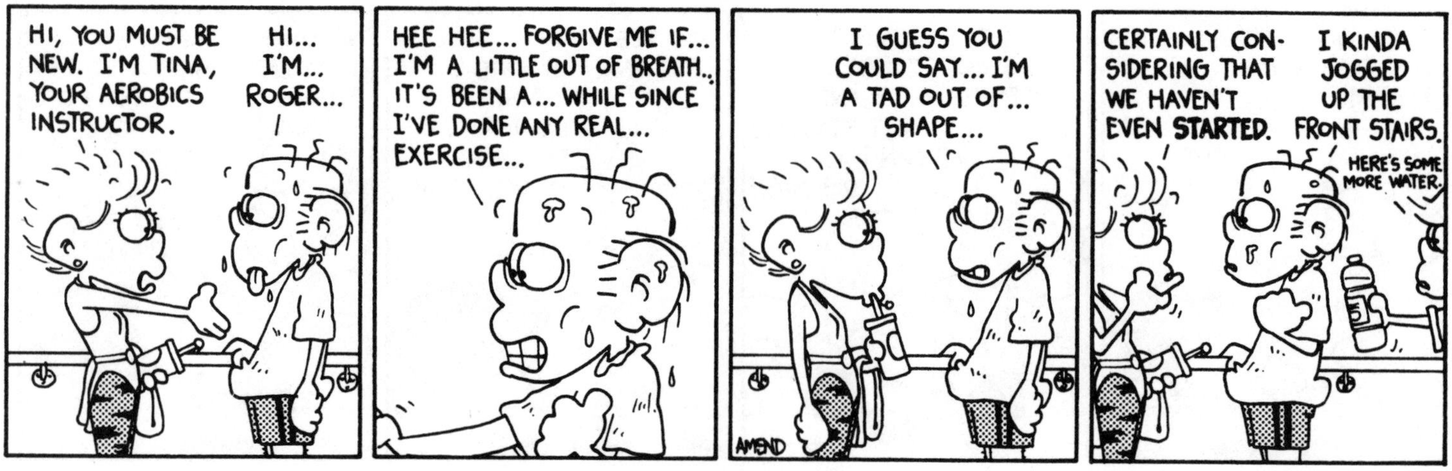
HI, YOU MUST BE NEW. I'M TINA, YOUR AEROBICS INSTRUCTOR.
HI... I'M... ROGER...
HEE HEE... FORGIVE ME IF... I'M A LITTLE OUT OF BREATH.. IT'S BEEN A... WHILE SINCE I'VE DONE ANY REAL... EXERCISE...
I GUESS YOU COULD SAY... I'M A TAD OUT OF... SHAPE...
AMEND
CERTAINLY CONSIDERING THAT WE HAVEN'T EVEN STARTED.
I KINDA JOGGED UP THE FRONT STAIRS.
HERE'S SOME MORE WATER.

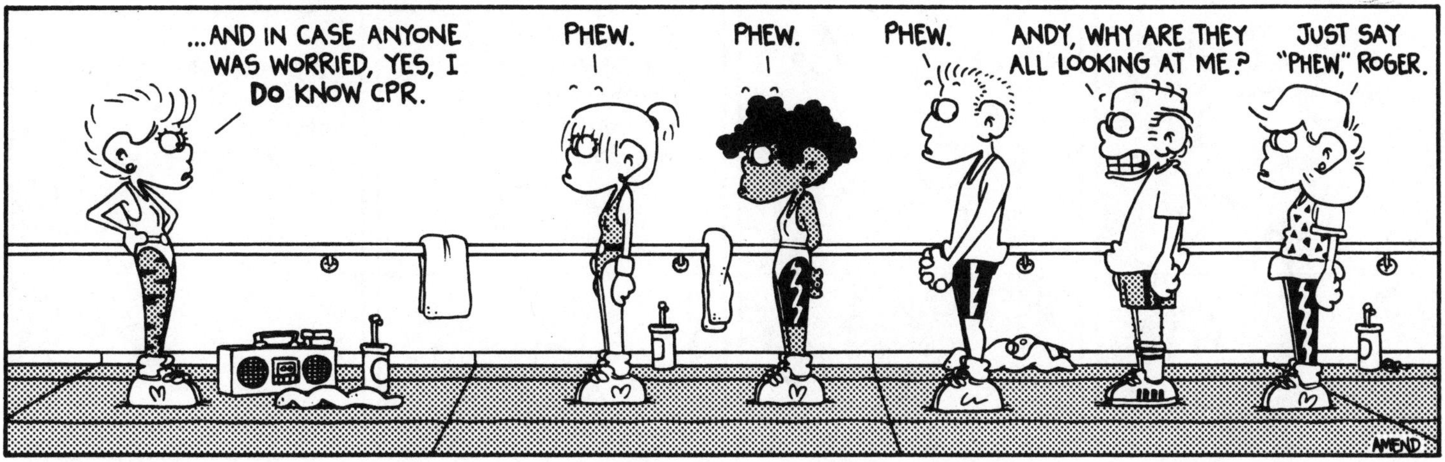
...AND IN CASE ANYONE WAS WORRIED, YES, I **DO** KNOW CPR.
PHEW.
PHEW.
PHEW.
ANDY, WHY ARE THEY ALL LOOKING AT ME?
JUST SAY "PHEW," ROGER.
AMEND

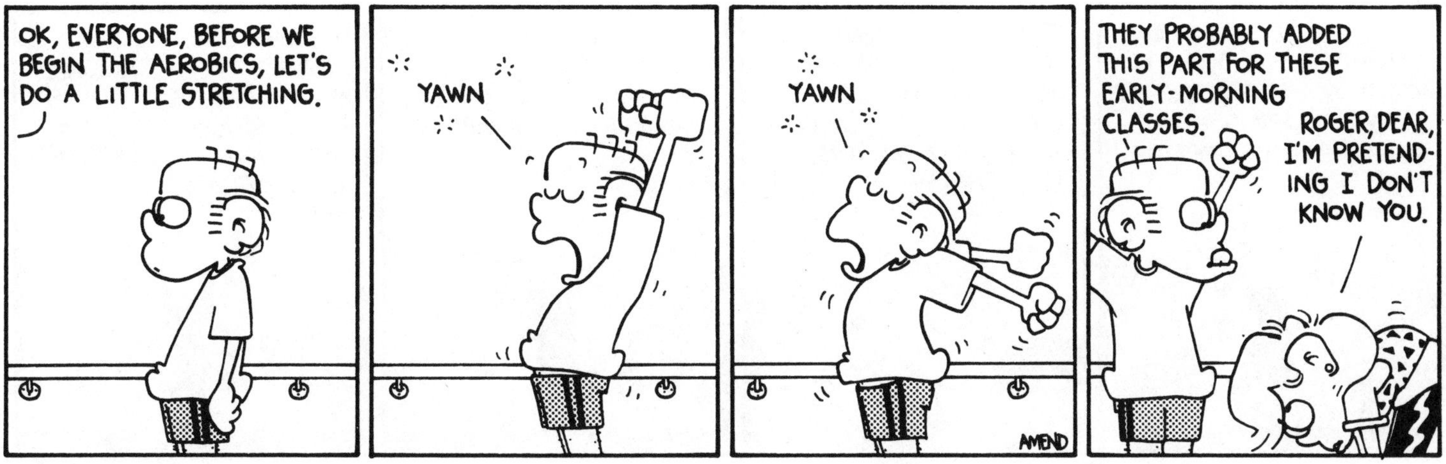
OK, EVERYONE, BEFORE WE BEGIN THE AEROBICS, LET'S DO A LITTLE STRETCHING.
YAWN
YAWN
AMEND
THEY PROBABLY ADDED THIS PART FOR THESE EARLY-MORNING CLASSES.
ROGER, DEAR, I'M PRETENDING I DON'T KNOW YOU.

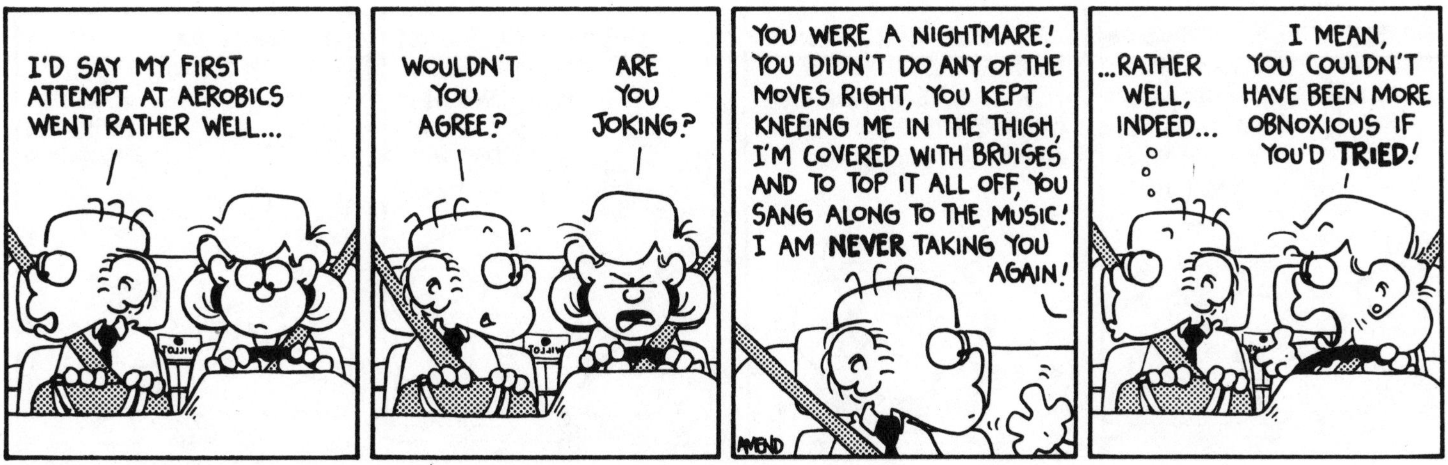
I'D SAY MY FIRST ATTEMPT AT AEROBICS WENT RATHER WELL...
WOULDN'T YOU AGREE?
ARE YOU JOKING?
YOU WERE A NIGHTMARE! YOU DIDN'T DO ANY OF THE MOVES RIGHT, YOU KEPT KNEEING ME IN THE THIGH, I'M COVERED WITH BRUISES AND TO TOP IT ALL OFF, YOU SANG ALONG TO THE MUSIC! I AM **NEVER** TAKING YOU AGAIN!
AMEND
...RATHER WELL, INDEED...
I MEAN, YOU COULDN'T HAVE BEEN MORE OBNOXIOUS IF YOU'D **TRIED**!

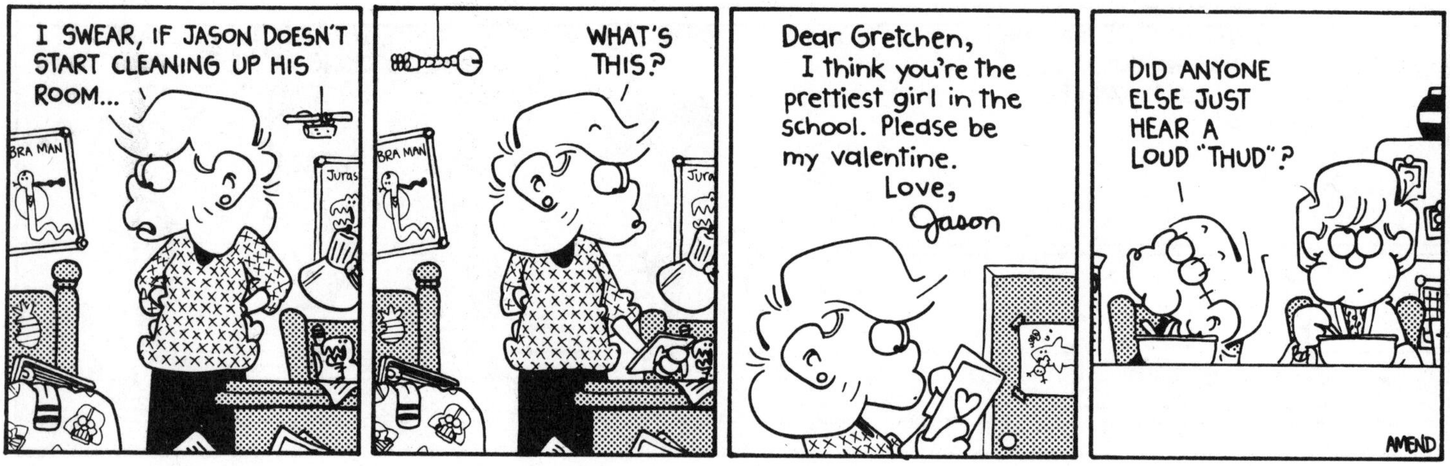
I SWEAR, IF JASON DOESN'T START CLEANING UP HIS ROOM...
WHAT'S THIS?
Dear Gretchen,
I think you're the prettiest girl in the school. Please be my valentine.
Love,
Jason
DID ANYONE ELSE JUST HEAR A LOUD "THUD"?
AMEND

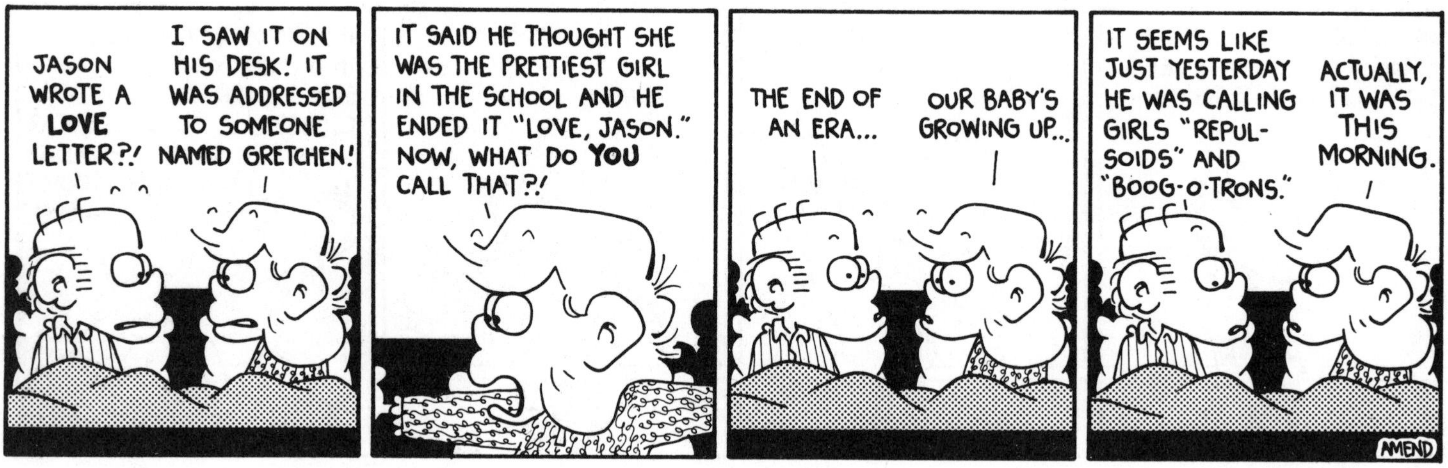
JASON WROTE A **LOVE** LETTER?!
I SAW IT ON HIS DESK! IT WAS ADDRESSED TO SOMEONE NAMED GRETCHEN!
IT SAID HE THOUGHT SHE WAS THE PRETTIEST GIRL IN THE SCHOOL AND HE ENDED IT "LOVE, JASON." NOW, WHAT DO **YOU** CALL THAT?!
THE END OF AN ERA...
OUR BABY'S GROWING UP...
IT SEEMS LIKE JUST YESTERDAY HE WAS CALLING GIRLS "REPULSOIDS" AND "BOOG-O-TRONS."
ACTUALLY, IT WAS THIS MORNING.
AMEND

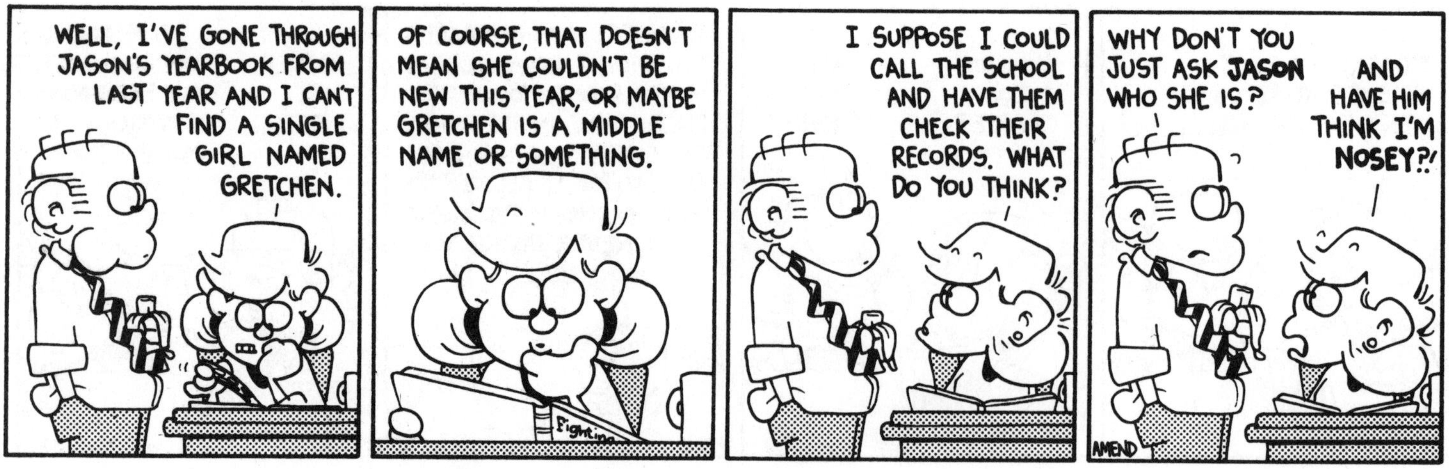
WELL, I'VE GONE THROUGH JASON'S YEARBOOK FROM LAST YEAR AND I CAN'T FIND A SINGLE GIRL NAMED GRETCHEN.
OF COURSE, THAT DOESN'T MEAN SHE COULDN'T BE NEW THIS YEAR, OR MAYBE GRETCHEN IS A MIDDLE NAME OR SOMETHING.
I SUPPOSE I COULD CALL THE SCHOOL AND HAVE THEM CHECK THEIR RECORDS. WHAT DO YOU THINK?
WHY DON'T YOU JUST ASK **JASON** WHO SHE IS?
AND HAVE HIM THINK I'M **NOSEY**?!
AMEND

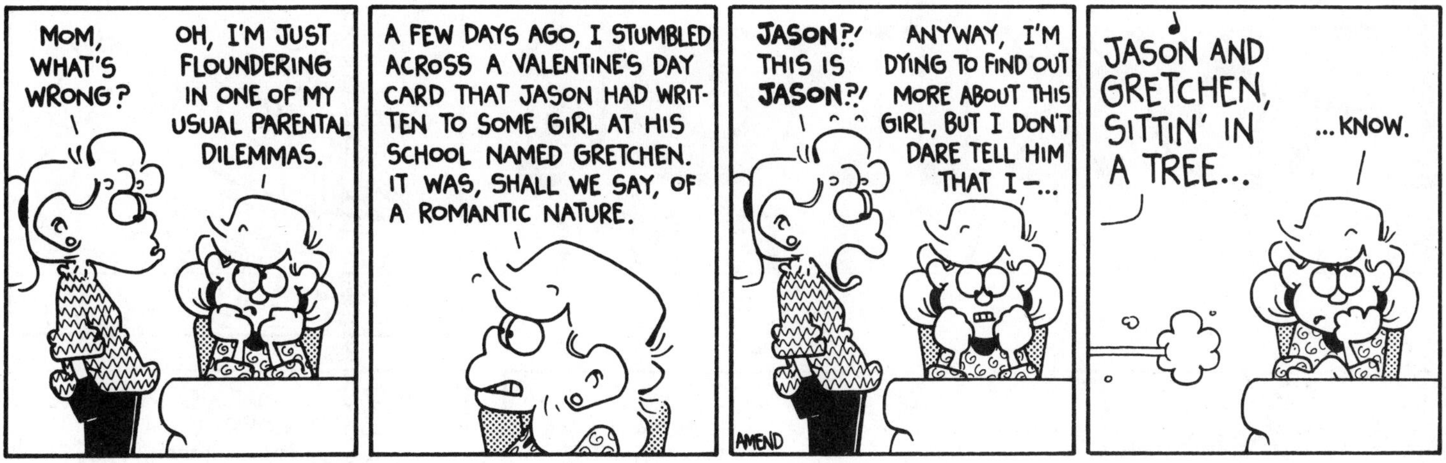
MOM, WHAT'S WRONG?
OH, I'M JUST FLOUNDERING IN ONE OF MY USUAL PARENTAL DILEMMAS.
A FEW DAYS AGO, I STUMBLED ACROSS A VALENTINE'S DAY CARD THAT JASON HAD WRITTEN TO SOME GIRL AT HIS SCHOOL NAMED GRETCHEN. IT WAS, SHALL WE SAY, OF A ROMANTIC NATURE.
JASON?! THIS IS JASON?!
ANYWAY, I'M DYING TO FIND OUT MORE ABOUT THIS GIRL, BUT I DON'T DARE TELL HIM THAT I–...
AMEND
JASON AND GRETCHEN, SITTIN' IN A TREE...
...KNOW.

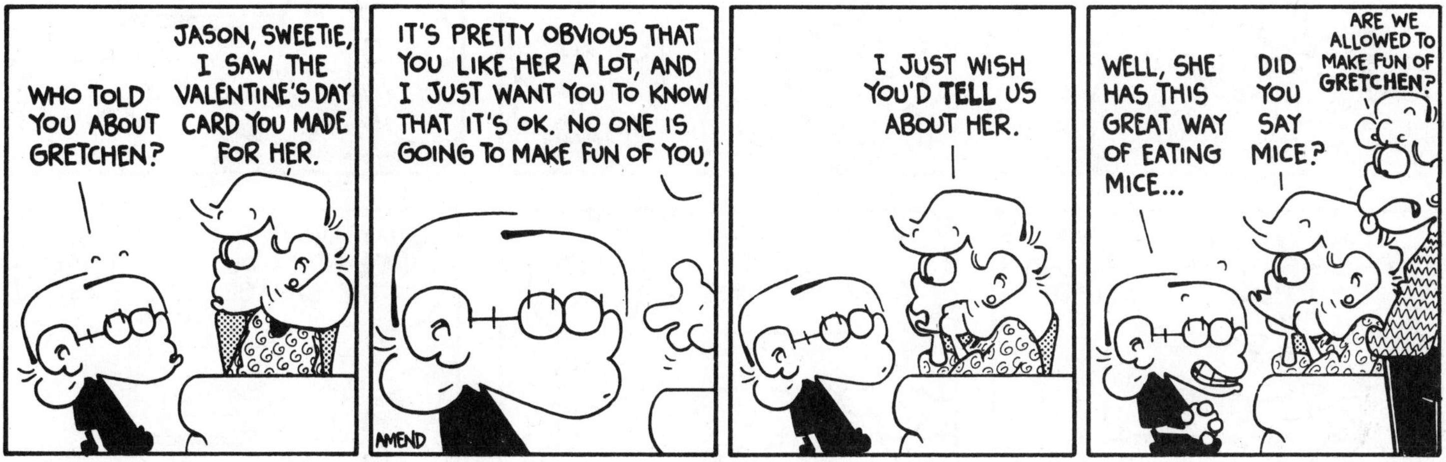
JASON, SWEETIE, I SAW THE VALENTINE'S DAY CARD YOU MADE FOR HER.
WHO TOLD YOU ABOUT GRETCHEN?
IT'S PRETTY OBVIOUS THAT YOU LIKE HER A LOT, AND I JUST WANT YOU TO KNOW THAT IT'S OK. NO ONE IS GOING TO MAKE FUN OF YOU.
AMEND
I JUST WISH YOU'D TELL US ABOUT HER.
WELL, SHE HAS THIS GREAT WAY OF EATING MICE...
DID YOU SAY MICE?
ARE WE ALLOWED TO MAKE FUN OF GRETCHEN?

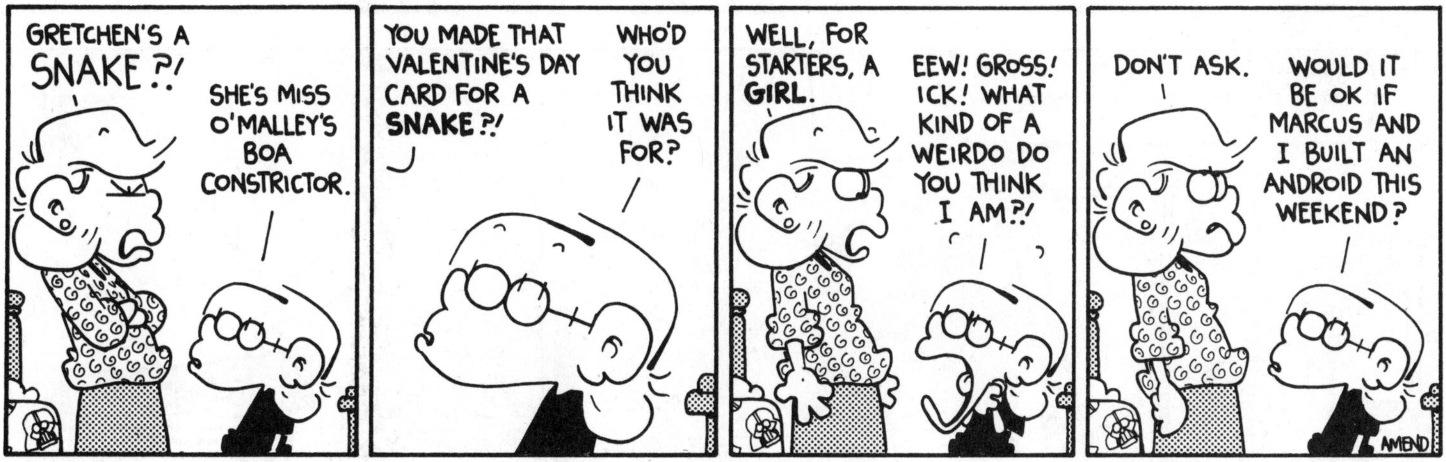
GRETCHEN'S A SNAKE?!
SHE'S MISS O'MALLEY'S BOA CONSTRICTOR.
YOU MADE THAT VALENTINE'S DAY CARD FOR A SNAKE?!
WHO'D YOU THINK IT WAS FOR?
WELL, FOR STARTERS, A GIRL.
EEW! GROSS! ICK! WHAT KIND OF A WEIRDO DO YOU THINK I AM?!
DON'T ASK.
WOULD IT BE OK IF MARCUS AND I BUILT AN ANDROID THIS WEEKEND?
AMEND

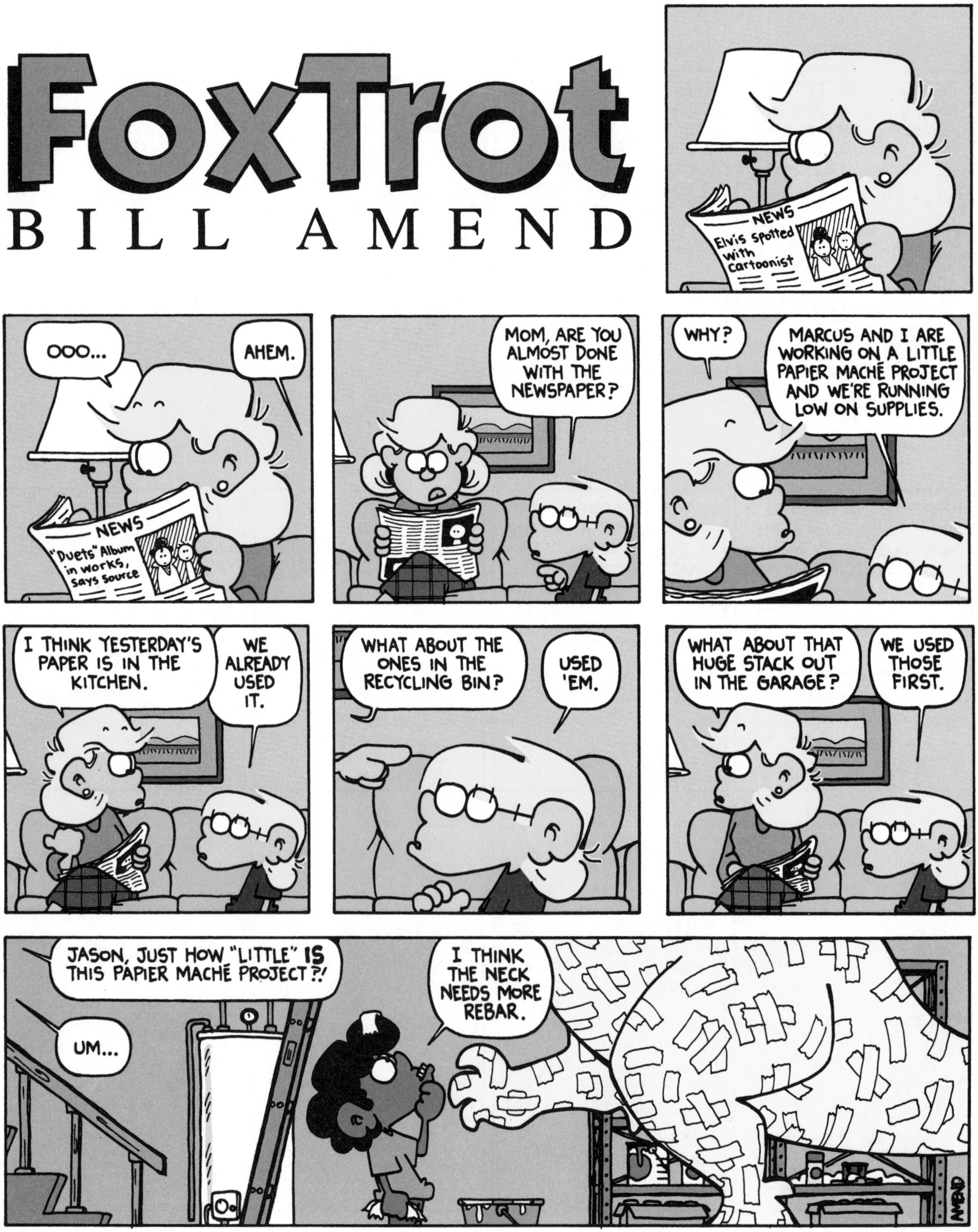
FoxTrot
BILL AMEND
NEWS
Elvis Spotted with Cartoonist
OOO...
AHEM.
NEWS
"Duets" Album in works, says source
MOM, ARE YOU ALMOST DONE WITH THE NEWSPAPER?
WHY?
MARCUS AND I ARE WORKING ON A LITTLE PAPIER MACHÉ PROJECT AND WE'RE RUNNING LOW ON SUPPLIES.
I THINK YESTERDAY'S PAPER IS IN THE KITCHEN.
WE ALREADY USED IT.
WHAT ABOUT THE ONES IN THE RECYCLING BIN?
USED 'EM.
WHAT ABOUT THAT HUGE STACK OUT IN THE GARAGE?
WE USED THOSE FIRST.
JASON, JUST HOW "LITTLE" IS THIS PAPIER MACHÉ PROJECT?!
UM...
I THINK THE NECK NEEDS MORE REBAR.
AMEND

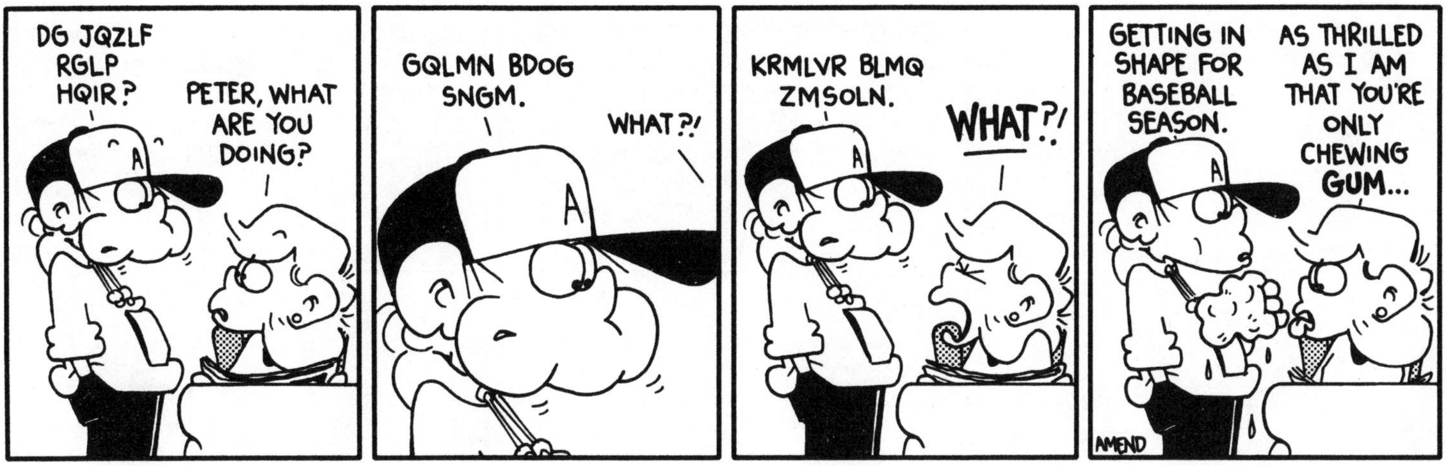
DG JQZLF RGLP HQIR?
PETER, WHAT ARE YOU DOING?
GQLMN BDOG SNGM.
WHAT?!
KRMLVR BLMQ ZMSOLN.
WHAT?!
GETTING IN SHAPE FOR BASEBALL SEASON.
AS THRILLED AS I AM THAT YOU'RE ONLY CHEWING GUM...
AMEND

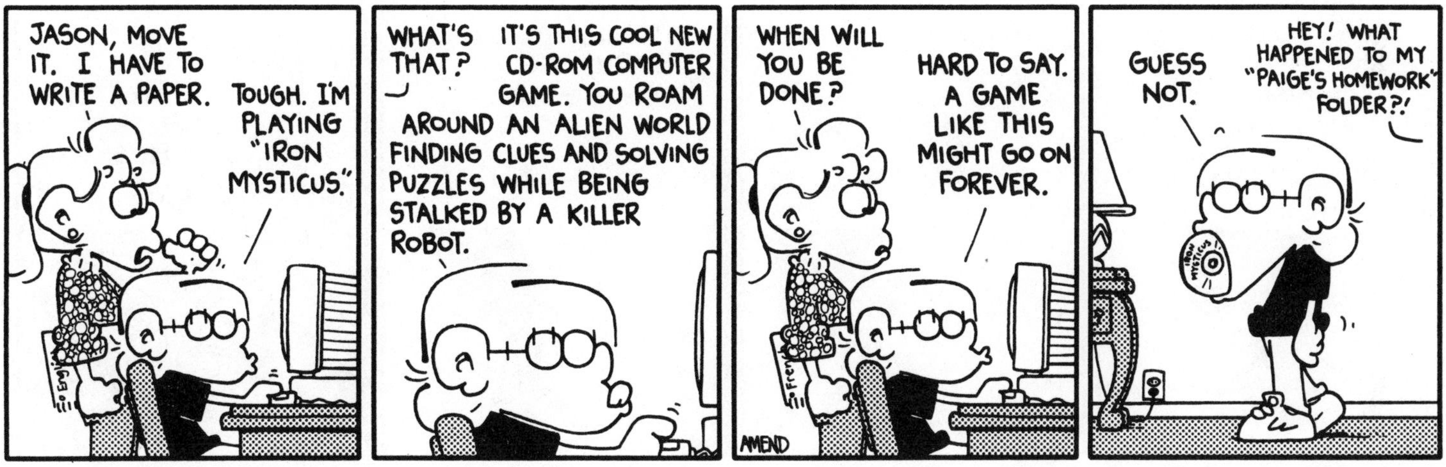
JASON, MOVE IT. I HAVE TO WRITE A PAPER.
TOUGH. I'M PLAYING "IRON MYSTICUS."
WHAT'S THAT?
IT'S THIS COOL NEW CD-ROM COMPUTER GAME. YOU ROAM AROUND AN ALIEN WORLD FINDING CLUES AND SOLVING PUZZLES WHILE BEING STALKED BY A KILLER ROBOT.
WHEN WILL YOU BE DONE?
HARD TO SAY. A GAME LIKE THIS MIGHT GO ON FOREVER.
AMEND
GUESS NOT.
HEY! WHAT HAPPENED TO MY "PAIGE'S HOMEWORK" FOLDER?!

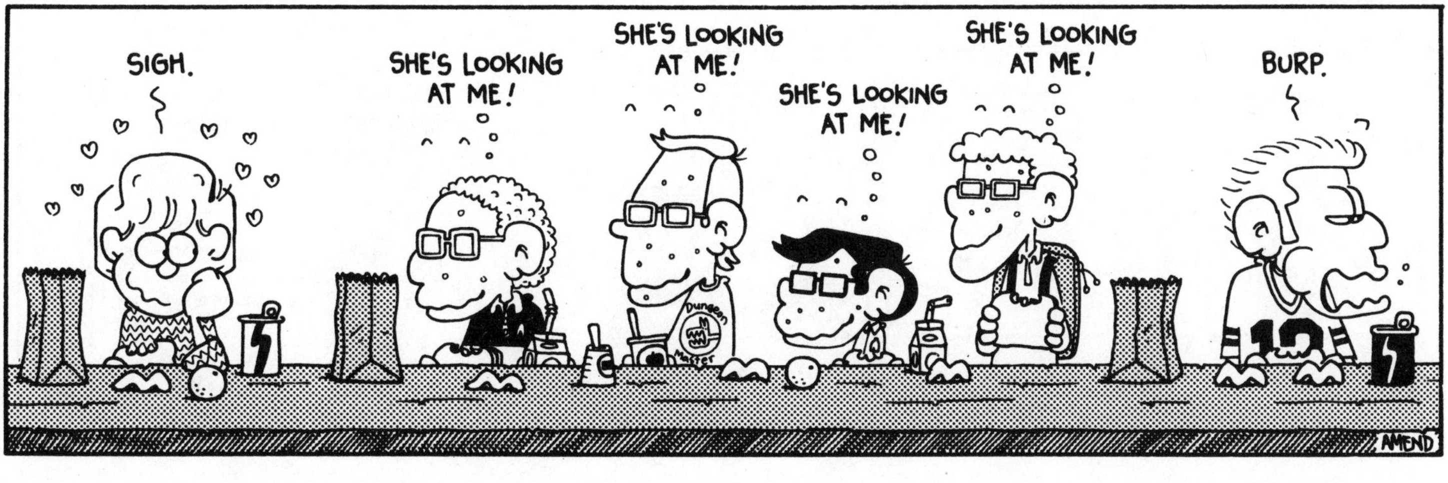
SIGH.
SHE'S LOOKING AT ME!
SHE'S LOOKING AT ME!
SHE'S LOOKING AT ME!
SHE'S LOOKING AT ME!
BURP.
AMEND

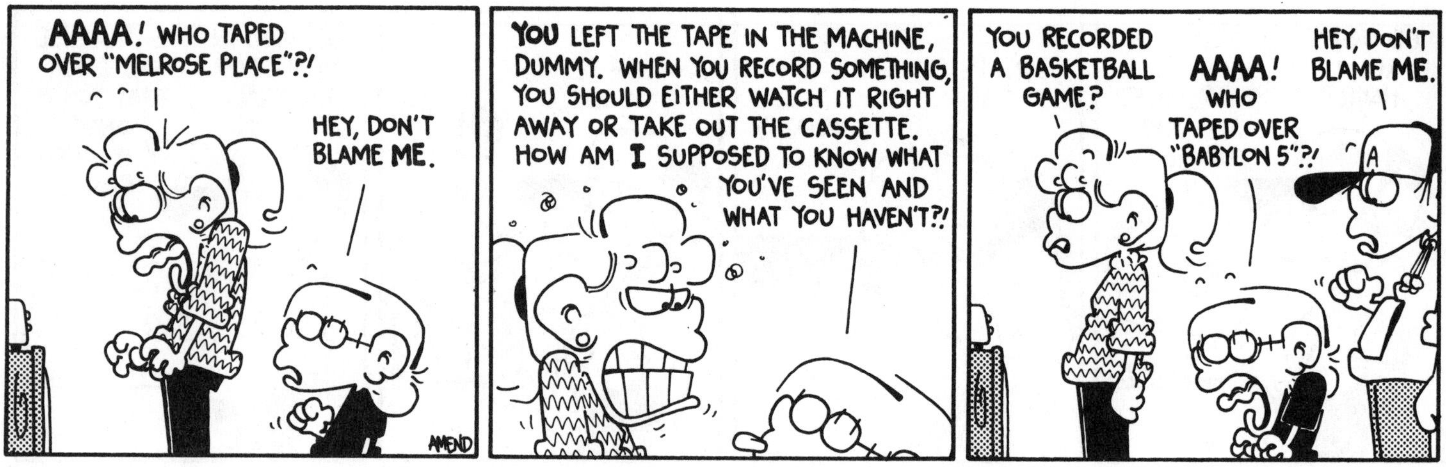
AAAA! WHO TAPED OVER "MELROSE PLACE"?!
HEY, DON'T BLAME ME.
AMEND
YOU LEFT THE TAPE IN THE MACHINE, DUMMY. WHEN YOU RECORD SOMETHING, YOU SHOULD EITHER WATCH IT RIGHT AWAY OR TAKE OUT THE CASSETTE. HOW AM I SUPPOSED TO KNOW WHAT YOU'VE SEEN AND WHAT YOU HAVEN'T?!
YOU RECORDED A BASKETBALL GAME?
AAAA! WHO TAPED OVER "BABYLON 5"?!
HEY, DON'T BLAME ME.

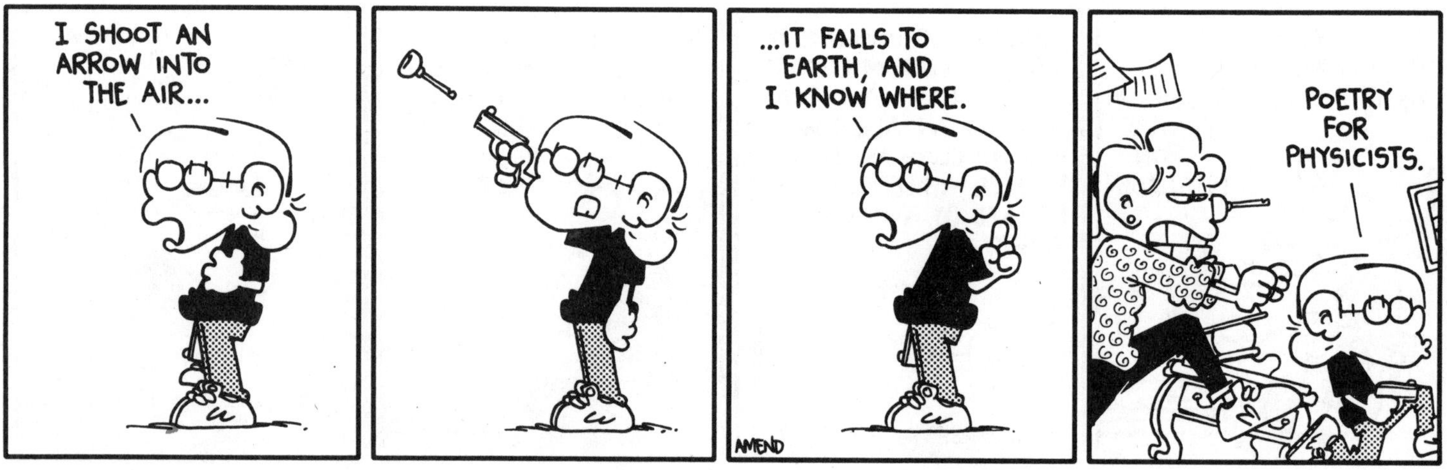
I SHOOT AN ARROW INTO THE AIR...
...IT FALLS TO EARTH, AND I KNOW WHERE.
AMEND
POETRY FOR PHYSICISTS.

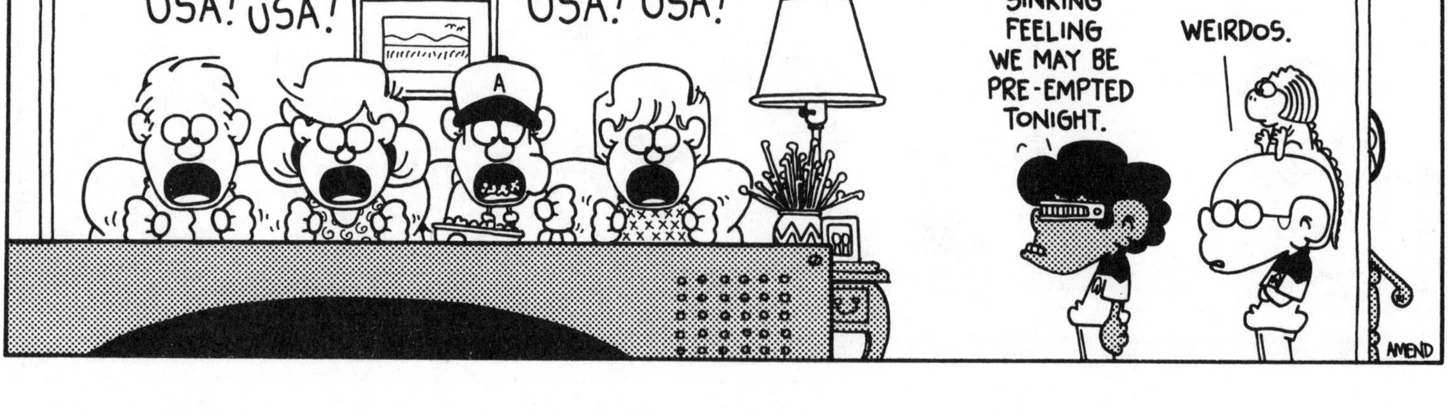
USA! USA! USA! USA! USA! USA!
USA! USA! USA! USA!
I HAVE A SINKING FEELING WE MAY BE PRE-EMPTED TONIGHT.
WEIRDOS.
AMEND

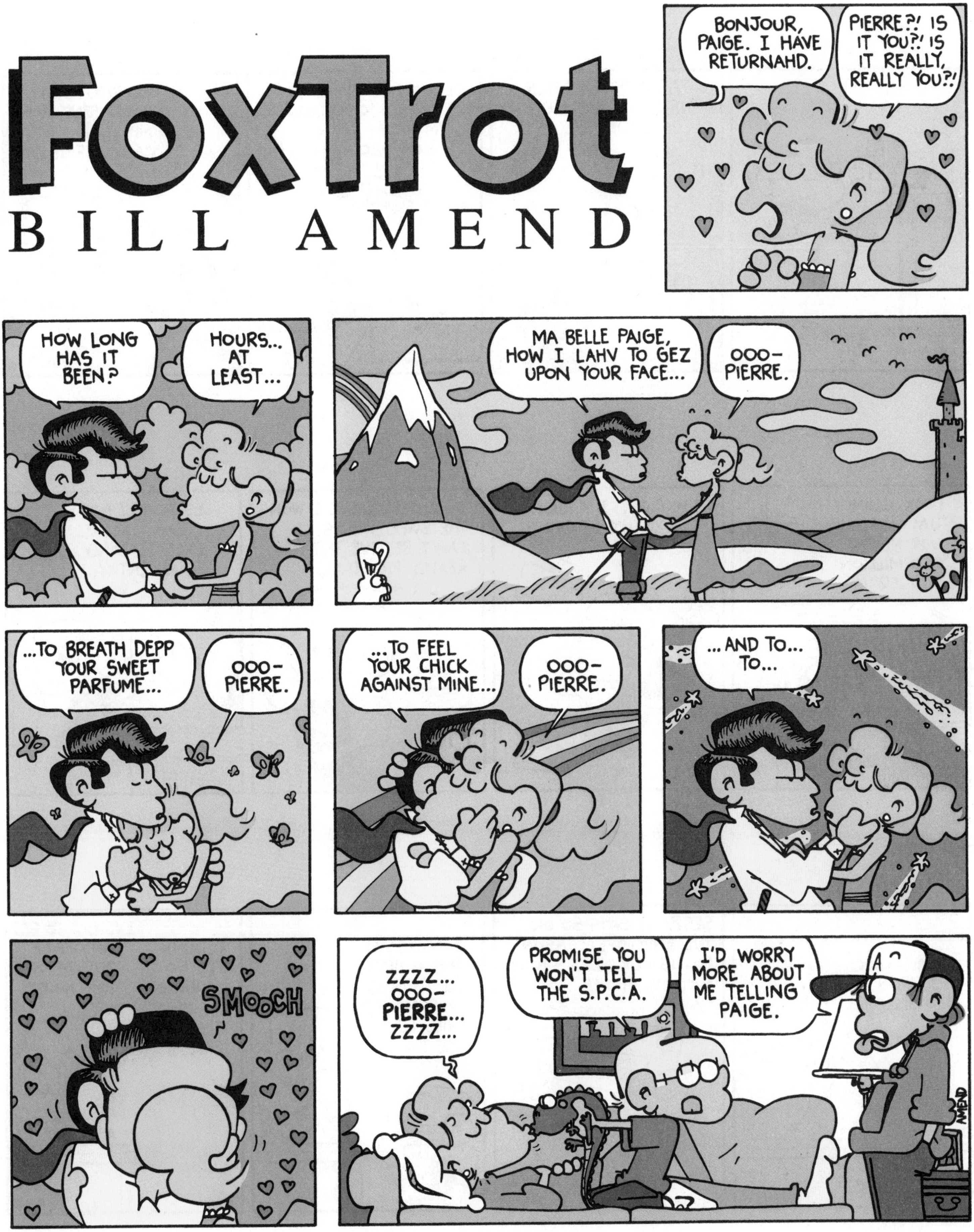
FoxTrot
BILL AMEND
BONJOUR, PAIGE. I HAVE RETURNAHD.
PIERRE?! IS IT YOU?! IS IT REALLY, REALLY YOU?!
HOW LONG HAS IT BEEN?
HOURS... AT LEAST...
MA BELLE PAIGE, HOW I LAHV TO GEZ UPON YOUR FACE...
OOO-PIERRE.
...TO BREATH DEPP YOUR SWEET PARFUME...
OOO-PIERRE.
...TO FEEL YOUR CHICK AGAINST MINE...
OOO-PIERRE.
...AND TO... TO...
SMOOCH
ZZZZ... OOO-PIERRE... ZZZZ...
PROMISE YOU WON'T TELL THE S.P.C.A.
I'D WORRY MORE ABOUT ME TELLING PAIGE.
AMEND

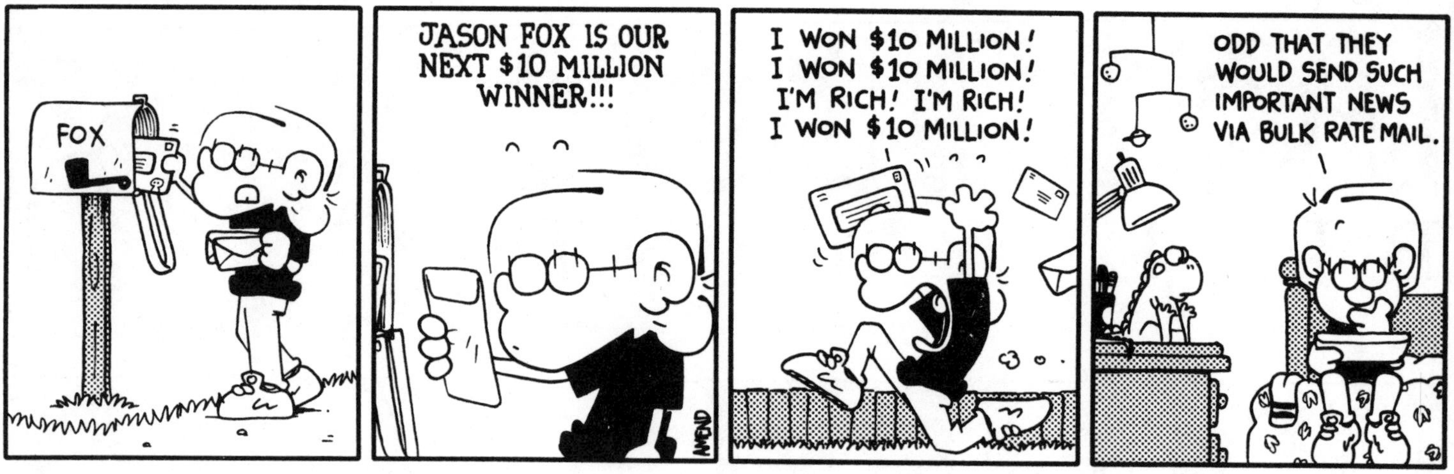
FOX
JASON FOX IS OUR NEXT $10 MILLION WINNER!!!
AMEND
I WON $10 MILLION! I WON $10 MILLION! I'M RICH! I'M RICH! I WON $10 MILLION!
ODD THAT THEY WOULD SEND SUCH IMPORTANT NEWS VIA BULK RATE MAIL.

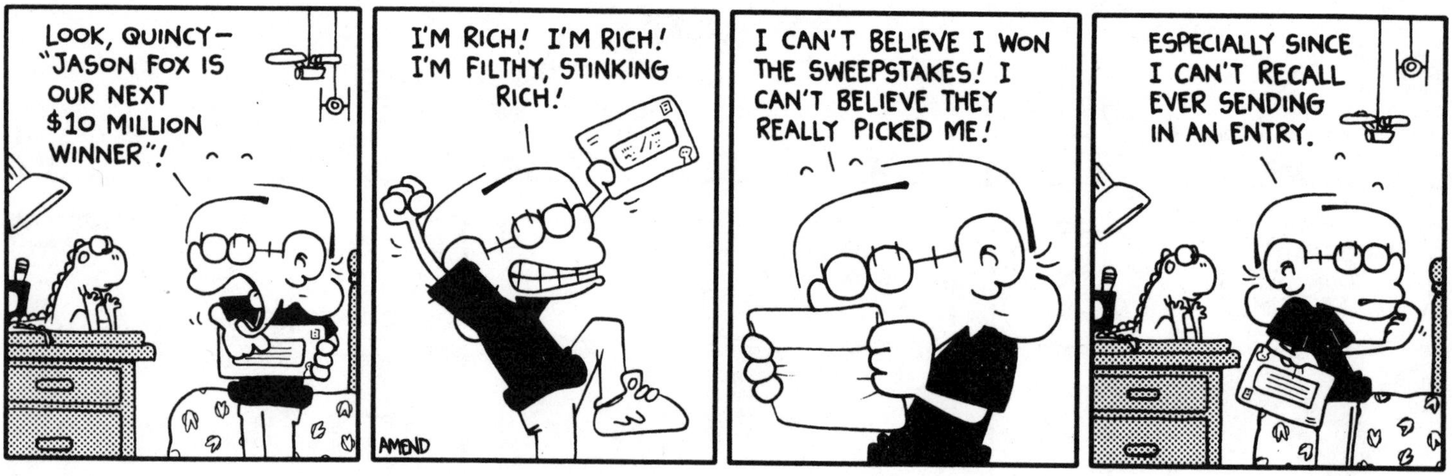
LOOK, QUINCY— "JASON FOX IS OUR NEXT $10 MILLION WINNER"!
I'M RICH! I'M RICH! I'M FILTHY, STINKING RICH!
AMEND
I CAN'T BELIEVE I WON THE SWEEPSTAKES! I CAN'T BELIEVE THEY REALLY PICKED ME!
ESPECIALLY SINCE I CAN'T RECALL EVER SENDING IN AN ENTRY.

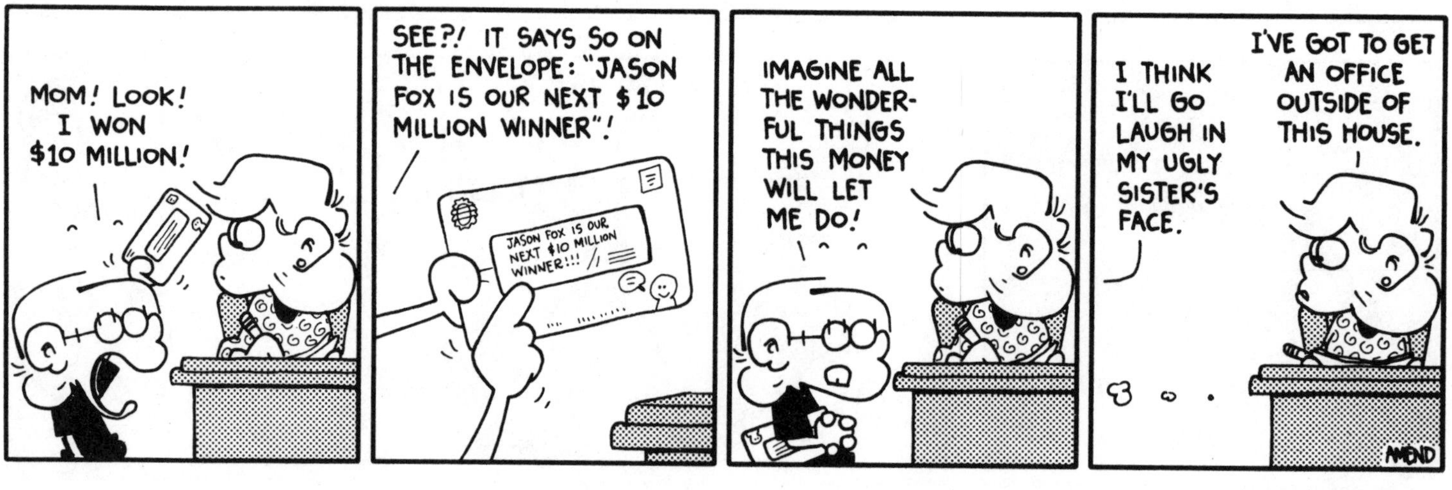
MOM! LOOK! I WON $10 MILLION!
SEE?! IT SAYS SO ON THE ENVELOPE: "JASON FOX IS OUR NEXT $10 MILLION WINNER"!
JASON FOX IS OUR NEXT $10 MILLION WINNER!!!
IMAGINE ALL THE WONDERFUL THINGS THIS MONEY WILL LET ME DO!
I THINK I'LL GO LAUGH IN MY UGLY SISTER'S FACE.
I'VE GOT TO GET AN OFFICE OUTSIDE OF THIS HOUSE.
AMEND

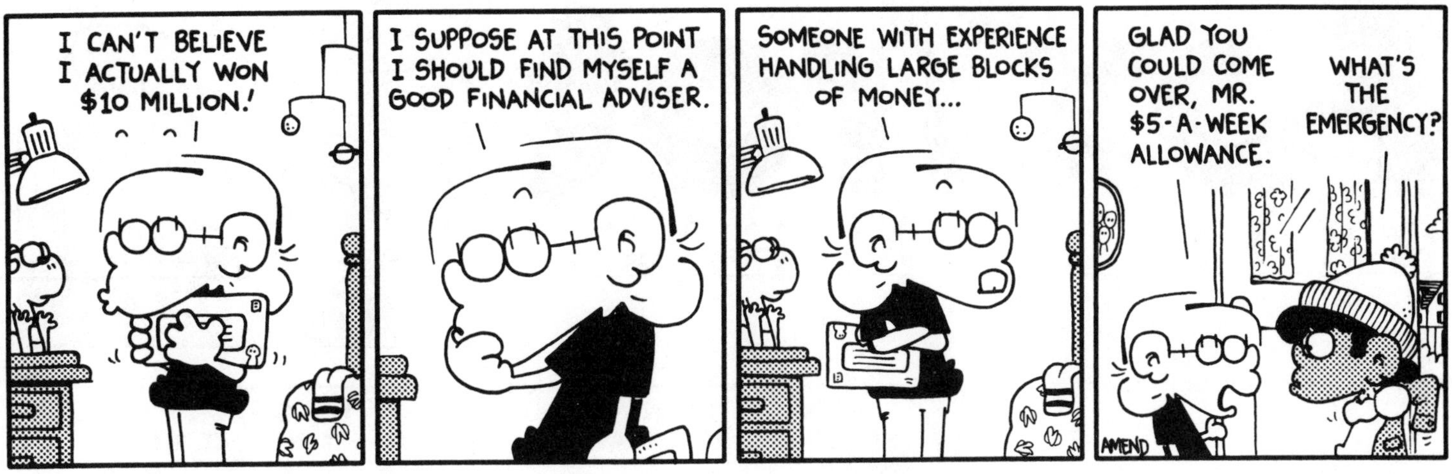
I CAN'T BELIEVE I ACTUALLY WON $10 MILLION!
I SUPPOSE AT THIS POINT I SHOULD FIND MYSELF A GOOD FINANCIAL ADVISER.
SOMEONE WITH EXPERIENCE HANDLING LARGE BLOCKS OF MONEY...
GLAD YOU COULD COME OVER, MR. $5-A-WEEK ALLOWANCE.
WHAT'S THE EMERGENCY?
AMEND

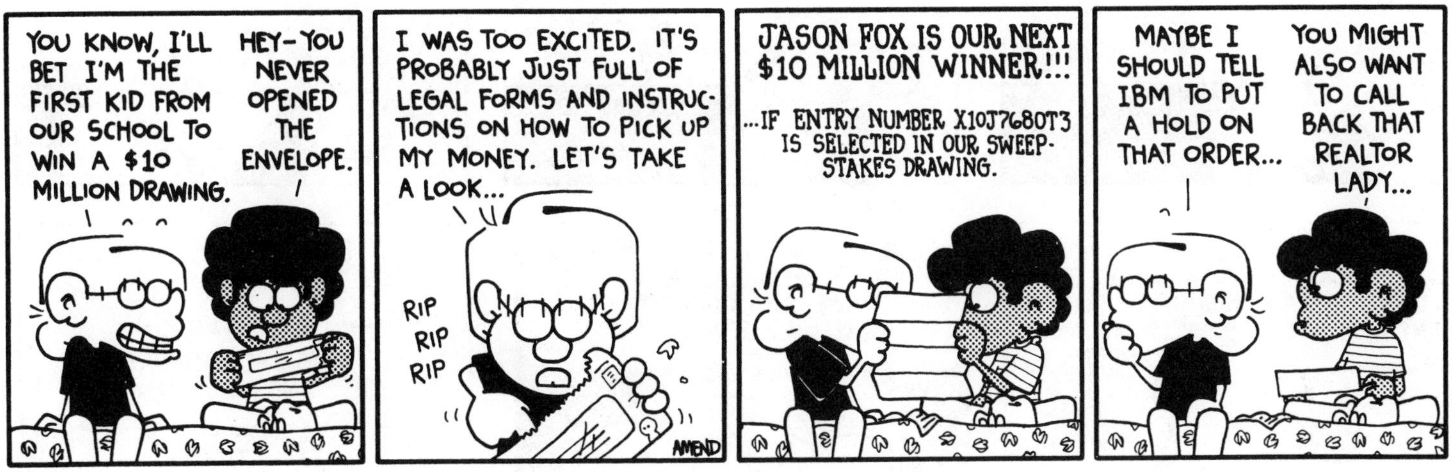
YOU KNOW, I'LL BET I'M THE FIRST KID FROM OUR SCHOOL TO WIN A $10 MILLION DRAWING.
HEY—YOU NEVER OPENED THE ENVELOPE.
I WAS TOO EXCITED. IT'S PROBABLY JUST FULL OF LEGAL FORMS AND INSTRUCTIONS ON HOW TO PICK UP MY MONEY. LET'S TAKE A LOOK...
RIP RIP RIP
AMEND
JASON FOX IS OUR NEXT $10 MILLION WINNER!!!
...IF ENTRY NUMBER X10J7680T3 IS SELECTED IN OUR SWEEPSTAKES DRAWING.
MAYBE I SHOULD TELL IBM TO PUT A HOLD ON THAT ORDER...
YOU MIGHT ALSO WANT TO CALL BACK THAT REALTOR LADY...

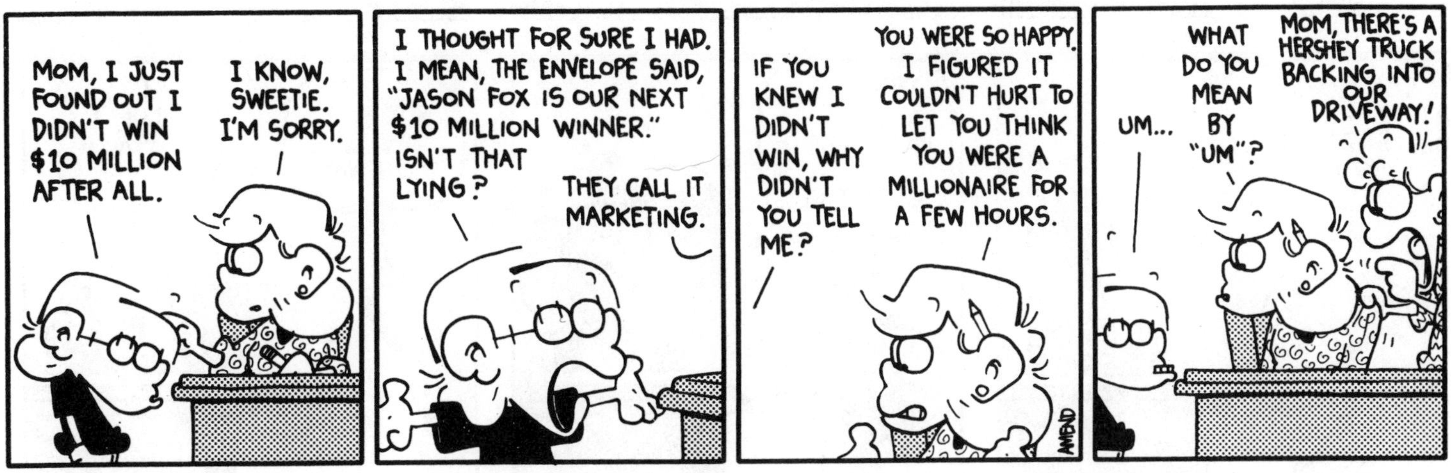
MOM, I JUST FOUND OUT I DIDN'T WIN $10 MILLION AFTER ALL.
I KNOW, SWEETIE. I'M SORRY.
I THOUGHT FOR SURE I HAD. I MEAN, THE ENVELOPE SAID, "JASON FOX IS OUR NEXT $10 MILLION WINNER." ISN'T THAT LYING?
THEY CALL IT MARKETING.
IF YOU KNEW I DIDN'T WIN, WHY DIDN'T YOU TELL ME?
YOU WERE SO HAPPY. I FIGURED IT COULDN'T HURT TO LET YOU THINK YOU WERE A MILLIONAIRE FOR A FEW HOURS.
AMEND
UM...
WHAT DO YOU MEAN BY "UM"?
MOM, THERE'S A HERSHEY TRUCK BACKING INTO OUR DRIVEWAY!

FoxTrot

BILL AMEND

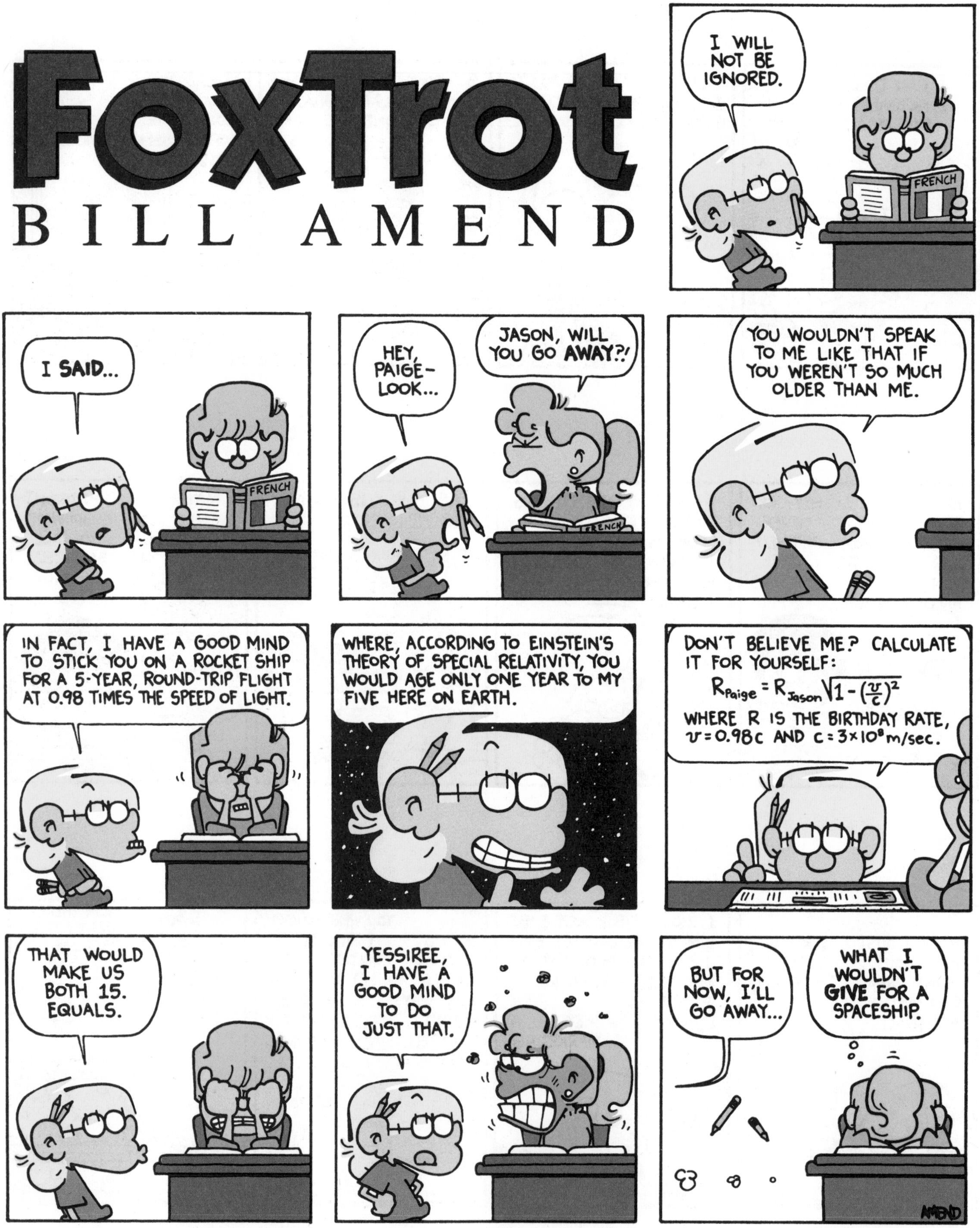
I WILL NOT BE IGNORED.
FRENCH
I **SAID**...
FRENCH
HEY, PAIGE- LOOK...
JASON, WILL YOU GO **AWAY**?!
FRENCH
YOU WOULDN'T SPEAK TO ME LIKE THAT IF YOU WEREN'T SO MUCH OLDER THAN ME.
IN FACT, I HAVE A GOOD MIND TO STICK YOU ON A ROCKET SHIP FOR A 5-YEAR, ROUND-TRIP FLIGHT AT 0.98 TIMES THE SPEED OF LIGHT.
WHERE, ACCORDING TO EINSTEIN'S THEORY OF SPECIAL RELATIVITY, YOU WOULD AGE ONLY ONE YEAR TO MY FIVE HERE ON EARTH.
DON'T BELIEVE ME? CALCULATE IT FOR YOURSELF: $R_{Paige} = R_{Jason}\sqrt{1-(\frac{v}{c})^2}$ WHERE R IS THE BIRTHDAY RATE, $v = 0.98c$ AND $c = 3\times10^8$ m/sec.
THAT WOULD MAKE US BOTH 15. EQUALS.
YESSIREE, I HAVE A GOOD MIND TO DO JUST THAT.
BUT FOR NOW, I'LL GO AWAY...
WHAT I WOULDN'T **GIVE** FOR A SPACESHIP.
AMEND

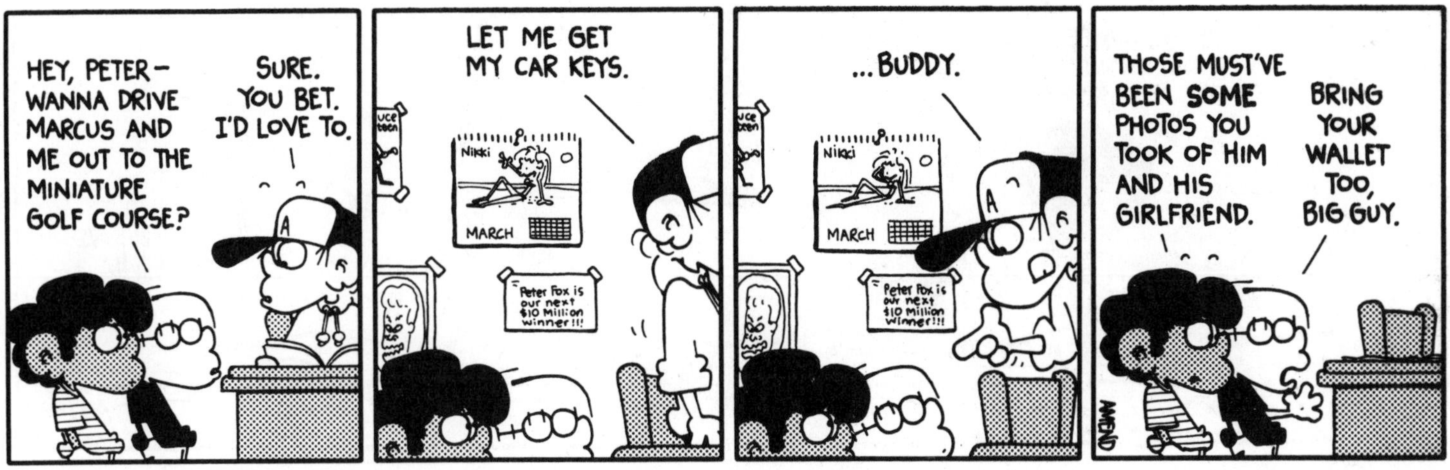
HEY, PETER— WANNA DRIVE MARCUS AND ME OUT TO THE MINIATURE GOLF COURSE?
SURE. YOU BET. I'D LOVE TO.
LET ME GET MY CAR KEYS.
Nikki
MARCH
Peter Fox is our next $10 Million winner!!!
...BUDDY.
THOSE MUST'VE BEEN **SOME** PHOTOS YOU TOOK OF HIM AND HIS GIRLFRIEND.
BRING YOUR WALLET TOO, BIG GUY.
AMEND

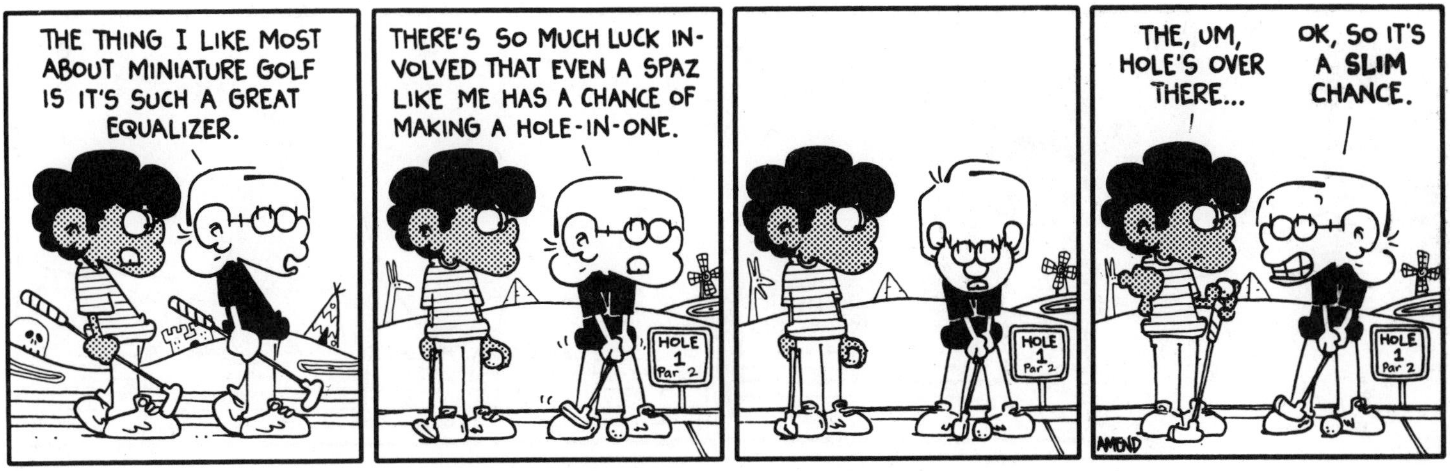
THE THING I LIKE MOST ABOUT MINIATURE GOLF IS IT'S SUCH A GREAT EQUALIZER.
THERE'S SO MUCH LUCK IN-VOLVED THAT EVEN A SPAZ LIKE ME HAS A CHANCE OF MAKING A HOLE-IN-ONE.
HOLE 1 Par 2
THE, UM, HOLE'S OVER THERE...
OK, SO IT'S A **SLIM** CHANCE.
AMEND

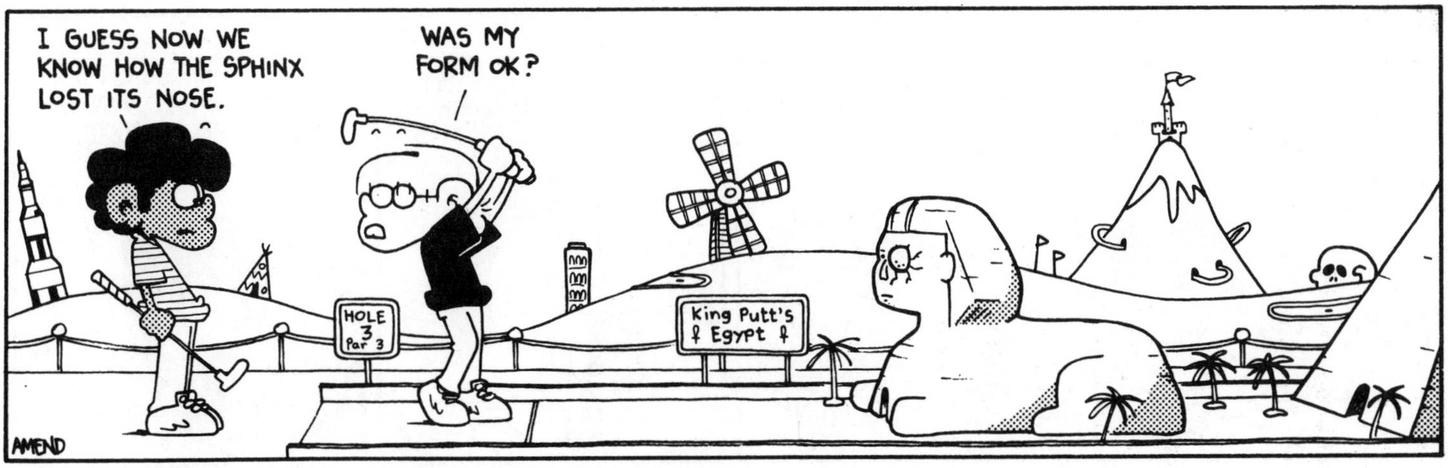
I GUESS NOW WE KNOW HOW THE SPHINX LOST ITS NOSE.
WAS MY FORM OK?
HOLE 3 Par 3
King Putt's Egypt
AMEND

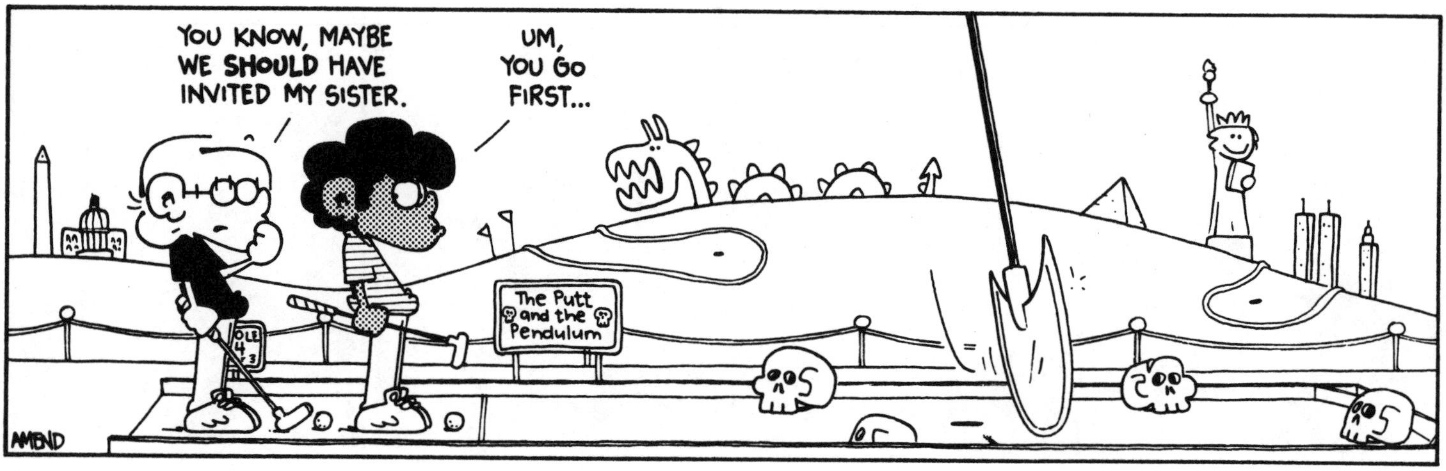
YOU KNOW, MAYBE WE **SHOULD** HAVE INVITED MY SISTER.
UM, YOU GO FIRST...
The Putt and the Pendulum
AMEND

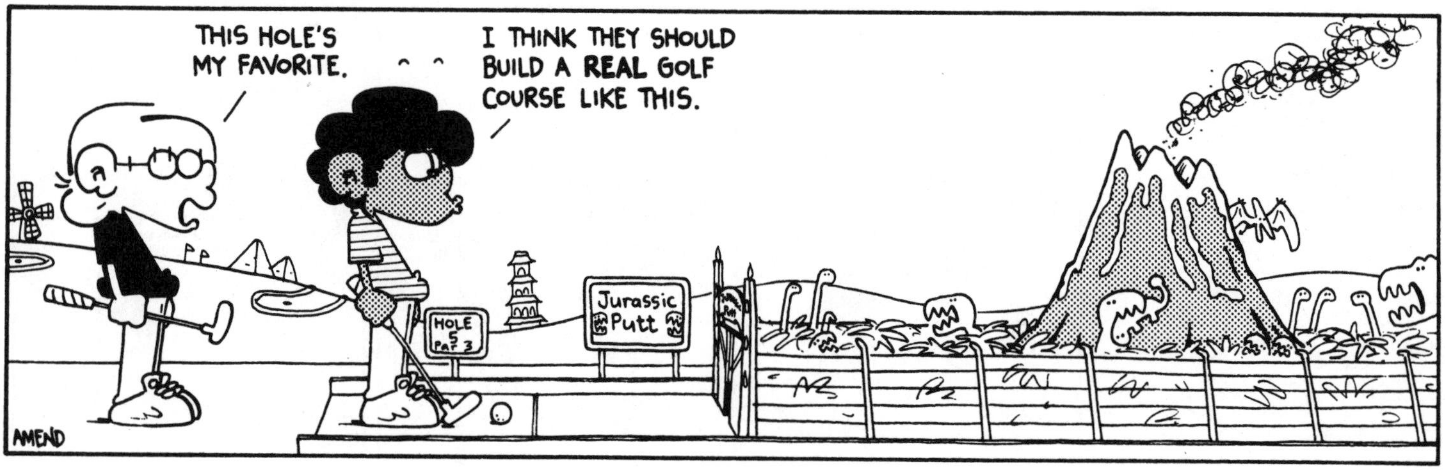
THIS HOLE'S MY FAVORITE.
I THINK THEY SHOULD BUILD A **REAL** GOLF COURSE LIKE THIS.
Jurassic Putt
HOLE 5 PAR 3
AMEND

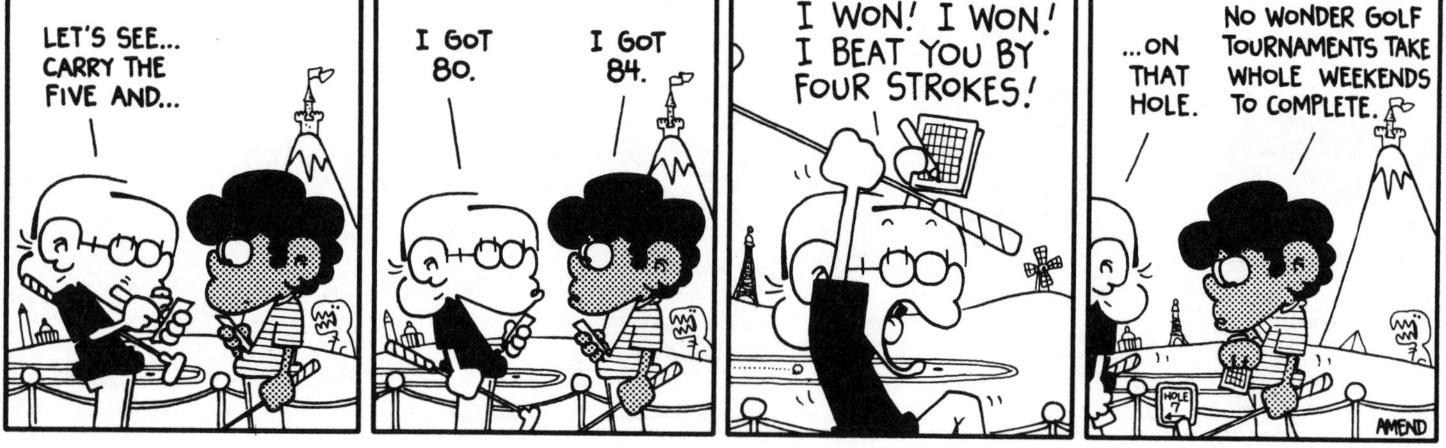
LET'S SEE... CARRY THE FIVE AND...
I GOT 80.
I GOT 84.
I WON! I WON! I BEAT YOU BY FOUR STROKES!
...ON THAT HOLE.
NO WONDER GOLF TOURNAMENTS TAKE WHOLE WEEKENDS TO COMPLETE.
AMEND

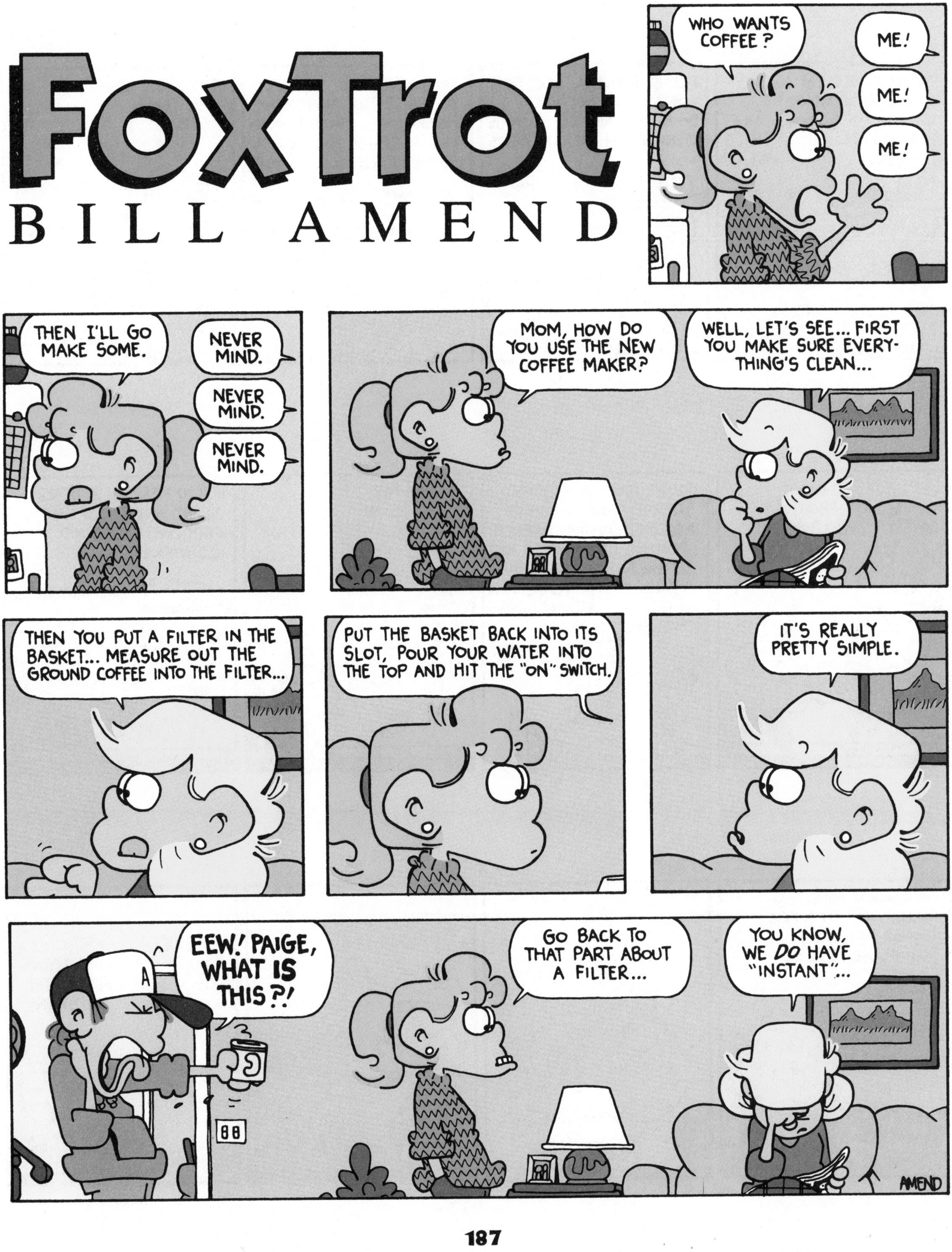
FoxTrot
BILL AMEND
WHO WANTS COFFEE?
ME!
ME!
ME!
THEN I'LL GO MAKE SOME.
NEVER MIND.
NEVER MIND.
NEVER MIND.
MOM, HOW DO YOU USE THE NEW COFFEE MAKER?
WELL, LET'S SEE... FIRST YOU MAKE SURE EVERY-THING'S CLEAN...
THEN YOU PUT A FILTER IN THE BASKET... MEASURE OUT THE GROUND COFFEE INTO THE FILTER...
PUT THE BASKET BACK INTO ITS SLOT, POUR YOUR WATER INTO THE TOP AND HIT THE "ON" SWITCH.
IT'S REALLY PRETTY SIMPLE.
EEW! PAIGE, WHAT IS THIS?!
GO BACK TO THAT PART ABOUT A FILTER...
YOU KNOW, WE DO HAVE "INSTANT"...
AMEND

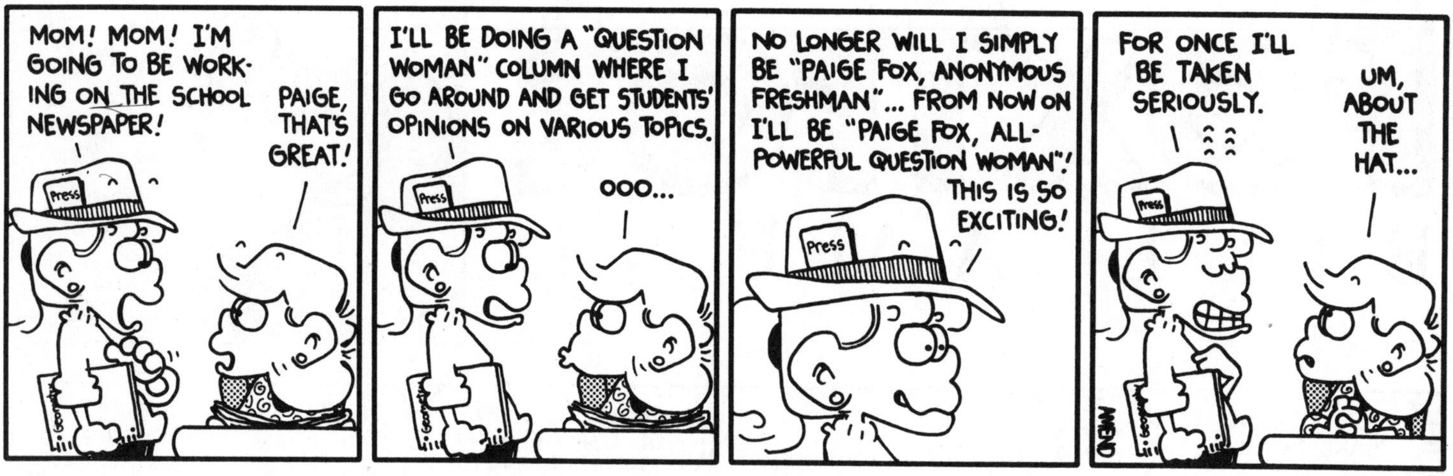
MOM! MOM! I'M GOING TO BE WORKING ON THE SCHOOL NEWSPAPER!
PAIGE, THAT'S GREAT!
Press
I'LL BE DOING A "QUESTION WOMAN" COLUMN WHERE I GO AROUND AND GET STUDENTS' OPINIONS ON VARIOUS TOPICS.
OOO...
NO LONGER WILL I SIMPLY BE "PAIGE FOX, ANONYMOUS FRESHMAN"... FROM NOW ON I'LL BE "PAIGE FOX, ALL-POWERFUL QUESTION WOMAN"!
THIS IS SO EXCITING!
FOR ONCE I'LL BE TAKEN SERIOUSLY.
UM, ABOUT THE HAT...
AMEND

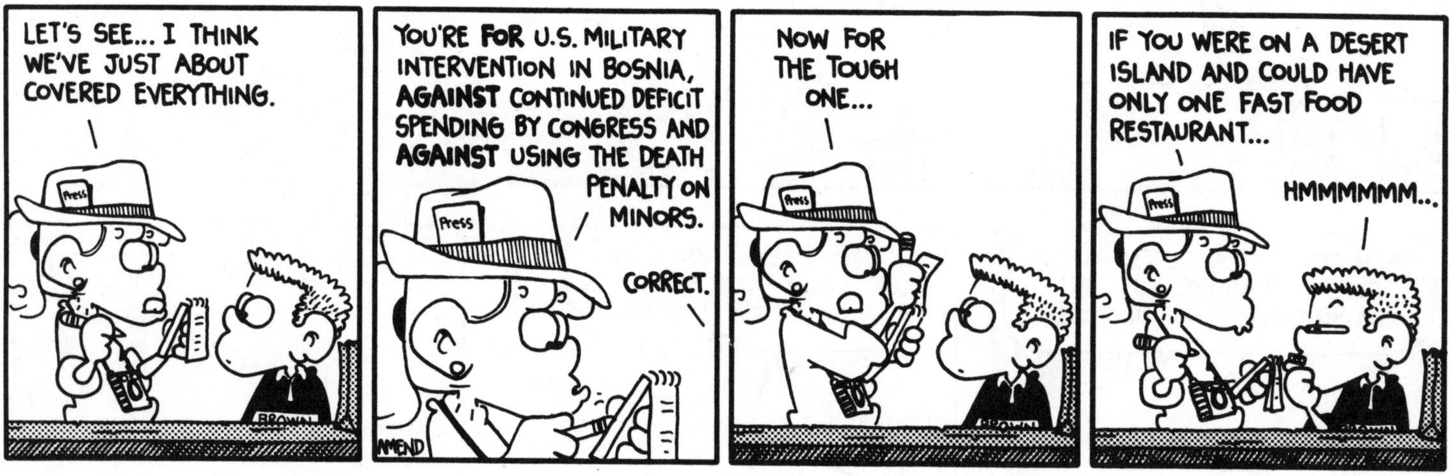
LET'S SEE... I THINK WE'VE JUST ABOUT COVERED EVERYTHING.
YOU'RE **FOR** U.S. MILITARY INTERVENTION IN BOSNIA, **AGAINST** CONTINUED DEFICIT SPENDING BY CONGRESS AND **AGAINST** USING THE DEATH PENALTY ON MINORS.
CORRECT.
NOW FOR THE TOUGH ONE...
IF YOU WERE ON A DESERT ISLAND AND COULD HAVE ONLY ONE FAST FOOD RESTAURANT...
HMMMMMM...
AMEND

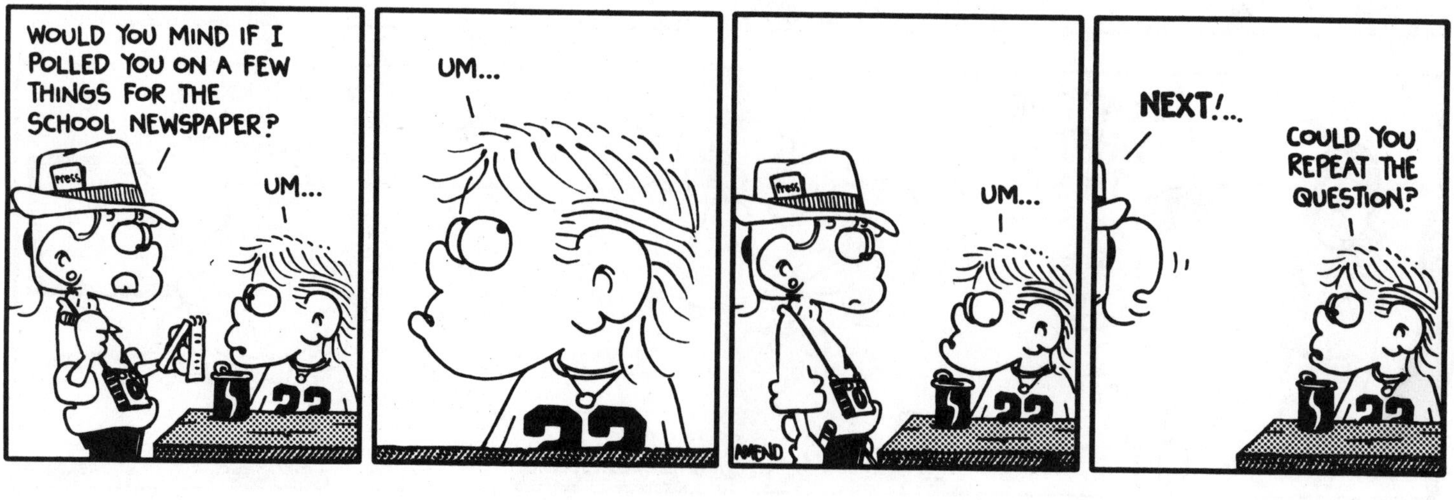
WOULD YOU MIND IF I POLLED YOU ON A FEW THINGS FOR THE SCHOOL NEWSPAPER?
UM...
UM...
UM...
NEXT!...
COULD YOU REPEAT THE QUESTION?
AMEND

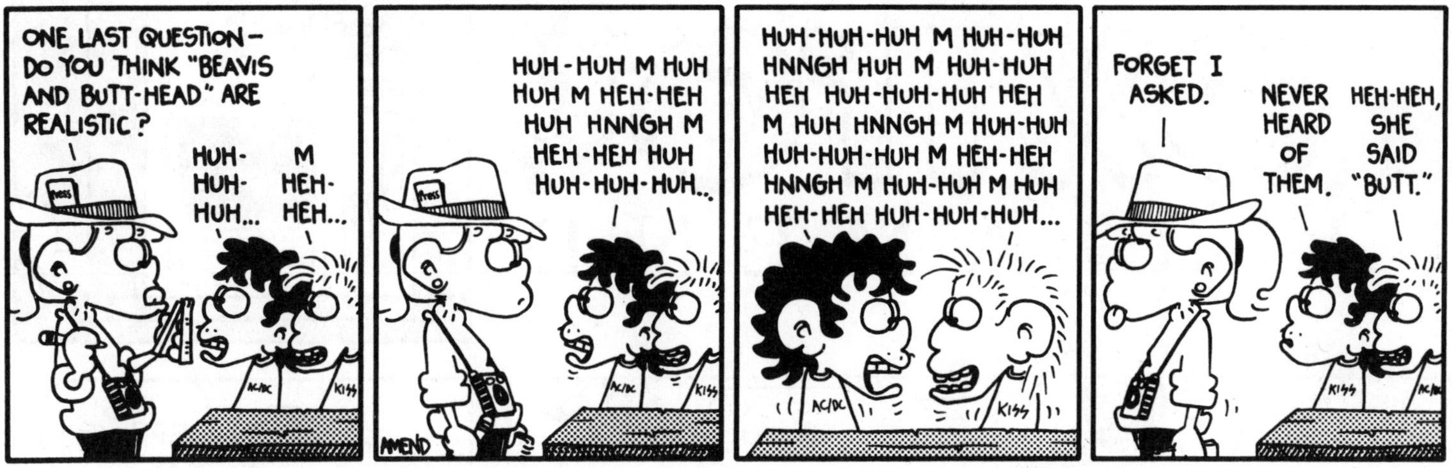
ONE LAST QUESTION—DO YOU THINK "BEAVIS AND BUTT-HEAD" ARE REALISTIC?
HUH-HUH-HUH...
M HEH-HEH...
HUH-HUH M HUH HUH M HEH-HEH HUH HNNGH M HEH-HEH HUH HUH-HUH-HUH...
HUH-HUH-HUH M HUH-HUH HNNGH HUH M HUH-HUH HEH HUH-HUH-HUH HEH M HUH HNNGH M HUH-HUH HUH-HUH-HUH M HEH-HEH HNNGH M HUH-HUH M HUH HEH-HEH HUH-HUH-HUH...
FORGET I ASKED.
NEVER HEARD OF THEM.
HEH-HEH, SHE SAID "BUTT."
AC/DC
KISS
AMEND

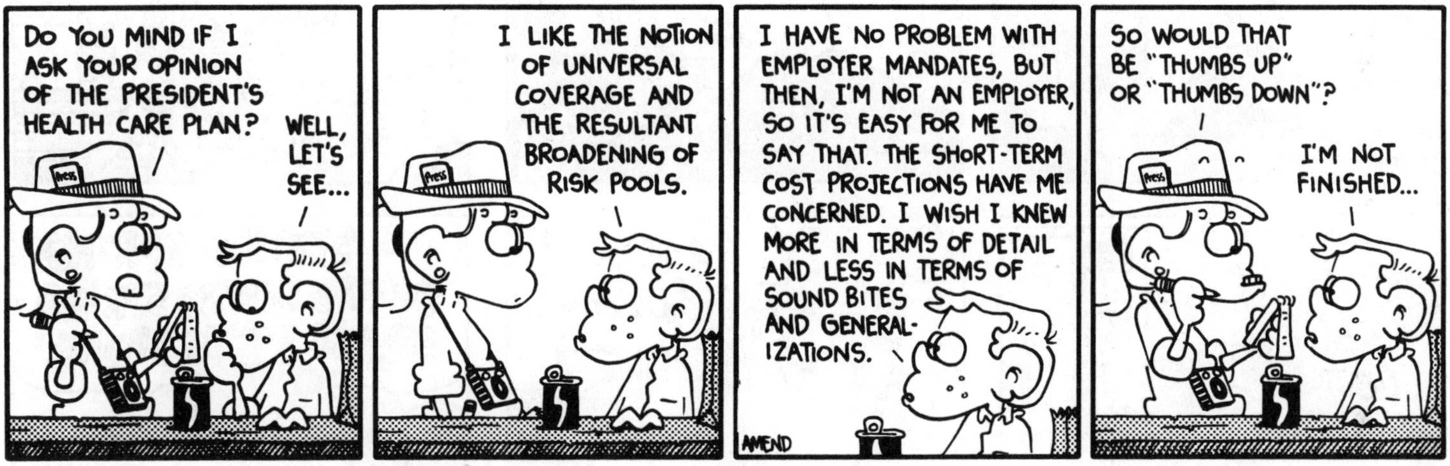
DO YOU MIND IF I ASK YOUR OPINION OF THE PRESIDENT'S HEALTH CARE PLAN?
WELL, LET'S SEE...
I LIKE THE NOTION OF UNIVERSAL COVERAGE AND THE RESULTANT BROADENING OF RISK POOLS.
I HAVE NO PROBLEM WITH EMPLOYER MANDATES, BUT THEN, I'M NOT AN EMPLOYER, SO IT'S EASY FOR ME TO SAY THAT. THE SHORT-TERM COST PROJECTIONS HAVE ME CONCERNED. I WISH I KNEW MORE IN TERMS OF DETAIL AND LESS IN TERMS OF SOUND BITES AND GENERAL-IZATIONS.
SO WOULD THAT BE "THUMBS UP" OR "THUMBS DOWN"?
I'M NOT FINISHED...
AMEND

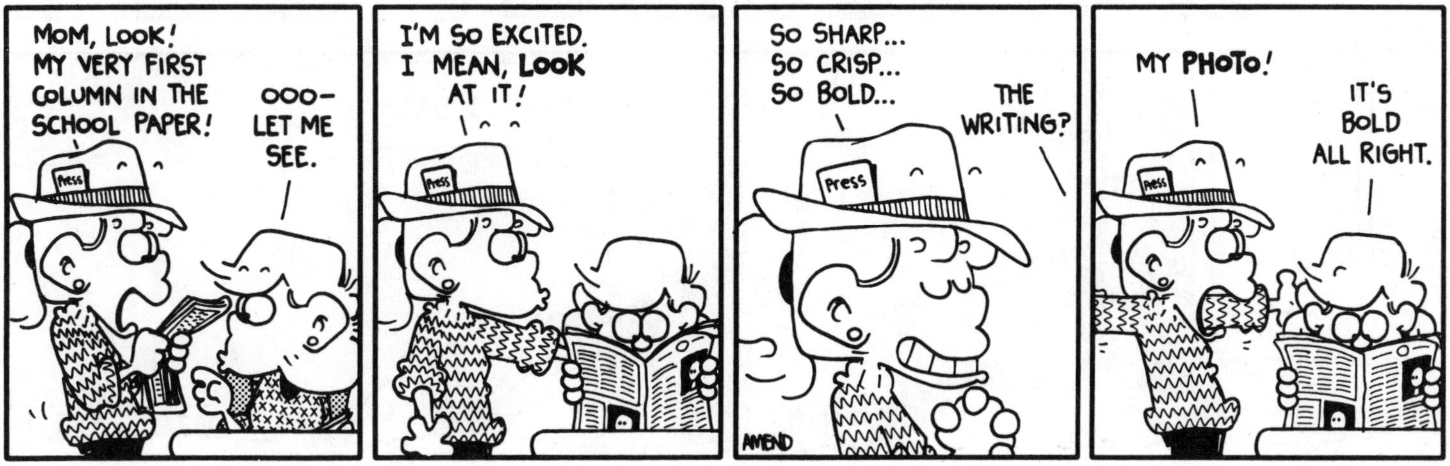
MOM, LOOK! MY VERY FIRST COLUMN IN THE SCHOOL PAPER!
OOO—LET ME SEE.
I'M SO EXCITED. I MEAN, LOOK AT IT!
SO SHARP... SO CRISP... SO BOLD...
THE WRITING?
MY PHOTO!
IT'S BOLD ALL RIGHT.
AMEND

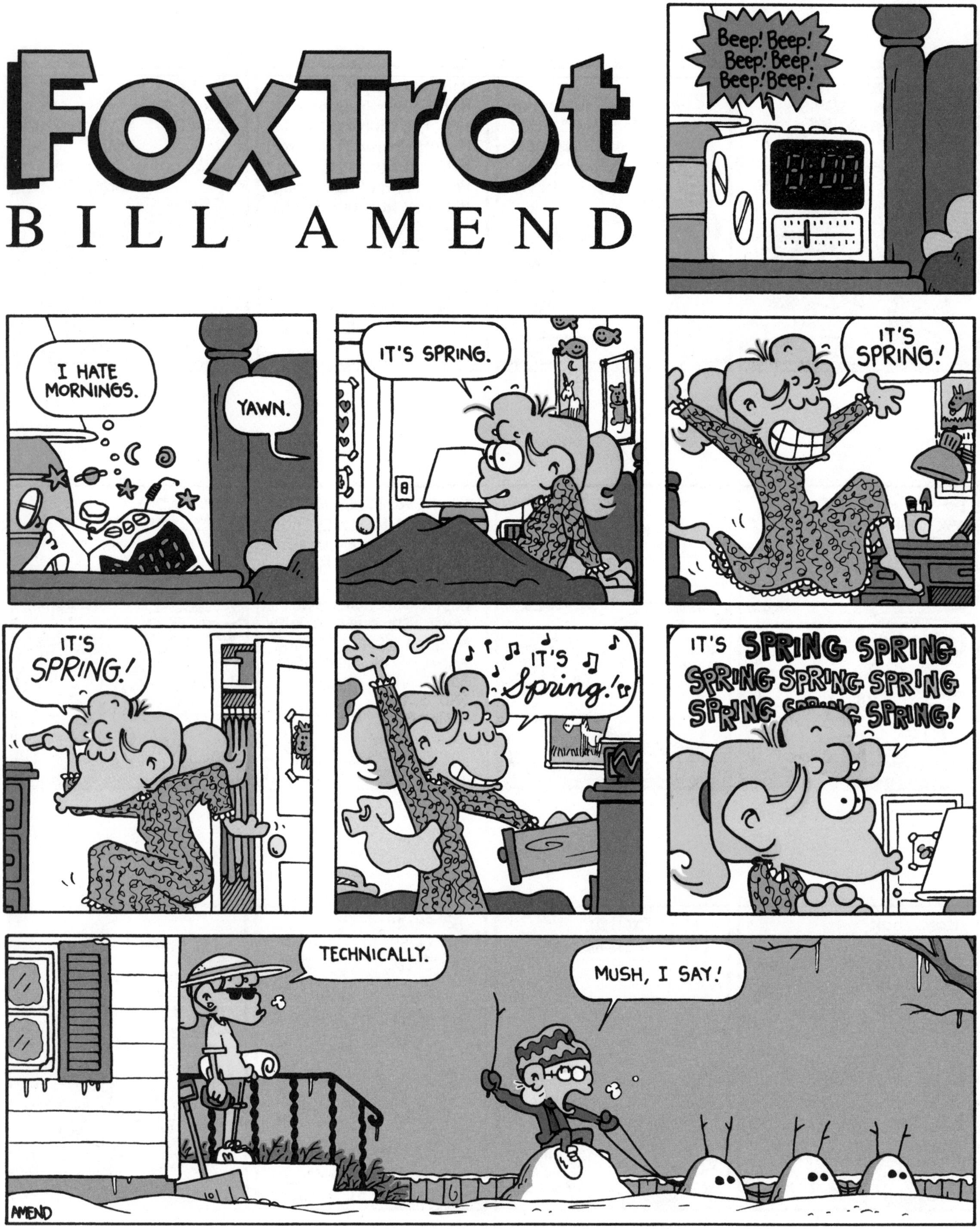
FoxTrot
BILL AMEND
Beep! Beep! Beep! Beep! Beep! Beep!
I HATE MORNINGS.
YAWN.
IT'S SPRING.
IT'S SPRING!
IT'S SPRING!
IT'S Spring!
IT'S SPRING SPRING SPRING SPRING SPRING SPRING SPRING!
TECHNICALLY.
MUSH, I SAY!
AMEND

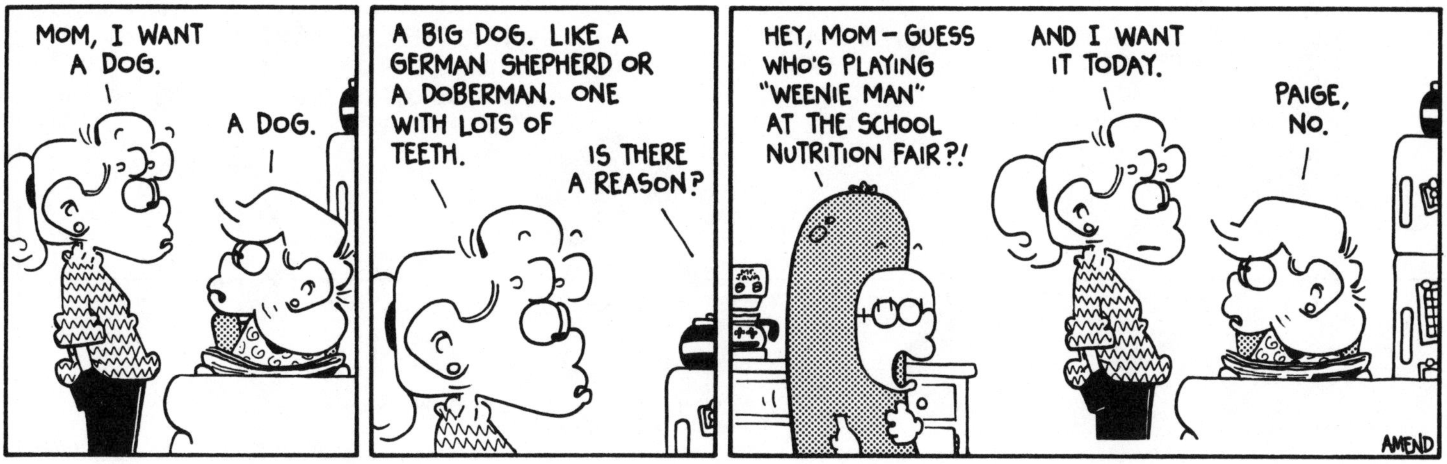
MOM, I WANT A DOG.
A DOG.
A BIG DOG. LIKE A GERMAN SHEPHERD OR A DOBERMAN. ONE WITH LOTS OF TEETH.
IS THERE A REASON?
HEY, MOM – GUESS WHO'S PLAYING "WEENIE MAN" AT THE SCHOOL NUTRITION FAIR?!
AND I WANT IT TODAY.
PAIGE, NO.
AMEND

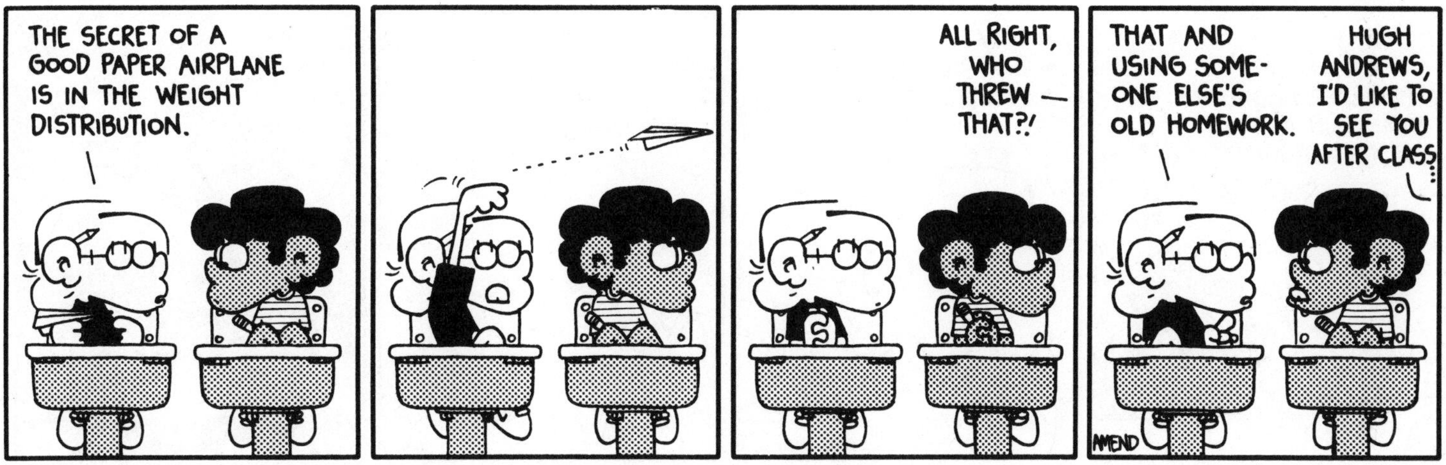
THE SECRET OF A GOOD PAPER AIRPLANE IS IN THE WEIGHT DISTRIBUTION.
ALL RIGHT, WHO THREW THAT?!
THAT AND USING SOME-ONE ELSE'S OLD HOMEWORK.
HUGH ANDREWS, I'D LIKE TO SEE YOU AFTER CLASS.
AMEND

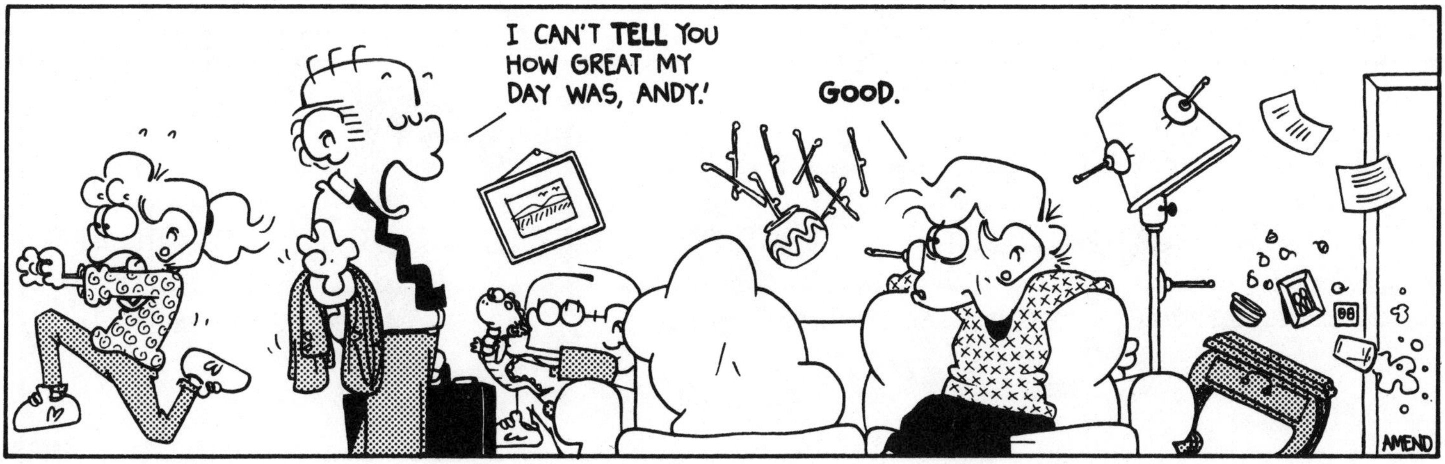
I CAN'T **TELL** YOU HOW GREAT MY DAY WAS, ANDY!
GOOD.
AMEND

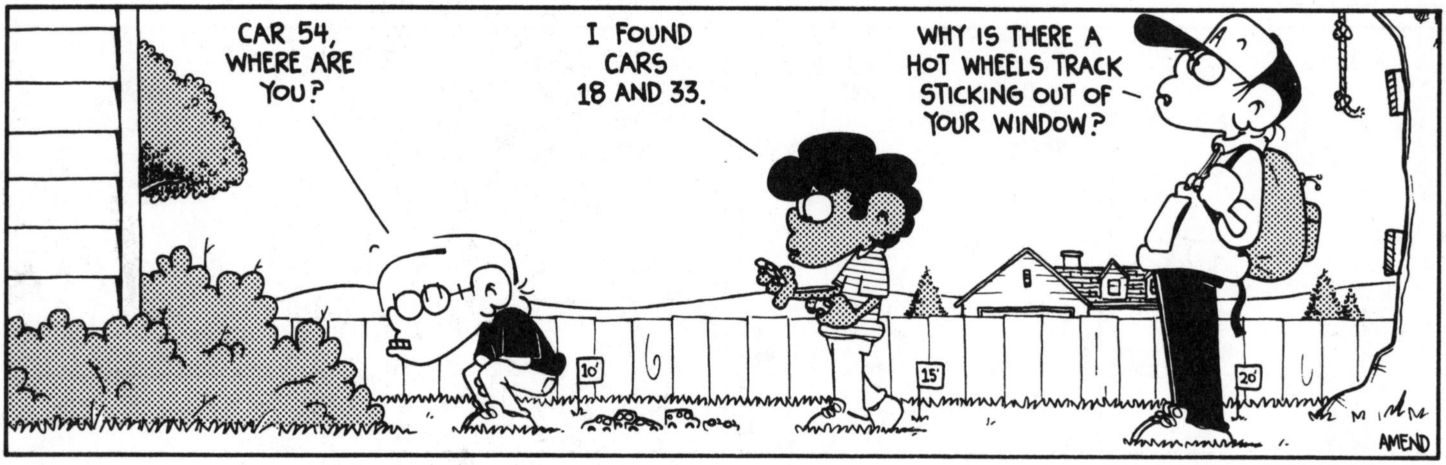
CAR 54, WHERE ARE YOU?
I FOUND CARS 18 AND 33.
WHY IS THERE A HOT WHEELS TRACK STICKING OUT OF YOUR WINDOW?
10'
15'
20'
AMEND

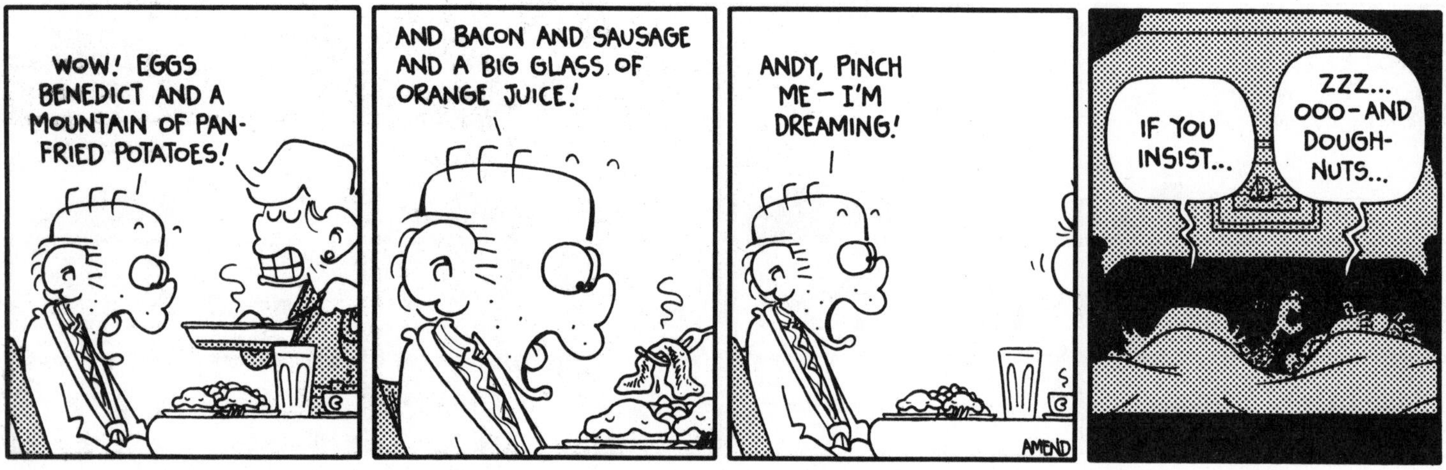
WOW! EGGS BENEDICT AND A MOUNTAIN OF PAN-FRIED POTATOES!
AND BACON AND SAUSAGE AND A BIG GLASS OF ORANGE JUICE!
ANDY, PINCH ME—I'M DREAMING!
AMEND
IF YOU INSIST...
ZZZ... OOO-AND DOUGH-NUTS...

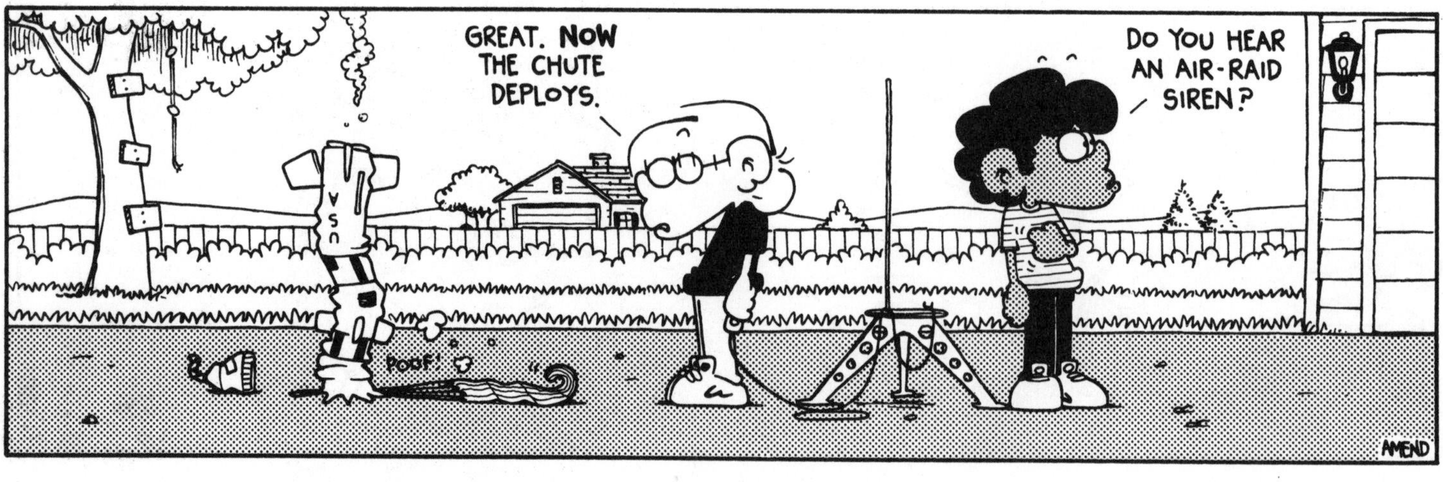
GREAT. NOW THE CHUTE DEPLOYS.
DO YOU HEAR AN AIR-RAID SIREN?
POOF!
AMEND

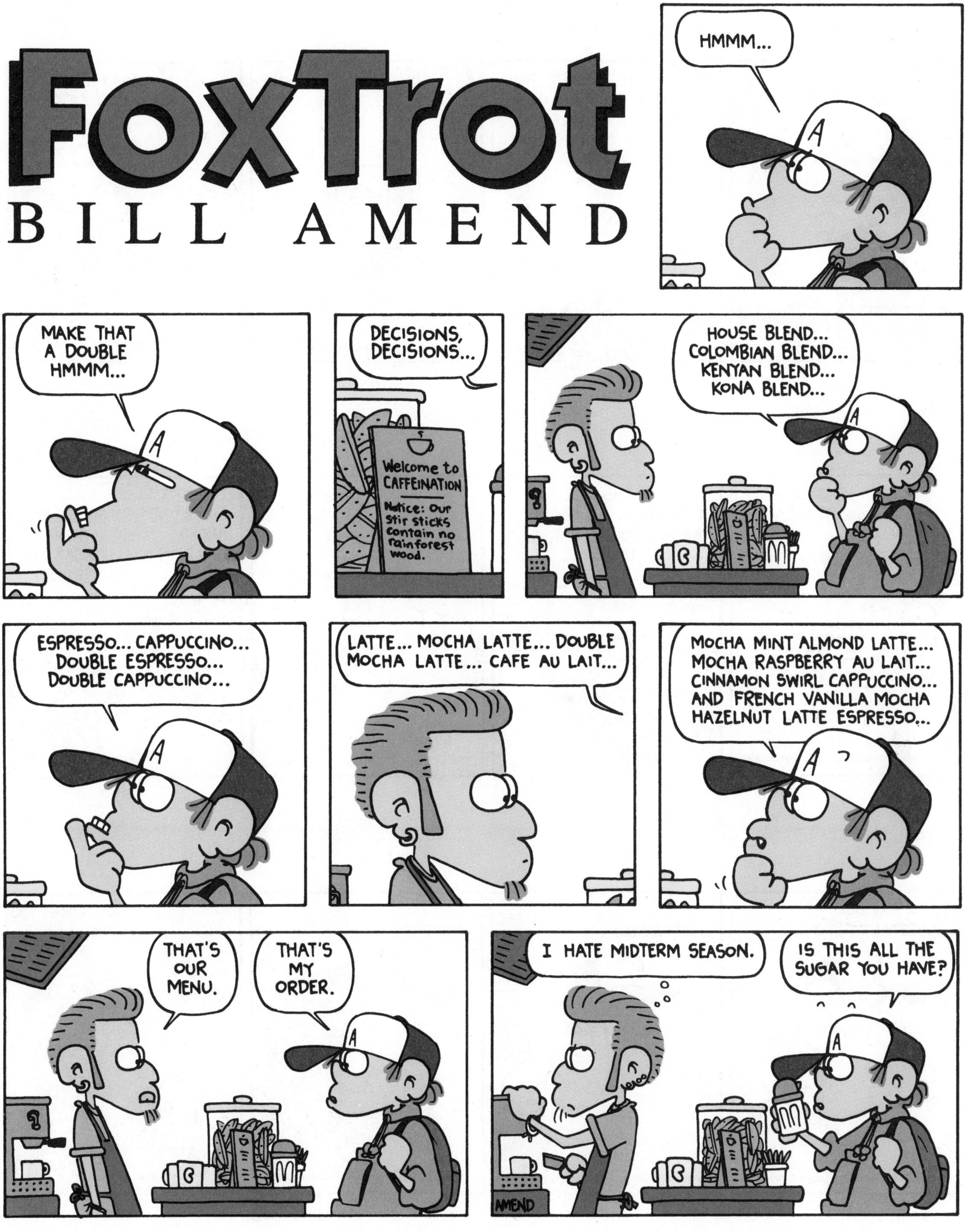
FoxTrot
BILL AMEND
HMMM...
MAKE THAT A DOUBLE HMMM...
DECISIONS, DECISIONS...
Welcome to CAFFEINATION
Notice: Our stir sticks contain no rainforest wood.
HOUSE BLEND... COLOMBIAN BLEND... KENYAN BLEND... KONA BLEND...
ESPRESSO... CAPPUCCINO... DOUBLE ESPRESSO... DOUBLE CAPPUCCINO...
LATTE... MOCHA LATTE... DOUBLE MOCHA LATTE... CAFE AU LAIT...
MOCHA MINT ALMOND LATTE... MOCHA RASPBERRY AU LAIT... CINNAMON SWIRL CAPPUCCINO... AND FRENCH VANILLA MOCHA HAZELNUT LATTE ESPRESSO...
THAT'S OUR MENU.
THAT'S MY ORDER.
I HATE MIDTERM SEASON.
IS THIS ALL THE SUGAR YOU HAVE?
AMEND

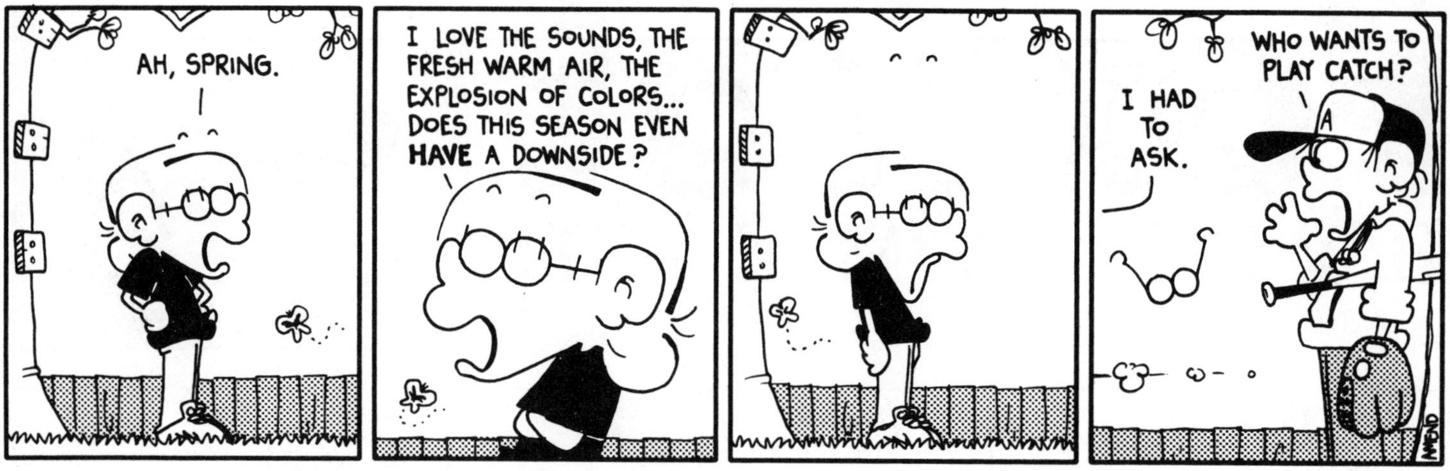
AH, SPRING.
I LOVE THE SOUNDS, THE FRESH WARM AIR, THE EXPLOSION OF COLORS... DOES THIS SEASON EVEN HAVE A DOWNSIDE?
I HAD TO ASK.
WHO WANTS TO PLAY CATCH?
AMEND

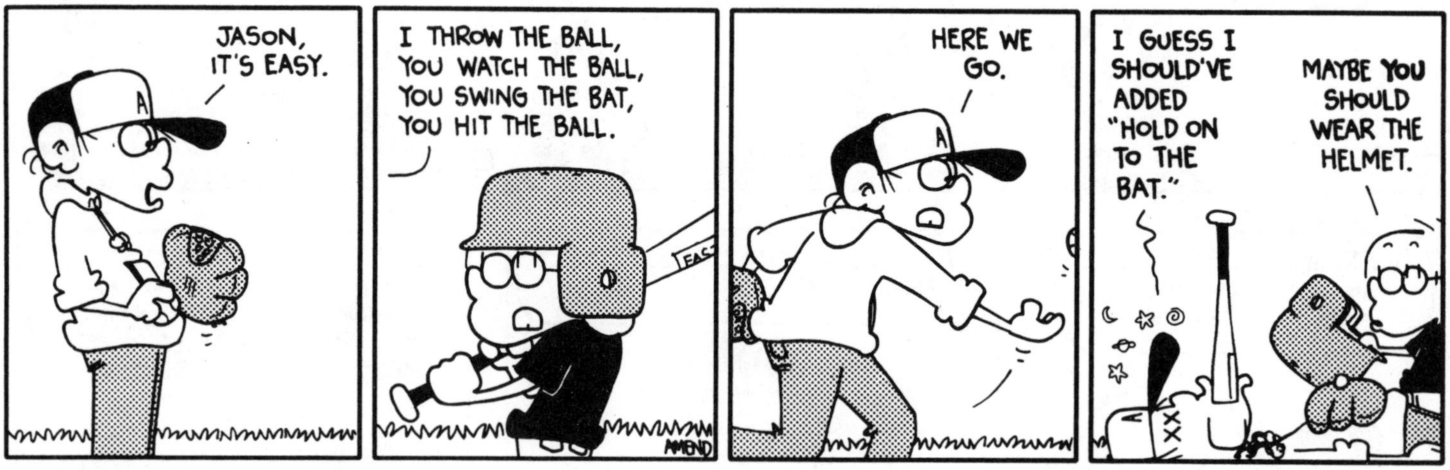
JASON, IT'S EASY.
I THROW THE BALL, YOU WATCH THE BALL, YOU SWING THE BAT, YOU HIT THE BALL.
HERE WE GO.
I GUESS I SHOULD'VE ADDED "HOLD ON TO THE BAT."
MAYBE YOU SHOULD WEAR THE HELMET.
AMEND

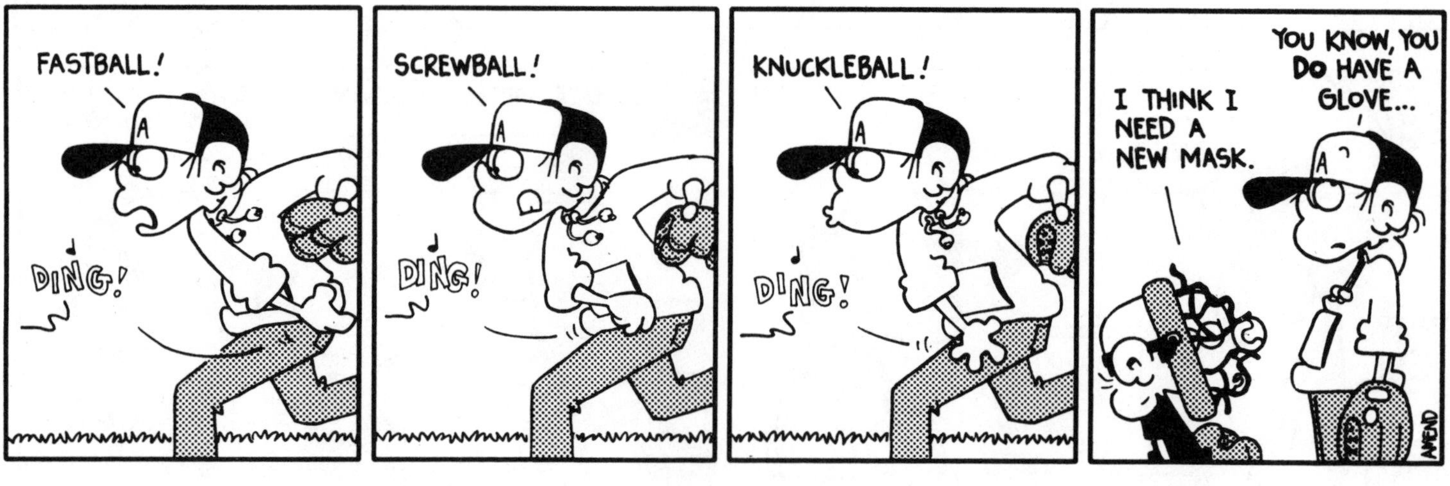
FASTBALL!
DING!
SCREWBALL!
DING!
KNUCKLEBALL!
DING!
I THINK I NEED A NEW MASK.
YOU KNOW, YOU DO HAVE A GLOVE...
AMEND

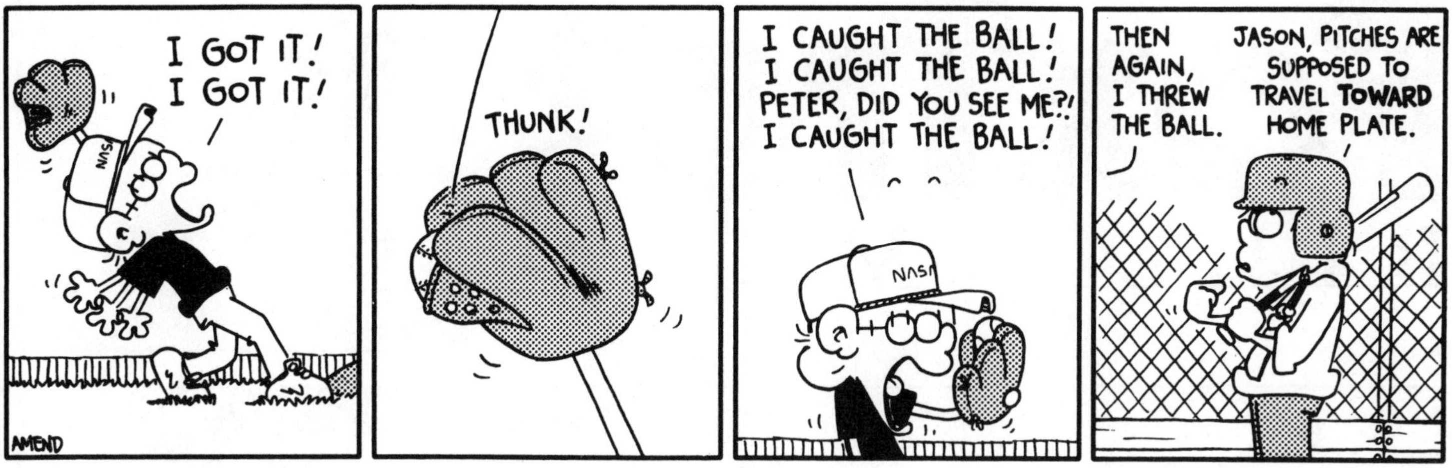

I GOT IT! I GOT IT!
AMEND
THUNK!
I CAUGHT THE BALL! I CAUGHT THE BALL! PETER, DID YOU SEE ME?! I CAUGHT THE BALL!
THEN AGAIN, I THREW THE BALL.
JASON, PITCHES ARE SUPPOSED TO TRAVEL **TOWARD** HOME PLATE.

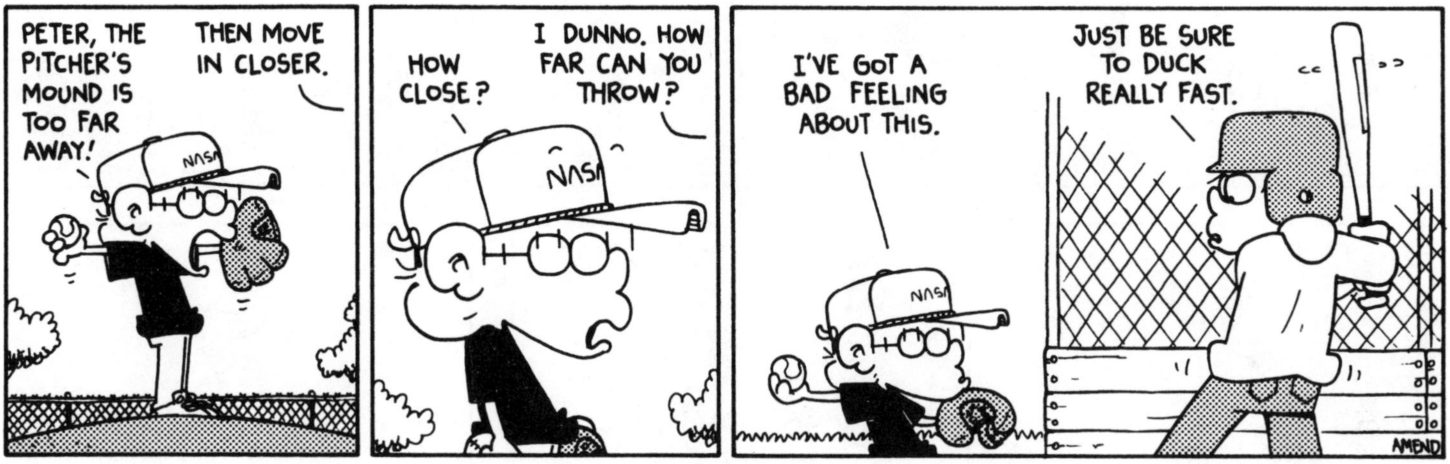

PETER, THE PITCHER'S MOUND IS TOO FAR AWAY!
THEN MOVE IN CLOSER.
HOW CLOSE?
I DUNNO. HOW FAR CAN YOU THROW?
I'VE GOT A BAD FEELING ABOUT THIS.
JUST BE SURE TO DUCK REALLY FAST.
AMEND

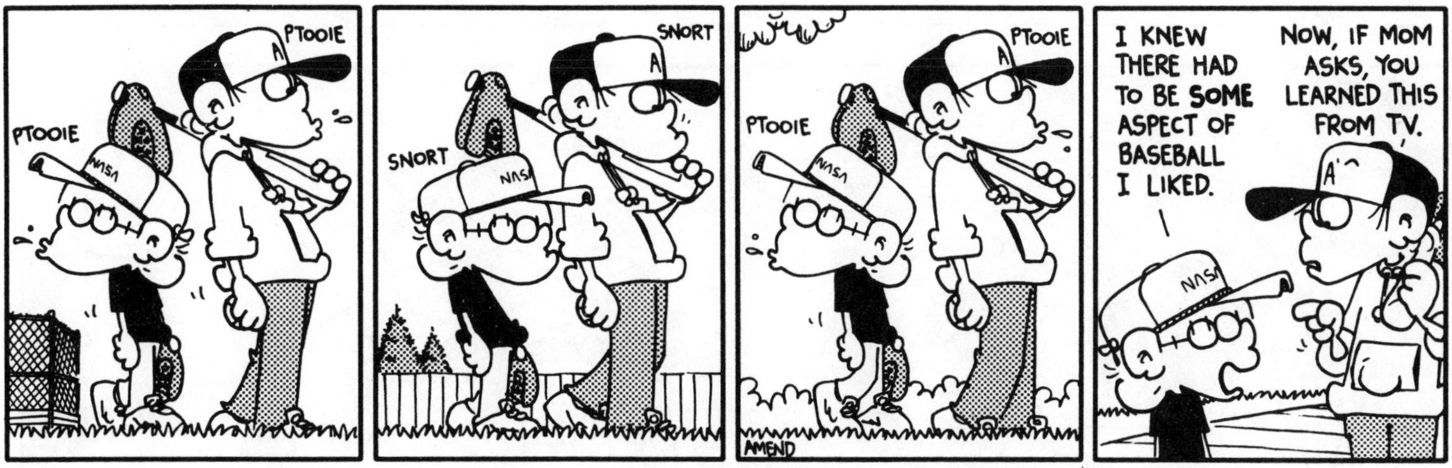

PTOOIE
PTOOIE
SNORT
SNORT
PTOOIE
PTOOIE
AMEND
I KNEW THERE HAD TO BE **SOME** ASPECT OF BASEBALL I LIKED.
NOW, IF MOM ASKS, YOU LEARNED THIS FROM TV.

FoxTrot
BILL AMEND

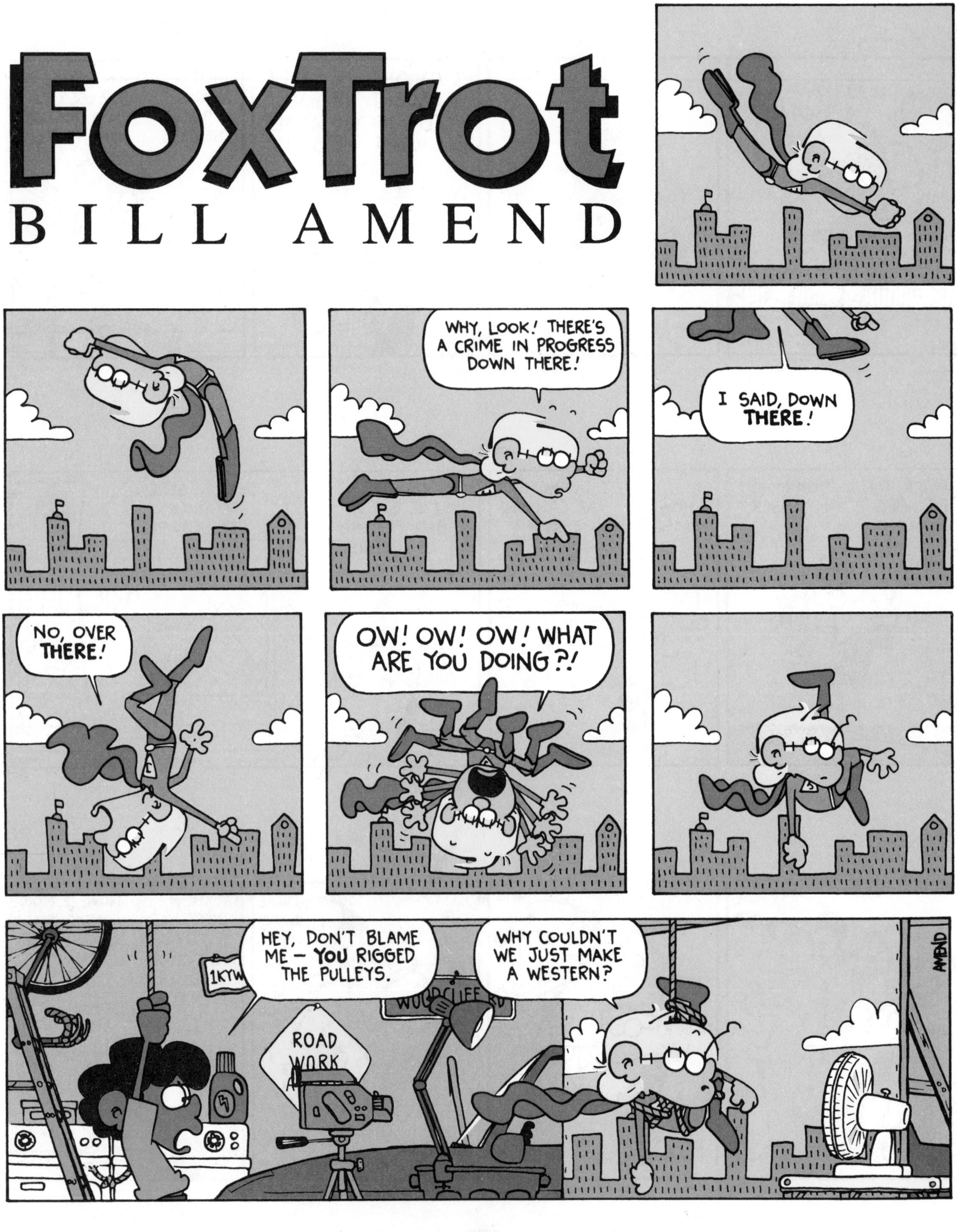

WHY, LOOK! THERE'S A CRIME IN PROGRESS DOWN THERE!
I SAID, DOWN THERE!
NO, OVER THERE!
OW! OW! OW! WHAT ARE YOU DOING?!
1KYW
HEY, DON'T BLAME ME — YOU RIGGED THE PULLEYS.
WHY COULDN'T WE JUST MAKE A WESTERN?
ROAD WORK
WOODCLIFF RD
AMEND

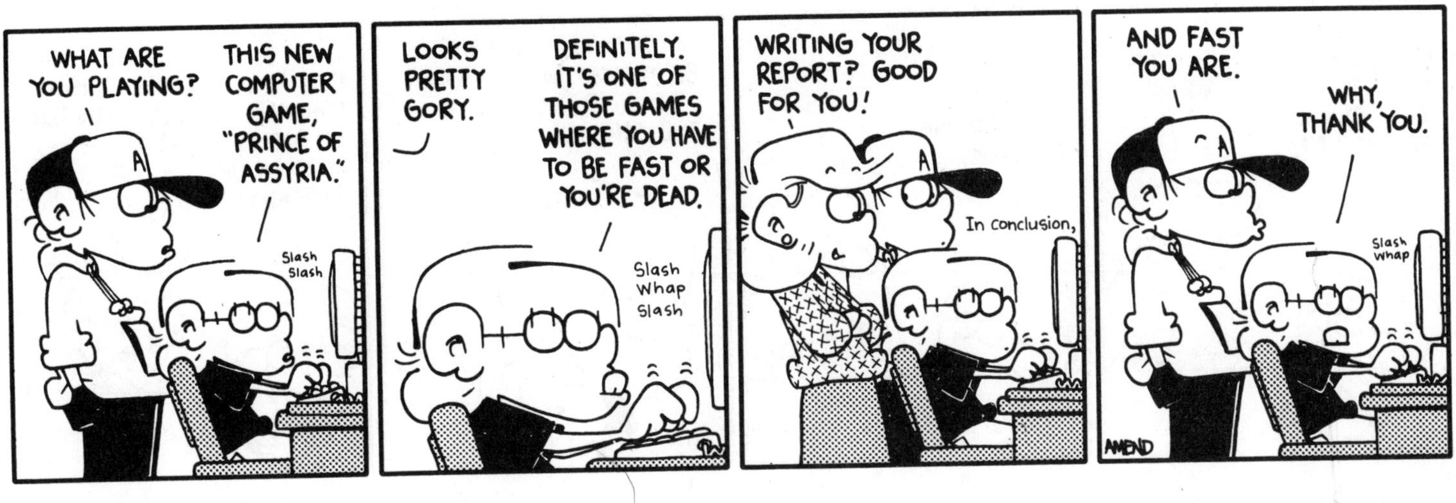
WHAT ARE YOU PLAYING?
THIS NEW COMPUTER GAME, "PRINCE OF ASSYRIA."
Slash Slash
LOOKS PRETTY GORY.
DEFINITELY. IT'S ONE OF THOSE GAMES WHERE YOU HAVE TO BE FAST OR YOU'RE DEAD.
Slash Whap Slash
WRITING YOUR REPORT? GOOD FOR YOU!
In conclusion,
AND FAST YOU ARE.
WHY, THANK YOU.
Slash Whap
AMEND

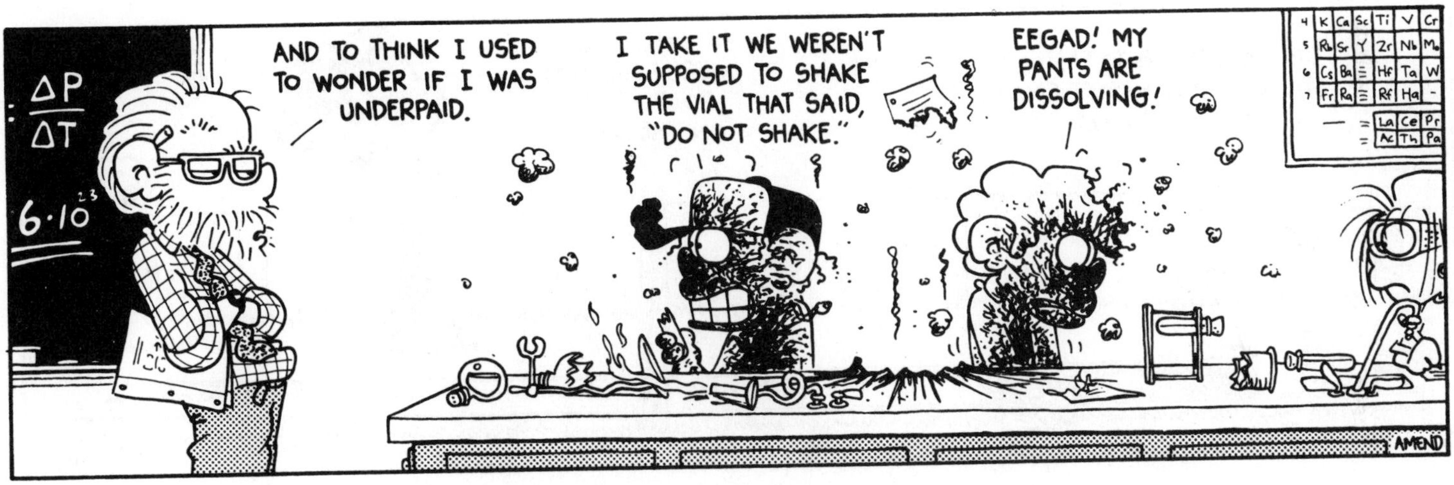
ΔP
ΔT
6·10²³
AND TO THINK I USED TO WONDER IF I WAS UNDERPAID.
I TAKE IT WE WEREN'T SUPPOSED TO SHAKE THE VIAL THAT SAID, "DO NOT SHAKE."
EEGAD! MY PANTS ARE DISSOLVING!
AMEND

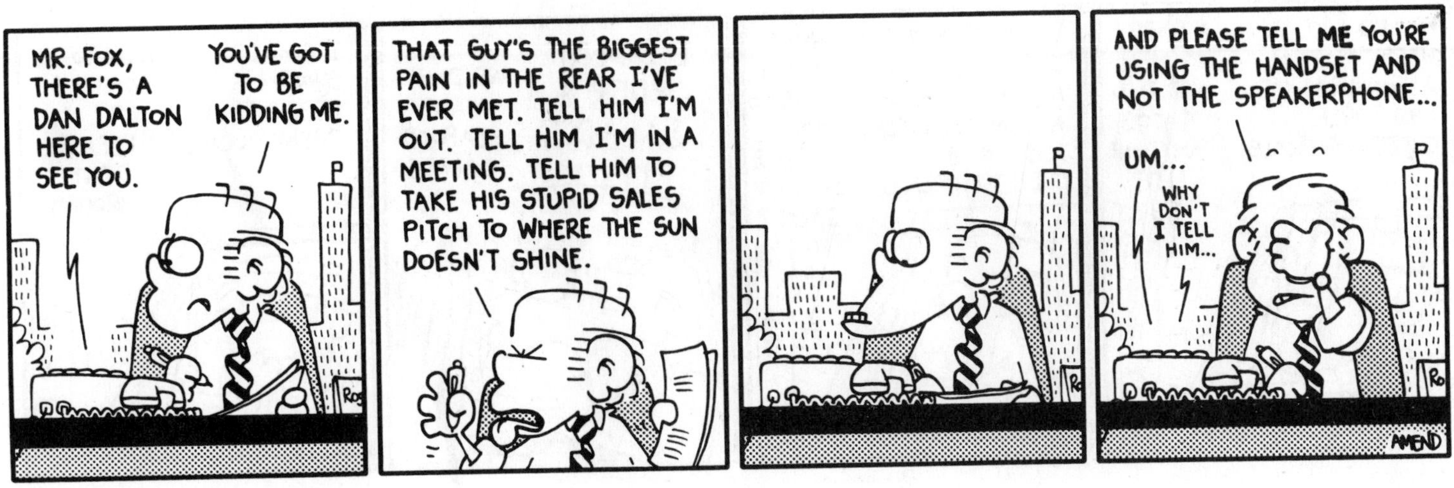
MR. FOX, THERE'S A DAN DALTON HERE TO SEE YOU.
YOU'VE GOT TO BE KIDDING ME.
THAT GUY'S THE BIGGEST PAIN IN THE REAR I'VE EVER MET. TELL HIM I'M OUT. TELL HIM I'M IN A MEETING. TELL HIM TO TAKE HIS STUPID SALES PITCH TO WHERE THE SUN DOESN'T SHINE.
AND PLEASE TELL ME YOU'RE USING THE HANDSET AND NOT THE SPEAKERPHONE...
UM...
WHY DON'T I TELL HIM...
AMEND

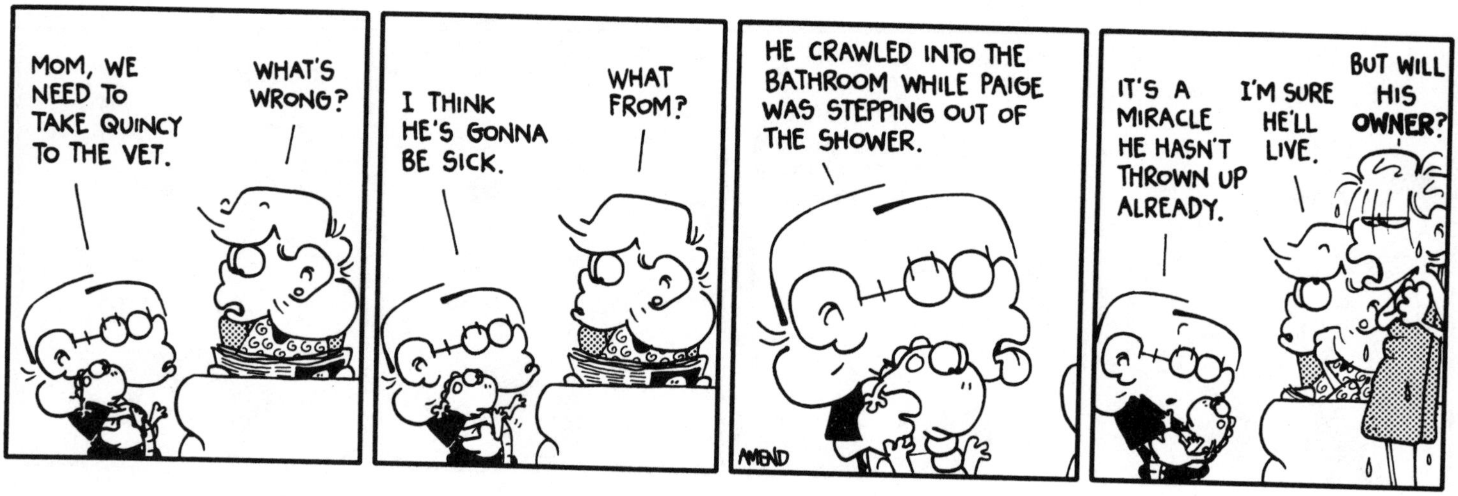
MOM, WE NEED TO TAKE QUINCY TO THE VET.
WHAT'S WRONG?
I THINK HE'S GONNA BE SICK.
WHAT FROM?
HE CRAWLED INTO THE BATHROOM WHILE PAIGE WAS STEPPING OUT OF THE SHOWER.
AMEND
IT'S A MIRACLE HE HASN'T THROWN UP ALREADY.
I'M SURE HE'LL LIVE.
BUT WILL HIS **OWNER**?

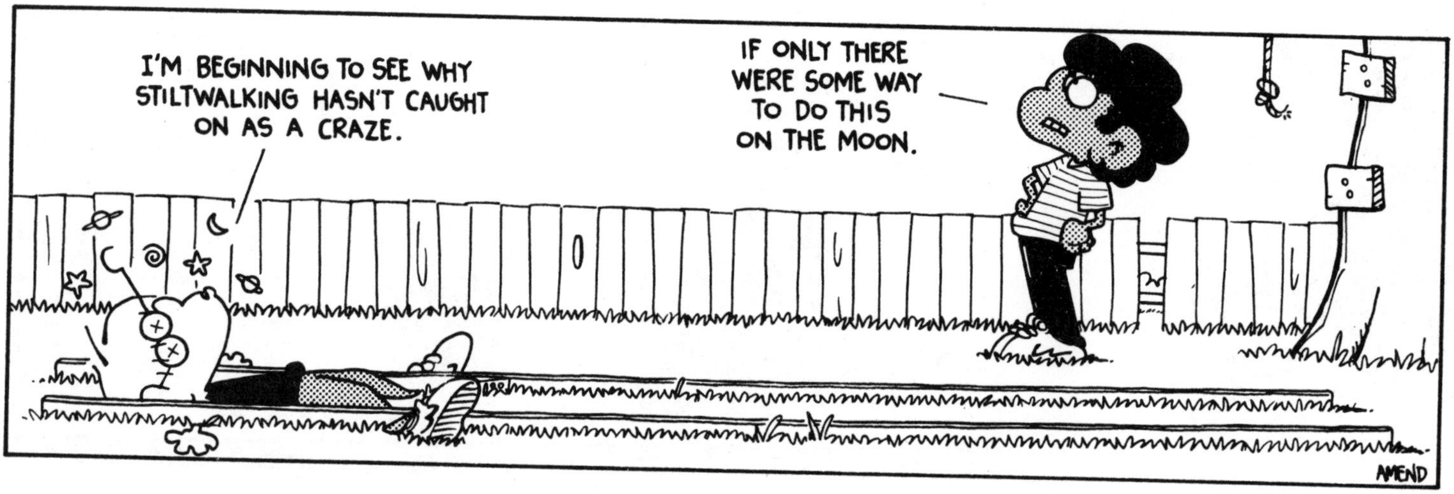
I'M BEGINNING TO SEE WHY STILTWALKING HASN'T CAUGHT ON AS A CRAZE.
IF ONLY THERE WERE SOME WAY TO DO THIS ON THE MOON.
AMEND

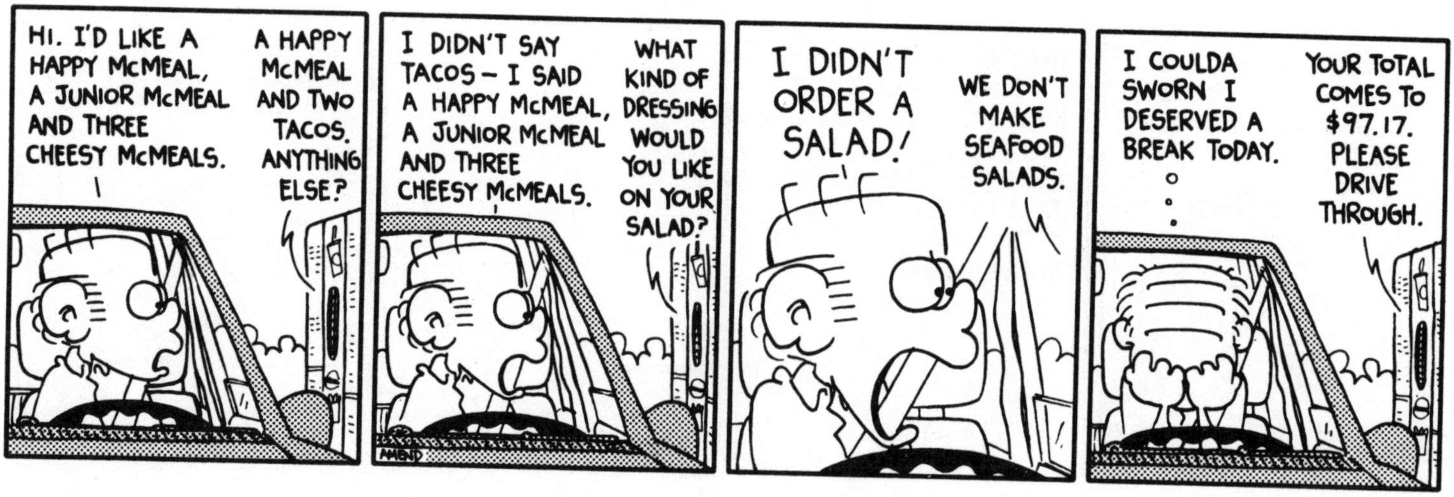
HI. I'D LIKE A HAPPY McMEAL, A JUNIOR McMEAL AND THREE CHEESY McMEALS.
A HAPPY McMEAL AND TWO TACOS. ANYTHING ELSE?
I DIDN'T SAY TACOS – I SAID A HAPPY McMEAL, A JUNIOR McMEAL AND THREE CHEESY McMEALS.
WHAT KIND OF DRESSING WOULD YOU LIKE ON YOUR SALAD?
AMEND
I DIDN'T ORDER A SALAD!
WE DON'T MAKE SEAFOOD SALADS.
I COULDA SWORN I DESERVED A BREAK TODAY.
YOUR TOTAL COMES TO $97.17. PLEASE DRIVE THROUGH.

FoxTrot
BILL AMEND

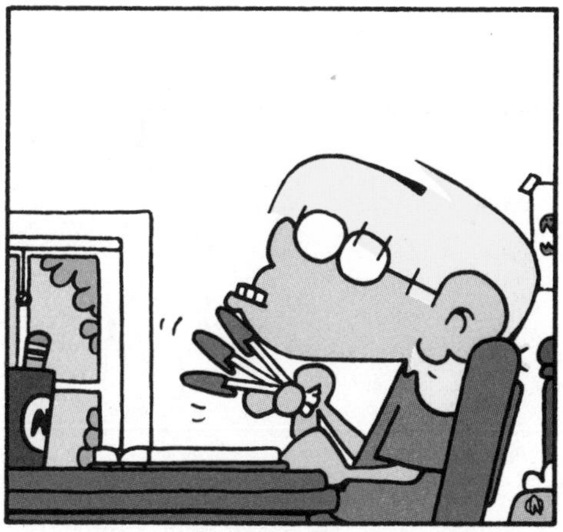

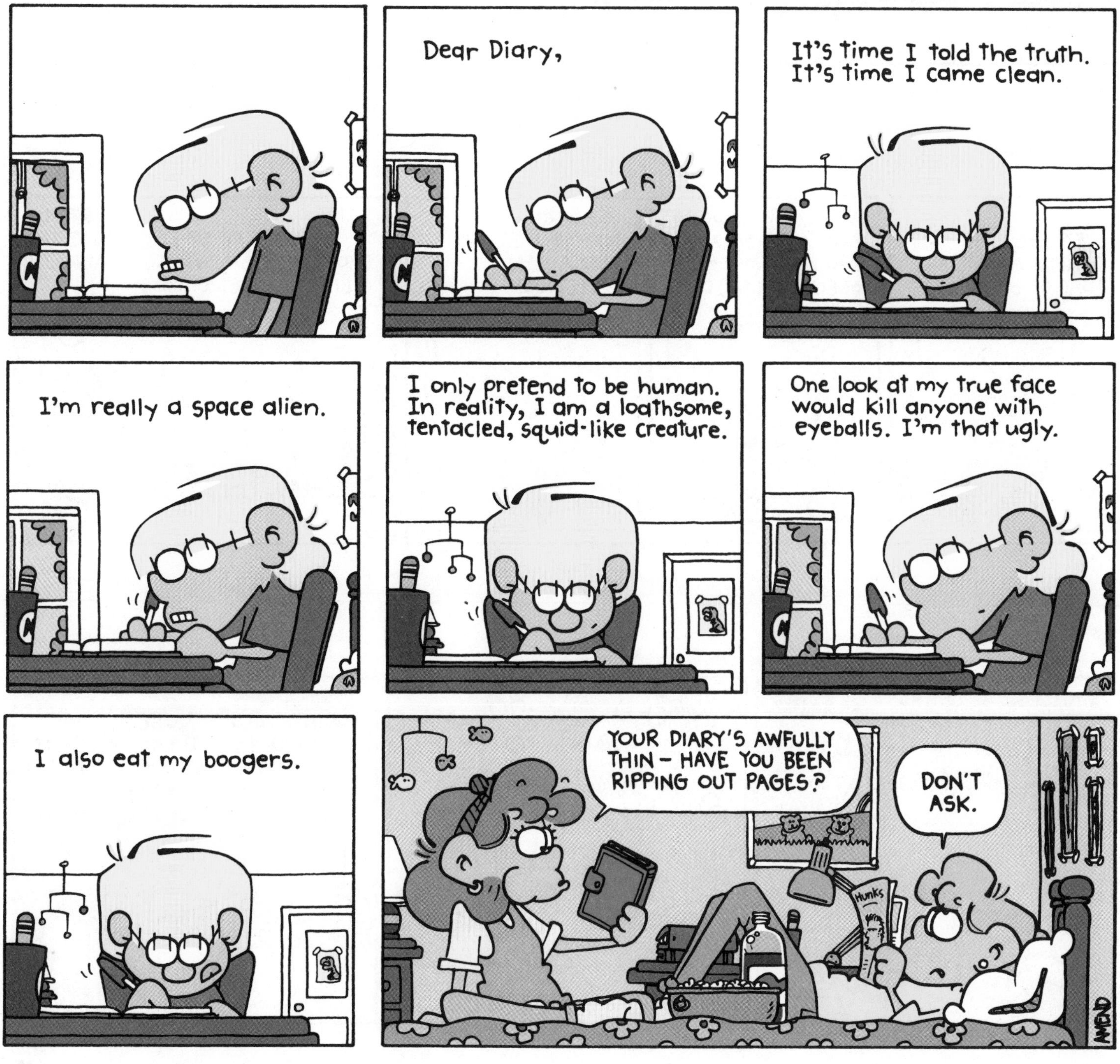

Dear Diary,
It's time I told the truth. It's time I came clean.
I'm really a space alien.
I only pretend to be human. In reality, I am a loathsome, tentacled, squid-like creature.
One look at my true face would kill anyone with eyeballs. I'm that ugly.
I also eat my boogers.
YOUR DIARY'S AWFULLY THIN – HAVE YOU BEEN RIPPING OUT PAGES?
DON'T ASK.
Hunks
AMEND

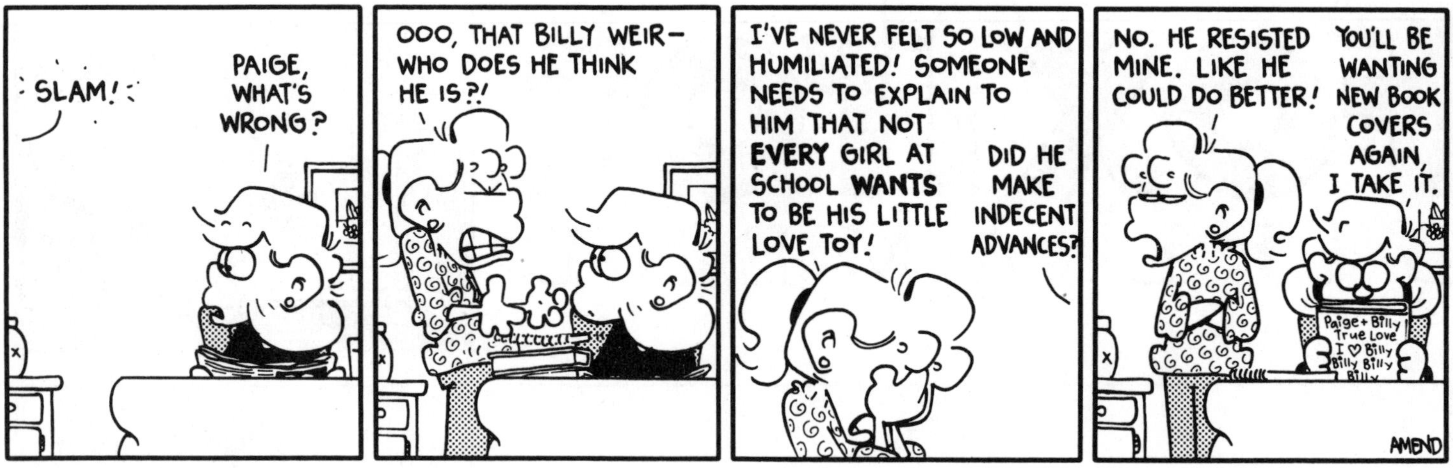
SLAM!
PAIGE, WHAT'S WRONG?
OOO, THAT BILLY WEIR— WHO DOES HE THINK HE IS?!
I'VE NEVER FELT SO LOW AND HUMILIATED! SOMEONE NEEDS TO EXPLAIN TO HIM THAT NOT EVERY GIRL AT SCHOOL WANTS TO BE HIS LITTLE LOVE TOY!
DID HE MAKE INDECENT ADVANCES?
NO. HE RESISTED MINE. LIKE HE COULD DO BETTER!
YOU'LL BE WANTING NEW BOOK COVERS AGAIN, I TAKE IT.
Paige + Billy
True Love
AMEND

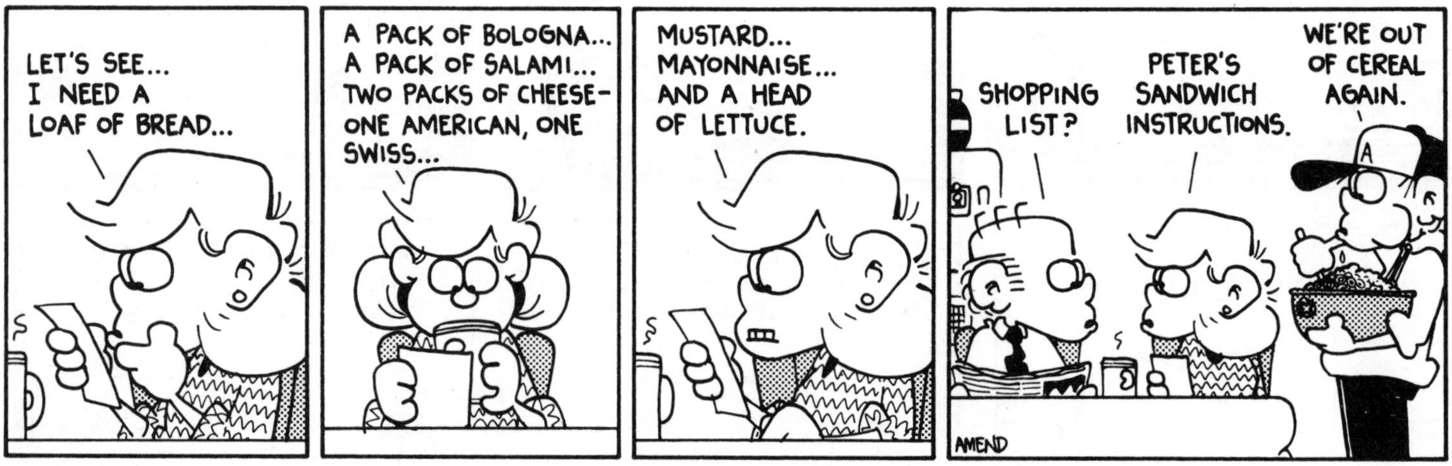
LET'S SEE... I NEED A LOAF OF BREAD...
A PACK OF BOLOGNA... A PACK OF SALAMI... TWO PACKS OF CHEESE-ONE AMERICAN, ONE SWISS...
MUSTARD... MAYONNAISE... AND A HEAD OF LETTUCE.
SHOPPING LIST?
PETER'S SANDWICH INSTRUCTIONS.
WE'RE OUT OF CEREAL AGAIN.
AMEND

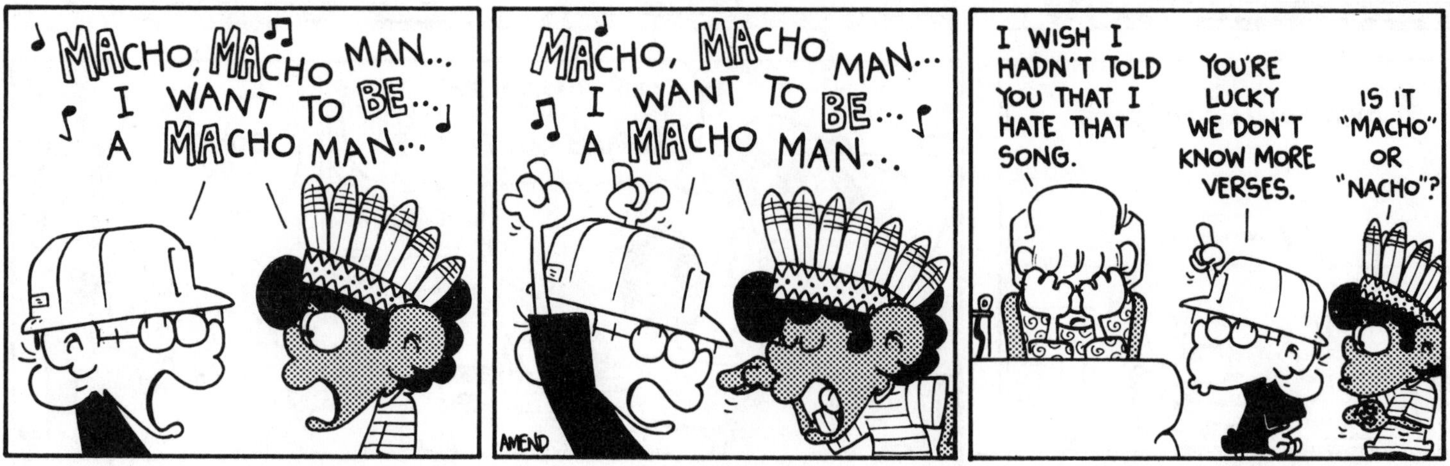
MACHO, MACHO MAN... I WANT TO BE... A MACHO MAN...
MACHO, MACHO MAN... I WANT TO BE... A MACHO MAN...
AMEND
I WISH I HADN'T TOLD YOU THAT I HATE THAT SONG.
YOU'RE LUCKY WE DON'T KNOW MORE VERSES.
IS IT "MACHO" OR "NACHO"?

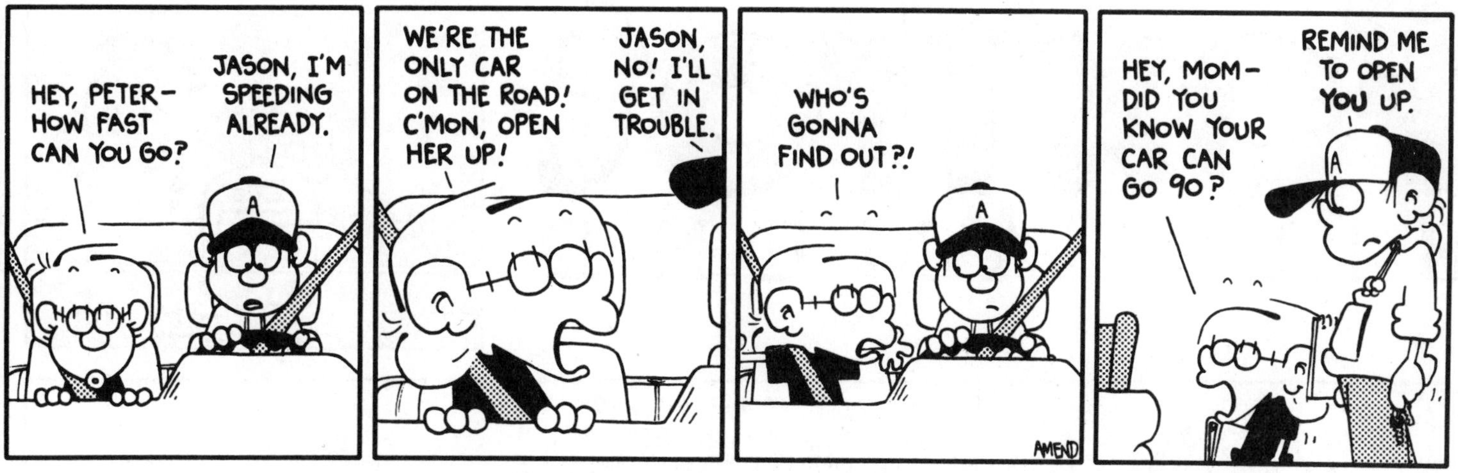
HEY, PETER- HOW FAST CAN YOU GO?
JASON, I'M SPEEDING ALREADY.
WE'RE THE ONLY CAR ON THE ROAD! C'MON, OPEN HER UP!
JASON, NO! I'LL GET IN TROUBLE.
WHO'S GONNA FIND OUT?!
HEY, MOM- DID YOU KNOW YOUR CAR CAN GO 90?
REMIND ME TO OPEN YOU UP.
AMEND

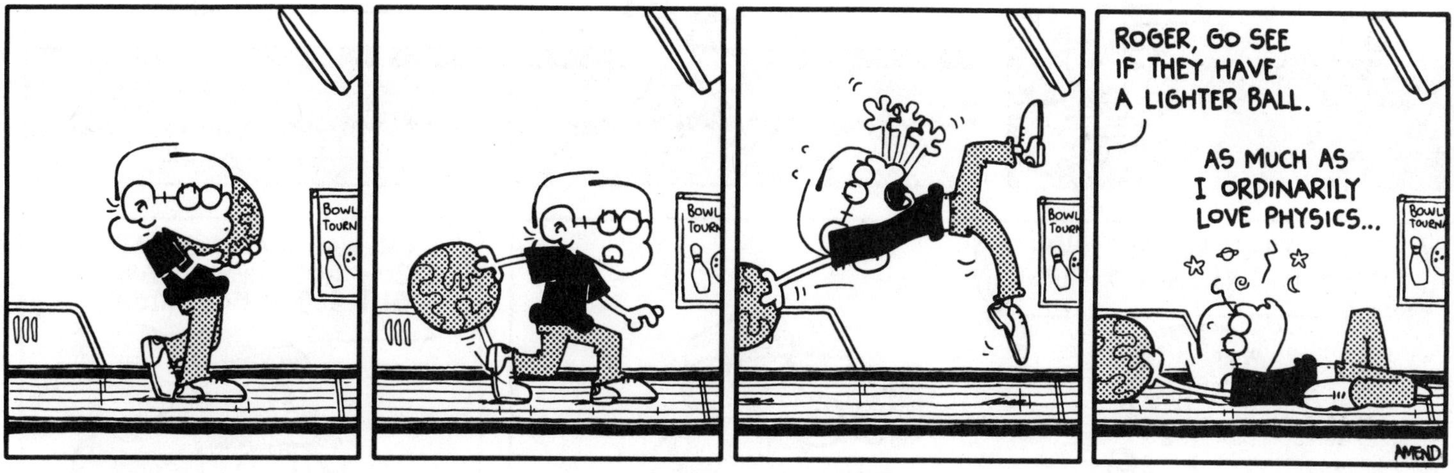
ROGER, GO SEE IF THEY HAVE A LIGHTER BALL.
AS MUCH AS I ORDINARILY LOVE PHYSICS...
AMEND

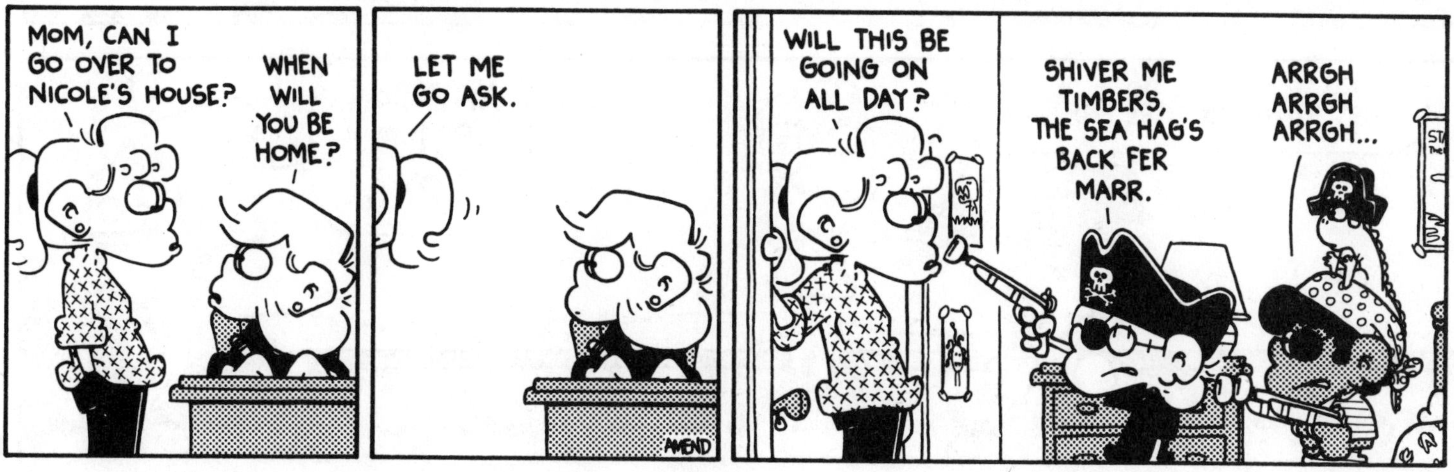
MOM, CAN I GO OVER TO NICOLE'S HOUSE?
WHEN WILL YOU BE HOME?
LET ME GO ASK.
AMEND
WILL THIS BE GOING ON ALL DAY?
SHIVER ME TIMBERS, THE SEA HAG'S BACK FER MARR.
ARRGH ARRGH ARRGH...

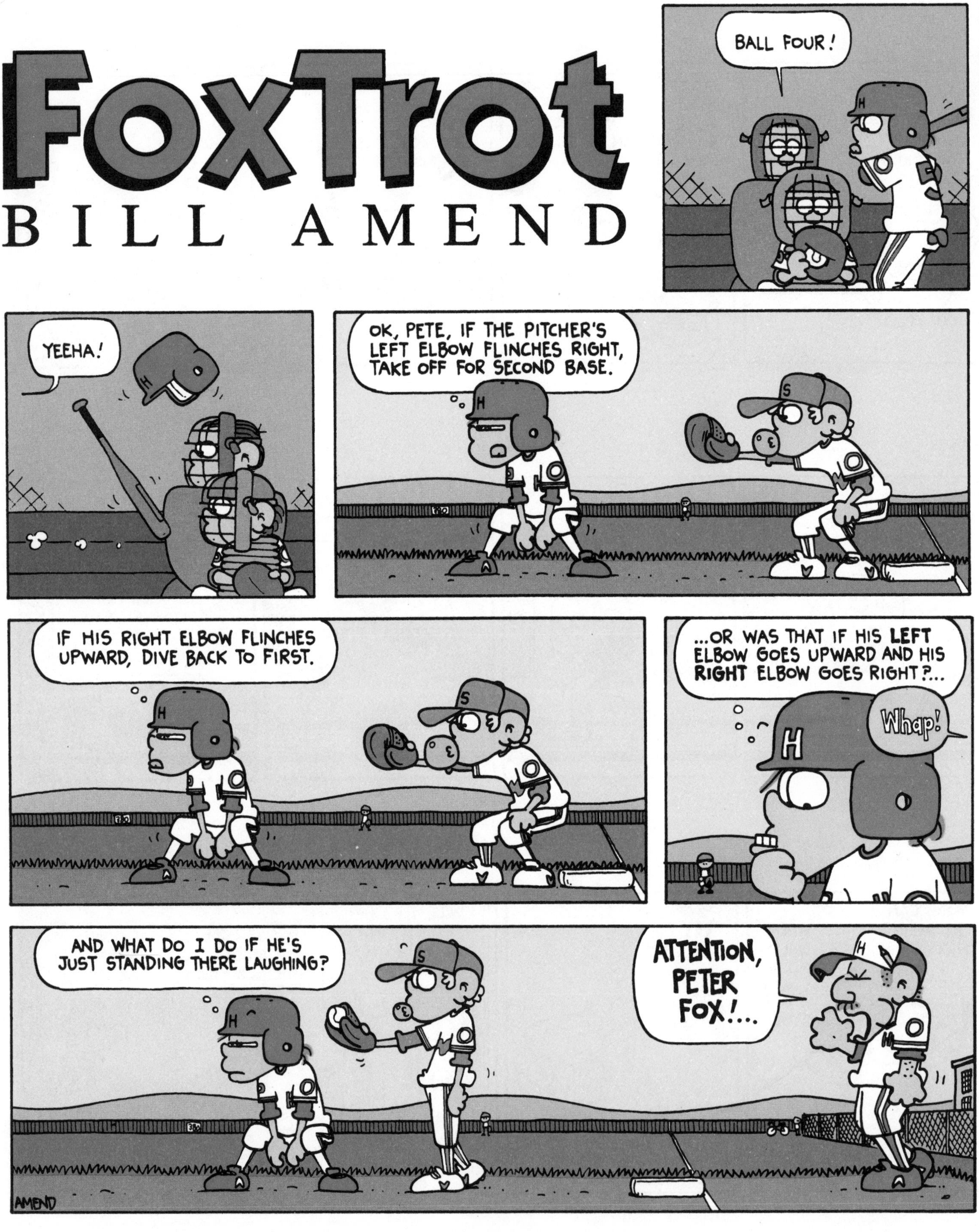
FoxTrot
BILL AMEND
BALL FOUR!
YEEHA!
OK, PETE, IF THE PITCHER'S LEFT ELBOW FLINCHES RIGHT, TAKE OFF FOR SECOND BASE.
IF HIS RIGHT ELBOW FLINCHES UPWARD, DIVE BACK TO FIRST.
...OR WAS THAT IF HIS **LEFT** ELBOW GOES UPWARD AND HIS **RIGHT** ELBOW GOES RIGHT?...
Whap!
AND WHAT DO I DO IF HE'S JUST STANDING THERE LAUGHING?
ATTENTION, PETER FOX!...
AMEND

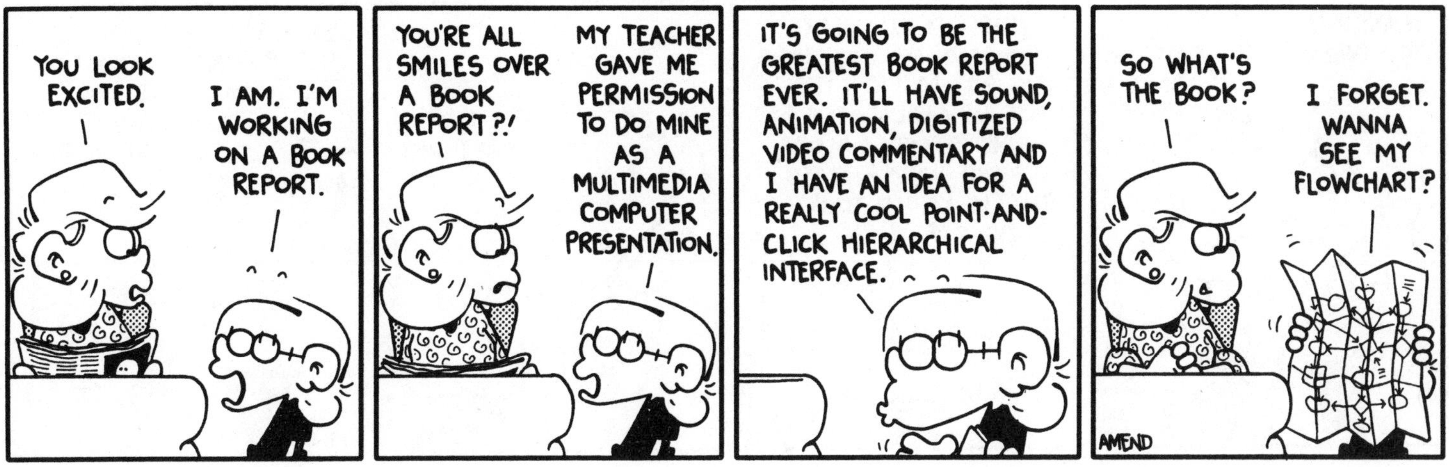
YOU LOOK EXCITED.
I AM. I'M WORKING ON A BOOK REPORT.
YOU'RE ALL SMILES OVER A BOOK REPORT?!
MY TEACHER GAVE ME PERMISSION TO DO MINE AS A MULTIMEDIA COMPUTER PRESENTATION.
IT'S GOING TO BE THE GREATEST BOOK REPORT EVER. IT'LL HAVE SOUND, ANIMATION, DIGITIZED VIDEO COMMENTARY AND I HAVE AN IDEA FOR A REALLY COOL POINT-AND-CLICK HIERARCHICAL INTERFACE.
SO WHAT'S THE BOOK?
I FORGET. WANNA SEE MY FLOWCHART?
AMEND

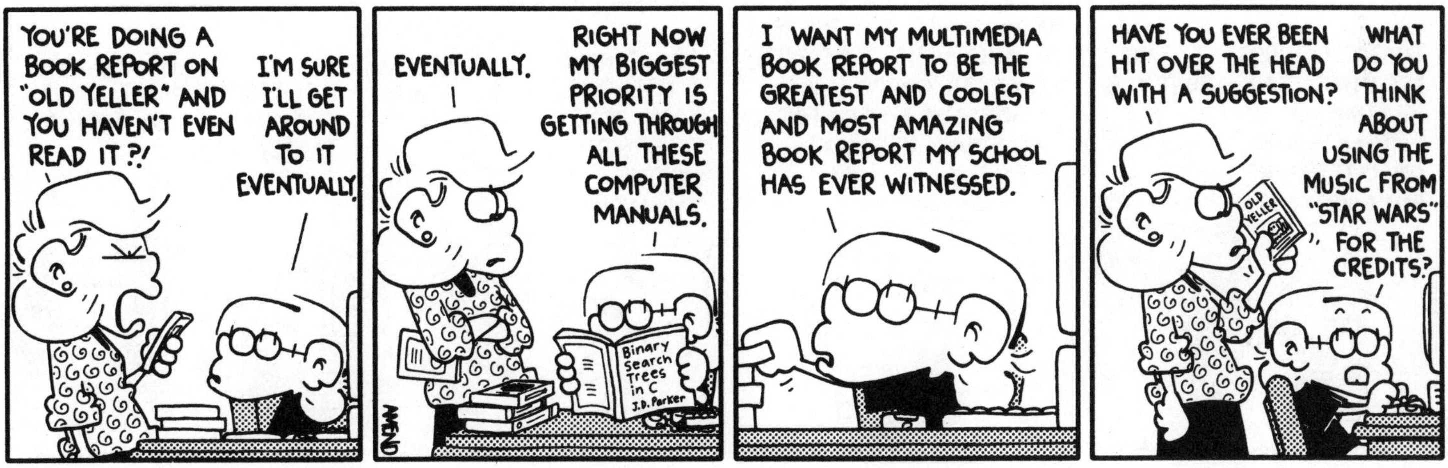
YOU'RE DOING A BOOK REPORT ON "OLD YELLER" AND YOU HAVEN'T EVEN READ IT?!
I'M SURE I'LL GET AROUND TO IT EVENTUALLY.
AMEND
EVENTUALLY.
RIGHT NOW MY BIGGEST PRIORITY IS GETTING THROUGH ALL THESE COMPUTER MANUALS.
Binary Search Trees in C
J.D. Parker
I WANT MY MULTIMEDIA BOOK REPORT TO BE THE GREATEST AND COOLEST AND MOST AMAZING BOOK REPORT MY SCHOOL HAS EVER WITNESSED.
HAVE YOU EVER BEEN HIT OVER THE HEAD WITH A SUGGESTION?
OLD YELLER
WHAT DO YOU THINK ABOUT USING THE MUSIC FROM "STAR WARS" FOR THE CREDITS?

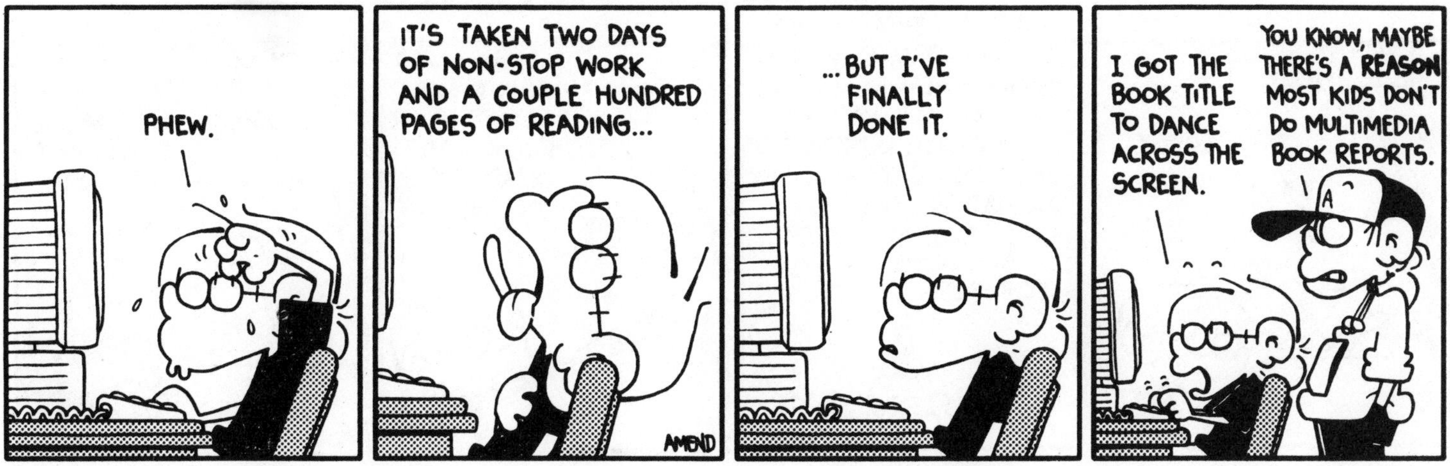
PHEW.
IT'S TAKEN TWO DAYS OF NON-STOP WORK AND A COUPLE HUNDRED PAGES OF READING...
AMEND
...BUT I'VE FINALLY DONE IT.
I GOT THE BOOK TITLE TO DANCE ACROSS THE SCREEN.
YOU KNOW, MAYBE THERE'S A REASON MOST KIDS DON'T DO MULTIMEDIA BOOK REPORTS.

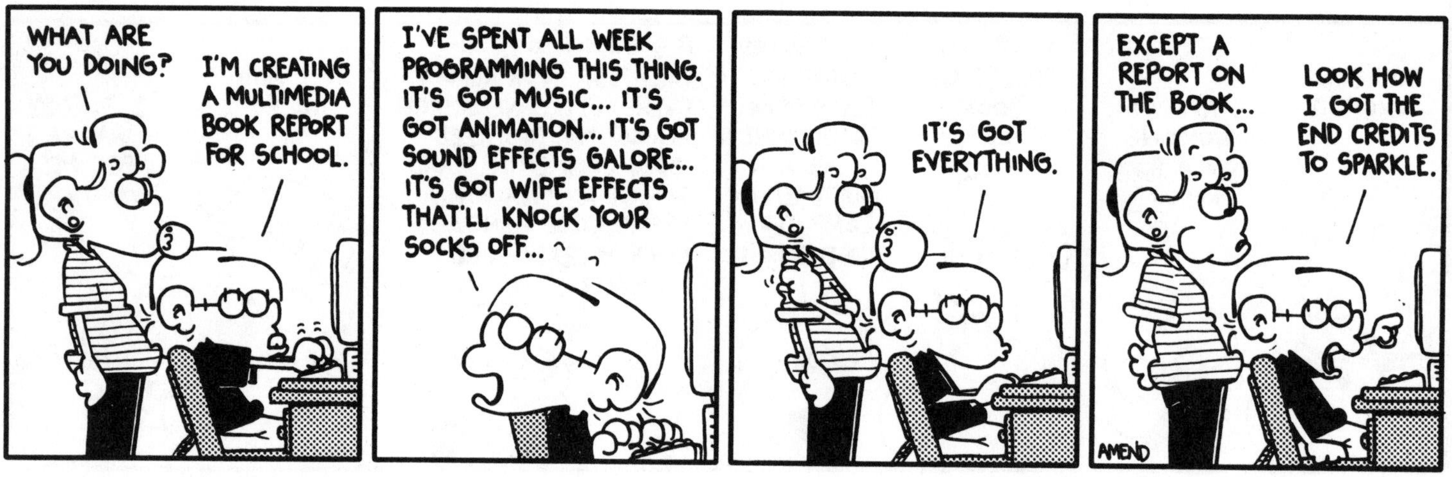
WHAT ARE YOU DOING?
I'M CREATING A MULTIMEDIA BOOK REPORT FOR SCHOOL.
I'VE SPENT ALL WEEK PROGRAMMING THIS THING. IT'S GOT MUSIC... IT'S GOT ANIMATION... IT'S GOT SOUND EFFECTS GALORE... IT'S GOT WIPE EFFECTS THAT'LL KNOCK YOUR SOCKS OFF...
IT'S GOT EVERYTHING.
EXCEPT A REPORT ON THE BOOK...
LOOK HOW I GOT THE END CREDITS TO SPARKLE.
AMEND

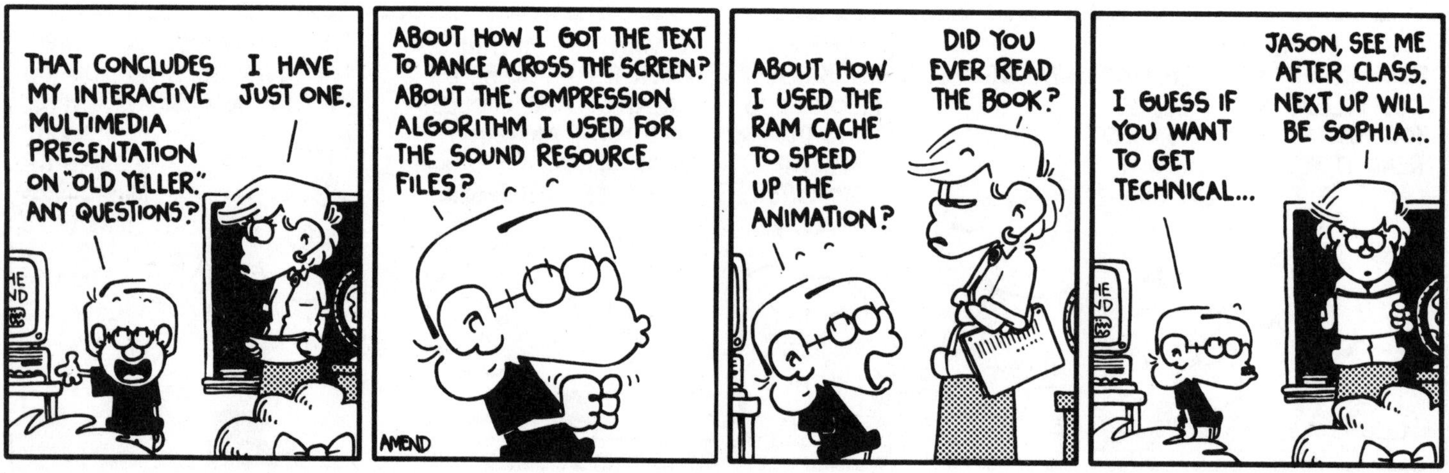
THAT CONCLUDES MY INTERACTIVE MULTIMEDIA PRESENTATION ON "OLD YELLER." ANY QUESTIONS?
I HAVE JUST ONE.
ABOUT HOW I GOT THE TEXT TO DANCE ACROSS THE SCREEN? ABOUT THE COMPRESSION ALGORITHM I USED FOR THE SOUND RESOURCE FILES?
AMEND
ABOUT HOW I USED THE RAM CACHE TO SPEED UP THE ANIMATION?
DID YOU EVER READ THE BOOK?
I GUESS IF YOU WANT TO GET TECHNICAL...
JASON, SEE ME AFTER CLASS. NEXT UP WILL BE SOPHIA...

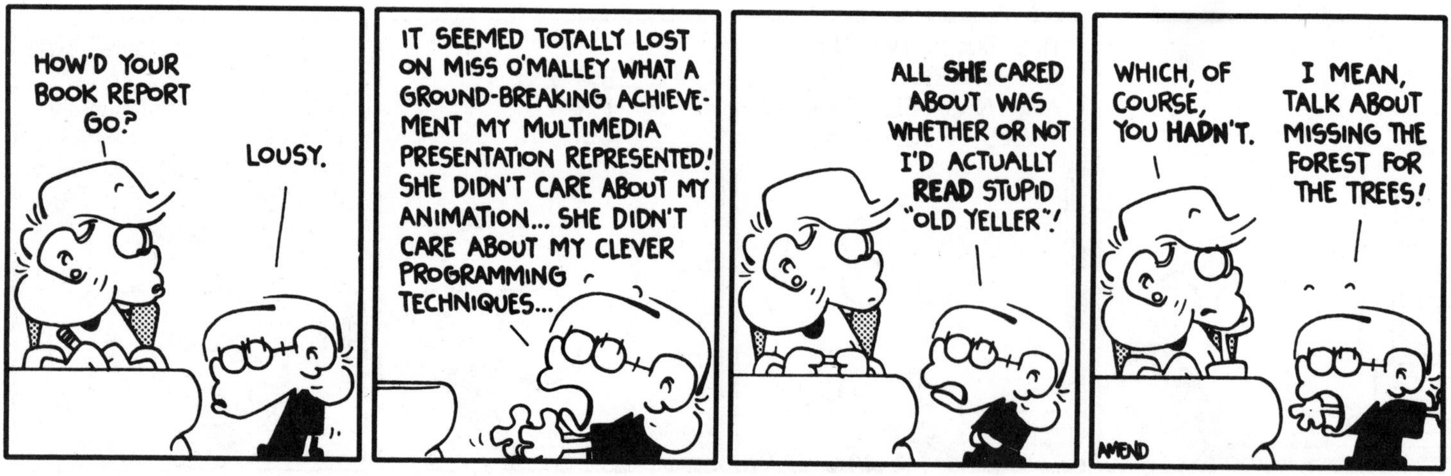
HOW'D YOUR BOOK REPORT GO?
LOUSY.
IT SEEMED TOTALLY LOST ON MISS O'MALLEY WHAT A GROUND-BREAKING ACHIEVEMENT MY MULTIMEDIA PRESENTATION REPRESENTED! SHE DIDN'T CARE ABOUT MY ANIMATION... SHE DIDN'T CARE ABOUT MY CLEVER PROGRAMMING TECHNIQUES...
ALL SHE CARED ABOUT WAS WHETHER OR NOT I'D ACTUALLY READ STUPID "OLD YELLER"!
WHICH, OF COURSE, YOU HADN'T.
I MEAN, TALK ABOUT MISSING THE FOREST FOR THE TREES!
AMEND

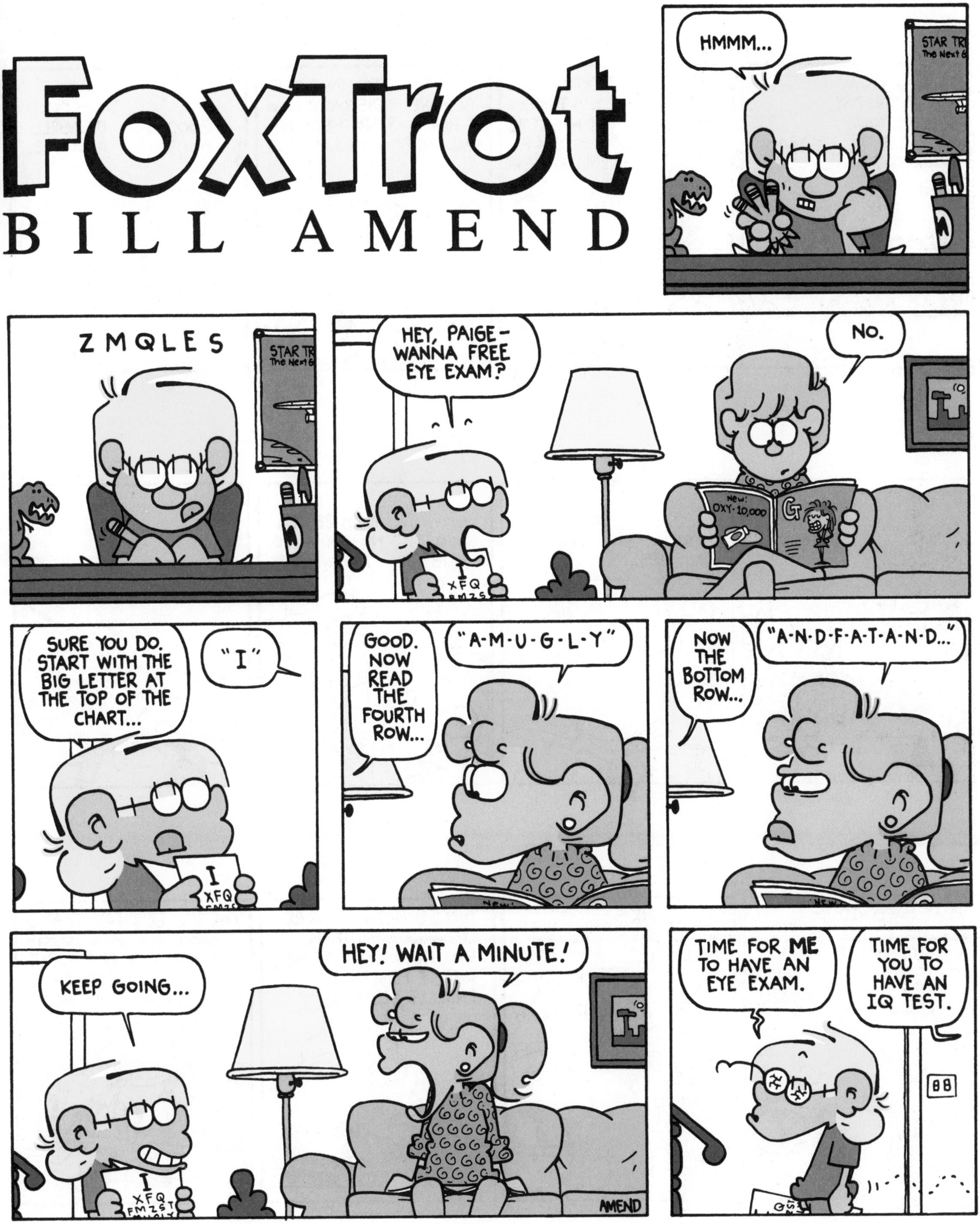
FoxTrot
BILL AMEND
HMMM...
STAR TR
ZMQLES
HEY, PAIGE- WANNA FREE EYE EXAM?
NO.
SURE YOU DO. START WITH THE BIG LETTER AT THE TOP OF THE CHART...
"I"
GOOD. NOW READ THE FOURTH ROW...
"A-M-U-G-L-Y"
NOW THE BOTTOM ROW...
"A-N-D-F-A-T-A-N-D..."
KEEP GOING...
HEY! WAIT A MINUTE!
AMEND
TIME FOR ME TO HAVE AN EYE EXAM.
TIME FOR YOU TO HAVE AN IQ TEST.

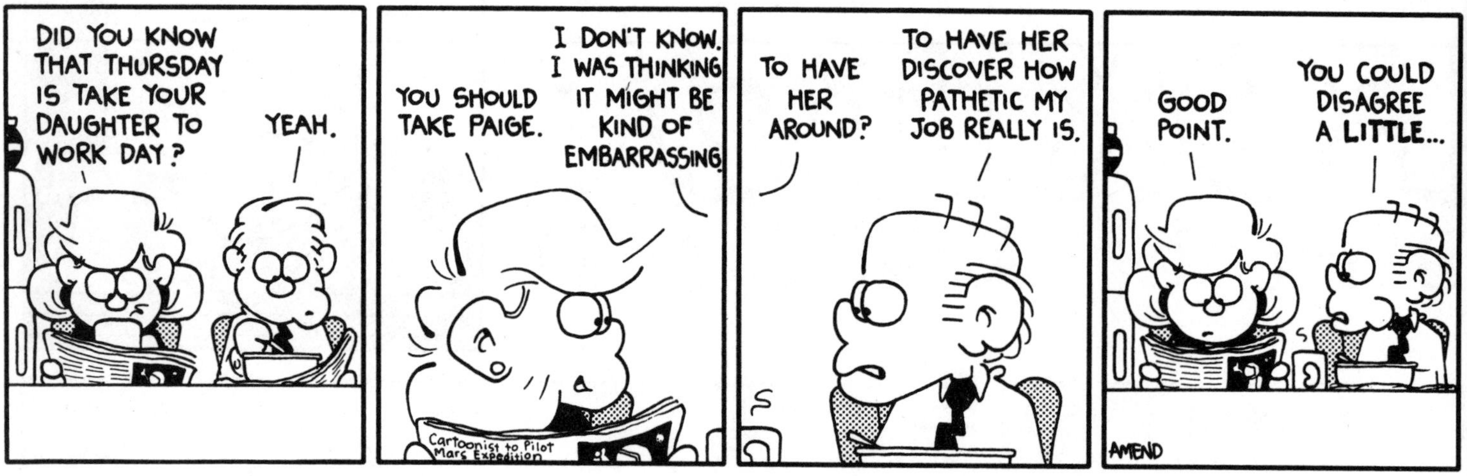
DID YOU KNOW THAT THURSDAY IS TAKE YOUR DAUGHTER TO WORK DAY?
YEAH.
YOU SHOULD TAKE PAIGE.
I DON'T KNOW. I WAS THINKING IT MIGHT BE KIND OF EMBARRASSING.
Cartoonist to Pilot Mars Expedition
TO HAVE HER AROUND?
TO HAVE HER DISCOVER HOW PATHETIC MY JOB REALLY IS.
GOOD POINT.
YOU COULD DISAGREE A LITTLE...
AMEND

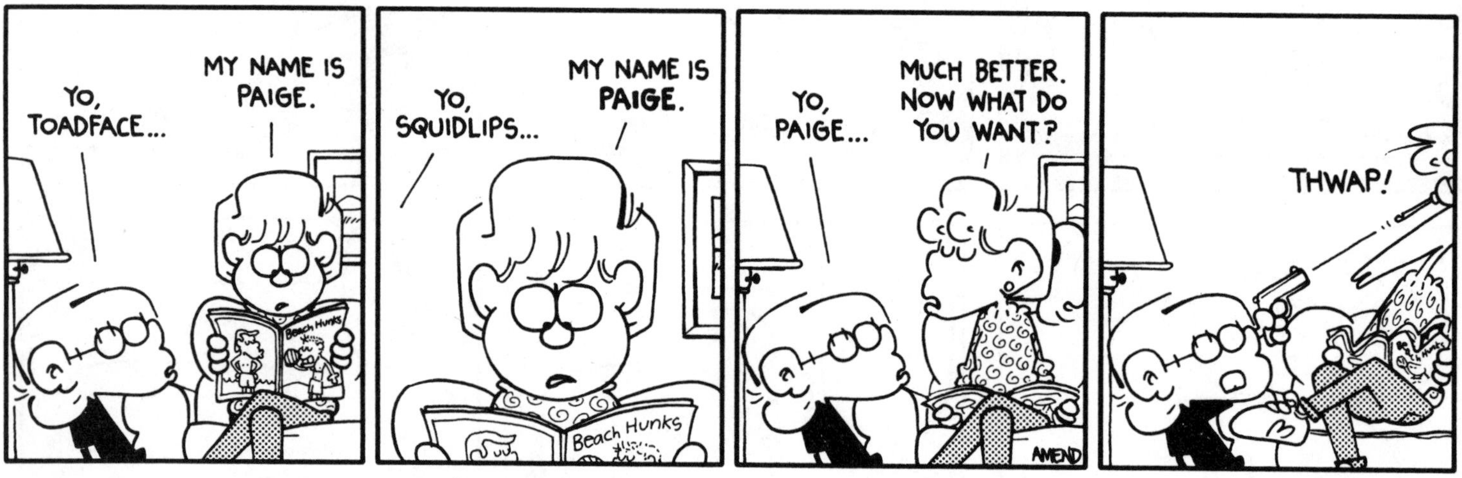
YO, TOADFACE...
MY NAME IS PAIGE.
Beach Hunks
YO, SQUIDLIPS...
MY NAME IS PAIGE.
Beach Hunks
YO, PAIGE...
MUCH BETTER. NOW WHAT DO YOU WANT?
AMEND
THWAP!

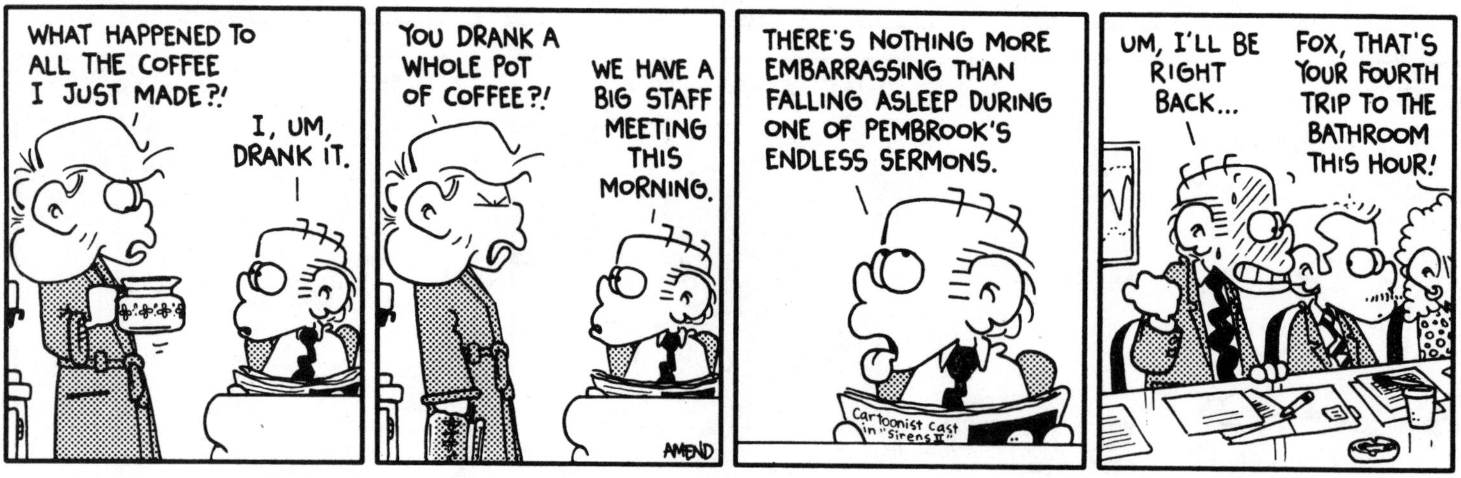
WHAT HAPPENED TO ALL THE COFFEE I JUST MADE?!
I, UM, DRANK IT.
YOU DRANK A WHOLE POT OF COFFEE?!
WE HAVE A BIG STAFF MEETING THIS MORNING.
AMEND
THERE'S NOTHING MORE EMBARRASSING THAN FALLING ASLEEP DURING ONE OF PEMBROOK'S ENDLESS SERMONS.
Cartoonist Cast in "Sirens II"
UM, I'LL BE RIGHT BACK...
FOX, THAT'S YOUR FOURTH TRIP TO THE BATHROOM THIS HOUR!

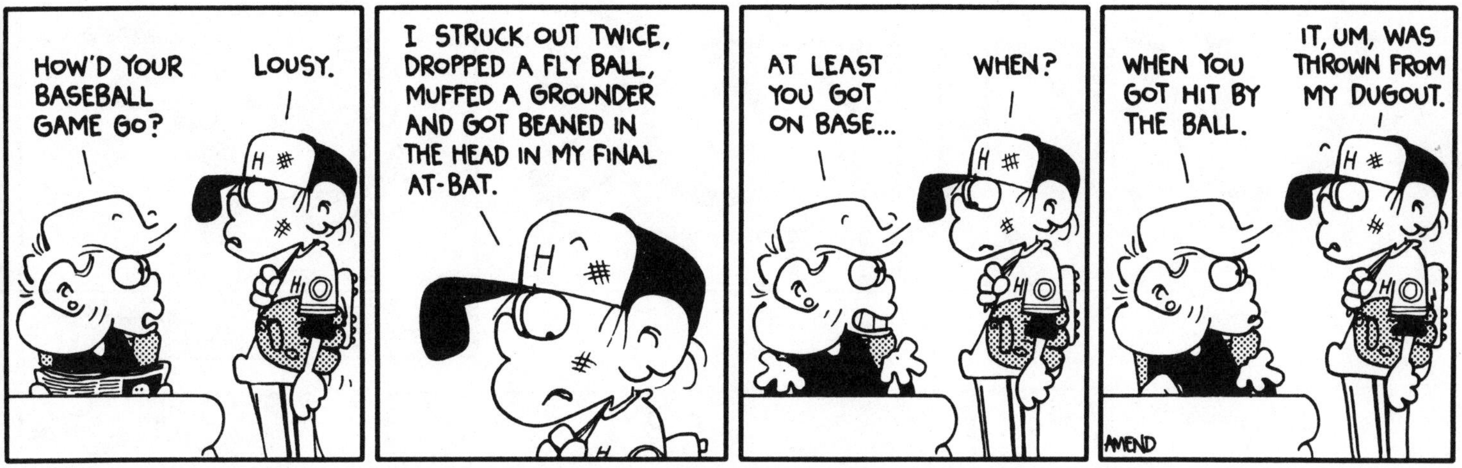
HOW'D YOUR BASEBALL GAME GO?
LOUSY.
I STRUCK OUT TWICE, DROPPED A FLY BALL, MUFFED A GROUNDER AND GOT BEANED IN THE HEAD IN MY FINAL AT-BAT.
AT LEAST YOU GOT ON BASE...
WHEN?
WHEN YOU GOT HIT BY THE BALL.
IT, UM, WAS THROWN FROM MY DUGOUT.
AMEND

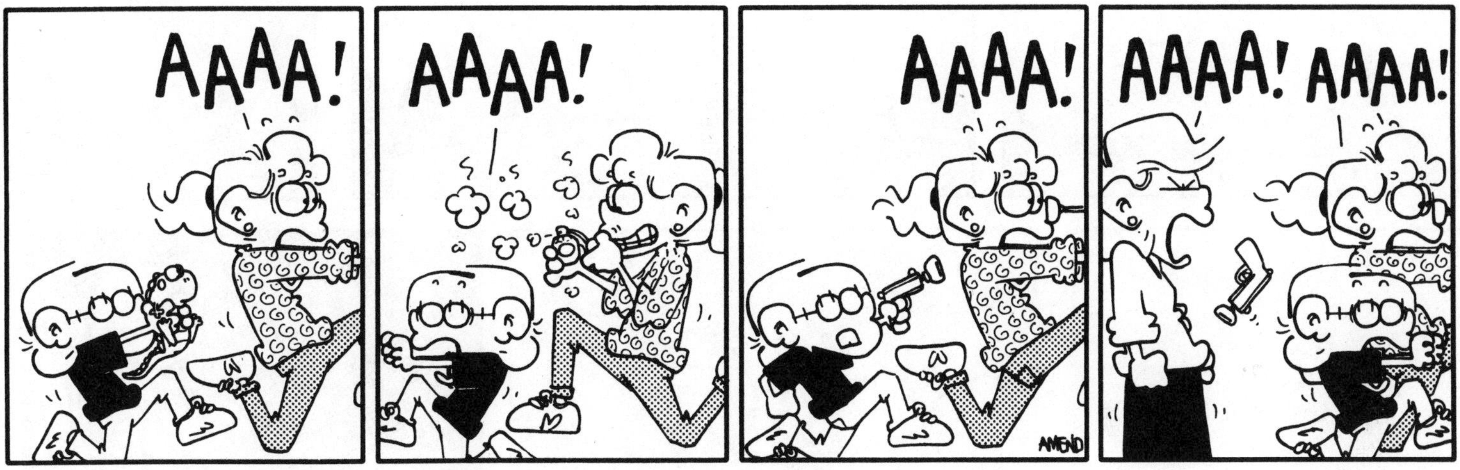
AAAA!
AAAA!
AAAA!
AMEND
AAAA!
AAAA!

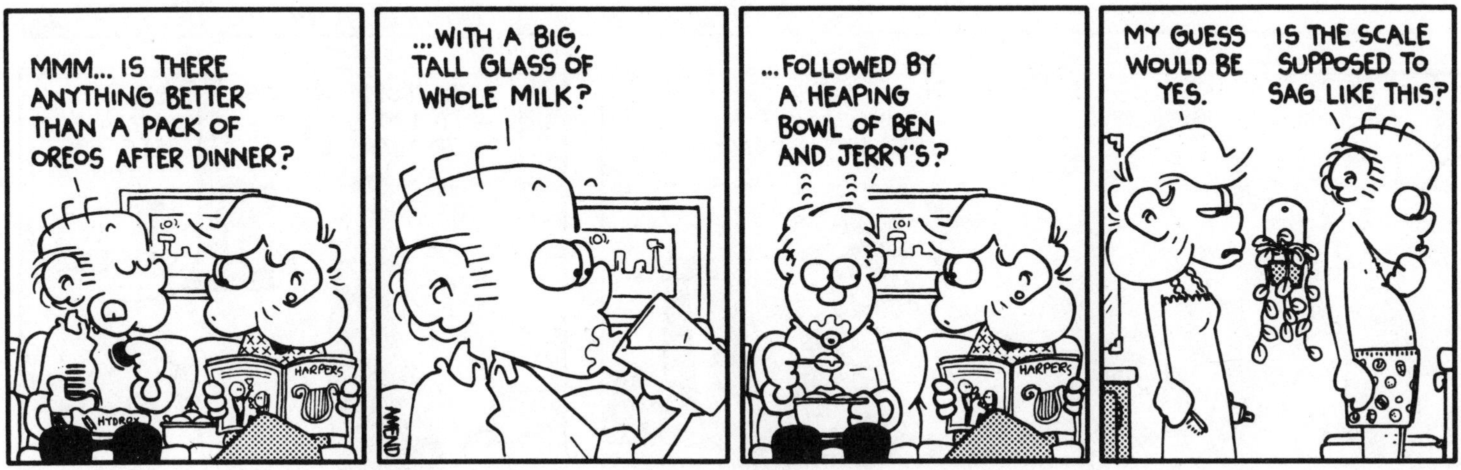
MMM... IS THERE ANYTHING BETTER THAN A PACK OF OREOS AFTER DINNER?
HYDROX
HARPERS
...WITH A BIG, TALL GLASS OF WHOLE MILK?
AMEND
...FOLLOWED BY A HEAPING BOWL OF BEN AND JERRY'S?
HARPERS
MY GUESS WOULD BE YES.
IS THE SCALE SUPPOSED TO SAG LIKE THIS?

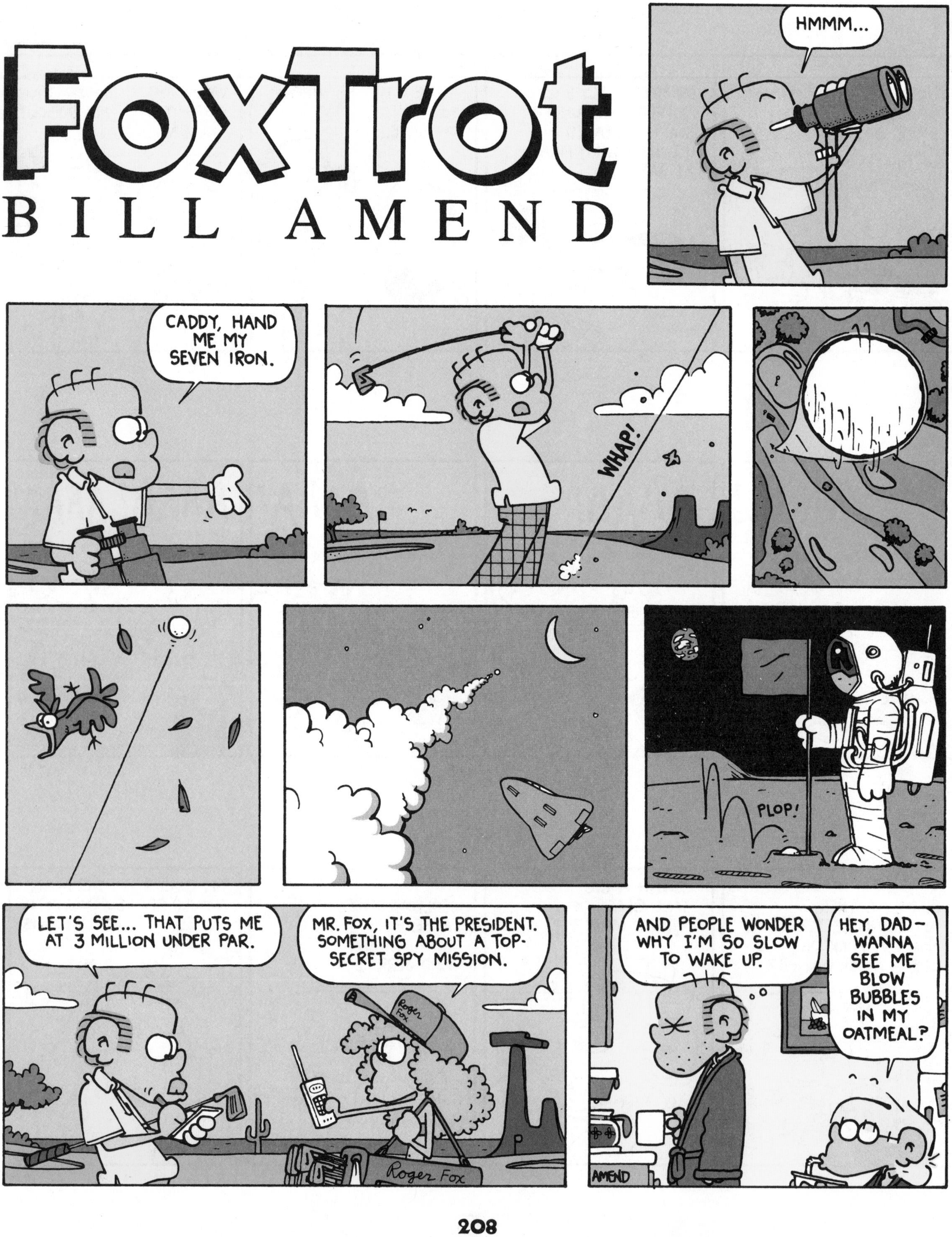
FoxTrot
BILL AMEND
HMMM...
CADDY, HAND ME MY SEVEN IRON.
WHAP!
PLOP!
LET'S SEE... THAT PUTS ME AT 3 MILLION UNDER PAR.
MR. FOX, IT'S THE PRESIDENT. SOMETHING ABOUT A TOP-SECRET SPY MISSION.
Roger Fox
AND PEOPLE WONDER WHY I'M SO SLOW TO WAKE UP.
HEY, DAD— WANNA SEE ME BLOW BUBBLES IN MY OATMEAL?
AMEND

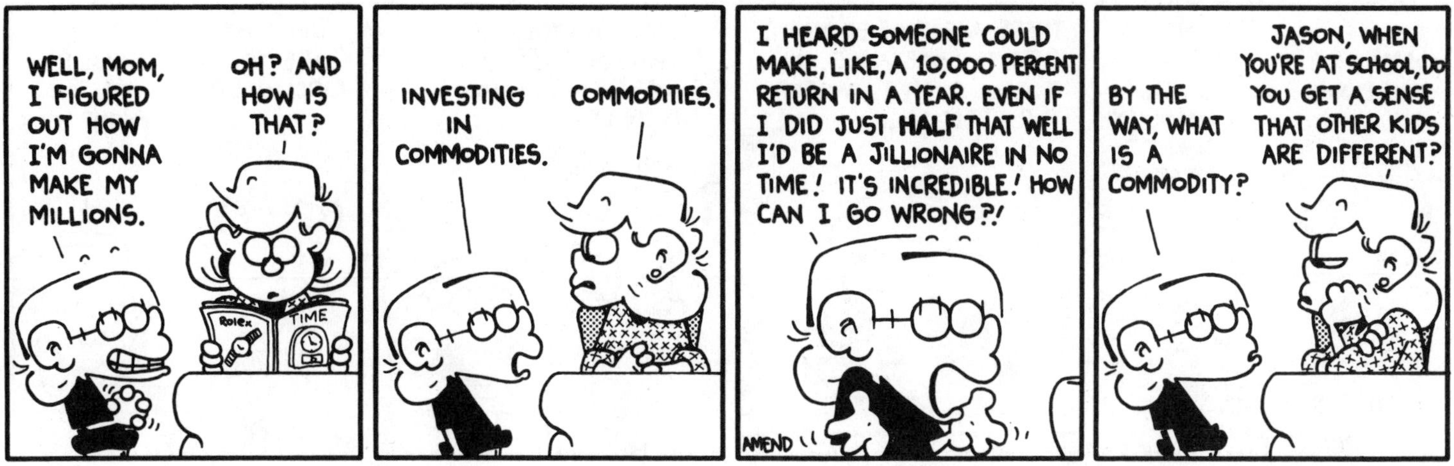
WELL, MOM, I FIGURED OUT HOW I'M GONNA MAKE MY MILLIONS.
OH? AND HOW IS THAT?
Rolex
TIME
INVESTING IN COMMODITIES.
COMMODITIES.
I HEARD SOMEONE COULD MAKE, LIKE, A 10,000 PERCENT RETURN IN A YEAR. EVEN IF I DID JUST HALF THAT WELL I'D BE A JILLIONAIRE IN NO TIME! IT'S INCREDIBLE! HOW CAN I GO WRONG?!
AMEND
BY THE WAY, WHAT IS A COMMODITY?
JASON, WHEN YOU'RE AT SCHOOL, DO YOU GET A SENSE THAT OTHER KIDS ARE DIFFERENT?

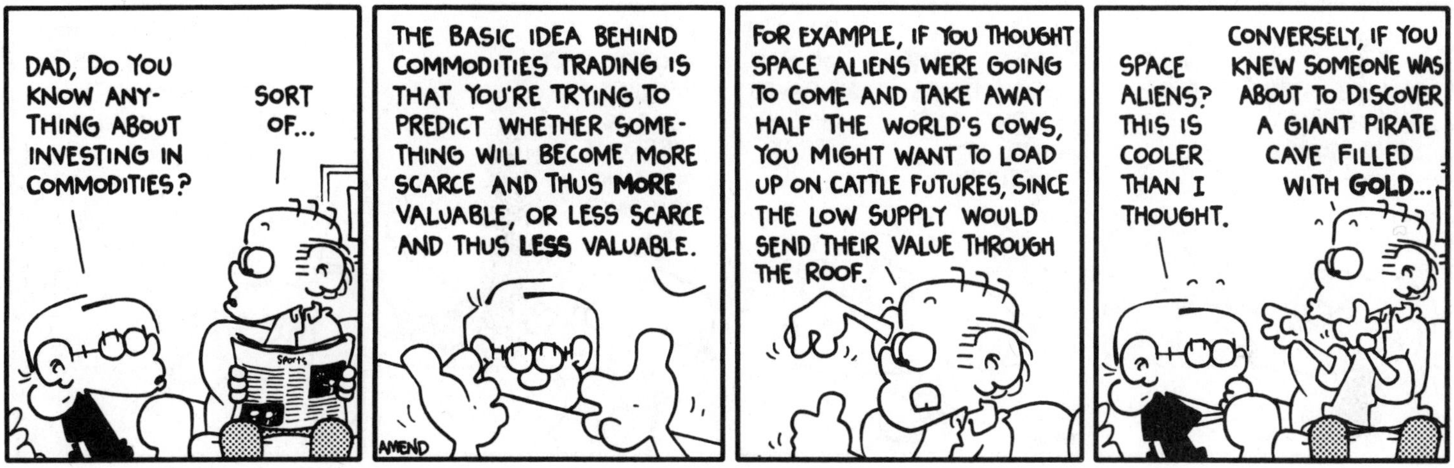
DAD, DO YOU KNOW ANYTHING ABOUT INVESTING IN COMMODITIES?
SORT OF...
Sports
THE BASIC IDEA BEHIND COMMODITIES TRADING IS THAT YOU'RE TRYING TO PREDICT WHETHER SOMETHING WILL BECOME MORE SCARCE AND THUS MORE VALUABLE, OR LESS SCARCE AND THUS LESS VALUABLE.
AMEND
FOR EXAMPLE, IF YOU THOUGHT SPACE ALIENS WERE GOING TO COME AND TAKE AWAY HALF THE WORLD'S COWS, YOU MIGHT WANT TO LOAD UP ON CATTLE FUTURES, SINCE THE LOW SUPPLY WOULD SEND THEIR VALUE THROUGH THE ROOF.
SPACE ALIENS? THIS IS COOLER THAN I THOUGHT.
CONVERSELY, IF YOU KNEW SOMEONE WAS ABOUT TO DISCOVER A GIANT PIRATE CAVE FILLED WITH GOLD...

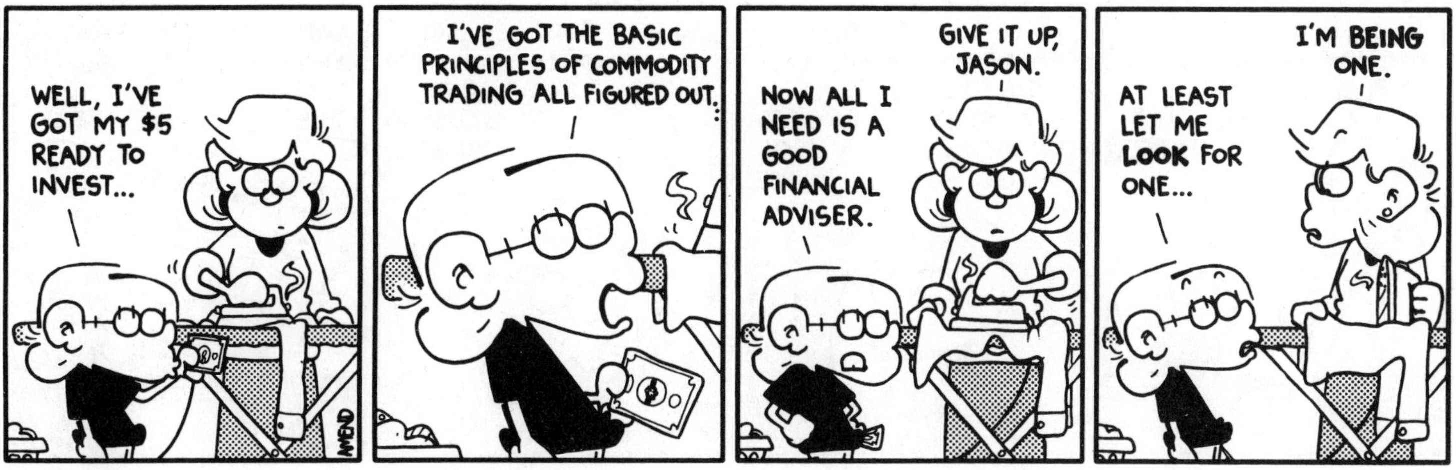
WELL, I'VE GOT MY $5 READY TO INVEST...
AMEND
I'VE GOT THE BASIC PRINCIPLES OF COMMODITY TRADING ALL FIGURED OUT.
NOW ALL I NEED IS A GOOD FINANCIAL ADVISER.
GIVE IT UP, JASON.
AT LEAST LET ME LOOK FOR ONE...
I'M BEING ONE.

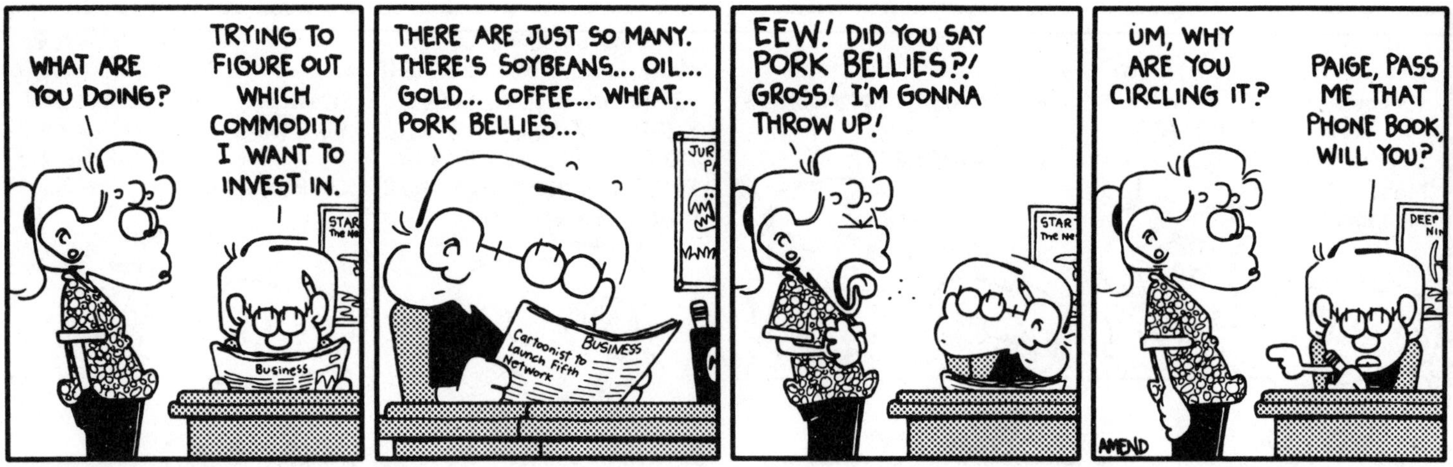
WHAT ARE YOU DOING?
TRYING TO FIGURE OUT WHICH COMMODITY I WANT TO INVEST IN.
Business
THERE ARE JUST SO MANY. THERE'S SOYBEANS... OIL... GOLD... COFFEE... WHEAT... PORK BELLIES...
BUSINESS
Cartoonist to Launch Fifth Network
EEW! DID YOU SAY PORK BELLIES?! GROSS! I'M GONNA THROW UP!
UM, WHY ARE YOU CIRCLING IT?
PAIGE, PASS ME THAT PHONE BOOK, WILL YOU?
AMEND

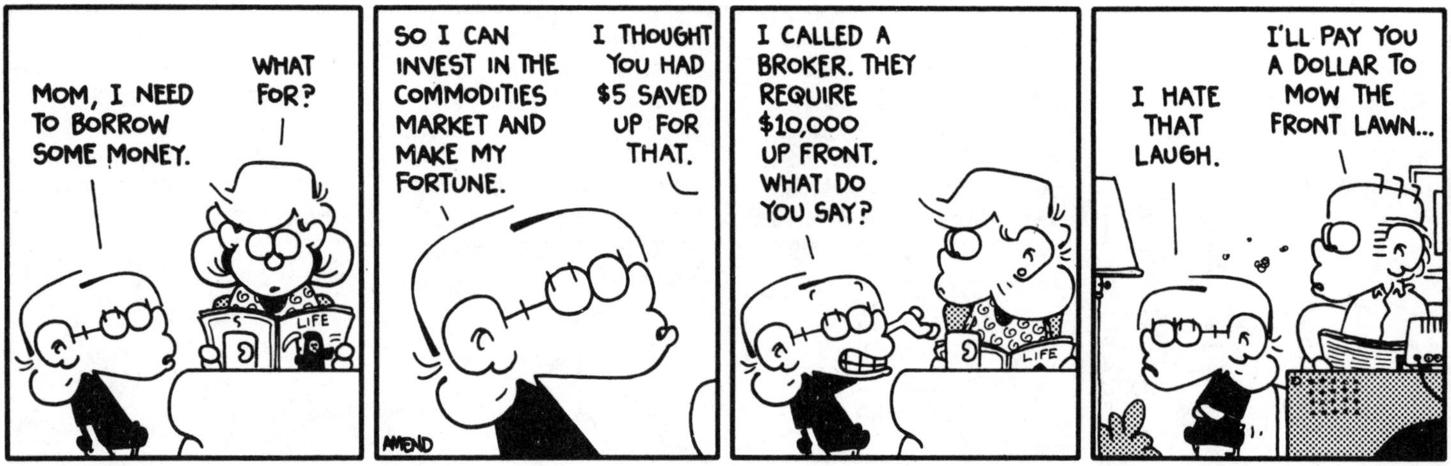
MOM, I NEED TO BORROW SOME MONEY.
WHAT FOR?
LIFE
SO I CAN INVEST IN THE COMMODITIES MARKET AND MAKE MY FORTUNE.
I THOUGHT YOU HAD $5 SAVED UP FOR THAT.
AMEND
I CALLED A BROKER. THEY REQUIRE $10,000 UP FRONT. WHAT DO YOU SAY?
LIFE
I HATE THAT LAUGH.
I'LL PAY YOU A DOLLAR TO MOW THE FRONT LAWN...

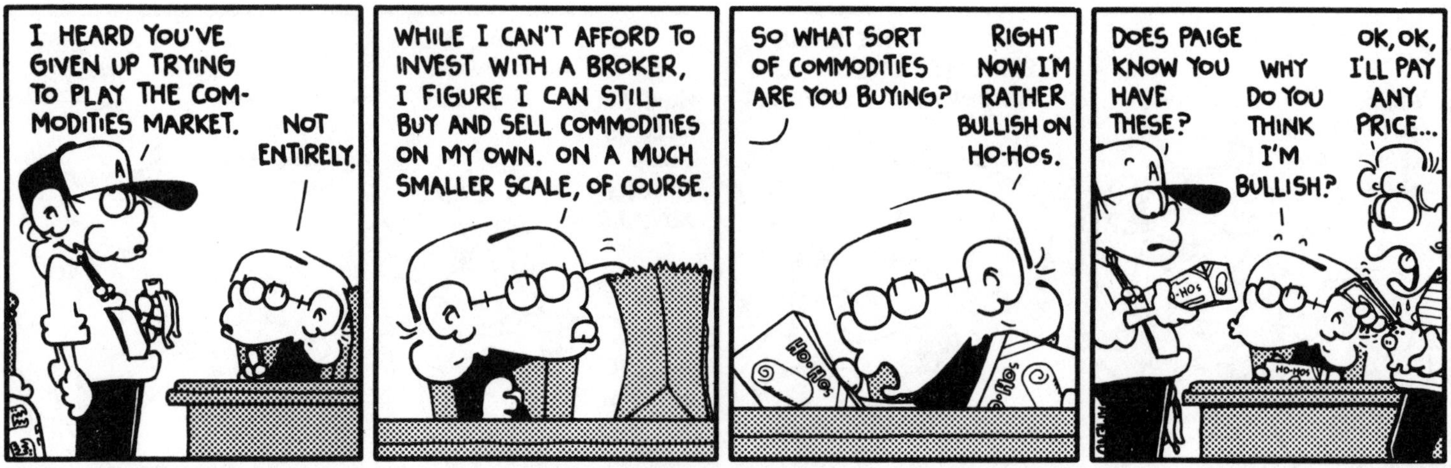
I HEARD YOU'VE GIVEN UP TRYING TO PLAY THE COMMODITIES MARKET.
NOT ENTIRELY.
WHILE I CAN'T AFFORD TO INVEST WITH A BROKER, I FIGURE I CAN STILL BUY AND SELL COMMODITIES ON MY OWN. ON A MUCH SMALLER SCALE, OF COURSE.
SO WHAT SORT OF COMMODITIES ARE YOU BUYING?
RIGHT NOW I'M RATHER BULLISH ON HO-HOS.
Ho-Hos
DOES PAIGE KNOW YOU HAVE THESE?
WHY DO YOU THINK I'M BULLISH?
OK, OK, I'LL PAY ANY PRICE...

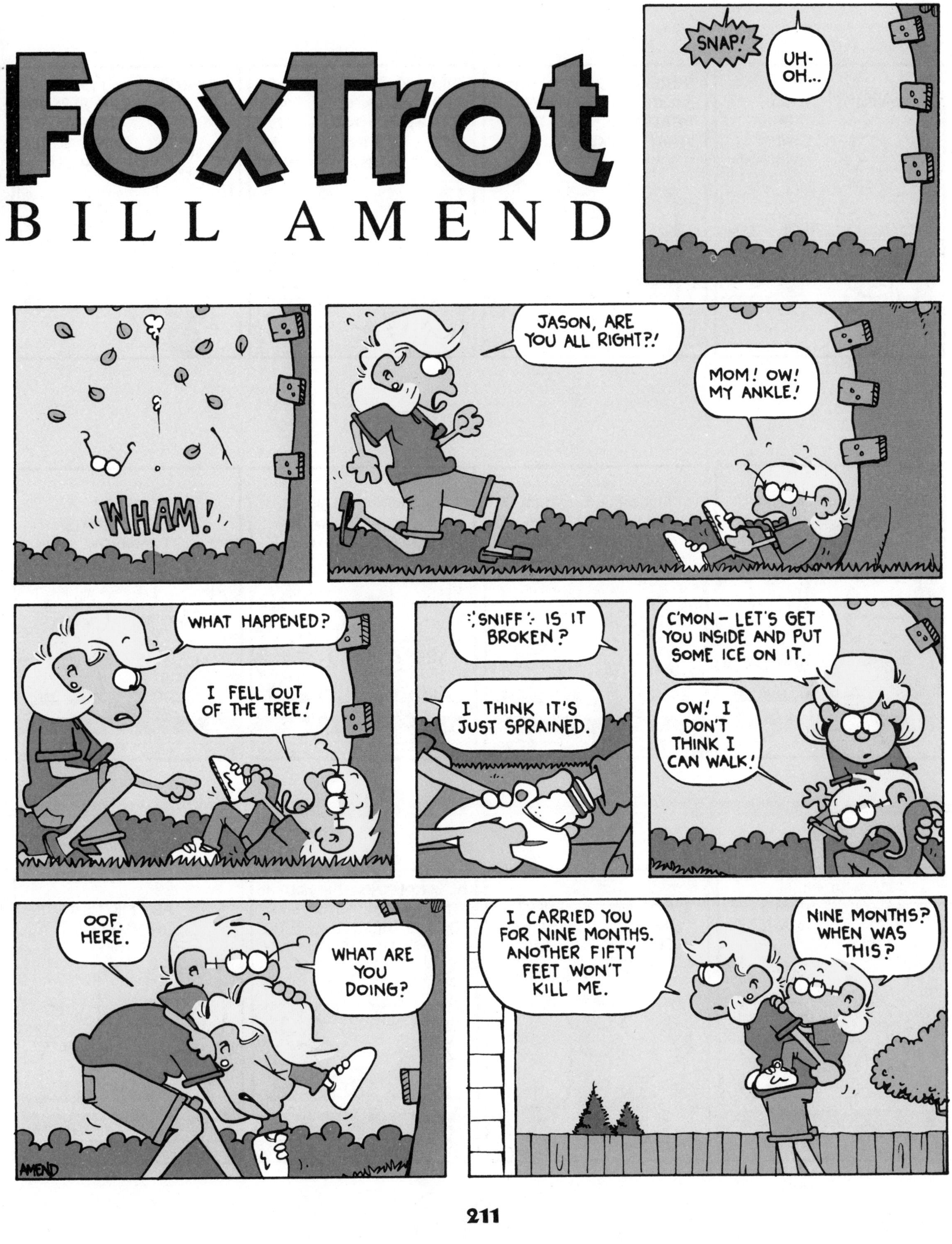
FoxTrot
BILL AMEND
SNAP!
UH-OH...
WHAM!
JASON, ARE YOU ALL RIGHT?!
MOM! OW! MY ANKLE!
WHAT HAPPENED?
I FELL OUT OF THE TREE!
SNIFF IS IT BROKEN?
I THINK IT'S JUST SPRAINED.
C'MON – LET'S GET YOU INSIDE AND PUT SOME ICE ON IT.
OW! I DON'T THINK I CAN WALK!
OOF. HERE.
WHAT ARE YOU DOING?
I CARRIED YOU FOR NINE MONTHS. ANOTHER FIFTY FEET WON'T KILL ME.
NINE MONTHS? WHEN WAS THIS?
AMEND

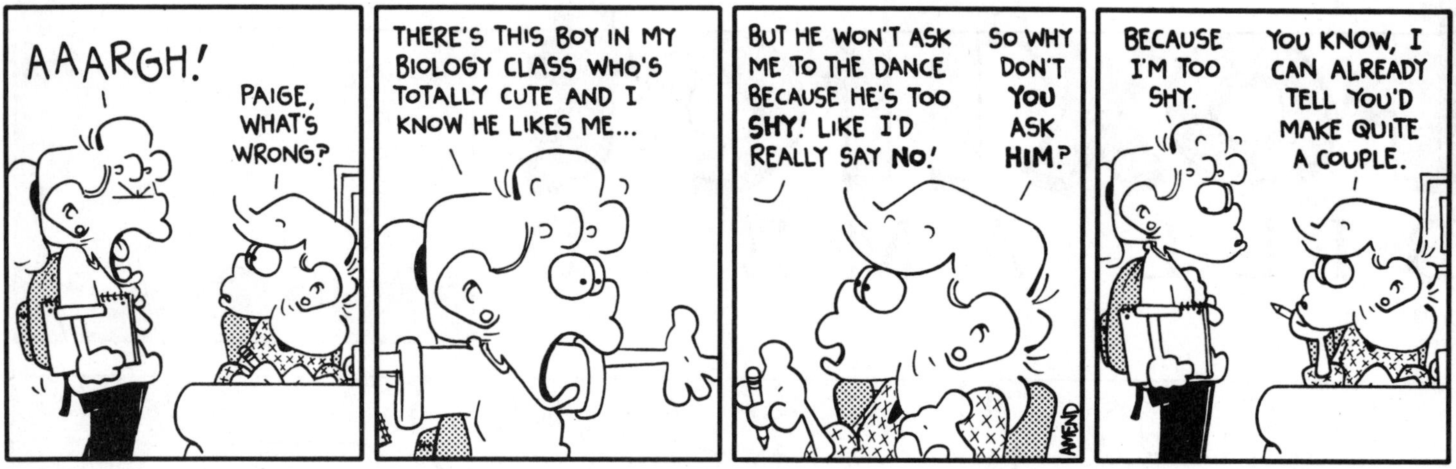
AAARGH!
PAIGE, WHAT'S WRONG?
THERE'S THIS BOY IN MY BIOLOGY CLASS WHO'S TOTALLY CUTE AND I KNOW HE LIKES ME...
BUT HE WON'T ASK ME TO THE DANCE BECAUSE HE'S TOO SHY! LIKE I'D REALLY SAY NO!
SO WHY DON'T YOU ASK HIM?
BECAUSE I'M TOO SHY.
YOU KNOW, I CAN ALREADY TELL YOU'D MAKE QUITE A COUPLE.
AMEND

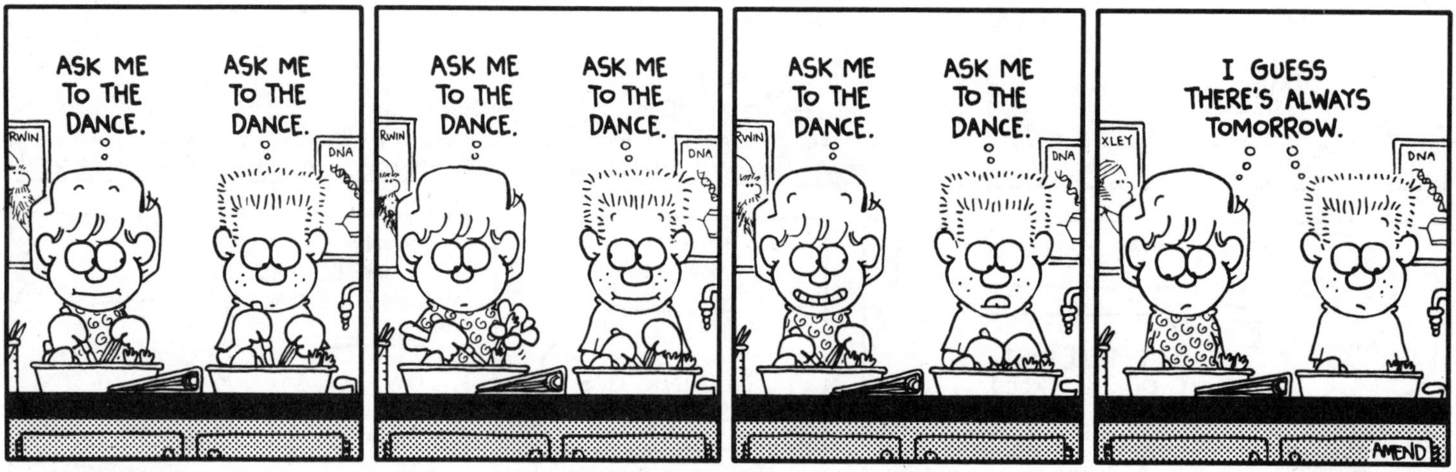
ASK ME TO THE DANCE.
ASK ME TO THE DANCE.
ASK ME TO THE DANCE.
ASK ME TO THE DANCE.
ASK ME TO THE DANCE.
ASK ME TO THE DANCE.
I GUESS THERE'S ALWAYS TOMORROW.
DNA
AMEND

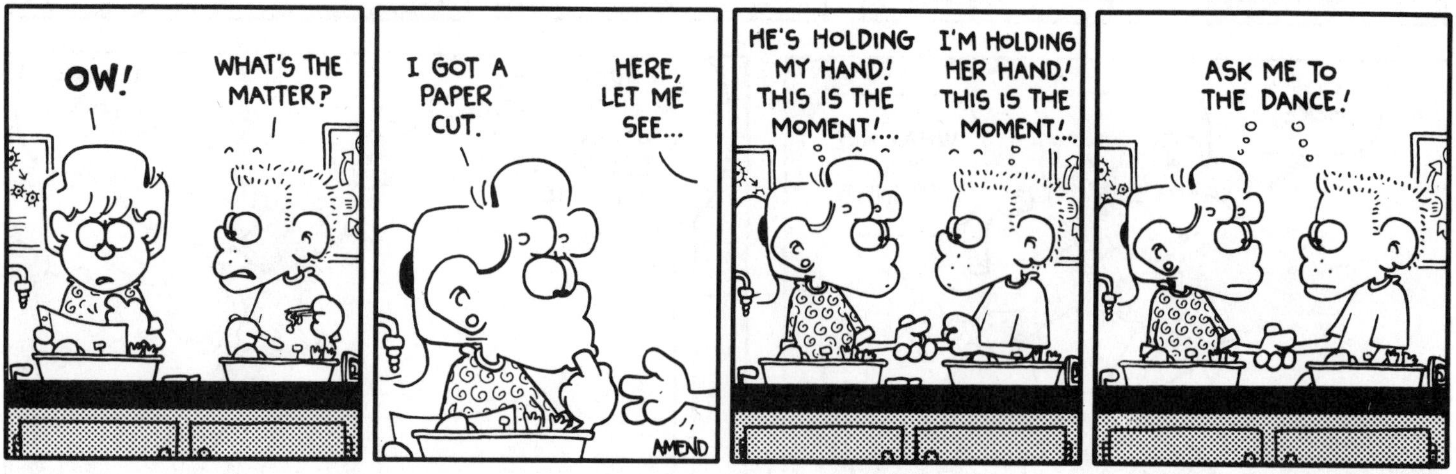
OW!
WHAT'S THE MATTER?
I GOT A PAPER CUT.
HERE, LET ME SEE...
AMEND
HE'S HOLDING MY HAND! THIS IS THE MOMENT!...
I'M HOLDING HER HAND! THIS IS THE MOMENT!...
ASK ME TO THE DANCE!

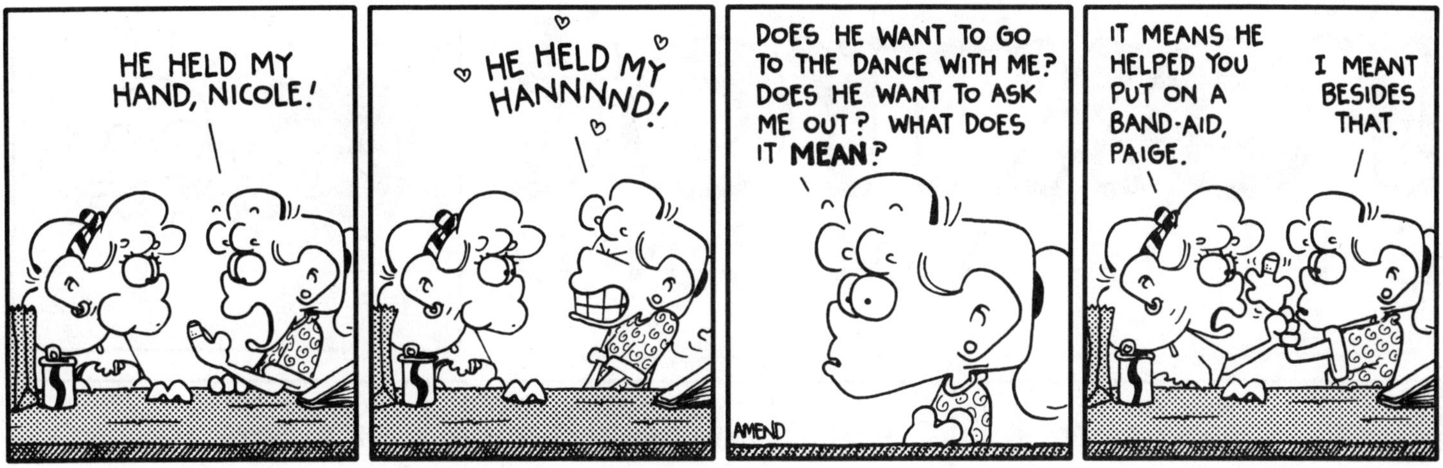
HE HELD MY HAND, NICOLE!
HE HELD MY HANNNNND!
DOES HE WANT TO GO TO THE DANCE WITH ME? DOES HE WANT TO ASK ME OUT? WHAT DOES IT **MEAN**?
AMEND
IT MEANS HE HELPED YOU PUT ON A BAND-AID, PAIGE.
I MEANT BESIDES THAT.

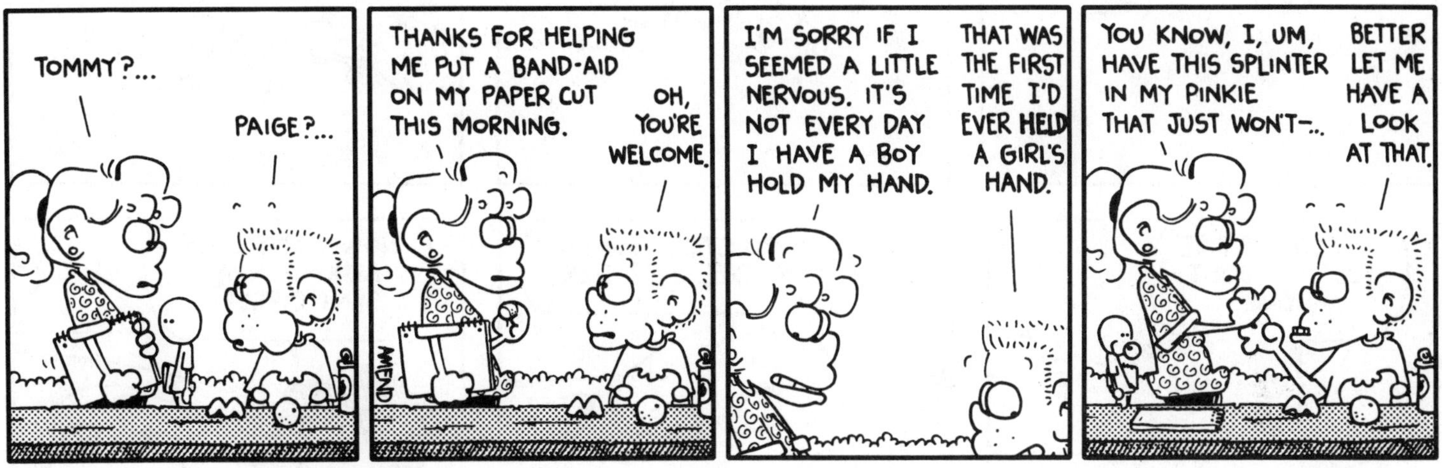
TOMMY?...
PAIGE?...
AMEND
THANKS FOR HELPING ME PUT A BAND-AID ON MY PAPER CUT THIS MORNING.
OH, YOU'RE WELCOME.
I'M SORRY IF I SEEMED A LITTLE NERVOUS. IT'S NOT EVERY DAY I HAVE A BOY HOLD MY HAND.
THAT WAS THE FIRST TIME I'D EVER **HELD** A GIRL'S HAND.
YOU KNOW, I, UM, HAVE THIS SPLINTER IN MY PINKIE THAT JUST WON'T-..
BETTER LET ME HAVE A LOOK AT THAT.

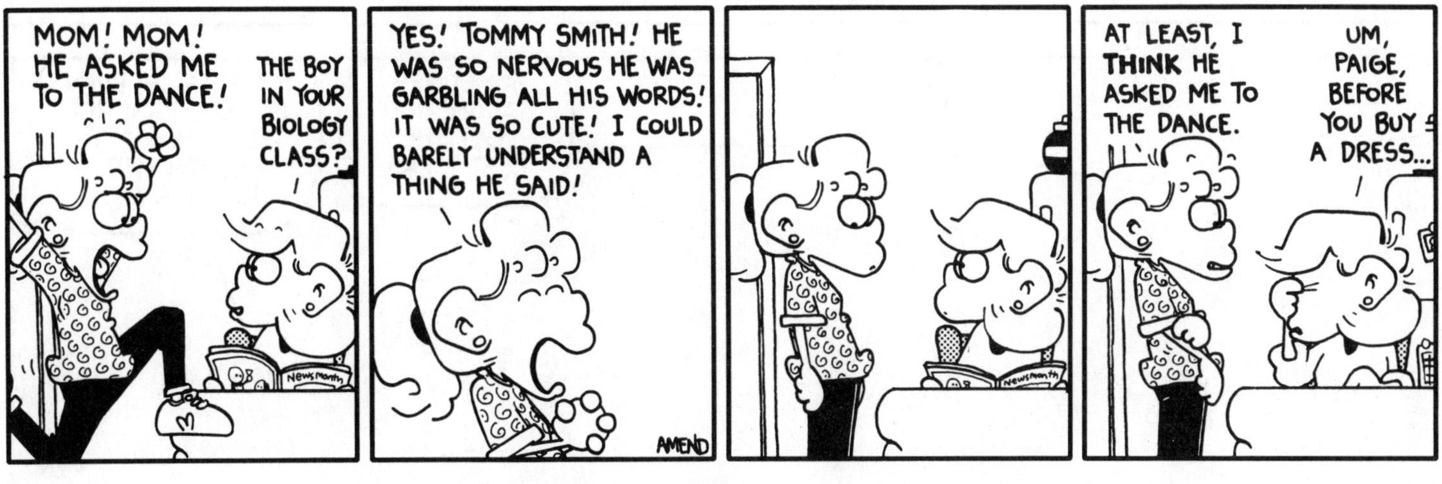
MOM! MOM! HE ASKED ME TO THE DANCE!
THE BOY IN YOUR BIOLOGY CLASS?
YES! TOMMY SMITH! HE WAS SO NERVOUS HE WAS GARBLING ALL HIS WORDS! IT WAS SO CUTE! I COULD BARELY UNDERSTAND A THING HE SAID!
AMEND
AT LEAST, I **THINK** HE ASKED ME TO THE DANCE.
UM, PAIGE, BEFORE YOU BUY A DRESS...

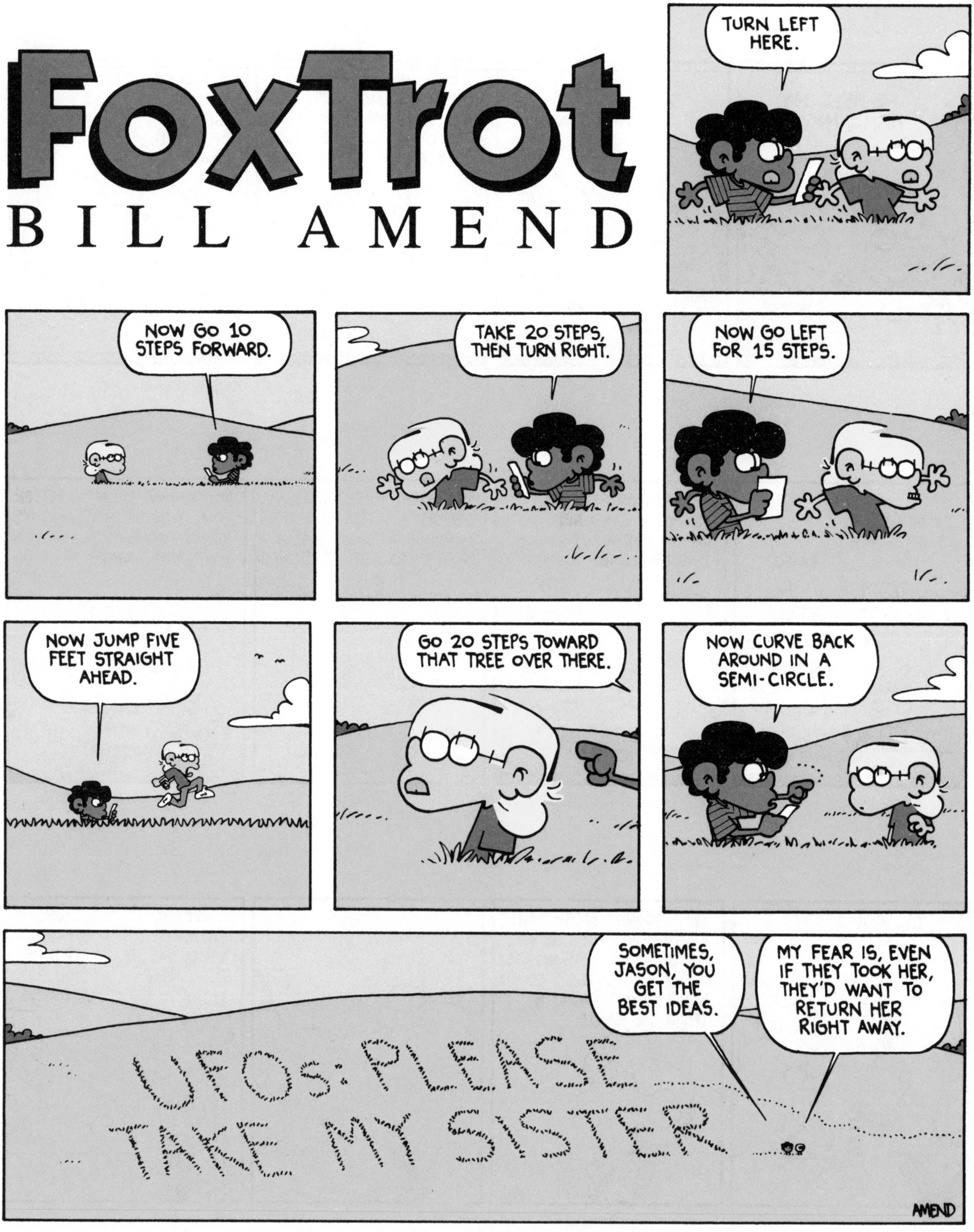
FoxTrot
BILL AMEND
TURN LEFT HERE.
NOW GO 10 STEPS FORWARD.
TAKE 20 STEPS, THEN TURN RIGHT.
NOW GO LEFT FOR 15 STEPS.
NOW JUMP FIVE FEET STRAIGHT AHEAD.
GO 20 STEPS TOWARD THAT TREE OVER THERE.
NOW CURVE BACK AROUND IN A SEMI-CIRCLE.
UFOS: PLEASE TAKE MY SISTER
SOMETIMES, JASON, YOU GET THE BEST IDEAS.
MY FEAR IS, EVEN IF THEY TOOK HER, THEY'D WANT TO RETURN HER RIGHT AWAY.
AMEND

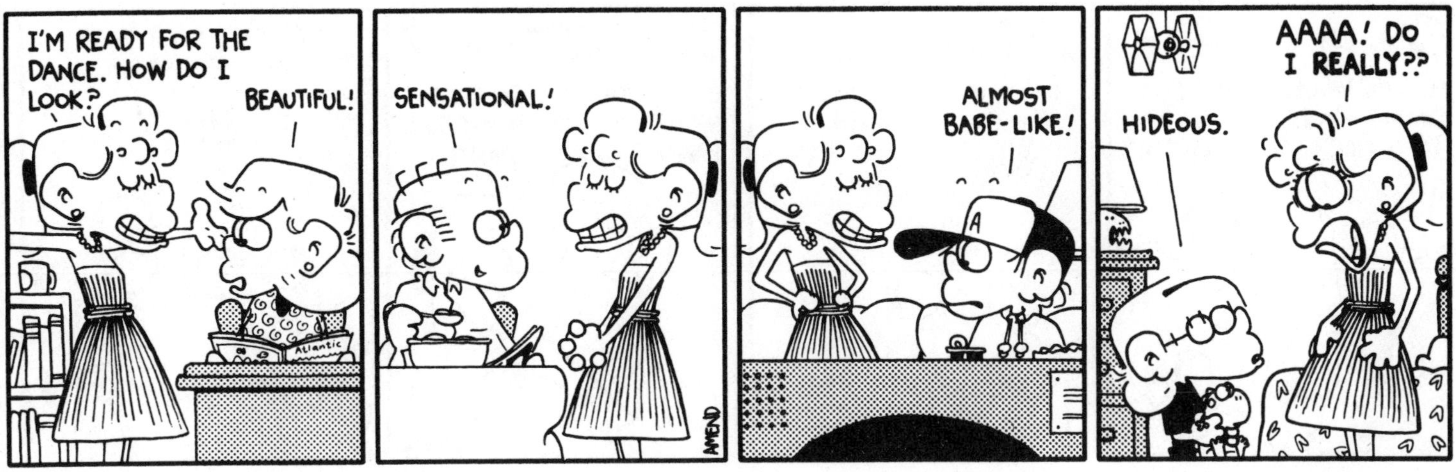

I'M READY FOR THE DANCE. HOW DO I LOOK?
BEAUTIFUL!
SENSATIONAL!
ALMOST BABE-LIKE!
HIDEOUS.
AAAA! DO I REALLY??
AMEND

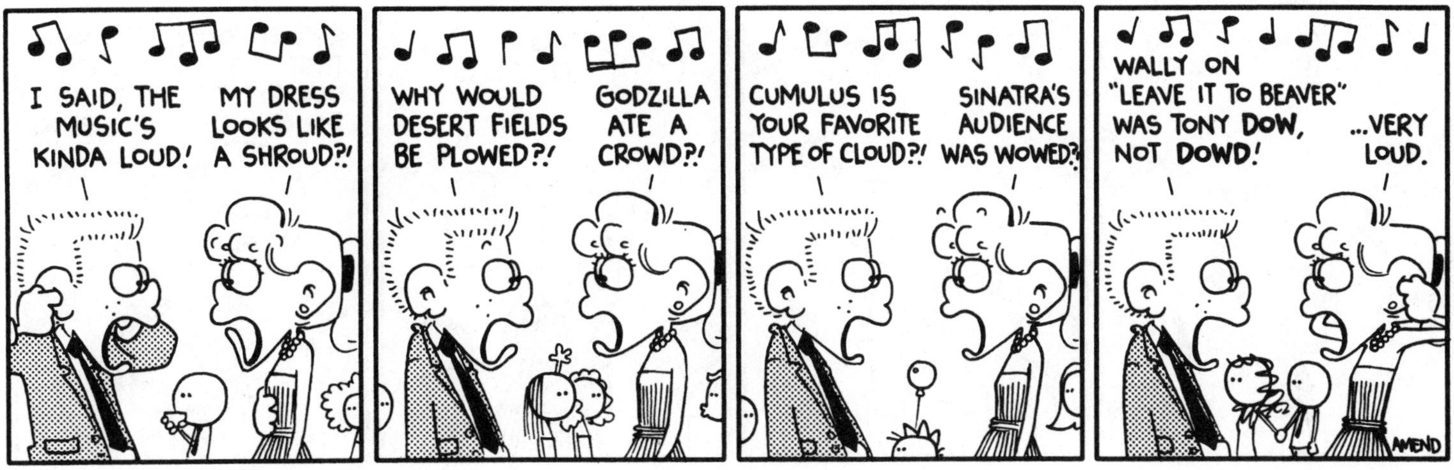

I SAID, THE MUSIC'S KINDA LOUD!
MY DRESS LOOKS LIKE A SHROUD?!
WHY WOULD DESERT FIELDS BE PLOWED?!
GODZILLA ATE A CROWD?!
CUMULUS IS YOUR FAVORITE TYPE OF CLOUD?!
SINATRA'S AUDIENCE WAS WOWED?!
WALLY ON "LEAVE IT TO BEAVER" WAS TONY DOW, NOT DOWD!
...VERY LOUD.
AMEND

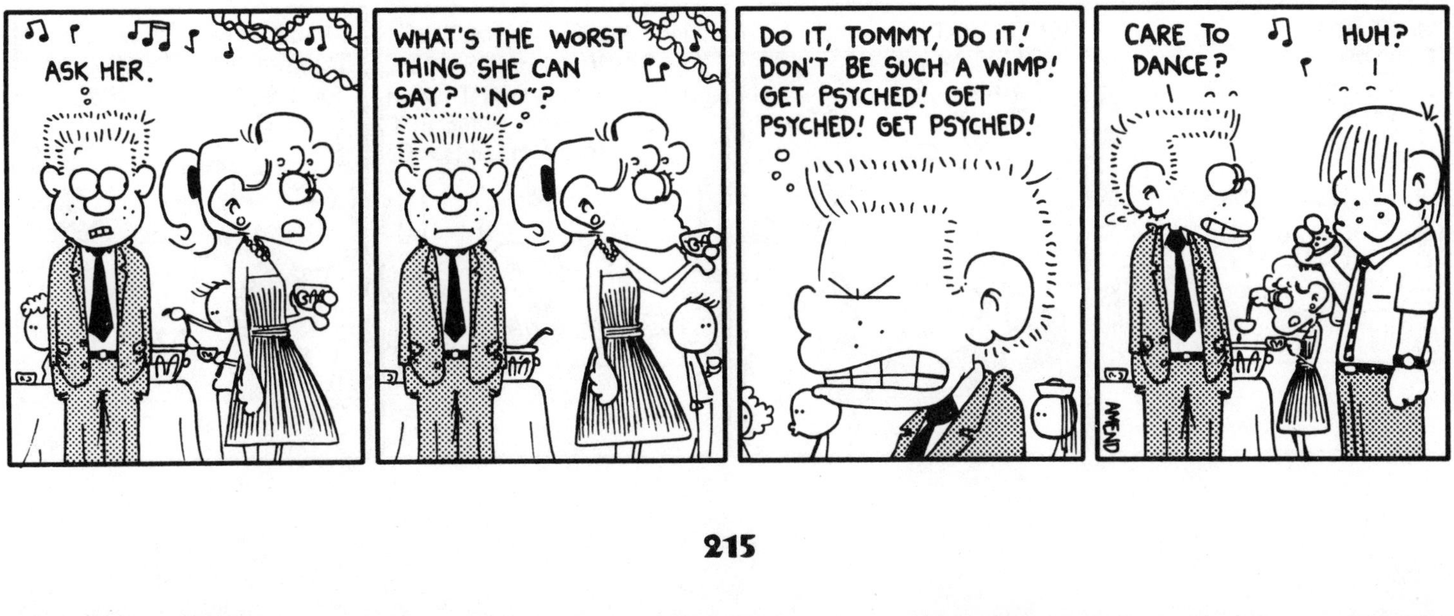

ASK HER.
WHAT'S THE WORST THING SHE CAN SAY? "NO"?
DO IT, TOMMY, DO IT! DON'T BE SUCH A WIMP! GET PSYCHED! GET PSYCHED! GET PSYCHED!
CARE TO DANCE?
HUH?
AMEND

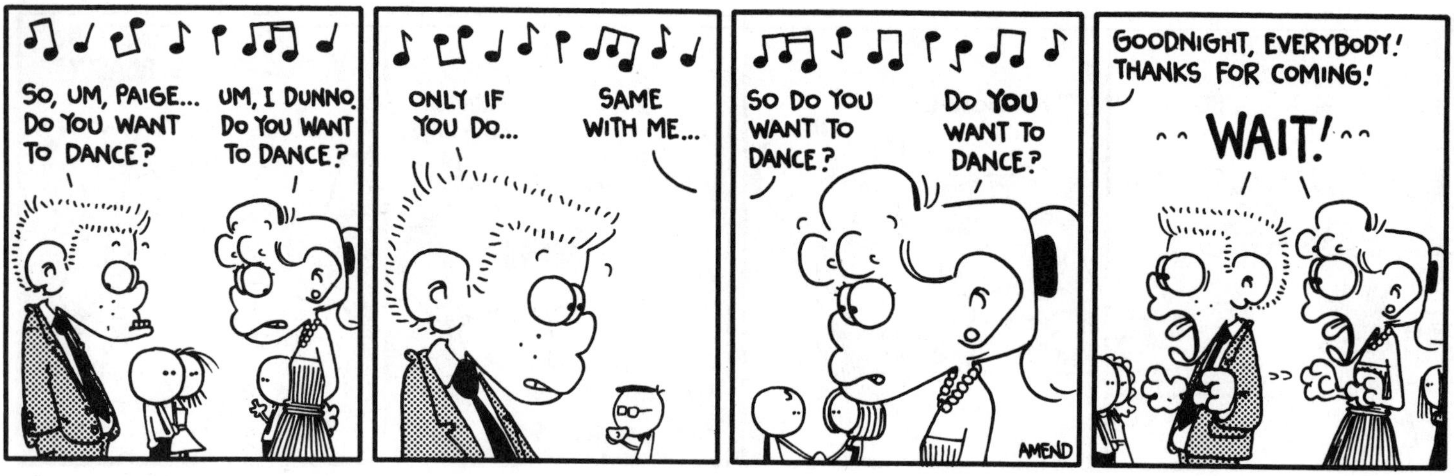
SO, UM, PAIGE... DO YOU WANT TO DANCE?
UM, I DUNNO. DO YOU WANT TO DANCE?
ONLY IF YOU DO...
SAME WITH ME...
SO DO YOU WANT TO DANCE?
DO YOU WANT TO DANCE?
AMEND
GOODNIGHT, EVERYBODY! THANKS FOR COMING!
WAIT!

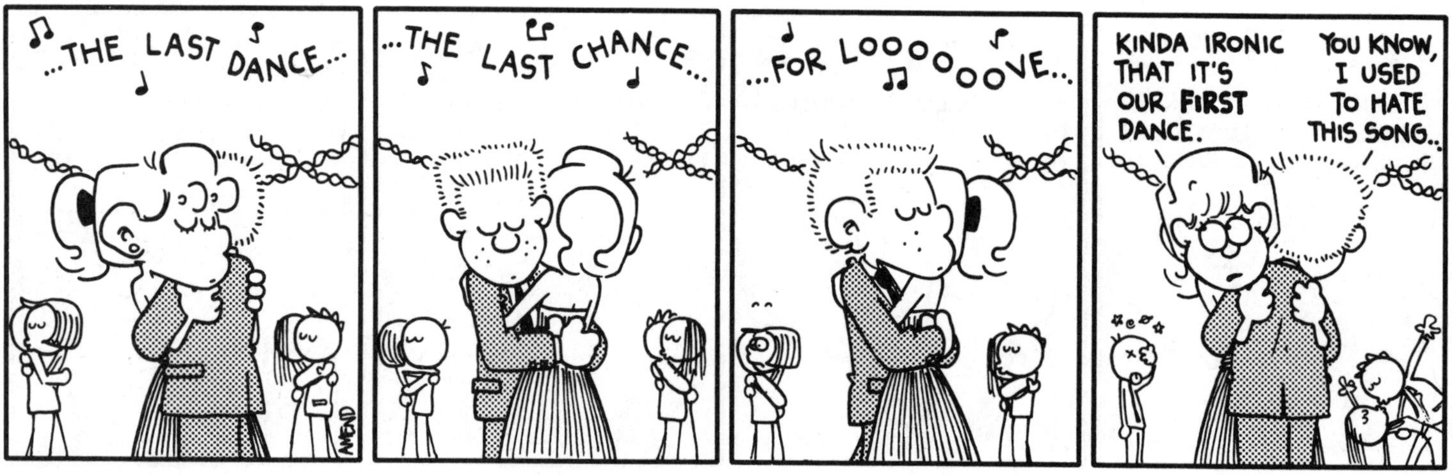
...THE LAST DANCE...
AMEND
...THE LAST CHANCE...
...FOR LOOOOOOOVE...
KINDA IRONIC THAT IT'S OUR FIRST DANCE.
YOU KNOW, I USED TO HATE THIS SONG..

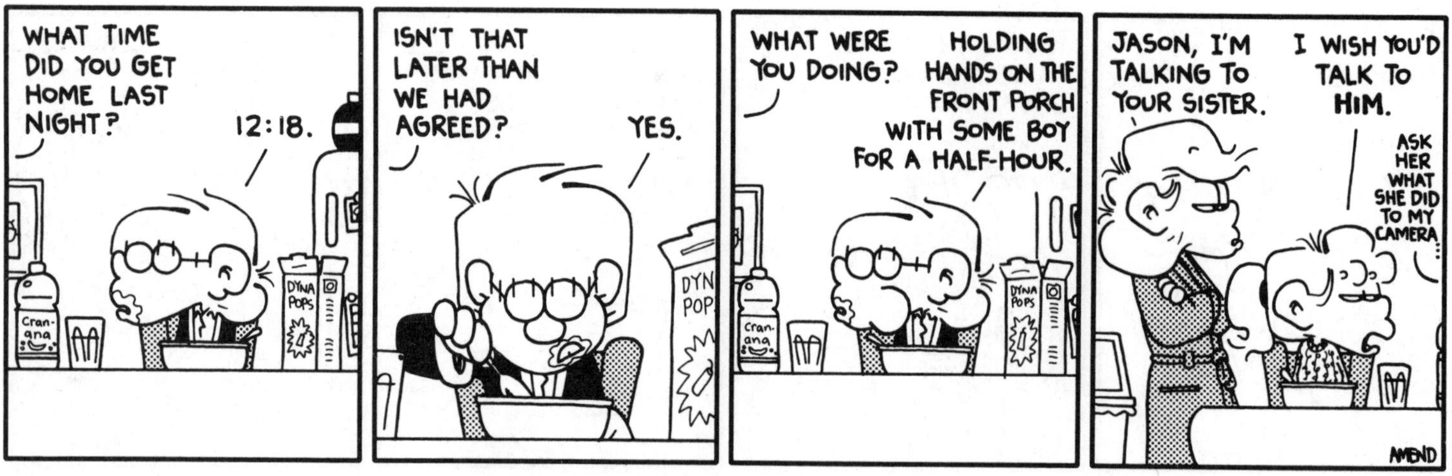
WHAT TIME DID YOU GET HOME LAST NIGHT?
12:18.
Cran-ana
DYNA POPS
ISN'T THAT LATER THAN WE HAD AGREED?
YES.
WHAT WERE YOU DOING?
HOLDING HANDS ON THE FRONT PORCH WITH SOME BOY FOR A HALF-HOUR.
JASON, I'M TALKING TO YOUR SISTER.
I WISH YOU'D TALK TO HIM.
ASK HER WHAT SHE DID TO MY CAMERA...
AMEND

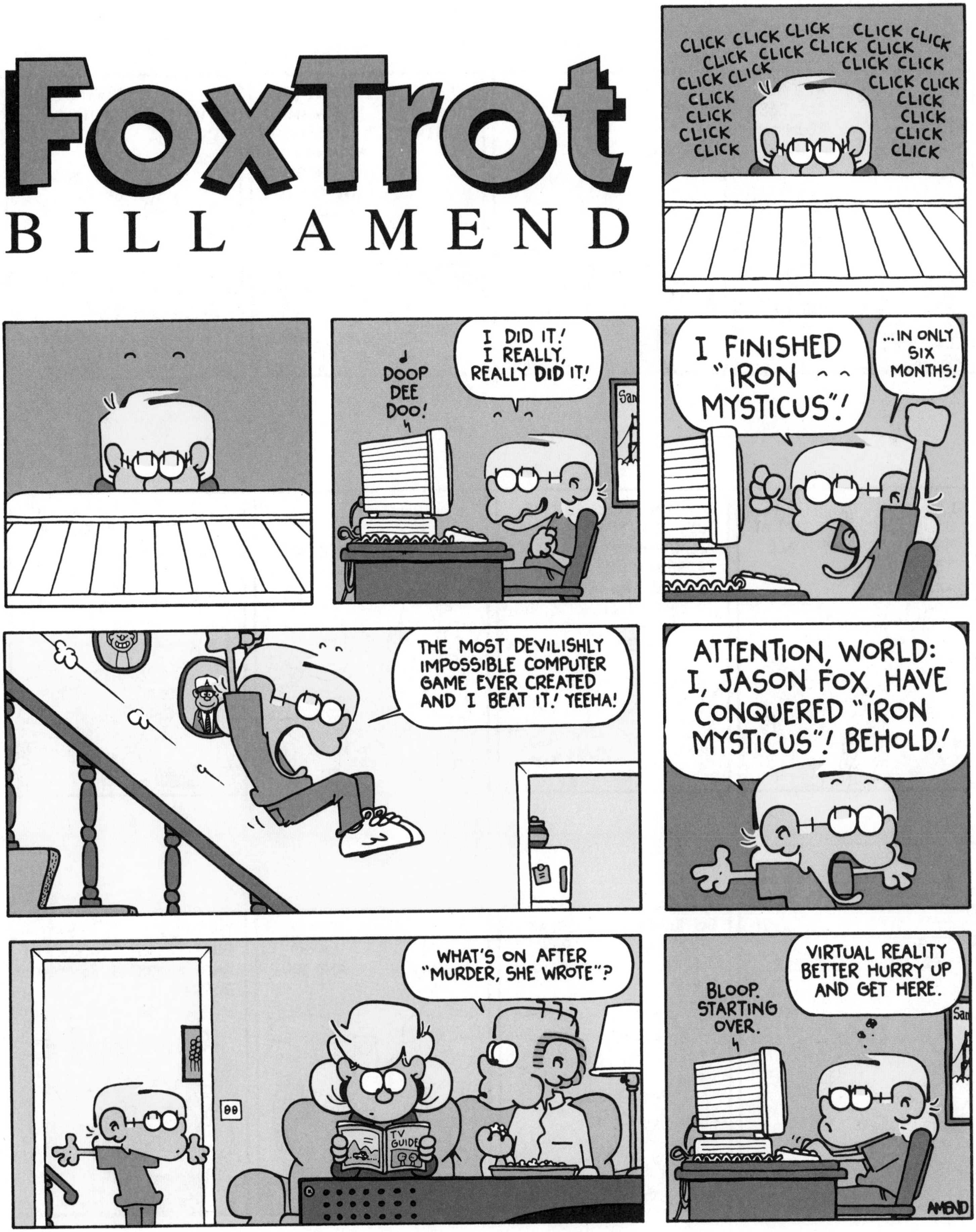
FoxTrot
BILL AMEND
CLICK CLICK
DOOP DEE DOO!
I DID IT! I REALLY, REALLY DID IT!
I FINISHED "IRON MYSTICUS"!
...IN ONLY SIX MONTHS!
THE MOST DEVILISHLY IMPOSSIBLE COMPUTER GAME EVER CREATED AND I BEAT IT! YEEHA!
ATTENTION, WORLD: I, JASON FOX, HAVE CONQUERED "IRON MYSTICUS"! BEHOLD!
WHAT'S ON AFTER "MURDER, SHE WROTE"?
TV GUIDE
BLOOP. STARTING OVER.
VIRTUAL REALITY BETTER HURRY UP AND GET HERE.
AMEND

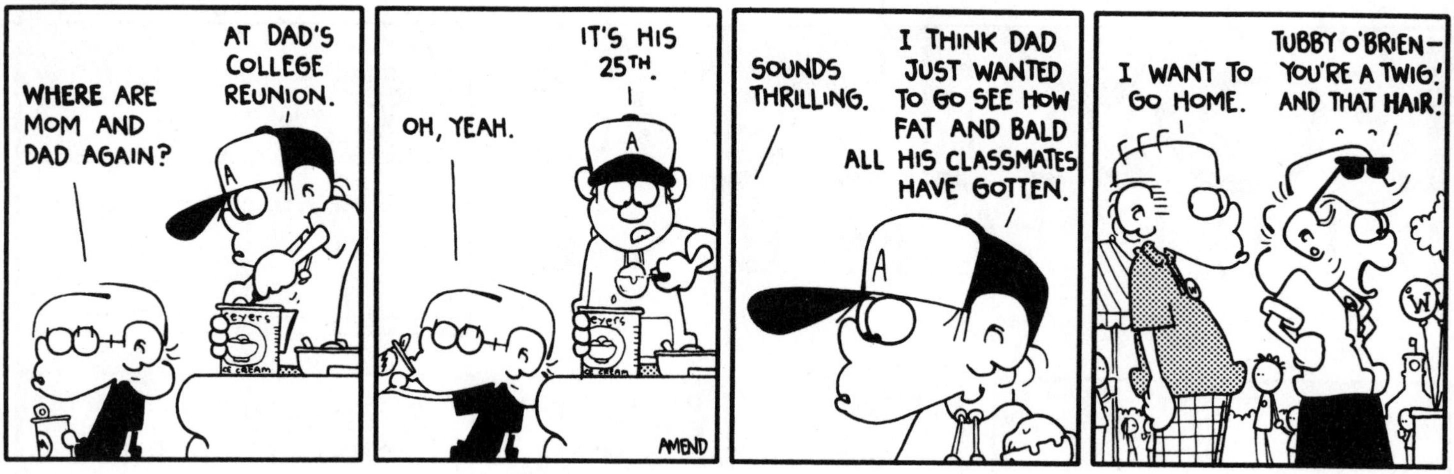
WHERE ARE MOM AND DAD AGAIN?
AT DAD'S COLLEGE REUNION.
OH, YEAH.
IT'S HIS 25TH.
SOUNDS THRILLING.
I THINK DAD JUST WANTED TO GO SEE HOW FAT AND BALD ALL HIS CLASSMATES HAVE GOTTEN.
I WANT TO GO HOME.
TUBBY O'BRIEN— YOU'RE A TWIG! AND THAT HAIR!
AMEND

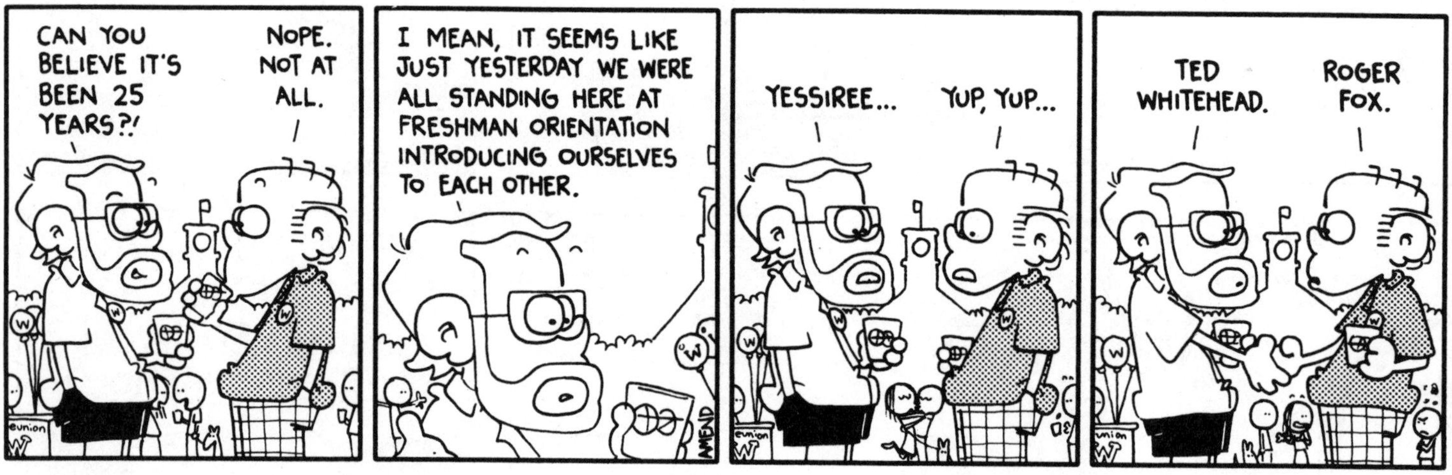
CAN YOU BELIEVE IT'S BEEN 25 YEARS?!
NOPE. NOT AT ALL.
I MEAN, IT SEEMS LIKE JUST YESTERDAY WE WERE ALL STANDING HERE AT FRESHMAN ORIENTATION INTRODUCING OURSELVES TO EACH OTHER.
YESSIREE...
YUP, YUP...
TED WHITEHEAD.
ROGER FOX.
AMEND

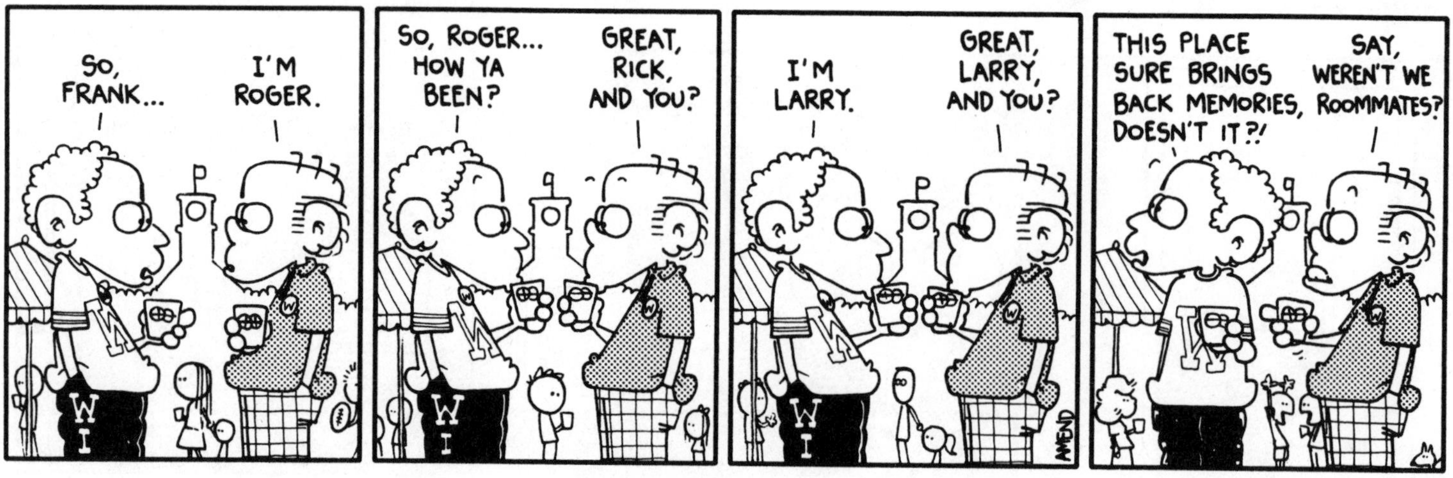
SO, FRANK...
I'M ROGER.
SO, ROGER... HOW YA BEEN?
GREAT, RICK, AND YOU?
I'M LARRY.
GREAT, LARRY, AND YOU?
THIS PLACE SURE BRINGS BACK MEMORIES, DOESN'T IT?!
SAY, WEREN'T WE ROOMMATES?
AMEND

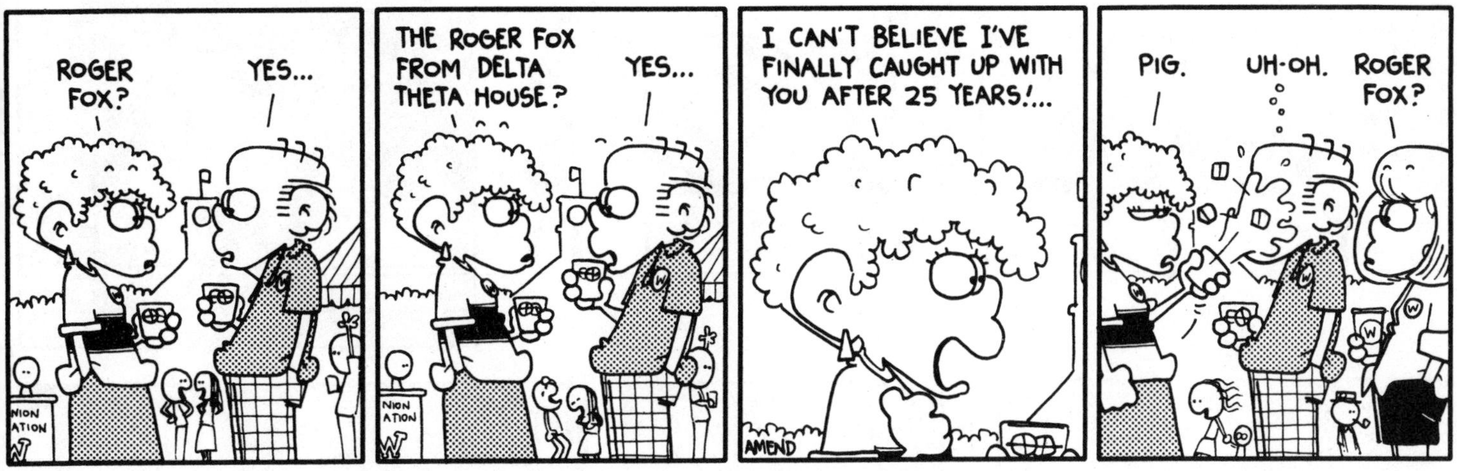
ROGER FOX?
YES...
THE ROGER FOX FROM DELTA THETA HOUSE?
YES...
I CAN'T BELIEVE I'VE FINALLY CAUGHT UP WITH YOU AFTER 25 YEARS!...
AMEND
PIG.
UH-OH.
ROGER FOX?

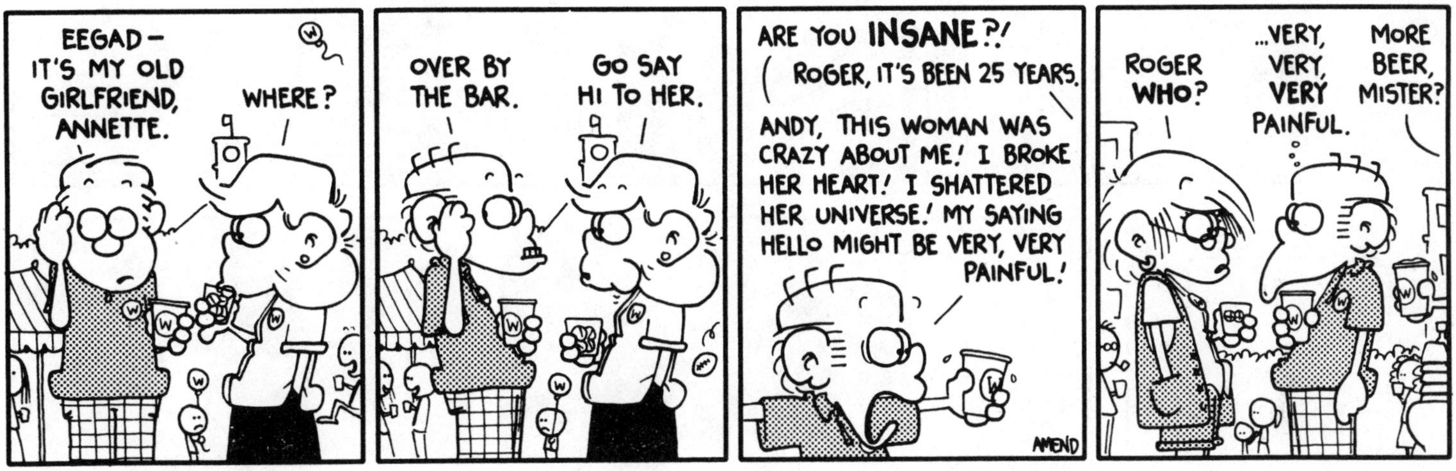
EEGAD – IT'S MY OLD GIRLFRIEND, ANNETTE.
WHERE?
OVER BY THE BAR.
GO SAY HI TO HER.
ARE YOU INSANE?!
ROGER, IT'S BEEN 25 YEARS.
ANDY, THIS WOMAN WAS CRAZY ABOUT ME! I BROKE HER HEART! I SHATTERED HER UNIVERSE! MY SAYING HELLO MIGHT BE VERY, VERY PAINFUL!
AMEND
ROGER WHO?
...VERY, VERY, VERY PAINFUL.
MORE BEER, MISTER?

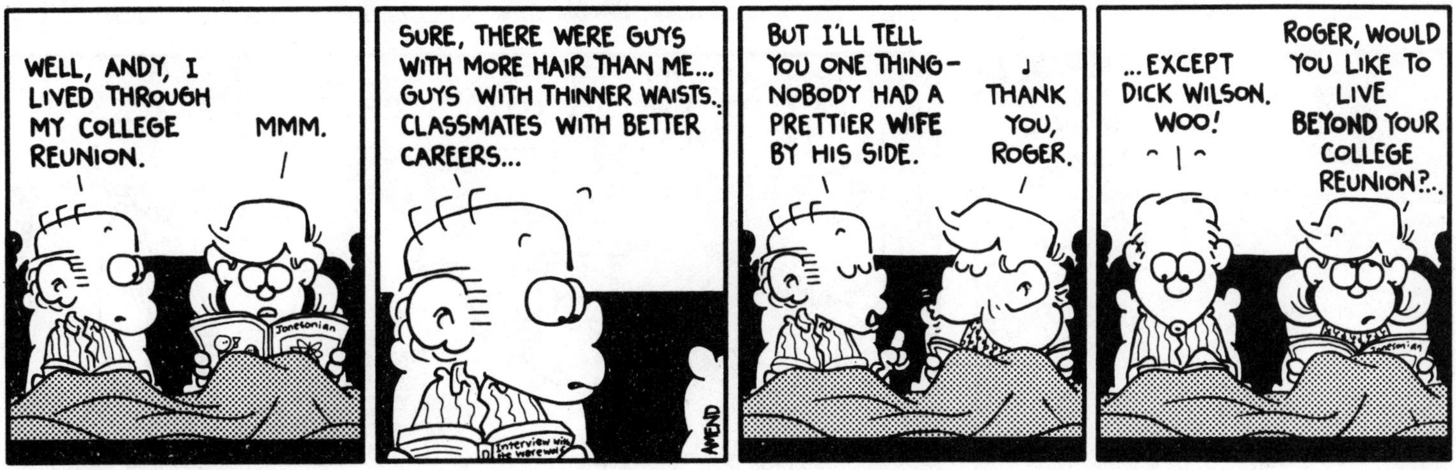
WELL, ANDY, I LIVED THROUGH MY COLLEGE REUNION.
MMM.
SURE, THERE WERE GUYS WITH MORE HAIR THAN ME... GUYS WITH THINNER WAISTS... CLASSMATES WITH BETTER CAREERS...
AMEND
BUT I'LL TELL YOU ONE THING – NOBODY HAD A PRETTIER WIFE BY HIS SIDE.
THANK YOU, ROGER.
...EXCEPT DICK WILSON. WOO!
ROGER, WOULD YOU LIKE TO LIVE BEYOND YOUR COLLEGE REUNION?..

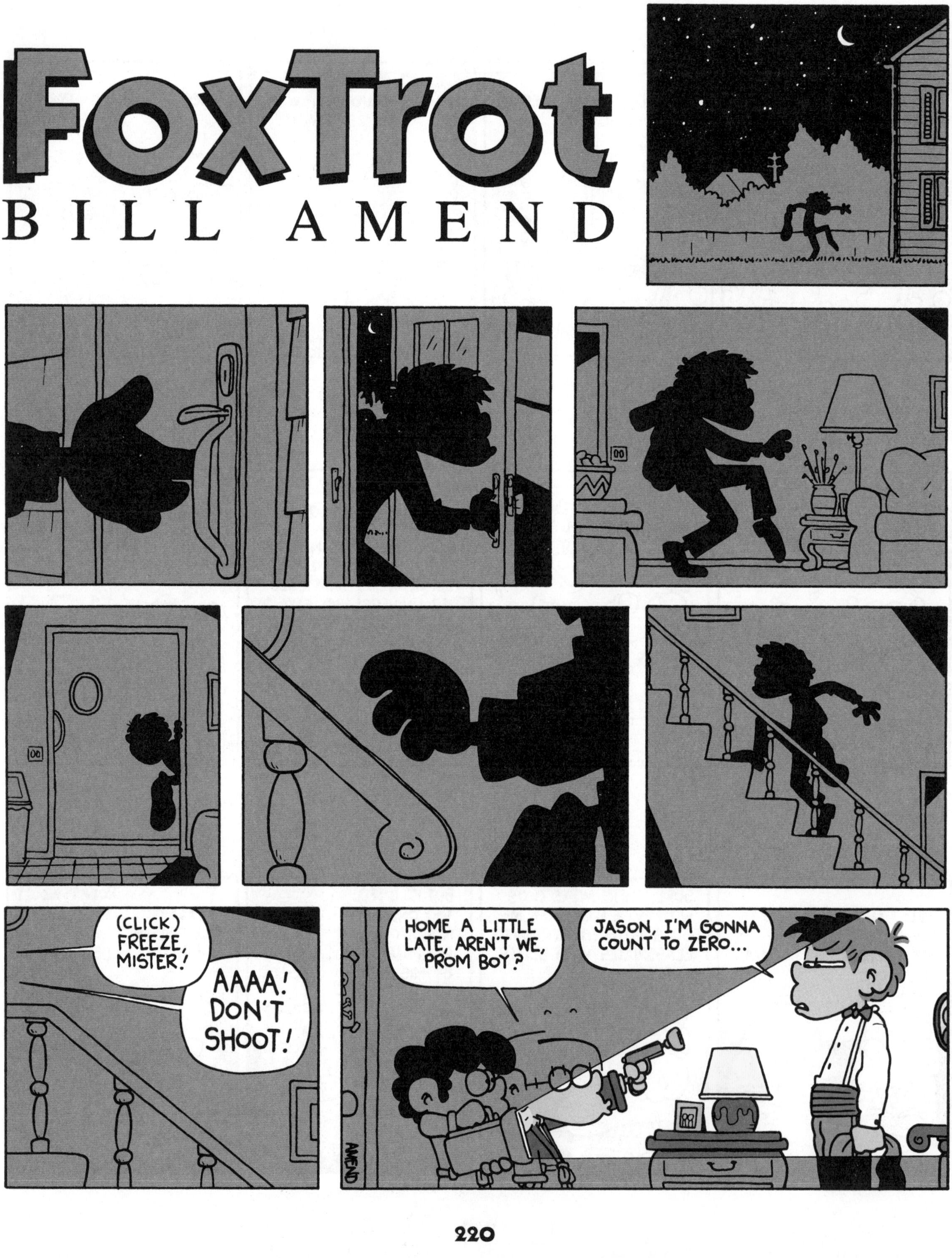
FoxTrot
BILL AMEND
(CLICK) FREEZE, MISTER!
AAAA! DON'T SHOOT!
HOME A LITTLE LATE, AREN'T WE, PROM BOY?
JASON, I'M GONNA COUNT TO ZERO...
AMEND

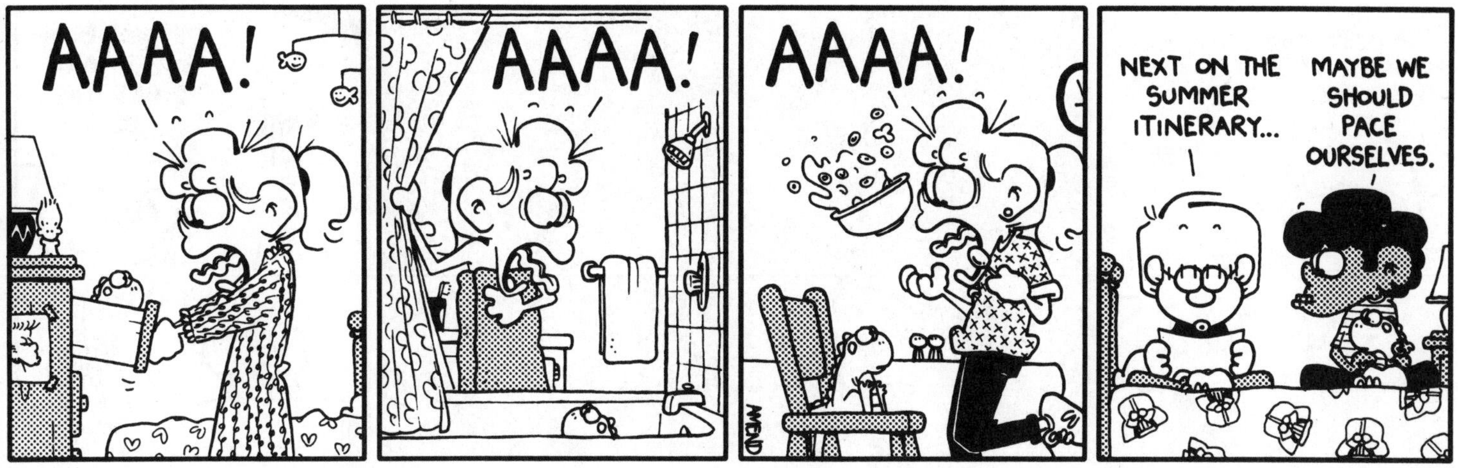
AAAA!
AAAA!
AAAA!
NEXT ON THE SUMMER ITINERARY...
MAYBE WE SHOULD PACE OURSELVES.
AMEND

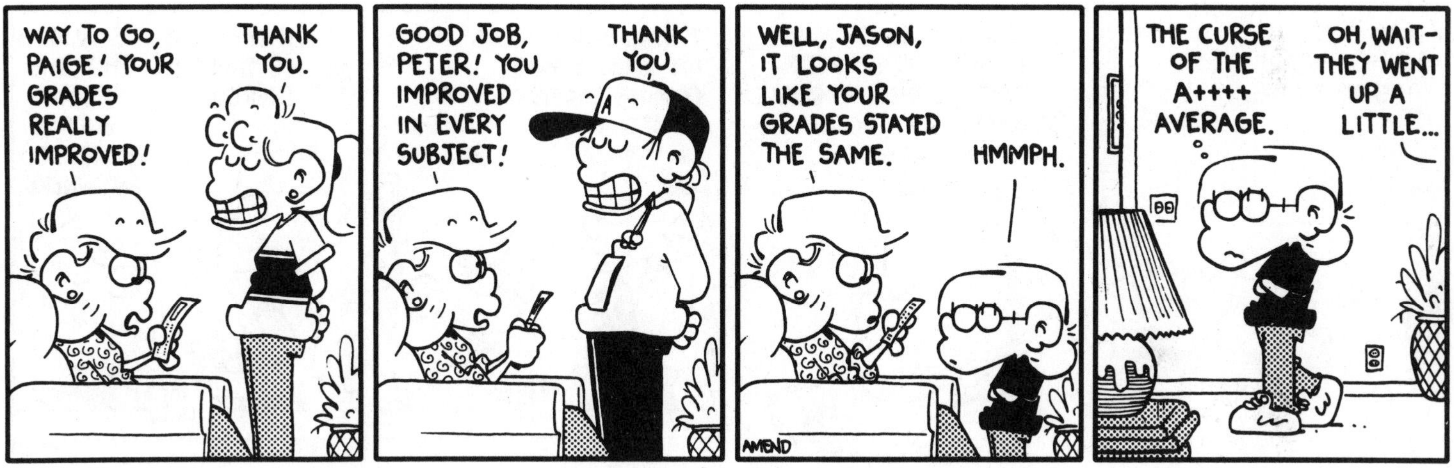
WAY TO GO, PAIGE! YOUR GRADES REALLY IMPROVED!
THANK YOU.
GOOD JOB, PETER! YOU IMPROVED IN EVERY SUBJECT!
THANK YOU.
WELL, JASON, IT LOOKS LIKE YOUR GRADES STAYED THE SAME.
HMMPH.
THE CURSE OF THE A++++ AVERAGE.
OH, WAIT- THEY WENT UP A LITTLE...
AMEND

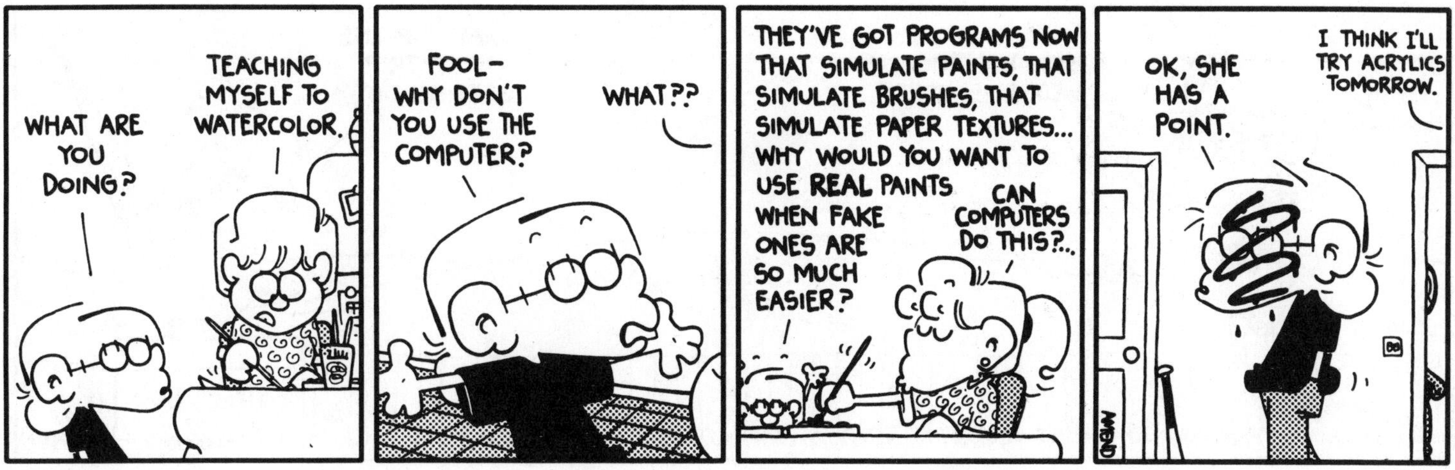
WHAT ARE YOU DOING?
TEACHING MYSELF TO WATERCOLOR.
FOOL- WHY DON'T YOU USE THE COMPUTER?
WHAT??
THEY'VE GOT PROGRAMS NOW THAT SIMULATE PAINTS, THAT SIMULATE BRUSHES, THAT SIMULATE PAPER TEXTURES... WHY WOULD YOU WANT TO USE REAL PAINTS WHEN FAKE ONES ARE SO MUCH EASIER?
CAN COMPUTERS DO THIS?..
OK, SHE HAS A POINT.
I THINK I'LL TRY ACRYLICS TOMORROW.
AMEND

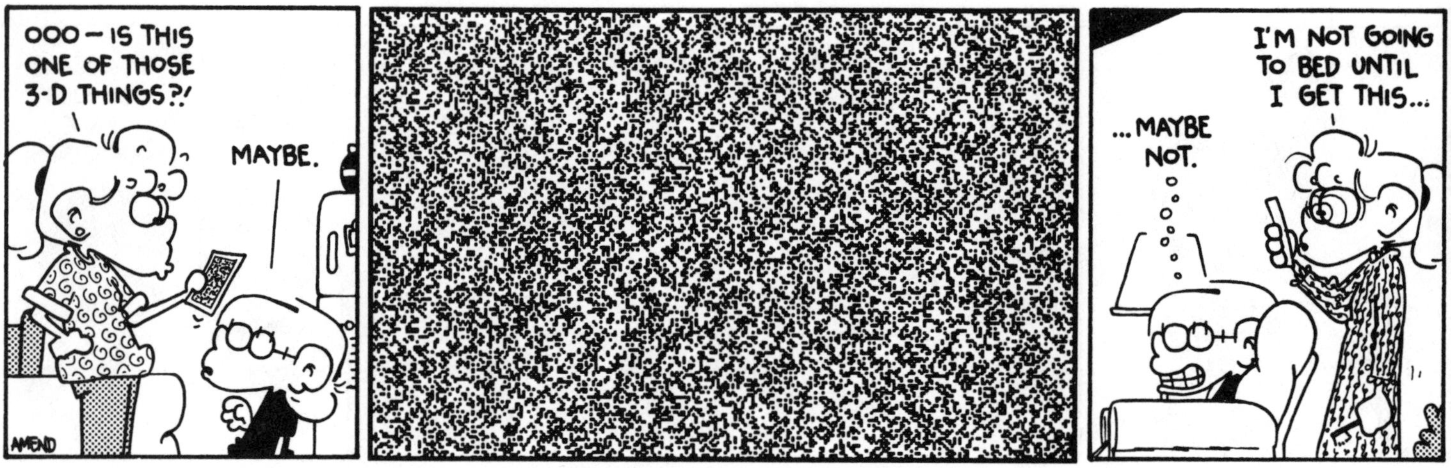
OOO – IS THIS ONE OF THOSE 3-D THINGS?!
MAYBE.
...MAYBE NOT.
I'M NOT GOING TO BED UNTIL I GET THIS...
AMEND

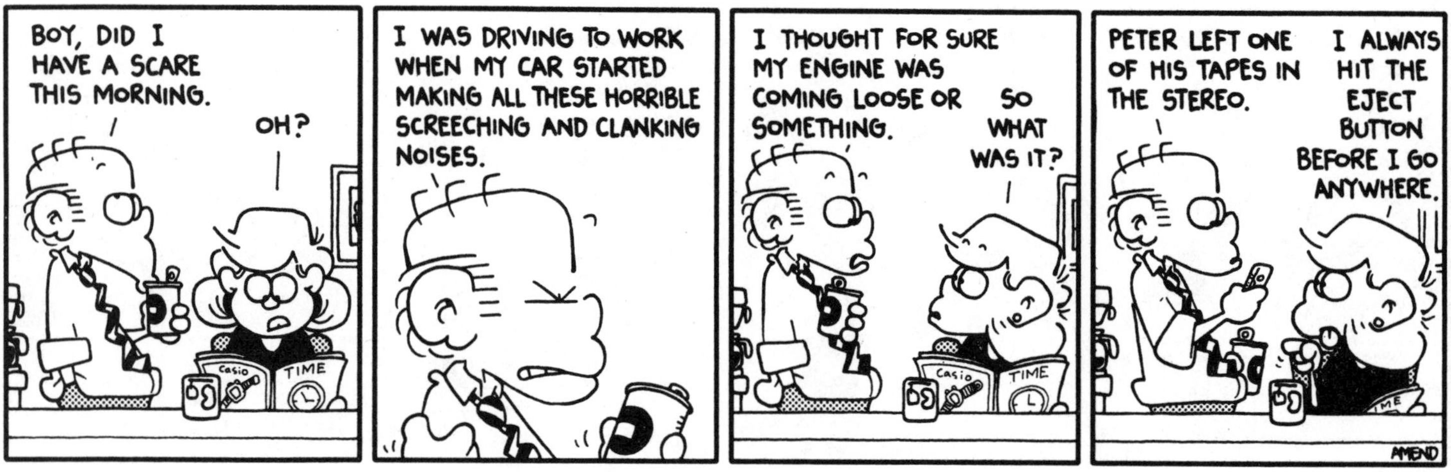
BOY, DID I HAVE A SCARE THIS MORNING.
OH?
I WAS DRIVING TO WORK WHEN MY CAR STARTED MAKING ALL THESE HORRIBLE SCREECHING AND CLANKING NOISES.
I THOUGHT FOR SURE MY ENGINE WAS COMING LOOSE OR SOMETHING.
SO WHAT WAS IT?
PETER LEFT ONE OF HIS TAPES IN THE STEREO.
I ALWAYS HIT THE EJECT BUTTON BEFORE I GO ANYWHERE.
AMEND

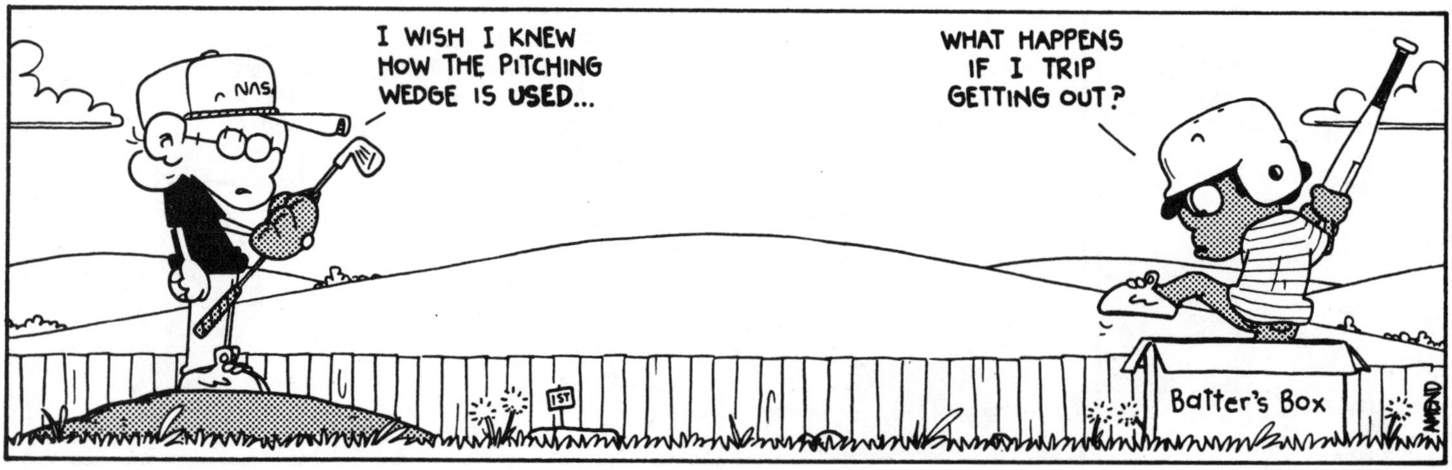
I WISH I KNEW HOW THE PITCHING WEDGE IS USED...
WHAT HAPPENS IF I TRIP GETTING OUT?
NASA
1ST
Batter's Box
AMEND

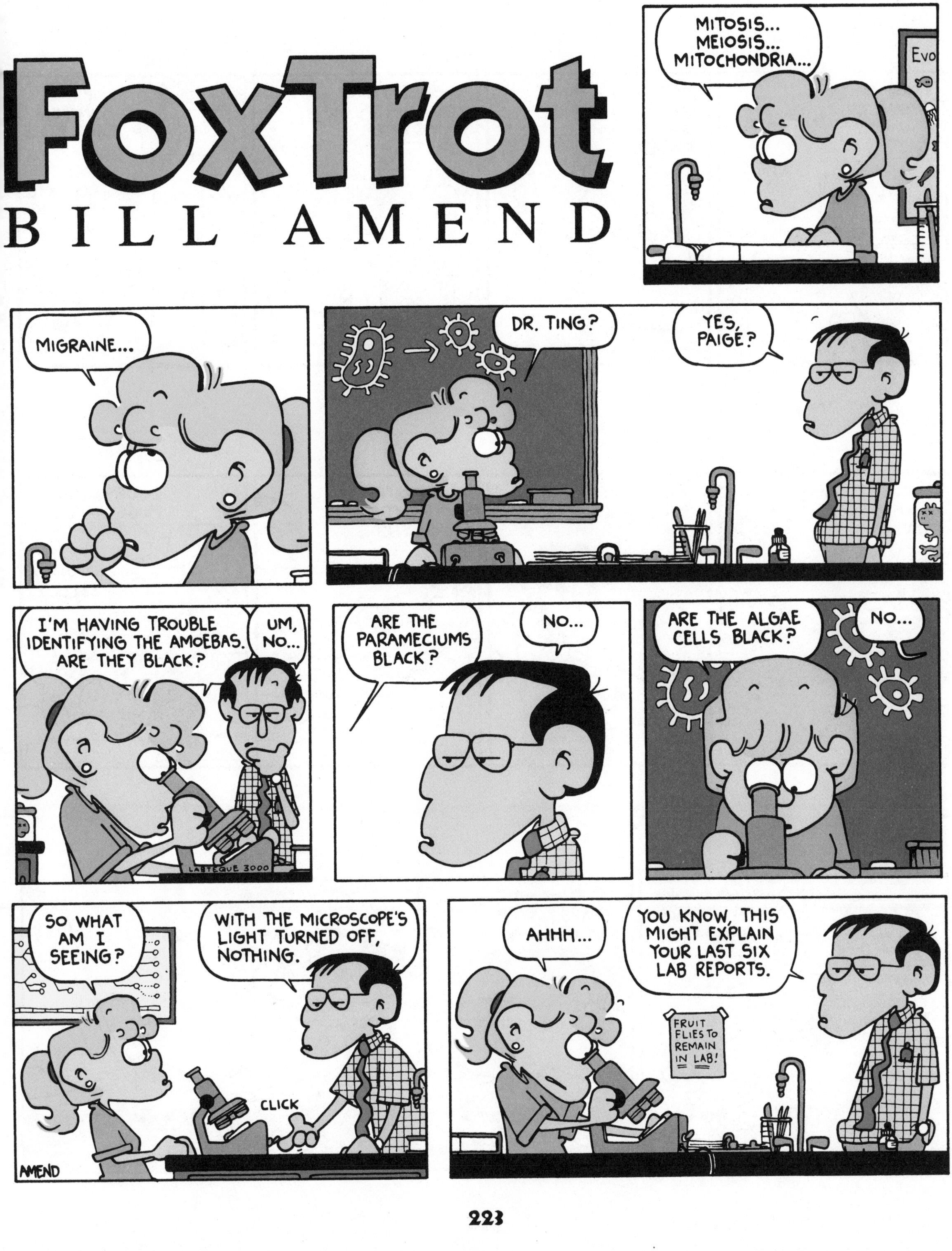
FoxTrot
BILL AMEND
MITOSIS... MEIOSIS... MITOCHONDRIA...
EVO
MIGRAINE...
DR. TING?
YES, PAIGE?
I'M HAVING TROUBLE IDENTIFYING THE AMOEBAS. ARE THEY BLACK?
UM, NO...
LABTEQUE 3000
ARE THE PARAMECIUMS BLACK?
NO...
ARE THE ALGAE CELLS BLACK?
NO...
SO WHAT AM I SEEING?
WITH THE MICROSCOPE'S LIGHT TURNED OFF, NOTHING.
CLICK
AMEND
AHHH...
YOU KNOW, THIS MIGHT EXPLAIN YOUR LAST SIX LAB REPORTS.
FRUIT FLIES TO REMAIN IN LAB!

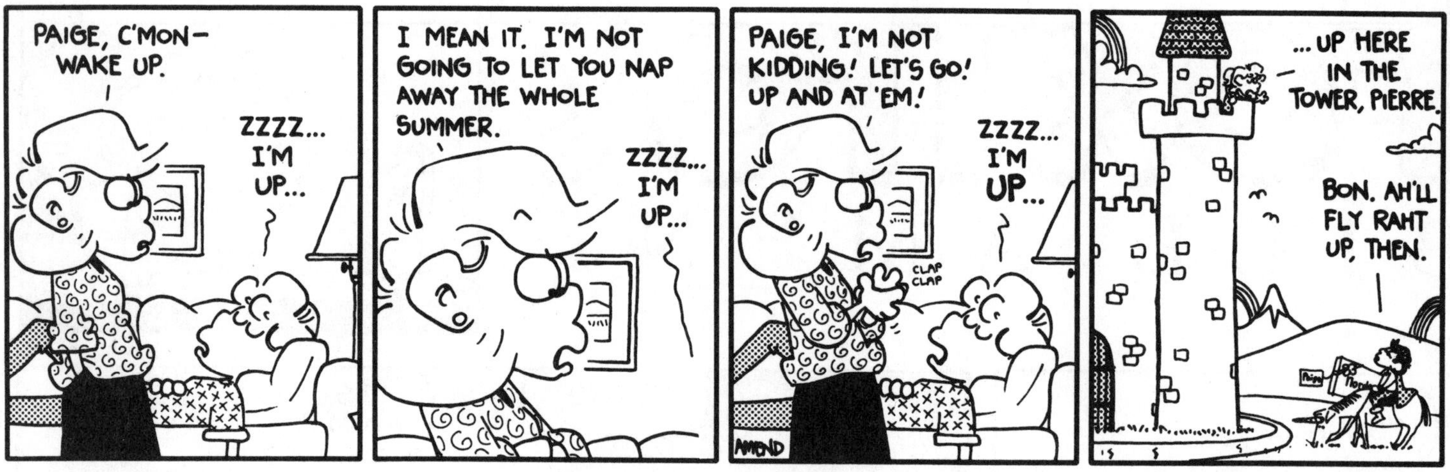
PAIGE, C'MON—
WAKE UP.
ZZZZ...
I'M
UP...
I MEAN IT. I'M NOT
GOING TO LET YOU NAP
AWAY THE WHOLE
SUMMER.
ZZZZ...
I'M
UP...
PAIGE, I'M NOT
KIDDING! LET'S GO!
UP AND AT 'EM!
CLAP
CLAP
ZZZZ...
I'M
UP...
AMEND
... UP HERE
IN THE
TOWER, PIERRE.
BON. AH'LL
FLY RAHT
UP, THEN.

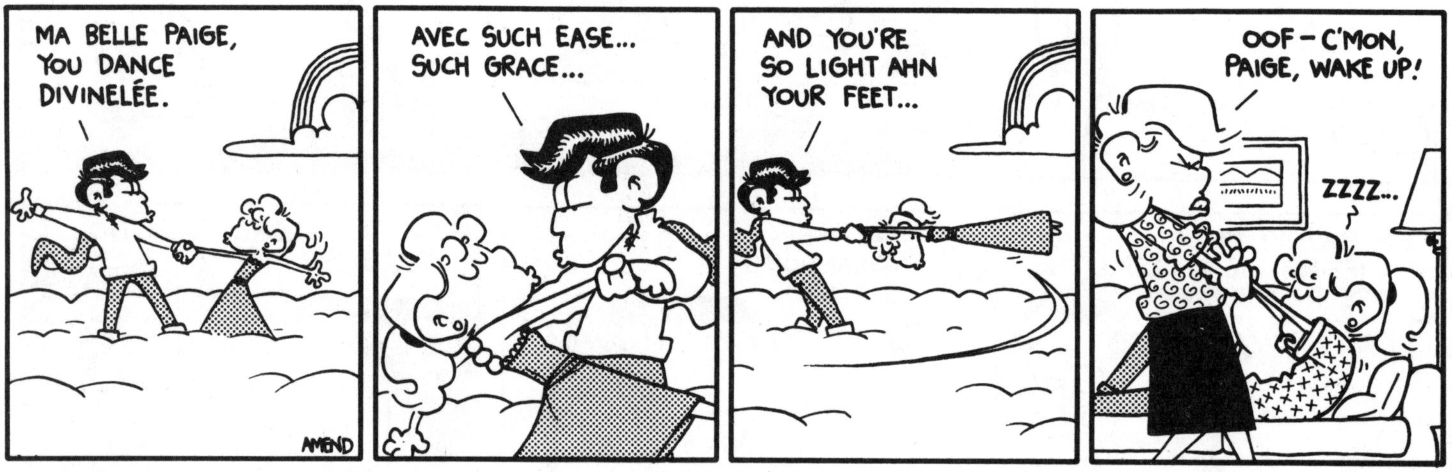
MA BELLE PAIGE,
YOU DANCE
DIVINELÉE.
AMEND
AVEC SUCH EASE...
SUCH GRACE...
AND YOU'RE
SO LIGHT AHN
YOUR FEET...
OOF—C'MON,
PAIGE, WAKE UP!
ZZZZ...

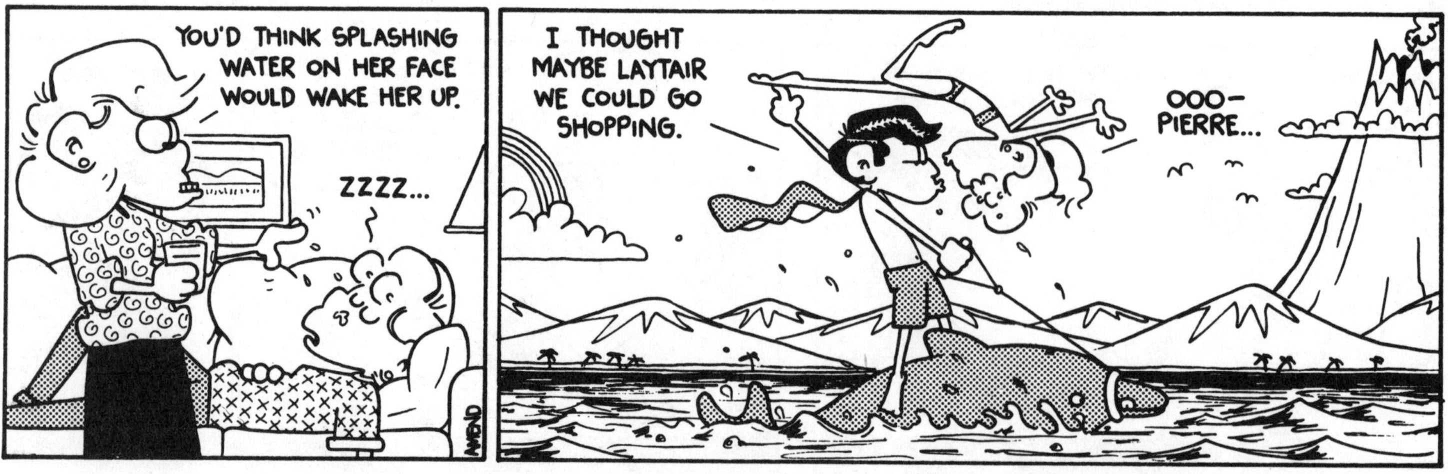
YOU'D THINK SPLASHING
WATER ON HER FACE
WOULD WAKE HER UP.
ZZZZ...
AMEND
I THOUGHT
MAYBE LAYTAIR
WE COULD GO
SHOPPING.
OOO—
PIERRE...

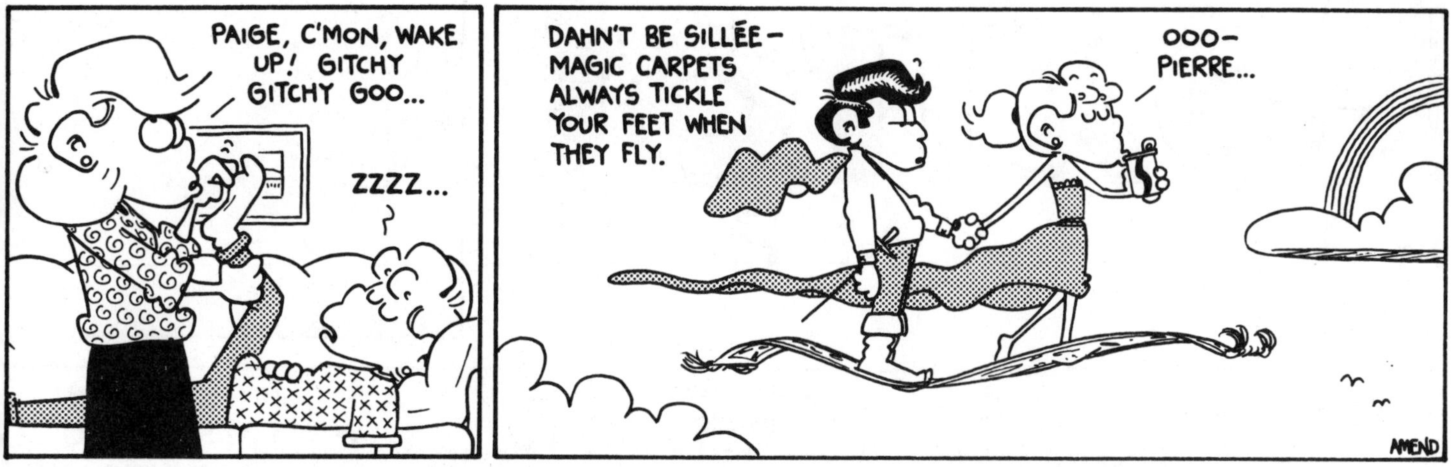
PAIGE, C'MON, WAKE UP! GITCHY GITCHY GOO...
ZZZZ...
DAHN'T BE SILLÉE– MAGIC CARPETS ALWAYS TICKLE YOUR FEET WHEN THEY FLY.
OOO– PIERRE...
AMEND

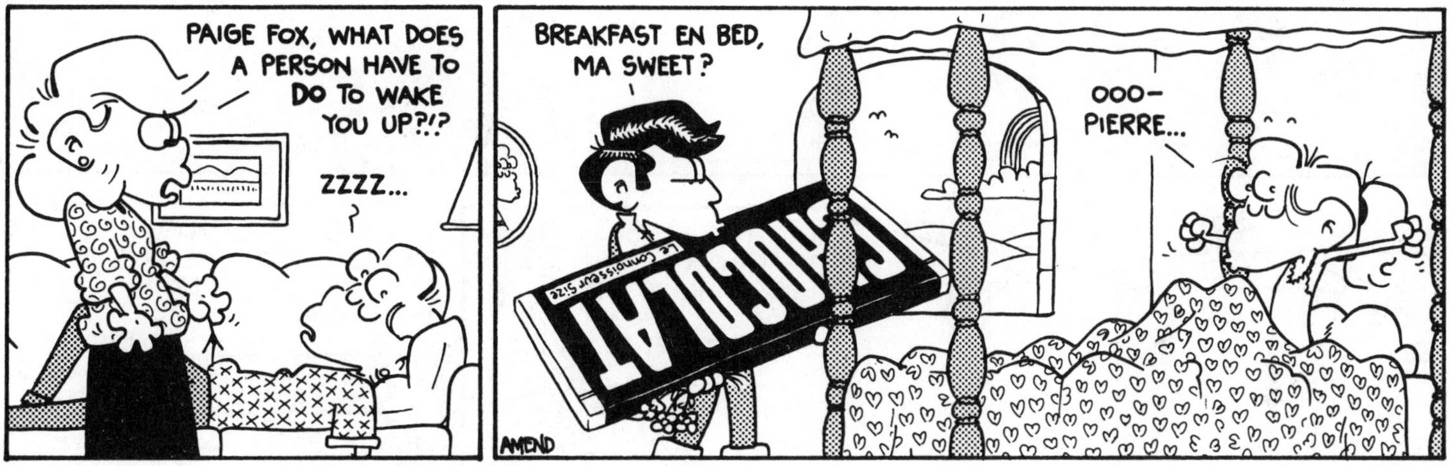
PAIGE FOX, WHAT DOES A PERSON HAVE TO DO TO WAKE YOU UP?!?
ZZZZ...
BREAKFAST EN BED, MA SWEET?
OOO– PIERRE...
CHOCOLAT
Le Connoisseur Size
AMEND

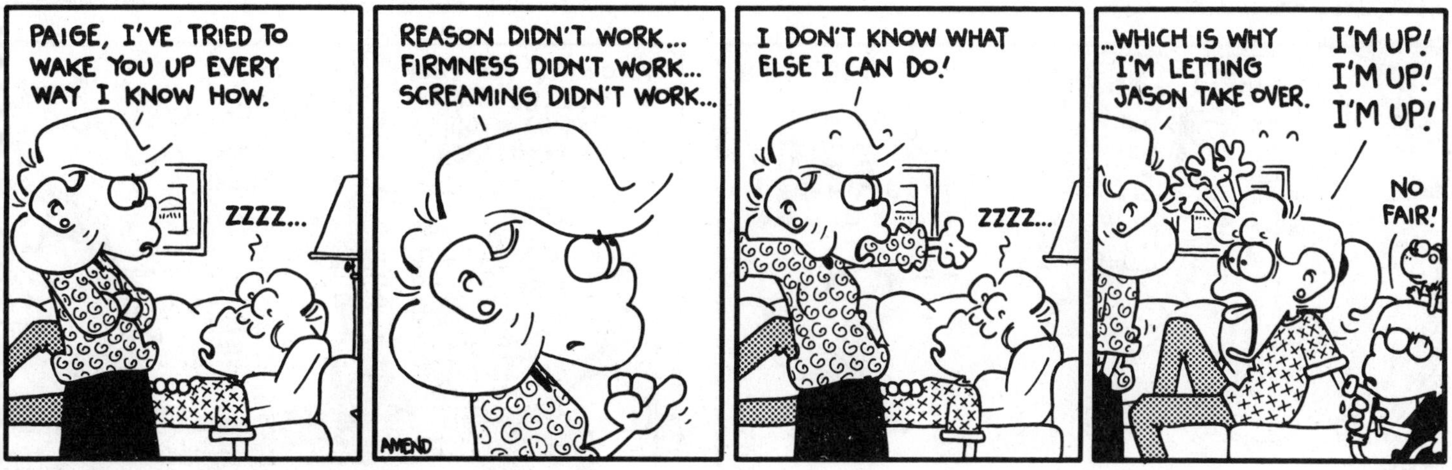
PAIGE, I'VE TRIED TO WAKE YOU UP EVERY WAY I KNOW HOW.
ZZZZ...
REASON DIDN'T WORK... FIRMNESS DIDN'T WORK... SCREAMING DIDN'T WORK...
AMEND
I DON'T KNOW WHAT ELSE I CAN DO!
ZZZZ...
...WHICH IS WHY I'M LETTING JASON TAKE OVER.
I'M UP! I'M UP! I'M UP!
NO FAIR!

FoxTrot
BILL AMEND

WHAT'S THAT FLYING AROUND UP THERE?
HOLY COW! IT'S A UFO!
AND IT'S LANDING! IT'S LANDING RIGHT HERE! THIS IS THE GREATEST MOMENT OF MY LIFE!
THE HATCH IS OPENING UP... I'M ABOUT TO COME FACE TO FACE WITH A SUPERIOR LIFE FORM...
PERHAPS I SHOULD KNEEL...
TAKE US TO YOUR MALL.
AAAAAA!
AMEND
KNOWING MY LUCK, THIS'LL BE THE ONE DREAM IN A MILLION I **DO** REMEMBER.
MOM SAYS STOP SCREAMING AND GET UP.
Jason

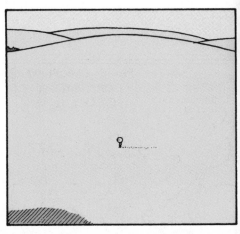

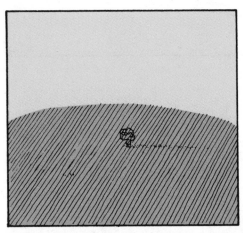

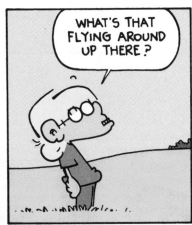

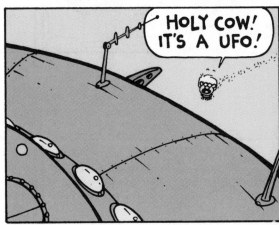

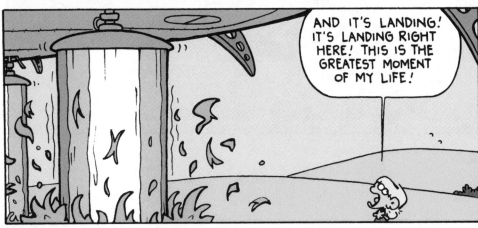

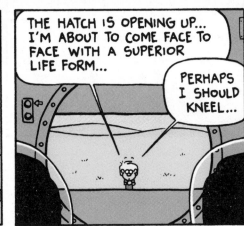

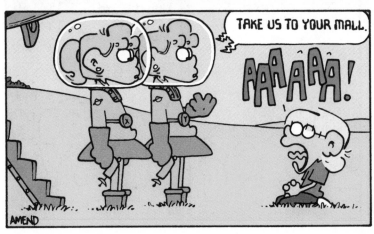

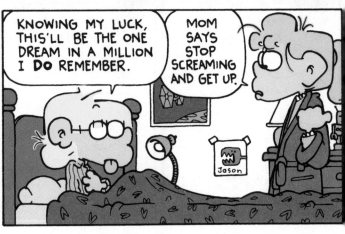

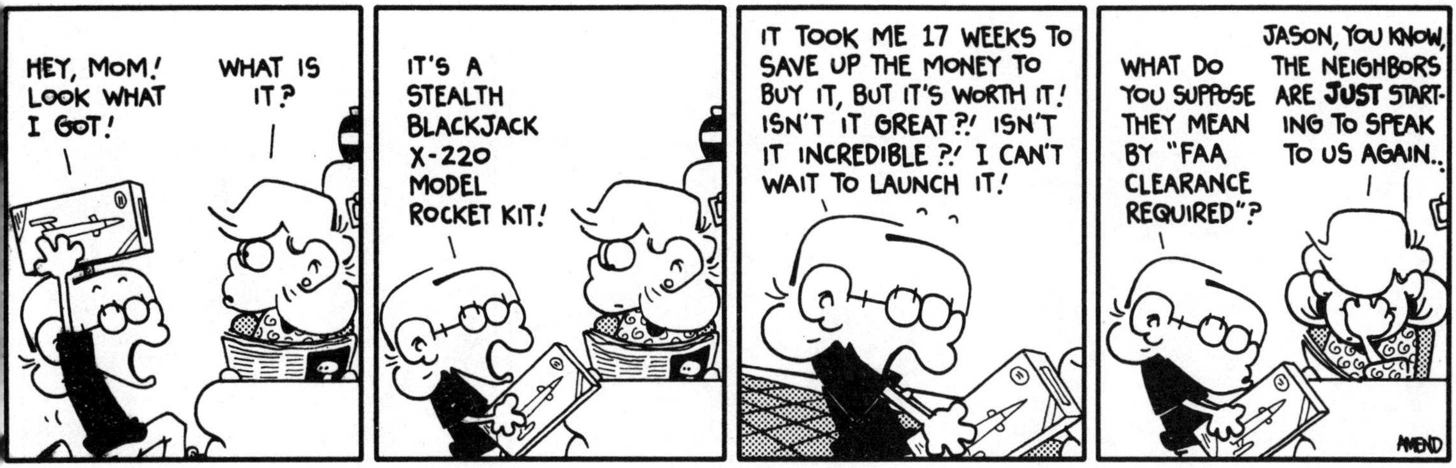
HEY, MOM! LOOK WHAT I GOT!
WHAT IS IT?
IT'S A STEALTH BLACKJACK X-220 MODEL ROCKET KIT!
IT TOOK ME 17 WEEKS TO SAVE UP THE MONEY TO BUY IT, BUT IT'S WORTH IT! ISN'T IT GREAT?! ISN'T IT INCREDIBLE?! I CAN'T WAIT TO LAUNCH IT!
WHAT DO YOU SUPPOSE THEY MEAN BY "FAA CLEARANCE REQUIRED"?
JASON, YOU KNOW, THE NEIGHBORS ARE JUST STARTING TO SPEAK TO US AGAIN...
AMEND

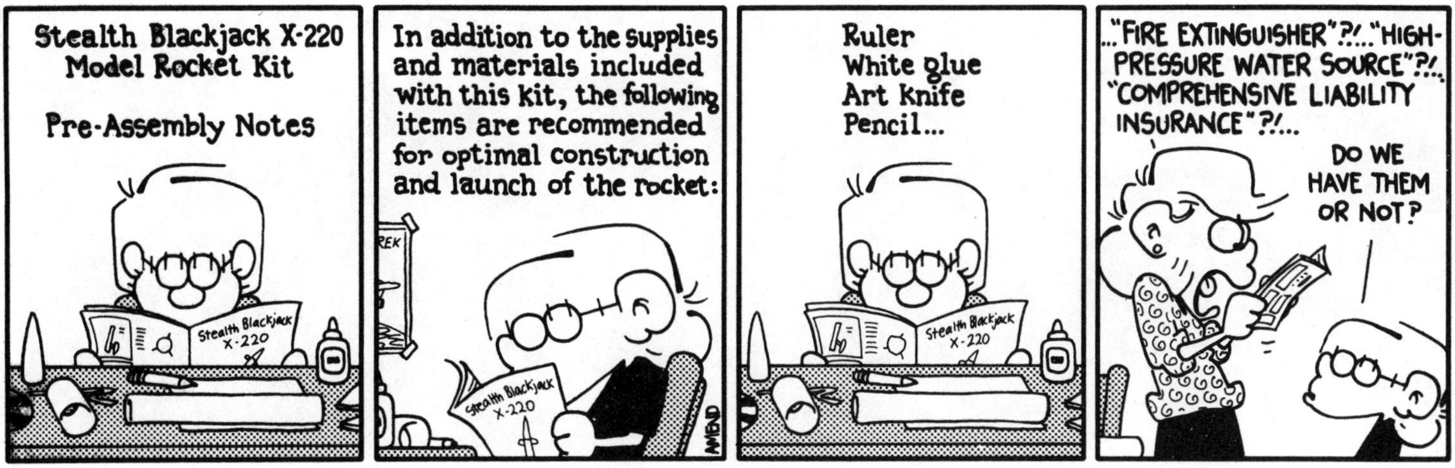
Stealth Blackjack X-220 Model Rocket Kit
Pre-Assembly Notes
Stealth Blackjack X-220
In addition to the supplies and materials included with this kit, the following items are recommended for optimal construction and launch of the rocket:
Stealth Blackjack X-220
AMEND
Ruler
White glue
Art knife
Pencil...
Stealth Blackjack X-220
..."FIRE EXTINGUISHER"?!..."HIGH-PRESSURE WATER SOURCE"?!.. "COMPREHENSIVE LIABILITY INSURANCE"?!...
DO WE HAVE THEM OR NOT?

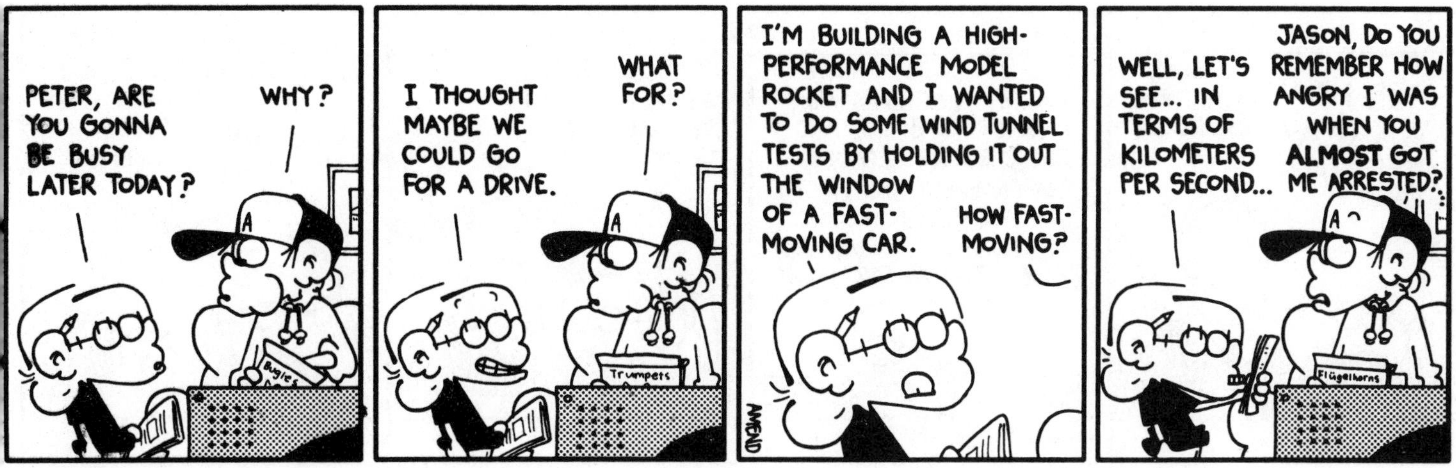
PETER, ARE YOU GONNA BE BUSY LATER TODAY?
WHY?
Bugles
I THOUGHT MAYBE WE COULD GO FOR A DRIVE.
WHAT FOR?
Trumpets
I'M BUILDING A HIGH-PERFORMANCE MODEL ROCKET AND I WANTED TO DO SOME WIND TUNNEL TESTS BY HOLDING IT OUT THE WINDOW OF A FAST-MOVING CAR.
HOW FAST-MOVING?
AMEND
WELL, LET'S SEE... IN TERMS OF KILOMETERS PER SECOND...
JASON, DO YOU REMEMBER HOW ANGRY I WAS WHEN YOU ALMOST GOT ME ARRESTED?
Flügelhorns

PETER... PAIGE... I'M GONNA GO LAUNCH MY ROCKET NOW.
NASA
A
NASA
I SAID...
WE HEARD YOU.
NASA
AMEND

UM, JASON, WHAT EXACTLY DID YOU MEAN BY "A FEW MODIFICATIONS"?
AMEND

WAAAA! YEE HA! WAAAA! YEE HA!
JASON, WHAT ARE YOU **DOING**?!
I'M CRYING BECAUSE I LOST MY X-220 MODEL ROCKET THAT TOOK ME FOREVER TO BUILD, AND I'M CHEERING BECAUSE I'M PROBABLY THE FIRST 10-YEAR-OLD IN HISTORY TO LAUNCH A CARDBOARD TUBE INTO LOW EARTH ORBIT.
OF COURSE, I PROBABLY BROKE ABOUT A ZILLION FEDERAL LAWS IN DOING THAT...
WAAAA! YEE HA! UH OH... WAAAA! YEE HA! UH OH...
LET ME TELL YOU WHAT LAWS **I'M** ABOUT TO BREAK...
AMEND

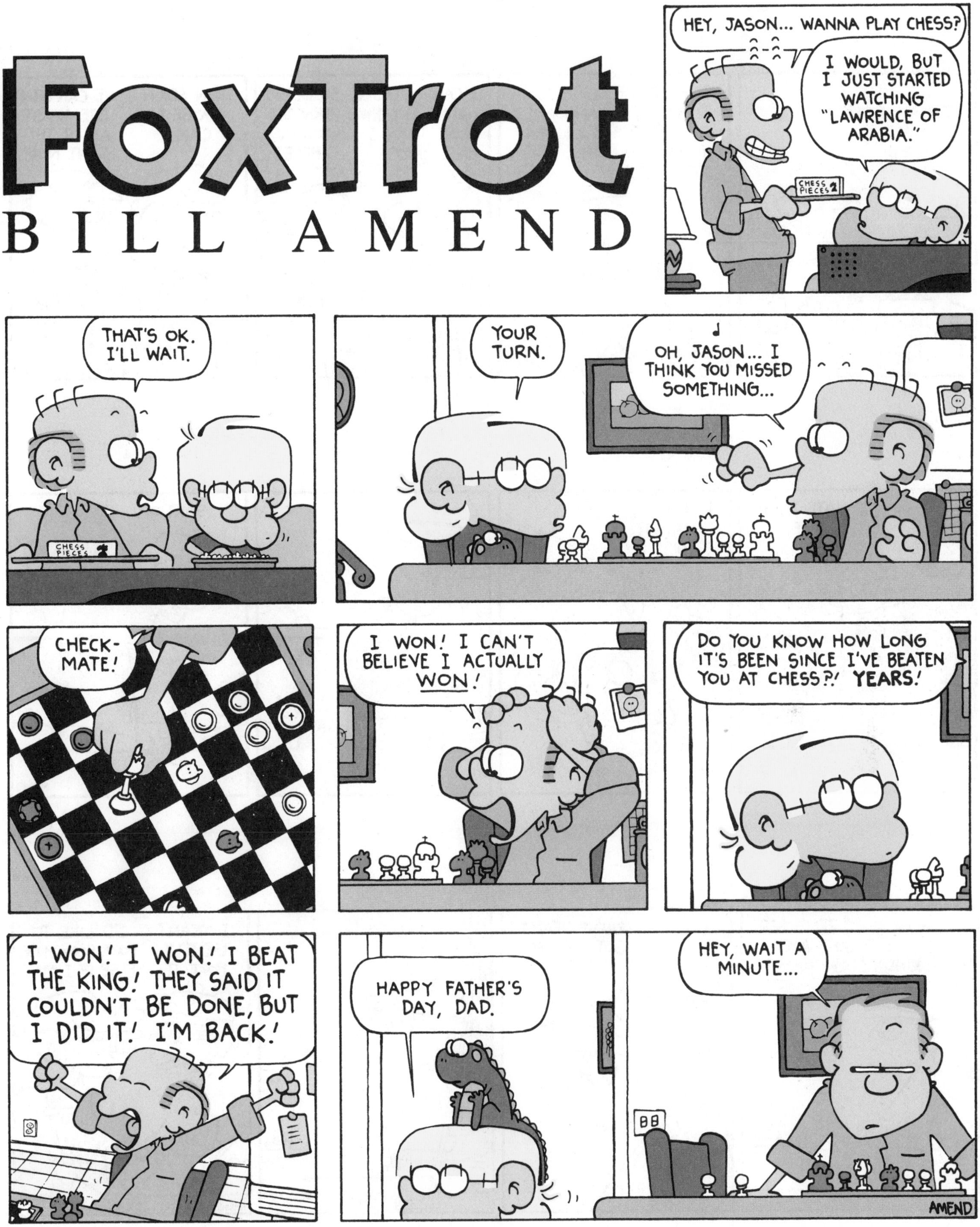
FoxTrot
BILL AMEND
HEY, JASON... WANNA PLAY CHESS?
I WOULD, BUT I JUST STARTED WATCHING "LAWRENCE OF ARABIA."
CHESS PIECES
THAT'S OK. I'LL WAIT.
CHESS PIECES
YOUR TURN.
OH, JASON... I THINK YOU MISSED SOMETHING...
CHECK-MATE!
I WON! I CAN'T BELIEVE I ACTUALLY WON!
DO YOU KNOW HOW LONG IT'S BEEN SINCE I'VE BEATEN YOU AT CHESS?! YEARS!
I WON! I WON! I BEAT THE KING! THEY SAID IT COULDN'T BE DONE, BUT I DID IT! I'M BACK!
HAPPY FATHER'S DAY, DAD.
HEY, WAIT A MINUTE...
AMEND

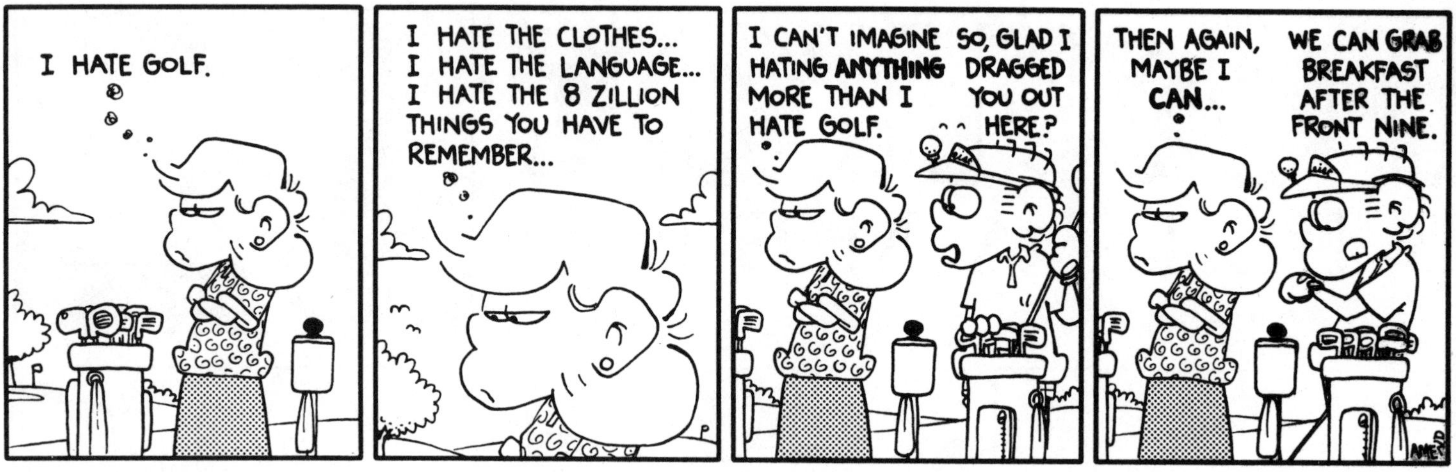
I HATE GOLF.
I HATE THE CLOTHES... I HATE THE LANGUAGE... I HATE THE 8 ZILLION THINGS YOU HAVE TO REMEMBER...
I CAN'T IMAGINE HATING ANYTHING MORE THAN I HATE GOLF.
SO, GLAD I DRAGGED YOU OUT HERE?
THEN AGAIN, MAYBE I CAN...
WE CAN GRAB BREAKFAST AFTER THE FRONT NINE.
AMEND

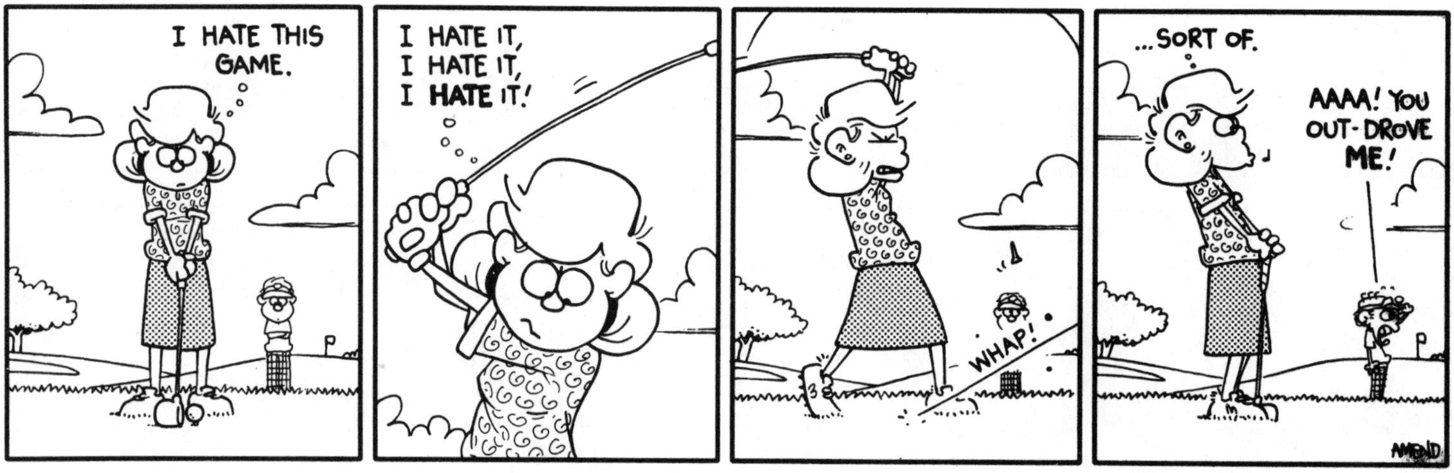
I HATE THIS GAME.
I HATE IT, I HATE IT, I HATE IT!
WHAP!
...SORT OF.
AAAA! YOU OUT-DROVE ME!
AMEND

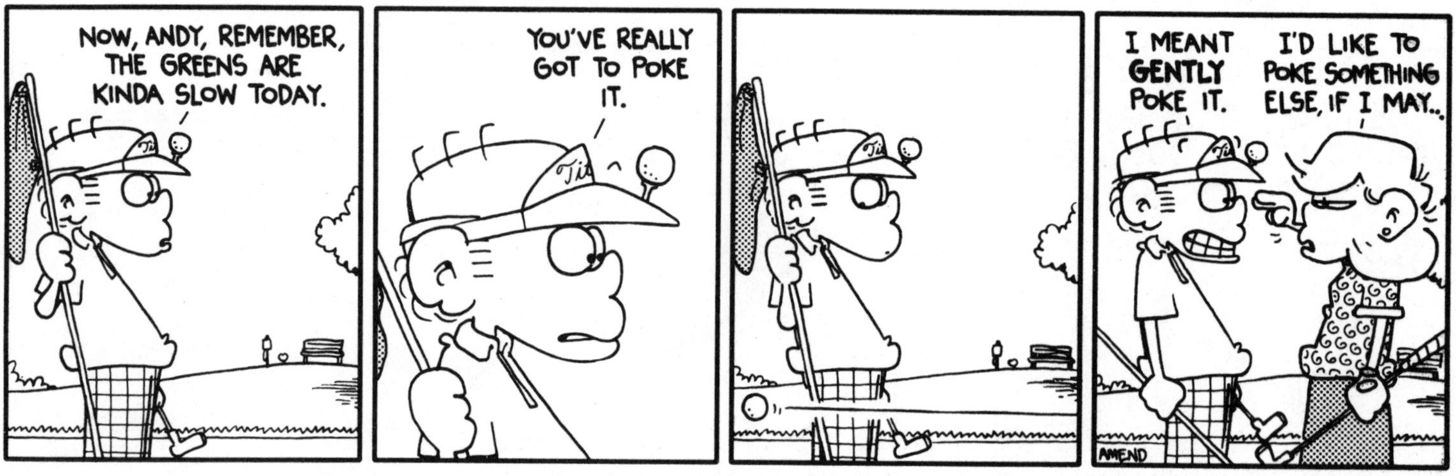
NOW, ANDY, REMEMBER, THE GREENS ARE KINDA SLOW TODAY.
YOU'VE REALLY GOT TO POKE IT.
I MEANT GENTLY POKE IT.
I'D LIKE TO POKE SOMETHING ELSE, IF I MAY...
AMEND

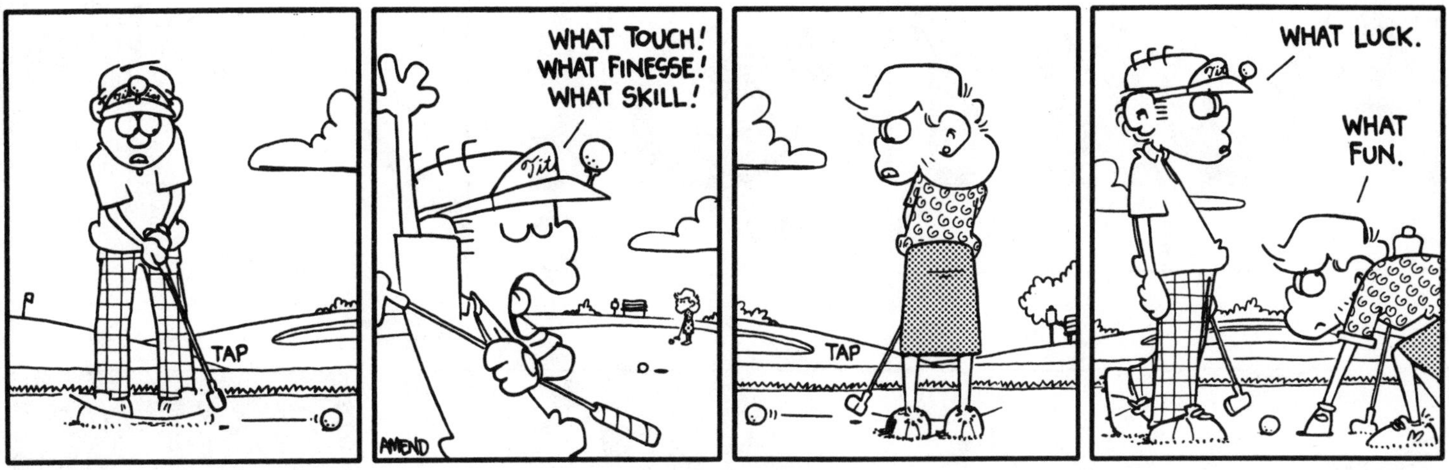
TAP
WHAT TOUCH! WHAT FINESSE! WHAT SKILL!
AMEND
TAP
WHAT LUCK.
WHAT FUN.

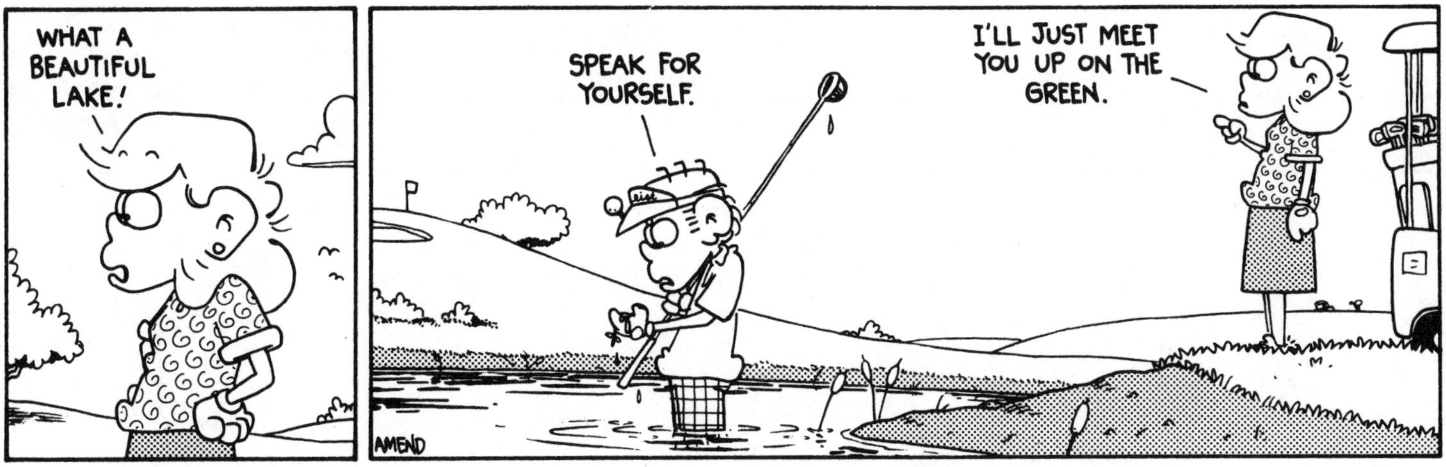
WHAT A BEAUTIFUL LAKE!
SPEAK FOR YOURSELF.
I'LL JUST MEET YOU UP ON THE GREEN.
AMEND

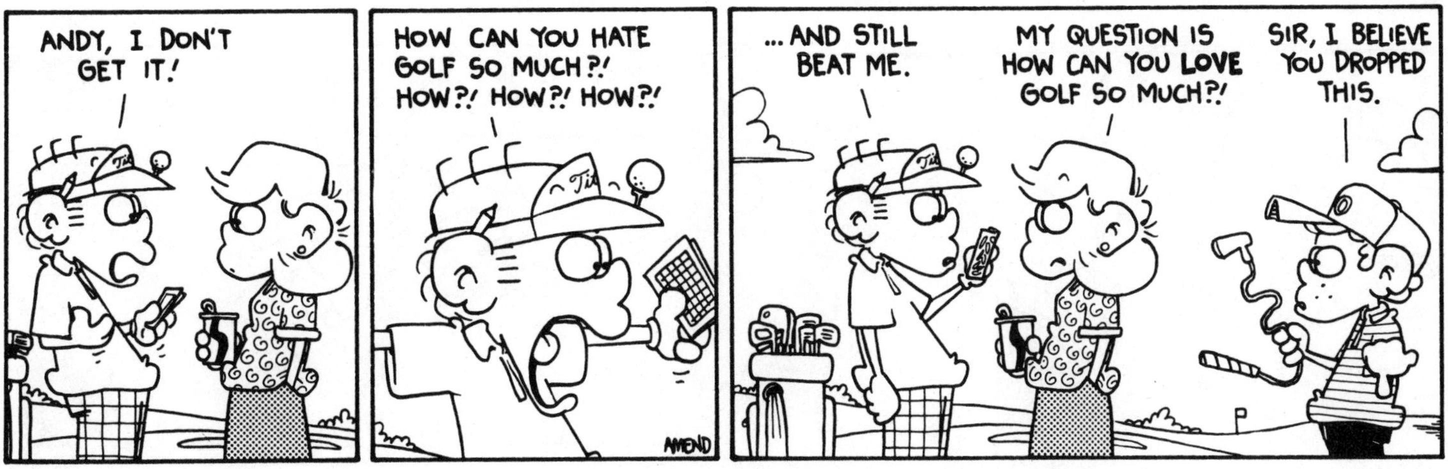
ANDY, I DON'T GET IT!
HOW CAN YOU HATE GOLF SO MUCH?! HOW?! HOW?! HOW?!
AMEND
...AND STILL BEAT ME.
MY QUESTION IS HOW CAN YOU **LOVE** GOLF SO MUCH?!
SIR, I BELIEVE YOU DROPPED THIS.

FoxTrot
BILL AMEND

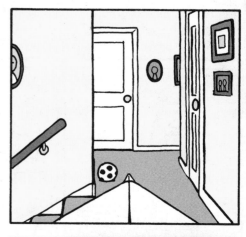

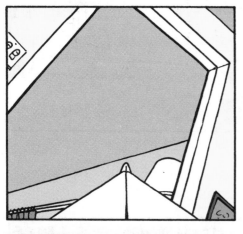

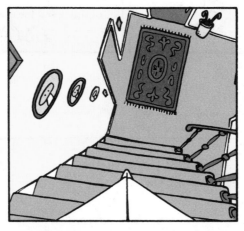

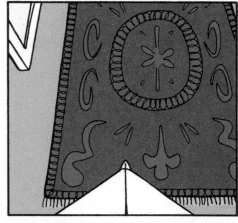

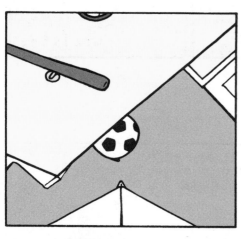

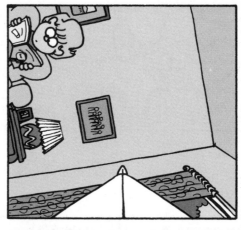

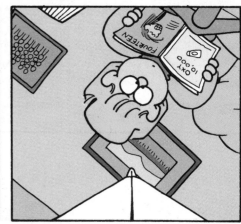

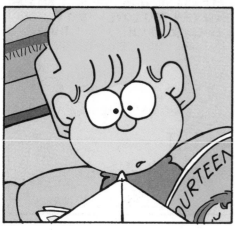

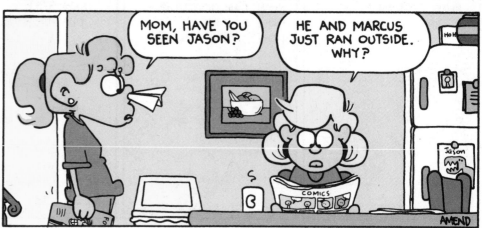

FOURTEEN
OXY 10,000
MOM, HAVE YOU SEEN JASON?
HE AND MARCUS JUST RAN OUTSIDE. WHY?
COMICS
Jason
AMEND

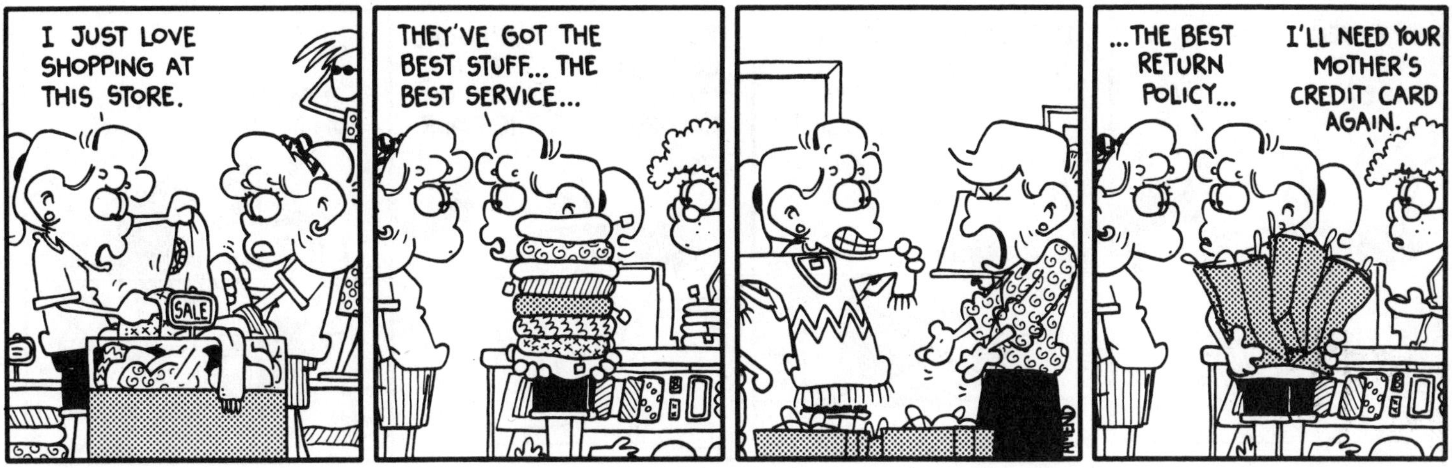
I JUST LOVE SHOPPING AT THIS STORE.
SALE
THEY'VE GOT THE BEST STUFF... THE BEST SERVICE...
...THE BEST RETURN POLICY...
I'LL NEED YOUR MOTHER'S CREDIT CARD AGAIN.
AMEND

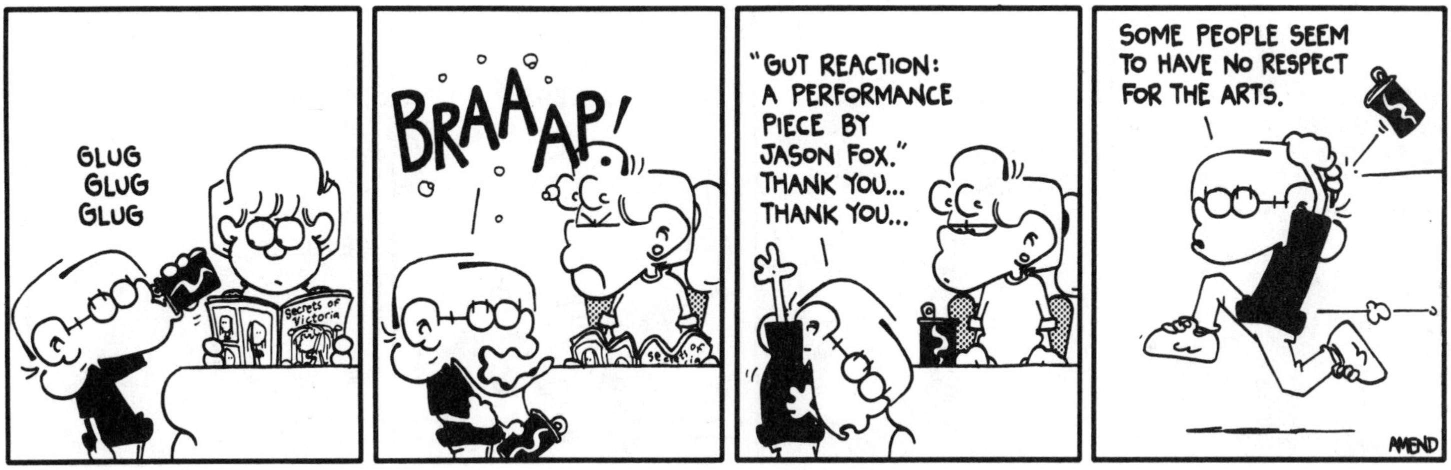
GLUG GLUG GLUG
Secrets of Victoria
BRAAAP!
"GUT REACTION: A PERFORMANCE PIECE BY JASON FOX." THANK YOU... THANK YOU...
SOME PEOPLE SEEM TO HAVE NO RESPECT FOR THE ARTS.
AMEND

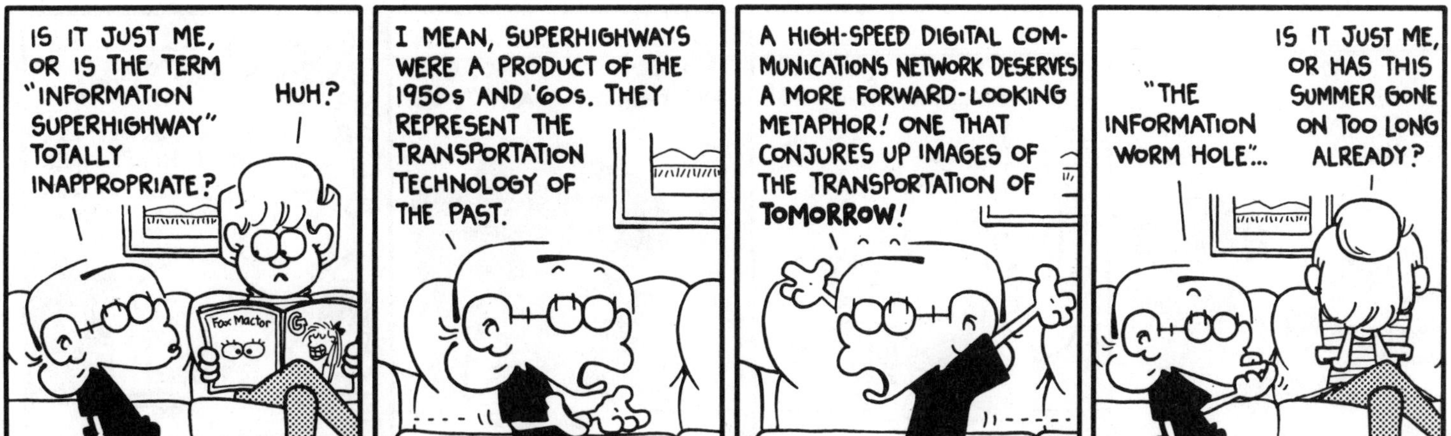
IS IT JUST ME, OR IS THE TERM "INFORMATION SUPERHIGHWAY" TOTALLY INAPPROPRIATE?
HUH?
Fox Mactor
I MEAN, SUPERHIGHWAYS WERE A PRODUCT OF THE 1950s AND '60s. THEY REPRESENT THE TRANSPORTATION TECHNOLOGY OF THE PAST.
A HIGH-SPEED DIGITAL COMMUNICATIONS NETWORK DESERVES A MORE FORWARD-LOOKING METAPHOR! ONE THAT CONJURES UP IMAGES OF THE TRANSPORTATION OF TOMORROW!
AMEND
"THE INFORMATION WORM HOLE"...
IS IT JUST ME, OR HAS THIS SUMMER GONE ON TOO LONG ALREADY?

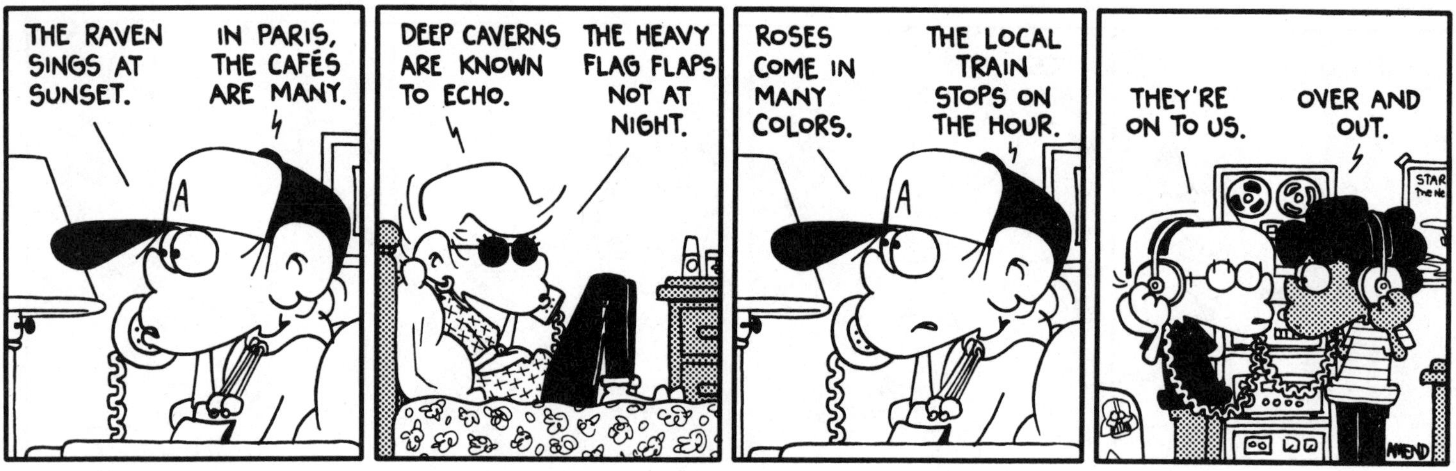
THE RAVEN SINGS AT SUNSET.
IN PARIS, THE CAFÉS ARE MANY.
DEEP CAVERNS ARE KNOWN TO ECHO.
THE HEAVY FLAG FLAPS NOT AT NIGHT.
ROSES COME IN MANY COLORS.
THE LOCAL TRAIN STOPS ON THE HOUR.
THEY'RE ON TO US.
OVER AND OUT.
AMEND

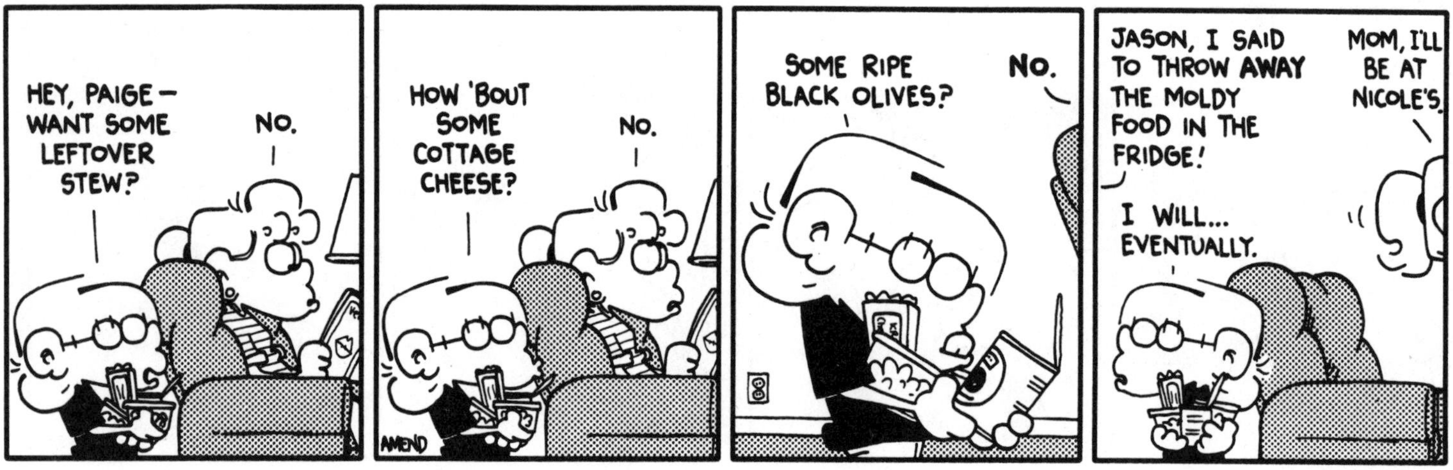
HEY, PAIGE— WANT SOME LEFTOVER STEW?
NO.
HOW 'BOUT SOME COTTAGE CHEESE?
NO.
AMEND
SOME RIPE BLACK OLIVES?
NO.
JASON, I SAID TO THROW AWAY THE MOLDY FOOD IN THE FRIDGE!
MOM, I'LL BE AT NICOLE'S.
I WILL... EVENTUALLY.

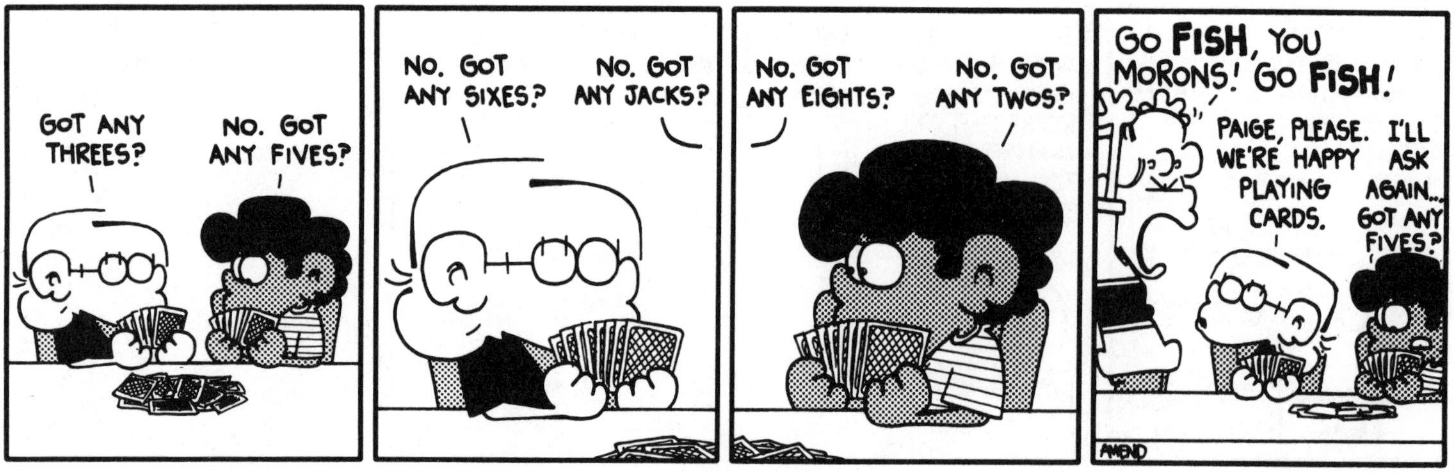
GOT ANY THREES?
NO. GOT ANY FIVES?
NO. GOT ANY SIXES?
NO. GOT ANY JACKS?
NO. GOT ANY EIGHTS?
NO. GOT ANY TWOS?
GO FISH, YOU MORONS! GO FISH!
PAIGE, PLEASE. WE'RE HAPPY PLAYING CARDS.
I'LL ASK AGAIN... GOT ANY FIVES?
AMEND

FoxTrot

BILL AMEND

WHAT A BEAUTIFUL DAY...
...FOR A PHYSICS LESSON.
NOW, PAIGE, AT THIS POINT WE'RE ESSENTIALLY NOTHING BUT POTENTIAL ENERGY, WHICH IS mgh.
Ride the DEATH DEMON 2
AS WE GO DOWN-HILL, THIS IS CONVERTED INTO KINETIC ENERGY, WHICH IS $\frac{1}{2}mv^2$.
SO A QUICK-AND-DIRTY APPROXIMATION OF OUR SPEED AT THE BOTTOM OF A DROP LIKE THIS MIGHT ASSUME $\Delta K.E. = -\Delta P.E.$ AND GIVE US $v = \sqrt{2g(-\Delta h)}$.
BUT, IN FACT, OUR CARS ARE CONSTANTLY LOSING ENERGY TO FRICTION. THIS IS WHY THE FIRST HILL HAS TO BE THE HIGHEST.
SEE WHAT I MEAN?
NOW, IN ORDER FOR OUR CAR TO NOT FALL OFF THE TRACK HERE...
JASON, PLEASE, THIS ROLLER COASTER MAKES ME SICK ENOUGH AS IT IS!
AAAA! MY CALCULATOR!
AMEND

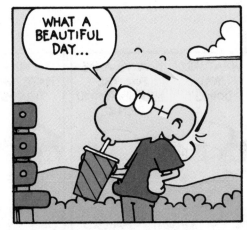

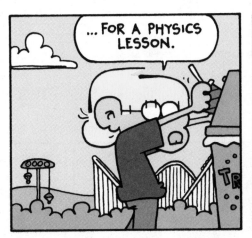

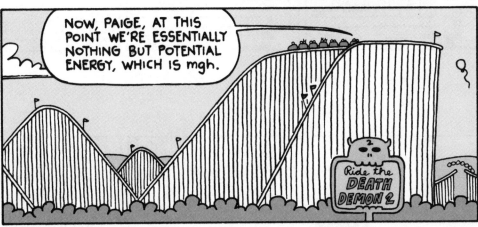

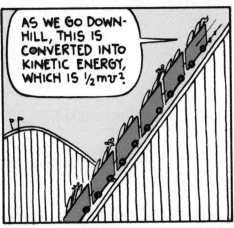

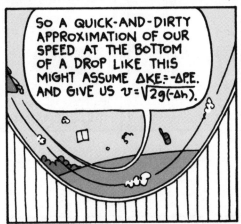

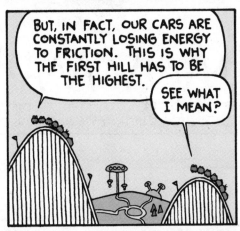

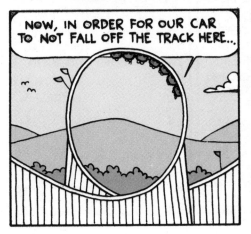

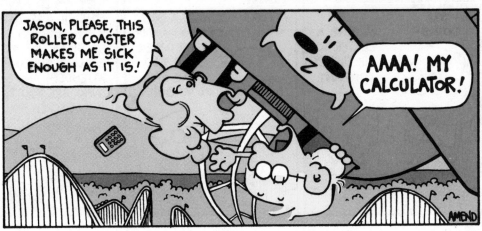

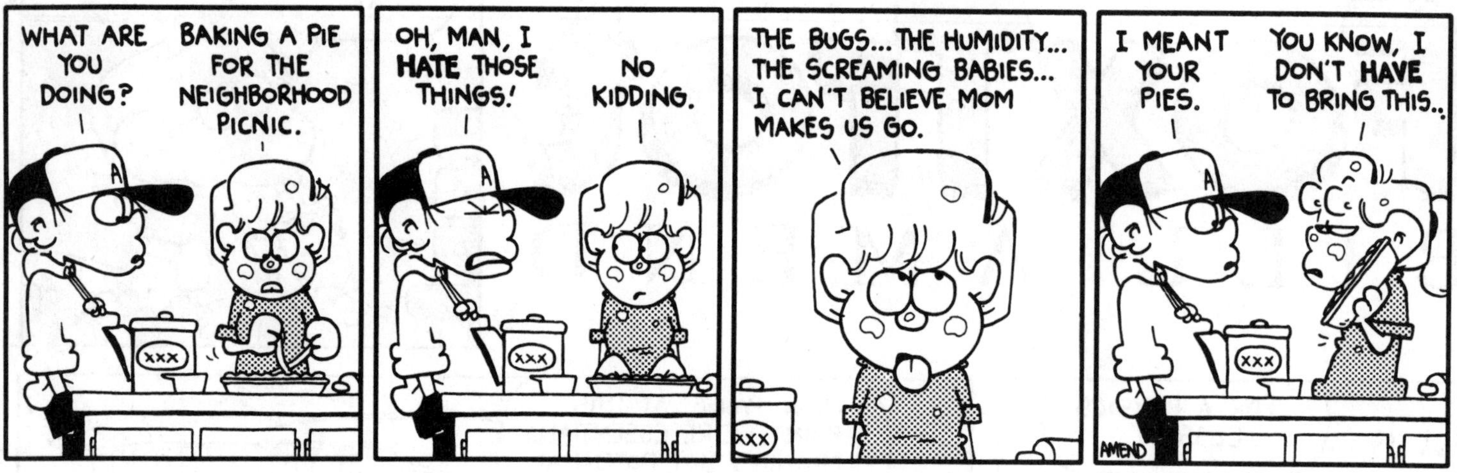
WHAT ARE YOU DOING?
BAKING A PIE FOR THE NEIGHBORHOOD PICNIC.
OH, MAN, I HATE THOSE THINGS!
NO KIDDING.
THE BUGS... THE HUMIDITY... THE SCREAMING BABIES... I CAN'T BELIEVE MOM MAKES US GO.
I MEANT YOUR PIES.
YOU KNOW, I DON'T HAVE TO BRING THIS...
AMEND

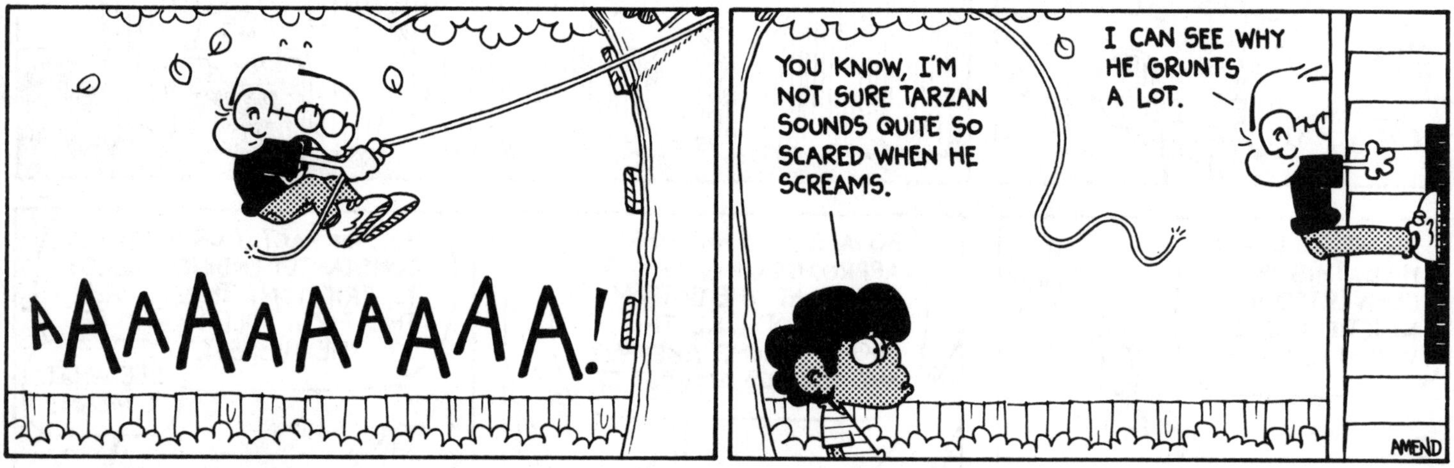
AAAAAAAAAAA!
YOU KNOW, I'M NOT SURE TARZAN SOUNDS QUITE SO SCARED WHEN HE SCREAMS.
I CAN SEE WHY HE GRUNTS A LOT.
AMEND

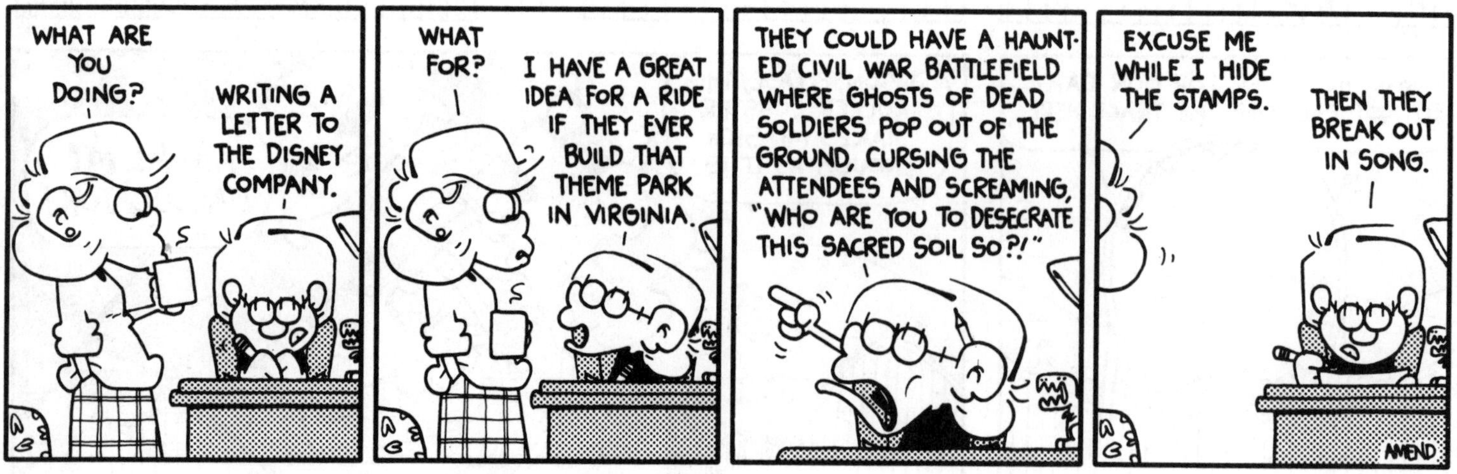
WHAT ARE YOU DOING?
WRITING A LETTER TO THE DISNEY COMPANY.
WHAT FOR?
I HAVE A GREAT IDEA FOR A RIDE IF THEY EVER BUILD THAT THEME PARK IN VIRGINIA.
THEY COULD HAVE A HAUNTED CIVIL WAR BATTLEFIELD WHERE GHOSTS OF DEAD SOLDIERS POP OUT OF THE GROUND, CURSING THE ATTENDEES AND SCREAMING, "WHO ARE YOU TO DESECRATE THIS SACRED SOIL SO?!"
EXCUSE ME WHILE I HIDE THE STAMPS.
THEN THEY BREAK OUT IN SONG.
AMEND

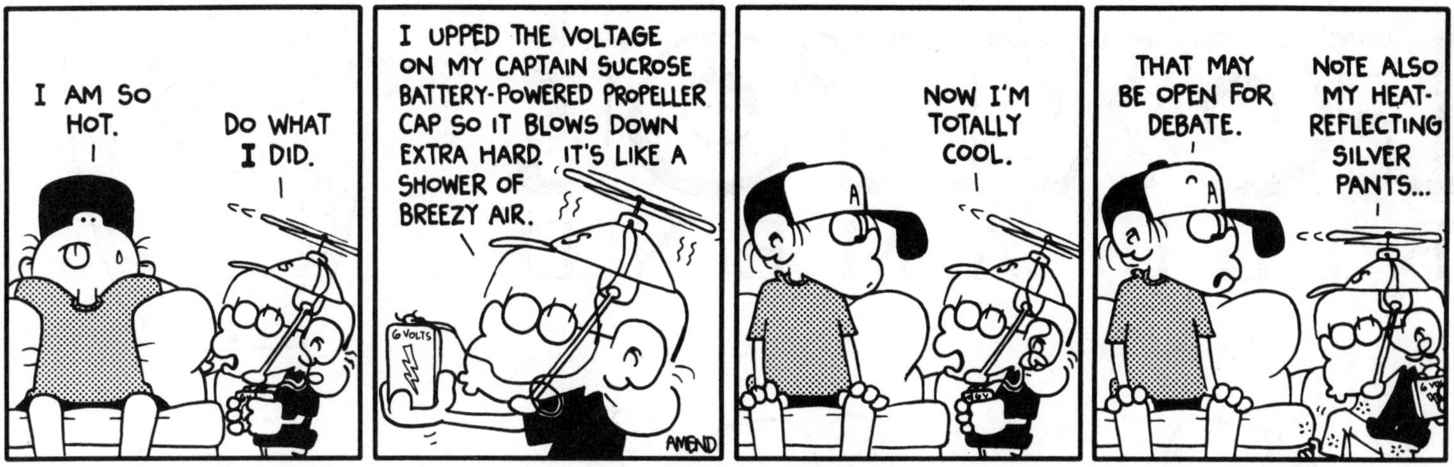
I AM SO HOT.
DO WHAT I DID.
I UPPED THE VOLTAGE ON MY CAPTAIN SUCROSE BATTERY-POWERED PROPELLER CAP SO IT BLOWS DOWN EXTRA HARD. IT'S LIKE A SHOWER OF BREEZY AIR.
NOW I'M TOTALLY COOL.
THAT MAY BE OPEN FOR DEBATE.
NOTE ALSO MY HEAT-REFLECTING SILVER PANTS...
AMEND

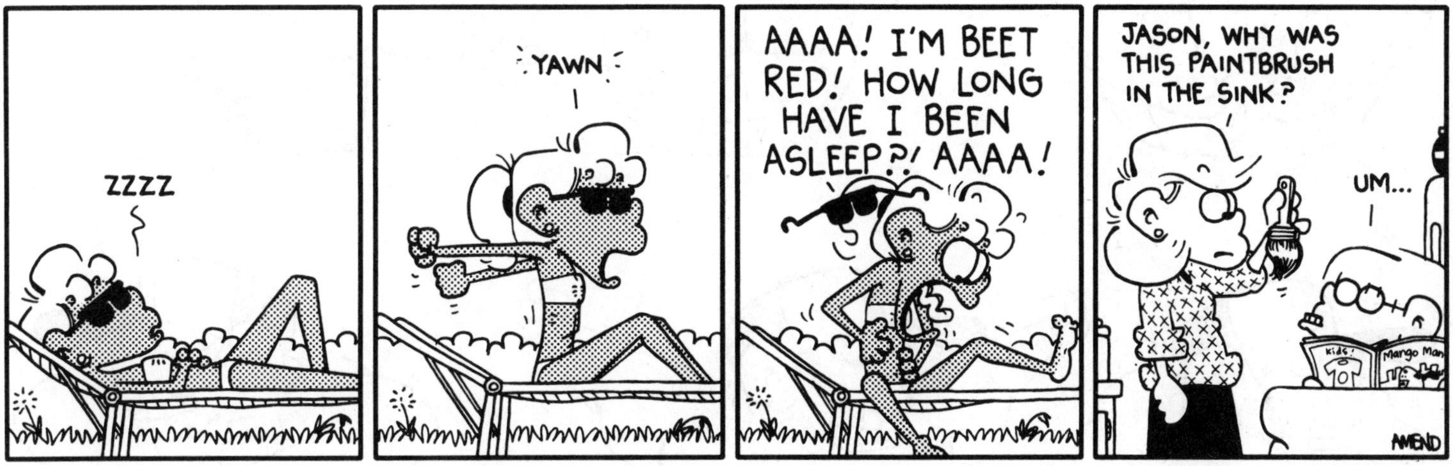
ZZZZ
YAWN
AAAA! I'M BEET RED! HOW LONG HAVE I BEEN ASLEEP?! AAAA!
JASON, WHY WAS THIS PAINTBRUSH IN THE SINK?
UM...
AMEND

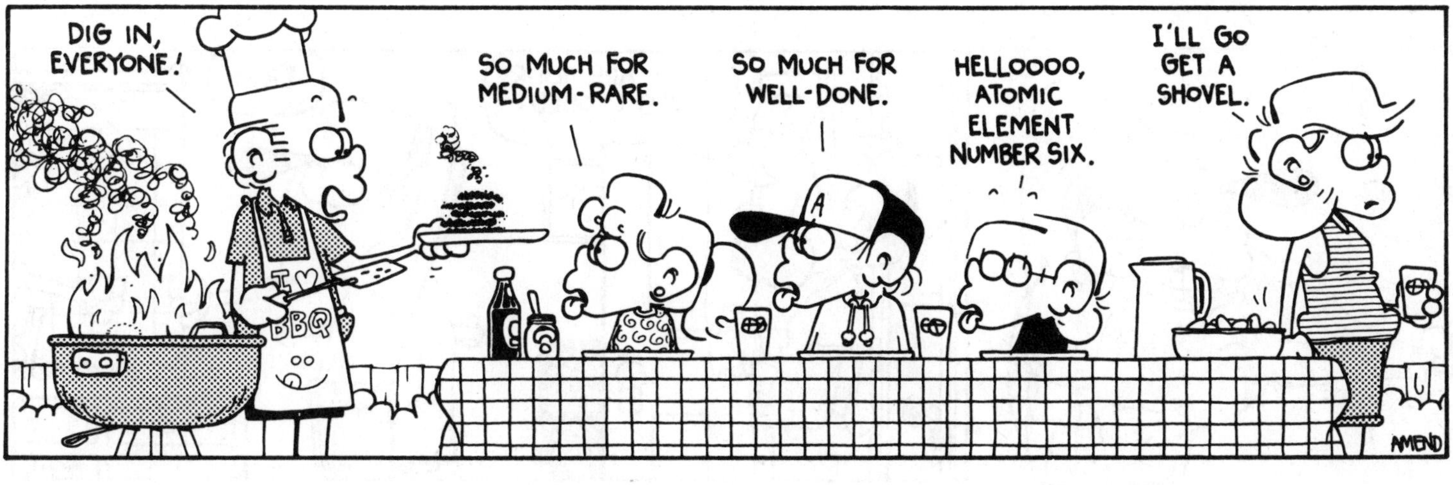
DIG IN, EVERYONE!
SO MUCH FOR MEDIUM-RARE.
SO MUCH FOR WELL-DONE.
HELLOOOO, ATOMIC ELEMENT NUMBER SIX.
I'LL GO GET A SHOVEL.
AMEND

FoxTrot

BILL AMEND

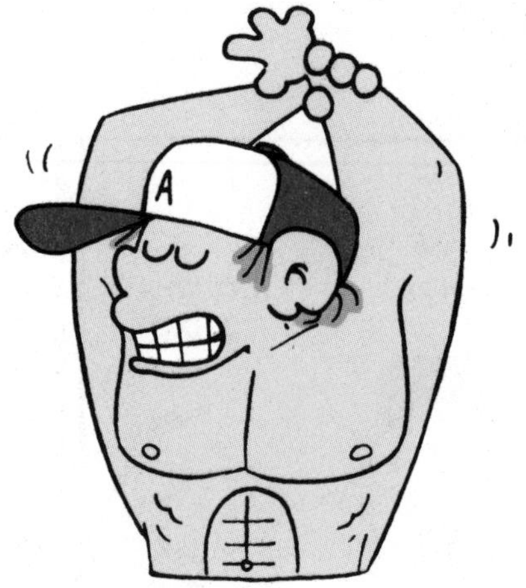

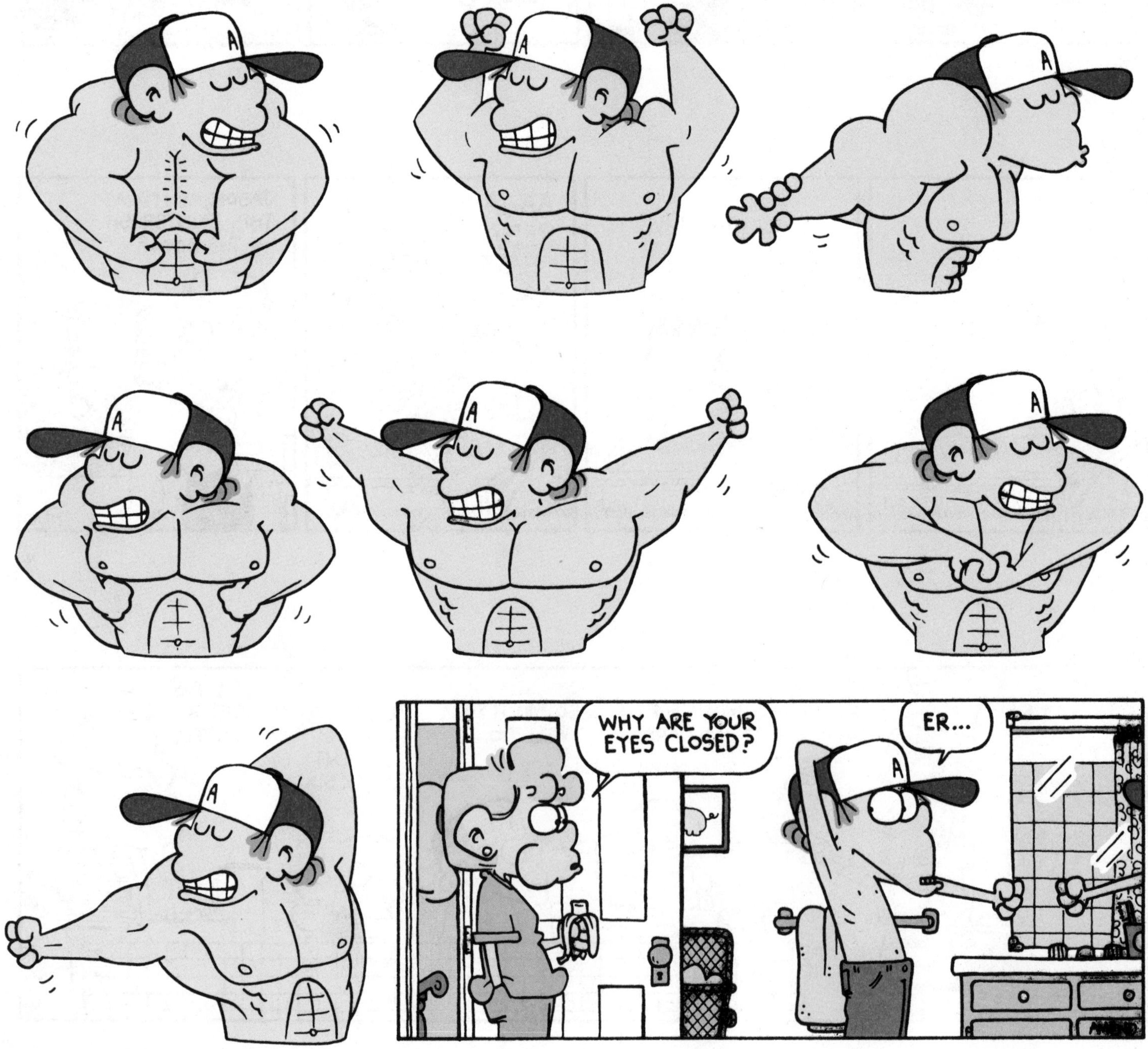

WHY ARE YOUR EYES CLOSED?
ER...

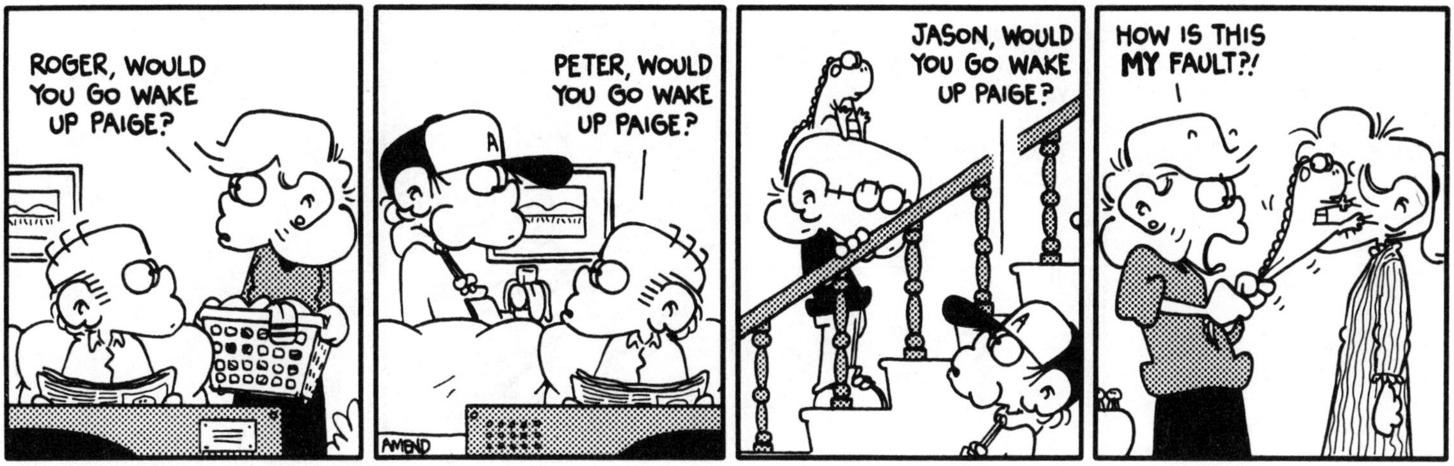
ROGER, WOULD YOU GO WAKE UP PAIGE?
PETER, WOULD YOU GO WAKE UP PAIGE?
AMEND
JASON, WOULD YOU GO WAKE UP PAIGE?
HOW IS THIS MY FAULT?!

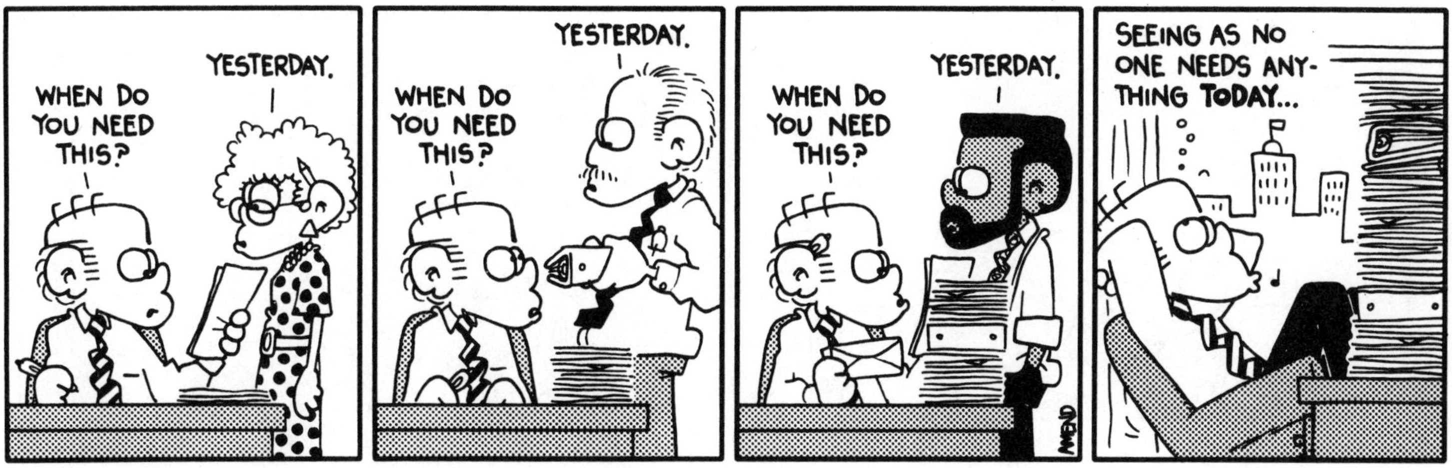
WHEN DO YOU NEED THIS?
YESTERDAY.
WHEN DO YOU NEED THIS?
YESTERDAY.
WHEN DO YOU NEED THIS?
YESTERDAY.
AMEND
SEEING AS NO ONE NEEDS ANYTHING TODAY...

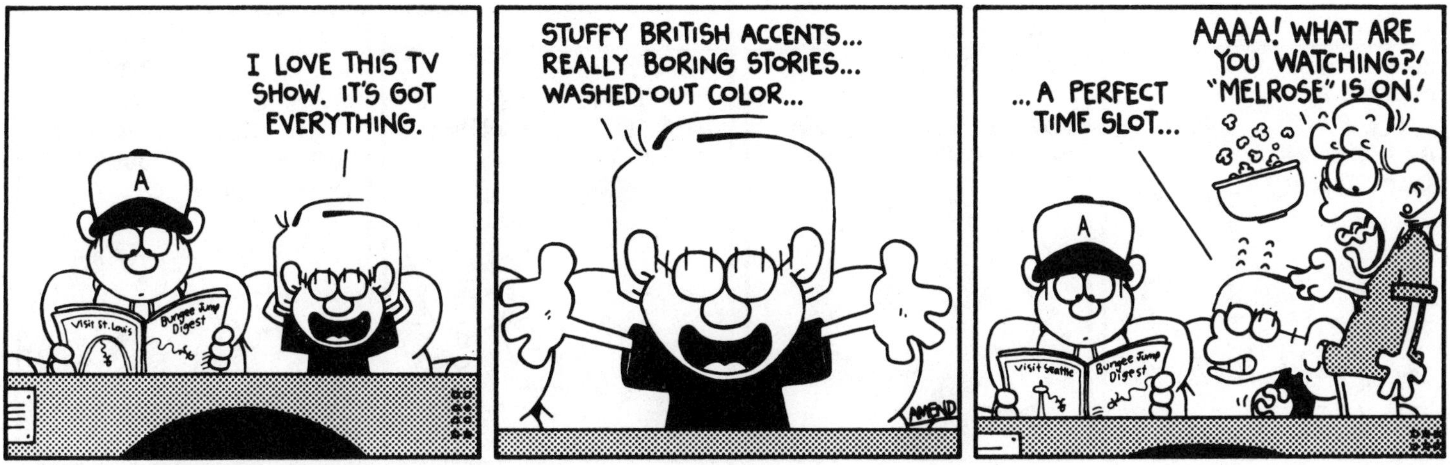
I LOVE THIS TV SHOW. IT'S GOT EVERYTHING.
STUFFY BRITISH ACCENTS... REALLY BORING STORIES... WASHED-OUT COLOR...
AMEND
...A PERFECT TIME SLOT...
AAAA! WHAT ARE YOU WATCHING?! "MELROSE" IS ON!

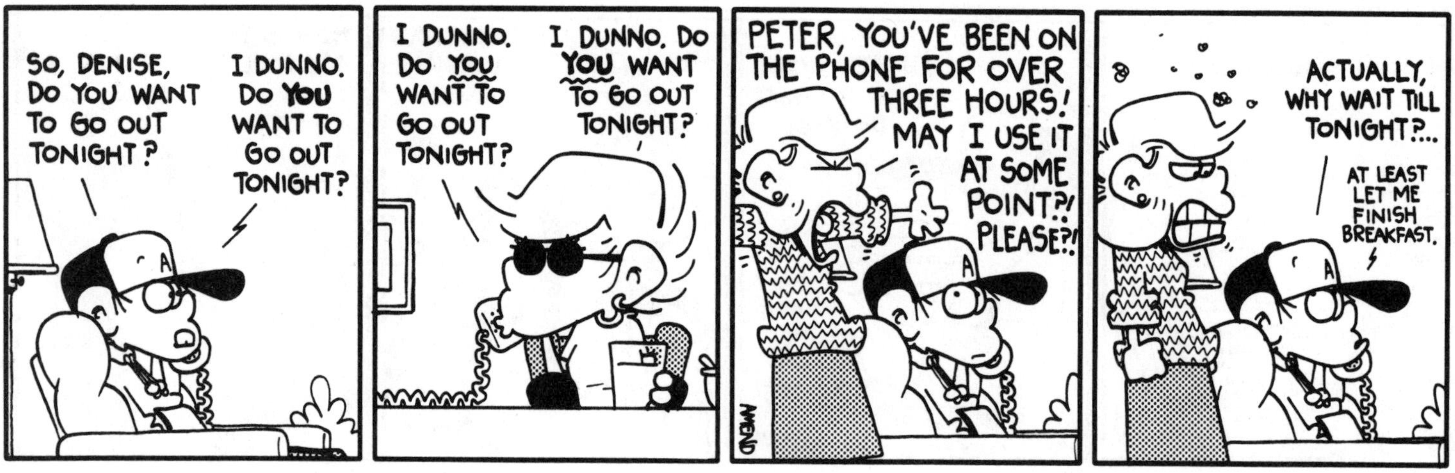
SO, DENISE, DO YOU WANT TO GO OUT TONIGHT?
I DUNNO. DO YOU WANT TO GO OUT TONIGHT?
I DUNNO. DO YOU WANT TO GO OUT TONIGHT?
I DUNNO. DO YOU WANT TO GO OUT TONIGHT?
PETER, YOU'VE BEEN ON THE PHONE FOR OVER THREE HOURS! MAY I USE IT AT SOME POINT?! PLEASE?!
ACTUALLY, WHY WAIT TILL TONIGHT?...
AT LEAST LET ME FINISH BREAKFAST.
AMEND

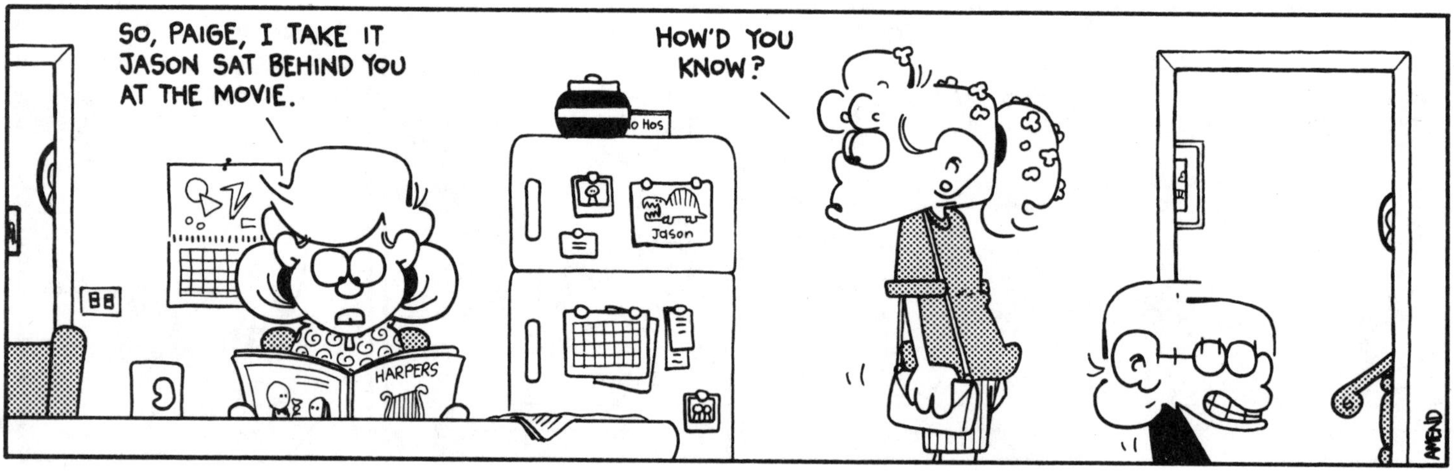
SO, PAIGE, I TAKE IT JASON SAT BEHIND YOU AT THE MOVIE.
HOW'D YOU KNOW?
Jason
HARPERS
AMEND

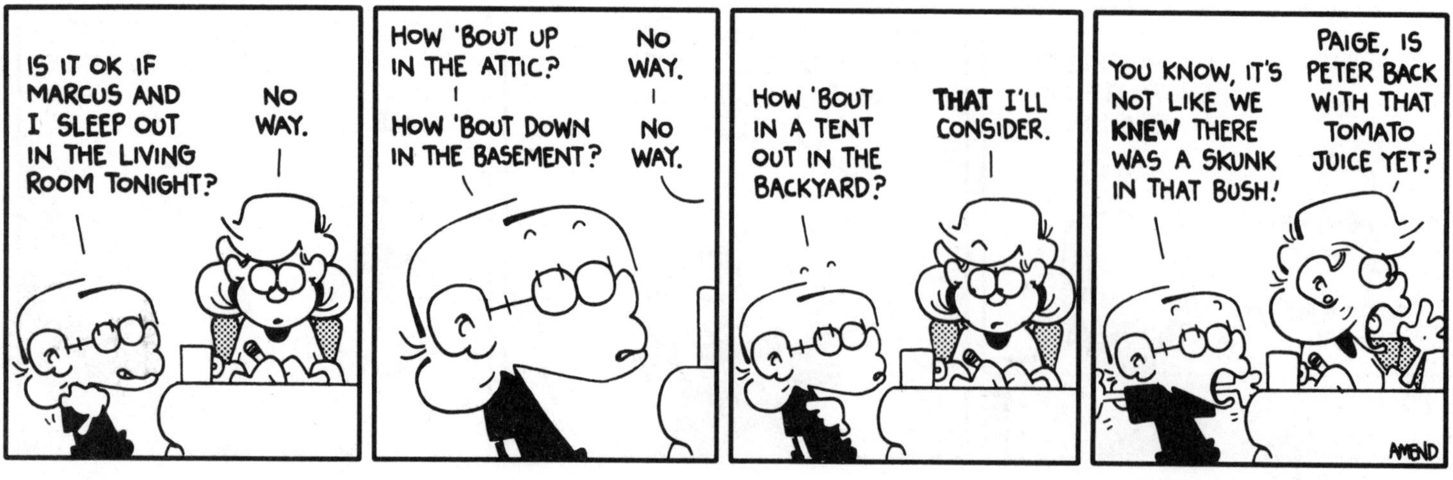
IS IT OK IF MARCUS AND I SLEEP OUT IN THE LIVING ROOM TONIGHT?
NO WAY.
HOW 'BOUT UP IN THE ATTIC?
NO WAY.
HOW 'BOUT DOWN IN THE BASEMENT?
NO WAY.
HOW 'BOUT IN A TENT OUT IN THE BACKYARD?
THAT I'LL CONSIDER.
YOU KNOW, IT'S NOT LIKE WE KNEW THERE WAS A SKUNK IN THAT BUSH!
PAIGE, IS PETER BACK WITH THAT TOMATO JUICE YET?
AMEND

FoxTrot

BILL AMEND

WHAT IS IT ABOUT BOYS AND TRAMPOLINES?
OPEN THE WINDOW ON "THREE"...
AMEND

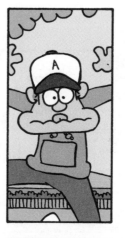

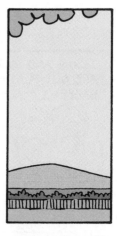

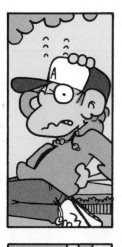

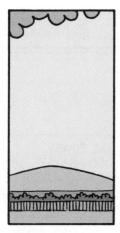

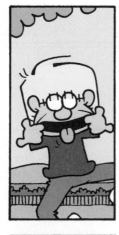

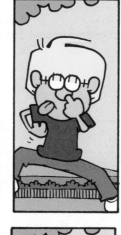

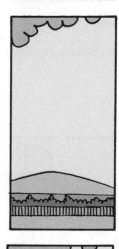

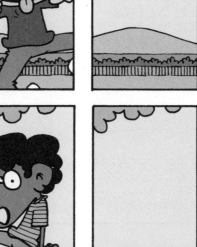

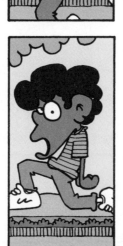

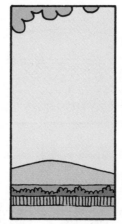

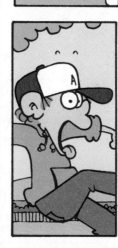

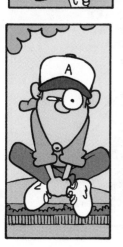

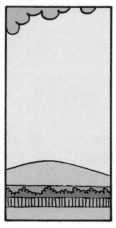

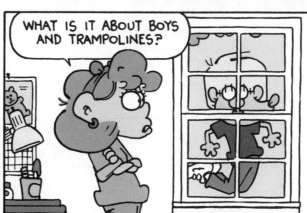

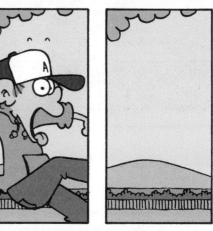

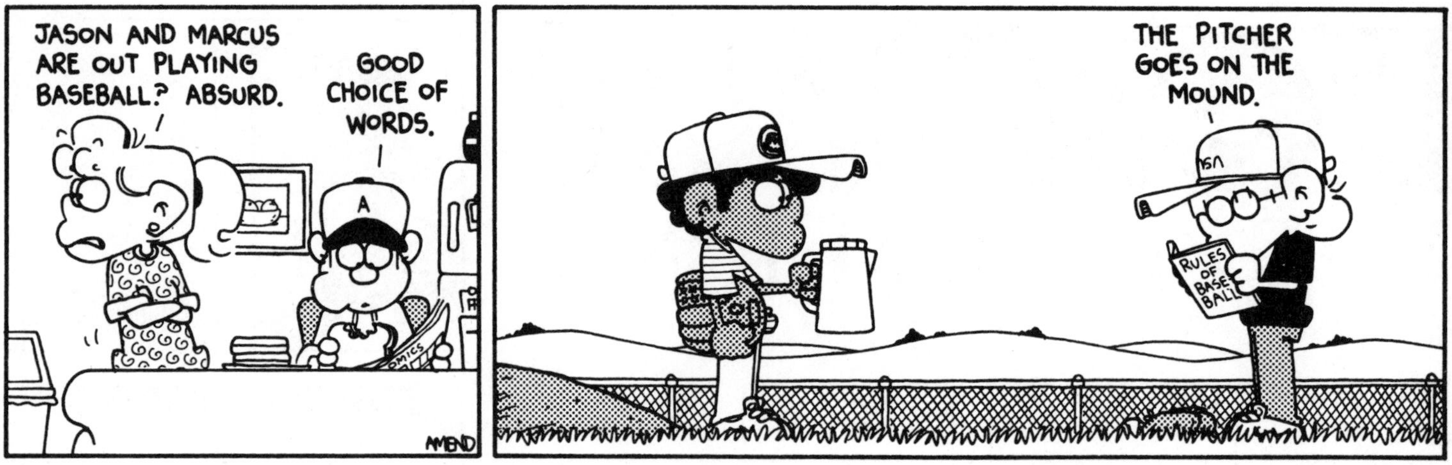
JASON AND MARCUS ARE OUT PLAYING BASEBALL? ABSURD.
GOOD CHOICE OF WORDS.
AMEND
THE PITCHER GOES ON THE MOUND.
RULES OF BASEBALL

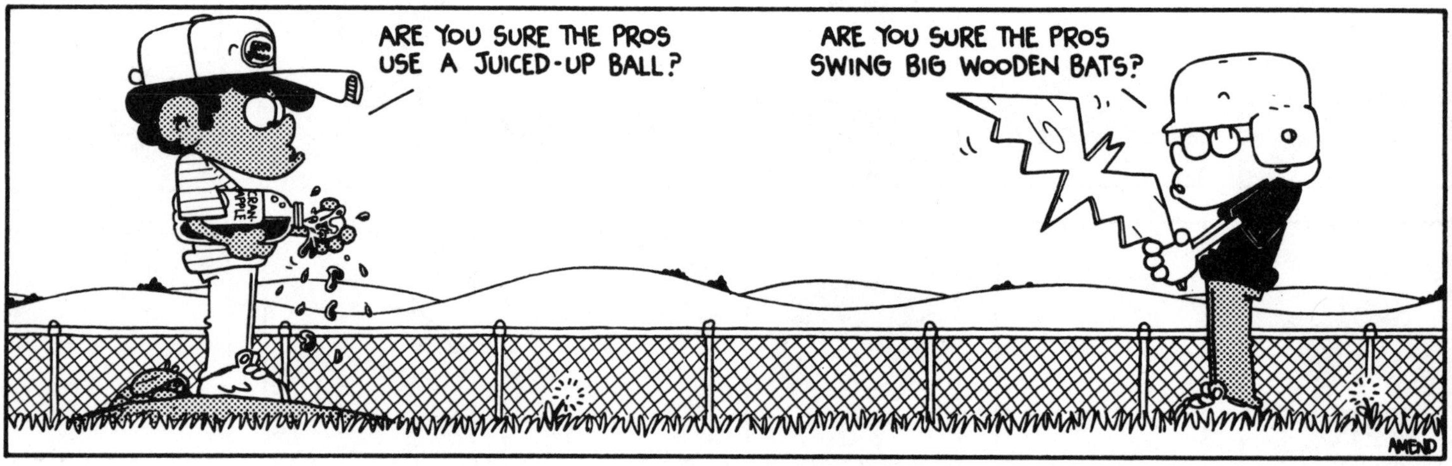
ARE YOU SURE THE PROS USE A JUICED-UP BALL?
ARE YOU SURE THE PROS SWING BIG WOODEN BATS?
AMEND

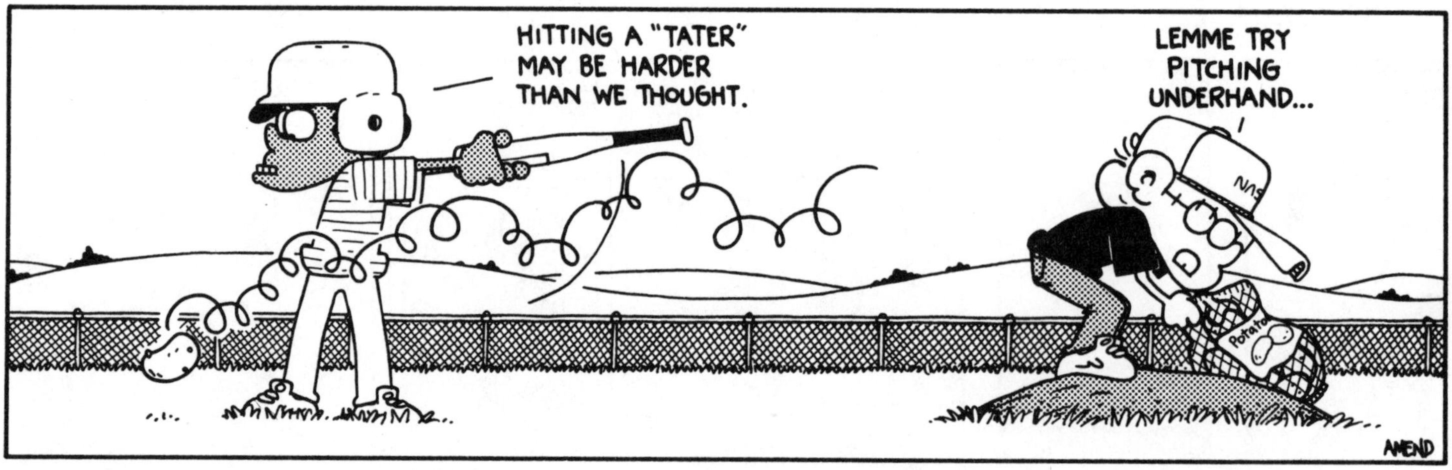
HITTING A "TATER" MAY BE HARDER THAN WE THOUGHT.
LEMME TRY PITCHING UNDERHAND...
Potato
AMEND

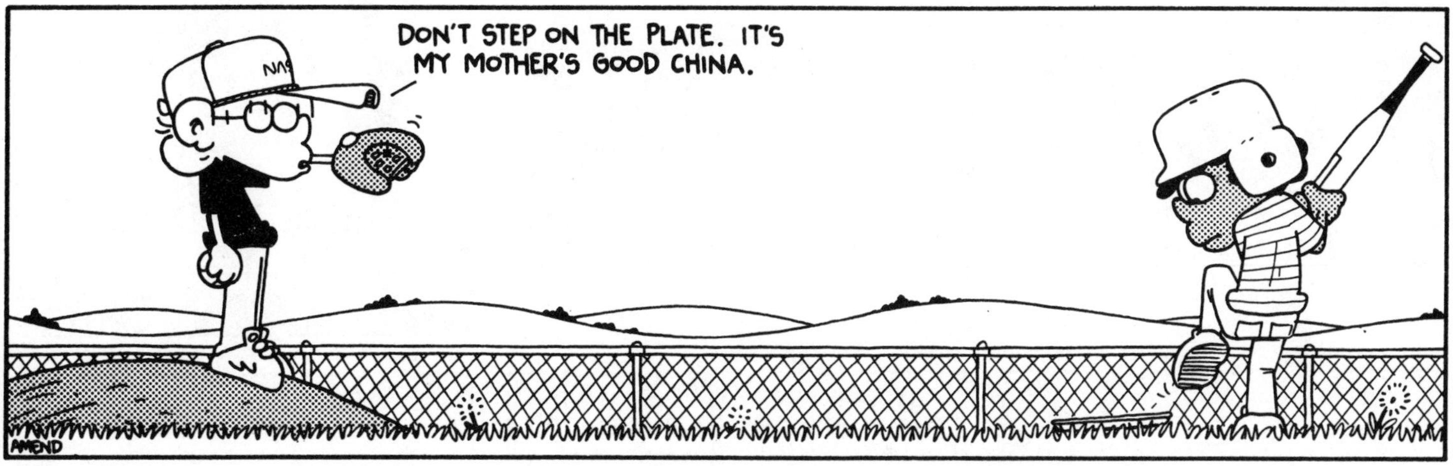
DON'T STEP ON THE PLATE. IT'S MY MOTHER'S GOOD CHINA.
AMEND

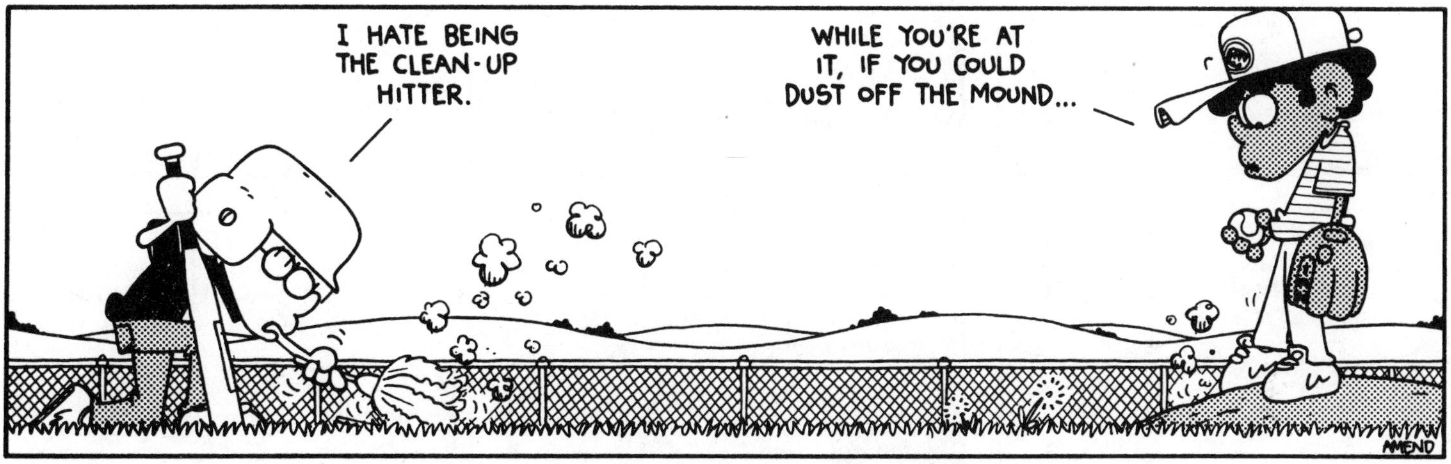
I HATE BEING THE CLEAN-UP HITTER.
WHILE YOU'RE AT IT, IF YOU COULD DUST OFF THE MOUND...
AMEND

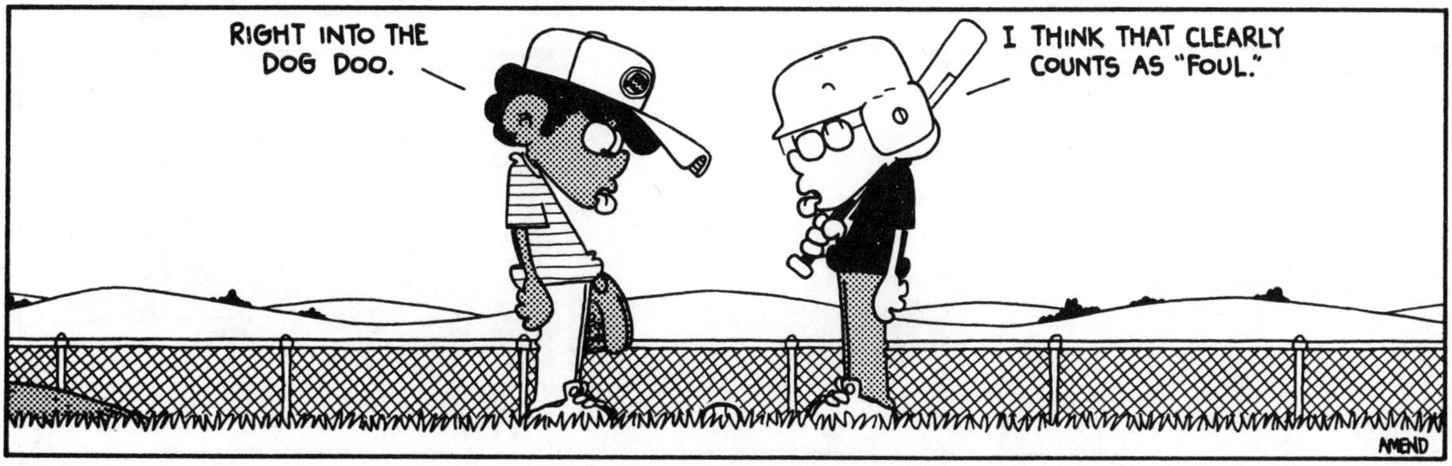
RIGHT INTO THE DOG DOO.
I THINK THAT CLEARLY COUNTS AS "FOUL."
AMEND

FoxTrot
BILL AMEND

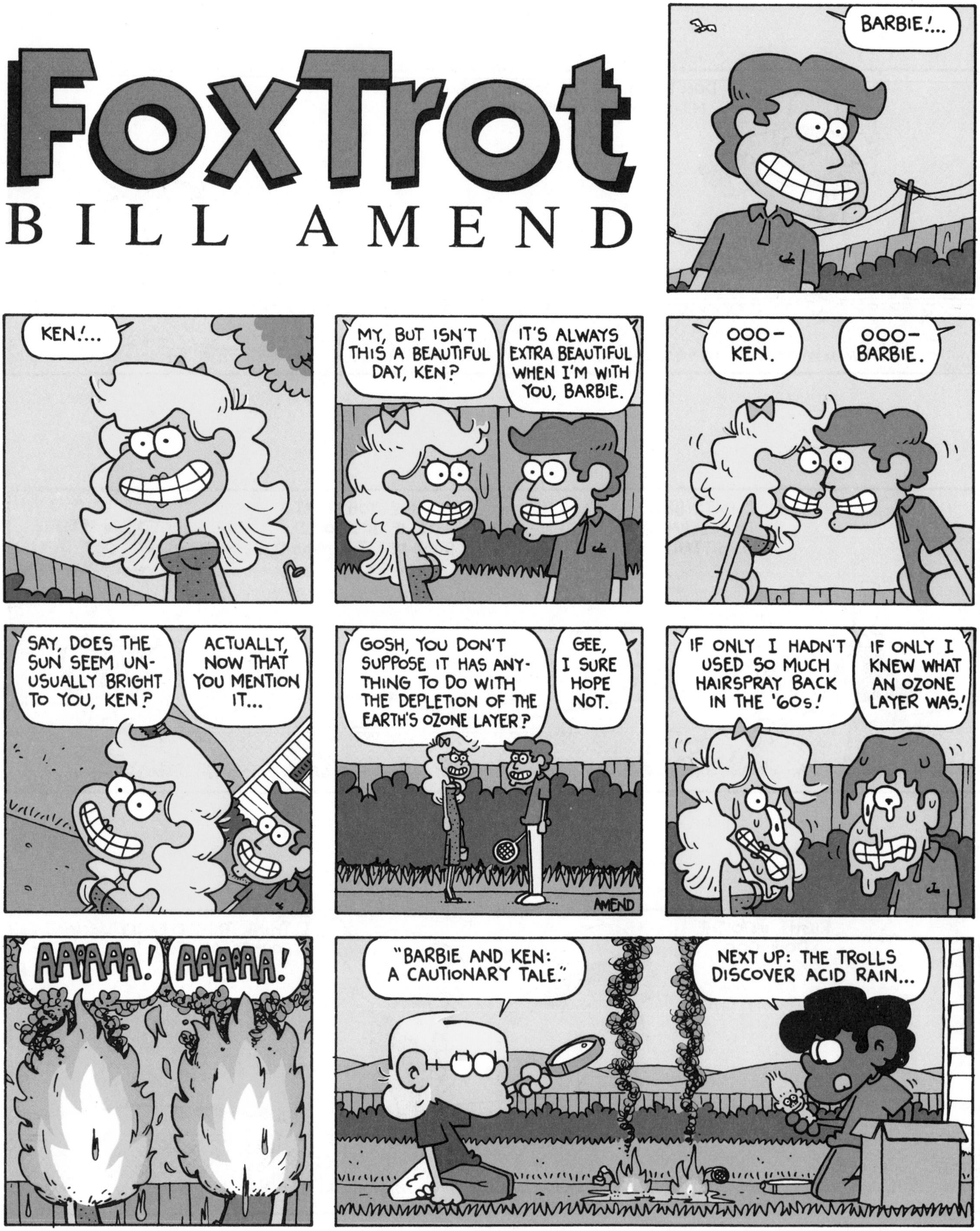

BARBIE!...
KEN!...
MY, BUT ISN'T THIS A BEAUTIFUL DAY, KEN?
IT'S ALWAYS EXTRA BEAUTIFUL WHEN I'M WITH YOU, BARBIE.
OOO- KEN.
OOO- BARBIE.
SAY, DOES THE SUN SEEM UNUSUALLY BRIGHT TO YOU, KEN?
ACTUALLY, NOW THAT YOU MENTION IT...
GOSH, YOU DON'T SUPPOSE IT HAS ANYTHING TO DO WITH THE DEPLETION OF THE EARTH'S OZONE LAYER?
GEE, I SURE HOPE NOT.
AMEND
IF ONLY I HADN'T USED SO MUCH HAIRSPRAY BACK IN THE '60s!
IF ONLY I KNEW WHAT AN OZONE LAYER WAS!
AAAAAA!
AAAAAA!
"BARBIE AND KEN: A CAUTIONARY TALE."
NEXT UP: THE TROLLS DISCOVER ACID RAIN...

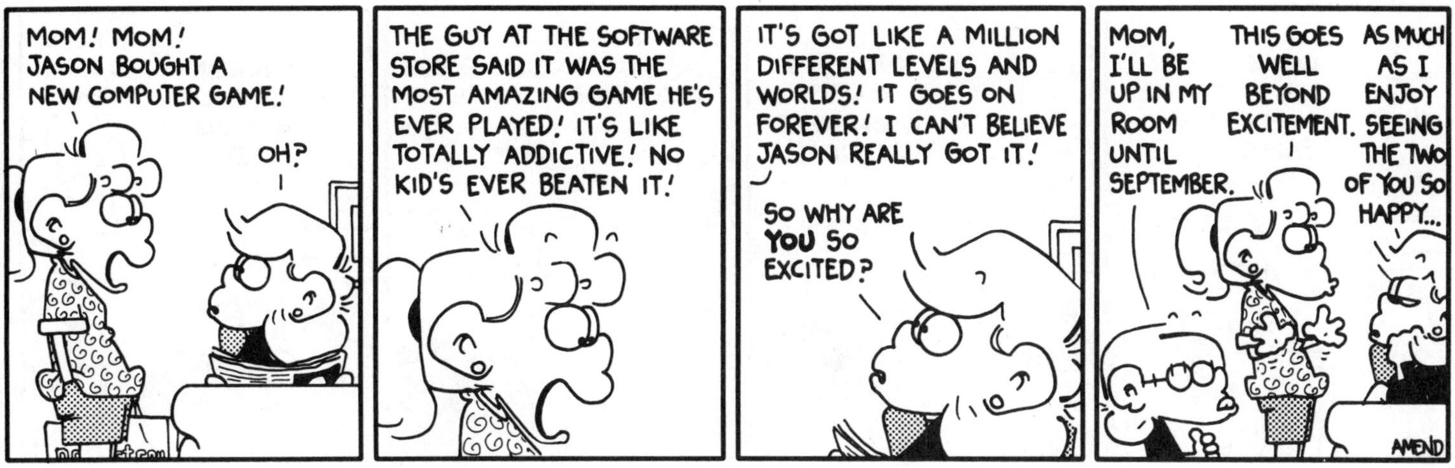

MOM! MOM! JASON BOUGHT A NEW COMPUTER GAME!
OH?
THE GUY AT THE SOFTWARE STORE SAID IT WAS THE MOST AMAZING GAME HE'S EVER PLAYED! IT'S LIKE TOTALLY ADDICTIVE! NO KID'S EVER BEATEN IT!
IT'S GOT LIKE A MILLION DIFFERENT LEVELS AND WORLDS! IT GOES ON FOREVER! I CAN'T BELIEVE JASON REALLY GOT IT!
SO WHY ARE **YOU** SO EXCITED?
MOM, I'LL BE UP IN MY ROOM UNTIL SEPTEMBER.
THIS GOES WELL BEYOND EXCITEMENT.
AS MUCH AS I ENJOY SEEING THE TWO OF YOU SO HAPPY...
AMEND

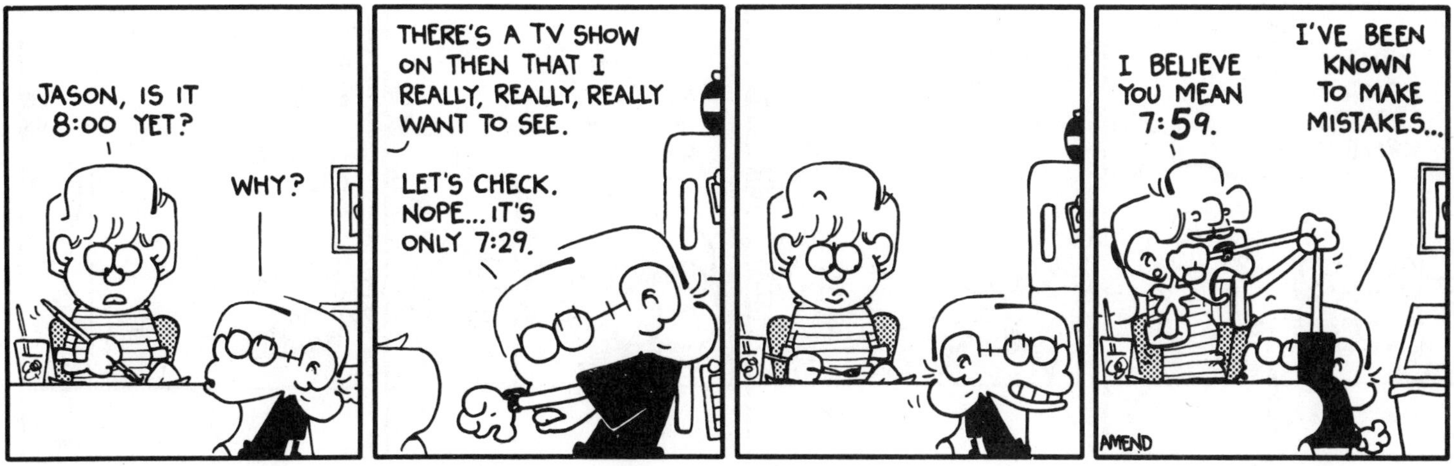

JASON, IS IT 8:00 YET?
WHY?
THERE'S A TV SHOW ON THEN THAT I REALLY, REALLY, REALLY WANT TO SEE.
LET'S CHECK. NOPE... IT'S ONLY 7:29.
I BELIEVE YOU MEAN 7:59.
I'VE BEEN KNOWN TO MAKE MISTAKES...
AMEND

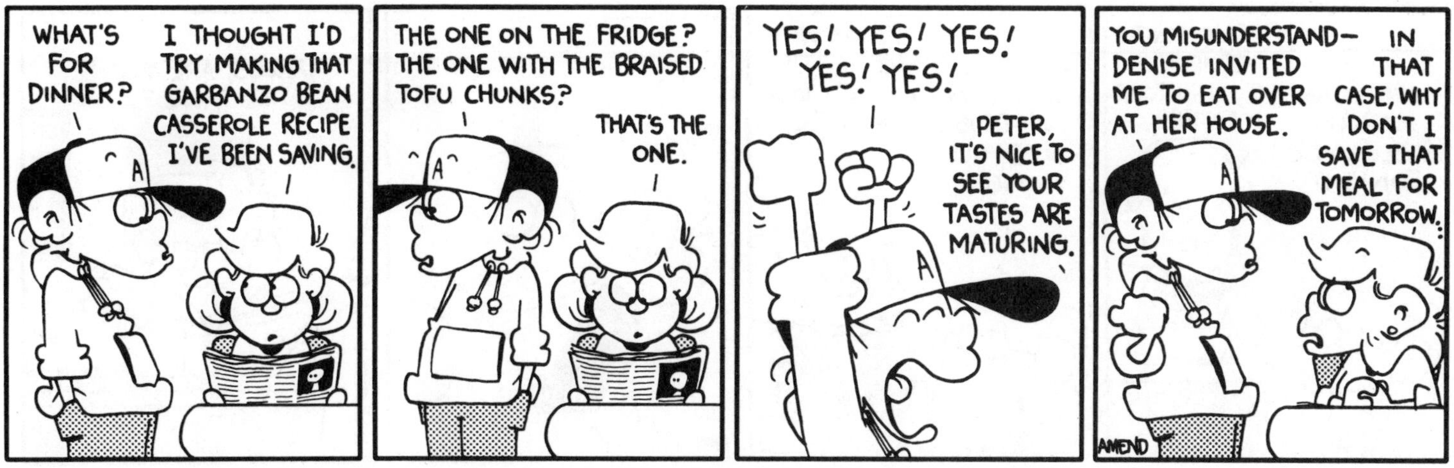

WHAT'S FOR DINNER?
I THOUGHT I'D TRY MAKING THAT GARBANZO BEAN CASSEROLE RECIPE I'VE BEEN SAVING.
THE ONE ON THE FRIDGE? THE ONE WITH THE BRAISED TOFU CHUNKS?
THAT'S THE ONE.
YES! YES! YES! YES! YES!
PETER, IT'S NICE TO SEE YOUR TASTES ARE MATURING.
YOU MISUNDERSTAND— DENISE INVITED ME TO EAT OVER AT HER HOUSE.
IN THAT CASE, WHY DON'T I SAVE THAT MEAL FOR TOMORROW.
AMEND

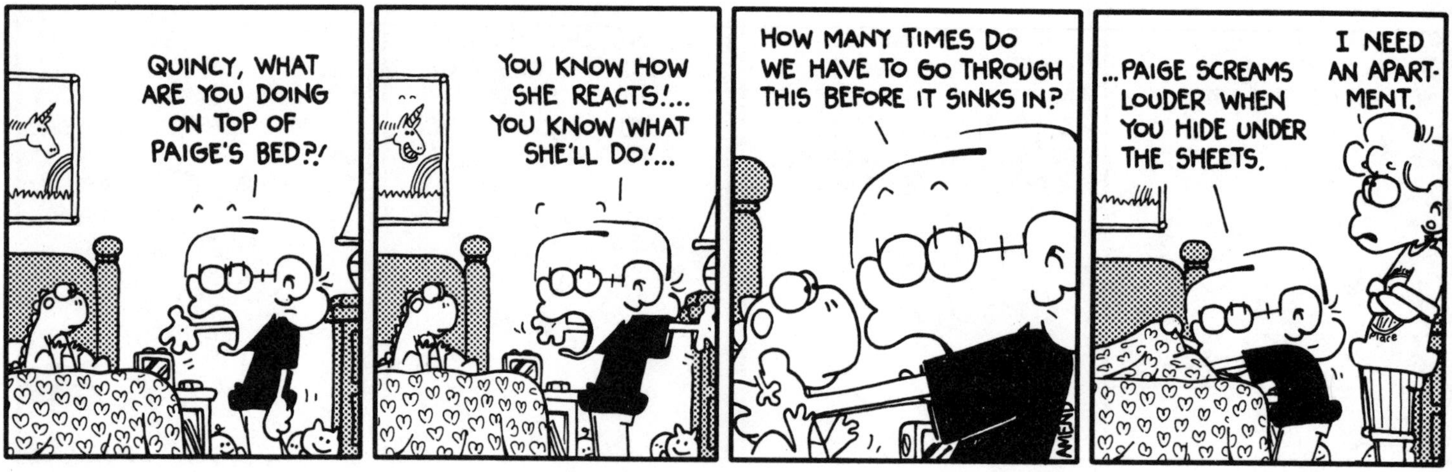
QUINCY, WHAT ARE YOU DOING ON TOP OF PAIGE'S BED?!
YOU KNOW HOW SHE REACTS!... YOU KNOW WHAT SHE'LL DO!...
HOW MANY TIMES DO WE HAVE TO GO THROUGH THIS BEFORE IT SINKS IN?
AMEND
...PAIGE SCREAMS LOUDER WHEN YOU HIDE UNDER THE SHEETS.
I NEED AN APARTMENT.

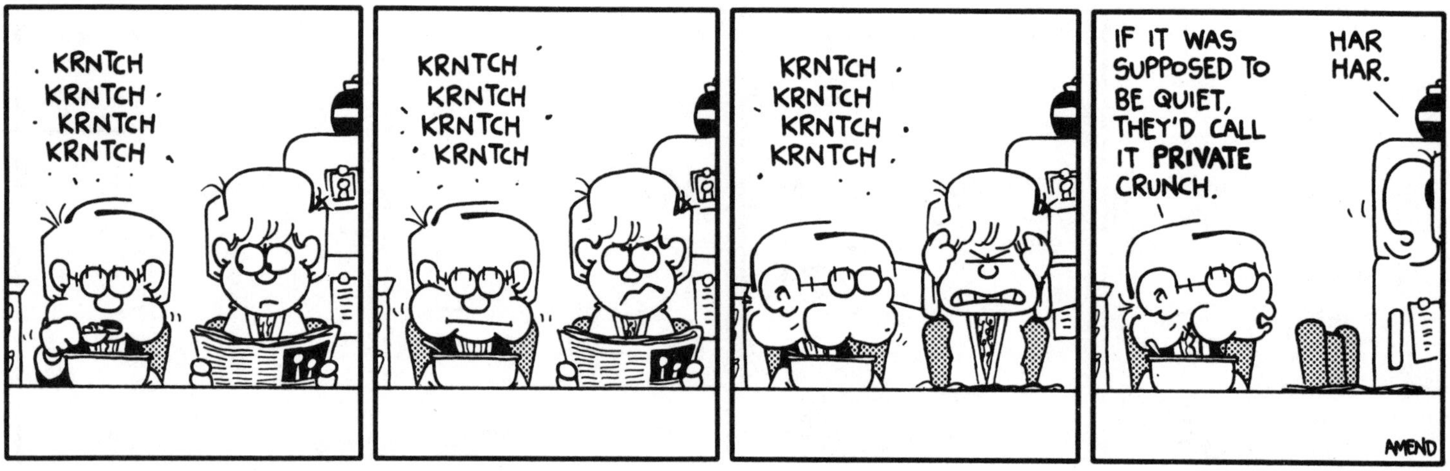
KRNTCH KRNTCH KRNTCH KRNTCH
KRNTCH KRNTCH KRNTCH KRNTCH
KRNTCH KRNTCH KRNTCH KRNTCH
IF IT WAS SUPPOSED TO BE QUIET, THEY'D CALL IT PRIVATE CRUNCH.
HAR HAR.
AMEND

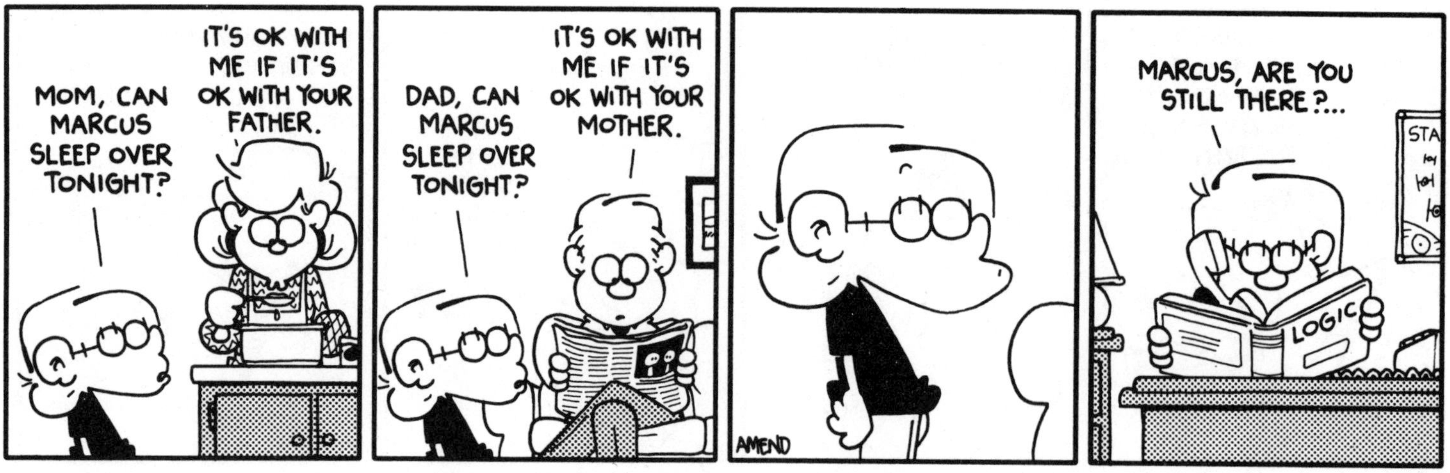
MOM, CAN MARCUS SLEEP OVER TONIGHT?
IT'S OK WITH ME IF IT'S OK WITH YOUR FATHER.
DAD, CAN MARCUS SLEEP OVER TONIGHT?
IT'S OK WITH ME IF IT'S OK WITH YOUR MOTHER.
AMEND
MARCUS, ARE YOU STILL THERE?...
LOGIC

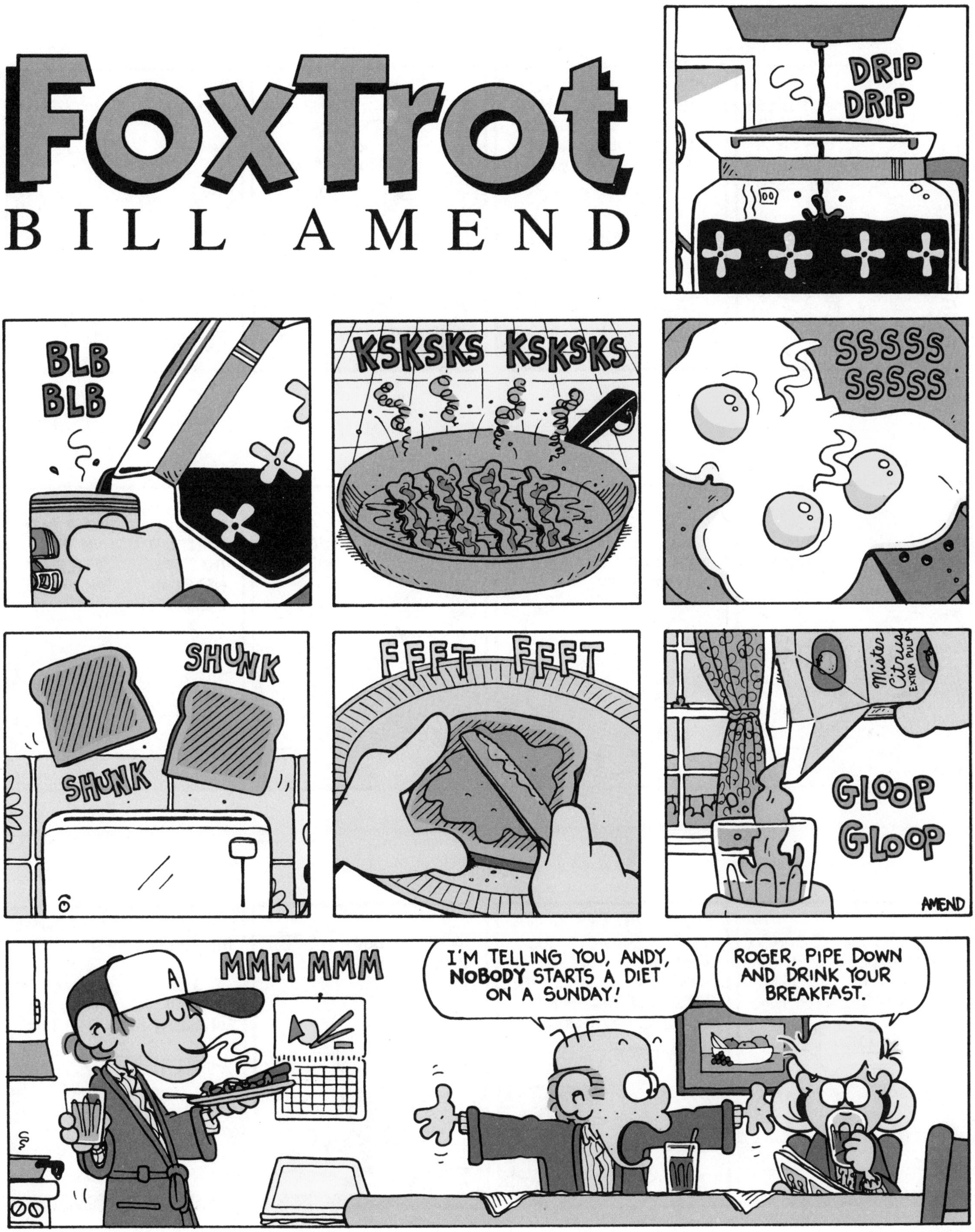
FoxTrot
BILL AMEND
DRIP DRIP
BLB BLB
KSKSKS KSKSKS
SSSSS SSSSS
SHUNK
SHUNK
FFFT FFFT
Mister Citrus EXTRA PULP
GLOOP GLOOP
AMEND
MMM MMM
I'M TELLING YOU, ANDY, NOBODY STARTS A DIET ON A SUNDAY!
ROGER, PIPE DOWN AND DRINK YOUR BREAKFAST.

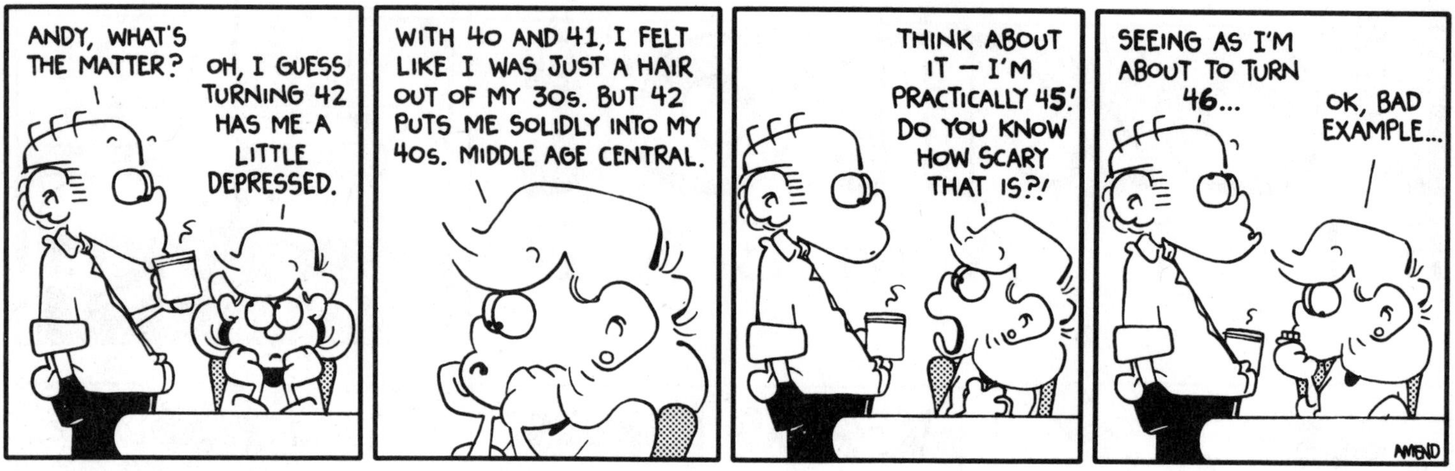
ANDY, WHAT'S THE MATTER?
OH, I GUESS TURNING 42 HAS ME A LITTLE DEPRESSED.
WITH 40 AND 41, I FELT LIKE I WAS JUST A HAIR OUT OF MY 30s. BUT 42 PUTS ME SOLIDLY INTO MY 40s. MIDDLE AGE CENTRAL.
THINK ABOUT IT — I'M PRACTICALLY 45! DO YOU KNOW HOW SCARY THAT IS?!
SEEING AS I'M ABOUT TO TURN 46...
OK, BAD EXAMPLE...
AMEND

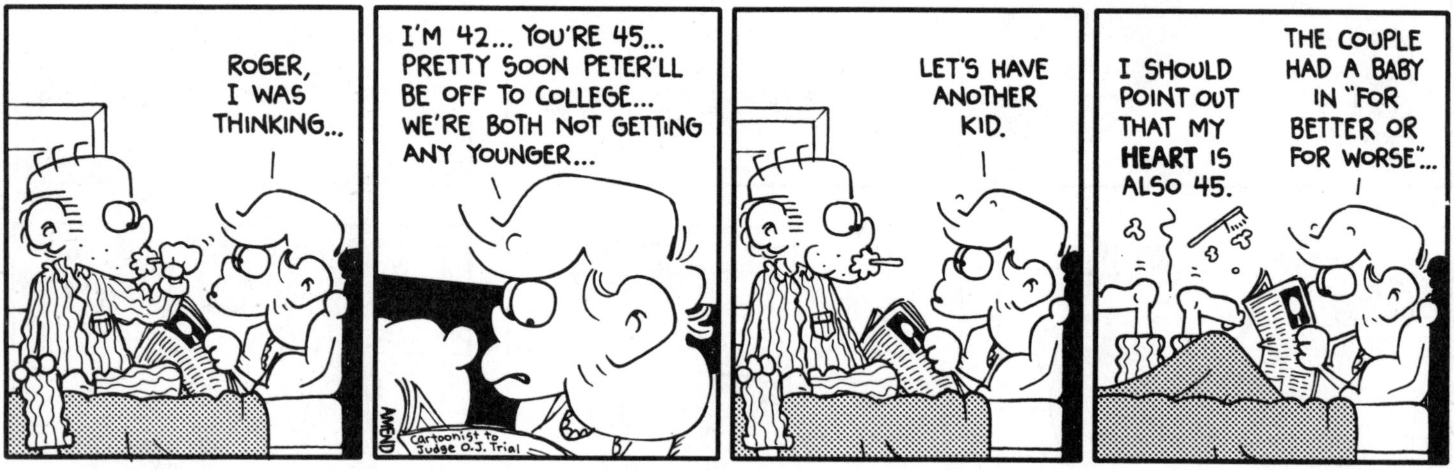
ROGER, I WAS THINKING...
I'M 42... YOU'RE 45... PRETTY SOON PETER'LL BE OFF TO COLLEGE... WE'RE BOTH NOT GETTING ANY YOUNGER...
AMEND
Cartoonist to Judge O.J. Trial
LET'S HAVE ANOTHER KID.
I SHOULD POINT OUT THAT MY HEART IS ALSO 45.
THE COUPLE HAD A BABY IN "FOR BETTER OR FOR WORSE"...

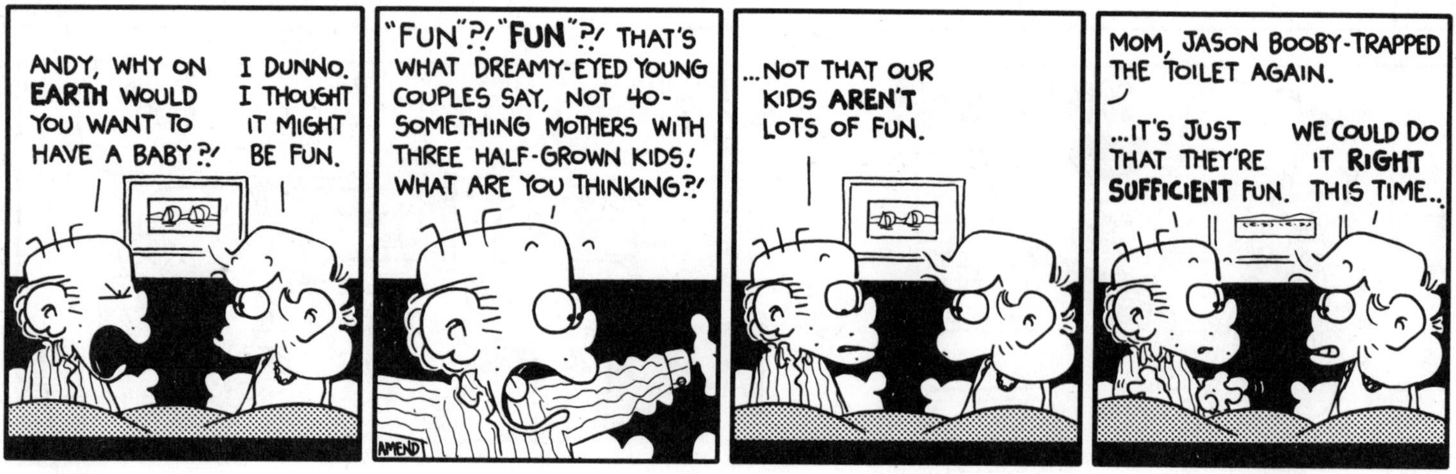
ANDY, WHY ON EARTH WOULD YOU WANT TO HAVE A BABY?!
I DUNNO. I THOUGHT IT MIGHT BE FUN.
"FUN"?! "FUN"?! THAT'S WHAT DREAMY-EYED YOUNG COUPLES SAY, NOT 40-SOMETHING MOTHERS WITH THREE HALF-GROWN KIDS! WHAT ARE YOU THINKING?!
AMEND
...NOT THAT OUR KIDS AREN'T LOTS OF FUN.
MOM, JASON BOOBY-TRAPPED THE TOILET AGAIN.
...IT'S JUST THAT THEY'RE SUFFICIENT FUN.
WE COULD DO IT RIGHT THIS TIME...

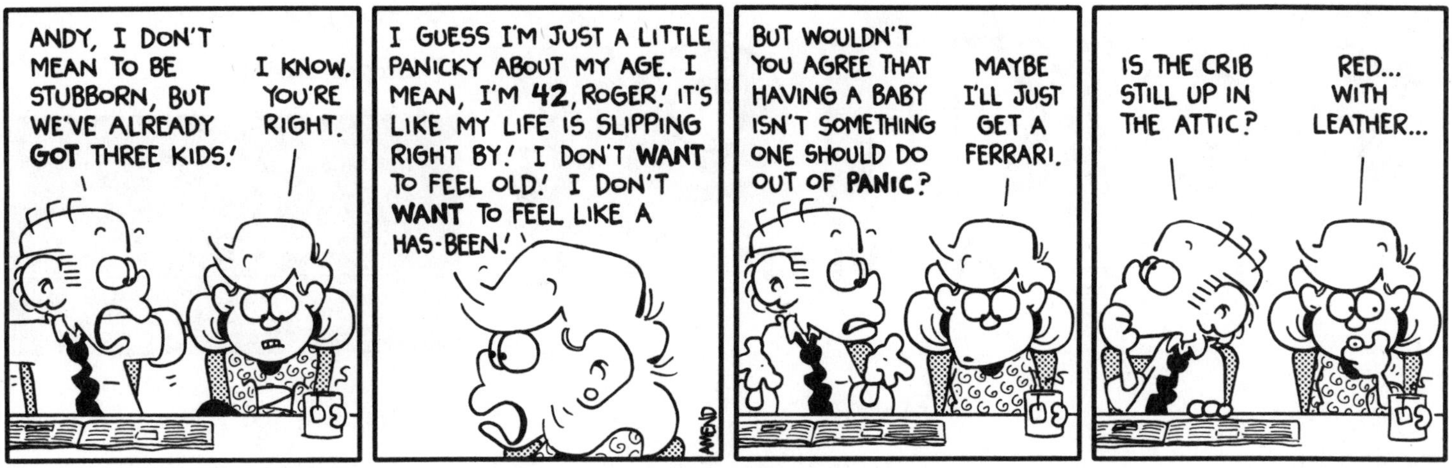
ANDY, I DON'T MEAN TO BE STUBBORN, BUT WE'VE ALREADY GOT THREE KIDS!
I KNOW. YOU'RE RIGHT.
I GUESS I'M JUST A LITTLE PANICKY ABOUT MY AGE. I MEAN, I'M 42, ROGER! IT'S LIKE MY LIFE IS SLIPPING RIGHT BY! I DON'T WANT TO FEEL OLD! I DON'T WANT TO FEEL LIKE A HAS-BEEN!
AMEND
BUT WOULDN'T YOU AGREE THAT HAVING A BABY ISN'T SOMETHING ONE SHOULD DO OUT OF PANIC?
MAYBE I'LL JUST GET A FERRARI.
IS THE CRIB STILL UP IN THE ATTIC?
RED... WITH LEATHER...

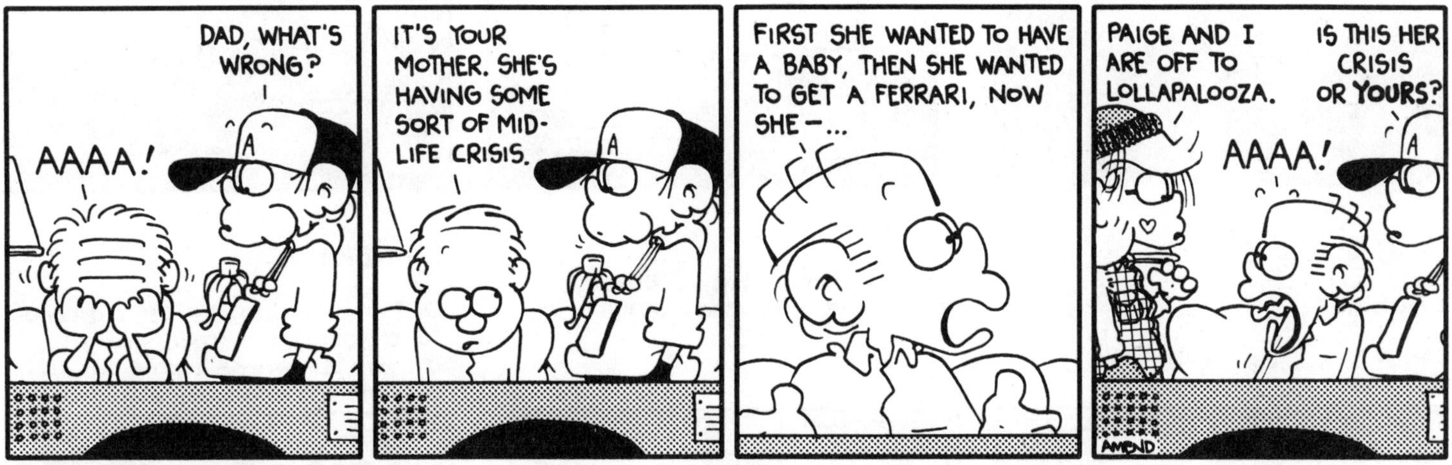
AAAA!
DAD, WHAT'S WRONG?
IT'S YOUR MOTHER. SHE'S HAVING SOME SORT OF MID-LIFE CRISIS.
FIRST SHE WANTED TO HAVE A BABY, THEN SHE WANTED TO GET A FERRARI, NOW SHE—...
PAIGE AND I ARE OFF TO LOLLAPALOOZA.
AAAA!
IS THIS HER CRISIS OR YOURS?
AMEND

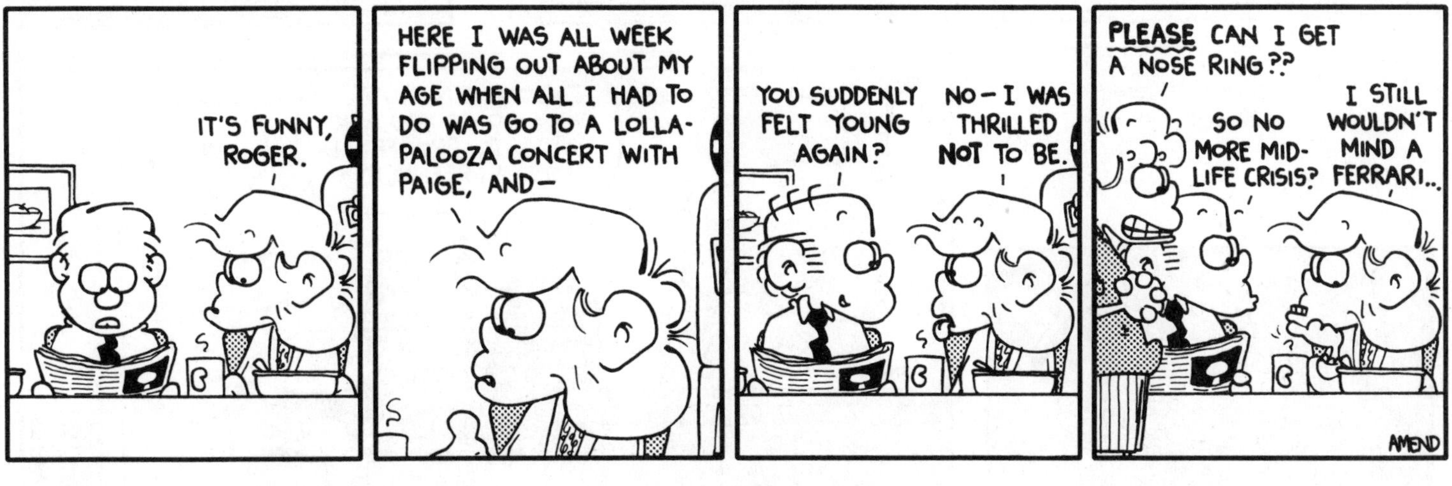
IT'S FUNNY, ROGER.
HERE I WAS ALL WEEK FLIPPING OUT ABOUT MY AGE WHEN ALL I HAD TO DO WAS GO TO A LOLLA-PALOOZA CONCERT WITH PAIGE, AND—
YOU SUDDENLY FELT YOUNG AGAIN?
NO—I WAS THRILLED NOT TO BE.
PLEASE CAN I GET A NOSE RING??
SO NO MORE MID-LIFE CRISIS?
I STILL WOULDN'T MIND A FERRARI...
AMEND

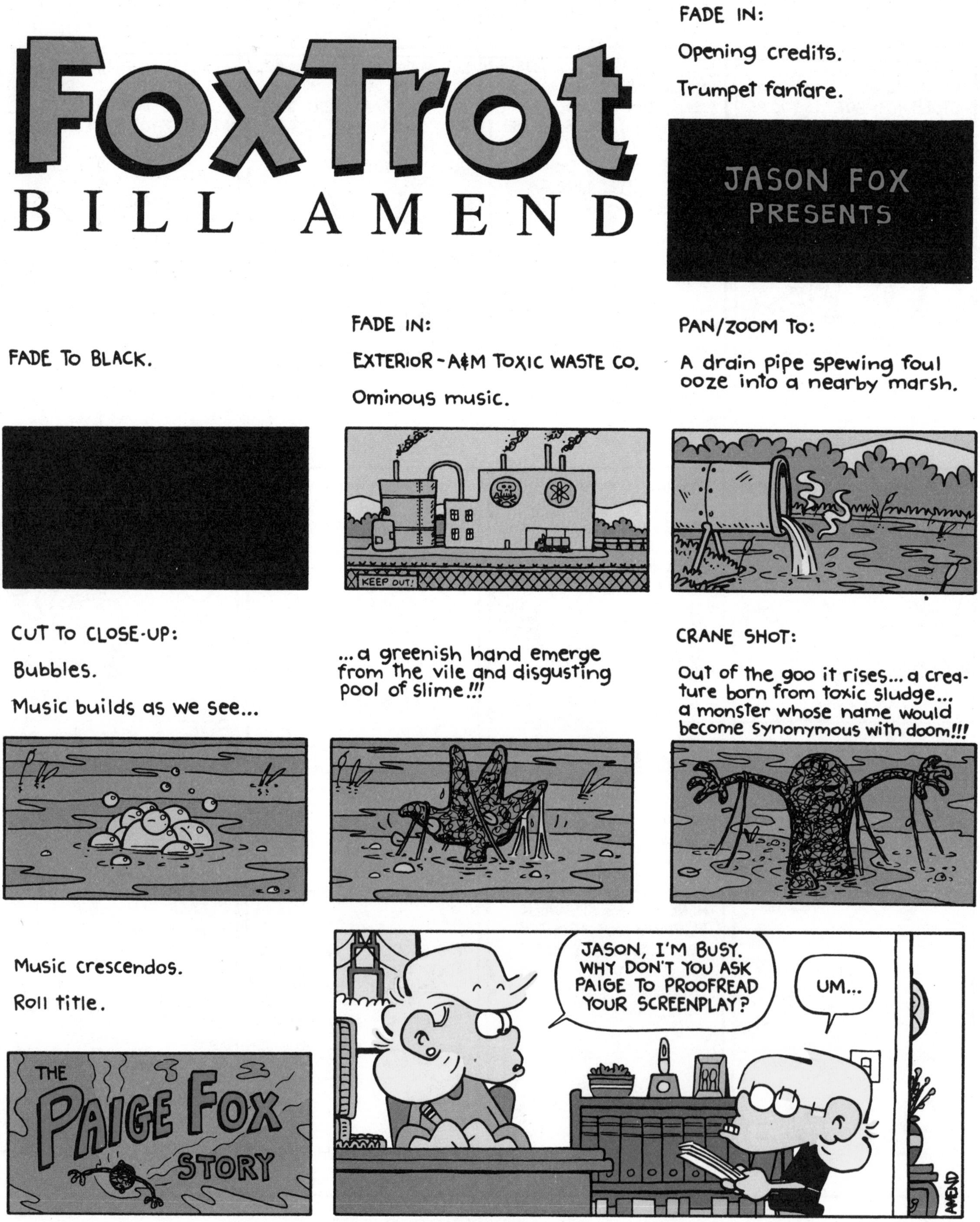
FoxTrot
BILL AMEND
FADE IN:
Opening credits.
Trumpet fanfare.
JASON FOX PRESENTS
FADE TO BLACK.
FADE IN:
EXTERIOR - A&M TOXIC WASTE CO.
Ominous music.
KEEP OUT!
PAN/ZOOM TO:
A drain pipe spewing foul ooze into a nearby marsh.
CUT TO CLOSE-UP:
Bubbles.
Music builds as we see...
...a greenish hand emerge from the vile and disgusting pool of slime!!!
CRANE SHOT:
Out of the goo it rises... a creature born from toxic sludge... a monster whose name would become synonymous with doom!!!
Music crescendos.
Roll title.
THE PAIGE FOX STORY
JASON, I'M BUSY. WHY DON'T YOU ASK PAIGE TO PROOFREAD YOUR SCREENPLAY?
UM...
AMEND

A BEHIND-THE-SCENES PEEK AT THE MAKING OF A SUNDAY FOXTROT COMIC STRIP

by Bill Amend

It all begins with me staring at a blank page on my trusty yellow legal pad. I do my best writing in the morning, on an empty stomach, with plenty of coffee coursing through my veins.

Daddy, have you seen Peter?
Not recently.
Jason, have you seen Peter?
He promised he'd drive me to the mall today!
Greetings, ugly human.
Jason, go away.
I wish to make a wager.
I will wager you a delicious dinner that I can hop into my spacecraft
you can count to ten.
and circle your planet 25 times
It's a bet.
No way can you do that.
You are faster than I thought, earthling. Here is your delicious dinner.
Meal Worms?!?
Yum Yum
Pffthth! Pffthth!

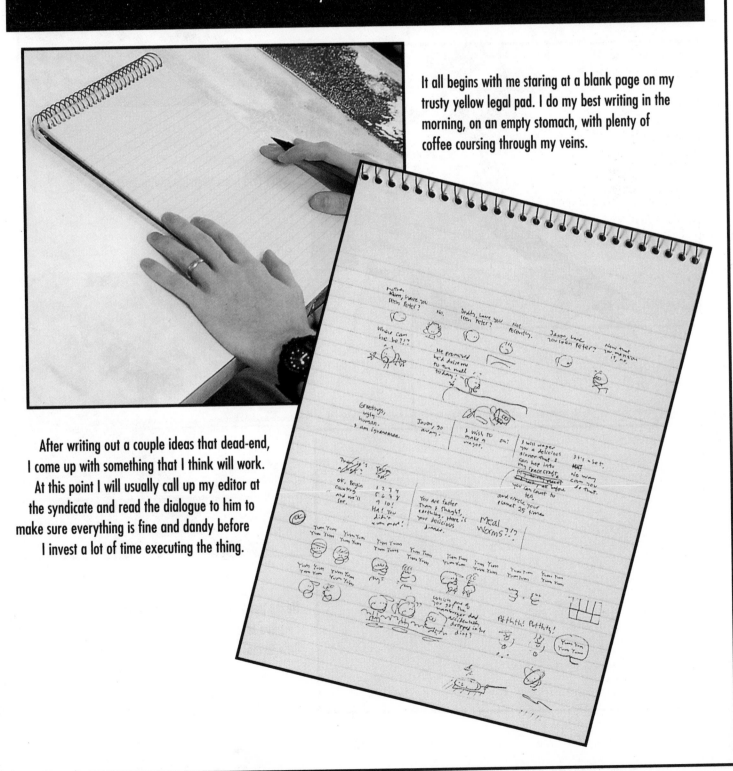

After writing out a couple ideas that dead-end, I come up with something that I think will work. At this point I will usually call up my editor at the syndicate and read the dialogue to him to make sure everything is fine and dandy before I invest a lot of time executing the thing.

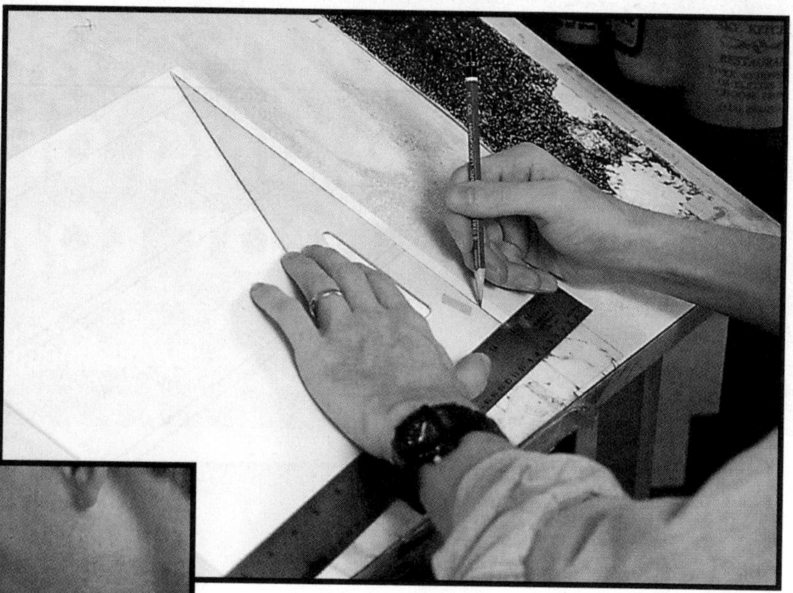

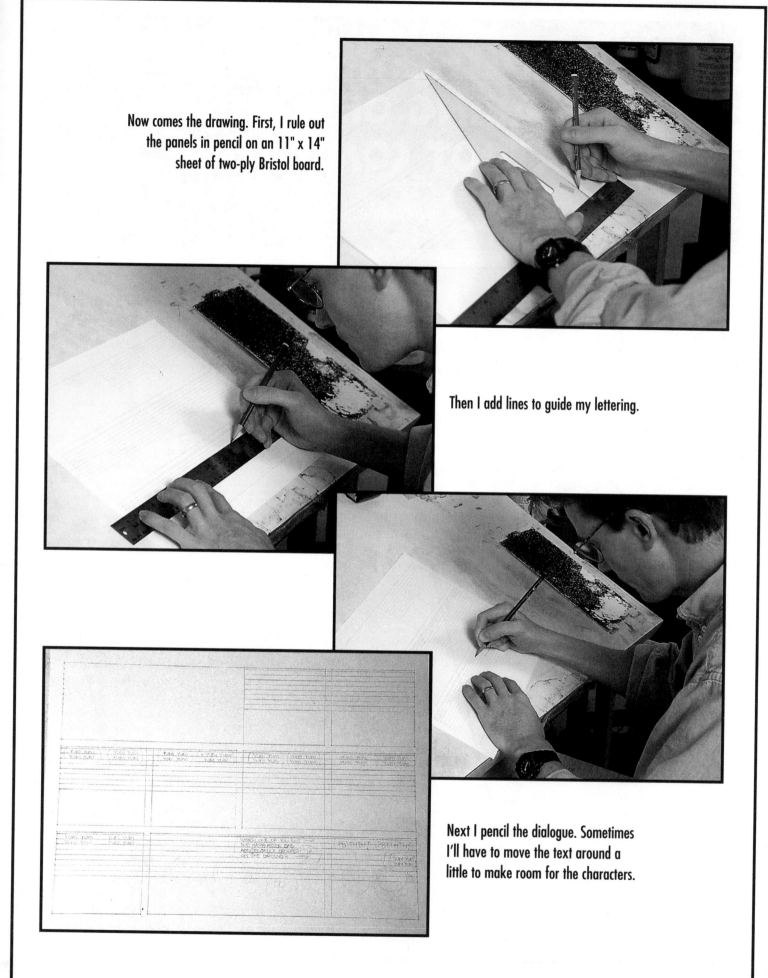

Now comes the drawing. First, I rule out the panels in pencil on an 11" x 14" sheet of two-ply Bristol board.

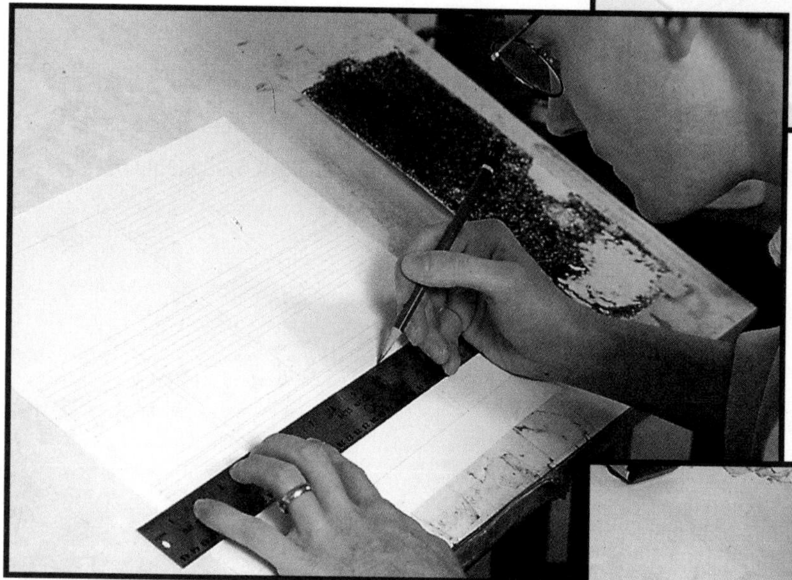

Then I add lines to guide my lettering.

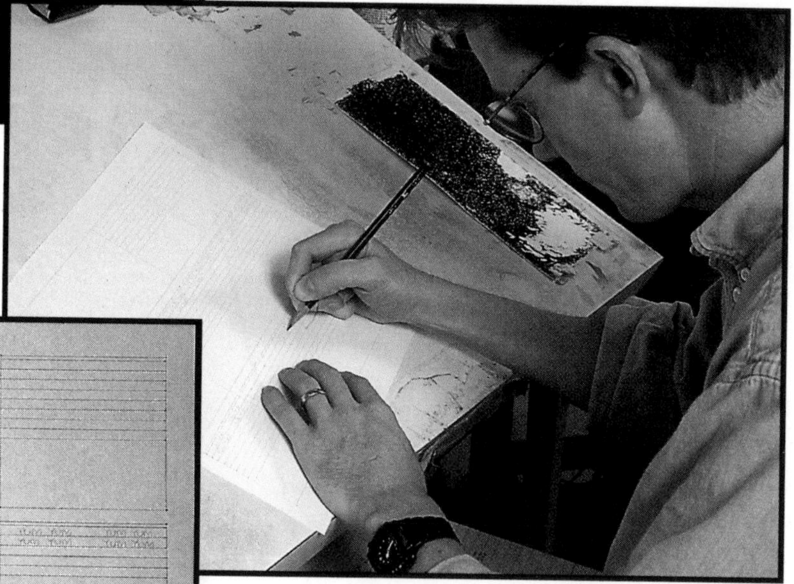

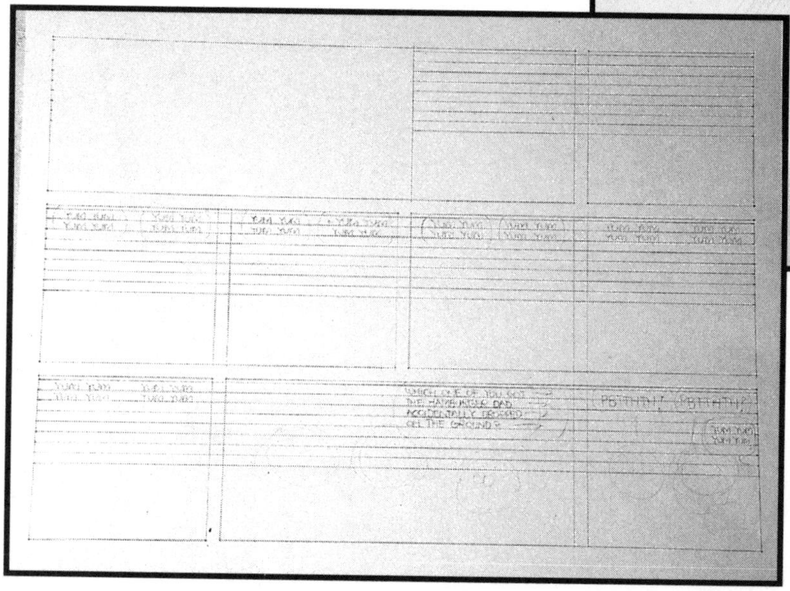

Next I pencil the dialogue. Sometimes I'll have to move the text around a little to make room for the characters.

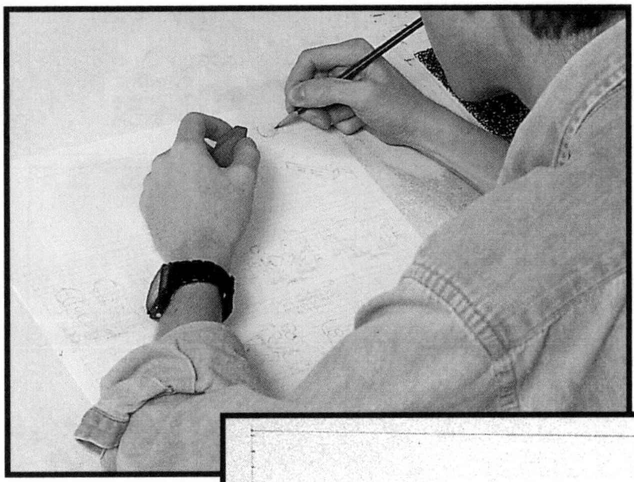

Now it's time to switch brain hemispheres and start drawing cartoons. I begin with really faint stick figures to block out where characters will be and then advance to very tight pencil renderings. This is my favorite part of the creation of a strip, but it's also the hardest for me. I use a 2H pencil and a kneaded rubber eraser.

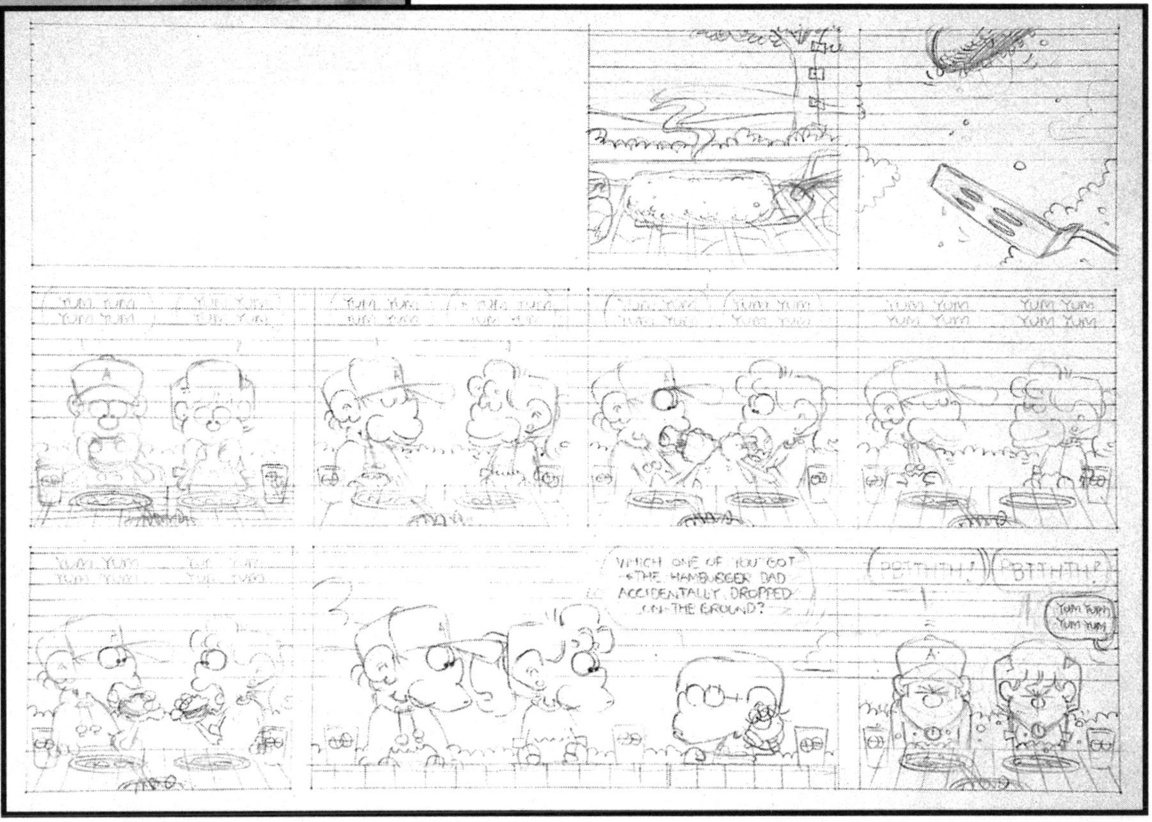

YUM YUM YUM YUM
WHICH ONE OF YOU GOT THE HAMBURGER DAD ACCIDENTALLY DROPPED ON THE GROUND?
PBTHTH!
PBTHTH!
YUM YUM YUM YUM

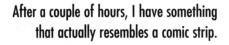

After a couple of hours, I have something that actually resembles a comic strip.

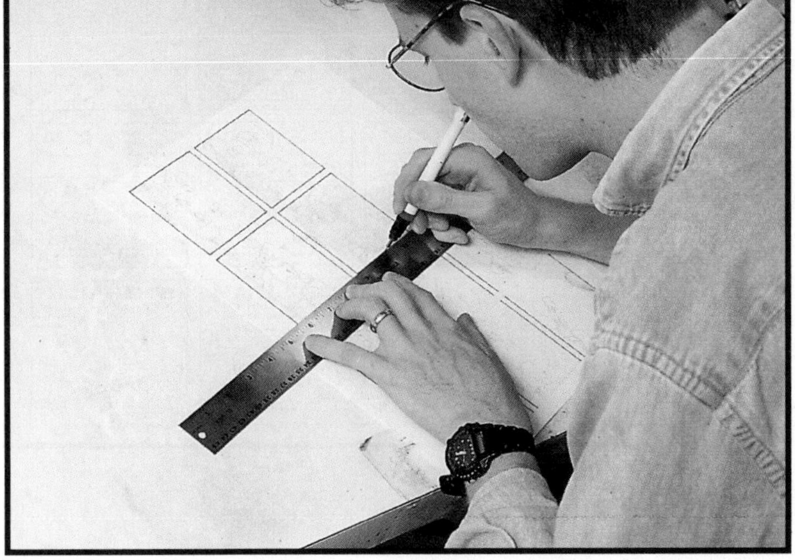

The first things I ink are the panel borders. I use a No. 2½ technical pen for this.

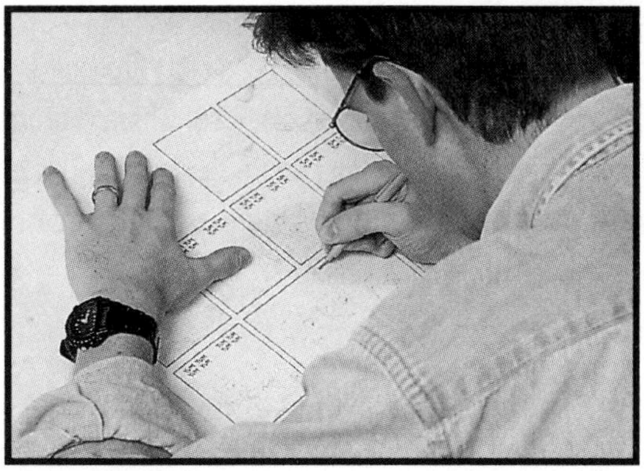

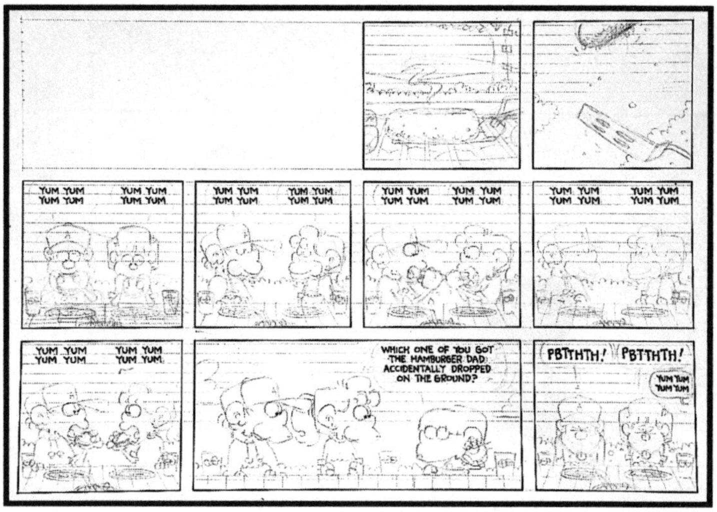
YUM YUM
YUM YUM
YUM YUM
YUM YUM
YUM YUM
YUM YUM
YUM YUM
YUM YUM
YUM YUM
YUM YUM
YUM YUM
YUM YUM
YUM YUM
YUM YUM
YUM YUM
YUM YUM
YUM YUM
YUM YUM
YUM YUM
YUM YUM
WHICH ONE OF YOU GOT THE HAMBURGER DAD ACCIDENTALLY DROPPED ON THE GROUND?
PBTTHTH!
PBTTHTH!
YUM YUM YUM YUM

Praying that all the coffee I drank before lunch has worn off and my hand isn't shaking too badly, I ink the lettering using a waterproof, permanent marker.

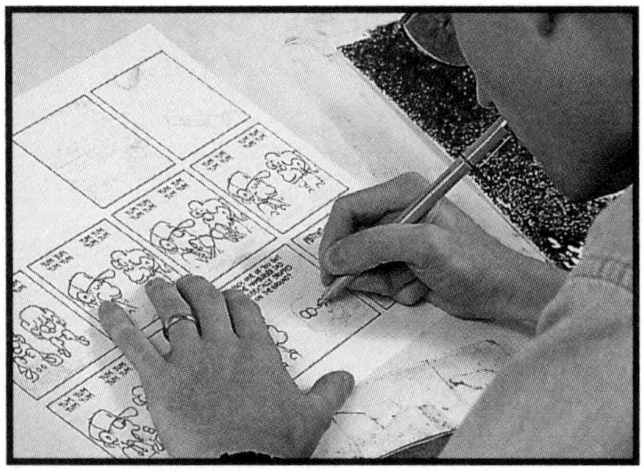

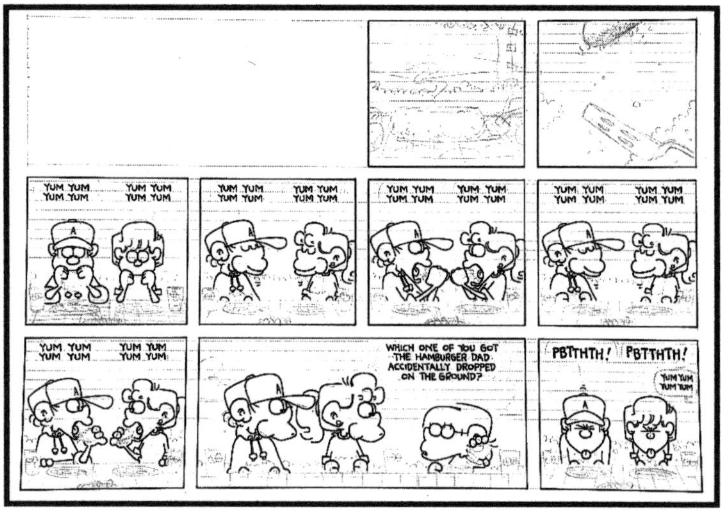
YUM YUM
YUM YUM
YUM YUM
YUM YUM
YUM YUM
YUM YUM
YUM YUM
YUM YUM
YUM YUM
YUM YUM
YUM YUM
YUM YUM
YUM YUM
YUM YUM
YUM YUM
YUM YUM
YUM YUM
YUM YUM
YUM YUM
YUM YUM
WHICH ONE OF YOU GOT THE HAMBURGER DAD ACCIDENTALLY DROPPED ON THE GROUND?
PBTTHTH!
PBTTHTH!
YUM YUM YUM YUM

Using the same pen, I trace over my art.
First, I ink the characters ...

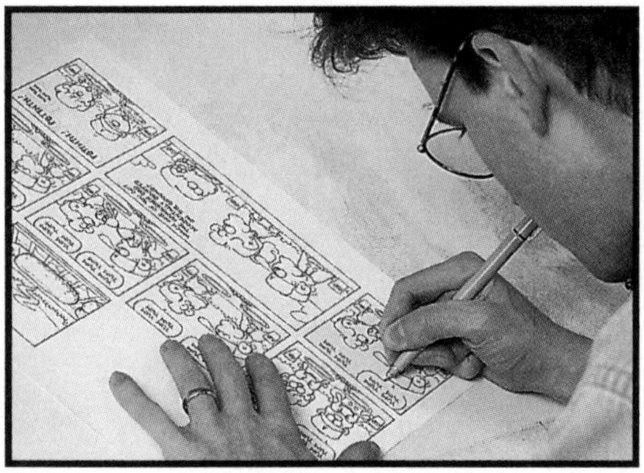

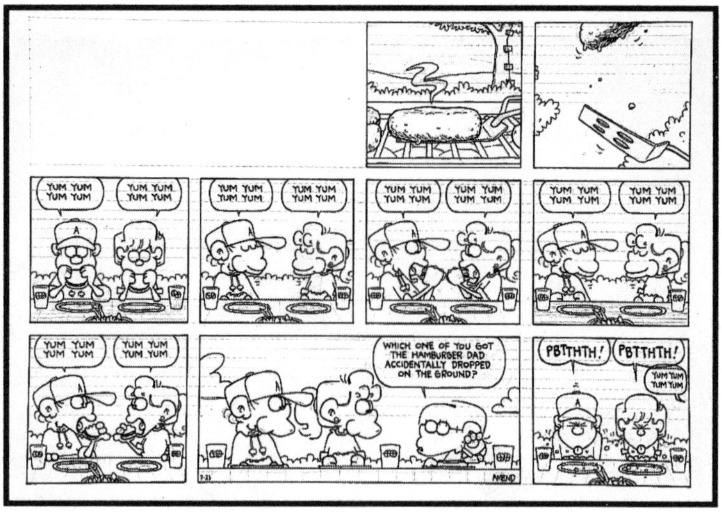
YUM YUM
YUM YUM
YUM YUM
YUM YUM
YUM YUM
YUM YUM
YUM YUM
YUM YUM
YUM YUM
YUM YUM
YUM YUM
YUM YUM
YUM YUM
YUM YUM
YUM YUM
YUM YUM
YUM YUM
YUM YUM
YUM YUM
YUM YUM
WHICH ONE OF YOU GOT THE HAMBURGER DAD ACCIDENTALLY DROPPED ON THE GROUND?
PBTTHTH!
PBTTHTH!
YUM YUM YUM YUM

...then I ink the background elements and the dialogue balloons. I use a No. 0 technical pen to ink any fine details.

We're into the home stretch now. I glue on a photocopy of my strip's logo using a spray adhesive.

Then I use opaque white paint to correct any inking mistakes I may have made.
(News flash: Even cartoonists goof up now and then.)

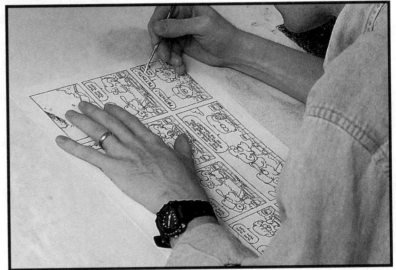

Finally, I erase my original pencil lines by gently going over everything with a kneaded eraser.

I specify color on a reduced-size photocopy with colored pencils and a key of numbers that correspond to particular colors.

For a Sunday strip, I have a palette of 125 colors to choose from.

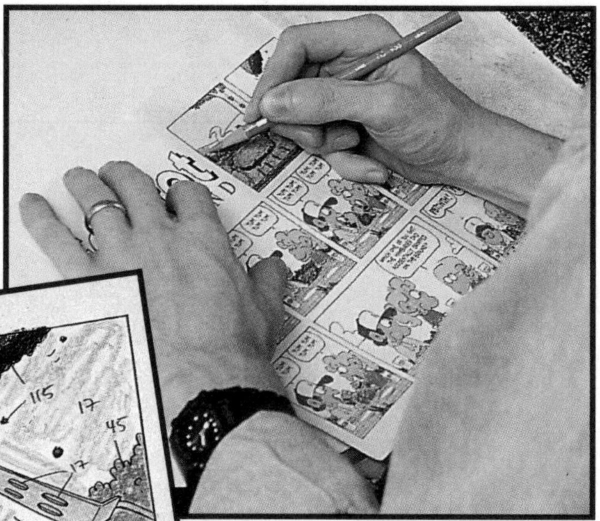

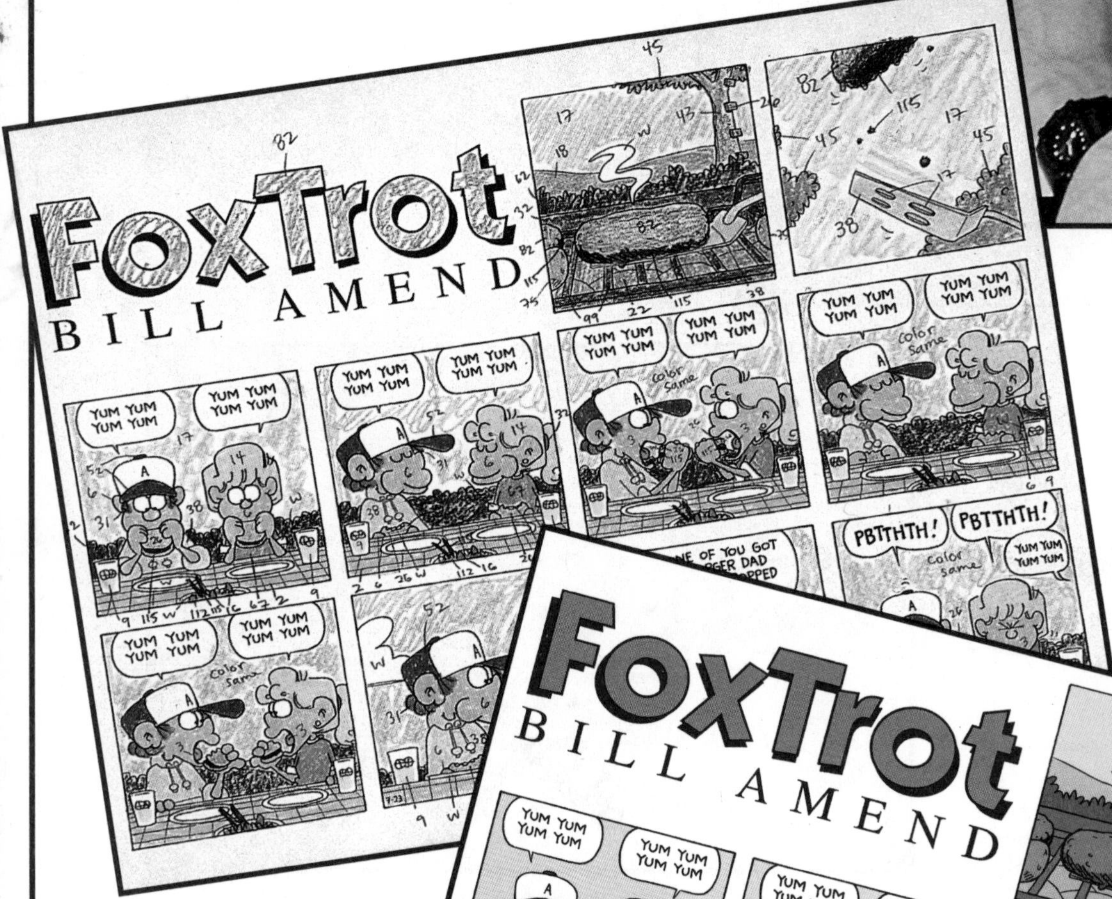
FoxTrot
BILL AMEND
YUM YUM YUM YUM
YUM YUM YUM YUM
color same
PBTTHTH!
PBTTHTH!
YUM YUM YUM YUM

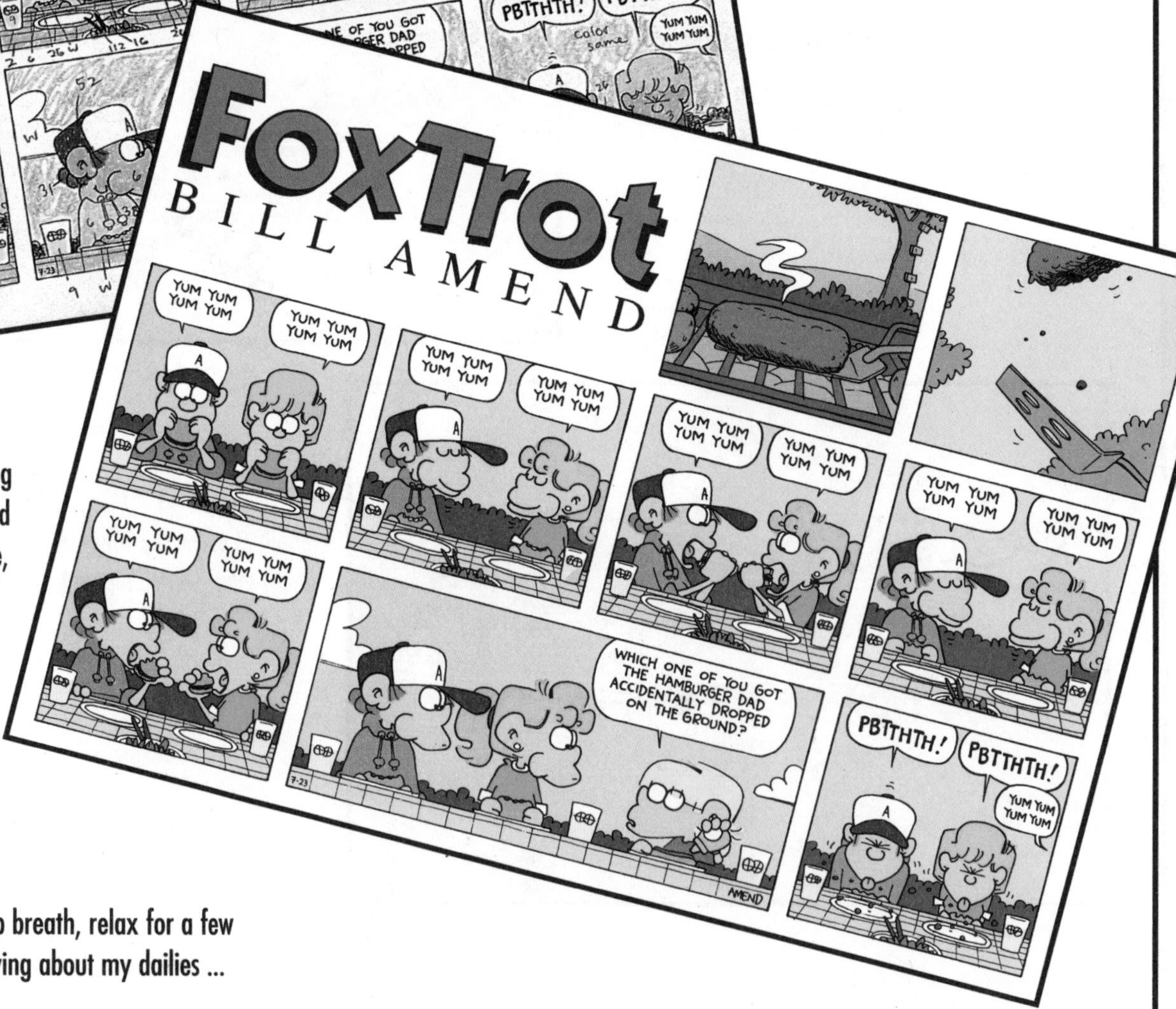
FoxTrot
BILL AMEND
YUM YUM YUM YUM
YUM YUM YUM YUM
YUM YUM YUM YUM
YUM YUM YUM YUM
YUM YUM YUM YUM
YUM YUM YUM YUM
YUM YUM YUM YUM
YUM YUM YUM YUM
YUM YUM YUM YUM
YUM YUM YUM YUM
WHICH ONE OF YOU GOT THE HAMBURGER DAD ACCIDENTALLY DROPPED ON THE GROUND?
PBTTHTH!
PBTTHTH!
YUM YUM YUM YUM
AMEND

After checking everything over one last time, I send the strip to my syndicate, where it is proofread and then forwarded for electronic coloring and distribution to newspapers where it will appear some six or seven weeks later.

Now I get to take a deep breath, relax for a few minutes, and start worrying about my dailies ...